AALUJA: Rescue, Reinte

Restoration of Major Ancient Egyptian Themes, Vol. I

AALUJA

"make, provide, to retrace one's steps, refer to the place of origin, restore!"

AALUJA:
Rescue, Reinterpretation and the Restoration of Major Ancient Egyptian Themes, Vol. I

Asar Imhotep
MADU-NDELA Institute for the Advancement of Science & Culture

MOCHA-Versity Press
Houston | San Antonio

2013

ABOUT THE AUTHOR

Asar Imhotep is a computer programmer and Africana researcher from Houston, TX whose research focus is the cultural, linguistic and philosophical links between the Ancient Egyptian civilizations and modern BaNtu cultures of central and South Africa. He is the founder of the MOCHA-Versity Institute of Philosophy and Research and the Madu-Ndela Institute for the Advancement of Science and Culture. He is also the author of *The Bakala of North America, the Living Suns of Vitality: In Search for a Meaningful Name for African-Americans, Passion of the Christ or Passion of Osiris: The Kongo Origins of the Jesus Myth* and *Ogun, African Fire Philosophy and the Meaning of KMT*. Asar is a noted speaker and philosopher and is currently organizing efforts in a nation-wide venture titled *The African-American Cultural Development Project*—a national project aimed at creating a framework for an African-American culture which will help vitally stimulate the economic, political, scientific and cultural spheres of African-American life in the United States.

A MOCHA-Versity Press Book
www.mochasuite.com

Cover Art: Harold Johnson
Interior & Cover Design and Composition: MOCHA Design Studios

ISBN-10: 1490956255
ISBN-13: 978-1490956251

FOR ELIJAH HERU JOHNSON

TABLE OF CONTENTS

LINGUISTIC ABBREVIATIONS

PB	Proto-Bantu
PWS	Proto-Western Sudanic (Westermann)
PWN	Proto-Western Nigritic (Mukarvosky)
PNC	Informal. No systematic reconstruction available
PCS	Proto-Central Sudanic (Bender)
PAA	Proto-Afro-Asiatic (Ehret, Diakonoff)
PPAB	Proto-Potou-Akanic-Bantu (Stewart)
Bantu	Proto-Bantu (Meeussen, Meinhof)
BANTU	Common Bantu (Guthrie)
“Bantu”	Bantu & Semi-Bantu (Johnston)
A-A	Afro-Asiatic (Diakonoff, Ehret, Greenberg)
ES	Eastern-Sudanic (Greenberg)
CS	Central-Sudanic (Greenberg)
CN	Chari-Nile (Greenberg)
NS	Nilo-Saharan (Greenberg)

[I have used Greenberg’s abbreviations (numbers & letters in brackets) to identify languages].

N-C	Niger-Congo
Mande	B Banbara, D Dioula, M Malinke (Delafosse,Westermann)
TogoR	Togo Remnant (Heine)
Polyglotta	Koelle’sPolyglotta Africana

PREFACE

This book aims to demonstrate the vitality and richness of ciKam (the ancient Egyptian language) by reexamining many of its core symbols and conceptualizations using modern African languages and cultures as sources for conceptual grounding and as fundamental points of intellectual departure. This particular project is part of an ongoing and larger endeavor called *The African-American Cultural Development Project*. I have undertaken this project as a son of the soil, a child of Africans who have lost their sovereignty and cultural memory as the result of the great holocaust of enslavement. The efforts of this project, in part, are directed toward recovering and reconstructing classical African cultures in an effort to utilize them as critical sources of paradigms for enriching and expanding modern African-African intellectual discourse and culture.

An endeavor of this magnitude demands that we have an accurate understanding of African cultural systems, concepts, history and values if we are to use the best of what Africa has to offer to help construct our own African-American culture. Egypt, then, becomes our starting point of analysis; primarily because it is one of the oldest African civilizations with an abundance of records written by the people of the Nile-Valley. This gives us historical grounding for which to measure the antiquity of these shared African traditions. As Dr. Cheikh Anta Diop has noted (Van Sertima, 1986), Ancient Egypt (and the Nile-Valley in general) becomes for Africa what Greece has been for Europe: a source of inspiration and cultural grounding.

It is this anchoring in African tradition that provides cultural authority for any claims to cultural authenticity for anything that we develop in this ongoing creative project. The great Senegalese scholar Diop—on his first and only visit to the United States, and in acknowledgment of our history and plight in America—charged us with the following task:

> We must reconstruct a new Afro-American cultural personality within the framework of our respective nations. Our history from the beginning of mankind, rediscovered and relived as such, will be the foundation of this new personality. (Van Sertima, 1986: 320)

In other words, as a result of the holocaust of enslavement and the great loss of cultural memory, a new African-American culture must be developed in order to regain our sovereignty and successfully march into the future (Wilson 1998, Imhotep 2009). This charge from Diop is part of the inspiration behind this book. In the process of examining various source materials on Egypt—for which to find inspiration—it became apparent that the vast majority of the literature was written by historians who did not belong to or studied African cultures and languages for which Egypt belonged and had commonalities. As a result of being cultural outsiders, many of the definitions of the concepts fossilized in the ancient Egyptian hieroglyphs (*mdw nṯr*) seemed a bit off and out of touch with what I knew about African cultures that shared the same vocabulary and cultural artifacts. But even with that said, it must be accepted that it is virtually impossible to fully translate ancient texts and concepts in terms which totally represent ancient approaches to thought and practice. As the Bamanan proverb states, "One can transfer all things from one place to another, except speech." There are limitations of time, space and culture that must be acknowledged. It is not to say that the Egyptologists were totally wrong in their assessments, but that they often missed the mark as a result of their cultural orientations that often "read into" the works instead of "drawing from" the texts.

Therefore, this study demanded the development of fresh methodologies and the careful reassessment of previous scholarship. I am interested and involved in the intellectual and practical project of concept generation and the development of new modes of analysis of ancient Egyptian (ciKam) texts. This has meant using old concepts and categories in new ways and creating new ones which more accurately and usefully serve the various analyses in this volume. The study of modern African languages and cultures has been a big help in the rescue and restoration of major Egyptian concepts. The essays included in this volume are just some of my reexaminations conducted in an effort to recover our lost traditions: those that have been fossilized in ancient Egyptian texts. Other volumes are to follow this publication, which build on the efforts of this volume.

There are many acknowledgments due when one's journey to wisdom has been supported by teachers from both the "Ivory Tower" of academia and the "school of initiation" of various African communities of memory. While it is not possible to mention each institution and individual who in one way or another contributed to making this book see the light of day, there are a few who cannot pass without mention. First and foremost I'd like to thank the Creator (*Mvidi-MuKulu*) and the ancestors (the *Bakulu/Egungun*) who have in subtle and not-so-subtle ways guided my research and who have opened paths to roads I would have probably never travelled if left to my own devices. To my *Ori* that has guided me towards my destiny, I say *àṣẹ*! I would like to give a warm thanks to brother Ádìsá Ájámú for looking over the *Introduction* and for providing his critical insights for that section and his sincere words of encouragement. A heartfelt acknowledgement of gratitude is extended to Kalia Glover who has also reviewed parts of this work and for allowing me to bore her to death with my linguistic ramblings. Youare very much appreciated. A special thanks goes to Evelyne Brener (Nzo Ma Kongo) of France (via Kongo) who has shared numerous scholastic resources with me—including translation work, scans and hard to find journal articles for independent researchers—for which many aspects of certain articles in this text could not have been written.

There are many friends whom I feel a special sense of gratitude and affection for their advice, moral support and for taking up the challenge of reviewing different aspects of the current text and providing their insights: Amun's Apostle, Ausar Wudjau, Sonjedi Ankh Ra, Amun Rah Apedemak Ptah and Malik Pasha of *The Ancient Kemetic Research Universite* (AKRU). Thank you all for your continuous inspiration, academic insights and critical challenges over the years on various subject matters. Much of what is written in this volume has been the fruit of many lively discussions among this group of enlightened gentlemen. A special shout-out is in order for Brother Bonotchi Montgomery (Detroit's master *sš* 𓏞 "scribe") who has always been a source of mutual exchange and inspiration for new areas of research.

Lastly, I am profoundly grateful to the following master teachers for their collegiality and creative challenges, which were indispensible in this project of rescuing, reinterpretation and the restoration of major Egyptian themes: Shushukulu[1] Dr. Mubabinge Bilolo (Egyptologist, Linguist, Philosopher), Shushukulu Dr. Alain Anselin (Egyptologist, Linguist, Anthropologist), Shushukulu Dr. Wade Nobles (Psychologist), Shushukulu Dr. Sylvain Kalamba Nsapo

1 *Shushukulu* in Tshiluba is a master teacher, a scholar, a scientist, a sophos who has the moral character and intellectual fortitude to get at the heart of a problem and unveil life's mysteries. A full examination of this term is provided in *Chapter 3.2*.

(Philosopher, Theologian), and Shushukulu Dr. Kipkoeech araap Sambu (Egyptologist, Coptologist). There is no doubt that their astute academic minds and critical eyes casted over this work in respective ways. Their uplifting compliments all helped in guiding, shaping and spurring me to this point. They, too, have taken the time to read through parts of this work and provided valuable commentary, suggestions and raised critical questions from the vantage points of their own areas of intellectual focus and competence. Any errors of commission and omission that may be found here are solely my own, though certainly unintended.

May Olódùmarè/Nzambi-a-Mpungu/Uqobo, to Whom we are most indebted for inspiring and overseeing things up to this stage, blaze your individual paths ever so brightly. Ume Njalo, "May you stand forever!"

Asar Imhotep (Ifamuyiwa Fagbemi)
The MOCHA-Versity Institute of Philosophy and Research
The Madu-Ndela Institute for the Advancement of Science and Culture
The African-American Cultural Development Project
San Antonio/Houston, TX
September 2013

Introduction

> Wisdom is the only thing that is eternal, but it takes human beings to build and pass it from generation to generation *–Shi proverb*
>
> *sḫꜥ.i nty gm(.i) fḳ ḥr st.s*
> *snfr.i nty ḫr ꜣhw r ḏr-ꜥ*
> *nn sw ḥr st.s*
>
> I made magnificent what I found ruined in its place
> I restored what was damaged long ago.
> And was no longer in its place
> (Tomb of Petosiris, New Kingdom)
>
> If we are going to reconstruct, we have to recognize what it is that we loss as it regards our relationship to other people. We reevaluate so we can understand what we gain by abandoning that which made us whole in the first place. *–Dr. John Henrik Clarke*

Aaluja: Rescue, Reinterpretation and the Restoration of Major Ancient Egyptian Themes Vol. I is a collection of essays which seek, in part, to situate current discourses concerning major Egyptian conceptual themes within their proper African contexts. Much of the reality as expressed in the ancient Egyptian writings has been distorted due, in part, to Eurocentric biases in interpreting the texts. Instead of drawing from the pool of shared African traditions from which emerged the Egyptian civilization,[1] researchers have instead sought inspiration outside of Africa among a (yet to be discovered) mythical Hamito-Asiatic race as the bringers of civilization to Egypt (ciKam).

This volume is located within the history of indigenous African traditions. I intend to explore the pre-colonial modes of knowing and being in Africa from their own epistemological orientations. I am interested in extracting from the available texts a reliable understanding of major ancient Egyptian concepts that reflect and have shaped their moral, cultural and theological universe. What is sought here is not merely seeking a place within a research process, which Europe has already begun, but the introduction of a process, which self-consciously begins and becomes a clear rupture with the European paradigm (Karenga 2006, Bilolo 2011). This calls for a radically different approach to ancient Egyptian studies than what prevails as convention in the Western academy (simply the collection of facts regarding artifacts and events).

In the West we are familiar with a concept called the *Three R's*: **r**eading, w**r**iting and a**r**ithmetic. This refers to the foundations of a basic skills-orientated education program within American schools. For our current discourse, the *Three R's* (3R's) refer to a particular operative sequence in the ongoing struggle of African agency and authenticity: ***R**escue*, ***R**einterpretation* and ***R**estoration*. In that sense this work can be seen as participating in the larger enterprise of re-establishing *mꜣꜥ.t* (ciLuba *malelela, bulelela*) in the field of African historiography started by

1 See Alain Anselin's article "Some Notes about an Early African Pool of Cultures from which Emerged the Egyptian Civilisation," in Exell (2011) for a list of such cultures.

the likes of Dubois, Shomburg, Jackson, Clarke, ben-Jochannan, Diop, Obenga and countless others. We must first *rescue* African concepts from the clutches of Western epistemological domination. We must then firmly establish the conceptual grounding for which to *reinterpret* these essential ancient Egyptian concepts as seen through African lenses. Finally, we must *restore* that which has been damaged as a result of an ongoing epistemological onslaught against competent African researchers who have exercised their agency in establishing new purposes, paradigms and possibilities in the various fields of Africology by Western educators.

It is often assumed that the cultural and religious paradigms of the Judeo-Greco-Romano world are superior to the African.[2] Its correlative assumption in regards to Egypt is that it is essentially a *pagan* project, undeveloped, prelogical, mythopoeic and without serious cultural depth or intellectual and ethical insight (Karenga, 2006: 13). For the Western mind what we find in Egypt are childish attempts at abstract thought and it is not to be taken seriously by critical thinkers and students of philosophy.

This frame of thought is suggested by Sir E. Wallis Budge in his book *Gods of the Ancient Egyptians: or Studies in Ancient Egyptian Mythology, 2 vols.* (1904), who stated that:

> The Egyptians, being fundamentally an African people, possessed all the virtues and vices which characterized the North African races generally, and it is not to be held for a moment that any African people could become metaphysicians in the modern sense of the word. In the first place, no African language is suitable for giving expression to theological and philosophical speculations, and even an Egyptian priest of the highest intellectual attainments would have been unable to render a treatise of Aristotle into language which his brother priests, without teaching, could understand. The mere construction of the language would make such a thing an impossibility, to say nothing of the ideas of the great Greek philosopher, which belong to a domain of thought and culture wholly foreign to the Egyptian. (Budge, 1904, vol. I: 143)

Although Budge can admit that the Egyptians are "fundamentally an African people," the African character of Egypt, in his eyes, is the basis for stripping the Egyptians of any kind of logical or rational faculties. In other words, they cannot think intelligently because they are Black. To reaffirm that this isn't an accidental reading on our part, in his attack on Brugsch's argument that the word *nṯr* "divine" was identical to Greek φύσις (physis) and Latin *natura*, Budge goes on to state that:

> It is difficult to see how the eminent Egyptologist could attempt to compare the conception of God formed by a half-civilized African people with those of such cultivated nations as the Greeks and Romans. (Budge, 1904, vol. I: 68)

In other words, the mere attempt at comparing African concepts with European concepts is grounds for dismissal. It is attitudes such as this that continue to permeate the scholastic literature concerning Egypt, even to the present day. An example can be gleaned from Stephen Quirke's book *The Cult of Ra: Sun-Worship in Ancient Egypt* (2001: 13). In *Chapter 1* of the text, Quirke makes the following statement as it regards the tale of Horus and Set:

> For it is difficult to read the tales as written here, with a knowledge of Egyptian myth, without laughing. The repetition of the episodes (the very feature absent in religious

2 Martin Bernal (1987), in part, attributes this to the *Aryan Model*. That is to say a model which purports that civilization started with the Greeks and that Greek civilization was an indigenous creation without any outside influences whatsoever. The world, therefore, is indebted to Greek (read European) culture for all serious advancements and civilization known to man.

> contexts) makes the gods, or rather the procedures described, look ridiculous. Most ludicrous of all is the behaviour of the sun god, who assumes the role of judge in the tale.

From what perspective is the story "laughable?" By what standards are their procedures "ridiculous?" The procedures as expressed in the tales reflect that which are inherent in the culture itself. To ridicule the procedures in the texts is to ridicule the culture itself, and by extension, the *people*. This, again, attempts to belittle the Egyptian way of life and make its *modes of being* seem childish in comparison to that which the Eurocentric writer understands from his own Western point-of-view. Neither on the empirical-historical, nor on the intellectual level have Africans been introduced into the world of modernity by Western writers as human beings who were involved (agents) in the many ordinary and extraordinary acts of work, thought and imagination that all human cultures undertake to cope with the one thousand and one challenges of its day. If the author looks at the subject (the people) with contempt and disdain, how can said author paint from the study a reliable portrait of the culture?

These are the types of limitations we attempt to bypass in this current study. Given the above considerations, I assume a need to go beyond the 'standard' approaches to interpreting ancient Egyptian cultural and theological phenomena, which are grounded in Eurocentric frameworks and paradigms. This "Western" approach often has a modern Greco-Judeo-Christian slant, which distorts the African meanings. It is therefore necessary to look at ancient Egyptian phenomena through a more culturally congruent lens. In the words of Ankh Mi Ra, we would therefore, "let the ancestors speak."

Rescue, Reinterpretation and Restoration

With regards to the task of reconstructing ancient Egyptian civilization, Maulana Karenga notes that "The fundamental human task becomes, then, one of rescuing and restoring the culture of Kemet and of exploring and expanding the human possibilities inherent in this process (Karenga & Carruthers, 1986: xiii). We therefore do not mean to minimize or neglect other African cultures. Egypt—as the most classical African civilization with countless records for analysis—becomes a point of departure that will allow us to reach out to explore other cultural centers in Africa in the developing and affirming of an African worldview.

This is the aim of this work and it is inherent in the title. The word *aaluja*, the title of this text, comes from the modern ciLuba-Bantu language of Congo. Its first historical attestation, however, can be found among the ancient Egyptians as the word *srwḏ*:

srwḏ "make secure, set right (a wrong), provide, fulfill (a contract)"; "to restore, repair, to make new again"; "to make grow, flourish."

This term is usually part of a phrase *srwḏ t3* "restoring the world." It is a polysemic phrase which carries with it the idea of raising up and restoring that which has been ruined; replenishing that which is lacking; strengthening that which has been weakened; setting right that which is wrong; and to make flourish that which is fragile and undeveloped (Karenga, 2008: 23). The underlying premise is not only to go back and fetch useful examples from history, but to make what we restore (and fetch) more beautiful and beneficial than it was before.

The word *srwḏ* (with *s*-causative prefix) derives from the root *rwḏ*  "strengthen, maintain, perpetuate, flourish, be prosperous, success, enduring, permanent, sturdy, steadfast, remain firm, firmness, consistency, be strong, prevail (over), competence, ability." One cannot "restore" anything without knowledge of how it was before; and one surely cannot improve on a model without a complete understanding of its historical stages and limitations. Therefore, a sense of history is built into the very fabric of the Egyptian term.

To get a sense of how *srwḏ*—as a key concept in *maatian* ethics—was used in the ancient Egyptian society, we can examine an excerpt from one of the *Declaration of Virtues* (DOV) given by Rediu Khnum who asserts that:

> I restored (*srwḏ*) that which I found ruined (*wsṯ*);
> I joined (*ṯs*) that which I found severed (*fdḳ*), and
> I replenished (*mḥ*) that which I found depleted (*iꜣṯ*) (cited in Karenga, 2006: 398)

This term (*srwḏ*) is used to identify an ongoing ethical obligation and practice that mandates that the body politic not only seek its own history, but continually builds and perfects the projects started by one's ancestors. This is imitative of creation itself as pressures in nature are always causing things to deteriorate (via the 1st law of thermodynamics). The ongoing process of evolution ensures that all things change, but also that all things are renewed in a more stable and more robust state. This is the inspiration for *srwḏ/rwḏ*. Thus, to *srwḏ/rwḏ* is to act in a divine manner that seeks to create stable and life-affirming environments in the midst of constant conflict, fluctuation and change.

As noted before, the root of *srwḏ* is *rwḏ* and this word finds its modern form in the ciLuba-Bantu language as the word *aaluja/aalwija* "restore, replace what had been removed or deleted"; *aaluka* "return, retrace (one's steps)"; *aaluja* "make, provide, to retrace one's steps, refer to the place of origin"; *-aalukija* "to think, reflect, consider, to render, to make"; *dyalukija* "reference, reaction, feedback"; *Aaluja* is related to the term *-aalabula* "change, modify, alter, return, extend, open"; *-aalabuka* "changed, alter, be modified, turn back, withdraw"; *aalula* "change (of place, position, shape), transformation, metamorphosis"; *-longolola* "repair, store with care, arrange methodically"; *-longa* "reward, give tip; *-longa* "arrange, put in order"; *bulongolodi* "administration, management"; *cilongolwelu* "garage"; *dilongolola* "preparation, preparing"; *ndongolwelu* "how to govern, how to arrange, arrangement, organization"; *-lukulula* "repair" (e.g., "a thread"); *-luka* "braiding, weave." Here we get a sense that the root not only deals with "repairing, restoring," but also with "organizing, putting something in its proper order and place."

Aaluja is synonymous with *sangula* "revive (in the next generation), ascendancy, reproduce in its descendants"; *busangù* "birthmark similar to that of a deceased relative"; *-sangulula* "reproduce, to revive in his descendants"; *-sàngula* "take out, pull out, remove"; *pingaji* "make, go back, refer, return" (<*pinga* "go back, return"); *dipingaja* "restitution, restoration"; *-pingana* "replace, successor." And these terms are synonymous with *Lundula* "activate", "to raise, grow", "stir (fire, life)." These terms also accurately describe the scope of this work and the ancestral mission to reestablish African agency. It is our ancestral obligation to restore the rich meanings and insights left in the sacred texts of *ciKam-ciKula* (ancient Egypt). The objective, then, is to *aaluja* "retrace one's steps, refer to a place of origin" in order to *aaluja* "restore, replace what had been removed or deleted."

I view this work as part of a sacred mission, an effort to restore that which had been damaged as a result of the holocaust of enslavement. I extract useful information from the Egyptian texts in an effort to find models of excellence worth emulating in modern times. The ancient Egyptian culture serves as a spring-board from which to launch a new African-American personality; a mission and task requested by our great ancestor and elder Cheikh Anta Diop.

> We must reconstruct a new Afro-American cultural personality within the framework of our respective nations. Our history from the beginning of mankind, rediscovered and relived as such, will be the foundation of this new personality. (Van Sertima, 1986: 320).

This work is an act of service and an ancestral obligation to the future. It is a self conscious restorative project, an attempt to repair that which laid in ruins for centuries. We seek also to explore the lessons our classical African civilizations offer us in conceiving and building our cultural future. King Kheti, father of Merikare, is quoted saying "Even one day is a donation to eternity and every hour is a contribution to the future" (Karenga & Carruthers, 1986: XV). If we wish to live for eternity, we must build for eternity and I hope this serves as a firm foundation from which to build on and expand. That is to say *rwḏ*  "strengthen, maintain, perpetuate, flourish, be prosperous, success, enduring, permanent, sturdy, steadfast, remain firm, firmness, consistency, be strong, prevail (over), competence, ability." Of course, this work is only possible as a result of standing on the shoulders of countless giants who have laid the initial groundwork and framing: e.g., Diop, Obenga, Karenga, Carruthers, Jackson, Houston, Dubois, Clarke, ben Jochannan, Bilolo, Pfouma, Ndigi, Nsapo, Mushete, Bimwenyi-Kweshi, Oduyoye, Lam, Beatty, Kajangu, Sambu, Finch, Browder, Epega and others. I pray this work expands upon their legacy.

Assumptions of the Study

The epistemological stance that grounds this work is rooted in African tradition. Out of this arises a commitment to the recovery of major African themes as expressed through ancient Egyptian tradition and concepts. Given this grounding in African tradition, this mission of recovery, reinterpretation and restoration is informed by several fundamental considerations and assumptions.

The first assumption is that ancient Egypt is an African country, its inhabitants were "Black" African people and its people spoke an African language traceable to *Negro-Africaines* (Homburger 1929, Obenga 1993, Bilolo 2011). While this may seem a given (even trivial to some researchers) these points cannot be stressed enough because it is on this grounding that ancient Egyptian culture, its institutions, its choice of vocabulary mapping and its unique forms of expression begin to make sense. It is the African context that gives texture to the ancient Egyptian society.

It is my observation that languages that are linguistically related, for the most part, share similar cultural ideas and expressions. The shared and related languages are the grounding for seeking shared traditions. This has allowed linguists to note common features of cultures separated by time and space. A few cases will help to illuminate the point. Julian Baldick's *Black God: The Afroasiatic Roots of the Jewish, Christian and Muslim Religions* (1997) establishes this premise almost immediately in the text as it regards the central thesis of his project:

> ...just as there is a common Afroasiatic language-family in this region [Africa and Arabia], so too there is a common family of religions, with an inner logic to be found in myths, folk-tales, rituals, customs and beliefs as far apart as Yemen and Nigeria: what is observable by anthropologists on the ground today goes back to an ancient past shared by the Bible and the pharaohs. (Baldick, 1997: 1)

In other words, the groups that belong to the Afro-Asiatic (Afrisan) super-family of languages have shared commonalities in religion, ritual and culture because they ultimately sprang from the same speech community in ancient times. The similarities in world-view are encapsulated in the language and since they share common vocabulary, they will often use the same vocabulary to refer to the same material and philosophical phenomena.

This argument is not limited to Afro-Asiatic. The case has been made also for Niger-Congo, a major branch of the Kongo-Saharan super family of languages (Gregersen 1972, Blench 1995[3]). In his work titled *Black Sumer: The African Origins of Civilisation* (2012), Hermel Hermstein does a historical comparative linguistic analysis to demonstrate that the ancient Sumerian language is a Niger-Congo language traceable to Proto-Bantu (PB), thus making the ancient Sumerians a 'Black' African people (at least initially before the Semitic incursions).[4] He too discusses the common features in religious concepts and culture as a result of a shared language between Sumerian and Niger-Congo speakers. He provides the following commentary:

> The religious traits common to both Niger-Congo speaking peoples and Sumerians can be found individually in many other cultures of the world. A distant supreme deity must occur in the culture of speakers of several hundred of the world's languages although this trait is not universal. There are almost seven thousand languages spoken in the world and each has its own culture. Each time another trait is added, the number of cultures around the world that would have both traits, and then all three traits, and so on, becomes progressively smaller. How likely is it that two cultures chosen at random would both have?
>
> 1. Distant supreme deity
> 2. Territorial spirits junior to supreme deity
> 3. Ancestral spirits junior to both supreme deity and territorial spirits
> 4. Ancestral spirits leading shadowy existence and requiring sustenance
> 5. Ancestral spirits [who] can tell the future and are consulted
> 6. Humans [that] require proper burial or else will return to haunt the living
>
> This group of traits cannot be said to be universal or common. The God of the Bible is actively involved in earthly affairs, as is Zeus of the ancient Greeks, and Jupiter of the Romans. It is, therefore, likely to be statistically significant that all six traits occur amongst the Sumerians and the speakers of Niger-Congo languages. (Hermstein, 2012: 122)

He is not alone in recognizing a common Niger-Congo religious and cultural tradition. Christopher Ehret's book *The Civilizations of Africa: A History to 1800* (2002) provides a similar commentary. However, he does this for basically all of the African language families discussed in this work. Moreover, this process is more or less repeated in the work *African Languages: An Introduction* (2000) edited by Bernd Heine and Derek Nurse.

This framework, however, is not limited to African languages. J. P. Mallory and D. Q. Adams in their work *The Oxford Introduction to Proto-Indo-European and the Proto-Indo-European World* (2006) operate within the same paradigm for Indo-European languages. For

3 However, fifteen years later Roger Blench's views had changed, with Blench (2011) proposing instead that the noun-classifier system of Central Sudanic, commonly reflected in a tripartite general–singulative–plurative number system, triggered the development or elaboration of the noun-class system of the Atlantic–Congo languages, with tripartite number marking surviving in the Plateau and Gur languages of Niger–Congo, and the lexical similarities being due to loans. Obenga (1993), however, provides a worthy case for the uniting of these two language families.

4 See also the second volume of his work titled *Black Sumer: The Physical Evidence (Part One)*(2013, Pomegranate Publishing. London) for the archeological evidence to support this premise.

them, the commonality in the languages of the Indo-Europeans provides the basis to assume shared cultural features as expressed in the vocabulary, which are then applied to common material and philosophical phenomena. The whole text is dedicated to the shared lexical and cultural features of Indo-European. As noted by Mallory and Adams:

> There is only one route to the reconstruction of Indo-European culture that offers any hope of reliability and that is *language*. Although we might compare cultural traditions, behaviour, or material culture among the different Indo-European groups, this exercise would be a very uncertain plunge into comparative ethnography or archaeology and we would be forced to compare peoples at vastly different time depths. (Mallory & Adams, 2006: 117) (emphasis mine)

In other words, if one is trying to reconstruct the proto-culture of a group of distant people, simply acknowledging shared cultural traits is not enough. Only by establishing a strong relationship via the languages can a real case be made for a common origin of a group of people. It is the language that ties all the pieces together. This is the basis for exploring the parameters of a shared mythology and cultural features among societies—living or ancient—who belong to the same language family. Mallory & Adams provide us with an example of a common religious feature as it regards this notion of a "final-battle" with the gods in the Indo-European world. They go on to state the:

> Celtic, Italic, Germanic, Indo-Iranian, Armenian, and Greek all reveal traces of an Indo-European eschatological myth, i.e. a myth that describes the end of the world in terms of a cataclysmic battle, e.g. the Battle of Kurukshetra from the *Mahābhārata*, the Second Battle of Mag Tured in Irish tradition, Ragnarök in Norse tradition, the Battle of Lake Regillus in Roman history, Hesiod's Titanomachy, and the Plain of Ervandavan in Armenian history. In all these traditions the end comes in the form of a major battle in which gods (Norse, Greek), demi-gods (Irish), or major heroes (Roman, Indo-Aryan, Armenian) are slain. The story begins when the major foe, usually depicted as coming from a different (and inimical) paternal line, assumes the position of authority among the host of gods or heroes, e.g. Norse Loki, Roman Tarquin, Irish Bres. In this position he exploits the labour of the protagonists until he is driven out and returns to his own people. A new leader then springs up among the protagonists (e.g. Irish Lug, Greek Zeus) often the **nepōt-* 'grandson' or 'nephew' of the deposed leader. The two sides then prepare for a major war (in Germanic and Iranian myth there is also a great winter) and the two forces come together and annihilate each other in a cataclysmic battle. Since a new order is called into existence after the battle, the myth may not be eschatological in the strict sense but rather represent a mythic encounter that brought a past golden age to an end. (Mallory and Adams, 2006: 439-440)

We better understand now why European movie producers are fascinated with making "end of the world" and "apocalyptic" films (e.g., *War of the Worlds*, *The Day the Earth Stood Still*, etc.). It is for this shared concept among the Indo-Europeans that I believe that it was Indo-Europeans who had a hand in creating the Bible.[5] We find echoes of this "final battle" in the book of *Revelations*; except in this book it is the gods (Jesus and the Angels) who win over man.

But what do you do when evidence supports the notion that the established boundaries for language categorization are in a sense arbitrary and non-existent? This is exactly the case as proposed by Oduyoye (1992, 1996), Diop (1977), Obenga (1992, 1993), Bilolo (2010, 2011)

5 See my upcoming work titled *Religious Proselytization as a Form of Violence: Infringement of the African Concept of Simultaneous Validity*, MOCHA-Versity Press, Houston, TX.

and Sambu (2011) among others. They have been able to demonstrate relationships between African languages that extend beyond established boundaries. The Egyptian vocabulary, grammatical, cultural and religious features betrays the notion that Egyptian is a language family by itself as a sort of isolate among the Afrisan family of languages. Its affinities with Wolof, Dagara, Bantu, Kalenjiin and Yorùbá alone defy the logic of such a categorization. The approach to spirituality and the name of the deities by the Egyptians alone would place it in the Niger-Congo family of languages given the criteria set out by Hermstein (2012) and Ehret (2000).

Obenga (1993) has put together, in my opinion, a more realistic classification model other than what has been proposed by Greensberg (1963). Obenga proposes three primary language families in Africa: Berber, Khoisan and Negro-Egyptian. The *Negro-Egyptian* family would consist of Egyptian, Cushitic, Chadic, Nilo-Saharan, and Niger-Kordofanian. This would better explain the non-accidental shared features belonging to both Niger-Congo and Nilo-Saharan and the ancient Egyptian languages, for example.

It is with this understanding that we are able to use languages such as Yorùbá and Tshiluba to gain insights into the ancient Egyptian language. As noted by Obenga (1992: 110-112) as it regards the criteria for comparing Pharaonic Egyptian and modern Black African languages:

a) Language has an oral tradition independent of writing. (Latin of the 3rd century BC and Lithuanian of the 16th AD, both present, however remote from each other in time or space, a faithful picture of Indo-European). We can therefore compare Egyptian and Coptic forms with correspondences in modern black African forms, even if we do not have all the successive stages of black African languages in the written forms. . .

b) The criteria of comparison are guaranteed by Pharaonic Egyptian which is the oldest witness of the languages compared. So the great time-span between pharaonic Egyptian and modern Black African languages, far from being a handicap, is, instead a strong criterion for comparison which must always make sure of having some ancient evidence for certain languages compared. This means that it is less worthwhile from the historical linguistic point of view to compare, for instance, Fongbe (Abomey, Benin) and Yorùbá (Nigeria, West Africa), but it is more pertinent to compare, for instance, Pharaonic Egyptian, Coptic and Yorùbá. Indeed, the oldest Egyptian hieroglyphic texts date back to around 3000 BC and the first written forms of Coptic as early as the third century BC.

c) Consequently, the enormous geographical discontinuity strongly favours the exclusion of borrowing in those ancient times, across the range of established similarities—morphological, phonetic and lexicological.

That is to say, that the very old separation between the Egyptian and Yorùbá languages, from the common predialectal block, eliminates the effects of convergence, and random, haphazard borrowing:

Pharaonic Egyptian	:*mi*, "take"
Coptic (Vocalized Egyptian)	:*mo, ma* "take"
Yorùbá	:*mú*, "take"
Pharaonic Egyptian	:*mw*, "water"
Coptic	:*mo, mē* "water"
Yorùbá	:*o-mi, omi*, "water" (Bini, Edo: *a-mē, amē*)
Pharaonic Egyptian	:*ḏ.t* "Cobra"
Coptic	:*adjo, ĕdjō* "viper"

Yorùbá	:*ejo, edjo*, "snake"
Pharaonic Egyptian	:*ir.t* "eye"
Coptic	:*ĕyĕr, yĕr* "eye"
Yorùbá	:*ri* "to see"

One would be hard pressed to assume that these basic vocabularies shared between Egyptian, Coptic and Yorùbá are somehow the result of chance look-a-likes. These are inherited terms from their shared predialectal parent. More Yorùbá and Egyptian examples are provided in the chapters that follow.

This study assumes that the Egyptians are Black-Africans and thus invests little energy in arguing their Africanness, which has already been conclusively established to this author's satisfaction (e.g., Diop 1991, Diop 1978, Lam 1994, Oduyoye 1996, Bilolo 2011, Sambu 2008, Bernal 1987). The deep cultural unity of Africa is already established (Diop 1987, 1989, 1991, Eglash 1999, Obenga 1993, Homburger 1929). We therefore move on to a different phase of this ongoing project into a phase to better understand ancient Egyptian cultural phenomena within its African context.[6]

How does the Africanness of ancient Egypt inform our understanding of that society? What lessons are the ancient Egyptians trying to teach us in their writings? What models of excellence can we observe that are worthy of emulation and are applicable in our times? The Blackness of the Ancient Egyptians are a given. Our focus now is on the intellectual, cultural and scientific life of the Egyptians and how these can illumine many of the modern Black African practices, and how modern Black African cultures can in turn provide insight into ancient Egyptian thought and praxis.

From here we then move on to critique much of the Western interpretations of Egyptian phenomena. To give a proper analysis of the various African world-views, one must first understand the qualities and aspects of its culture. This idea is reaffirmed in Calvin C. Hernton's "Introduction to the Second Addition" of Janheinz Jahn's seminal work *Muntu: African Culture and the Western World* (1990):

> Human beings create culture to bring sense to existence and meaningful ways of viewing the world and living in it. Sense and meaning are salient qualities and vital functions of African culture. But you have got to feel, comprehend, understand, and respect the fundamentals of African culture before you can see the sense and appreciate the meaning.

This helps us to understand more clearly why Stephen Quirke (2001) could not fully grasp the stories of Horus and Set: He did not "respect the fundamentals of African culture." As a result, he could not therefore "see the sense and appreciate the meaning" inherit in the story, which for him was "laughable."

Toward this end, it must be understood that Egyptian culture is very similar to most African cultures, but differs drastically than what we find in Europe or Asia. Quirke (2001: 13), for instance, confirms the vast difference between the psychology of Europe versus the psychology of the ancient Egyptians in the realm of art.

> For us, ancient Egyptian art carries a strange familiarity, in the succinct rendering of human and animal figures, yet the underlying conventions of this art differ markedly from European tradition. The immortalizing purpose of Egyptian art stands at odds with

6 See for instance Karen Exell. (ed.) (2012). *Egypt in Its African Context: Proceedings of the Conference Held at The Manchester Museum*. British Archaeological Reports. London.

> the bodily perspective developed by the ancient Greeks, and the spatial perspective refined in the Western European Renaissance.

Our assertion is that this is the case because the ancient Egyptian artistic expression belongs to the greater African artistic sphere and that it is the difference of environment, language and history that provides a different psychology among the Egyptians (*rmṯ*) as expressed through their *art*. The Egyptians are different because Black Africans are fundamentally different than Europeans.

Many researchers have acknowledged this difference. Paul Masson-Oursel (French orientalist and philosopher) has pointed out, cogently, that "black mental attitudes" were "the backdrop of pharaonic civilization" (cited in Obenga, 2006: 85). While Serge Sauneron (Egyptologist) writes, "Thus the revelations of Ogotemmeli, or of 'Bantu Philosophy', turn out to contribute precious information which helps us better understand certain aspects of Egyptian religious thought. But in this connection, there is little, if anything, we can expect from a reading of Plato..."[7]Along a similar vein, Fredric Portal informs us that, "The religious practice of the Black people is the latest expression of the doctrines of Ethiopia and Egypt."[8] In other words, what we see commonly expressed in modern African cultures are extensions and in many ways continuations of the practices and thoughts as expressed by the ancient Ethiopians and Egyptians.

During the famous Cairo International Colloquium organized by UNESCO in 1974, two prominent European Egyptologists had this to say as it regards the character of ancient Egyptian society:

- Professor Vercouter declared that in his opinion, Egypt was African in its writing, its culture and its way of thinking.
- Professor Leclant acknowledged the same African quality in the Egyptians' temperament and in their way of thinking[9]

Emile Amelineau (Coptologist, Archaeologist and Egyptologist), in the same spirit, writes:

> Egyptian cosmogonies are for the most part legends which resemble those of Uganda quite closely, with this difference: one senses that the Egyptians tried to grasp the intangible, that they wanted to achieve knowledge of the ultimate meaning of things... Egyptian ideas have an air of profound antiquity. No other people, apparently, could possess such a long historical consciousness.[10]

Gerald Massey asserts that the late explorer Dr. David Livingstone stated that "the typical negro found in Central Africa is to be seen in the ancient Egyptians, not in the native of the west coast" (Massey, 1975: 24). Sir. E. Wallis Budge, in his *Hieroglyphic Dictionary Vol. I,* provides one of the most insightful commentary on the difference in Egyptian thought with that of Europe and Asia. This not only includes the particular world-view, but the psychology of the language and its reflection in the *mdw nṯr* (hieroglyphic) writing script.

---

7 S. Sauneron, *Les pretres de l'ancienne Egypte* (Mo. 6 in the series "Le Temps Qui Court"), Seuil, Paris, 1957. p. 4.

8 Frederic Portal, *Des Couleurs symboliques dans l'Antiquite, le Moyen Age et les Temps moderns*, Editions de la Maisnie, Paris, 1979. p. 4.

9 Unesco, *Le peuplement de l'Egpte ancienne et le dechiffrement de l'ecriture meroitique*, Paris, Unesco, 1978. p. 87.

10 Emile Amelineau, *Prolegomenes a l'etude de la religion egyptienne*, Part Two, Ernest Leroux, Paris, 1916. p. 106.

> Now no one who has worked at Egyptian can possibly doubt that there are many Semitic words in the language, or that many of the pronouns, some of the numbers, and some of its grammatical forms resemble those found in the Semitic languages. But even admitting all the similarities that Erman has claimed, it is still impossible to me to believe that Egyptian is a Semitic language fundamentally. There is, it is true, much in the Pyramid Texts that recalls points and details of Semitic Grammar, but after deducting all the triliteral roots, there still remains a very large number of words that are not Semitic, and were never invented by a Semitic people. These words are monosyllabic, and were invented by one of the oldest African (or Hamitic, if that word be preferred) peoples in the Valley of the Nile of whose written language we have any remains. These are words used to express fundamental relationships and feelings, and beliefs which are peculiarly African and are foreign in every particular to Semitic peoples. The primitive home of the people who invented these words lay far to the south of Egypt, and all that we know of the Predynastic Egyptians suggests that it was in the neighbourhood of the Great Lakes, probably to the east of them. The whole length of the Valley of the Nile lay then, as now, open to peoples who dwelt to the west and east of it, and there must always have been a mingling of immigrants with its aboriginal inhabitants. These last borrowed many words from the newcomers, especially from the "proto-Semitic" peoples from the country now called Arabia, and from the dwellers in the lands between the Nile and the Red Sea and Indian Ocean, but they continued to use their native words to express their own primitive ideas, especially in respect of religious beliefs and ceremonies....As none of the literature of the peoples who lived on each side of the Valley of the Nile has been preserved, we have no means of finding out how much they borrowed linguistically from the Egyptians or the Egyptians from them, but I believe the Egyptians were as much indebted to them as to the Semites. I do not for Value of one moment suggest that such literature as the modern inhabitants of the Valley of the Nile and the neighbouring countries possess, dialects for whether it be those on the east or those on the west of the Nile, can be utilized for explaining ancient Egyptian texts, but the comparatively small amount of attention which I have been able to devote to the grammars and vocabularies of some of the languages now spoken in the Eastern Sudan has convinced me that they contain much that is useful for the study of the language of the hieroglyphs. The ancient Egyptians were Africans, and they spoke an African language, and the modern peoples of the Eastern Sudan are Africans, and they speak African languages, and there is in consequence much in modern native Sudani literature which will help the student of ancient Egyptian in his work. From the books of Tutschek, Krapf, Mitterutzner, and from the recently published works of Captain Owen and Westermann, a student with the necessary leisure can collect a large number of facts of importance for the comparative study of Nilotic languages both ancient and modern.[11]

Expanding beyond Egypt to the rest of Black Africa, we now look to some fundamental differences between the African and European worldview(s). In the book *Symposium of the Whole: A Range of Discourse Toward an Ethnopoetics* (1983), there is an excerpt by *Negritude* poet Leopold Sedar Senghor (pp. 119-120) that illuminate how we should approach the study of African languages and symbolism. The excerpt is from his work *Prose & Poetry* translated by John Reed and Clive Wakei (1976: 84-85). The title of the excerpt is *Speech and Image: An African Tradition of the Surreal.* I will quote at length:

> The African languages are characterized first of all by the richness of their vocabulary. There are sometimes twenty different words for an object according to its form, weight, volume and colour, and as many for an action according to whether it is single

11 E. A. Wallis Budge, *An Egyptian Hieroglyphic Dictionary Vol. I*, John Murray Publishers, London, 1920. pp. lxviii-lxx

> or repeated, weakly or intensely performed, just beginning or coming to an end. In Fulani, nouns are divided into twenty-one genders which are not related to sex. The classification is based sometimes on the meaning of the words or the phonetic qualities and sometimes on the grammatical category to which they belong. Most significant in this respect is the verb. On the same root in Wolof can be constructed more than twenty Verbs expressing different shades of meaning, and at least as many derivative nouns. While modern Indo-European languages emphasize the abstract notion of time, African languages emphasize the *aspect*, the concrete way in which the action of the verb takes place. These are essentially *concrete* languages. In them words are always pregnant with images. Under their value as signs, their sense value shows through.
>
> The African image is not then an image by equation but an image by analogy, a surrealist image. Africans do not like straight lines and false *mots justes* [correct words]. Two and two do not make four, but five, as Aime Cesaire has told us. The object does not mean what it represents but what it suggests, what it creates. The Elephant is Strength, the Spider is Prudence; Horns are the Moon and the Moon is Fecundity. Every representation is an image, and the image, I repeat, is not an equation but a symbol, an *ideogramme*.[12] Not only the figuration of the image but also its material... stone, earth, copper, gold, fibre—and also its line and colour. All language which does not tell a story bores them, or rather, Africans do not understand such language. The astonishment of the first Europeans when they found that the "natives" did not understand their pictures or even the logic of their arguments!
>
> I have spoken of the surrealist image. But as you would suppose, African surrealism is different from European surrealism. European surrealism is empirical, African surrealism is mystical and metaphysical. Andre Breton writes in Signe Ascendant: "The poetic analogy (meaning the European surrealist analogy) differs functionally from the mystical analogy in that it does not presuppose, beyond the visible world, an invisible world which is striving to manifest itself. It proceeds in a completely empirical way." In contrast, the African surrealist analogy presupposes and manifest the hierarchized universe of life-forces.[13] (emphasis mine)

Jordan Ngubane, in his book *A Conflict of Minds* (1979) cites the Rev. Sabelo Ntwasa's attack on the albification (the imposition of Caucasian values on the African) in the Christian church. Ntwasa suggest that:

> We must also remember that the individualistic approach of the missionaries is due to their having come from an individualistic society; hence their failure to understand our communal and man-centred society, which is the hallmark of the Black world. . . Blacks, therefore, with their tremendous sense of community in their culture, have the responsibility of building this into the very fabric of the life of the Church.

Again, the focus is on the apparent distinction between the cultural paradigms that dominate on the landmasses of Europe and that of the continent of Africa. Even in the nature of language we get a sense of the different approach to seeing the world. J. Torrend in his book *A Comparative*

12 An *ideogram* or *ideograph* (from Greek ἰδέα *idéa* "idea" + γράφωgráphō "to write") is a graphic symbol that represents an idea or concept. Some ideograms are comprehensible only by familiarity with prior convention; others convey their meaning through pictorial resemblance to a physical object, and thus may also be referred to as pictograms.

13 This excerpt is good information to keep in mind throughout this whole volume as it helps to explain why we must utilize African cultures and languages as resources for better understanding Egyptian and for better understanding the underlying philosophy that permeates throughout ancient Egyptian thought and expression.

Grammar of the South-African Bantu Languages (1891: 122)—as it regards the nature of Bantu locative classifiers and prepositions—notes the following:

> This is a subject which we must consider apart from European views concerning the cases of substantives[14] in general and locatives in particular, because they would be an obstacle to a correct perception of the Bantu mind. To explain myself when we say for instance, "It is dark in the house", "he lives above me", "he lives below me", etc, we are accustomed to consider the expression "in the house" as a locative which has no influence at all on the verb "it is dark"; and likewise the words "above, below are not substantives, but prepositions otherwise we should say "above of me, below of me", etc. On the contrary in the larger number of the Bantu languages such expressions as "in the house", "above", "below", etc., are substantives of the same type as those we have examined in the preceding articles, and require after them the same constructions as if we had "the-inside-of-the-house", "the-place-above", "the-place-below", etc. Thus we have in Tonga.
>
> Mu-*ganda* mu-*la-sia*, lit. "the-inside-of-the-house it-is dark," i.e., "it is dark in the house"
> U-*kede*ku-*tala*ku*angu*, lit. "he lives the-place-above that-of-me", i.e., "he lives above me"
> U-*kede*ku-*nsi*ku-*angu*, lit. "he lives the-place-down that-of-me", i.e., "he lives below me"

This is important to note as the way cultures phrase their sentences also speak to the underlying logic of their message. Dr. Kimbwandende Fu-Kiau provides us with another example of the importance of words to the interpretation of a phenomenon in the Bantu languages. In his work *African Cosmology of the Bantu Kongo* (2001: 69-70), he gives the following statement in regards to the Bantu-Kongo concept of "crime" and how the language is important to understanding their worldview.

> One talks about "committing a crime" in western judiciary language. But in most African cultures, and that of the Kongo in particular, one says "Natan'kanu," bearing a crime. One must discuss the contrast between these two concepts in order to more easily understand the African concept of crime. This distinction is basically linguistic-cultural. Understanding "les-jeux-des-mots" [the game of words], wordgames, is very important in any study of two or more distinct cultures. A wordgame is a key word to intellectual or scientific understanding. In English one "feels a pain"; in Kongolese (Kikongo), one "sees a pain,"[15] [mona mpasi]. When an Englishman "smokes a cigarette," a Mukongo will "drink a cigarette" [nwasaka/nsunga]. In English one "smells a certain perfume," the Mukongo will "hear it" [wansunga]. When western school defines man as "an intelligent animal, an imperial animal" or as a "toolmaker," as do the non-initiated African scholars, the westernized, i.e., the "kiyinga" in the African way of thinking; the "Nganga," the initiated African man in the African way of thinking, who is a specialist of perceiving the world's things, will, himself prefer to say that the human being is a system of systems [Muntu i kimpakia bimpa]. He is also variably called "n'kingu a n'kingu"—a principle of principles, i.e., the pattern of patterns. Because "muntu," the human being, is the key system of systems, he is able as such to produce materially and technologically other mechanical systems.

14 A *substantive* is a broad classification of words that includes nouns and nominals; *Grammar* denoting, relating to, or standing in place of a noun.

15 On page 116 of the same work, Fu-Kiau further clarifies, "There is a fundamental relationship between hearing, seeing and feeling/reacting [wa, mona ye sunsumuka]. Feeling is understanding. The Bantu do not "feel" pain, unless they "see" them [mona mpasi]."

If the scholastic material consistently informs us that there are very significant differences in the psychology, language, culture and world-view of the African and Indo-European people, then why do we rely on European methods and psychology to analyze and interpret ancient Egyptian cultural phenomena when the Egyptians are African people? The many misconceptions and resulting transubstantive errors concerning Egypt by Western scholars are due, in part, to the drastic differences between the two world-views and cultures (Diop 1991, Wobogo 1976, Thiong'o 1993).[16] To interpret Egyptian phenomena from the African perspective provides little to no difficulty for African researchers as these ancient expressions and ideas are present in the living traditions of Black African people.

The theoretical assumption here is that because the ancient Egyptian society arose out of the same speech and cultural communities as most of the rest of Black African societies, to better understand this ancient culture it would be most beneficial to examine the very cultures that the Egyptians share strong affinities with and use them as resource centers to better understand the Egyptian. This text employs an *African-Centered* approach to the study of ancient Egypt.

Toward an African-Centered Approach

Karenga (2006: 15) asserts that an African centered approach to the study and interpretation of ancient Egyptian culture offers a rich source of parallels and foci for comparative analysis, which have been consistently overlooked to the detriment of critical and comprehensive analysis. The *Afrocentric method* is derived from an Afrocentric paradigm, which deals with the question of African identity from the perspective of African people as centered, located, oriented and grounded. Such a paradigm, as applied to ancient Egyptian studies, recognizes and respects the geographical and cultural reality of Egypt in Africa and departs with the notion that somehow ancient Egypt was a West Asian country and enterprise.

When discussing ancient Egyptian culture, it is important to link it historically and culturally with other African societies. This is due, in part, because 1) it was an indigenous African society composed of African people, 2) it had trade relations with other African people for which this act of trading becomes the fertile ground for cultural and material exchange, and 3) its language is African and is related to such languages as Wolof (Diop 1977, 1991), Bantu (Obenga 1992, 1993, Bilolo 2010, 2011, Ndigi 2002), Kalenjiin (Sambu, 2008, 2011), Fulani (Lam, 1994) and Yorùbá (Oduyoye, 1984, 1996). But with all comparative work, one must caution against drawing unnecessary conclusions concerning relationships between cultures that exist in far reaching geographical spaces and in vastly different time periods. We must not confuse relationship with parallels; parallels with origins.

There are five fundamental characteristics of the Afrocentric method. They are as follows:

1. The Afrocentric method considers that no phenomena can be apprehended adequately without locating it first. A *phenom* must be studied and analyzed in relationship to psychological time and space. It must always be located. This is the only way to investigate the complex interrelationships of science and art, design and execution, creation and maintenance, generation and tradition, and other areas bypassed by theory.

2. The Afrocentric method considers phenomena to be diverse, dynamic, and in motion and therefore it is necessary for a person to accurately note and record the location of phenomena even in the midst of fluctuations. This means that the investigator must know where he or she is standing in the process.

16 This subject will be fully explored in my upcoming work *Religious Proselytization as a Form of Violence: Infringement of the African Concept of Simultaneous Validity* (forthcoming).

3. The Afrocentric method is a form of cultural criticism that examines etymological uses of words and terms in order to know the source of an author's location. This allows us to intersect ideas with actions and actions with ideas on the basis of what is pejorative and ineffective and what is creative and transformative at the political and economic levels.

4. The Afrocentric method seeks to uncover the masks behind the rhetoric of power, privilege, and position in order to establish how principal myths create place. The method enthrones critical reflection that reveals the perception of monolithic power as nothing but the projection of a cadre of adventurers.

5. The Afrocentric method locates the imaginative structure of a system of economics, bureau of politics, policy of government, expression of cultural form in the attitude, direction, and language of the phenom, be it text, institution, personality, interaction, or event[17]

Queeneth Mkabela, in her article "Using the Afrocentric method in researching indigenous African culture" (2005: 178), asks the questions, "How can the Afrocentric method as advanced by Asante (1987, 1988, 1990, 1995) be used in researching African indigenous culture and can African research refrain from sticking to the pathways mapped out by the colonial or neo-colonial experts?" These are very important questions, which can be directed towards ancient Egypt as an indigenous African culture; thus inviting a methodology that allows us to accurately represent the culture.

The issues concerning ancient Egypt are compounded by several factors. The first is that the state of ancient Egypt is no longer a living reality in that location: it is currently governed by Arabs who migrated from Arabia and whose cultural paradigm is Islam. It has been that way since the year 642 AD. As a result, the ancient Egyptian language (*tshiKam*) is no longer spoken in this area as it has been replaced with Arabic. This poses a problem for researchers because one cannot simply go to Egypt currently and ask native Egyptians information about the meaning of the ancient symbols and the proper pronunciation of the words associated with these concepts carved in stone. This is exacerbated by that fact that the records that are left by the indigenous Egyptians did not employ vowels for vocalization. Only during the Greek invasion, with the development of the Coptic script, were vowels integrated into the system. But by this time there was significant change in the language and we don't know how previous invasions by foreign powers and migrations affected the language through contact.[18]

Because of the loss of sovereignty, starting with the invasion of the Hyksos and later with the Persians, Assyrians, Greeks, Romans, British and Arabs, the culture of Egypt has drastically changed and has lost, in many respects, much of its African character. It has now been replaced with cultures that developed outside of the African cultural, social and historical experiences. This is why we look to modern Black African cultures to provide us with the cultural keys that will allow us to unlock the hidden mysteries of ancient Egyptian thought and philosophy. Using

---

17 Molefi Kete Asante "Afrocentricity" :http://www.asante.net/articles/1/afrocentricity/ (retrieved May 26, 2013)

18 See Sarah Grey Thomason & Terrence Kaufman (1988) *Language Contact, Creolization and Genetic Linguistics* (University of California Press. Berkeley and Los Angeles, CA); Also, Bernd Heine & Tania Kuteva (2004). *Language Contact and Grammatical Change* (Cambridge University Press. Cambridge, New York, Melbourne, Madrid, Cape Town, Singapore, Sao Paulo) for issues concerning language contact and its possible effects on language change. See also essays in the *Journal of Language Contact: Evolution of languages, contact and discourse*, Brill Publications. http://cgi.server.uni-frankfurt.de/fb09/ifas/JLCCMS/ (retrieved May 31, 2013).

a *locational theoretical model*[19] (Bekerie, 1997: 12-18) we locate ourselves in the rich soils of mother Africa and center ourselves in the whole of the Nile-Valley so we are properly oriented in our line of questioning and centered in ourselves as agents of our own history. We will operate from the inside out, instead of by the traditional model that operates from the outside in.

Methodology

This study employs various methods to articulate both deconstructive and reconstructive approaches. As this work primarily deals with concepts as expressed in the lexical inventory of ancient Egypt, the primary tool of analysis will be historical comparative linguistics and philology. As noted previously, the linguistic affinities have already been established by numerous scholars (named and unnamed), so demonstrating the relatedness of Egyptian to other Black African languages is unnecessary here: it is part of the overall assumptions. I will also utilize various tools in the fields of comparative religion, mythology and cultural anthropology. This will provide symmetry to the findings we discover through the linguistic analyses.

As a first step in my analysis, I explore and examine modern African languages for cognate terms for the Egyptian concepts under investigation. This ensures that we are on solid grounds by which to go further and seek cultural connections between the various African centers of wisdom. Although I rely on modern renditions of vocabulary shared between Egyptian and Black African languages, I also utilize reconstructed forms to reduce the off-hand dismissal of the proposed shared cognates as "chance coincidence."

The vast majority of the Kongo-Saharan reconstructions derive from Campbell-Dunn (2009a, 2009b; one can check his sources in those texts for the reconstructions). The Proto-Bantu reconstructions derive from the *Bantu Lexical Reconstruction* (BLR3) online database.[20] The Afro-Asiatic reconstructions derive from the *Tower of Babel* (TOB) online dictionary. The Kalenjiin language vocabulary will come from the *Kalenjiin Online Dictionary*.[21] The ciLuba-Bantu terms derive from the *Ciluba Research Center for African Languages* online database.[22] The primary source for the Egyptian terms derives from the *Mark Vygus Egyptian Dictionary* (2012). Any other sources will be specifically cited in the text.

To gain better insight into indigenous pre-Western African cultures, I have also engaged in dialogues of mutual enrichment with knowledge-holders of various African traditions. I have also engaged in dialogues of mutual enrichment with scholar-initiates[23] who are doing cutting-edge research in the field of Africology. These scholars are primary resources for better understanding pre-Western modes of thought and being. They have the distinctive advantage of also being trained in Western academies. Many of these scholars have also done their own comparative work and they have been most helpful in these current explorations. Initiated scholars provide valuable insights, which are not available to the scholar who is not steeped and invested in the culture(s) under examination.

I view studies written by initiated scholars of greater methodological usefulness than those by anthropologists who are not a part of the tradition. The initiated scholar writes from the perspective of an insider of the culture. Many researchers have been labeled 'experts' in the

19 This, in short, refers to the study of African peoples and their philosophy of life from their origin, grounded in their diversity and creativity. It is a means that places or locates African people in their own center stage.

20 Currently located here: http://www.africamuseum.be/collections/browsecollections/humansciences/blr

21 http://www.africanlanguages.com/kalenjin/

22 http://www.ciyem.ugent.be/

23 Scholars who have been formally initiated into African ways of being and culture.

academy as it regards the study of a group of people and have only spent a small amount of time with the people (if any time at all). For our research, no one is going to be more of an expert on a people and a tradition than the people themselves who live the tradition. Also, much information is not given to outsiders and much of the information given to anthropologists may be unreliable (which also fuels the distortion). Initiated elders do not give freely that which you have not earned the right to know (as tested through initiation).[24]

Throughout this text I have used the Tshiluba-Bantu language and culture as a sort of control group when comparing the *r n km.t* (language of ciKam - ) with other African languages. I found inspiration to go in this direction by examining the works of Dr. Mubabinge Bilolo. In his book titled *Invisibilité et Immanence du Créateur Imn (Amon-Amun-Amen-Iman-Zimin): Exemple de la Vitalité de l'Ancien Égyptien ou CiKam dans le CyenaNtu* (2010: 18), he claims that:

> Chemin faisant, donc après la traduction systématique de quelques lettres, j'avais constaté que le vocabulaire ciLuba était presqu'à 85% identique au vocabulaire de ciKam antique et que presque la totalité des concepts majeurs sont encore en usage jusqu'à ce jour. En outre, j'avais découvert que certaines règles grammaticales devraient être revues. La transcription et la lecture de beaucoup de mots sont très problématiques. Mieux vaut y aller tout doucement que de prolonger les conventions problématiques de lecture et de transcription. Un doute méthodologique m'accompagne et m'oblige de revoir signe par signe.
>
> Along the way [in his research], after the systematic translation of some of the letters, I found that the Ciluba vocabulary was almost 85% identical to the vocabulary of ancient ciKam [Egypt/km.t] and that almost all of the major concepts are still in use to this day. In addition, I discovered that certain grammatical rules should be reviewed. The transcription and reading of many words are very problematic. [It is] better to go slowly than to prolong the problematic conventional reading and transcription(s) [of the Egyptian writing script]. A methodological doubt is with me and forces me to do a sign by sign review. [my translation]

Employing a research method using Tshiluba as a control, I have since been able to verify the claims made in this text (and others). Prior to my knowledge of Tshiluba, I would often compare Egyptian with Kikongo and IsiZulu. So I was already on a firm Bantu foundation. I still use these languages for comparisons with Egyptian, but I have found better answers to certain Egyptian conundrums using the Tshiluba-Bantu language. I contend this is so because Tshiluba is one of the more conservative Bantu languages[25] and retains much of the old proto-Bantu features. As a procedure I like to cross-check my findings in Tshiluba with the Yorùbá

24 Hermstein (2012) and Scranton (2006) does an excellent job, in my opinion, in demonstrating the limitations of anthropological research conducted by outsiders in the case of Walter Van Bleek and the Dogon people of Mali. Van Bleek was very dismissive of Marcel Griaule & Germain Dieterlen (1986) and accused them of fabricating data because he (Van Bleek) was unable to extract the same sacred information from the Dogon as Griaule and Dieterlen were able to. Van Bleek could not get the same information from the Dogon because he was not initiated into Dogon culture. Griaule got access to the deeper meanings of Dogon lore only after approximately 16 years of being around the Dogon and fighting the French on their behalf. Van Bleek never gained the trust of the Dogon as he was not initiated into their culture. Therefore, he was unable to reduplicate the findings of Griaule and Dieterlen because he was an outsider. This demonstrates the importance and value of the insider who can provide more accurate information on a particular cultural world-view.

25 See for instance Gloria Cocchi, "Locative Constructions in Bantu." In *Quaderni del Dipartimento di Linguistica* - Università di Firenze 10 (2000): 43-54.

(Niger-Congo) and Kalenjiin (Nilo-Saharan) languages. You will find many comparisons in these texts with these two groups. These two languages, for me, verify the grammatical features that are often fossilized in Egyptian.

Bilolo's method is to use a single language to do comparisons with Egyptian. I prefer to use one language as a primary, and then others and reconstructed forms for added insight. Much of the details and nuances can be missed by multiple language comparisons *en masse*. Many researchers miss insights into the language and the deeper meaning of concepts because they do not concentrate on one language and they very seldom, if ever, search for the synonyms of these terms in the respective language. "The advantage is that a synonym sometimes reveals some better graphs of the ciKam script" (Bilolo, 2010: 29). In other words, a synonym of a cognate term from the living language (which may also be found in the ancient) may reveal something missed as a result of convention, which was created during the colonial period and by researchers who first assumed that the Egyptian language and writing script was an Asian enterprise.

Much of the sacred writing script is symbolic and hides a deeper meaning than what is first suggested in the narratives and assertions in the text (Karenga 2006, Bilolo 1986, Obenga 2004). This is why we look to modern African languages to observe how the people utilize the cognate terms in everyday life in order to gain insight into the ancient phenomenon as expressed in the Egyptian writing script (*mdw nṯr*). As I (2008, 2011) and other African researchers have noted, the traditional way of transcribing the glyphs, and its subsequent grammar are paralyzing to the advancement of research and creativity.[26] In many people's eyes the hieroglyphs have revealed all that they can reveal. This is not the mindset of the African researcher who understands that we've only just scratched the surface. But as long as we continue to use European logic and approaches to *mdw nṯr*, we will always be in a box that we cannot get out of and we will never get to the core of how the script actually functioned. Only the natural, cultural and linguistic richness of Africa will help reveal the mysteries embedded in this writing script.

When the Baluba of Congo sees an Egyptian sign, they do not have go through a modern Egyptian language dictionary to find the words for them. All they have to do is access their ancestral memory bank alive in their language. The thesis of Bilolo is that a Luba child, who has spent ten years in the village, can name most of the signs and develop a list of words without any knowledge of Egyptology. This is because, again, the lexical and cultural inventory is already present in their everyday lives. *Table 1* below provides an example of what we mean.

Table 1:[27]

Glyph	ciKam	ciLuba
	*Kʿp, kp*	Kapia; Kam(onyi)
	*ḫt, sḏt; rkh; tȝ; psi; ȝbw; tkȝ; srf, psi<fš(i)*	Ta, oTa, yoTo>Ḫiota; Hyoto; Ciota; Kota; Ket(a,e); ciPisha; mPisha, Tuka; nTooka; nKang; Lukang; Lukeka; Lukekesh; Lakuka; Kalanga (rkh>krh); Kangila (khr); Aba; ci-Aba; -abw>Baba, Boba, Buba (w>b)
	*nsrsr, nšršr*	Nsonsol, noshel, nosheshel; Losheshel(a,e); Shila

26 See the discussion in "Introduction On Egyptology Seminary" by the eminent Cameroonian Egyptologist and linguist Dr. Dou Kaya on his website: http://doukaya.over-blog.com/ (retrieved May 29, 2013)

27 Kalamba and Bilolo (2010: 118-119).

	*šntr; bꜣ*	Ntole-Ntole, Ntola-ntola; Ntolesh; Ba, Bwa, Kam(onyi), Kam (onyia); Sundula, Sentedi
	*ḏꜣ; wḏꜣ*	Endu, Inda, Ndu> mw-Endu; mw-Inda;,Tumba; Banda (w>b); Undu>m
	*tꜥ; h̲t*	Ta, Ota; Cioto; Kioto; Kota; Twa; Cianga
	*ꜣh̲; ꜣh̲ꜣh̲*	Kank(a,u), Kanga; Kangala (dikangala); Kenke; Keka; ci-Minyi, ci-Munyi; ci-Keka, diAnga (*ꜣh̲.t*)
	*bꜣ*	Buta, (lu-, ka-)Buta. Nyunyi wa Bwa-Bwa-Bwa; Ba (ka-Ba ka nyunyi; mu-Ba; bu-Ba); La-Ba; Bemba; Owa>Cyoa
	*wbn, ꜣh̲w, psḏ*	Ubala; ubanda; banda; anga; wang, wenga
	*Rꜥ; hrw; ššw; ìtn*	Lo(u,a,i)>Li-L(u,o)>DiLu, Di-Lo, Ri-Ro; u-Lilu; Li-Ba>Di-Ba; Kulu; Sese; Shosha; Tanya; Tanga

The African researcher should not be bound by the limits of European paradigms. The vast majority of the research dollars may currently be in the hands of the European schools, but the African school still has the cultural advantage which allows the one properly trained in research methodology, and initiated into African cultural world-views, to provide better insights into the Egyptian world whereas the outsider cannot. The African researcher must utilize his/her culture, traditions, training and creativity to unlock what has been hidden or obscured due to European and Asian colonialism, and a disdain for African culture which has often introduced bias into research methods and writings.

The Afrocentric method suggests cultural and social immersion as opposed to scientific distance as the best approach to understanding African phenomena (Mkabela, 2005: 179). In this regard, I also draw on my own experiences as a student and practitioner of the Yorùbá system of Ifa to provide additional insight into cultural parallels with the ancient Egyptian. There are many parallels in the Yorùbá and the ancient Egyptian religious traditions. The Yorùbá culture is a valuable resource for expanding our understanding as it regards current African spiritual discourses: e.g., in the practice of installing the king. Many of the families in Nigeria, in their oral traditions, trace their lineage back to the Nile Valley. Research conducted by myself and the likes of Oduyoye (1984, 1996) and Campbell-Dunn (2006, 2008) would imply that these oral traditions are in fact plausible and true.

And lastly, while part of my analysis of the various topics of this volume will be concerned with deconstruction, a major segment of these examinations will be focused on creative reconstruction of the meanings of Ancient Egyptian motifs and ethos. This effort in reconstruction is not done arbitrarily, but is grounded in comparative linguistic methods that allow for us to find the same or similar concepts in living African languages and to use these living concepts as conceptual grounds for interpreting ancient Egyptian thought and praxis. Of course primary Egyptian texts must be consulted to give context and support for the comparisons.

Overview

The essays collected in this volume were written at different time periods over the last couple of years and though they have now been compiled into one volume, they are not meant to be considered as a single narrative. As a result, one might note that many concepts and items are repetitive throughout the different essays. However, because the topics and the information contained within these essays seemingly overlap with each other in terms of scope and application, I found it beneficial to bring them together in one volume so that the reader may get the most out of them.[28] I found that questions left unanswered in one text would be answered in another in an unrelated topic. Instead of referring to the loose articles, it was best to compile them here. However, not all of the essays included in this volume were written and released prior to this publication. Chapters 1, 2 and 8 were written specifically for this volume.[29]

Chapters 1 and **2**: *Did the God Ra Derive from Arabia? An examination of Wesley Muhammad's claim in Black Arabia and the African Origin of Islam*—are concerned with an argument that Wesley Muhammad advanced in his 2009 book *Black Arabia and the African Origins of Islam*. He asserts that the ancient Egyptian god Ra was an import into Egypt from an anonymous group of Black Semites from Arabia (what he calls Afrabia). He also claims that the god Ra is an Egyptionized version of the Semitic god Allah. *Part I* of this series takes a critical look at Muhammad's thesis by first examining and tracing the origins of the god Ra of ancient Egypt. *Part II* in this series is focused on the definition and origins of the god Allah among the Semites. The details from both essays are considered and a conclusion is posited in *Part II* of the series.

Chapter 3: *African Origins of the Word God*. This, in many respects, is a continuation of the first two chapters. This essay takes a fresh look at the question of the origins of the word "god" in the English language. I posit that this term is actually African and was inherited into the Proto-Indo-European language.

Chapter 4: *Understanding Àṣẹ and its Relation to Èṣù among the Yorùbá and ꜣst in Ancient Egypt*, explores the relationship between the Yorùbá concept of *Àṣẹ* and its relationship to leadership and good governance. The assertion advanced here is that this term is at the heart of the names for *Èṣù* among the Yorùbá and *ꜣst*/*Wsr* (Isis and Osiris) among the ancient Egyptians. By understanding the Yorùbá concept of *àṣẹ*, we can better understand the function and role of *ꜣst* and *Wsr* in the ancient Egyptian tradition.

The *Reinterpretation of the Word Ankh*, Parts I and II make up **Chapters 5** and **6** respectively. These essays are concerned with a reevaluation of what the word *ꜥnḫ* means in Egyptian anthropology and how it is applied in the Egyptian context. *Part I* focuses on the etymology of the word itself and *Part II* is concerned with the inspiration behind the *ꜥnḫ* symbol. As can be expected, African languages are consulted to expand our conceptualization of this very recognizable concept and symbol.

Chapter 7: *Reevaluation of the Word Hotep*. This chapter examines with greater scrutiny the ancient Egyptian concept of *ḥtp* "peace," commonly vocalized as *hotep*, and its many applications. By comparing the Egyptian with the Tshiluba-Bantu and Kalenjiin languages, we get a more expansive understanding of the concept.

Chapter 8: *Tying Knotty Ropes as a Way of Knowing in Ancient Egyptian* is the final chapter and it is concerned with the ancient Egyptian concept of *knowing* and its possible traces to a prehistoric notion of tying "ropes." In some unrelated studies I noticed that many of the ancient Egyptian words for "writing" carried with them determinative signs of knotted ropes or strings. The same thing holds true for words dealing with "knowledge" and I wanted to know how the sign for "ropes" was connected, in any way, with words having to do with "knowledge" and "writing." I immediately recalled a similar connection among the Bantu-Kongo of central Africa and after comparing the cultural themes between the two groups and languages, it inspired me to examine this relationship further and expand my research

28 It also makes it easier to reference the material when one can see the discussions side-by-side to better understand the interrelatedness and parallels of the themes examined in the texts.

29 Note also that the footnotes for items in tables are given at the end of each article and they have their own reference numbers separate from the ones at the bottom of each page.

parameters. This chapter contains my preliminary results.

DID THE GOD RA DERIVE FROM ARABIA?

An examination of Wesley Muhammad's claim in Black Arabia and the African Origin of Islam

This essay takes a critical look at the possible origins of the god *Rʿ* in the ancient Egyptian spiritual tradition. It also takes a critical look at the claim by Wesley Muhammad (2009) that the god *Rʿ* is 1) really the Semitic god *Allah* (P.Sm. *ʾḷ*) and 2) *Rʿ* was imported into Egypt from Arabia by Black Semites. Based on anthropological research and comparative linguistic data from across the continent of Africa, it is this author's contention that both of these statements cannot be substantiated by the evidence and that *Rʿ* was an indigenous name and concept of the Egyptian people. In Part I of this series we will focus on the dynamics and history of *Rʿ* as expressed by the Egyptians, as well as other African people. In Part II of this series we will research the origins and meanings of the name *Allah* and we will combine our research from both essays to come to a more definitive conclusion in regards to the origins of *Rʿ* and *Allah* historically.

Major points of disagreement

Muhammad's overall hypothesis (2009: 114) is that: "The sun-god of Egypt is an eastern deity [read Arabian] with a Semitic name." The following are some major points of contention I have with Wesley Muhammad's thesis in *Black Arabia.*

- **Issue 1:** Does not point to where exactly this "deity" came from or provide an explanatory thesis for how it entered Egypt. Moreover, he doesn't explain why native Egyptians would adopt a foreign deity and make it its most senior god.
- **Issue 2:** Doesn't provide lexical data to support his claim. We know in Egyptian the word *Rʿ* is used for the anthropromorphic conceptualization of the Divine, and it is the name for "sun, day" in the Egyptian language. Was this the case among Semitic speakers? In other words, does Ra = Sun in Semitic? His conclusion is based on the similarities of phones that make up the lexical unit, but he doesn't provide shared homonyms to establish the relationship, nor does he provide the original term for which was used to define the Divine in Egyptian that was replaced with *Allah* from the Semites. In other words, his proposed cognates do not stand on two legs: *form* and *meaning*.
- **Issue 3:** His association of Ta-Neter (*tȝ-nṯr*) with Arabia.
- **Issue 4:** The Semitic exclusivity of Allah. Muhammad presents the data in regards to *Allah* as if *Allah* (*ʾḷ*) was 1) a Semitic invention and 2) exclusive to Semitic people. As we will see throughout this presentation, this root is all over Africa and older than the Afro-Asiatic language family: it is in fact a global root and cannot be the exclusive domain of the Semitic speakers.

The first two issues will be addressed in this essay. Issue four will be addressed in Part II which focuses on the origins of the god *Allah*.

Much of Muhammad's argument is based on the notion that *Allah* is best represented by the articulations of cultures that lived in pre-Islamic southern Arabia. Muhammad (2009: 84) argues that the goddess *Shams* (P.Sm **šmš* "sun") was an import into Southern Arabia from Mesopotamia along with other "nature" gods which disrupted the historical associations of the Divine. He doesn't, however, argue that there was a sun-god by the name of *Allah* in Southern Arabia and it appears that sun-worship, according to Muhammad, was introduced into Southern

Arabia by Mesopotamian immigrants. In other words, Muhammad doesn't argue that *Allah* the sun-god was replaced by *Shams* the sun-goddess. There is no claim for an Arabian sun-god by the name of *Allah*. This is going to be very important to note later on in our discourse.

In this series we argue that the so-called "sun-god" of Egypt is actually a crystallization of concepts that are brought together by reason of perceived commonalities in conceptualizations and similarities in pronunciations for the concepts being crystallized. In linguistics we call this process *paronymy,* "A word linked to another by similarity of form." Although the most elevated symbol of *Rᶜ* is the sun, we will discover that the focus has never been the sun at all, but a different idea for which the Egyptians used many symbols to convey. This *Deitic Polysemy*[1] is quite common in Egyptian theology and is a practice that is wide-spread across the continent of Africa.

The Egyptian writing is in the typical Kongo-Saharan thinking (like Sumerian) which uses the *rebus principle* to maximize usage of common terms that sound alike. A common example usually given in literature to explain the rebus principle is presented below:

> "To name one custom, the Yorùbá of Africa have always used pebbles as indexical symbols; these could even assume homophonic value (an important component of some phonetic writing), whereby one word sounds identical to another with a different meaning. To arrange a tryst, for example, A Yorùbá man would leave six pebbles for a woman to find - Yorùbá *efa*, or 'six', also means 'attracted'. If the woman was willing, she left eight pebbles as an answer: Yorùbá *eyo*, or 'eight', also means 'agreed'." *History of Writing* by Steven Roger Fisher, Reaktion Books (2001: 21)

This practice among the Ancient Egyptians is acknowledged by other prominent Egyptologists. The great Egyptologist Serge Sauneron highlights this feature of Egyptian linguistic "punning" in his work *The Priest of Ancient Egypt* (2000:125-127):

> The Egyptians never considered their language – that corresponding to the hieroglyphs – as a social tool; for them, it always remained a resonant echo of the vital energy that had brought the universe to light, a cosmic force. Thus study of this language enabled them **to "explain" the cosmos.**
>
> It was word-play that served as the means of making these explanations. The moment one understands that **words are intimately linked to the essences of the beings or objects they indicate,** resemblances between words cannot be fortuitous; they express a natural relationship, a subtle connection that priestly erudition would have to define...
>
> This practice can seem childish and anything but serious. Yet its logic emerges if we try to understand the value the Egyptians placed on the pronunciation of words. **Any superficial resemblance between two words was understood as conveying a direct connection between the two entities invoked.** It thus became a general practice, employed in all periods and in all areas of inquiry, and in priestly lore it was the basic technique for explaining proper nouns, essentially the very means of defining the nature of the deities. This was the case with Amun, the great patron of Thebes. We do not know just what his name meant, but it was pronounced like another word meaning "to be hidden," and the scribes played on this resemblance to define Amun as the great god who hid his real appearance from his children...**The mere similarity of the sounds of the two words was enough to arouse a suspicion on the part of the**

1 The *Theory of Deitic Polysemy* is an interpretational framework and method designed to properly deconstruct, educe and explicate the meaning and purpose behind the characters in African myths and spiritual traditions based on a traditional praxis of synthesizing (linguistically) similarly pronounced lexemes into a singular representative we call a "deity."

> **priests that there was some close relationship between them,** and to find in it an explanation of the god's name: "thus addressing the primordial god…as an invisible and hidden being, they invite him and exhort, calling him Amun, to show and reveal himself."[2] (emphasis mine)

With such simplistic elegance, Sauneron provides the framework for a better understanding of the nature of Egyptian deities. The truth to his statements will be made more apparent to the reader by the end of this essay. Before there is deification, there is experience. Deification of *people, objects, actions* and *ideas* happen after a people has had some experience in the real world with these concepts within their own cultural framework.

The names of the deities come directly from the objects or concepts themselves. For instance, the Yorùbá "god" *Èṣú* is, in part, the deity of "rulership, kingship, authority and power." This is because the name is a by-form of the word *àṣẹ* which means "authority, power, law, work, etc." Deification helps to keep important concepts in the public memory. Myths serve as cultural encyclopedias which creatively articulate important themes in ways that allow for easy reference of the concepts. The name for all deities are in reality simply epithets, descriptive adjectives that describe an important feature of the Divine.

Epithets outline a deity's character, describe his/her physical appearance and attributes and give information about the cult. In his essay "Epithets, Divine" (2011),[3] Dagmar Budde discusses, in-depth, the nature of ancient Egyptian epithets for the Divine. Budde classifies Egyptian epithets into three domains: 1) nature and function, 2) iconography (physical characteristics, posture, and attributes), and 3) provenance and local worship; to which can be added the following subdomains: 4) genealogy, 5) status and age, and 6) myths and cosmogonies. The domains that will concern us in this discourse are *iconography* and *status and age*. It is from these two domains for which we argue *Rᶜ* and *Allah* get their names.

Nature and function. Here, a deity's *nature* can be expressed in his/her name: e.g., *'Imn* "the hidden/secret one"; *ḫns* "the traveler"; and *sḫmt* "the mighty one." Epithets, however, provide more information about its character and spheres of influence. When a people formalize epithets for the Divine, they create an ideal image of humans and project it on the world of the gods. As John S. Mbiti notes in his *African Religions & Philosophy* (1989: 50):

> It is to be noted also that ultimately everything we say about God is in one way or another anthropomorphic, since it is expressed in human terms and human thought forms. Man does not know the language by which God describes Himself. Whatever mental picture we make of God, it is at best a human image.

Epithets, therefore, can refer to human traits like "wisdom, friendliness, honesty, and a sense of justice." Further themes articulate the Divine's ability to change shape, to regenerate, and to create as well as physical strengths and weaknesses, freedom of movement and the closeness to humans.[4] This is illustrated by the following: *Rᶜ* is the "Lord of rays" (*nb-ḫḏdwt*); in his role of moon deity, Khons appears as he "Who repeats rejuvenation" (*wḥm-rnp*). Osiris, as the dying and eternally reborn spirit, was worshipped as "Lord of Life" (*nb-ᶜnḫ*; ciLuba *Bwena-Anga*).

Status and age. With adjectives like "great," "small," and "first" (*wr/t, ᶜ3/t, nḏs/t, šrj/t,*

2 We also note that the word *jmn* in Egyptian can mean "create." Thus *jmn* "hidden" and *jmn* "create" combine to give us the deity *'Imn* who is at once the hidden power behind all things and the creative agent behind all evolutions.

3 Dagmar Budde, 2011, "Epithets, Divine." In: Jacco Dieleman, Willeke Wendrich (Eds.) *UCLA Encyclopedia of Egyptology*, Los Angeles, CA. http://digital2.library.ucla.edu/viewItem.do?ark=21198/zz0028t1z4

4 C.f. Otto, Eberhard. (1964). *Gotta und Mensch nach den agyptishen Templinschriften der griechish-romischen Zeit*. Heidelberg: C. Winter. pp. 11-40.

tpj/t), epithets can indicate the status of a deity or his/her position within a hierarchy. Many label the Divine as "unique" (*wˁ/t*), while others distinguish the Divine with formulations such as, "Whose like does not exist (among the gods)" (*jwtj-sn.nw.f/.s, jwtj-mjtt.f/.s, n-wnn-mjtt.f, nn-ḫr-ḫw.s-m-nṯrw*) and "Beyond whom nobody exists" (*jwtj-m33-ḥrj-tp.f/.s*). These epithets are rooted in metaphor, more specifically ones with spatial dimensions and will be discussed in-depth in *Part II*. The epithet can also establish a relationship with a comparative construction like, "Who is greater than all other gods" (*wr-r-nṯrw-nbw*). Belonging to this category are epithets regarding "age" such as: "Small child" (*ẖrd-nḫn*) and "Eldest one" (*j3w/smsw*).

I argue in this essay that the name *Rˁ* is not a generic name for "god" as proposed by Muhammad (2009), but is a personification of abstract concepts which are symbolized by concrete realities as metaphors. I argue here that *Rˁ* represents three (3) major concepts primarily: wisdom/knowledge, creation and the force of change (time) in the universe. The association between *Rˁ* and creation is well attested in other works. But not much is written concerning *Rˁ* as a source of knowledge and the very cause of time itself. These themes we will explore in this essay.

Ra as a Source of Knowledge

"Knowledge" is conceptually associated in many world languages with being able to "see." For instance, a word in the French language for "to know, knowledge" is *savoir*. The root of this word is *voir* "to see." This root is also present in the word *apercevoir* "see, perceive, observe, notice." By way of metaphor, "light" is also associated with "knowledge" and "wisdom." This is why in English, when we have an epiphany, a "bright light turns on" in our heads. *Light* becomes a symbol for *awareness* as light allows us to actually *see* the phenomena around us. We become conscious of things due to the presence of light in the physical world.

When you have knowledge of something, it is as if *light* is being shed on the matter. When you are ignorant of something, it is if you were being kept in the *dark* (where you cannot *see*). A few English statements will *illuminate* this point for us:

- Allow me to **shed/throw some light** on the matter.
- Can you **enlighten** me as to what your intentions are?
- There are a couple of points that I'd like you to **clear up**.
- He kept us **in the dark** about his plans.
- I haven't got the **foggiest/faintest** idea.

It is my argument that these types of metaphoric extensions are present in the Egyptian language, and more so in reference to the god *Rˁ*. What we will often see in African languages is that the same words for "fire, sun and vision" are often represented by the same consonant root. For instance, in the ciLuba-Bantu language we have the consonant cluster *m-n* in association with *light*: *munya* "shine", *muunya* "sun, heat of the sun, light, day" *mwinya* "same as *muunya*," *cimunyi* "light", *mwndu* "lamp". This same *m-n* cluster can be seen in the following terms dealing with "vision."

> *-mòna* "see, perceive, feel, experience, experiment, have, in possession of"; *bumònyi(u)* "act, see, testimony"; *cimwènenu* "representation, spectacle"; *cimwènu* "control by sight, by observing, visible sign, purpose, intent"; *dimòna* "act, see, vision,

show"; *-dìmwèna* "see for yourself, see by yourself"; *kadìmòna* "mirror" [see one's reflection]; *kamònyì kàà dîsu* "pupil of the eye"; *lumòno(u)* "sense of sight, views"; *lumònyi* "apple of the eye"; *-à/-a lumònyi* "worth seeing, luxurious"; *lumwènu* "mirror, glass"; *mumònyi* "a seer, witness, one who owns property."

As we can see here in Tshiluba, the *m-n* root is used for "the sun, day, the heat of day, light, a lamp and to shine." But this same root is used for words dealing with "sight, perception, witnessing, seeing, acting, possession, observation and testimony."[5] It is the phenomenon of light that allows us to perceive any reality; and it is this natural fact that we argue is being articulated by the ancient Egyptians when they invoke the name of the god *Rʿ*, who for the Egyptians was that Divine spirit which "reveals" that which was unknown. The *m-n* root may be a serial noun. The *m* morpheme may derive from *b* and the *n* from *l* [m<b<p; n<l] from an original root: **pVl* "fire, light."

<u>FIRE</u> Sumerian *ne-mur* "fire"

NA "fire"
MU "fire" -r

PWS *ná* "fire", Kebu *ná-wo* "fire" Sumerian *bún* "lamp"
PWN *MUAL* "to shine"
Atlantic *na, nak* "sun, day" (Westermann 1928 : 85 – 86) [Arabic *nar* "fire"]
PWN *PHI* "burn" (fire)
Bantu *pía* "fire"
"Bantu" *–ωmu* "fire" (195), but *bu, bi* (259, 267, 187, 184, *buri* 121, 222 etc), without nasalisation of *b* to *m.*
Mande *mana* "fire"
Mande *wumbe* "fire"
Mangbetu *mudé* "heat"
PCS **pVl, *pVr* "light"

*N = n *A = e *B = m *U = u

The *m-n* root is an ancient root and can be seen in these words dealing with "knowledge" (a byproduct of vision, witnessing, etc.) from the TOB database:

Proto-Afro-Asiatic: *(ʔV-)*mVn-*
Meaning: know, test
Semitic: **mVnVw-* 'count; test, try' ~ **ʔVmVn-* 'be certain, believe'
Western Chadic: **man-* 'know'
Central Chadic: **ma/un-* 'analyze' 1, 'understand' 2 ,'surely' 3
East Chadic: **min-* 'warn'
Central Cushitic (Agaw): **ʔamVn-* 'believe' (?)
Low East Cushitic: **man-* 'mind'
Warazi (Dullay): **Hemen-*

5 We witness a similar phenomenon in Tshiluba with another cognate term for *sun* in the Egyptian language: Egyptian *ššw, šw* "sun, sunlight", *šw* "the empty eye"; Tshiluba *sese; shosha; nsêse*(a) "sunlight, rays of the sun" [See also *nkêke(*a) "rays of the sun"]; *di-su* "eye" (*me-su* "eyes"; *ka-isu* "small eye"; *tu-isu* "small eyes"). The sun (*rʿ, itn, ḥrw, šw*) is also used for words dealing with "time." Egyptian: *r šw* "forever" (with sun determinative), *sw* "day, dates." In ciLuba we have *shòò* "late, tardy, too late, delayed, length"; *kushòò* "too late, sooner or later, eventually, in the end, finally." It should be noted that in the *Coffin Texts* (80 B1C) it states, "Shu is eternal time and Tefnut infinite time" (Obenga, 1992: 40).

Borean (approx.) : *MVNV*
Meaning : to think
Eurasiatic : **manu*
Afroasiatic : **man-*
Sino-Caucasian : ST **ṅV̌m* 'mind, think'
Austric : PAA **miŋ* 'hear' (> PST *mVn?), PAN **maŋmaŋ* 'stare, look', **nemnem* 'think'
Amerind (misc.) : **ma(n)* 'know, see' (R 412 **ma(k)*); **muni* 'see, look' (R 610) [+ A]; **mena* 'wish' (R 859) [+ A K]
African (misc.) : Bantu **-màn-* 'know'.
Reference : МССНЯ 339, ОСНЯ 2, 42-43, Peiros 1989, 1998, 223; GE 9 **mena* (+ ?Khois., NiC, Kord., NS; dubious SC).

It is with this understanding of this *m-n* root that we can get a more accurate interpretation for the god *Imn* among the ancient Egyptians. It is assumed that *Amen/Amun/Imn* is always to be rendered as "the hidden one." It is our argument that Amen *can* be interpreted as a distant and invisible force, but also, in contrast to its popular meaning, can be interpreted as the spirit that "reveals" and makes "known" that which was once *hidden*. The Egyptians highlighted this feature of the Divine by juxtaposing the sun glyph (*rˁ*) to the root *Imn* (*jmn-rˁ*). In the ciLuba-Bantu language we find applications of this combination that reinforce this aspect of the name given to the Divine among the ancient Egyptians. More importantly, it provides new interpretations that provide an expanded set of meanings which can be associated with the god *Imn*.

Table 1: *Ỉmn-Rˁ* among the Baluba[6]

Egyptian Sign	***Pronunciation***	**CiLuba**	**Meaning**
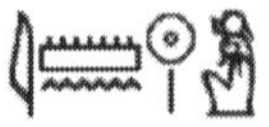	*Imn-ra*	*Amanda* (n+ra=nda)	"That which belongs to the west, to the valley", "what is below/downstream."[1] Nb. For the Nile-Delta, *manda* is the *mutu* "head" of the Great Lakes region.
		mwindila	"He/She is expected" (and on whom rests the hopes)
(babala)	*Ra-Imn*	*Alamina*	"Watch, be on the watch, spy, monitor the movements of the enemy"; "hatching" (of eggs) [in other words "revelation, revealing, coming into being"]
		lamuna	Drawn from sleep, awake, raise up, be careful
		Lamina	"Monitor, ensure, maintain, keep, observe, be in a constant manner, to have a habit"
		muLaminyi	"He / she who guards, watches, monitors and is protected for"
		lemena	"Bend" (bow or spring); paste, fix, bulging, nail, tie, take (someone) to the ground after terrace"
		lumina	"Eater, swallower "
		lumwenu	"Mirror, glass, spectrum"
	Imn-bai	*Amwenibwa; Amenyibwa*	"Whether it is seeing", "Whether it is to know"

6 Kalamba and Bilolo (2009: 127-128)

It is our contention that *'Imn-Rᶜ*, based on the name, is the one who "watches over, monitors, spies, ensures, protects by monitoring, observes, reveals, and knows." Even without the *-ra* extension, the *m-n* root still operates within the domain of "revelation, sight, and experience." If our insights are correct, and we think they are, this may demonstrate that the sun glyph in *imn-rᶜ* may at times be considered as a determinative and not part of the core word. The TOB database for Afro-Asiatic provides us with the following information that supports the above hypothesis:

> Proto-Afro-Asiatic: *(*ʔV-)man-*
> Meaning: sun, day
> Egyptian: *i͗mny* 'Sun-god' (reg)
> Western Chadic: **myan-* 'day'; Montol: *mene* [Fp]
> East Chadic: **myan-* 'day'; Dangla: *mena* [Fd]; Migama: *méènè* [JMig]
> Notes: **ʔi-* may be a prefix.

In other words, the *m-n* root references the "sun" and/or "day" without the suffix *-rᶜ* which could mean that the suffix could, in many cases, be a determinative to reinforce the association between the sun and daylight. This would give us fuel to associate other derived meanings of the root that can be associated with 'sight' as can be seen in the ciLuba examples below:

Table 2: *mnw*[7]

Egyptian Sign	ciLuba	Meaning
 =*mnwj*²	(<-*mwena*)	"things (*Bi-*) views (*mweni*)", the verb -*Mwena* = -*monena, monyina*
	= *malu maMona*	"Business/problems (*malu*) encountered, experienced (*maMona*)"
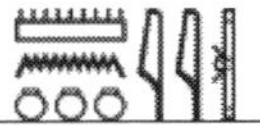	= *bi-mwe(ne) nu*	"visible monuments, visible memories, statues"
	= *Cimwenu*	"monument, memories", "by which we continue to see a person, has something to remember her by," "mirror, manifestation"
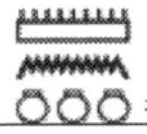 = *mnw*	= *Bi-monu*	"property, possessions," "property we saw (*bi-Mwena*) = one possesses"
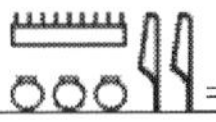 = *mnwj*	= *Bi-moni*	"those who see it, watch"; "the beings who possess = who see"

As noted in Obenga (1992: 73), *Imn* is represented by the light of the moon and is associated with the "left eye" of the Divine (*Aton* being the right eye; daylight sun). This could be symbolic of *Imn's* ability to reveal and reflect what is in the spiritual (hidden) world by examining what can be seen in the physical.[8] It is apparent that *Imn* can be a source of revelation (without the *-rᶜ* determinative) when we note that the Ogdoad (*ḫmnyw*) of Hermopolis (*ḫmnw*) consisted of eight "gods" (or ten principles) that were relative opposites of each other. These were the cosmogonic forces responsible for all the phenomena of the universe by the action of the laws

7 Kalamba and Bilolo (2009: 120)

8 Which is why the text cited in Obenga discusses the moon's light deriving from the sun's light. It becomes a metaphor for *metaphysics* ("the work beyond the physics"). In other words, in order to study what can't be seen, one must study that which can be observed. This is the basis of science which looks for laws (which cannot be seen or detected) by studying the physical objects which can be observed, which in reality is the reflection of the laws at work (just like the moon light is the reflection of sun light).

of opposites. They were:

> *Nun and Nunet* = the eternally uncreated primordial matter and its opposite, thus, in the most rigorous logic, being in general and non-being; in other words, matter and nothingness. Nothingness does not signify the absence of matter, but rather matter in its chaotic state.
>
> *Hehu and Hehut* = temporal eternity and is opposite; others say: the spatial infinite and the finite.
>
> *Kuk and Kuket* = the primordial darkness and its opposite, thus darkness and light.
>
> *Gareh and Garehet* = night and its opposite, thus night and day.
>
> *Niaou and Niaouet* = movement and its passive opposite, therefore movement and inertia, according to Amelineau; others translate: "spatial emptiness" and its opposite.
>
> *Amon and Amaunet* = the hidden and its opposite, thus rigorously; the noumenal world, inaccessible to the senses, and the phenomenal world: the noumenon and the phenomenon in the Kantian sense. (Diop, 1991: 353)

Imn's counterpart in the Hermopolin tradition was *Imn.t* and *Imn.t* was the "revelation" aspect of *Imn* "the hidden." In the ciLuba language this is reflected in the term *diManya* "knowledge, science, information, concept" (*jmn.t* <> *t.jmn*).

A word for "sun" in the Egyptian language is *ḥrw* (which uses the same glyph as *rꜥ*: ☉). Its cognate in ciLuba, when attached to the *m-n* root, also reveals similar interpretations as *jmn-rꜥ*.

Table 3: *Ỉmn-ḥrw*[9]

Egyptian Sign	Pronunciation	**CiLuba**	**Meaning**
	*Ỉmn-ḥrw*	*mwenekela*	appear, being seen, become visible, perceptible; to reveal a/ for; to show
		mwenekelu	appearance
		di-mwenekela	Emergence, birth, occurrence, shape, color, vision
		mumwenekedi / *umwenekela*	Whoever shows, turns out, appears to / for.
	*Ỉmn-ḥrw*	*Imane-Kulu*	Snaps upright, he straightens upright, he climbs up
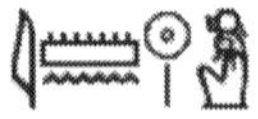	*Ỉmn-ḥrw*	*Ammwena-Kulu*	He looks at me/ seen from above/ up there
		Mwena-Kulu	Lord of Heaven, Master of the Sun, of all that is above
		Mwinangila	*Batamine* = he looks attentive

9 Bilolo (2010:75)

	*'Imn-ḥrw*	*Amwenekela*	He shows
		Ammwenekela	He appears, he shows me

The name *jmn* is pronounced in various ways across Africa. It is used among the Igbo of Nigeria as a conceptual extension to the name of the Divine (*Chukwu*). God is known among the Igbo as *Chukwu Abia-**ama*** "God the revealer of Knowledge and Wisdom." In other words, it is God—the knowledge and wisdom—that reveals himself (Umeh, 1997: 135). It should be noted that *Chukwu* is also represented by the *sun*. The word *ama* "know, be familiar with" among the Igbo is comparable to the word used for God among the Dogon: *Amma*. The word *ama*/*amma* is comparable to Proto-Afro-Asiatic (PAA):

> PAA **yam-* "day"; Semitic **yawm* "day"; Egyptian *jmy* (Middle Egyptian) "sun (as an eye)"; Western Chadic **yam*(m) "evening (before sunset)" (Hausa *yàmmā* "west; afternoon [when the sun is in the west]); East Chadic **yam-* "day"

In the *Pale Fox* (1986) Griaule and Dieterlen reveal that when *Amma* opens his *eye*, a whirlwind came into being and out came a bright *light*.

> Amma, having thus positioned the *yala* for the prefiguration of the universe, acted upon them. He "opened his eyes." This act provoked the emergence of the *yala* from the spiral which, turning in the other direction, will prefigure, inside the egg, the future expansion of the universe. Because of this, it is said that Amma "pushed aside the *yala* of the *gaba* and of the *anu*," in order that the spiral turning on its axis might be able to reverse itself. **Thus Amma had pierced the envelope of his own womb, and his "eye," as it burst forth from the hole, had become a light that illuminated the universe and revealed the existence of all things in formation**. (Griaule and Dieterlen, 1986: 125-126) (emphasis mine)

Here we should note that, just like in our Baluba and Igbo examples, the "light" is a symbol of revelation, of consciousness, of the inner workings and the formations of existence. *Amma*, as a result of opening his "eye," becomes for man the *revealer* of knowledge and wisdom among the Dogon. We see this same type of correspondence among the Ancient Egyptians with *'Imn-rʿ*/ *'Imn-ḥrw*. It is said more specifically in plain language as it regards the *nṯr Rʿ*. In the "Myth of Ra and Isis," *Rʿ* states that:

> I am he who, if he openeth his eyes, doth make the light, and, if he closet them, darkness cometh into being. (Budge, 1904, vol. 1: 362)

This is direct confirmation that the Egyptians are using *paronymy*[10] *to make correlations between concepts based on the similar sounding of words (e.g., Egyptian jrj, rj* "eye"; *rʿ* (Coptic *rei*) "day, light, sun").[11]

An example from West Africa may also give us a possible correlation with the Egyptian

10 *Paronymy*: The relationship between two or more words partly identical in form and/ or meaning, which may cause confusion in reception or production. In the narrow sense the term *paronymy* refers to 'sound-alikes' (cognate near-homophones such as affect/effect or feminine/ feminist), but in the wider sense it covers any 'lookalike' or 'meanalike' confusable words." (R. R. K. Hartmann and Gregory James, *Dictionary of Lexicography*. Routledge, 1998).

11 We will discuss this phenomenon in greater detail in the section "Ra and the divine eye" below.

god *Rʿ*. We spoke of "light" (from the sun) being a metaphor for "knowledge," but it can also be a sign for the dispelling of evil. Umeh (1997: 114) informs us that among the Igbo the Divine (*Chukwu*) is symbolized by the sun. In his form as the God-of-Light, *Agwu*, he is known as the "Divine Light" who "disperses and/or extinguishes danger, evil or darkness." In this context *Agwu* is seen as a protector and his rays are the weapons which dispel evil which is symbolized by darkness. The sun-god *Rʿ* is also seen as a protector and dispeller of evil (*isft*; Isizulu *uzibuthe* "spirit of conflict"). These characteristics were passed on to the kings of Egypt as they were the *sʿw Rʿ* "sons of Ra." A Middle Kingdom text affirms the king's political and moral role. The text says that, "Ra installed the king . . . to judge humans, satisfy (*sḥtp*) the divine ones, realize (*sẖpr*) Maat (rightness) and destroy (*sḥtm*) *isfet* (wrongness)" (Karenga, 2006: 32). The divine king is a representative of the sun on earth and as the sun dispels darkness (evil), so does the king in his role as the commander-in-chief and protector (*ẖwi*) of the land. Again, the rays of light are used to symbolize intelligence and it is intelligence that defeats ignorance (darkness). For African people, the fundamental hurdle that man has to get over, to realize his divine power, is the overcoming of *ignorance*, not sin as in the Abrahamic traditions.

The association of the sun with the Divine is a common African theme. Mbiti (1989: 52) discusses the relationship between the sun and God in African traditions:

> Among many societies, the sun is considered to be a manifestation of God Himself, and the same word, or its cognate, is used for both. Examples of this may be cited from among the Chagga (*Ruwa* for both God and sun), peoples of the Ashanti hinterland (*We* for both), Luo (*Chieng* for both), Nandi (*Asis* for God, *asista* for sun) and Ankore (*Kazooba* for both[12]). Among others, like the Azande, Haya, Igbo and Meban, the sun is personified as a divinity or spirit, and thought by some to be one of God's sons. There is no concrete indication that the sun is considered to be God, or God considered to be the sun, however, closely these may be associated. At best the sun symbolizes aspects of God, such as His omniscience, His power, His everlasting endurance, and even His nature.

We should also add that among the Ingassana of Sudan, God and the sun is represented by the word *Tel*. C. G. Seligman[13] argues that this term (*till, tel*) for sun is present in West Africa and in ancient Christian texts of Nubia where it meant "Lord" or Master" (Seligman, 1934: 16). In the Kalenjiin language this root is present in the title for the Divine *Asiis Cheptaleel: Chee-po-Tel* or *Tie-po-Tel* "she, the girl of Tel" (She of the Sun now in common expression as "white girl") (Sambu, 2008: 75).

The cited excerpt from Mbiti (1989) informs us that in Africa the sun is only used as a metaphor for some attribute of the Divine: it is not the Divine itself. So this begs the question, if the Egyptians had borrowed *Rʿ* from the Semites, how did the Semites conceptualize *Rʿ* (*Aḷah*) prior to this adoption and did these attributes transfer over once the Egyptians adopted the deity? Moreover, what makes us assume the Egyptians had not already recognized and conceived of these attributes prior to meeting the Semites? What did the Semites introduce to the Egyptians that they didn't already have in terms of concepts and the words to represent those concepts? What were these concepts known as in the Egyptian language prior to the adoption of the lexemes from the Semites?

---

12 In ancient Egypt this word was *sbꜣ* "star, teacher, wisdom" without the *ka-* prefix. The Divine is seen as the source of enlightenment (like a sun or a star is a source of light) and the universe's greatest "teacher."

13 C.G. Seligman (1934) *Egypt and Negro Africa: A Study in Divine Kingship*. George Routledge and Sons Ltd. London.

Plato and the Metaphor of the Sun

This notion that the sun is the ultimate symbol for "visibility" and "knowledge" finds symmetry among the ancient Greek philosophers. We begin with Plato (423 – 347 BCE) who actually studied in Egypt. We are told by Hermodores of Syracuse, a direct disciple of Plato, that Plato, "At the age of twenty-eight ... went to Megara, to see Euclid, accompanied by a few other pupils of Socrates. Then Plato went to Cyrene, to see the mathematician Theodorus and to his home in Italy, to Philolaos and Eurytos, both Pythagoreans; then to Egypt, to see the prophets" (Obenga, 1992: 95). It is from Egypt for which he may have found inspiration, through the articulation of the God *Rʿ*, for his *Metaphor of the Sun* given that much of Greek philosophy (according to the Greeks themselves) derives from Egyptian philosophy.

Plato, in the *The Republic* (507b-509c; book VI), uses the sun as a metaphor for the source of Illumination (arguably the source of intellectual illumination); which he held to be the form of the Good.[14] Most scholars argue that this is Plato's notion of God (although there are some who find this interpretation problematic). The *eye*, Plato says, is unusual among the sense organs in that it needs a medium, namely light, in order to operate. Here we can see the relationship between the "eye" and "light" in the Greek tradition as has been explored in this essay in regards to African philosophy. We know that the strongest and best source of light (in our everyday experience) is the sun. With it, objects can be discerned clearly. Analogous things, he writes, can be said of intelligible objects (i.e., the fixed and eternal forms that are the ultimate objects of scientific and philosophical study):

> When [the soul] is firmly fixed on the domain where truth and reality shine resplendent it apprehends and knows them and appears to possess reason, but when it inclines to that region which is mingled with darkness, the world of becoming and passing away, it opines only and its edge is blunted, and it shifts its opinions hither and thither, and again seems as if it lacked reason. (The Republic bk. VI, 508d; trans. Paul Shorey)

The "world becoming and passing away" alludes to the visual and perceptual world. For Plato, by contrast, "the domain where truth and reality shine resplendent" is none other than Plato's world of forms--illuminated by the highest of the forms, that of the Good. For Plato, in order to have knowledge, we must direct our intellect to forms. It is the highest form (the Good) that *illuminates* all other forms. Anything less would be mere opinion.

Plato also informs us that the sun and the Good ("the object of knowledge") are both sources of "generation":

> The sun ... not only furnishes to those that see the power of visibility but it also provides for their generation and growth and nurture though it is not itself generation. ... In like manner, then ... the objects of knowledge not only receive from the presence of the good their being known, but their very existence and essence is derived to them from it, though the good itself is not essence but still transcends essence in dignity and surpassing power. (509b)

It is important to reflect on the fact that according to Plato, the sun provides for the generation, growth and nurture of forms. This is not only a scientific fact (as all of the elements and life

14 Plato describes "The Form of the Good" (τοῦ ἀγαθοῦ ἰδέαν) in his dialogue, *the Republic*, speaking through the character of Socrates. The Sun is described in a simile as the child or offspring (ἔκγονος ekgonos) of the Form of the Good (508c-509a), in that, like the sun which makes physical objects visible and generates life on earth, the Good makes all other universals intelligible, and in some sense provides being to all other Forms, though the Good itself exceeds being.

in our galaxy were once cooked in dying suns/stars), but is also the reality as expressed by the ancient Egyptians—for *Rʿ* is the "creator" aspect of the Divine Totality. The sun was the single most important creation of Deity, the only one of the Deity's creations that was able to create further life and sustain life (Sambu, 2008: 71).

The following is a summary of the metaphoric relationship between the sun and the Good as expressed by Plato:

Analogy of the Sun (506d-509c)

	The Sun	**The Good**
is ...	a visible object	an intelligible object
that makes ...	objects visible	objects intelligible
to the ...	eye	soul
through the power of ...	sight	understanding
by providing ...	light	truth

It is our argument that these same ideas are behind the symbolism of *Rʿ* as the so-called "sun-god." The sun is only a metaphor, a source domain, to represent the seat of intellectual light: the light of knowledge, wisdom and understanding. The ancient Egyptians, as mentioned earlier, played on similar sounding words that, for the Egyptian sages, represented a meaning chain of associated relationships. The order of this relationship is as follows:

Sun → Light → Eye → Seeing → Knowledge

Each concept in the chain, as far as lexical representations go, are represented by an *-r-* (*-l-*) consonant root (or equivalent phoneme due to sound mutation; e.g., l>d) in the Egyptian language. In order to add validity to the claim that the "god" *Rʿ* came from the "Middle East," one would have to demonstrate these types of relationships among the anonymous Semites who allegedly introduced the Egyptians to the god *Rʿ*, for which they would have adopted these meanings as well. Does *Rʿ* (*Allah* according to Muhammad), for example, mean "sun, eye, light, knowledge, etc." in the Semitic languages? We will see that there are a few cognates with the *-r-* consonant root in the Semitic languages (as Semitic languages ultimately derive from Kongo-Saharan languages and share many lexemes), however, the most important lexeme is missing for these associations; and the other concepts that do share a common lexical root were not elevated to the level of deity to be imported as a deity among the ancient Egyptians.

There is another possible conceptual relationship between *vision, revelation* and the *sun*, this time, however, in regards to general life science. We are familiar with *Rʿ* as the creator aspect of the Divine. But where does this association come from? I argue that this is based on the fact that *fire* (ra/la/na/da) is an *activating* agent for all biological life. The *fertilizing* agent is water.

As an example, the earth's soil, although dry and lifeless, has the potential to develop life (in the more familiar sense). The life is dormant in the soil. Water is the fertilizing/fructifying agent for the soil but this alone will not bring out the life potential in the soil (or seeds). There must be a power source to ignite the life potential hidden in the black/red soil. The light from the sun is that power source. It is the activating agent which jump-starts the life potential into forms we are commonly familiar with. In this sense, we are still connected to this concept of *revelation*, as it is the sun's rays that reveal the soil's life potential. We know what type of life can grow out of this type of soil because the sun reveals its nature. This, I argue, is one of the meanings behind the dynamic plethora of associations of the 'sun-god' *Rᶜ*.

Light is a symbol for *consciousness* in the human psyche. In the realms of quantum mechanics, consciousness is also a creative agent in the universe. Those familiar with quantum theory will note that the properties of an electron or a photon do not exist until they are perceived and measured. The electron/photon is either a *wave* or a *particle* and its form depends entirely on how and when it is measured; it comes into existence as one or the other only by virtue of being measured.[15] In other words, things exist because they are perceived. The nature of quantum mechanics is beyond the scope of this essay, but I would encourage the reader to read-up on the "double slit" experiment which proved the above revelations in the laboratory.[16]

However, we note the above to point out that modern scientific experiments support the ancient Egyptian notion that consciousness is a creative, activating force as symbolized by the "eye" and the "sun" in Egyptian iconography. This may lead to the answer for a 'proof' of God (if one needs one), for if forms exist without human observation, what is observing the universe to give form to photons and electrons in the first place (ciLuba *Ammwena-Kulu* "He looks at me/ seen from above/ up there"; *mwenakela* "appear, being seen, become visible, perceptible; to reveal a / for; to show" ; *muLuminyi* "Monitor, ensure, maintain, keep, observe, be in a constant manner, to have a habit"; Egyptian *'Imn/Imn-Rᶜ/Imn-ḥrw*)?

Ra as the Divine Eye

The ancient Egyptians often depicted the God *Rᶜ* as an "eye." This is, in part, due to the associations already mentioned above and also the similarity in pronunciation between the word *rᶜ* "sun" (Coptic *rei, ri, re*) and the words *ᶜr* "to see"; *ir.t/ri* "eye" (Yorùbá *ri* "to see"; *ori* "head, consciousness"[17]). This relationship can also be seen in the word *mr.t* "eye" and *mrr* "fire, flame" in Egyptian.[18] The eye/sun (fire) relationship is not only associated with the God *Rᶜ*, but is also associated with *Hr(w)* (which we could also argue is just another form of *Rᶜ* which is predynastic). In the Egyptian literature, *Hrw's* right eye was the sun and his left eye the moon (Wilkinson, 2003: 200). An Egyptian text informs us that these concepts were also associated with the gods Amon (as we have already discussed) and Aton:

> (God-Moon) Light of the night, image of Amon's left eye which rises in the East while Aton (the sun) is in the West. Thebes is inundated by its brilliance, for the left eye receives the light of the right eye…" (Obenga, 1992: 73)[19]

15 See J. Jorgan, "Quantum Philosophy," in *Scientific American*, July 1992, pp. 94-104.

16 See Gary Felder and Kenny Felder, (1998), "The Young Slit Experiment." http://www4.ncsu.edu/unity/lockers/users/f/felder/public/kenny/papers/quantum.html (retrieved May 06, 2012).

17 Often the word "head" in African languages can also be the same word for the "parts of the head"; features such as eyes, nose, etc. Even verbs such as "biting" are actions of the "head" and often have the same root (PWS **li* "head"; **li* "to eat"). Modern verbs derive from primal nouns in early African languages. (see Campbell-Dunn 2009a, 2009b: 148).

18 *-r-* root with *m-* prefix; Kalenjiin *leel* "white, new, young, immature, empty"; used in the name *Cheptaleel* (and *tiliil "clean, holy"*), an epithet for the Divine *Asiis* represented by the sun: *aisiista*. We note also in Kalenjiin: *laal* "light fire"; laay "start fire, light a fire"; *liil* "flash light at, dazzling light at"; *luu* "light, give off light, gleam, glow, radiate"; *luuwu* "shine, beam, emit light."

19 This is a clear scientific document that notes that the moon's source of light is the sun.

This is a theme that expands beyond Egypt. We witness this same theme among the Balese (Walisi, Balissi, Lesa, etc.) of the Congo of Central Africa. As Mbiti (1989: 52) notes, "The Balese regard the sun to be God's right eye, and the moon His left eye." Among the Kalenjiin of Kenya "the sun is the daytime eye of Asiis while the moon is Her night eye" (Sambu, 2008: 35). Among the Dogon, "The center of the sun is like the pupil of the eye called *giri dege*, 'person of the eye' " (Griaule and Dieterlen, 1986: 508).[20] Because of the orb shape of the sun and the moon—and the oneness of the Creator—the ancient Africans metaphorically viewed these celestial bodies as "eyes" of the Divine, which are "monitoring" [Egyptian *imn-rᶜ*; ciLuba *La-mina*] all of Creation and man's actions.

When you look at the primary glyph for the sun in the *mdw ntr* [☉], it looks more like the pupil of an eye than an actual sun orb. While we can explain the outer circle shape of the sun, it is difficult to rationalize, based on images of the actual sun, the smaller circle inside the sun "disk." However, one could argue that the outer circle is simply the halo surrounding the sun.

When we understand this from the perspective of an actual eye, then we can see the inspiration behind the glyph and its "visual pun" which becomes the image of the sun.

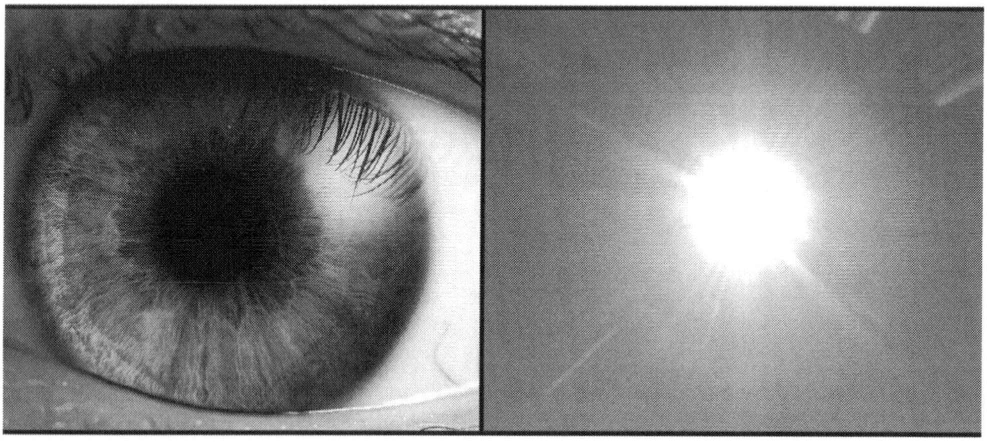

Figure 1: Human eye and the sun as seen from the surface of the earth[21]

When you look at an actual human eye, extending from the pupil at the center are tiny wave-like features that resemble "rays of light" radiating (*wdi*) from the sun. It is from this living "glyph" that we get the symbol for the sun in the Egyptian hieroglyphs. We can better understand now the symbolic and physical relationship between fire, sun, light, the eye, vision and knowledge. Also, we understand better the relationship between the *-r-* linguistic root for fire, eye and sun and its association with the God *Rᶜ* in the Egyptian language. Where ever there could be logical and meaningful associations between concepts, the ancient Egyptians didn't hesitate to make them. This practice is called *paronymy*.

The Semitic languages carry this *-r-* root in relationship to *vision* and *knowledge*. Arabic

20 The sun among the Dogon is considered to be female. Its name *nay* also means "four," the female number; it has the same derivation as the words for "mother" and "cow" (*na* and *nā* and implies the concepts of fecundity and reproduction. Because one sees a small image of oneself in the pupil of another person, this is why the center of the sun is called "person of the eye." The iris is called *giri geu* "dark (black) eye" and the white of the eye is *giri pili* "white eye" (Griaule and Dieterlen, ibid.)

21 Eye image courtesy of Petr Novák, Wikipedia.

provides the best examples in regards to the root meaning and its metaphoric extensions:[22]

> *rā'aā*: observe, to give something its rightful dues, to regard in the right spirits, to see something in the right light. ; *r-'-y* "to see, to behold, to sight, in full view; spectator; mirror; to show vanity; to cause to see, to make a show before others, to act hypocritically, to demonstrate, to come into view; to conceive, to consider, to deem, an opinion; a dream, a vision, outer appearance.; *ra'ā* : to see, to realize, to see as, to consider, to take something to be, to perceive, to dream, to see in a dream, to judge, to examine, to evaluate, to behold, to observe, to reflect upon, to remember; *yurā* : to be seen, to be examined, to be judged, to be scrutinized; *'arā*: to show someone something; *ri'a'*: hypocrisy, acting hypocritically, in order to be seen, to show off; *ra'y*: vision, sight; seeing, sighting, opinion; *ri'y*: show, appearance; splendor; *ru'yā*: dream.

In the Tigrigna language of Ethiopia/Eritrea (a Semitic language) we have *raəy* "sight"; *awräyä* "make known"; Hebrew *ra'a* "to look"; Kalenjiin (Nilo-Saharan) *i-roo* "to look"; Yorùbá (Niger-Congo) *alá* "vision." Compare the above to forms in the Omotic (Afro-Asiatic) languages (Bengtson, 2008: 113):

> **KNOW**: Om.: (N) * *'ar-* > Ometo **'er(r)-*; Chara *ár-*; Gimira **'er-*; Gonga **'ar(r)i-*; Hozo *arɛti*, Seze, Mao *'àl-* id. ||| Cush.: (E) Dullay**'ar-* id. || (S) **'ar-* "to see" (Ehret 1980, 286; E 364, #729).

This is an old Kongo-Saharan/Afro-Asiatic root, as can be seen from the following reconstructions from the TOB database:

> Proto-Afro-Asiatic: **riʔ-*
> Meaning: eye;
> Semitic: **rVʔVy-*
> Western Chadic: **riH-* 'eye'
> Notes: Cf. **ʔir-* eye

This is important to note because this root finds no special exclusiveness in the Semitic languages, a language family for which Egyptian does not belong. It is found in practically all African language families under different dialectical variations. If Muhammad (2009) would have argued from the standpoint of *Rˁ* deriving from the conceptualization of "vision," his thesis would have been on more solid ground. However, he provides no context for the borrowing. If we assume the Egyptians borrowed *Rˁ* from Arabian Semites, he still would have to answer as to why would the Egyptians abandon a concept that they already had for a Semitic one and replace these concepts with words that they already possessed in their language? Especially when these terms were similarly pronounced like the Semitic ones (assuming that the Egyptians would have borrowed the *-r-* root for *vision, eye, sight*, etc., which is highly improbable).

Let's do a thought experiment to see exactly what we're saying here. Let's say that someone claims that the Old English (O.E.) speakers had a god by the name of *Regn* who was the personification of "rain." It just so happens that the word *regn* in O.E. actually means "rain" (i.e., it is an earlier pronunciation of "rain"). Later a historian argues that the god *Regn* was borrowed from the Old Norse (O.N.) speakers who have a term *regn* in its lexicon which also means "rain." The task for the historian is to demonstrate how, why and when this exchange could have come about. The astute historian, one who is familiar with historical linguistic

22 Most of the words in this essay, in regards to the Arabic language, will derive from: Badawi, Elsaid M., and Haleem, Muhammad A. (2008). *Arabic-English Dictionary of Qur'anic Usage.* Koninklijke Brill NV. Leiden, Netherlands.

methods, would immediately run into several problems for this hypothesis.

The first problem is that the term *regn* in O.N. (in our hypothetical example) was never elevated to the status of a god in that community. So why would the O.E. speakers borrow a term from O.N. and then personify it as a deity when the people who they borrowed the term from did not personify the lexeme in their own culture? The second problem is that the O.E. speakers have the *exact same word* in their language and it is not due to borrowing (*regn* vs. *regn*). This term was inherited from its predialectical parent. We know this by examining other well attested related languages for the same term: P.Gmc. **regna-* (cf. O.S. *regan*, O.Fris. *rein*, M.Du. *reghen*, Ger. *regen*, Goth. *rign* "rain").[23] If the O.E. speakers borrowed the term *regn* from the O.N. speakers, they wouldn't have replaced anything as it is the exact same word. If there was a slight pronunciation difference, it was only dialectical. We couldn't conclude, based on the evidence, that our hypothetical god *Regn* is present in O.E. due to borrowing. The best answer is that the god *Regn* is a local cultural artifact and the name derived from a native word it inherited from its predialectical parent: that it wasn't an "Angloization" of an O.N. word. This type of scenario is what we posit for *Rˁ* among the ancient Egyptians.

What sets our hypothetical scenario apart from the real one we are currently engaged in is that the Semites never had the matching lexemes like in our hypothetical scenario above: Egyptian *rˁ* "sun," Semitic **šmš* "sun." We assume that if you borrow a concept from a people you would not only borrow the name of the concept, but also its meaning and application. The Semites never had a sun-god *Rˁ*[24]*;* they never had an "eye of Ra"; they never had a hawk deity named Ra. Remember Muhammad's (2009: 117) argument is that Allah = *Rˁ* and *Rˁ* was imported into Egypt from the "east." If these concepts (the sun, eye, hawk, etc.) were not deified concepts among the Semites (with the aforementioned vocabulary), what would motivate the Egyptians to borrow these terms from the Semites and then deify them when they were not deified among the Semites?

The problem with the thesis that *Rˁ*, as the Sun-God, was imported from Arabia is that in Arabia (in the Semitic languages) the word for "sun" doesn't match the Egyptian form (neither is the word for *eye*: e.g., Semitic **ʕayn-* 'eye').[25] But we find these forms in Africa and they pose no morphological or phonological difficulties. In African languages, abstract concepts derive from concrete realities as we have seen throughout this **essay.** The following table compares the word for sun in Egyptian with other languages to see which languages, in regards to this term, more closely align with the Egyptian.

Table 4: Words for "sun"

Semitic: Akkadian: *samas, shamash*; Ugaritic: *sps*; Hebrew: *semes*; Arabic: *shams*
Berber Siwa: *tfokt;* Nefusa: *tufut*; Ghadames: *tufet*, *thafath*; Mzab: *tfuit*; Tachelh'it: *tafukt*; Tamazir't: *tafukt*; Zenaga: *tufukt*, etc.[3]
Egyptian Ancient Egyptian: *Ra;* Coptic: *re, rei, ri*

23 From http://www.etymonline.com/ (retrieved April 6, 2012).

24 However, the Semites had a sun-goddess *Śamšu*. However, Akkadian has *Šamaš* as a male-god.

25 For example, compare Semitic **ʕayn-* 'eye' to the following reconstructions from the TOB database: Proto-Afro-Asiatic: **ʔir-* "eye"; Egyptian: **ʔir-* 'eye'; Western Chadic: **yir-* (<**ʔir-*) 'eye'; Central Chadic: **ʔiray-* 'eye'; East Chadic: **ʔEr-* 'eye'; Beḍauye (Beja): *iray* 'see'; South Cushitic: **ʔar-* 'to see'.

The Rest of Black Africa: Sidamo (Kushitic): *arriso;* Saho-Afa (Kushitic: *ayro;* Rendille (Kenya): *orr'ah;* Songhay (Niger): *ra;* Vai (Liberia): *ra;* Susu (Guinea): *ra;* Gbin: *ra;* Kono: *ra;* Numu: *re;* Ligbi: *re;* Samo: *re;* (from Obenga 1992)[4]
Languages of the Bahr el Ghazal Ndogo: *ri;* Sere: *ri*; Tagbu: *ri* and *li*; Bviri: *li*; Mondu: *ra*
Other African Languages: Zande : *u.ru* ; Hausa : *ra-na* ; Gouro : *iri* ; Baoulé : *u-ro* ; Sango : *la* ; Banda : *o-lo* ; Bantou : *ta* , *te* ; Baya : *soe* ; Fang : *zô* , Dogon : *naa-ge* ; etc. **Kushitic**: Saho : *aryo* ; Harari : *ir* ; Gurage : *aher* ; Caffino : *are - do* , « light, days »
-NC: Mande: "la, de"; Gur: "da, tyã"; **[Adamawa Eastern]:** "ula, lo, ela, ora, la" (from Campbell-Dunn 2009b)
[Mande]: Dyula *la*, Mano, Dan *de;* Dagari *da*; Mossi *da* (*re*); Minianka *tya*(*ga*); Ga *la* "fire"; Abe *la* "fire"; Idoma *ola* "fire" **[Adamawa Eastern]:** Boritsu *ula* "fire"; Vere *ula* "day"; Mumuye *la* "sun"; Mbum *lo* "day"; Sango *la* "sun"; Mayogo *ela* "sun"; Barambo *ora* "day" (from Greenberg 1963)

We see that the prehistoric -*r*- initial is treated differently in the Egyptian (r/l : râ, rê, rĕ, rĕi, ri in the different Coptic dialects) and the Negro-African languages (r/l/n : aryo, are, ri, ra, ru, ro/li, lo, la, lu, le/na ; r/s/z : sa, se/za, zô, etc.).

The word *rᶜ* "sun" in Egyptian derives from an old Kongo-Saharan root **rV* "fire, flame." It can be seen in the Egyptian words: *rᶜi* "light, flame, fire" (Budge 419a); *rwy* "evening" (Budge 420b), *rwy* "flame." The myth of Ògún among the ancient Africans was the way that our ancestors came to terms with the natural phenomenon of a volcano. The ancestors explained the fire in the volcano by postulating an agent at work on top of the volcanic mountain. On top of the mountain they posited a town of fire—symbolically named *Ìrè*. This name is cognate with Yoruba *àårò* "fire pot," Arabic *'araa* "to burn," Hebrew *'ir* "heat," Afar *ur* and Bari *yur* "set on fire."

What we don't come across in the literature, in regards to Arabia, is *Rᶜ* "the sun" used to denote God. However, in Black-Africa this is precisely the case outside of Egypt. A few examples will make this clear: *Iruwa* (ra) = Sun (Chagga-Bantu), also a god (see Mbiti, 1989: 52; Chami, 2006: 71; *riwa/ruwa*); *Ora* = sun, God (Igbo) (Umeh, 1997: 98); *We* = sun, God (Ashanti) [r>w] (Mbiti, 1989: 52; Issa and Faraji, 2006). We note also Nembe Ijo *irua* "sun." However, the word for sun here has been demythologized.

In East Africa among the Venda-Bantu speakers of Zimbabwe and South Africa, the Divine is known as Luvhimba and is also thought to be *Rᶜ* (connected with the idea of "father"). The Divine's respectful name in full is *Ra-Luvhimba*. *Luvhimba* is symbolized by the *eagle*; the bird that soars aloft. According to custom, *Raluvhimba* was wont to manifest himself by appearing from time to time as a great **flame** on a platform of rock above a certain cave.[26] In Botswana, in the Setswana language, the name *RaRa* means "God." If the root -*ra*- is not repeated, it simply means "father" and is often pronounced as *rre*.[27]

Another word for *sun* and *god* in West Africa is also in Egyptian: *Anyanwu* "sun, God" (Igbo) (Agu, 1997:12). Umeh (1997: 131) pronounces the term in Igbo *Anwu* which is closer to

26 Edwin W. Smith, 'The Idea of God among South African Tribes' in Smith (ed.), *African Ideas of God, a Symposium* (2nd Ed. London, 1950) pp.124-126.

27 A reflex in Egyptian is the term *dꜣ*  "copulate." Here r>d.

the Egyptian *iwnw*. In Egyptian we have *ink* "Heliopolis" (On), *iwnw* "Heliopolis" (On) ["City of the sun"], *iwn*  "sun God." We should note: PWS *ná* "fire" [l > n?]. Compare this to Jukun *yunu* "sun"; Idoma (Nkum dialect) *yeno* "sun"; Efik *Nnyan* "the name of the sun-god." These terms are cognate with Yorùbá *ìyàn* "famine" (i.e., "drought") and *yan* "to roast." Umeh (1997: 114) notes that among the Igbo, Agwu is the "God of light," *Anwu*, whose "Eye is the Sun (*Anyanwu*). The word for "eye" in Igbo is *anya*. So *anyanwu* is the "eye of the sun" (*anya + anwu*).

If anything we could argue that *Rʿ*, as the sun-god, was imported from West Africa and not Arabia as its forms match more closely to Egyptian than it does with Semitic. One could argue, although unsuccessfully, that *Rʿ* was imported into Egypt by the Inca of Peru as their name for the "sun" is *Ra* and the name of the great festival of the Sun is *Rami* (Garnier, 1094: 143).[28] The Inca reality is closer to the African than is the Semitic for which Muhammad claims imported *Rʿ* into Egypt. But it is our contention that *Rʿ* was a native concept which used a lexeme inherited from its predialectical parent and there was no "Egyptianizing" a Semitic term and concept.

As we will see, *-r-* is the root and throughout world languages a prefix was added to this root and they have all gone through their own evolution of sound mutations. Remember that r/l/n and r/l/d are common sound shifts in Africa. Some forms, however, are the result of serialization of the noun.

<u>LIGHT</u> **Sumerian** *ra* "light"

LA, DA, RA "fire"

PWS *la* "day", *d.a* "day"
PWN *DÌNÁ* "fire"
Bantu *tango* "sun" ?
PNC **la, ra* "sun, day", Barambo *ora* "day" (daylight)
Dyula *la* "day, sun", Gã *la* "fire", Abe *la* "fire", Dagari *da* "day, sun" (Greenberg)
Egyptian *ra* "sun"
Mande (Delafosse 1929) *lā, dā* "day"
Mangbetu *tiane* "day" (loss of *n*) ?
Mangbetu *ro* "sky"
CS Kreish *kadda,* Bagirmi *kada* "sun, day", Mangbutu *kora* "day" (compare to Eg. *hrw* "sun, day")
CN Didinga *kor* "sun", Dinka *ako,l* "sun", Bari *ko,lo,ŋ,* Turkana *ekoloŋ* "sun" (Greenberg)

["Sun", "day" and "fire" have the same etymology]

***L = r** ***A = a**

<u>FIRE</u> Sumerian *izi* "fire"

DI "fire" [R]

PWS *lim, (dim),* Temne *lim, dim* "to extinguish", Bowili *diná* "to extinguish"
Bantu (Meinhof) *lima, ndima* "to extinguish"
PWN *DIM* "extinguish"
PWN *DÌNÁ* "fire"
PWS *tùà, (tò̩)* "to roast" (of the sun)

28 Cited in Sambu (2008: 11)

Bantu *dido* "fire"
Bantu *jadi,* "lightning"
"Bantu" *didi* "fire" (204), *dite* "fire" (225), *iji, bu-iji* "fire" (82) are possible candidates for producing *izi.* Lack of a prefix is common on Sumerian nouns.
Mande M *gã-ndi, kã-ndi* "fire"
Eastern Sudanic: Dongola *masi(1)* "sun", Dagu of Darfur , Sila *ma:si* "fire", Modob *ussi* "fire"
Chari-Nile: Central Saharan: Maqdi *asi* "fire", Lega *kasi* "fire"

*D = z(s) *I = i

FIRE Sumerian *ne-mur* "fire"

NA "fire"
MU "fire" -r

PWS *ná* "fire", Kebu *ná-wo* "fire" Sumerian *bún* "lamp"
PWN *MUAL* "to shine"
Atlantic *na, nak* "sun, day" (Westermann 1928 : 85 – 86) [Arabic *nar* "fire"]
PWN *PHI* "burn" (fire)
Bantu *pía* "fire"
"Bantu" *–ωmu* "fire" (195), but *bu, bi* (259, 267, 187, 184, *buri* 121, 222 etc), without nasalisation of *b* to *m.*
Mande *mana* "fire"
Mande *wumbe* "fire"
Mangbetu *mudé* "heat"
PCS **pVl, *pVr* "light"

*N = n *A = e *B = m *U = u

The Semitic languages have this *-r-* root, but by the time Semitic forms as a language family, this root has taken on a prefix which is no longer operative and that initial consonant sound has weakened into /*ʔ*/ or /*ʕ*/ as can be seen in these examples:

Proto-Afro-Asiatic: *ʔu/ir-[29]
Meaning: **fire, to burn**
Semitic: **ʔūr- ~ *ʔirr* 'fire' ~ **ʔry* 'set fire to'
Egyptian: *ỉr.t* (gr) 'flame'
Western Chadic: **yar-* 'burn'
Central Chadic: **ʔur-* 'burn'
East Chadic: **ʔyar-/*ʔwar-* 'burn' 1, 'warm oneself' 2
Saho-Afar: **ʔur-* 'burn'
South Cushitic: Maʔa *iʔora* 'ashes'
Notes: Cf. **war-* 'to burn, roast', **rVwVy-* 'fire; burn', **ḥr* 'burn'.

Proto-Afro-Asiatic: **ʔur-*
Meaning: **day**
Semitic: **ʔVr-* 'day, light, sun'
Central Chadic: (?) **wur-* 'morning'
Saho-Afar: SaAf *ayro*
High East Cushitic: **ʔor-* 'midday'
Notes: Related to **ʔur-* 'burn, be hot'? Or to **ʔVr-* 'moon'?

29 Sergei Anatolyevich Starostin "The Tower of Babel" (TOB) website (Afro-Asiatic Etymologies database): http://starling.rinet.ru/

It is my contention that the Semitic variations of the root derive ultimately from the p-r/b-r roots where the *p-/b-* initial consonants became a glottal stop and even *w-* in Chadic. As stated before, this is an ancient root and this can be found in Indo-European languages as well. The following examples come from *The Nostratic Macrofamily: A study in distant linguistic relationship,* Walter de Gruyter & Co. Berlin by Allan R. Bomhard and John C. Kerns (1994: 525):

> 376. Proto-Nostratic **ʕal-/*ʕəl-*
>
> A. Proto-Indo-European **ʕɦəl-* [**ʕɦal-*] 'to burn': Sanskrit *alāta-m* 'a fire-brand, coal'; Latin *altar, altāre, altāria, altārium* 'that which is placed upon an altar proper (*āra*) for the burning of the victim; a high altar (more splendid than *āra*)', *adeleō* 'to burn a sacrifice': Swedish *ala* 'to blaze, to flame, to flare up, to burn'. Pokorny 1959:28 **al-* 'to burn'; Walde 1927-1932.I:88 **al-*; Mayrohofer 1956-1980.I:55.
>
> B. Proto-Afroasiatic **ʕal-/*ʕəl-* 'to make a fire, to light, to ignite, to kindle, to burn': Proto-Semitic **ʕal-aw/y-* 'to burn' > Hebrew *ˀōlāh* 'burnt offering'; Biblical Aramaic *ˀelāθ* 'burnt offering'; Palmyrene *ˀlt'* 'altar'. Proto-Semitic **ʕal-ak-* 'to make a fire, to light, to ignite, to kindle' > Arabic *'alaka,* to catch fire, to kindle'; Mehri *ˀālōk* 'to make a fire', *hālōk* 'to light, to kindle'; Jibbali *aˀlek* 'to light, to kindle'; Harusi *ˀalok* 'to light, to kindle'.
>
> Buck 1949:I.85 burn (vb.); 22.14 altar; 22.15 sacrifice, offering. Illic-Svityc 1971-.I:276, no. 140(?) *?ʌLʌ

The Indo-European forms meaning "blaze, sacrifice and burning" are closer to the Egyptian form than is the Semitic, however, these terms were never elevated to represent the "sun" in Indo-European. Therefore, *ra* (*ala*) "sun" couldn't have come from Europe either. Less work is needed to match the Egyptian forms and applications of *rˤ* to the forms found in the Black African languages. Not only do you have the *rˤ* forms, but you also have the forms which have been subject to change over time.

The forms attested in Semitic do not match the forms found in Egyptian. However, the TOB database has the following entry:

> Proto-Afro-Asiatic: **raʕ-*
> Meaning: sun, god
> Semitic: **rayʕ-* 'daylight'
> Egyptian: *rʕ* 'sun, Sun-god' (pyr) (?)
> Western Chadic: **(*ʔa-)riʔ-* 'sky' 1, 'cloud' 2
> East Chadic: **raH-* 'god' 1, 'sky' 2
> Notes: Cf. Eg rʕ 'sun; god', rather <*lVʕ-.

However, when we open the entry on Semitic we have the following:

> Number: 2666
> Proto-Semitic: **rayʕ-*
> Afroasiatic etymology:
> Meaning: 'daylight'
> Arabic: *rayʕ-*

The only Semitic language provided by this database is Arabic. However, going through the Strong's Dictionary for Hebrew provides the following: *'owr* "illumination or luminary, bright, clear, day, light (-ning), morning, sun." [SH215, SH216]; *'uwr* "flame, fire, light"; *'owrah* "luminousness, light"; *halal* "to be clear, to shine, to rave, glory, give (light)"; *nharah* [נְהָרָה] "daylight, light"; *niyr* "candle, lamp, light" (Arabic *nar* "fire").[30] Akkadian has *urru* "light, daylight"; *seru* "daybreak, daylight"; *umu* "day"; *namru* "bright"[31] (O'Connor and Freedman, 1987: 142).

Looking into the Canaanite language (from which Hebrew derives) we have the following entries: Canaanite *ym* (pronounced "ya^{w}m") "day"; *'c* (Pronounced "ec") "fire"; *cmc* (Pronounced "camc") "sun."[32] This leaves me to suspect that the *r*-forms in Hebrew are loans and are a result of areal contacts. The entry *'owr* "morning, sun" derives from *'owr* which is a causative for "to be or to make luminous." So this isn't a word for "sun, morning" in Hebrew, but is a *verb* for "to make shine, to illuminate."

Words for "to light, shine, illuminate" in Egyptian are the following: *ꜥbꜥb, itn, sp, siši, ḥꜣy, psḏ, swbḫ, sḥḏ, ḥḏ, sti, ṯhn, wbn, ꜥbꜣ, wbg, wgb, ḫbs*. Although Egyptian has *rꜥi* "fire," it doesn't have an *-r-* root specifically meaning "to shine, to illuminate" in the dictionaries I have access to. I contend that in Egyptian this *-r-* root (meaning "to shine") was fossilized with an old prefix *m-* in the word *mꜣ.wt*[33] "rays (of light), sheen, light" (*ꜣ* = *l*; <*mrr* "flame"; Yorùbá *màrè* "shining, splendor," *imọlẹ* "light, brightness, glow"; ciLuba *ciMunyi* "torch, light"). This root no longer existed as a single morpheme meaning "to shine."

The Egyptian term *rꜥ* "sun" derives from an ancient word *ra/la* meaning "fire." As Campbell-Dunn (2009b) notes, "fire, day, sun" have the same etymology in Kongo-Saharan languages which more closely matches the Egyptian than does Semitic with no morphological difficulty.

In Akkadian, one of the oldest attested Semitic languages, the word for fire is *iš*: see also *iš?tum*, "fire" (written as *i-ša-tum* or *i-ša-tu-um* or with a logogram which corresponded to the Akkadian word *izi*, instead of *iš?tum*, "fire").

Fire: Semitic:
Proto-Afro-Asiatic **ʾis-* ("fire"). Descendents → Akkadian: (išātu); Amharic: እሳት (əsat); Aramaic: Syriac: ܐܫܬܐ ('ešāṯā'), Hebrew: אשתא ('ešāṯā'); Ge'ez: *əsat*; Hebrew: אֵשׁ (ʾēš); Phoenician: 𐤀𐤎 (ʾs) Tigre: *əsat*; Ugaritic: (išt)

The word for "sun" in world languages often derives from words for "sky" or "fire." Searching the TOB Semitic database only gave one entry for "sky" and it is obvious that this is where we get the Semitic term for "sun" (P.Sm **šmš*): (entry number 911); Proto-Semitic: **šamay-* "sky"; Akkadian: *šamû;* Ugaritic: *šmm*; Hebrew: *šamayim*; Syrian Aramaic: *šemayy-;* Arabic: *samāʔ-;* Geʕez (Ethiopian): *samāy*; Mehri: *semē`*; Harsusi: *semē*. It is my contention that the Semitic word for "sun" (*šmš*)[34] is a reduplication of the biconsonantal root of the type **pl* > *plpl* > *plp* (see E. Vernet 2008: §4.8).

The Semites never associated *fire* alone with the sun or with the *-r-* root. It is for this

30 Arabic *nar* "fire" is cognate with Yoruba *oòrùn* "sun," *erùn* "dry season"; Hausa *rana* "sun, daytime, *rani* "dry season." Yoruba also has *ran* "to shine" which is also built from the same root. As we can see, the cognates cited in Semitic reverse the *r-n* consonant order.

31 In other literature the definition given to *namaru* is "to dawn, shine brightly."

32 http://canaanite.org/

33 The word *ꜥbꜣ* "light, glistening" may be an alternate variation (a doublet) of *mꜣ.wt*; both originating from PCS **pVl, *pVr* "light" [p>b>m; r/l > ꜣ]. The forms *wbn* "to brighten, to rise, to shine, to dawn. glitter"; *ꜥbꜥb* "appear, shine (of the sun)"; *brg* "to light up"; *bꜣḫ* "bright, light"; may also derive from this root as well.

34 The TOB database has Proto-Semitic **šm* "sun." Edward Lipiński in his *Semitic languages: outline of a comparative grammar* notes: *šam?š→*šamš 'sun'. You will get slight variations depending on what source you use.

reason, and others to be discussed in Part II of this essay, that I am not convinced that the Egyptian *Rʿ* was imported from Arabia and was an Egyptianization of Proto-Semitic *ʾḷ* (Allah). It is clear from the Egyptian texts that *Rʿ* has been associated with the sun from the moment he was attested in the Egyptian records. We cannot find such attestations among the Semites. I will demonstrate that Allah, among the Semites, was associated with the "sky" and most importantly "rain/water."

The Dynamic Aesthetics of Ra

We noted at the beginning of this essay—quoting Serge Sauneron (2000:125-127)—that the Egyptians had a habit of associating concepts whose names had a similar pronunciation with each other (paronymy). I argued in Imhotep (2011) that the god *Rʿ* was depicted often with various motifs primarily because they have the *-r-* root and are similar in pronunciation to *rʿ* (Coptic *re, ri, rei*). The following image will demonstrate this fact among the Ancient Egyptians.

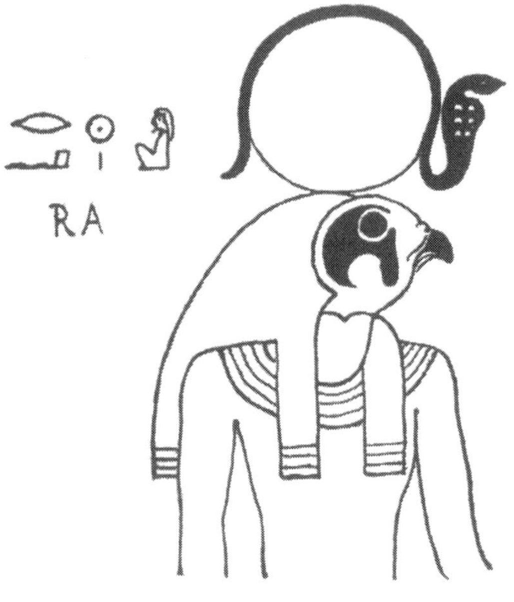

Figure 2: The God *Rʿ*

What we are seeing above is the name *ra* "written" three times in one motif: Egyptian *r* "snake"; *rrw* "snake," *wrw* "large snakes," *ra* "sun, day"; *ra* "hawk?" As we can see, each aspect of the image above of the god *Rʿ* is associated with an *-r-* root. The most difficult aspect to support is that of *rʿ* = hawk. This is because in the modern dictionaries we do not find entries of *rʿ* "hawk or falcon."

It is my contention that a root *-r-* for "hawk" more than likely existed in Egyptian in predynastic times and was replaced with *bjk* "falcon"; *ṯnḥr* "hawk"; *gmḥsw* "hawk." This root was fossilized with an *ḥ-* prefix and simply became known as *ḥr/ḥrw* "the god Horus who is depicted as a falcon." We can see this form in the word above *ṯn-ḥr* "hawk." Other notable forms for "falcon" in Egyptian are:

> *ḏrjt* (= {*ḏrt*}) "Falcon" [Wb V 600]; *ḏrtjt* Falk females [Wb V 597]; *ḏrtj* "falcon" [Wb V 597]; *ḏrt* "hawk, harrier" [Wb V 596]; *šf* "small birds, from hawks hunted" [Wb IV 455]; *šnbtj* "Hawk" [Wb IV 514]; *ʿẖm* "idol, Falcon" [Wb I 225]; *bjkt* "female falcon"

> [Wb I 445]; *bjk* "Falcon" [Wb I 444]; *kmk* "falcon-headed god" [Wb V 131]; *ḳbḥ-snw.f* "falcon-headed Horus son" [Wb V 31]; *sjꜣw* "sacred falcon" [Wb IV 29]; *sẖꜣ* "Falcon idol" [Wb IV 235]; *whnnwtj* "name of a falcon pair" [Wb I 346].

The *ṯn-* prefix could be a number of things. Egyptian has *ṯn* "border guard"; *ṯnḥ* "to look, to observe." Could *ṯnḥr* have been seen as a type of "guardian spirit?" We also have *ḥrḥr* "to guard, to keep watch." We would have to see a textual example to see if that interpretation is warranted. We also have *ṯni* "lift up, promote, distinguish, be distinguished, elevated (of speech)." This would be more fitting given that a common determinative for a "god" in the Egyptian hieroglyphs is the falcon on a raised platform [𓅆] which signals someone of high rank, authority and divinity; for which we could successfully argue is a person (spirit) of great "distinction." The term *ṯnḥr* could possibly mean "watcher from on high."

It is my opinion that the *-r-* root was simply an old word for "bird"[35] in general and was given specific associations to certain birds as time evolved: i.e., Mangbetu *ri* "animal or bird" (Egyptian *wr* "animal"); Proto-Bantu **kodi* "bird of prey, hawk"; Sumerian *hurin* "eagle"; Wolof *cooli, ceeli* "kite"; Akan (Kwa) *koli* "hawk"; Songhai *k'úrò* "bird"; Dogon *ene* "fowl" (l>n); Yorùbá *arawo, àkàlà* "vulture"; ciLuba *mv-ulu, mf-ulu* "hawk" (v, f < p), *ciMi-Nyi* "eagle" [Egyptian *mnw* "pigeons, doves"; *mnt*, singular form]; ciLuba *Nkulu, Nkole, Ngal, nGole, Cyal,* "Prominent or powerful man, hawk"; *Kal, ciKololo*[36] *"raven"; Kalenjiin (Nilo-Saharan) keereet* "kind of hawk."

We can see the *-r-* root associated with general words for *bird* in the Egyptian language: *rw* "geese"; *wr* "swallow, rock martin" (Wb I 326); *wr/wꜣr* "young bird" (Cerny: CED S 98); *ḏpr* "bird" (Vygus); *gry*[37] "a bird" (Vygus); *ḏryt* "a kite." We are supported in our assumption with the entry *-ꜣ-* "vulture, bird (in general)" [Vygus 2011: 483]. The glyph is of Gardiner Sign G1 𓄿. As we have noted before, *ꜣ* = *l* or *r*.

When we look into the Afro-Asiatic language family as a whole, we can see further evidence that *rʿ* is associated with a "bird" or specifically "birds of prey."

> Proto-Afro-Asiatic: **raHaw/y-* "bird"; Semitic: **rahw-* or **raʔ-* 'crane' or 'red kite'; Western Chadic: **ray(aw)-* 'bird'; East Chadic: **rāy-* < **raHay-* 'vulture'; Low East Cushitic: **raHaw-* 'large bird' ; Hebrew *rāʔā* 'red kite'; Arabic *rahw-;* Proto-Semitic: **rahw-* or **raʔ-;* Proto-WChadic: **ray(aw)-* 'bird'; Bolewa: *rayo, yaro* [Bn:22], met. *yàró* [CLR]; Karekare: *ràỳí* [ShV]; Ngamo: *ràỳí* [ShV]; Bele: *ràawí* [ShB]; Proto-EChadic: **ray-* 'vulture'; Migama: *ráàyà* [JMig] {Notes: cf. Dangaleat *úríyà* 'heron' [Fd]}; Proto-Low East Cushitic: **raHaw-* 'large bird'; Arbore: *raw.*

As we can see above, the G1 𓄿 sign is more than likely a generic term for a "large bird of prey."[38] This association became attributed to the God *Rʿ* (*Ḥrw*) who was depicted as a hawk (a large bird of prey). It should be noted that among the Igbo of Nigeria, a term for the Divine is *Agwu* which is described as a kite, which is also the Sun-God/God of light. The first son of

---

35 Or "flight" that was deverbalized. See *Part II* of this series this volume.

36 Other names are *NyemBwa*, *KwAngala*, and *Ngole*. The last two words have the *g-l* root which would be consistent with the *k-l* in *Kulu/Hrw*.

37 Could *gry* "bird" just be another form of *ḥrw*? We argue that the Egyptian form, *ḥrw*, derived from a form *kulu* where *k* > *ḥ*. That same *k-* could have weakened and became *g-*. This is quite common as /k/ and /g/ interchange in Egyptian: e.g., *gnw/ḳnw* "golden oriole" (a bird) [r>l>n?].

38 In modern-times we classify a certain species of bird as *Accipitridae* (birds of prey with very hooked beaks and varying diets). Included in this group are hawks, eagles, kites, harriers and Old World vultures. It appears as *rʿ* or *ꜣ* represents any bird belonging to this group. In other words, *rʿ/ꜣ* may be a "class" or "type" of bird more so than a specific bird.

Agwu is named *Aro* (Egyptian *Rꜥ?*) and he appears as a "falcon-headed or hawk-headed sky spirit that saves like his father the Kite-headed Savior Holy Spirit" (Umeh, 1997: 115).

In addition to *rꜥ* being equated to a "hawk" or "large bird of prey," one could speculate an additional association with that of the "eye" of the hawk which has a similar pronunciation to *ra/re/ri/rei* (Egyptian *ir.t*; Coptic *alō*, *alooue* "pupil, eye"[39]; Lingala/Kituba *kutala* "to look, to watch, to see"; *(ki)talatala* "mirror"). The falcon and hawk are known all over the world for their great vision and for their ability to see their prey from far distances. The trait being illuminated here is the bird's "visual acuity" and its ability to make fine discriminations. Hawks can distinguish their prey at upwards to three-times the distance a human being can. We argue that the eye of the falcon is being used as a metaphor to highlight the themes of "prudence, precision, accuracy, insight, and forethought."

These are all traits of someone who is highly "skilled" and "wise" (*jḳr* "excellence, skillful, superior, trustworthy"). We are supported in our analysis by the depiction of the snake on top of the head of *Rꜥ*. Snakes are often associated with bad omens and disaster, but it is also a sign of "wisdom" in many ancient traditions. It reminds us of the verse in Matthew 10:16 - "Behold, I am sending you out as sheep in the midst of wolves, so be **wise as serpents** and innocent as doves."

C. Staniland Wake in his article "The Origin of Serpent Worship,"[40] describes the association between wisdom and snakes in ancient traditions around the world. He informs us that:

> One of the best-known attributes of the serpent is **wisdom**. The Hebrew tradition of the fall speaks of that animal as the most subtle of the beasts of the field; and the founder of Christianity tells his disciples to be as wise as serpents, though as harmless as doves. Among the ancients the serpent was consulted as an oracle, and Maury points out that it played an important part in the life of several celebrated Greek diviners…The serpent was associated with Apollo and Athene, the Grecian deities of Wisdom, as well as with the Egyptian Kneph (Warburton supposes that the worship of the One God Kneph was changed into that of the dragon or winged-serpent), the ram-headed god from whom the Gnostics are sometimes said to have derived their idea of the Sophia. This personification of divine wisdom is undoubtedly represented on Gnostic gems under the form of the serpent. In Hindoo mythology there is the same association between the animal and the idea of wisdom. Siva, as Sambhu, is the patron of the Brahmanic order, and, **as shown by his being three-eyed, is essentially a god possessing high intellectual attributes**. Vishnu also a god of wisdom, but of the…type which is distinctive of the worshippers of truth under its feminine aspect. The connection between wisdom and the serpent is best seen, however, in the Hindu legends as to the Nagas. Mr. Fergusson remarks that "the Naga appears everywhere in the Vaishnava tradition. There is no more common representation of Vishnu than as reposing on the Sesha, the celestial seven-headed snake, contemplating the creation of the world…The *Upanishads* refer to the science for the serpents, by which is meant the wisdom of the mysterious Nagas who, according to Buddhistic legend, reside under Mount Meru, and in the waters of the terrestrial world. One of the sacred books of the Tibetan Buddhists is fabled to have been received from the Nagas. (Bolded emphasis mine)

We argue that the association between "snakes" and "wisdom" is, again, grounded in this

---

39 See Johanna Brankaer. (2010). *Coptic: A Learning Grammar* (Sahidic). Otto Harrassowitz GmbH & Co. KG, Wiesbaden. p.146.

40 Wake, C. Staniland. "The Origin of Serpent Worship." In: *Serpent and Siva Worship and Mythology, in Central America, Africa and Asia and the Origin of Serpent Worship*. Hyde Clarke, M.A.I., and C. Staniland Wake, M.A.I. J. W. Bouton Publishers. New York, NY. (1877) pp. 39-43.

concept of "vision." Snakes do not have vision characteristics like the hawk or falcon. Some snakes have what we call "infrared vision." Infrared light has longer wave lengths than that of the visible spectrum of light seen by humans. It is also known as "heat vision" and it allows the snake to signify the presence of warm-blooded prey in 3-dimensions, which helps the snake aim their attack.[41] The actual image is not as clear as that of a human's, but the image is a general composite of the object which allows it to get a general depiction of what the object looks like. It reminds us of the scene in the movie *Matrix Revolutions* where Neo lost his eye-sight in a battle with Baine (a.k.a. Agent Smith). Because Neo reached such a high level of consciousness throughout the series, in the "real world" Neo was able to see objects as they "really" were: as variations of "light" and "heat" without all of the details such as contours and the like.

This is how snakes see. The snake's brain creates an image profile based on the heat distribution of the object. All of this is possible because of "heat." Did the ancient Egyptians have a working understanding of the correlation between a snake's vision and heat? Is this why we see many depictions in Egypt of a snake wrapped around the sun, as is the case with our image of *Rˁ* above? Further research would have to be conducted to see if the Egyptians understood the science of infrared light and the snake's ability to see using infrared. It is clear, however, that the Egyptians understood light to be waves (see Finch, 1998: Pl. 20), so this level of questioning is within range of known empirical facts.

What isn't in dispute is the notion that snakes symbolize wisdom and I argue that this is partly based on the unique seeing capabilities of snakes that allow them to strike with "precision." The ancients may have seen this as a sort of "sixth sense" and sought to embody this characteristic and thus why numerous priesthoods used the snake as a symbol for their respective centers of wisdom. A snake's infrared vision is especially helpful at night where, due to the evolution of its particular eye design, its vision would basically be useless in such dark conditions. But because it can see an object's heat profile, it sees at night clearly[42] and this may have been the inspiration for an association between the symbolism of a snake with esoteric and "hidden" knowledge (*jmn*). To see the unseen, one has to be able to have a certain type of vision that ordinary people do not have and this is what the priesthood embodies.

Malidoma Somé, a shaman of the Dagara people in Burkina Faso, in his work *Of Water and the Spirit* provides the best explanation, in my opinion, as to the purpose of initiation (education) in the African schools of wisdom (a.k.a., *priesthoods*) that informs our discussion here.

> Traditional education consists of three parts: enlargement of one's **ability to see**, destabilization of the body's habit of being bound to one plane of being, and the ability to voyage transdimentionally and return. Enlarging one's vision and abilities has nothing supernatural about it; rather, it is "natural" to be part of nature and to participate in a wider understanding of reality (Somé 1994: 226).

We are seeing a theme here, in regards to the common images of the "sun-god" *Rˁ*. We are seeing a correlation between *light, vision* and *wisdom* and all of these concepts are symbolically represented as the *sun*, the *falcon* and the *snake* respectively. Besides the conceptual relationship between the symbols mentioned above, the names for these concepts all have an *-r-* linguistic root.

Can this relationship be demonstrated among the Semitic speakers for which the claim is made for its origin? Can these relationships be made, with the same words, in the Semitic

41 See Andreas B. Sichert, Paul Friedel and J. Leo. van Hemmen, "Snake's Perspective on Heat: Reconstruction of Input Using an Imperfect Detection System." In: *Physical Review Letters*. 97, 068105 (2006).

42 Think of a snake having built-in night vision goggles like the troops in the U.S. military.

languages and cultures of Arabia? Since all of these symbols, we argue, have the same connotation, it could be argued that *R*ᶜ may have been known by the other symbols prior to the sun being the most dominant.

Ra as a snake

When we look at terms for "snake" in the Semitic languages, we do not find a matching *-r-* root for this association either. Here are the Proto-Semitic words for snake given by the TOB database:

> **taman-* "snake, dragon"; **ʔar(a)w-* "snake, chameleon"; **šVmm-* "kind of reptile" (snake, lizard); **ŝarap-* "kind of snake or worm"; **ḥVm(V)ṭ-* "kind of snake/lizard"; **bat_an-* "snake"; **ʔapʕaw-* "kind of snake" (viper?); **hVwVy-* "kind of worm, snake"; **ṣV[ʕ]Vr-* "snake" (Akkadian *ṣēru*); **tVnnVn-* "(mythical) snake, dragon"; **naḥaš-* "snake"; **ʔaym-* "snake"; **ṣipaʕ-* "snake"; **šib(šib)-* "(water)worm; snake"; **šVpp-* "kind of snake, worm"

The only reconstructed term that comes close to the Egyptian forms (*r, rrw, wrw*) is **ʔar(a)w-* "snake, chameleon." However, this form is not present in Arabia, but found only in the African branches of Semitic: Geʕez (Ethiopian): cf. *ʔarwe mədr* 'snake; Tigre: *ʔərawito* 'chameleon' [LH 359], *ʔarwe* 'snake'; East Ethiopic: Sel Wol *wäro*, Sel *woro*, Zw *wäru* 'python'; Gurage: Msq *oro* id. LGur 660: <Cush. Thus, the association between *R*ᶜ and snakes didn't come from Arabia either.

Cambpell-Dunn (2009b) argues that *r*(a) "snake" derives from *ra* "crawl"

> <u>SNAKE</u> ? — **Sumerian** *a-lá* "harmful being"
>
> **LA, DA, RA "snake", "crawl" a-**
> PWS *la* "lie, sleep" — **Sumerian** *alad* "protective spirit"
> PWN *DAD* "crawl"
> Mande *bida* "black snake"
> Mangbetu *tatala* "snake"
>
> [Snakes were both harmful beings and protective spirits].

The word for snake in Egyptian (*r, rrw, wrw*; ciLuba *lwèlè*(à) "serpent"; syn. > *lwasa*) may also derive from roots meaning to "go" as can be seen in the following:

> <u>GO</u> — **Sumerian** *du* "to go, come"
>
> **LU, DU**
>
> PWS *lu* "knee"
> PWN *DUI* "knee"
> Bantu *du,(i)* "knee"
> Bantu *du,* "come out"
> Bantu *tu(u) duk* "descend"
> Mande *dyulã* "descend"
> Mangbetu *adrue* "to follow"
> PCS **lu* "motion", **oru, oro* "motion"

***D = d** ***U = u**

<u>GO</u> **Sumerian** *rá* "to go"*(re$_7$, ri$_6$)*

LA, RA, LI, RI "go"

PWS *là* "earth, ground" ?
Bantu (Johnston 1922: 535) *lāā* (16), *laba* (1), *laγa* (120), *la* (199), *ala* (204, 205) "go"
"Holoholo" *lah* "to flee", *lak'* "to march"
PCS **la* "motion", **li, ri* "motion"
Mande *tar̕a* "to go"
Mangbetu *ôli* "to march", *oro* "to flee"
Mangbetu *ri* "animal"
Eastern Sudanic : Merarit *la* "to go" (elsewhere *lo*)
Chari-Nile: Lendu *ra* "to go"
***L = l** ****A = a**

<u>GO ABOUT (GO)</u> **Sumerian** *du-du* "go about"

LU, DU "knee" **[R]**

PWS *lu* "knee", *(ru, du)*
PWS *DUI, LÚNKU, DÚNKU* "knee"
Bantu *du,* "come out'
Ngombe *duli* "knee", *dua* "come"
Mande *gyēru, dyēru* "to go'
Mangbetu *adrue* "to pursue"
PCS **lu* "motion"
Chari-Nile : Berta *kudu* "knee"
Afro-Asiatic : Chad : Gerka, Ankwe (1) *duk* "near"

***D = d** ***U = u**

<u>GOING</u> **Sumerian** *a-rá* "way of going"

LA, DA, RA "go" **(<u>h</u>)a-** **-n**

PWS *là* "earth", "under" **Sumerian *<u>h</u>a-ra-an*** "road"
PWN *LIAT, (LAT)* "tread", PWN *DAD* "to crawl"
Bantu *diat* "tread on"
Bantu *jidá* "road"
Bantu *dai,* "long"
BANTU *DÀ* "long"
Mande *gyā, dyā* "long"
Mande *sīra, sīla* "road"
Mangbetu *hi* "road", *oro* "to flee"
PCS **la* "motion"
Eastern-Sudanic: Merarit *la* "to go", Tama *lo* "to go", Masai *lo* "to go"
Chari-Nile: Lendu *ra* "to go"

[Maori has *ara* "road"}[*-an* is an article]

***D = r** ***A = a**

The snake may have been named after its unique motion. The snake becomes the personification of motion as objects in motion move in the pattern of "waves" and the form of a snake's body when moving becomes the perfect symbol for this concept of motion.

Ra and the measurement of time

Another form of the *-r-* root in regards to snakes is in the form *ꜥrꜥt* 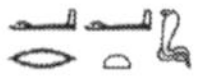 "Uraeus." This is the feminine form of the word, making the masculine form *ꜥrꜥ* (*ala*). The Arat snake is a symbol of a "goddess" and is often depicted as a cobra with a sun disk on its head and a set of cow horns surrounding the sun disk. This informs us that Arat is another form of Isis and Het Heru.

ꜥrꜥ.t "Uraeus" (goddess)

These are important connections we are making because this leads us to another connection between the snake motif (*r, rrw, wrw, rꜣ, ꜥrꜥt*) and of the sun (*rꜥ, ḥrw*), and that is the concept of "time." In many traditions, like the Yorùbá (Nigeria) and the Fon (Benin) systems of West Africa, time is depicted as a snake uncoiling from a center (in Kongo it is simply a spiral series of circles).[43] Snakes are also symbols of "transformation" and in many respects this is also a symbol of "time," but more so "cyclical time" (seasons). We see the snake determinative in a couple of words dealing with *time* or certain gods in the Egyptian lexicon.

Table 5:

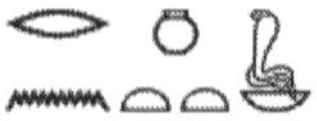	*rnnwtt* "The goddess *Rnnwtt*"
	*rnnwtt* "lunar month, feast, harvest festival, goddess of the harvest"
	*rnnt* "wet nurse, wardress, nurse goddess"
	*rnnt* "fortune, destiny, riches"
	*wnwt* "hour goddess" (of Uraeus snake)
	*wrt* "Great One" (of Uraeus, of goddess) [remember *wrw* means "great snake"; *rrw* "snake"; *ꜥrꜥrt* "uraeus"; ciLuba *lwèlè*(à) "serpent"; syn. > *lwasa*)
	*nṯrt* "goddess"

The goddess *rnnwtt* was popular among agricultural workers (Wilkinson, 2003: 226). We

43 See K. Bunseki Fu-Kiau (2001). *African Cosmology of the Bantu Kongo: Principles of Life & Living*. Athelia Henrietta Pr; 2 edition. New York, NY.

would assume so given that *rnnwtt* is also associated with lunar months which help to time the proper planting and harvesting of crops (which is why she is the goddess of harvests). We argue here that the snake becomes an emblem of *time* and the word *rnnwtt* probably originated from a word meaning "snake." The following in the Kalenjiin language is interesting: *eereen* "villain, snake"; *eereenet* "snake."[44]

In the word *wnwt* "hour goddess (of Uraeus snake)" it is clear that the *ʿrʿt* snake is associated with "time," as we can see it accompanied as a determinative with two other symbols of time: the *star* ⋆ and the *sun* ⊙ . We use the sun and the stars to measure time and predict the coming seasons. The snake (*r, rrw, wrw, r3, ʿrʿt*), we argue, is a symbol of "motion" as there is no "time" without "motion" (PCS **la* "motion").

Aristotle speculated that time was just a measure of motion, where by 'motion' he means change of any sort, including qualitative change. We are reminded of our great science-fiction writer Octavia Butler who declared that, "All that you touch You Change. All that you Change Changes you. The only lasting truth is Change." God is "change" (*ḫpr*) according to Butler in her most famous work *The Parable of the Sower*. In order to define the uniformity of time, that is, the notion of equal intervals of time, Aristotle was guided by astronomical practices, which in antiquity provided the most practical and accurate measures of time. He identified uniform motion with the rate of motion of the *fixed stars* ⋆ ; a choice for which he found a dynamical justification in his celestial physics. [45]

The *-r-* root for "snake" becomes a source for a play on words with the theme of "motion and going." In Egyptian this root is *ʿr* "to leave, to go out, mount up, ascend, extend, penetrate, lead, carry away, come on." When this root is reduplicated we have *ʿrʿr* "to accomplish, to perform, to effect, to supply, to improve." This root in ciLuba is *eela* "to exit, go from self (sound, idea, word, or object), to issue, to express." It is seen in the word *lwendu*(o) "walk, travel, facing" (<*enda* "walk, go, function") [n+l > nd].

The word *pr*(i,u) in Egyptian is a serial verb consisting of *-p-* "come, become" and *-ʿr-* "ascend, extend, lead, carry away, come, to go out." We see variations of the *-p-* root in the following Egyptian terms:

ppi	"unknown" [verb]{used about movement}
pwy	"to fly, to flee, to escape, to flutter"
pt	"to flee, to run"
ptpt	"tread (roads), trample (enemies), smite" (reduplication)

The following table displays some terms for relative motion in the Egyptian language consisting of the *p-r* root.

44 This relationship between "snake" and "bad character" can be seen also in Egyptian with the terms: *r/r3* "snake" and *t3 r3* "slanderer, gossiper."

45 Rynasiewicz, Robert, "Newton's Views on Space, Time, and Motion", *The Stanford Encyclopedia of Philosophy (Fall 2011 Edition)*, Edward N. Zalta (ed.), http://plato.stanford.edu/archives/fall2011/entries/newton-stm/

Table 6:  = prt

Egyptian	**ciLuba**[5]
pr "come" ***pri*** " to go forth, to emerge, to escape, to issue, to leave, to proceed" *prr* "to go forth, to emerge, to escape, to issue, to proceed" *wꜣ* "to go" (*ꜣ* = *l* ?) *ʿr* "mount up, ascend, extend, penetrate, lead, carry away, come on"	**vwa** "come, become" **lwa** "come" (out) **liya** "come"
prj "to emerge, arise"	**vwija** "to come, make happen, to become" **divwa** "came, advent"
pri "to display, to show, be visible, be apparent" *pri* "go, come out, escape (from), issue, proceed, leaving"	**vwila** "come by, occur, reaching" (towards something)
pri "come forth" *pri* "go, come out, escape" *pr* "go up, ascend"	**civwilu** "arrive, to become, because of the arrival" **mvwilu** "approach, grounds for coming, how come"
prw "motion, procession, (child)birth, outcome, result"	**cidìvwilè** "to be pregnant while not having a period" (to become pregnant)
prw "motion, procession, outcome, result"	**kavwidìlà** "reason (for coming), because of the coming"
	vwavwa "days to come or coming days"

This becomes vitally important if we want to begin to understand the root and nature of the god  *ẖpr/ẖprr* in ancient Egypt. *H̱pr* is the god of "change, transformation, evolution and becoming." The word *ẖpr* is simply the word *pr* "come, go forth, issue, leave, proceed, emerge, motion, ascend, etc.," with the *ẖ*- prefix. The god *ẖpr* is attested as early as the 5th dynasty (2494-2345 BCE) from a pyramid text that evokes the sun to appear in the form of *ẖpr*. However, he may have been one of the very earliest gods of Egypt, yet there is no record of him having an actual cult. Crude objects resembling scarabs have been discovered dating from as early as the Neolithic period (7000-5000 BC).[46]

This is important to note because it is assumed by Muhammad (2009) that the god *rʿ* was "introduced" into Egypt during the third dynastic period from Arabia when it is clear that the concepts, the terminology and study of *rʿ* goes back at least 7000 years BCE. There is corroborative evidence from the Ptolemaic period on this question of Ra through the *nṯr ẖpr*.

Loprieno, in his book *Ancient Egyptian: A Linguistic Introduction* (1995: 24), introduces to us the *acrophonic principle* in the Ptolemaic age of Egyptian writing. *Acrophony* is the naming of letters of an alphabetic writing system so that a letter's name begins with the letter itself. For example, Greek letter names are acrophonic: the names of the letters α, β, γ, δ, are spelled with the respective letters: ἄλφα (alpha), βῆτα (beta), γάμμα (gamma), δέλτα (delta). In the Ptolemaic period, this method of writing was used especially when it came to the name of deities (Loprieno, ibid.). Sir E. Wallis Budge in his *Hieroglyphic Egyptian Dictionary Vol. I* has a late rendering of Osiris that is instructive here.

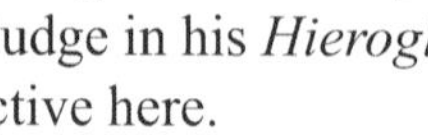

Wsr "Osiris" (Budge, 181a)

46 "Egypt: Khephir, God of the Sun, Creation, Life and Resurrection" http://www.touregypt.net/featurestories/khephir.htm (retrieved April 8, 2012)

This variation of the word Asar is given by the consonants *w-s-r* [quail chick (*w* - G43) + duck (*sꜣ* - G39) + dung beetle (*ḫpr* - L1). In the cryptic (acrophonic) way of spelling, all that matters is the first consonant in the name of the glyph being used. If the dung-beetle was always rendered as *ḫpr*, by the acrophonic principle, the L1 glyph would render the [*ḫ*] sound because this is the first letter. But it is not being used for /*ḫ*/, as this would render the word *wsḫ*. But instead the glyph represents the [r] sound. This would imply that the L1 glyph was not always rendered as *ḫpr* but also as *rʿ*. This is why the god *ḫpr* is associated with *rʿ* because the beetle glyph has the same phonetic value as *rʿ*.[47] It is not uncommon in Egyptian for a single glyph to have two or more phonetic values. With this being the case, the 7000 BCE renderings of *ḫpr* in the archeological record should be seen as *rʿ* also, pushing *rʿ* to predynastic times which would coincide with the linguistic evidence of *rʿ* "God, sun, etc." in other African languages (PWS, PWN, PCS, etc.).

It is possible to honor and worship a spirit/god without there being a cult center dedicated to it (e.g., *Oludumare* among the Yorùbá does not have a cult center). *Rʿ* is a composite of homonyms and homophones that has been present in the language since predynastic times. Which term is to be utilized depends on the nature of the Divine they want to highlight at that moment. In the case of *ḫpr/ḫprr*, or *rʿ* in the form of a snake, it is the process of "motion" that denotes "time" that is the subject of Egyptian discourse. It is expressed in plain "English" in a Theban hymn for *Rʿ* (Assmann Hymn-D) which states, "Hail overlord of circling time, Atum the great one of the line of eternity" (Quirke, 2001: 68). *ỉtm* is another form of *Rʿ*. In Hymn-F (ibid., 70) we have another form of *Rʿ* as "Atum-Khepri" (*ỉtm-ḫprj*).

We find support for our analysis among the Baluba of Central Africa. The term for scarab/ beetle (*Scarabaeus sacer*) in ciLuba is:

ḫprr

kapepu, kapepwela, kapepula, kapulupulu, kaholoholo, kampulu, cipepu, cipepwela, cipepula, ciholoholo, cipulupulu; cimpulu[6]

We note that the image of *ḫpr* is of him raising the sun (Ra) in the eastern horizon. There are a few terms in ciLuba that are of importance for us here. To "raise" in ciLuba is *shu-la*. The root of the word *ḫpr* has the meaning of "wind" or to "blow." In ciLuba "blown" is *pupa, peeps, pepula, pupwila*. In Luba *Cipepu* or *Cipepewela* can also be rendered *ku-ku-Pepa* or *pepula* "blow, being carried by the wind."[48] We should note that *Cipepu-la* means "strong wind," "Breath bearer of Ra." The key words are *Pa* "to give, to sponsor, to award; blow *Pe/ Pa* "wind" (also *cipepa, cipepela*) and *Pela-Ditem* "friction or making fire by rubbing with stone or wooden flint." We are supported by the fact that many of the depictions of *ḫpr* are with

47 Many words for "bugs" or "snakes" derive from a verb meaning to "go" or "crawl." Take for instance Proto-Afro-Asiatic: **tak*ʷ- "bug, beetle; fly." The concept of "flying" (motion) is what gives the bug/beetle its name in this case. With that said, compare *Rʿ* with the following: PWN *DAD* "to crawl"; PB **dànd* (LT) "crawl, creep, spread (as a vine); PB *dù* "come (or go) out; ooze, bleed"; **Sumerian** *dal* "fly"; **[Egyptian** *ʿr* = mount up, ascend, extend, penetrate, lead, carry away, come on]; Kalenjiin *laa* "carry"; PWN *LIAT, (LAT)* "tread"; Mangbetu *oro* "to flee"; Mangbetu *oda* "go ahead"; PCS **la* "motion," **oro* "motion"; Eastern-Sudanic: Merarit *la* "to go", Tama *lo* "to go", Masai *lo* "to go"; Chari-Nile: Lendu *ra* "to go." We will further confirm these attributes below in our continued discussion on *ḫpr*.

48 Remember our Egyptian term: *ppi* "unknown"[verb]{used about movement}

stretched out "wings" which focuses our attention on "flight, movement."

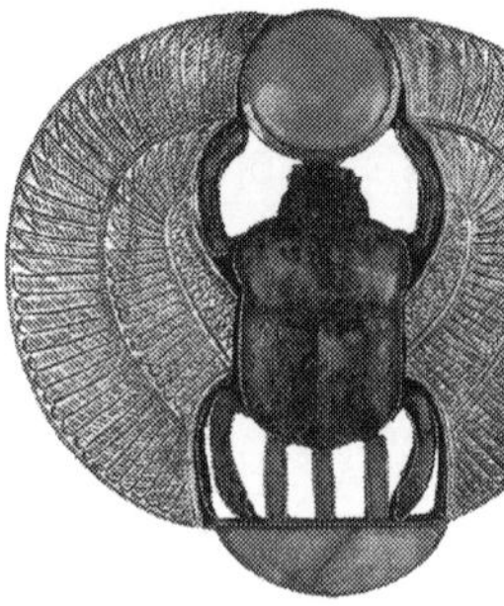

Figure 3: Lapis Winged Scarab from the Global Museum, with King Tut's coronation name: *Neb-Kheper-u-Re*

The form of *rꜥ* as *ḫprr* represents the force that compels the sun and its light rays to "move" across the universe. This *pe/pa, pepu,* etc., root is an ancient Niger-Congo root meaning *wind* or to *blow.*[49]

> PWS *pi* "to fly", *pí* "to throw", "feather"; PWN *PAPA* "wing"; PWN *PHET* "blow," *PHUPH* "wind, blow", *PHUP* "pigeon, dove" (flap wings), I Yorùbá *a-fefe* "wind," III Lefana *o-fe-fe* "wind," V Temne *a-fef* "wind," VI Mende *fefe* "wind, breeze," Mangbetu *mbimbato* "wind," Bantu *pepo* "wind", Swahili *upepo* "wind," Bantu (Meeussen) *peep* "blow"; Fula *fufede* "blow" (forge); Bantu *padad* "fly"; Kongo *epapi* "wing", Ngala *lipapu* "wing" etc.; Mande *pã* "to fly" (with wings), also *dama* "to fly"; Mangbetu *kupapa* "wing"[50]

All of these forms have to deal with relative "motion" and we argue here that *Rꜥ*, in relationship to time, is characterized by his "motion" (traversing) across the sky. The word *rꜥ* is built into the word *ḫpr/ḫprr* and if *ḫpr* is attested between 7000-5000 BCE, then one couldn't argue a dynastic importation of *rꜥ* into Egypt. Here are a few lexical items that reinforce the notion that *rꜥ* is associated with time:

> Sumerian *u-na* "heaven" (Wanger), "time, night" (Delitzsch); Sumerian *en* (*én, èn*) "time", "until"; Mangbetu *êda* "to make endure" (with other reflexes); Bantu *deedó* "today", *i,dó* "tomorrow, yesterday"; PWS *la, da* "sun, day", "always"; Sumerian *a-ra* "times" (Campbell-Dunn, 2009b).

In the following image we see all of the aspects of *rꜥ* reinforcing this aspect of "time" and "motion."[51]

---

49 See Westermann's Index B (1927 : 310 f) for reconstructed PWS and Bantu roots; **pap* "wind."

50 See GJK Campbell-Dunn (2006: 88). *Who Were the Minoans: An African Answer*. Author House Publishing. Bloomington, IN. Also Campbell-Dunn (2009b).

51 For a more in depth discussion on Ra's association with time, see Chapter II "The Sun Cult and the Measurement of Time" in Quirke (2001: 41-72).

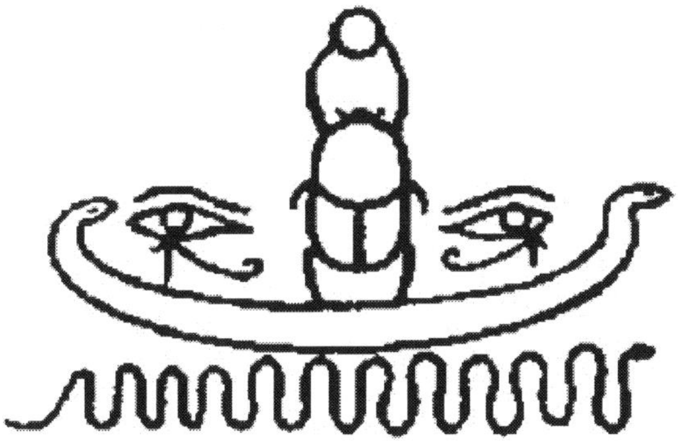

Figure 4: The god *Rʿ* in the form of *ḫpr* traversing the night sky on the boat of *Rʿ* on top of the god *ʿ3pp*. Replication from the *Egyptian Book of the Dead.*

What we see above is the god *Rʿ*, in the forms of *ḫprr* and *wḏt*, sailing on the boat of *rʿ* on the "waves" of *ʿ3pp* "the god of chaos" (see Wilkinson, 2003: 221). Even the boat used to sail through time is a double-headed snake. This is confirmation that the snake is a symbol of time. As we can see here, the god *ʿ3pp* (bottom snake) is used to propel creation forward. This would make sense given its root *pp* which in the Egyptian language (*ppi*) deals with "motion."

I argue that *ʿ3pp* (*3* = *l*) is simply the term *pepula* "blown, being carried away by wind" (*ḫ-pr*) in ciLuba reversed. Or it can be rendered in ciLuba *lupeepèlè*(à) "wind."[52] It is the element that causes change (*ḫpr*) and time to exist. In modern scientific language we call this force *entropy* (also the *second law of thermodynamics*):

> **Entropy** is a thermodynamic property that can be used to determine the energy not available for work in a thermodynamic process, such as in energy conversion devices, engines, or machines. Such devices can only be driven by convertible energy, and have a theoretical maximum efficiency when converting energy to work. During this work, entropy accumulates in the system, which then dissipates in the form of waste heat.
>
> In classical thermodynamics, the concept of entropy is defined phenomenologically by the second law of thermodynamics, which states that the entropy of an isolated system always increases or remains constant. Thus, entropy is also a measure of the tendency of a process, such as a chemical reaction, to be entropically favored, or to proceed in a particular direction. It determines that thermal energy always flows spontaneously from regions of higher temperature to regions of lower temperature, in the form of heat. These processes reduce the state of order of the initial systems, and **therefore entropy is an expression of disorder or randomness.**[53]

Also noted in the Wiki article:

---

52 To confirm the correspondence, we note in Egyptian *ppt* "a plant"; ciLuba *cipùpù* "foliage" (*pp.t* > *t.pp*) (Egyptian *-t* suffix is prefixed in ciLuba as *ci-*). Therefore in ciLuba we have: *pee* "wind"; *-peepa* "blow hard, be impetuous; shake in the wind; blow"; *cipeepè*(à) "wind"; *lupeepèlè*(à) "wind"; *cipeepèlè*(à) "violent wind, storm"; *Cipùpu* (*mpuupija*) "storm, hurricane, tornado, strong wind, violent storm.; disaster." It is where we get the name Typhon from in Greek, the god of violent storms, the whirlwind and tornados: Typhon < Cipupu = Tshipupu > Typupo. It should be noted that Typhon was depicted as having a lower body consisting of snakes (*ʿ3pp*?). This is ultimately where we get the concept of a "typhoon" (a violent storm of the sea).

53 http://en.wikipedia.org/wiki/Entropy (retrieved April 8, 2012). Remember that *ʿ3pp* is "the god of chaos/disorder."

> **The Arrow of Time**: Entropy is the only quantity in the physical sciences that seems to imply a particular direction of progress, sometimes called an *arrow of time*. As time progresses, the second law of thermodynamics states that the entropy of an isolated system never decreases. Hence, from this perspective, **entropy measurement is thought of as a kind of clock**.[54]

Again, we are reintroduced to this notion of time, and if our connections are sound (and we think they are) then this reinforces, from our Egyptian perspective, the association between *snakes* and *time*. We should also note that the word *prt* (root of *ḫpr*) is the name for the *autumn equinox*, a key time marker for the ancient Egyptians.

The god *R*ʿ has had many forms and associations since before predynastic times. The study of the sun's movements has been observed since predynastic times. Robert Bauval and Thomas Brophy in their work *Black Genesis: The prehistoric origins of ancient Egypt* (2011) discuss the ancestors of the ancient Egyptians (who come from Chad, the Sahara and Sudan) and their scientific astronomical observations.

One of the old predynastic sun temples is found in the Dhakla oasis and is commonly known as the Djedefre (*ḏdfr*) water-mountain, which may have been the inspiration for this glyph: 𓈌. This mountain served as a natural solar calendar and had three horizon stations which marked the solstices and the equinoxes of the sun (Bauval & Brophy, 2011: 143-145). We see this reflected later on in Egyptian history in a Hymn to Ra which states:

> Hail Ra in your rising
> Atum Ra-Horakhty.
> I adore you, your perfection in my eyes.
> May your radiance come to be upon my breast.
> You proceed, you set in the Evening Barque,
> Your heart elated [after battle] in the Morning Barque.
> You traverse the sky in peace, all your enemies are felled.
> The Unwearying stars rejoice for you,
> The Indestructible stars adore you.
> **You set in the horizon of the Horizon Mountain,**
> Perfect as Ra every full day,
> Living and stable as my lord,
> Ra the true of voice (Quirke, 2001: 68) (emphasis mine)

It's hard to imagine that a people who have been following the motion of the stars (see the predynastic calendar at Nabta Playa) and the sun since predynastic times would all of a sudden, a thousand years later, decide to deify the sun by inspiration of wandering Semites who didn't have the term *r*ʿ "sun" in their vocabulary.

The Nabta Playa site in Sudan was known as a ceremonial and astronomical site. It, like the Djedefre water-mountain, was a calendar with solar alignments to the summer solstice and the equinoxes (Ibid., 307). The earliest calendar of ancient Egypt is dated to around 4200 BCE and there is evidence that the ancestors of the Egyptians have been star gazing and recording their observations as early as 26000 BCE (see Finch, 1998: 167-202). Not to sound repetitive, but *R*ʿ (symbolized by the sun, snake, falcon and beetle) has been an important part of the imagination and culture of the Nile Valley inhabitants for more than 30000 years. On what empirical grounds can one assert that the Semites introduced *R*ʿ (*‘ḷ*) as a theological and astronomical concept to

54 For an expanded discourse, I recommend Morris H. Shamos (Ed.) (1959). *Great Experiments in Physics. Henry* Hold and Company, Inc. and John Clark (1994). *Matter and Energy: Physics in Action*. Oxford University Press. New York, NY. More recent articles can be obtained from http://www.entropylaw.com/.

the ancient Egyptians so late in their history?

Conclusion

Part I of this series sought to examine the linguistic and conceptual origins of the Ancient Egyptian god *Rˤ*. We also sought to find validity in the claim that the Egyptian god *Rˤ* could have been imported from Arabia during the 3rd Dynasty as the god Allah, a claim made by Muhammad (2009). Our analysis concludes that it is highly unlikely that *Rˤ* was an import by Semites from Arabia into Egypt during the 3rd Dynasty for several reasons. 1) *Rˤ* has been a part of Egyptian culture since before predynastic times, 2) *Rˤ* is a polysemous domain that has been represented by different symbols throughout Egyptian history (and at other times all combined into one image), 3) these iconographic emblems are all pronounced as *rˤ* (re, rei, ri, r(w)) and each of these emblems (sun, snake, eye, etc.) are not pronounced as such in the Semitic languages, and lastly 4) *Rˤ* and Allah have two different etymologies and thus two different conceptualizations.

Much of the latter points has been addressed in Part I of this series, but will be given a more distinctive argumentation in Part II. It is our argument that *Rˤ* (primarily), as the sun-god, derives from a word *rˤ* "sun" (< "fire"), while *Allah* among the Semites derives from a root that means "sky" (< "length, height"). While *Rˤ* is associated with *knowledge, creation, light, motion* and *time*, the Semitic god *Allah* is primarily associated with "rain." With the evidence provided in this essay, and with more to come in Part II, it appears to us that the claims made in Muhammad (2009) cannot be substantiated by the evidence. We will now examine the origins of the god Allah beyond the Semitic linguistic and cultural group.

(Table Footnotes)

1 I posit that this phrase *Amanda* is also cognate with Egyptian *imnt* "the west, the western, secret, hidden place, crypt, right side, realm of the dead."

2 The final *-j* (yy) in Egyptian is often the *bi-* prefix in ciLuba.

3 Note: the skeleton of the word for "sun" in Berber generally entails considerably more consonants (3 or 4) than in ancient Egypt where there is only one.

4 We also add: Yorùbá : *ala* (white light - of a star or sun - reflex); *ra~* "shine" (as sun and moon) (< PB **-dang-* "shine")

5 http://www.ciyem.ugent.be

6 Bilolo (2008: 201).

DID THE GOD RA DERIVE FROM ARABIA?

An examination of Wesley Muhammad's claim in Black Arabia and the African Origin of Islam Part II: Allah the sky-god

We continue our examination of the assertion made by Wesley Muhammad in his book *Black Arabia: The African Origin of Islam* (2009) in that the ancient Egyptian God *Rʿ* was an import into the Nile Valley by Semites from Arabia. In *Part I* of this series we took a look at the etymological origins for the word *Rʿ*, as it pertained to the sun-god, and did a cross linguistic comparison to see if there were linguistic grounds to make such a claim. We concluded that there were no linguistic grounds for this exchange as Semitic words for *sun* were totally different than the Egyptian: Egyptian *rʿ/ḥrw* "sun"; PSm. **sms* "sun." As a result of the examination of this question in *Part I*, a suggestion was made for a possible correlatation for the presence of the name *Allah* in the Egyptian records in relation to the "sky, heavens." *Part II* of this series explores this possibility. Before we get into the meat of our exploration, we must introduce the reader to the linguistic field of *semantics*. Understanding some key aspects of the relationship of *metaphor* to the development of words and concepts will be critical in understanding the basis of our argument in these two essays. We will now take a look at semantics and the importance of its understanding to the argument that *Allah* of the Semites is a 'sky-god'.

Semantics

Semantics is a branch of linguistics that studies *meaning* as communicated through human language (i.e., *words* and *sentences*). A person who studies semantics is a *semanticist*. Semanticists often have to have a nodding acquaintance with other disciplines such as philosophy and psychology which also investigates the creation and transmission of meaning. Therefore, semantics in of itself is a multi-disciplinary field of inquiry. Space will not allow for a deeper discussion of semantics here. So we will only take a cursory look at key concepts that pertain to this discussion. I recommend the reader review the book *Semantics* by John I. Saeed (now in its third edition).

The verb *mean* has several uses for us here. This includes inferences based on *cause* and *effect* and on the knowledge about the arbitrary symbols used in public signs (Saeed, 1995: 5). Human beings have a habit of identifying and creating signs: of making one thing stand for another. This practice of signification is argued by scholars such as Ferdinand de Saussure to be part of a larger discipline called *semiotics*. Semioticians investigate the types of relationship that may hold between a sign and the object it represents (a **signifier** and its **signified**). One basic distinction is between *icon, index* and *symbol*. These terms are identified as such:

- An **icon** is where there is a similarity between a sign and what it represents (e.g., a portrait and its real life subject)

- An **index** is where the sign is closely associated with its signified, often in a causal relationship (e.g., *smoke* is an index of *fire*)
- A **symbol** is where there is only a conventional link between the sign and its signified (e.g., as in the case of insignia to denote military ranks, or wearing black at a funeral). Words would be considered, then, verbal symbols.

These concepts will become very important for us throughout this discussion. It is the knowledge of these types of distinctions that will inform us how terms become *polysemous*, meaning that one word has many senses which extend the root into more expansive schemas. Before we expand into this aspect of the subject, we must first explore *literal* and *non-literal* meaning since it is *meaning* that is important for us in this discourse.

Literal and Non-Literal Meaning

Literal meanings distinguish between instances where the speaker speaks in a neutral, factually accurate way (e.g., "I'm hungry"). A *non-literal* meaning distinguishes instances where the speaker deliberately describes something in untrue or impossible terms in order to achieve a special effect (e.g., "I'm starving"). Non-literal uses of language are typically called "figurative" language which is described by a host of rhetorical terms (i.e., metaphor, irony, metonymy, synecdoche, hyberbole, and litotes).

The line between *literal* and *non-literal* meanings is difficult to demarcate. One of the ways by which language changes over time is by the speakers shifting the meanings of words to fit new conditions. One such shift is caused by *metaphoric extension.* This is where some new idea is depicted in terms of something more familiar. For a time, the metaphoric nature of the expression remains clear. However, after a while such expressions become fossilized and their metaphorical quality is no longer apparent to the speaker. When we speak of Washington, DC being the *capital* of the United States, Americans no longer conjure up images of a physical "head." The word capital "head" is now fossilized in the English lexicon. In many instances, historical comparative linguistics is the only tool available to us that allow us to trace the original lexical roots, their meanings and their metaphoric extensions.

Categorization

As a result of the development of non-literal meanings, words extend themselves to create a *field* of meaning anchored in a central *theme*. The underlying theme unites all of the extended meanings and gives them sort of a conceptual family relationship (i.e., categories). Often words can be polysemous: e.g., to *call* someone's name from across the street vs. to *call* someone on the phone. The former use of *call* implies actually using ones voice to identify the person across the street. The latter usage of the word *call* refers to the act of actually dialing numbers with your fingers on the dial pad of a phone. One can technically make a call, in this sense, without using one's voice. A *call* is made even if the other person doesn't pick-up on the other end of the line and verbally replies back.

Words belong to never-ending chain sequences, to phrases, sentences, and contexts which become the fabric of the entire language (Lord 1966: 241). Words have no meaning until they become joined together in a linguistic whole. As long as there's no clash of context, this range of associations can coexist (like in the case of *homophones*). Whenever homophones exist, the homophones will acquire different spellings wherever possible (e.g., person—parson; soul—sole; maze—maize; bell—belle). When *homonymy*—words that sound the same but are spelled differently—begins to cause confusion in a language, often the root word takes on a different shape to make clearer the distinction: e.g., cloth—clothe; brothers—brethren; shade—shadow). A word will either adjust itself dynamically in a field or be rejected. Meanings build up composite meanings in a larger "field of tension."

Categories represent a complicated network of similarities overlapping and criss-crossing: sometimes overall similarities, sometimes similarities of detail. When categorizing an entity, it is not so much a question of ascertaining whether the entity possesses a strict set of attributes (this or that feature), but how closely the dimensions of the entity approximate to the optimum dimensions. Categorization makes it possible for an organism to reduce the limitless variation in the world to manageable proportions. It can also reject themes that do not fit into the category; so it can be a tool of distinction as well as a unifying tool. The notion of *similarity* underlies all categorization processes. Things are similar to the extent that a human being, in some context and for some purpose, chooses to regard them as similar. Details of the categorization process can be found in Taylor (1995) chapters 2-3.

What's important for us to note here is that human beings have a need to find similarity between phenomena. When we capture these similarities in language, we create a category for which different words can be used to represent items in the category (e.g., category = *animal*; thus a *canine* becomes a domain for which a *dog* or a *wolf* would be subentries or *schemas* under the category of *canine*). I argue in this paper that word roots can also be categories and by a process of agglutination, inflection and metaphoric extension, new concepts can arise and these new terms would all belong to the same category while sharing the same lexical root. This is what I argue is ultimately going on in regards to the word *Allah* in the Arabic language.

Allah belongs to a *polysemous category*. Polysemous categories exhibit a number of more or less discrete, though related meanings, clustering in a family resemblance category (Taylor, 1995: 122). What's important to note in this discourse, and for this model of polysemy in particular, is the notion of *meaning relatedness*. It is, namely, relatedness of meaning which permits different meanings to get associated in the first place. There are many ways in which different meanings find symmetry in polysemous categories, but we will discuss two very important ways that this process occurs: that is by *metonymy* and *metaphor*.

Metonymy

Metonymy is a process of transferred reference. It is a figure of speech whereby the name of one entity e^1 is used to refer to another entity e^2 which is contiguous to e^1. There is a referring function which permits the name of a container to refer to the contents of the container, as when we say *the kettle's boiling* (Taylor, ibid.). In the same type of process the referring function permits the name of a producer to refer to the product (e.g., *Does he own any Picassos? Diop is on the top shelf*). A subcategory of metonymy is *synecdoche*. Here the reference to the whole is made by referring to a salient part of the whole: e.g., *We need some new faces around here.* Often the name of an institution may stand for an influent person or influential group (*The Government has stated…; According to the White House…*). This is a highly conventionalized process.

I argue that in many respects the name *Allah* can be considered a form of metonymy. As will be demonstrated later on, *Allah* derives from a word for "sky, rain." The original referent has been fossilized and is now considered a proper name for the Divine among Arabs. In ancient times, referring to the heavens meant referring to the Divine. It is no different than referring to the White House (a location) to mean the people who work and run the White House (the object). In our case, as regards *Allah*, He is the force or spirit that "runs" things from the location of the *sky*. We will see that this level of *metonymy* derives ultimately from *metaphor* as it regards *Allah*. But there are many aspects to *Allah* and they all derive and are articulated through the process of *metaphoric extension*.

Metaphor

For the cognitive semanticist, *metaphor* can be seen as a means whereby ever more abstract and intangible areas of experience can be conceptualized in terms of the familiar and concrete. This notion of metaphor is thereby motivated by a search for understanding. The word *metaphor* literally means to "transfer over" or "carry over" (meaning). It is an important form of figurative language which is seen usually as reaching its most sophisticated forms in literary, mystic, religious or poetic language (rappers, I argue, are masters at metaphor).

Metaphor is somewhat like a *simile* in that it involves the identification of resemblances (Saeed 1997: 302). However, metaphor goes a step further by causing a transference where properties are transferred from one concept to another. The starting point or described concept is often called the **target** domain (the *tenor*). The comparison concept or the analogy is called the **source** domain (the *vehicle*).

In African mythology (and we can argue mythology in general) the mythological characters are the source domains (the vehicles) that "drive, carry" us to the target domain. In *Part I* of this essay, we discussed the ancient Egyptian God *Rʿ* having many different associations, icons and symbols. One of his symbols given to him by the Egyptians is that of the *sun* which also goes by the same name (*rʿ*). In relation to this topic of metaphor, the *sun* would be the *source domain*.

We mentioned that one of his associations is with "enlightenment, intelligence, wisdom and the ability to see." The symbol of the sun becomes the "vehicle" that carries us to the *target domain* which is "wisdom, intelligence, etc." The concrete phenomenon of "light" (given off by the sun) is then "transferred" to the abstract concepts of "wisdom, intelligence and knowledge." Just as light allows us to "see" with our physical eyes, knowledge, wisdom and understanding allows our mind's "eye" to "see" (comprehend) the world around us.

Metaphor expands our use of concepts and helps to add many layers to a given domain or theme. We will now look at some specific examples in regards to the context by which metaphor is used and how the study of polysemous roots informs our current discussion.

Category Extension

Metaphors allow us to understand one domain of experience in terms of another. In order to serve this function, there must be some grounding, some concepts that are not completely understood via metaphor to serve as the source domain (Saeed, 1997: 304).[1] Lakoff and his colleagues discuss the possibility that many areas of experience are metaphorically structured by means of a rather small number of image schemas. Amongst these image schemas are the following:

a) **Containment.** The image schema profiles a container, with its inside and outside, in the domain of three-dimensional space. The image schema is applied metaphorically to a large number of non-spatial domains. Linguistic forms are conceptualized as containers (*put ideas into words, the contents of an essay, empty words*), as are emotional states (*be in love, fall out of love*).

b) **A journey and its component parts** (i.e. *origin, path, and destination, with possible obstacles and detours on the way*). Life itself is frequently conceptualized as a journey (*My life isn't getting anywhere, He's come a long way, We're going round in circles*), as is, for instance, the progress (i.e. moving forward) of society (*He's a progressive, He's ahead of his time, He's a*

1 Citing Lakoff, George and Turner, Mark. (1989). *More than Cool Reason: a field guide to poetic metaphor*. University of Chicago Press. Chicago, IL. p. 135.

fellow traveler).

c) **Proximity and distance.** Once again, a schema based on spatial relations is projected on to non-spatial domains. Thus degree of emotional involvement and the possibility of mutual influence are understood in terms of proximity (*a close friend, a close adviser, to keep one's distance*).

d) **Linkage and separation.** Closely related to the proximity-distance schema is the schema of linkage and separation. Again, basically spatial notions can be applied to abstractions. We make *contact with people*, we *keep in touch*, and we *break social and family ties*.

e) **Front-back orientation.** This schema is applied, in the first which major sensory organs, especially where the eyes are located. The front particularly widespread conceptual metaphor applies this schema to orientation in time. The future lies in front (*look forward to the future*), while the past is at one's back (*look back on the past*). Events, too, have fronts and backs. Many languages make no formal distinction between 'in front of' and 'before', and between 'behind' and 'after'. What is in front of an event is what happens before; what is behind, happens after.

f) **The part-whole relationship.** The whole consists of parts arranged in a specific configuration. The separation or rearrangement of the parts results in the destruction of the whole. Primarily, this schema is applied to discrete, concrete entities. Metaphorically, it can be applied to a range of abstract notions, for example, interpersonal relations. A married couple forms a whole; on divorce they *split up*, or *break up*; later, they may *come together* again.

g) **Linear order.** Primarily, this schema arranges objects in a one-dimensional line in terms of their increasing distance from an observer. Metaphorically, it can be applied to temporal sequence. What occurs *first* happens before, what comes *second* occurs later.

h) **Up-down orientation.** Primarily, this schema has to do with spatial orientation within a gravitational field.

i) **Mass vs. multiplex conceptualizations.** Some aspects of these alternative ways of viewing objects/events have already been mentioned. (Saeed, 1997: 134-135)

Space will not allow us to examine every image schema discussed by Lakoff above. However, the most important schema for our discourse is **h) Up-down orientation**. This type of metaphor is described as a spatial category because the schema is understood within a three-dimensional spatial context. Lakoff and Johnson provide us with common examples that would fall under this schema.

a) **HAPPY IS UP; SAD IS DOWN**
I'm feeling *up*. My spirits *rose*. You're in *high* spirits. I'm feeling *down*. I'm *depressed*. He's really *low* these days. My spirits *sank*.

b) **CONSCIOUS IS UP; UNCONCIOUS IS DOWN**
Wake *up*. He *fell* asleep. He *dropped* off to sleep. He's *under* hypnosis. He *sank* into a coma.

c) **HEALTH AND LIFE ARE UP; SICKNESS AND DEATH ARE DOWN**
He's at the *peak* of health. He's in *top* shape. He *fell* ill. He's *sinking* fast. He came *down* with the flu. His health is *declining*.

d) **HAVING CONTROL OR FORCE IS UP; BEING SUBJECT TO CONTROL OR FORCE IS DOWN**
I have control *over* her. He's at the *height* of his powers. He's in a superior position. He ranks *above* me in strength. He is *under* my control. He *fell* from power. He is my social *inferior*.

e) **GOOD IS UP; BAD IS DOWN**
Things are looking *up*. We hit a *peak* last year, but it's been *downhill* ever since. Things are at an all-time *low*. He does *high*-quality work.

f) **VIRTUE IS UP; DEPRAVITY IS DOWN**
He is *high* minded. She has *high* standards. She is an *upstanding* citizen. That was a *low* trick. Don't be *underhanded*. I wouldn't *stoop* to that. That was a *low-down* thing to do. (Saeed, 1997: 394)[2]

---

2 Citing George Lakoff & Mark Johnson. (1980). *Metaphors We Live By*. University of Chicago Press. Chicago, IL. pp. 14-21

Many of the earlier mentioned schemas, and especially the *up-down* orientation schema, clearly derives from the most immediate of all of our experiences, our experience of the human body. The experiential base of containment is the human body with its surface separating the inside from the outside (Taylor, 1995: 135). In regards to the *up-down* schema, it is our gravitational field which provides the bases for these metaphors.

Our bodies or the ground beneath us provides the zero point for which the *high* entity is implicitly compared. This is going to be very important to keep in mind when we start talking about the name *Allah* deriving from a word for "sky"; as the root of the word *Allah* is a metaphor that is anchored in the *up-down* schema. The *-l-* root derives from a word that denotes "height, length, measure, and linearity." From this category derives other meanings on the root which creates a *meaning-chain* that links all of the concepts together to form a greater network of concepts. We will now move forward and examine the etymology of the name *Allah* in Arabic.

The -r- root and its spatial orientations

According to convention, the Arabic word *Allah* consists of two words in the Arabic language: *il* (def. article) "the" + *ilāh* "god" meaning "the [sole] God." This name *Allah* exists in other Semitic languages such as Hebrew *'eloah*, *'Ĕlāhā* ܐܠܗܐ (in Biblical Aramaic) and *'Alâhâ* ܐܠܗܐ in Syriac. The Proto-Semitic form is given as *‘ḷ "god, deity." Other texts suggest that it can also be written as *‘ḷh*.[3] The problem with most etymologies as concerns the name *El, Illāh, Ilu*, etc., is that they never define what 'god' means within a Semitic context. What is the Semites saying when they utter *‘ḷh*? What were the earliest conceptions? Words for the Divine have humble origins. What common words were used to denote 'god' among the Semites?

As noted by the Hebrew scholar Ludwig Koehler:

> The theological, and also the more far-reaching religious world of ideas grew out of the non-theological, the common, and whatever one wished to say theologically was expressed in language drawn from the common world of ideas.[4]

So it must be kept in mind that no matter how "sacred" a name for the Divine, or its divinities, is projected to be by practitioners of a particular faith, the terms given to those concepts derive from ordinary, common words in the vocabulary. It is the "lexeme" that gets personified and the accompanying myths are developed around the meaning behind the names given to the deities.

Muhammad (2009: 84) argues that Old South Arabian is the place that has kept the old Semitic religious tradition. Maybe we can get some clues as to what these Southern Arabians thought about when they thought about the Divine. Citing Ulf Oldenburg's text *Above the Stars*

---

3 W. S. LaSor in his article "Proto-Semitic: Is the Concept No Longer Valid?" (1990: 205) suggesst that both *'l* and *'lh* were part of the proto-Semitic lexicon.

4 Ludwig Koehler, in the preface to Koehler-Baumgartner's *Lexicon in Veteris Testamenti Libros* (E. J. Brill, Leiden, 1953) p.xiv., cited in Oduyoye (1996: 29). We can see an example with the word in Hebrew *ba'al*. A wife calls her husband *ba'al*, her "lord, master." But the Canaanites called the Divine *Baal*. In the Yorùbá language this word does not have a religious connotation. Like the Hebrews, the Yorùbá wives call their husbands *baále*. In the ancient Egyptian the /b/ sound has become /w/ and our term is given as *wr*  "lord, master, god, great one, chief." Here we have in language evidence of the concept of the man being "head of household" (a lord, master, etc.). As the Divine is considered the "head" of the world and all things, the common term **b-l* was used to label the Divine's role as master of all things. We note in Yorùbá: *bála* "a title of honor among the Ogboni people"; *bále* "a house holder, master of a house"; *bále-ero* "host, landlord"; *bále* "president, chief, governor" ; *bále-idilé* "head of a household or family, patriarch"; *baále-ilé* "father/head of the household"

of El, Muhammad provides us with all of the characteristics associated with this pre-Islamic god *Allah*. He informs us that:

> The numerous theophorous names composed with the proper name of 'El [read: **Aḷah**] illuminate the distinct character of El and his original glory. He was called '***the first***' and '***exalted***', the king ***above*** all, and therefore his title ***the King*** became another name for El. He was characterized by his strength...As the almighty king of creation he ruled in righteousness, and Righteousness became the name of El, by which he is invoked in the oldest class of personal names; it reveals El as the author and standard of righteousness[...] The terms of kinship '***father, uncle, brother***', which are so abundant in the oldest names reflect a patriarchal social organization typical of nomadic tribes. El belonged to the clan as ***head*** of it, and his function was that of a guardian defending the rights of its members...Another important name of EL was ***Savior***. (Muhammad, 2009: 84-85) (**bolded** and ***italicized*** emphasis mine)

I highlighted certain key terms in the above quoted paragraph to act as conceptual markers which are going to become real important for us throughout this discourse. Keep in mind our notes from the previous discussion on *polysemous categories*, *metaphoric extensions* and the *up-down* image-schema. We will discover that all of these attributes and conceptualizations are represented by the *-l-(-r-)* root in both Kongo-Saharan and Afro-Asiatic languages.

As discussed in *Part I* of this series, traditional methods of deification often crystallized a set of seemingly related concepts into one representative entity. This entity (the deity) becomes a *category* which encompasses many different concepts, and often these concepts share the same consonantal root. In other words, because there is a similarity in how these words are pronounced AND there appears to be a relationship between the concepts, these terms are then combined and represented as one entity: in our case here, the name of the Divine.

For example, let's say in some hypothetical ancient tradition we have a God by the name of DADA "god." Some of his attributes includes: 1) king (authority), 2) god of fire, and 3) savior. Let's say that in this hypothetical tradition, in the language of this ancient people, the lexemes that represent each concept are as follows: *idada* "fire"; *ododa* "king"; and *dadala* "savior." As we can see here, each term has a similar pronunciation. What's common to each term is the /d/ sound in the C_1 and C_2 positions (d-d) which forms the skeleton.

All of these concepts are united under the theme of "power": the *power* to *rule*, the *power* of *fire/life*, and the *power* to *save*. In this respect, these are attributes that could rightfully be associated with the Almighty. So, in the process of creating a mythology for the people to easily grasp the nature of the Divine, instead of calling the Divine by each variation of these terms, they simply combine all of these terms and call him DADA. They then create a story which includes different scenarios by which each of these attributes can be highlighted. The myth then becomes an oral encyclopedia which helps to define the key aspects of the Divine. This is roughly what we are arguing is going on with *Allah* among the Semites.

Ultmately this leads to folk-etymology which genuinely becomes part of the tradition. This is something that linguists struggle with when trying to get at the heart of the meaning of the names for deities from the ancient past. Walter von Warburg in his book *Problems and Methods in Linguistics* (1969) observed that "religious concepts can also be influenced and even completely transformed by the form of words associated with them. The effects of this process of re-interpretation are particularly noticeable in the case of the names of saints and divinities. The re-interpretation of names can also give rise to popular legends" (Von Wartburg, 1969: 124-125). What is being stated here is that legends are built around the meaning behind the name of deities or heroes. Over time these names can be reinterpreted and new legends can emerge as a result of the new interpretation. What I argue here is that these reinterpretations are often fueled by the process of paronymy and it is this process which gives the appearance of polysemy when in fact the similar sounding, or homophonic, terms may have distinctive roots.

The ancients weren't concerned about distinquishing paronymy and homonymy and making clear distinctions between concepts when it came to spiritual concepts. The ancient mind had a bias towards synthesis. The modern researcher has a bias towards compartmentalization. This is why we use comparative linguistics and philology to filter through the layers in order to get to the heart of the concepts.

> Ancient Rabbinic interpretation differs from the modern approach. Firstly, there was a certain striving for the production of multiple meanings...Secondly, interpretation might not only fasten on the literal form of the text but might attach meaning to segments of it which are, from our point of view, at a sub-meaningful level...Thus, while the acceptance of multiple meanings diminished the centrality of a clear procedure from linguistic evidence, the finding of meaning in sub-meaningful elements enable interpretation also to be closely literal. This linguistic-form allegory, both literal and allegorical at the same time, favoured the multiplicity of meanings. A philological treatment...elucidates the meaning of the existeng text through the application of linguistic evidence hitherto ignored...The principle evidence used in a philological treatment is the linguistic usage of the cognate languages and with it the usage of the other stages of the same language...This consideration, if successful, may suggest...a meaning other than that which has normally been acknowledged...[5]

Contrary to Islamic beliefs, the so-called proto-Semitic *‘ḻ "god, deity" is not an exclusively "Semitic" word for the Divine. This term is older than Afro-Asiatic and is found in many world languages. The *-l-* root, without the aid of the Arabs or Hebrews in Africa, was already a staple term associated with the Divine.

Muhammad (2009) argues that the Arabic *Allah* is found in the Egyptian spiritual system as the god *Rˁ*. As we argued in *Part I* of this series, the god *Ra* and *Alah* of the Semites belong to two different roots; and by having two different roots, there are ultimately two different conceptualizations for each representative term. The name *Ra* in Egyptian, associated with the "sun-god," ultimately derives from a word for "fire" and it is the concept of fire and its radiating light that is at the center of this association. However, the name *Allah* derives from a root that means "sky" and it ultimately derives from a more ancient root that means "length, top, distance."

The ciLuba-Bantu language provides us with some much needed insight into this root. This root in ciLuba is given as follows:

> ***eela*** "remove, send away, clear out, dismiss"[6] or "to exit from the self (sound, idea, word, object ...) make, express, speak." [*eela*[1] 15/0 verbe transitif V.: *-eela*[2], *-eela*[3] *>ejil, esh, eshangan, ulul, elangan, el, angan, iibw, akaj, akan, ek, ekan, ekej* [1+i>di] ⇒*-eela* Luvulè [2006-07-10 11:08:08]].[7] All of the following words in ciLuba derive from the root *eela* (remember l>n, l>d, d>t; [n + l> n, n + i> nyi]):
>
> V.: bipendu, butà, byonù, cibingu, cidya, cilà, dîyi, -eela[1], kààlumbandì, kabòòbò(ù), kalele(a), kalèlè(à), kankundulwila, kashìbà, lubìlà, lukòndò(ù), lukonko(u), lusanzu2, lusùmwìnù, mapìkù, mbìlà, meeji, milawu, mpatà1, mukòsò(ù,à), mukundulwila,

5 James Barr (1968). *Comparative Philology and the Text of the Old Testament* (O.U.P.) pp. 44, 46.

6 This root is present in the Egyptian word *srw*  "remove" where *s-* is a causative prefix.

7 See http://www.ciyem.ugent.be/index.php?qi=3707 (Retrieved January 31, 2012)

mukunda1, mulandù, mulawu, mulengu[2], mulùngà, munda, munkundulwila, musha, mwâwù, mwònzò(ù)2, mwoyo(i)[1], ngonga, nnyàshì, nsènsè(à), nshinga1, twasàkidila >esh, eshangan, ulul, elangan, el, angan, iibw [l+i>di] ⇒-eela Luvulè

In other words, *eela* denotes anything that propagates from a zero point. This provides us with, in essence, a sense of "measurement" given by "length" or "distance." When you measure something, you find a zero-point which is your starting position to measure the distance outward from point-zero. You then count the intervals until you reach the desired *length*. The *image-schema* associated with this term is *linear order* which arranges objects in a one-dimensional line in terms of their increasing distance from an observer (whether vertical or horizontal).

The *ela/le* roots give us the following variations in ciLuba:

-le(a)	"long, large, above"
lee-, le	"big, tall, high"
-leepa	"stretch, become longer, grow, last"

In the ciLuba language, the concept of "height" (*le/lee*) is combined with one of "length, distance" to give us "very long, very deep, ancient or very old, very large (*male*, *maalabale*), etc."[8] This is from an old root: PWS **la* "old, elder." Through the process of affixation we expand the root meanings of *eela/le.*

bu-le(a)	"length, height, depth, duration"
ba-le (*-le*(*a*))	"above, long, large"
ka-le	"history" (reaching far back in time)
pabule(a)	"remote"
kulu/dyulu	"sky, heavens"

The root *-le/-la* "long, large, above" (with the underlying theme of *distance*) is extended, with a bit of prefixation, to mean "stretch, grow, depth, history, remote, sky, heavens, duration, etc." As we can see, this root crosses many domains such as "measurement, time, and space." As we can also see, besides the *linear order* image-schema, this root encompasses the *up-down* schema as well: "above, sky, heavens, height, tall, high." We observe this root as reflected in the following ciLuba terms:

Table 1: *ʿḷ* in ciLuba-Bantu

peewulu	the attic (the top part of the house)
kuulu	above, in the air, standing, time (atmospheric conditions)
muulu	up above, in the air (also means "exalt")
Kulu	old, ancient, elder, primary, principal, supreme, older (adult): *Mvìdi Mukulu* Supreme Spirit
bukùlukulu	decay (over time), being outdated, conservatism; also "archeology"
cikùlukùlu	old custom, ancient practice
mukùlù	elder (god); old, grandfather; Chief, Director, President

8 This can be seen in Egyptian, as it regards aspects of time and history: 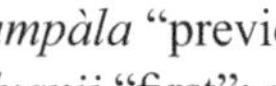 *mr* "earlier, previously, before, yonder, beyond"; *Yorùbá ní ìbẹ̀rẹ̀* "early"; ciLuba *kumpàla* "previously, before"; *-à/-a kumpàla* "first, initial" (<*mpala* "front, opposite, face"; *-à/-a mbedyanji* "first"; *mbedi* "first, initial"). The morpheme *m-* is a prefix and *-r-* is the root.

-kola	grow, grow old
bukola	holy spirit, holy, force, energy, expressly
cikolelu	how to educate (pedagogy) [from *-kola* meaning "grow, raise"]
kolesha	raise, educate, grow [with causative *-esha* suffix]
Kale	long, above, large
kale	history
kale	formally (thus relation to ancestors), once, long
kale	long ago, long time ago, in old times, remote or distant times,
a kale	old, ancient, aged (*bena kale* = forefathers)

The cognate term in Egyptian for the ciLuba root *eela/le* is *ʿr*. The underlying connotation of this term directs our attention "upwards" and in the process denotes "height."

ʿr	"elevated, prominent" 
ʿr	"mount up, ascend, come on" [9]
ʿr	"mount up, ascend, extend, penetrate, lead, carry away, come on, approach" 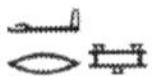
ʿr	"stairs, steps" 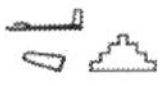
ʿr	"abode of the god" (Vygus)  (*jʿrj.t* "God's home" [Wb I 42])

The same prefixation process in ciLuba is present in Egyptian and these prefixes add various shades of meaning to the root. The following examples utilize the *-r-* root which denotes a spatial dimension or measurement.

ḥr	"distant"	Vygus
m-ḥrw	"above"	Wb III 142
m-ẖrw	"down"	Wb III 393
m-ʿrw	"near"	Wb I 41
n-ḥrw	"up"	Wb III 143
n-ẖrw	"down"	Wb III 393
wr	"size"	Wb I 330
wr	"large"	Wb I 328
wr	"big, be big"	Wb I 326
wr	"large quantity"	Wb I 331
wr	"highly"	Wb I 330
wr	"how much?"	Wb I 331

As we can see, the underlying theme of "distance" evokes concepts of "large, many, up, down, and high." It is this underlying theme that gives rise to the meaning behind the name of the Egyptian god *ḥrw* (Horus) which comes from an ancient root that means "distant, height, old, sky, etc." Here is a fuller list of the relevant terms with the *ḥ-r* biconsonental root that denotes our concept of "distance" and its *metaphoric-extensions* in Egyptian.

ḥr/ḥrw	"Horus"
ḥr	"distant"
ḥrw	"sky, heavens"

9 Kalenjiin *telel* "rise up"; Egyptian/Coptic *toile* "rise up"

ḥrw "day, sun"[10]
ḥrw "top, upper"
ḥr/ḥry "be far (from), awe"
ḥr "plot, plotting, to prepare"[11]
r ḥry "up, onwards"[12]
ḥry "upper, topside"
r ḥrw "up above"
r ḥr "before"
ḥr "face, sight, front, mask, surface (of building), attention, head, mind"
ḥrw "faces, people"
ḥrw "top"
ḥry "superior, chief, upper, who or which is upon, who is higher, having authority over, Headman, Master"
ḥr.ty "travel, journey"; *ḥrytuw* "travel" (by land)
ḥryt "terror, dread, respect" (of someone in an authoritative position)

Alternate variations with consonant losses and/or sound mutations:

hr.t "sky, heaven"
ꜣr.t "heaven, sky"
ḫw.t "sky"
ḳꜣi "tall, high, exalted, be raised on high, uplifted"
kꜣ "long, height, length, to be long (of time)"
(ciLuba *kale* "long time ago, long, history, above, large"; Egyptian *ꜣ* = l)
ḫy "high"
ḫy "height"
ḫy "to be high, be exalted, be loud (noise)"

All of these terms are related and derive from the same root: -r-/-l-. These are perfect examples of the concept of *metaphoric-extension* by which many different terms can be derived from the same root which belongs to a central theme. The concept of "distance" also gives way to "road" and "travel" in African languages. This root in Egyptian is given as *ḥrt* "way, path, road" (Kalenjiin *oreet*). Since "length, distance" can be associated with "time," this same root gives way to words denoting "age" and "seniority" as well:

DISTANT, REMOTE
Sumerian *ul* —be distant, remote
KU —big -l
PWS *ku, kul* —old
PWS *kua* —road
PWN *KUA* —go (from **kula*)
PWN *KWUL* —be big
Bantu *kúdú* —adult
Bantu *kulu* —big (Meinhof)
Bantu *buk* —go away
Mande *ku* —return
Mangbetu *eku* —to return

10 Often the word for "sun, day" in world languages is the word for "sky, heavens." Another form is *ḥrꜣr* "sun, day" (see Budge 417, 450).

11 Metaphorically extended from the concept of "distance" or "forward in time" (*linear-order* schema).

12 *r* [preposition] "to, towards, at, concerning, regarding, according to, more than, from, apart, into, against."

ES Dilling *okul*, Kondugr *oŋgul* —road
CS Bulala *kori, gõri* —road
Khoisan /Nusan (S) *!nu* —foot
[Sumerian has lost initial *k* and final *a*]

The word for "sky, height, above" is usually also the same word for "head" as we can see below with these reconstructed forms.

PWS *LI, DI* "head, spirit, hand" ; GI "sky" *n- -r*
PWS *li (di)* —head,
PWS *ti* —head, —roofing straw
PAC (Proto-Atlantic-Congo, Stewart 1973) *-li-, -lu-* "head"
CS Lendu *ra, arra* "sky"
ES Tama *ar* "sky, rain",
Mangbetu *ro* "sky"
PWS *la, (dā)* —day (sky, rain)
PB **gudu, *godo* (PWN *GULU* —sky)
PWS *lu, (du)* "head" PWS *lé,(dé, dó)* "one'" (total), with *dó* as common reflex Sumerian *dù* "totality"
PCS **d.u* —head
ES Dongola, Kenuzi, Mahas, Gulfan *ur* —head
CS Madi *oru* —up, Moru *kuru* —up, Lendu *ru(na)* —up
PWS *lu* —head*(du, ru);* Yorùbá *o-ri, o-li*—head (one head),
PWN *TÚI* —head
[Greek *ana* — "up, on" is probably related].
PWS *na* —above

I argue here that the equivalent term for *Allah* in Egyptian, in terms of a "god," is not the sun-god *Rˁ*, but the god *ḥr/ḥrw* which is associated with the "sky, heavens" (and also the "sun" and "day"). Although *Rˁ* and *ḥrw* are practically one and the same, they represent different concepts (save for the association with the sun) and these differences will be made clearer in the upcoming sections.

As stated before, the *l* root in ciLuba (Bantu) has many prefixes which give it different shades of meaning. One prefix is *k-* and this morpheme becomes *ḥ-* in Egyptian. To prove it, the chart below displays cognate terms between ancient Egyptian and ciLuba in regards to the *k-r* root. The best way to do this is to compare shared homonyms.

Table 2: Lexical Correspondences with Egyptian /ḥ/ with ciLuba velar /k/ initial, and alveolar liquid /r/ with ciLuba /l/ secondary position

Egyptian /h/	**ciLuba /k/**
ḥrw "mountain"	*mu-kuna* "mountain" (ciLuba) [l>n]
ḥrw "top, upper"	*kale, kule, kulu* "top, upper, highest"
ḥrw "heavens, sky"	*kuulu* "heavens, sky"
ḥrw "hawk, bird" (*tnḥr*) [Coptic *haliit* "bird, kite")	*Nkulu, Nkole, Ngal, nGole, Cyal, Kal; ciKololo* "hawk, bird, raven" (also "prominent man")
ḥrw "be cut when ripe" (of corn)	*kole* "ripe, mature, grow (<*kola*)"
ḥꜣꜣ r "to decide"	*kàla* "decide at once"
ḥrw "those above" (in heavens, especially of the stars)	*kulu* "ancestors"

ḫrpw “director, governor, chiefs, foremen, wardens, superiors, overseer of the landlords"	*Mukulu* (***pukùlù, tukùlù***) “Elder, old, grandfather, Chief, Director, President (*Mukulu wa Cipangu* Parish Council President), principal wife of a polygamist household”; ***Kùlula*** “use, age” (V:-***Kulu***, ***kùlumpa***-[l + i> di] ⇒-sèlela;[1]
ḥrw “be quiet, at peace” *grw* “silent” [Wb V S 180]	*le-kela, kua-kala* “silence, quiet”, *hola* “silent, peace, quiet”, *akula* “quiet”
hr "be pleasing, soothing, to be continent"	*Kalolo*: goodness, amiability, kindness, attractiveness, obedience, fairness, justice, honesty, integrity, faithfulness, gentleness, humanity, humility, modesty, reverence, tracetableness, meekness, docility, deference, civility, decorum, politeness, courtesy. *-a kalolo*: good, amiable, kind, attractive, obedient, fair, just, honest, faithful, gentle, humane, humble, modest, reverent, tractable, meek, docile, deferential, decorous, courteous, polite, civil.
ḥrw “be pleased, be satisfied, be content”	*mu-hole* (<*hola*) “satisfied, content”
kh “difficult, strong, wild”	*hale* (also *kule*) “to be crazy, deranged, wild, foolish, mad, reckless, vicious, violent” (to become…<*hala*)
knỉ (*ḳnỉ*) “mighty, capable, active, strong, valiant, conquer, eager” *ḥr* “terror, dread” *r ḥr* “combat” *ḥr* “anguish, agony, fear”	*kale, kala*[2]: to be strong, strong, well, vigorous, arduous, firm, steady, solid, hard, immovable, fixed, steadfast, powerful, robust, tough (as meat), violent, severe, serious (matter),
hrw “voice, sound, noise”	*cy-ono* “noise, snoring” *lw-ono* “noise” *kale* “loud voice” *orò, ariwo* (Yorùbá) “roar, noise”
ḥrw “battle, war” *ḫrw.yt* “war” *ḫrw.yt* “war” *ḫrwyw* “war, rebellion, revolt” *kn* “brave man, hero, soldier, mighty, capable, active”	*bu-kole* “force, energy, strength” *kola* “become difficult, hard, force, energy, strengthen” *Kanda* “prohibit, prevent, defend, be blocked, ” *kala* “strength, power” *nkama* “force, might, power, strength”
ḥrw [drink] Wb III S 148	*nwa* “drink” [r>n] (elision of *k*- prefix?) *munù≈munwì* “drinker” *-pùùkila* “absorb, drink” (*pùù*- “diminutive”)
ḥrw “apart from” [Wb III S 146]	*Mu-kàlu* “boundary line, border, limit”

Sound correspondences

Egyptian /*ḥ*/ = ciLuba /k/[13]
Egyptian /*ḥ*/ = ciLuba /h/
Egyptian /r/ = ciLuba /l/
Egyptian /r/ = ciLuba /n/
Egyptian /n/ = ciLuba /n/

The correspondences between ciLuba *k-r* and Egyptian *ḥ-r* are regular. The roots of the words *ḫr/ḫrw* in Egyptian are: *ʿr, wr, rw*. This root, in other African languages, can be given as *li, la,*

13 We can also argue for an Egyptian /g/ = ciLuba /k/.

le, lu, ro, ri, ru, re, ra, di, du, da, do, tu, ti, and thu (also *sa, se/za, zô,*). As we will see later on, the r/l/d/n common sound change will be important.

We go through these exercises to build a case that we can use languages such as ciLuba to gain insight into ancient Egyptian lexemes. As we can see, as a result of these comparisons, the Egyptian word *ḥrw* consists of two morphemes: the *ḥ-* prefix and the *-r-* root. The -r- root is associated with a category-theme of "distance." This root then gives rise to other concepts by way of metaphoric-extension defined as "large, big, top, high, heaven, sky, head, etc." As we will see, it is this second level of meaning that gives rise to a third level of meaning which is associated with "age, authority, rulership, and mastery"; and it is on this level that this root is associated with God (or a king). The next section will explore the latter associations in more detail as they relate to *Allah* in Arabic and *Ḥrw* in the ancient Egyptian.

The up-down schema and the Divine

We mentioned earlier that the *up-down* schema, discussed by Lakoff, deals with spatial orientations in a gravitational field. Our existence in a gravitational field provides the inspiration for the *up-down* schema and it is living in this type of orientation for which we draw our metaphors in relation to the Divine. When we think of the Divine we think in terms of the word "high" which is characterized against the domain of three-dimensional space.[14]

There are two distinct spatial senses, extensional *high* (*high*^{1}), as in *high building*, and positional *high* (*high*^{2}) as in *high ceiling* (Taylor, 1995: 136). The first sense (*high*^{1}) denotes the greater than average **vertical extent** of an entity; and the second (*high*^{2}) denotes the above average **location** of an entity on the vertical dimension. These meanings are related through metonymy. If, for instance, an entity is *high*^{1}, then its upper surface is *high*^{2}. It is the second sense of *high* that is subject to extension by way of metaphor.

When we discuss an entity's position in a vertical space, *high*^{2} normally implies a zero-point or origin, from which vertical distance is measured, as well as a norm with which the high entity is implicitly compared. The floor or ground is usually the zero-point when we speak of *high telegraph wires* or *high ceilings*. But the sea level would more than likely be the zero-point when one speaks of a *high plateau*. The sky is high in comparison to man which is on the ground. As we have seen, the entity being profiled and the means by which we describe it are one and the same word in Egyptian: *ḥrw* "sky, top, upper" and *ḥr* "distant, be far."

The three major conceptual metaphors that involve the up-down schema concern the domains of *quantity* (MORE IS UP, LESS IS DOWN), *evaluation* (GOOD IS UP, BAD IS DOWN), and *control* (POWER IS UP, POWERLESSNESS IS DOWN). We do not have space to explore the first two domains in depth, but they will be hinted on throughout this essay. However, it is the third domain (control) that is important for us at this point in the discussion.

The third conceptual-metaphor (POWER IS UP) maps the *up-down* schema on to power relations. We tend to think of persons or groups with power to be *higher* than those without power. We also tend to think of status, at times, in terms of the *up-down* schema: *high society, high class, high born,* and of course, *high status.* A more limited expression of high status can be seen in phrases such as *high command, high priest,* or *high position in a company*. Positions of higher status are generally thought of as positive. But this isn't always the case. Thus we have phrases like *high-handed* and we get upset if someone doesn't get off of their *high horse*.

The conceptual domain of *control,* which informs our POWER IS UP schema, is lexically represented by our *-r-* and *-l-* roots in African languages. We see this theme expressed in the Yorùbá language as: *Olu* "great, lord, God"; *enu* "top, high"; Igbo *enu* "top of, up." A related Yorùbá word *Olá* means "elevated status, fame, honourable estate." It can be seen in such names

14 We also think in terms of "vastness" and "remoteness."

as *Olásení* "fame is not unachievable," *Oladŭnní* "high status is sweet to have," *Olánrewájú* "status is progressing forward," and *Oláitán* "honour never gets used up."

This root in Egyptian is given as the word *wr,* which has many associations with "authority" as we can see in the following table.

Table 3: ʿl in Egyptian

Hieroglyphs	Meaning	Yorùbá	ciLuba
	*wr* = great one, great man, **god**, chief, elder Budge 170b	*Olu, Oluwa, Elu, El* "God" *Olu* "great, lord"	*K-ulu* (A) old, ancient, elder (B) primary, principal, supreme *Mvìdi Mukulu* Supreme Spirit (C) eldest, older (adult)
	*wr* = master		*mukùlù* (A) Elder (god) (B) old, grandfather (C) Chief, Director, President
	*wr* = great one	*Olá* "elevated status, fame, honourable estate"	*cikùlukùlu* ancient practice, old custom *bukùlukulu* (A) decay (B) being outdated (C) conservatism also "archeology"
The Uraeus			
	*wr.t* = great one, title of Osiris Faulkner pg. 64		
	*wr.t* = great one (of uraeus, of goddess)		
	*wrr.t* = crown		

As we can see here, Egyptian *wr* (also known as *ba'al, baal, baále*, etc.) means "great, god, lord, chief, master, great one, elder, great man" (Kalenjiin *oor* "great"). All of these terms are given vitality by the *up-down* schema, and more specifically the control domain (POWER IS UP). It is this root which is included in the word *ḥr*(*w*) which at times was the Supreme Being (ciLuba *Nkulu, Nkole* "prominent or powerful man"; *nGole* "God") and more often the Divine as represented as the son of *Wsr* (Osiris).

We know the name *ḥrw* is associated with the *up-down* schema and the POWER IS UP domain because the hieroglyphic script gives us a clue. Often the determinative for the *nṯrw*, denoting a divine attribute or person of *high status*, is depicted as a falcon (*ḥr*) standing on an elevated platform  as can be seen in the name *ḫprr* below.

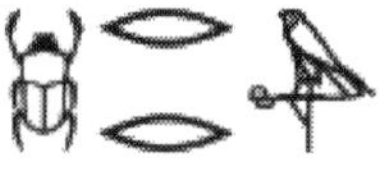

Egyptian	*ḫprr*	"god of evolution, time and the sun";
Kalenjiin	*khipirir*	"the red one, the dawning one";
Kalenjiin	*khiprur*	"the one who is blossoming, is ripe, is roasted";
CiLuba:	*Cipepu-la*	"strong wind," "Breath bearer of Ra."

As we can see from the depiction of the determinative (*Mfulu-CiTapa, Mvulu-Citapa/-ciTaha* "exalted spirit, high chief"), the ancient Egyptians are trying to focus our attention to the fact that this being is one of *high status*; one that has the power to make change. The Egyptians deliberately created motifs to redirect (transfer) our attention to abstract concepts (the target domain) by showing us concrete images (the source domain) from common experiences that denote the ideas through the living symbols of nature.

The Kalenjiin name for *nṯr* also supports this analysis. Among the Pokoot the name for the Divine *Tororrot* means "sky, the on high, the heavens" and the conceptual symbology is articulated as a mix between a man and a bird, a being with two opposing natures (Sambu, 2008: 135). *Tororrot* derives from *toror* "elevate"; *toroor* "massive and high, elevated"; *Netoroor* "the exalted, the Almighty One"; *Netiliil* "the Holy One." In ciLuba-Bantu the Egyptian *nṯr* can be rendered *Ntalù* "excellence" (<*tala-ma* "to protrude, be prominent, be far distant from, be cautious, be careful, pay attention be careful, be smart"). Mervyn Beech during the first decade of the Twentieth century, while discussing the Kalenjiin concept of *Tororrot*, notes that:

> Torôrut is the Supreme God.[15] He made the earth and causes the birth of mankind and animals. No man living has seen him, though old men, long since dead, have. They say he is like a man in form, but has wings—huge wings—the flash of which causes lightning, *kerial*, and the whirring thereof is the thunder, *kotil*. (Beech, 1911: 19).

This symbol [Gardiner sign G7] is used for many words dealing with divine concepts. We already know the bird on top of the platform is *ḥrw/ḥr*. This may be related to Kalenjiin *tariit* "bird, kite," but given in Egyptian/Coptic as *dryt*, *trii* and *haliit*. It should be noted that the common word in Egyptian for "falcon, kite" is *bik*. This word has our determinative. This may correspond to the ciLuba word *-bììka* "get up, stand up." The names for totem items may not be the representative of the object, but more so its actions. The focus of *ḥrw*, represented by the falcon, may be more in line with *hri* "to fly, to ascend." It contains the *-ri-* root for "flight, ascent" (Egyptian *ꜥr* "ascend, elevated, abode of the god") as seen in Kalenjiin *tiriren* "flying," *tiriit* "bird." Thus in ciLuba *-bùùka* "flight, take flight, fly, take off, fly away, stealing" (Egyptian *bik* "falcon, kite"); Kiswahili *-ibuka* "emerge, resurface, spring up, rise"; PB (Meeussen) **-búuk-* "wake up, and/or rise"; **-buuk-* "fly (away, up)"; **-buk-* "go away."

The *-r-* root of elevation is present in the Egyptian term *sr* "noble, Office, Magistrate"; Kalenjiin *siir* [a panther skin garment worn by priests. It is the attire of an *accomplished* man; semantic shift].[16] *Siir* in Kalenjiin also means "go yonder, come to senses (wake up), cross, jump over."

Allah the *Òrìṣà*?

In the Yorùbá language the word for "head" comes in two primary forms: *orí* and *òrìṣà/òrìsà*. Oduyoye (1996: 29-30) is of the opinion that these are two separate words: that the word *orí* is not a part of the word *òrìṣà*. He warns against trying to separate the word *òrìṣà* into two

15 It is a title for Asiis, the Supreme Being among the Kalenjiin.

16 Kalenjiin *sere* "blessed, prosper, plenty" may be related as well.

separate components: *orí* + *ṣa*. *Òrìṣà* is one word and so is *orí*. However, I disagree with Oduyoye on the point that the root of *Òrìṣà* is not *orí*. I argue here that these are doublets in the Yorùbá language. The *-ṣa* 'suffix' is an old Kongo-Saharan morpheme that is no longer productive in Yorùbá and fossilized in the language as a result of metathesis.

The *-s* 'suffix' is a variant of *-k* which is prefixed in Bantu and found in CN Bertat *alu, kulu* "head"; Mande *ku-n.golo, -n.kolo* "head"; PWN (*GHIDU*) "head"; PB **-cɔdi* "tip of something, top, hill" (<PWS *lu* "head" (*du, ru*); Yorùbá *o-ri, o-li* "head"; PWS *LI, DI* "head, spirit, hand"; PAC (Proto-Atlantic-Congo, Stewart 1973) *-li-*, *-lu-* "head"). We have in the Ijebu dialect *orúwo* "head"; Egyptian *ḥrw* "upper part, top." There is a liquid consonant interchange in the *-r-w-* root to *-l-w-*. The concrete "head" is metaphorically extended to the status found in *Olúwo* (*Olíwo*) "the first title in the Ọṣùgbó, in order of preference," "a head priest of Orúnmìlà" (Oduyoye, 1996: 29). The highest application of this root is *Olúwa* "lord, master."

I suggest here that the *k-l/g-l* consonant root became reversed (*l-k/l-g*) by a process of metathesis. The velar consonant became palatalized to eventually become /*s*/.[17] To demonstrate the first variation, observe the following with the *k-l* form from the TOB database:

> PAA **ḳʷaʔVl-* "back of head, nape"; W.Chadic **ḳwal-* "brain, skull"; **kwakVl-* (redupl.) "brain"; Lower E.Cushitic **ḳawl-* "nape" (Oromo *qolee* "nape"; **kol*); High E. Cushitic **ḳoʔl-* "nape, back of neck"(Hadiya *ḳoʔlo*; Kambatta *ḳoʔlu*); Omotic **ḳVllaw-* "head" (Kafa *ḳɛllo*; P.Omotic **ḳVll-* "head").

> PAA **gVl(gVl)-* "head, skull"; Semitic **ga/ulga/ul-at-* "skull, head" (Akkadian *gulgullu, gulgullatu*; Hebrew *gulgōlät*; Judaic Aramaic *gulgultā*, *gulgaltā* (also 'head') *gwlglh*, det. *gwlglth* [Sok 123]; Arabic *ǧalaǧat-* 'crâne; tête' [BK 1 311] (< **ǧalǧal-at-?*)) Central Chadic **gVl-* "head" > **n-gul-* "temple" (Proto-CChadic: **gVl-* , **n-gul-* "head, temple"; Mulwi: Muktele *gəl*; Zime-Dari: *ŋ-gəlā* [Cpr]; Zime-Batna: *ŋ-gəla* 2 [Sa]); East Chadic **gVl* "head" (Kwang: *gólò* ; Mobu (dial. Kwang): *gòló*; Notes: Cf. Sokoro *geltim* 'thy brain'.); Omotic **gayl-* "head" (Ometo: Dizi *gayli, geli* "head").

We find the consonantal reversal (with sound change) in the following African languages: Yorùbá *òrìṣà/òrìṣẹ́* "head"; Ijebu-Ode *Olísà* "chiefs in the rank of Ilamuren"; Edo *Olisakeji* "title used in addressing the *ọba* when he wears a certain attire"; Igbo *Olisa* "God"; Dahomey *Mawu-Lisa* "God." In Malawi (among the Ambo, Barotse, Bemba, Kaonde, Lala, Lamba and Luapula) *Lisa* "God"; Among the Baluba (Congo), the Ila (Zambia), Nyanja and Tonga (both found in Zambia and Malawi) it is *Leza* "God" (see Oduyoye, 1996: 28). The name *Orisa* can be seen in the Igbo name *Nwaorisa* "son of a deity."

Among the Afro-Asiatic speakers we have the following: Egyptian *rš* "head, summit," Hebrew *ro'sh*, Arabic *ra's*, Aramaic *re'sh*, Akkadian *rishu* "head." Hebrew *ro'sh* metaphorically means "first in rank" or "head in status." The *r-s* root is in the Hebrew word *ri'shon* "first." Practically all forms of this root have this extended or derived meaning. In Arabic we have *ra'is* "President, Prime Minister"; Ethiopic *Ras* "President, King"; Nilotic *Reth/Rwot/Ruoth* "Chief, King." Among the Edo we have *Oliha* "a chief, first in rank at the Uzama"; Shilluk (Nilo-Saharan) *Reth* "King."

A fuller treaty of the *r-s* root is given by the TOB database for Semitic as follows:

> PAA **raʔ(i)s-* "head" (Proto-Semitic: **raʔ(i)š-* {} **raʔ(i)s-* "head"; Akkadian: *rāšu* 'Kopf, Haupt' OAkk, *rēšu* OB on [AHw 973]; Eblaitic: *rí-še6* /riʔši/ [Kr 46; Bl E No. 79]; Ugaritic: *rʔiš*, pl. *rʔašm* [Aist 285]; Canaanite: MOAB *rš* [Segert 267], AMARNA

17 The phenomenon in linguistics is known as *bleeding and feeding*: the output of one change serves as the input for another. For example: **Change A**, *x* > *y*. **Change B**, *y* > *z*.

> *ru-šu-nu* (with 1 pl. pron suff.) [HJ 1042]; Phoenician: *rʔš* [T 297]; Hebrew: *rō(ʔ)š* [KB 1164]; Aramaic: DALLA OLD OFF NAB *rʔš*, PLM OFF *rš*, OFF NAB *ryš* [HJ 1042]; Biblical Aramaic: *rē(ʔ)š* 'Kopf, Anfang' [KB deutsch 1777]; Judaic Aramaic: *rēšā* [Ja 1477]; *ryš* [Sok 510]; Syrian Aramaic: *rēšā* [Brock 728]; Modern Aramaic: MAʕLULA *rayša* [Bergsträsser Maʕl 77] MAL *raiša* 'Kopf' [Berg 77] BAH **rayša* 'Kopf' [Cor 183] TUR *rīs,ō* 'head, top' [R Ṭūrōyo 118] MLH *rišo* 'Kopf' [J Mlah 188] HRT *reša* 'Kopf' [J Hert 197] NASS *rīšä* 'head' [Tser 0191] URM *ris,ə* 'head' [R Urmi 102] MMND *rīš*, emph. *rīša* 'head' [M MND 505] GZR *réša* 'head, top' [Nak 84] IRAN **rīša* 'la testa; il capo' *rīšihçyβ* (suff.) 'la mia testa' [Pen 120]MAʕLULA *rayša* [Bergsträsser Maʕl 77]; Mandaic Aramaic: *riš, riša* [DM 434]; Arabic: *raʔs-* [BK 1 793]; Epigraphic South Arabian: SAB *rʔs1* [SD 112]; Geʕez (Ethiopian): *rəʔ(ə) s* [LGz 458]; Tigre: *räʔas* [LH 155]; Tigrai (Tigriñña): *rəʔ(ə)si* [Bass 151]; Amharic: *ras, əras* (also 'top') [K 381]; Harari: *urūs* [LHar 32]; Mehri: *ḥə-rōh* (-ō- <*ā) [JM 310]; Jibbali: *réš* [JJ 201]; Harsusi: *ḥé-rīh, ḥerīh* [JH 101] (<**ḥa-rīš*); Soqotri: *réy, reʔ, réh*, pl. *ʔírʔeš* [LS 390] (cf. also [SSL LS 1468; SSL 4 96])).

As we can see from the data above, Semitic has two words for "head": **ga/ulga/ul-at-* and **raʔ(i) š- {}* **raʔ(i)s-*. These are doublets with the first variation being a reduplicated form. The *r-s* to *s-r* forms can be seen in the following:

> Proto-Afro-Asiatic: **carw-* "elder, chief"; Semitic: **sarw(-ay)-* ~ (?) **sVran-* '(military) chief, prince; Proto-Berber: **zVwVr-* "'precede, be the first'"; Ayr: *əžwər*; Ahaggar (Tahaggart): *əhwər*; Tawllemmet: *əžwər*; Taneslemt: *əšwər*; Qabyle (Ayt Mangellat): *zwir*; Proto-WChadic: **car*(am)- "chief"; Warji: *cārá* [SNb]; Daffo-Butura: *sàràm* [JR]; Proto-EChadic: **sVr-* (<**n-sVr-*) "adult"; Tumak: *sə̄rí* [Cp] [Notes: Ch *s-> Tum h-, *ns- > s-, for initial prefix cf. CCh Mafa *nʒar-* `be older then (person, thing)' [BMaf] (nʒ- < *nc- is normal)].

There is a concept in linguistics called *directionality*. The known directionality of certain sound changes is a valuable clue for reconstruction. Directionality notes that some sound changes, which recur in independent languages, typically go in one direction: e.g., (a > b). However, this type of change is usually not found in the other direction (sometimes never): i.e., (b > a). For example, many languages have changed *s > h*, but the change in the other direction is almost unknown (i.e., *h > s*). In cases such as this, if we find in two related or sister languages the sound correspondence /s/ in Language_1 and /h/ in Language_2, then we reconstruct **s* and postulate that in Language_2 **s > h*. The reverse is highly unlikely since it goes against the known direction of change. It is with this knowledge that we know *òrìṣà* is the earlier form of *ilāh* (Edo *oliha*) because the directionality is from *s > h*.[18] We can witness this phenomenon in Semitic where the **r-s* root for "head" morphs into *r-h* in the following languages: Mehri: *ḥə-rōh* (-ō- <*ā); Harsusi: *ḥé-rīh, ḥerīh* (<**ḥa-rīš*); Soqotri: *réy, reʔ, réh*, pl. *ʔírʔeš*.

As we have stated previously, the root is *-li-/-lu-* and it represents a theme of dimensionality in time and space (e.g., up, length, tall, height, great, expanse, etc.; PB *-*dai* "far"; Sumerian *ri* "be distant"). From this root we get "head" (**li*, **lu*) as a concept. This notion of "height, up, head" extends itself to be associated with *leadership* and we find this association lexically with *lu* in Sumerian.

In discussing the Sumerian determinatives, Campbell-Dunn (2009a: 50) notes that the *lú* determinative in Sumerian is used to denote "professions and official positions."[19] This can be

18 However, *s > k* is common.

19 *lu* [PERSON] (12429x: ED IIIa, ED IIIb, Ebla, Old Akkadian, Lagash II, Ur III, Early Old Babylonian, Old Babylonian, uncertain, unknown) wr. lu_2; *mu-lu*; $mu\text{-}lu_2$; lu_{10}; lu_6 "who(m), which; man; (s)he who, that which; of; ruler; person" Akk. *amēlu*; *ša*.

seen in the Sumerian word *lu-gal* "king" ("lord; master; owner; a quality designation").[20] He derives this term from PWS *lu* "head." As noted by Campbell-Dunn, "Head has a long history as a metaphor indicating leadership, importance, chiefly position, etc. The head was particular in Africa. Hence it tended to be enlarged on works of art." We get confirmation in the Zwana (Setswana?) language of South Africa. In Zwana, the word for "lord" or "master" is *ra* or *raey*. If one were to say, for instance, "Mr. Hurtak" in Zwana, one would say "Rahurtak" (Mutwa, 2003: 161). This root is reflected in PB **-jɛnɛ* "owner, chief"[21]; Sumerian *en* "lord, master, ruler"; Yorùbá *Olá* "elevated status, fame, honourable estate."

To further substantiate the status of the "head" in African tradition, we can look to Yorùbá philosophy to shed some light on these associations. In her work *African Voices in the African American Heritage,* Betty M. Kuyk, as it regards the Yorùbá concept of the head, notes that:

> The Yorùbá, who had some degree of hierarchal organization, used a crown as a symbol of leadership. The head contains the mind, and Thompson quotes a Yorùbá diviner who said that traditional Yorùbá philosophy held that God's spirit was in each person's head. It is, Thompson explains, the "source of his character and destiny." With that power one can control one's behavior – especially "evil impulses." The head is the most important part of the body, and the crown was referred to as "the House of the Head." (…) In the African context the crown symbolized the leader's responsibility for the whole community, for being its link with its ancestral leaders, for preserving knowledge of its traditions, for maintaining balance in all spheres within it. (Kuyk, 2003: 144)

This concept has survived among African-American spiritualists in Louisiana. As Kuyk further notes (ibid):

> We glimpsed the supreme importance of the mind of humans in African philosophy when we looked at the importance the Dogon ascribe to speech. A root doctor in Louisiana revealed the same concept in African American thought. Hyatt asked if he used an altar, "I don't need no altar," he declared, "because my altar, which is myself, is in my brain – you see, because I was gifted for that."

The name Allah is simply a word for "head, chief, up, highest" and this is why, as we will see later on in our discussion, Allah is associated with the *sky*. To get a grasp on how this could be, we must first understand the nature of "concrete nouns" and how they have shaped our early human vocabulary. As Campbell-Dunn notes:

> The original "nouns" which we see behind Sumerian, however, were not the nouns that we recognise today. Today we define the noun by contrast with the verb. The "primal" noun, if we may call it such, knew no such contrast. The ARM was used alike for a limb of the body and for ACTIONS OF THE ARM. The HEAD was used alike for the physical organ, and for ACTIONS OF THE HEAD, eating and drinking, for example, even for the water that was drunk. Each primal noun was a cluster of associations, some more concrete and separable than others. But a concrete noun, we think, was at the core. Something similar happens in child language : ("moon" = "streetlight" = "baloon"). And concepts were not discrete units. They overlapped and flowed into each other. The MOUTH was part of the HEAD. The SKY was the HEAD of the world, from which the RAIN fell. Even the distinction between ARM and LEG is blurred. (Campbell-Dunn, 2009a: 148)

20 See the University of Pennsylvania Sumerian Online Dictionary: http://psd.museum.upenn.edu/epsd1/nepsd-frame.html

21 PB **jènì* "forehead," **cènì* "forehead, face" might be relevant.

The same root **li*/*lu* (and its variants) give us the word for "sky" in African languages and Indo-European. A few examples from the TOB database reinforce this premise.

> PAA: **raw*- "sky"; Egyptian *rw* "sky" (pyr); W.Chadic **ruw* "sky" (Proto-WChadic: **ruw*- (var. *ray*) "sky"; Karekare: *rəwì* [Kr N 116]; Fyer: *rúrùwê* [JgR]; Sha: *ʔarè* [JgR]); S.Cushitic **raw*- "sky" (Burunge (Mbulungi): *raw*)
>
> PAA: **ḥar*- "sky"; Egyptian *ḥr.t* "sky" (pyr); W.Chadic **ḥar*- "sky" (Hausa: *gàrī*); Low E.Cushitic **haror*- "cloudy weather" (Oromo (Galla): *harooressa*).
>
> PAA: **liw*- "cloud, sky"; Egyptian *nw.t* "sky" (pyr); W.Chadic **liw*- "cloud" (Mupun: *llùú* [FrM]; Sura: *ìlúu* [JgS]; Chip: *lìwu* [Kr N 105]; Ankwe-Goemai: *low-ɨn* [Kr N 105]; Boghom: *līlyu , lwai* [Sm ?]);

Note the *ḥ*- prefix in the second set of examples. We see in Hausa that the *ḥ*- initial is *g*- and we argue that this *g* (<*k*) became *j-/s-* in initial position as well. Stewart's (2002: 219)[22] PPAB reconstructions provide us with the following examples to reaffirm our hypothesis: Common Bantu **-judu* "top, sky"; Proto-Bantu **-jʊlʊ*; Proto-Potou-Akanic-Bantu **- jʊlʊ*; Proto-Potou-Akanic **-tʊlʊ*; Proto-Akanic **-sʊlʊ*; Akan *ɔ-sʊrʊ, -sʊ*. We note also from Campbell-Dunn (2009b): PB **gùdù* "sky, top, heap, hill"; **jùdú* "top, sky"; **gùdú* "upstream, rainbow."

It is this notion of "up, top" that is reflected in PB **túè* "head"; **túade* "chief"; **túadi* "hero, chief"[23]; ciLuba *mu-salu* "dignitary"; *n-sala* "top, summit, extreme top"; *mu-sala* "boundary, terminal, edge"; Egyptian *sr* "noble, Office, Magistrate"; Kalenjiin *siir* "jump, pass, excel, win" (semantic theme: distance); *siir* "a panther skin garment worn by priests" [It is the attire of an *accomplished* man; semantic shift?].

It is these underlying themes that are behind the consonant cluster representing this Egyptian sign: *wsr* . The focus of this sign is the "head" (the upper most part of the body) and it is why it is associated with the word *wsr*  "make strong, powerful, wealthy, and influential." A *wsr* is someone/something of high prestige, someone with authority (the ability to make something happen). I believe this term is a variant of the word *sr* "noble, Office, Magistrate." The *wsr* form is just a variant of the word *swr*  "promote (an official), increase (herds), extol, to augment, to multiply." The theme behind this term is "elevation, exaltation" and "expansion." The *Law of Belova*[24] *may be at play here.*

The focus of this glyph *wsr*  "head and neck of canine"; [Gardiner sign F12] is the "head" and it is used in the word *wsr.t*  "part of the head" (Budge 182b). We see a similar focus on another word in Egyptian with the same consonant root: *sr*  "giraffe". The same word is used to mean *sr* 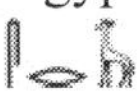 "foretell, prophesy." The giraffe is a source domain to refer us to the

22 STEWART, John M. "The potential of Proto-Potou-Akanic-Bantu as a pilot Proto-Niger-Congo, and the reconstructions updated." *JALL 23*. Walter de Gruyter. (2002), 197-224.

23 The Proto-Bantu /t/ corresponds to Yoruba /r/: e.g., PB *-*tUe* "head," Yoruba *o-ri* "head"; PB *-*tope* "mud; marsh," Yoruba *E-rOf-O* "mud; marsh"; PB *-*tUe* "ashes," Yoruba *ee-ru* "ash"; PB *-*tud*- "hammer; forge," Yoruba *rO* "forge (pre-nas. theory, irr)"; PB *-*taano* "five," Yoruba *a-ru~* "five" (irr).

24 "According to this rule, the first *w*- and *j*- in Eg. triconsonantal roots cannot always be treated as morphological prefixes, but in many cases rather reflect the original PAA [Proto-Afro-Asiatic] internal root vocalism *-u-, *-i- (i.e. Eg. wC_1C_2 and jC_1C_2< AA *C_1uC_2- and *C_1iC_2- respectively). As for PAA (C_1aC_2, it may eventually yield Eg. jC_1C_2, but $ꜣC_1C_2$ as well though the examples for it are of very limited number." Takacs in (Rocznik, 1998: 115)

target domain of being able to "see" far into the future like a giraffe; who because of its height, can see danger a mile away before it comes. The word also means to "promise" which has implications for the "future." The underlying semantic theme is "distance." The giraffe has a tall body-frame due to its long neck and this "high head" becomes the metaphoric starting point to denote being able to see far into the future.

Another extension on the theme of "head" is the concept of "beginnings" or "the source." We see this theme expressed in the following terms from the TOB database:

> PAA **tuṗ-* (?) "begin"; Egyptian *tp* (pyr) "beginning" (<*tp* "head"); W.Chadic **twab-* "begin" (Tangale *tobi* "begin").

The head is the "top" of the body, the upper most part of our being. The concept of "beginning" stems from our ancestral observations of child birth in that it is the "head" that comes out of the womb "first." We *begin* our life here on earth with our "head" leading the way and this is how this term extends metaphorically to mean "leadership." All of our actions begin with a "thought" and it is believed our thoughts originate in the "head." In other words, our head (thoughts) is the beginning of our actions (thought > word > deed). It is our "head" that controls the body and this is another source for the notion that "leadership" is associated with the "head." These are the underlying themes present in Egyptian *tp*  "head, tip (of toe etc), top part of a pot, spit (of land), peak"; *tpw* "tips, ends"; *tp* "top, upon"; *tp* "person."

The same term is used in words dealing with "ancestors" in the Egyptian language. The ancestors are our "beginning." These persons or spirit beings came "before" and "lead the way" for our existence today. Since we come after them, with the human-body as our frame of reference, they would be the "head" and we the body. Those yet to come (our descendants) would be the feet: those agents of life that move creation forward.

We see the word *tp* in the following: *tp ꜥwy*  "predecessors, ancestors"; *tp ꜥwy* "ancestors"; *tpw ꜥw*  "ancestors, forebears, those of former times"; *tpw ꜥ 3ḫw*  "ancestors of light"; *tp ꜥwy rꜥ*  "ancestors of Ra." We find the same connotation in the words *òrìṣà* "head" and *òrìṣà* "patron saint(s), ancestors." As noted by Oduyoye (1996: 30): *Ènìyàn ni í d' òrìṣà*, "It is human beings who become *òrìṣà*." The *òrìṣà* are venerated as first in rank. They are considered to be first in time. This is one of the many connotations of Allah: he is the first, our primary ancestor, the beginning of us all, our father (who art in heaven).

We see another variant of *òrìṣà* and *Allah* in Egyptian with the word *ḥ3t*  "front, forehead, forepart (of animal), prow (of ship), vanguard (of army)"; *ḥ3t*  beginning (of region), foremost, the best of, first"; *ḥ3t*  "chief"; *ḥ3t*  "lead." More expanded forms include *ḥ3wtyw* 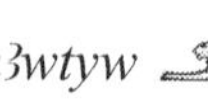 "ancient"; *ḥ3wty*  "ancestors, forebears"; *ḥ3wtyw*  "Leader, Captain"; *ḥ3wtyw* 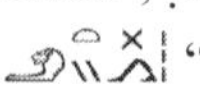 "the First, Commander"; *ḥ3wty*  "the foremost." We note that the  glyph is the "head" or the "beginning" of the lion which reinforces its definitions. Every connotation we have associated with *òrìṣà* and *Allah* are present in these forms of *ḥ3t* above. We argue that the *-t* is a grammatical suffix on the root *ḥ3*, which in reality is a variant of *ḥr* "face, head; upon, on, in, at, from, on account of, concerning; Horus; be distant, be far; sky."[25] The ultimate root is *-r-/-3-* and we see this reflected in Egyptian with the word

25 Take note of the following: *k3* "to plot, to plan" > *ḥr* "to plot, plotting" (*šnw* "to plot, to question, to investigate" may also be relevant). These are all activities of the "head." Compare also *k3* "kingship: with *ḥ3t* "chief, lead."

irw "ancestors" (< PWS **lu* "head, person").

Other connotations are given by this root as well. We have in Egyptian *ḥ3wt* "secondary gods"; *ḥ3ty* "a Prince." The secondary "gods" are in reality the prominent people or priests of a society (those of immense knowledge, skill and prestige). Among the Yorùbá, for example, the *ọba* "king" is considered *èkejì òrìṣà*, "second only to the *òrìṣà*." Among the Igbo of Nigeria, the priests are called *Dibia* "father of knowledge." They have a similar saying: *Chukwu welu, Olu Dibia* "After God, Dibia comes next." While *ḥ3t* denotes that which comes first, it also signifies those second in rank, those who will in time become first in rank: thus "secondary gods, a prince, etc."

We also note the word *ḥ3t* "Nile mouth." Unlike in our modern Western conceptualization, the *mouth* of the river is its "source," not its place of "exit." Again, the notion of "head" is at play. The head has a mouth that "eats." Anything that is eaten travels "down" the pathway into the stomach.[26] This anatomical fact became the source for the word *ḥ3wtyw* "Nile." The source of the Nile would be the "head" and the extent of the Nile would be the neck or body. I am reminded of the word *dikoshi/nkoshi* (ciLuba-Bantu) which means "neck, nape." It is also the word used to mean "second in command after the *Mpala.*" *Mpala* is the "chief, face, head, front" (*mwènàmpalà* "ambassador, Lieutenant, replacement, substitute, person commissioned"; *bedi* "first, primary") and is cognate with Egyptian *pr-3ʿ* "Pharaoh."

Semantic extensions for "head" are also found in the idea of classification of types under heads or headings. It is this conceptualization that we have "chapters" in books; the word deriving from Latin *caput* "head." The Yorùbá have this same conceptualization, for the word *orìṣisi* "different types" falls into the schema of "groupings" and "classifications" (headings). This is important to note as the cognate term in Hebrew for the Yorùbá word *òrìṣà* is *ri'shon* "first." In the Bible the book of Genesis is known in Hebrew by the word: *bəre'sit* (*bə* + *re'sh-it*) "in the beginning."

This root is cognate with Egyptian *š3ʿ* "begin, start, be the first, spring, originate, to elapse" (*r-š* <> *š-r*).[27] A variant of this form is *ẖrp* "start, begin, be the first, manage, to master, be preceded"; *ẖrp* "controller, Governor, Administrator, govern, control, administer, act as controller, direct (someone), head, scepter" (of authority)[28]; Arabic *Calif/Caliph* "ruler"; ciLuba *mukùlù* (*pukùlù/tukùlù*) "old, ancient, grandfather, forefather, Chief, Director, President, chief wife of a polygamist (household)"; *kùlumpa* "grow up, getting older, aging, old" (*-kùluba/-kùlupa*); *bakùlù* "ancient, antique, older, primordial, primary, supreme" (<*kulu*).[29] Its other variant is *z3b* or *s3b* "judge, dignitary, senior (in titles)." Wilkinson (2001: 116) defines *z3b* as "noble, official." We note the following in Semitic from the TOB database:

> Proto-Semitic: **sVrw(-ay)-* ~ (?) **sVran-* "(military) chief, prince"; Ugaritic: Cf. *srn* 'prince' (DUL, 770); Hebrew: Cf. *sərānīm* 'Stadtfürsten' (pl.) (KB deutsch,

26 The Nile River's source is in Ethiopia and Uganda. The flow of the river travels "north" and empties into the Mediterranean Sea.

27 Compare the root to ciLuba *iikija* "start, make"; *cyaShilu* "start, at the beginning, foundation, realization."

28 Note the semantic implications of its root: *ẖ3* "office, bureau, hall"; *ḥ3t ẖ3* "herdsmen."

29 The *Grammar and Dictionary of the Buluba-Lulua Language* by W. M Morrison (1906: 232) informs us of a variant of this root *kulu* (*kelenge*) and its relationship to leadership: "Office, n. The name of the office is made by prefixing *bu-* to the root of the title; as, *mukelenge*, *bukelenge*, "chieftship." appoint to, v. see APPOINT." This prefix can be seen in the word *bulongolodi* "administration, management." We note that this feature is fossilized in Semitic and this is how we get the *-f* or $-p^h$ in the C_3 position in *calif/caliph* from the root *-cal-* in the Egyptian word *ẖrp*.

727); Arabic: *sarīr-* 'dignité royale, royauté' BK I 1076, *sarw-* 'chef, prince', *srw* 'ê. genéreux et d'un caractère mâle' BK I 1085; Epigraphic South Arabian: Sab *s1rwyt* 'campaigning force' (considered a Gz loanword by Müller) (SD, 128); Geʕez (Ethiopian): *sarwe* 'army, troops; military leader; virile, robust' (LGz 515); Tigre: *sərot,* pl. *särwat* 'relation, tribe, kind' (LH, 178); Tigrai (Tigriñña): *särawit* 'army' (KT, 678); Amharic: *särwe* 'leader' (LGz 515, K 491) (< Gz?); East Ethiopic: Zwy. ṭor *särawit* 'army' (LGur, 563); Gurage: End ṭōr *särawit,* So *sərayət* 'army' (LGur, 563); [Notes: Highly problematic. Ugr and Hbr are considered non-Sem loanwords. Arb is otherwise related to Akk *šarru* 'king' < Sem **šarr-* < Afras **sarr-*.]

All of these forms derive from the same ultimate source: PWS **li*/**lu* which means "head." Allah (*'ḷh*) is just a dialectical variant of the word *òrìṣà* found in the modern Yorùbá language. My proposal for the sound-shift is *k-l > s-l > l-s > l-h.* This change happened before Proto-Semitic. I do not treat the glottal stop [ʔ] before */ḷ/* as part of the root historically. Most languages tend to insert glottal stops before vowel-initial words (Garellek, 2013: 2). Glottal stops before word-initial vowels are often optional in a language, though for some languages they are obligatory. So we posit a root *-ḷ-* with a variant *-ḷ-h-* in a similar manner as Yoruba *orí* with variant *òrìṣà/òrìsà.*

Allah refers to the "head, beginning, source, leader, chief, king, primary ancestor, lord and master" of all that exist. He is "father" or the "supreme being." Allah is a title of leadership and is found in virtually all African languages which work against the notion that Allah is somehow a privileged creation of the Semites.

The -r- root of distance in the Semitic languages

The -r-/-l- root denoting a spatial reference frame within a three-dimensional space is also found in the Semitic languages as regards the *up-down* schema. A few examples are warranted here. We compare the ancient Egyptian *ḥr* « upon, above » to the Semitic:

« upon, above »
Akkadian *'l,*
Ugaritic *'l,*
Syriac *'al,*
Hebrew *'al,*
Arabic *'ala,*
Ethiopian *la'la*

[Berber has *iggi* « upon »]

This *-l-* root denoting distance is present in many popular names in the Arabic language. For example, the Arabic name **Ali** (Arabic: عليّ, *'Alī*) is a male name, derived from the Arabic root *'-l-y* which literally means "high". Islamic traditional use of the name goes back to *Ali ibn Abu Talib*, the Islamic leader and cousin of Muhammad, but the name is identical in form and meaning to the Hebrew: עֵלִי, *Eli*, which goes back to the *Eli* in the Books of Samuel: **Eli** (Hebrew: עֵלִי, Modern *'Eli,* Tiberian *'Ēlî,* "Ascent"; Ancient Greek: Ἠλι; Latin: *Heli*).

In Hebrew, the name *Aaliyah* means "going up, ascending." An alternative spelling variation is *Aliyah.* This name in Arabic, the feminine form, is found in many variations and all belong to the same theme.

Aaliyah:	Feminine form of Arabic *Aali*, meaning "the high, exalted one."
Alia:	Variant of Arabic *Alya*, meaning "heaven, sky."

Aliah:	Variant of both Arabic *Alya*, meaning "heaven, sky," and Arabic *Aliyah*, meaning "the high, exalted one."
Alina:	Arabic name meaning "noble."
Aliya:	Variant of Arabic *Aliyah*, meaning "the high, exalted one."
Aliyah:	Feminine form of Arabic *Ali*, meaning "the high, exalted one."
Aliyya:	Variant of Arabic *Aliyah*, meaning "the high, exalted one."
Aliyyah:	Variant of Arabic *Aliyah*, meaning "the high, exalted one."

This is ultimately where I argue that the Arabic name *Allah* (*il'ilāh*) derives. It is this root from which we get Yorùbá *Olu, Elu, El* "God," *Oluwa* "lord"; Sumerian *ulu* "Holy" (Turkish *ulu* "Holy"); Hebrew *Eloah* "God," *Eloh'iym* "Gods"; Canaanite *El* "God"; Babylonian *Ilu* "God"[30] The Semitic root *ʾlh* (Arabic *ʾilāh*, Aramaic *ʾalāh*, *ʾelāh*, Hebrew *ʾelōah*) is *ʾlu* with a so-called parasitic *h*. The Semitic forms are simply variations of the *òrìṣà* (r-s) found in modern Yorùbá. The Edo cognate of *òrìṣà* is *oliha* "a chief, first rank at the Uzama."

As mentioned previously, this root often carries a prefix. Another form in Arabic of this root is *tali* "high, tall." The Yorùbá cognate is the word *tálá* (Kalenjiin *toror* "elevate"; *Tooroorut* "the exalted, the on high, the heavens" (Egyptian *ṯrt* "goddess"); *tooroor* "tall, elevated and massive") and is found in one of the names of the divine known as *Obàtálá* "the exalted king."[31] M. Lionel Bender, in his article "Nilo-Saharan" (Heine & Nurse, 2000: 69), notes that the *t-r* root in Nilo-Saharan (**tAr*) means "sky, up, god, lightning, outside" and provides the following examples:

A Gao, Kaado	'outside': *tar-Ey*	Fc	*tor-o ~ dar-a*
B Kanuri	*tol-ila*	Ek	*tell-i*; *dOr*
Zagawa	*tao*, 'outside': *terr-i*	En	*tel*; *der*
C Maba, Mimi	*ta(a)-l*	I	Komo 'outside': *-til-a*
Masalit	*dol-e*	L	Krongo 'lightning': *tal-* 'outside': *-taar-a*
D Fur	'lightning': *taur-a*		
Amdang	*terr-e*		

This *t-l* root denoting "height" and "distance" is even found in European languages. Allan R. Bomhard's article "The Glottalic Theory of Proto-Indo-European Consonantism and Its Implications for Nostratic Sound Correspondences," in the book *The Mother Tongue* (2007), provides us with a few examples.

> **Proto-Nostratic** **t'al-* (~ **t'ǝl-*) '(vb.) to stretch out, to extend; (n.) length; height; (adj.) long, tall; high':
> **A. Afrasian**: Proto-Semitic **t'a/wa/l-* 'to stretch out, to extend'; Proto-Semitic (reduplicated) **t'al-t'al-* 'to throw'; Proto-Semitic **na-t'al-* 'to lift';
> **B. Proto-Indo-European** (**t'el-/*t'ol-/*t'C-* 'to stretch, to extend, to lengthen':) (extended forms) **t'C-H-g*^{o}*-* 'long', **t'l-e-Eg*^{o}*->*t'lēg*^{o}*-* '(vb.) to stretch, to extend, to lengthen; (n.) length'.

In addition, I contend that this root is present in the Egyptian word *tr* "time, season," which focuses on timelessness, of time seen as the right season or period of something (Obenga,

30 We will come to see later on in *Chapter 3* that the very word "god" derives from this *-l-* root [kulu > godo > god].

31 Obàtálá, like Allah of the Arabs, was more than likely historically associated with the sky and lightning and thus his association with "white" and the folk-etymology that he is the "King of white cloth." See the Nilo-Saharan correspondences in Heine & Nurse (2000: 69) for the *t-r* root with these associations.

2004: 202). *tr* in ciLuba would be *diba* "sun/star, show/demonstrate, time, hours, moment" [Lo(u,a,i)>Li-L(u,o)>DiLu, Di-Lo, Ri-Ro; u-Luilu; Li-Ba>Di-Ba]. The root is *lo*(u,a,i) (Egyptian *rˁ*) and the schema of *linear-order* is at play here, as well as the *up-down* schema.

Allah embedded in different names for the Divine

Many outsiders to African languages would think that *'l* is foreign or not native to African languages and is solely a Semitic phenomenon. But as we can see, this is not the case. The confusion arises here because the layman is unaware that many native names for the Divine in African languages actually incorporate the very name which became *Allah* in Arabic. *Allah* is not a proper name; it is a descriptor, an adjective.

As noted before, Arabic *ilāh/alāh* is ciLuba *ulu*. This root is prefixed with *k-, h-, m-,* and *d-*. The following are common names for the Divine in the Kongo. As we are to see, the root (in Tshiluba) is encompassed in a larger context by way of being included in a larger sentence; most names in Africa are really short sentences.

- ***Mvidi-Mukulu wa Cimpanga***: God Supreme, Ram (Aries)
- ***Mvidi-Mukulu wa kumana kumona:*** primordial God who sees the ends of everything
- ***Mvidi-Mukulu kamana kumona:*** Supreme God who sees everything to perfection
- ***Mvidi-Mukulu kwena umumone to***: The Supreme God you do not see
- ***Mfidi-Mukulu:*** Supreme Being
- ***Ndele-Mukulu*** (Egyptian, *Ntr-Wr*): first (principle, primordial) God
- ***Mwene-Kuulu:*** master on high, owner of heaven

The Egyptians, the Yorùbá and the Baluba have been worshipping "Allah" without any introduction by Semites. The name has just been "hidden" within a larger name, as a process of agglutination, and unless one knows how names are constructed in these respective languages, one will not be able to recognize the name when they see it. The *-l-* root is either used as an adjective to denote the "high" position of the Divine, or is used in terms of the perceived "location" of the Divine.[32]

An example of the latter is given in Igbo. John Umeh (1997: 133) provides us with a few praise names for Chukwu (God): Obasi-di-***enu***, Obasi-no-n'***enu*** and Obasi-di-***elu*** (God is very near and with us, while simultaneously being very high or living very high up depending on which of the praise names are being used above). Another praise title for Chukwu also associates him with the heavens: Eze-Chita-Oke-bi n'enu-ogodo-ya-na-akpu n'ana (the High, share-bringing-King-that-lives-up-in-the-Heavens-while-His-clothes-are-sweeping-the-ground). The expression "His clothes sweeping the ground" refers to the material manifestation (of matter) which is metaphorically conveyed as "His clothes." In other words, He is never totally out of reach.

Often the focus is not on location, but on the *age* of the Divine relative to man and creation in general. In essentially all spiritual traditions, God is the *oldest* entity in existence. Nothing existed before God and all things derive from It, which would make the Divine the "Father" (or Mother) of all things. Many names reflect this frame of thought with the same words used for "height, high, sky, and time." As we have noted throughout, the underlying connotation of the -r-/-l- root is "distance" and "remoteness."

This notion of "age" is reflected in one Amazulu and Ndebele name for the Divine: *Unkulunkulu* "the oldest of the old." This root is present in the following ciLuba terms:

32 However, when one discusses the "bigness" or "vastness" of the Divine, then the term speaks more to the Divine more directly as it is meant to convey the idea that God is and is in everything: i.e., infinite (<long, stretch, extend, etc.).

> ***-Kulu*** "old, ancient, elder," "primary, principal, supreme" *(Mvìdi Mukulu* Supreme Spirit), older (*Taatu Mukulu* "big brother of the father, paternal uncle older than the father"); ***bukùlù***[1], ***bukùlù***[2], ***bakùlù,***[2] ***bikùlù***[2] "primogeniture, seniority rule, precedence, rule, birthright"; ***-Kùlumpè(a)*** "old; eldest principal large, old, middle, adult"; ***Bukùlukulu*** "decay, being outdated, conservatism, archeology (***-à/-a bukùlùkulu*** "archaeological")"; ***cikùlukùlu*** "ancient custom"; ***mukùlù***[1] (***pukùlù, tukùlù***) "Elder, old, grandfather, Chief, Director, President (*Mukulu wa Cipangu* Parish Council President), principal wife of a polygamist household"; ***Kùlula*** "use, age" (V:-***Kulu***, ***kùlumpa***-[l + i> di] ⇒-sèlela; ***Lukulu*** word ☛ V. 11:-kulu; ***Makulu*** word ☛ 6 V.:-kulu; ***mikùlù*** word ☛ 4 V.:-kulu).

Remember that the root *eela/le* is polysemous, with meanings of "to make, express, to exit from the self (sound, idea, word, object, etc.)." From this root, with extended meanings of *age* and *adulthood*, the notion of "progenitor" enters our discourse. The Divine is seen as the primordial progenitor of all things in existence. In other words, God is the "source" of all things (the cosmic parent). This fact is reaffirmed in John S. Mbiti's seminal work *African Religions and Philosophy* (1989) as he notes,

> Many visualize God as Father, both in terms of His position as the universal Creator and Provider, and in the sense of His personal availability to them in time of need. The Akamba consider the heavens and the earth to be the Father's 'equal-sized bowls'; they are His property both by creation and the rights of ownership; and they contain His belongings. The Lunda, Bemba and others in the same region, speak of God as 'the universal Father' and mankind as His children. The Suk and Baganda hold that God is Father not only to men but also to the divinities and other spiritual beings. The idea of God being a Father of creation is reported among other African peoples, some of whose only or major personal name for God simply means 'Father'. (1989: 48-49)[33]

E. Bólájí Ìdòwù, in his seminal work *Olódùmarè*, informs us that the Supreme Being *Orìṣànlà* is sometimes said to be the:

> … father of all the *orìṣà* of Yorùbáland and that it was he who gave each one of them the name *orìṣà*, thus naming them after himself. Thus, the title "father" here denotes his relationship to the other divinities as well as suggests that he was the original divinity from whom at least a number of them derived. He is automatically the **senior** and **head** of them all. (Ìdòwù, 1994: 71). (bolded emphasis mine)

The root of the name *orìṣà* is a word that means "head." Often the same name for the Divine is used as a word for the King. Among the Yòrúba the word *Oba* means "king." It belongs to the same root as *iba* "father." A diviner is known as a *babalawo* "father of mysteries." When we talk about *Obàtálá*, on one level, the name means "exalted king," but on another level it can be interpreted as "The Primordial Father."

Among the Ba'ila of Zambia, the chief's relation to his people is given by the term *kulela*, which some have defined as "to rule." This is a secondary meaning. The word *kulela* is primarily "to nurse, to cherish" and the word is applied to a woman caring for her child. The chief is the father of the community; they are his children and what he does is *lela* them (Eglash, 1999: 29). This word itself is a term that has been metaphorically-extended and derives from the same proto-Bantu root that is reflected in the following terms in ciLuba:

---

33 For a detailed study, see Mbiti's larger work, *Concepts of God in Africa* (1970), chapters 8-13.

> *Baledi* "parents" (Der.:-*Lela*[1]; Sing.: *Muledi* "parent, mother father"); *buledi* "is to generate, maternity, paternity, parent"; *bulelà* "relationship, relationship characterizing those who cannot marry them, charity, kindness, generosity"; *ciledi* "cause, origin, source"; *cileledi* "matrix"; *cilelelu* "time of birth, date of birth"; *cilelelu*[2] "placenta"; *dilediibwa* "birth, Christmas" (the *birth* of Christ); *dilela* "child, children, birth, complicated thing"; *Ndedi* "cause"; *ndelelu* "descendants, generation"; *Mulele* "member of an extended family, parent" < *lelela/lela* "give birth, produce, cause, a family, adopt, educate, raise."

The Egyptian words *mry* "beloved, to love" and *nṯr* "god, the divine, generative aspects of nature" all derive from this root.[34] The name for the goddess *mꜣꜥt* also belongs to this root. Historically, in the Egyptian language, the phoneme transcribed as /ꜣ/ was actually an /l/ sound. *Maât* (righteousness, reciprocity, truth, balance, harmony, justice) was originally pronounced something more like *mala*(*t*). In ciLuba this is *mulele* "member of an extended family, parent." The terms *malelela, malela* "righteousness, justice, truth" and *malanda* "love, friendship and fraternity" also derive from the same root as Egyptian *mryw* "lusty youth lovers" and *mry* "suitor, beau" (Egyptian *mꜥhwt/mhwt* "family, kith, kin, tribesmen, generations").[35]

The Egyptian *bw mꜣꜥ/mꜣꜥ.t* "truth" in the ciLuba-Bantu language is *Bulelela* "actuality, truth" (*malelela, malela*). You can also say in ciLuba *Cyama/Cama* or *Meyi-malelela* or *Meeyi* (= *Mꜣꜥt*). The root of the word *mꜣꜥ.t* is *ꜣꜥ* with an ***m-*** prefix (ciLuba *lelèlà* "actual, real, authentic, true, genuine, veritable"; Egyptian *rri* "really, truly"; Yorùbá *ododo* "truth, fact, justice, equality, right, righteousness" [r>d]). All of these terms exist because of the process of metaphoric-extension.

The concept of "truth" is a tertiary meaning, again, deriving from the root *eela* "make, express, to exit from the self (sound, idea, word, object, etc.)." The projecting outward from a point gives way to the concept of "measurement." The following provides more proof of the *ꜣ* to *l* correspondence. In the Egyptian language the word *mꜣ* means "measure."[36] This word in ciLuba is *mwanda* "an amount, measure, extent, far." Here the sound rule is [n+l>nd]. In other words, when the /l/ is nasalized, *l* > *d*. This relationship can also be seen in ciLuba by way of comparison with Egyptian *mꜣꜥ* "truth"; ciLuba *munda* "true" where *-nd* was *l* (Kalenjiin *iman* "it is true," "so be it"; *imanda* "justice, right"; *imanit* "the truth"); also in ciLuba *-à/-a milòwo*(*u*) "agreeable, true, sincere, good." The idea of truth, in this context, derived from demonstrating that one has taken "accurate measurements" of something. We see the word *eela* reflected in the ciLuba words:

eelejila	"add, in addition to"
eelekeja	"measure, to gauge, take stock"

From this sense of *addition*, which falls into our *linear-order* schema, we get this concept of "truth" deriving from the field of mathematics. As Karenga (2006: 6) notes about its etymology, *mꜣꜥt* suggests an evolution from a physical concept of "straightness, evenness, levelness,

---

34 We explore the relationship of the *-r-* root and *nṯr* in more detail in the chapter on *Ntr* in Vol. II of this book series.

35 The -r-/-l- root may also be seen in the Egyptian word *ẖr* "relatives (of family), household members, underlings, inhabitants (of land)." The word *hnw* "associates, family" may be a morphological variant: *ẖ>h*; *r>n*.

36 We also reaffirm this in Egyptian with our root *lee-/le-* "distant, remote, far, long, large, above" (measured to be as such) by the following: *wꜣ* "far, distant"; ciLuba *b-ule*(a) "length, height, depth, duration"; *pabule*(a) "remote") [w>b]; *ꜣw* "time span, length, range (of time)"; *ꜣwt* "length, range, forever"; ciLuba *k-ale* "history" (reaching far back in time)

correctness," as the wedged-shaped glyph suggests. We understand now that the *m-* in *mꜣꜥt* is a prefix, and that the root is *ꜣꜥ* (*ꜣ* = l). With that said, in ciLuba we have the following: *-oolòlòke*(a) "straight, correct" (<*-oolola* "extend, stretch"; *-oolwela*). This confirms the suggestions made by Karenga (2006).

The underlying idea of *mꜣꜥ.t*—as it pertains to the concept of lineage, parenthood, generations, etc. (*lela*)—is that you treat people how you would treat *family*.[37] In another sense, given that the root deals with *additions*, this can also refer to the ever expanding nodes of human "generations" (ciLuba *ndelelu*; Egyptian *nṯrw*) from the primordial mother and father.

In the Kalenjiin language *maat*[38] means "fire; a *relationship* term for and between: paternal relations, circumcision-mates, age-mates, members of one military regiment" (Sambu, 2008: 272). The word *mat* in Kalenjiin means "don't" and introduces all teachings of the "don'ts" of the code of conduct (laws of *mꜣꜥt* in Egypt). The word *mat* also means "path, way" and is used among the Kalenjiin speaking people in the same way we would use the word "lineage" in English. The English root is "line" and it reinforces this theme of "projection, distant" from a zero-point: *linear-order* schema.

We can also see the *ꜣ* = *l* in another Egyptian term *mꜣꜥ* "leader" that also has the "*ala*" (*eela/le*) root and it too relates to the *up-down* schema. In ciLuba we have *mwadi* "chief, leader, president"; [l + i>di]. Here *m-* is the prefix and *ꜣꜥ* is the root. We know this because the root is isolated in Egyptian as *ꜥꜣ* (*ala*) "leader, chief workman, commander, Elder, Noble, Master."[39] In Yorùbá this term is *Oluwa* "master," *Olu* "chief, captain, God." Remember that the terms for "authority" often derive from words that mean "large, big, and grand"[40] and in the Egyptian language we have *ꜥꜣ* which means "great, grand"; *ꜥꜣ* "great (of size), many, greatly, greatness, influence"; "distinguished, genteel, noble"; *ꜥꜣ.t* "a great thing"; *ꜥꜣi* "big, important, heavy, sublime, plentiful, much, rich, senior." This term is also cognate with Yorùbá *n-la* "great, grand" (as in the name *Orìṣànla* "The Great Orìṣà" or "Chief of the Orìṣàs"[41]; PWS **la* "old, elder" (the elders were the leaders of traditional societies; those up in *age*; those with the *greatest* knowledge). 'Allah' is embedded in the name for God in Yorùbáland as *Orìṣànla*.

Remember that a "leader" is often viewed in terms of a "father" (the head of household) and among the Yorùbá this root is *baálé*/*balé* "father, leader"; "householder, master of a house"; "governor, president, chief of a town or village"; m>b. The name of the Canaanite God *Baal* "lord, master, husband" (Akk. *bēlu* "lord; proprietor") is cognate with this term. *Baal* simply means "father" and denotes the Divine as the "Chief spirit," "The progenitor of all life," "The ruler of all that exist." The TOB database has the following reconstructions:

> Proto-Afro-Asiatic: **baʕVl-*
> Meaning: elder male relative in-law, husband
> Semitic: **baʕl-* 'husband, master, owner'
> Central Chadic: **bVlaw-* 'man' (?)
> Saho-Afar: **ball-*'father-in-law'
> Low East Cushitic: **HVbbVl-* 'brothers and sisters; relatives' ~ **bVHVl-* `husband, lover'

---

37 Among the *Bakala* (African-Americans) we still greet each other (more so to our age-mates) as "brother" or "sister." Any older woman of our parents or grandparents age is called "Big Mama" (regardless of physical size).

38 In Egyptian it is possible that the *l* > *a* in this example, or the *l* was dropped all together. The Kelenjiin people would have separated at the time of the loss of *l* in *mꜣꜥt*.

39 Phonemes were often reversed in monosyllabic words, especially where the /r/ or /ꜣ/ consonant is the root.

40 Think of the English phrases "large and in charge" or "big man on campus."

41 A third title for the Supreme Being, also called *Obàtálá*. See Epega (2003: 48) and Ìdòwù (1994: 71).

(<Sem?)
High East Cushitic: **bVHil-* 'master' [1], 'friend' [2]
South Cushitic: **balaʔ/ʕ-* 'cross-cousin'
Notes: Related to **baʕVl-* 'rule, command; own; be able'.

Here *Baal* is another form of the word *Allah* and this root has come to form a great number of words which have been used to represent the Divine: all by way of metaphoric-extension [e.g., PWS *lu,* (*du*) "head"; PWS *lé,*(*dé, dó*) "one'" (total), with *dó* as common reflex; Sumerian *dù* "totality"].

Table 3: Baal[42]

	Canaanite	**Lu-ganda**	**Yorùbá**	**Hebrew**
"Divinities"	*Ba'al*	*Lu-baale* *ba-lu-baale*		*B*^{e}*'al-iym*
"husband"			*baálé*	*ba'al* (*ha-'išš-ah*)
"land lord"			*Bale ilé*	*ba'al* *hab-bayit*
"chief of rural settlement"			*baálé*	

The Hebrew word *ba'al* "lord, master" was too close to the name of the Canaanite God *Ba'al*, and as a result, the Hebrew's 'God' banned usage of the word *ba'al* in relation to him. Hosea 2:16-17 tells us that:

In that day, says Yahweh
You will call me "My *'iyš*"
No longer will you call me "My *ba'al*"
For I will remove the names of the *b*^{e}*'al-iym* from her mouth
And they will be mentioned by name no more.

As a result of the rejection of *b'l*, the Hebrews adopted the Afroasiatic root *'lh* (*alah*) "lord" for "divine lord" (Hebrew *'eloah* "God," *'eloh'iym* "lords" (Gods); Yorùbá *olúwa* "lord, master," *olúwo* "head of the Osugbo, the council of chiefs," *orúwo* "head" (Ijebu dialect); Egyptian *wr* "lord, chief, master, great one," *m3ᶜ* "leader"; ciLuba *mukulu* "chief, director, president"; Sumerian *lú* "lord, chief"). Little did they know that they were replacing one word for a dialectical variation of the same word. The Hebrews could have benefited greatly from the field of comparative historical linguistics.

In the same spirit, the b-l root was reversed by a process of metathesis and survives in Yorùbá as the word *Àràbà* "the title of the chief priest of Ifá" in Ile Ife. As noted by Oduyoye (1997: 101), the connotation of the title can be seen in the fact that the silk cotton tree, the largest tree in Africa, is in Yorùbá called *igi àràbà.* This word means "big, great" and is built on the sonsonantal root -r-b- which underlies the reduplicated ideophone ribiribi (*iṣé ribiribi* "great deeds"), *réberèbe* "extensive." This range of meaning can be found in Hebrew rab "great, many, numerous," from the same root as rabbi, the title of the Jewish religious teacher. A Rabbi is a Rab "master," Rabbi "my lord." The root is reduplicated in Biblical Aramaic *rabrᵊban* "big words" (Daniel 7:8), magnate, chief. The word *àràbà* is not confined in use to the title of the chief priest of Ifa: when a man has grown big in wealth and power, the Yoruba say *O d' àràbà* "He became an *àràbà*." Therefore, *àràbà* is used to mean *great power* and *wealth.* In Arabic *rabb* is used even of God in *Suratu-l-Fatiha*: the vocative *ya rabbi* is used to call on God. The

42 Saakana (1991: 72).

r-b root is cognate with Egyptian *w-r* (b>w) and may be a dialectical variation of the word *nb* "Lord, Master, Owner, Possessor, Lady Mistress" (r>n).

We reiterate here that the Divine is described in the following terms: "the all, high, large, big, master, chief, head, owner, progenitor, the eldest, the source, the mother, father, parent, the remote, the distant, the way (path), the highest, most exalted, primordial, supreme, great, most ancient, lord, etc." All of these terms in African languages derive from the -r-/-l- monosyllabic root whose underlying theme is "distance, length, remoteness, and up" (concepts within three-dimensional space).

We go into this amount of detail to demonstrate that *Allah* (*ʾḷ*) is only one dialectical form among many from a root that is more ancient than Semitic and even Afro-Asiatic. To claim *El, Alah, il-ilāh* is a "Semitic" god is not keeping with the facts. "Allah" is indigenously African and is embedded in many names for the Divine all across the continent of Africa. As we can see here, *la*(e,i,o) is used primarily as a descriptor, not a proper name. In the final sections of this essay we will demonstrate under what context *Allah* in the Arabic became a proper name and why *Allah*, in relationship to all of the other pre-Islamic "gods" in Arabia, became the sole representative of the Divine in that area.

Allah as the sky-god/god of rain

Earlier we cited Ulf Oldenburg's text *Above the Stars of El* (2010: 84-85). We highlighted the attributes of *El* (*Aḷah*) which were given as "the first, exalted, the king above all, head, father, uncle, brother and savior." All of these terms, as we have demonstrated, are the by-products of the process of metaphoric-extension to the very ancient root of -r-/-l- (*eela/le/la*) which has the underlying theme of "distance, remoteness, length and height."

In this section we will demonstrate that *Allah* was historically associated with "rain" and the "sky." These words also belong to the -r-/-l- root. Wesley Muhammad provides various sources that give us clues to *Allah*'s earliest associations. Muhammad (2009: 84) argues that *ʾḷ/ ʾḷh* was eventually "crowded out" of Old Southern Arabia by "nature" deities of the North. But it would seem that *Allah* himself is a nature deity (of the heavens).

Muhammad, in describing the ancient Arabian religions, starts out with a comparison and then ultimately equates the Sumerian God *An/Enki* with the Arabic God *Allah* (Muhammad, 2009: 91-98). On pg 93 he notes that the Akkadian god *Anu* (who he equates with *Allah*) is also known as the "first (god), the heavenly father, the greatest one in heaven and earth, and the one who contains the entire universe." We know these attributes are represented by the *-l-* root and we will demonstrate below that l>n and this is how *Al* becomes *An*.

It has been demonstrated conclusively, to this author's satisfaction, that the Sumerian people were a Niger-Congo/Kongo-Saharan speaking people.[43] Their vocabulary matches many of the lexemes found in Kongo-Saharan languages (along with other grammatical features). With that said, the Sumerian *An* and Akkadian *Anu* are just dialectical variations of the Kongo-Saharan **ra* (as both the "sun" and the "sky."). Muhammad notes that *An* was considered to be a "luminous" god as his ideogram was that of an asterisk 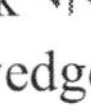, a cuneiform star with eight points (written DINGER), which was later modified to a wedge cross (a sign for "God,

43 See the works by Rev. W. Wanger (1935). *Comparative Lexical Study of Sumerian and NTU ("Bantu"): Sumerian the "Sanscrit" of the African NTU Languages*. W. Kohlhammer. Berlin.; GJK Campbell-Dunn (2009a). *Sumerian Comparative Grammar*, and (2009b) *Sumerian Comparative Dictionary*. Penny Farthing Press. New Zealand; and Robin Walker (2011). *When We Ruled: The Ancient and Mediaeval History of Black Civilisations*. Black Classic Press. UK. The latest work confirming the Niger-Congo origins of the Sumerians is by Hermel Hermstein (2012) *Black Sumer: The African Origins of Civilization*, Pomegranate Publishers. Kindle Edition.

heaven"). *Enki* (a variation of *An*) is called "the bright light in the heaven" and "Great Light of the Apsu."[44] For Muhammad, *An* is a 'star-god' *par excellence* and *Enki* is the 'star-god of the waters' (as he was encompassed in the primordial waters).

I argue that the reason *An* and *Enki* are associated with both "light" (stars) and "water" is that the word *An* is just the word for "sky" and in African languages the word for "sky" is also the word for "rain" and sometimes the "sun" (a *sun* is a *star*). We should note that the Etruscans worshipped a "sky god" called *Ani* who resided in the heavens and depicted with two faces (Jordon, 2004: 20). The Etruscan language is commonly considered a language-isolate, but GJK Campbell-Dunn now considers this a Niger-Congo language.[45] The Celtic (Irish) people, before Christianity, used to worship a chthonic mother goddess by the name of *Anu* (also *Ana*) and was associated with fertility and the primordial mother of the *Tuatha de Danann* (Jordan, 2004: 22).[46] This may prove to be relevant upon further investigation. In comparison, we note that the Igbo goddess of the earth is named *Ala* and she is responsible for morality, the ancestors and fertility.

The same root for "sky" is the same root for "God" in Sumerian: *en* "god," *an* "sky" [Daniel A Foxvog, *Intro to Sumerian Grammar* (2009:7, 9)]. We also have the following notes from Foxvog that reaffirm our association of the Sumerian word for "sky" deriving from roots meaning "high, long, above, etc."

> The Sumerian sign *AN* can represent:
> - the logogram *an* in the meaning "sky, heaven"
> - the logogram *an* in the meaning "high area"
> - the logogram *an* in the meaning "(the sky-god) An"
> - the logogram *diĝir* "god, goddess"
> - the determinative for deities, as in *den-líl* "(the god) *Enlil*"
> - the syllable *an*, as in *mu-na-an-šúm* "he gave it to him"
> - the syllable *am6* (in Old Sumerian), as in *lugal-am6* "he is king" (Foxvog, 2009: 15)

An is equivalent to the Egyptian word *iwn* "sun." The sun was deified among the ancient Egyptians as *iwn* "sun God" . Before one begins to speculate that this may be a loan from the Sumerians into Egyptian, one has to consider the Igbo *Anwu* "sun-god," *Anyanwu* "eye of God (the sun)"; Jukun (Wukari dialect) *yunu* "sun"; Idoma (Nkum dialect) *yeno* "sun"; Efik *Nyan* "the Sun-God." This root is reflected in Yorùbá in the verb *yan* "to roast" and the noun *ìyàn* "famine, drought." Yorùbá *òrùn* "sun" may be a variation of this term (*orùn* "sky"). *Rʿ* and *iwn* are variations of the same word. The words *ink/iwnw* are the names of the ancient Egyptian city the Greeks called *Heliopolis* "city of the sun" (*On* of the Bible). This was the cult center of *Rʿ* throughout Egyptian history (in its physical and spiritual senses). It was an astrological center and probably was the place where they measured the sun's movement to anticipate the seasons associated with agricultural activities. The city of Denderah was also

44 Citing Tony Nugent, "Star God: Enki/Ea," 269; Andrew George "Babylonian texts from the folios of Sidney Smith, Part Two: prognostic and diagnostic omens." ***Revue d'assyriologie***, 83 (1991): 152 [art.=137-167].

45 See Campbell-Dunn's paper "The Etruscan Decipherment" currently located here: http://home.clear.net.nz/pages/gc_dunn/Etruscans.html. You can also see Campbell-Dunn *The African Origins of Classical Civilization* (2008). Author House. Bloomington, IN.

46 The *Tuatha de Danann* (peoples of the goddess Danu; Anu/Ana) is a collective name for a pantheon of deities among the Celtic speaking people of Ireland. The deities include the DAGDA, LUG, GOBNIU, Nuadu Argatlam and others and represent a possibly non-tribal hierarchy of the supernatural joined against a common foe, the powers of destruction and misfortune, the *Fomoire*, and the *Fir Bolg* who were allegedly an agricultural tribe from Greece.

called *iwnt* and this too was a major center of astrological institutions (think of the temple of *Ht Hrw* (Hathor) Denderah).

Dendera Zodiac, temple of Hathor

We see this *iwn* root reflected in the following terms which are associated with our -r-/-l- root which simply morphed into *-n-* (and *-t-*):

PWS *na* "above" [n < r]
PWN *NI* "rain" (from on high) [Proto-Western-Negritic, Mukarovsky 1976/77]
PWS *NI* "rain, high"
Bantu *niin* "ascend"
Swahili *nya* "rain"
Mande *yire* "ascend"
Mande *mi* "rain"
Mangbetu *ênie* "to raise" (child)
Mangbetu *onie* "to reign"

<u>FIRE</u> **Sumerian** *ne-mur* "fire"

NA "fire"
MU "fire" -r

PWS *ná* "fire", Kebu *ná-wo* "fire" **Sumerian** *bún* "lamp"
PWN *MUAL* "to shine"
Atlantic *na, nak* "sun, day" (Westermann 1928 : 85 – 86) [Arabic *nar* "fire"]
PWN *PHI* "burn" (fire)
Bantu *pía* "fire"
Bantu *–ωmu* "fire" (195), but *bu, bi* (259, 267, 187, 184, *buri* 121, 222 etc), without nasalisation of *b* to *m.*
Mande *mana* "fire"
Mande *wumbe* "fire"
Mangbetu *mudé* "heat"
PCS **pVl, *pVr* "light"

*N = n *A = e *B = m *U = u

<u>HEAVEN</u>
(Wanger)

Sumerian *u-na* "heaven"

"time, night" (Delitzsch)

TU "fire" **u-**
NA "above"

Sumerian *an* "heaven"

PWS *tùà, (tọ̀)* "to roast" (of the sun)
PWS *na* "above"
Or PWS *tu, tua* "water" (rain from sky) ?
PWN *THU, THUA* "water place"
Bantu *tu,mb* "to roast" (compare *utu* "the sun")
"Bantu" *tuna* (273), *tuwana* (256), "sky"
Bantu *to* "river"
Mande *Nala* "God" ?
Mangbetu *anana* "climb tree" (to sky ?)
Khoisan : Naron (C) */am, /gam* "on" ?
Afro-Asiatic : Chad : Hausa (1) *sama* "above", Logone (2) *sama* "rain", Mandara (6) *samaya* "sky"[47] (Greenberg)

***T = #** ***U = u** ***N = n** ***A = a**

[Igbo has the prefix seen in Sumerian: *ka-* = *h̲a-* : but *ka* is an old N-C word for "fire". We also have *da* = *ta,* but PWS *la, (dā)* "day" from "sun," "fire" etc].

[Greek *ana* — "up, on" is probably related].

The word **na/*ni* (Egyptian *iwn*) is simply a 'catch-phrase' for the "sky" and its important features: "the sun, stars" and "rain" (e.g., Yorùbá *orùn* "heaven, sky", *òrùn* "sun."). A relevant example is given by Campbell-Dunn as it regards Indo-European: "One is reminded of Latin *diēs, dius, divus* and also of Greek *dios, dia* etc. "Day", "rain", "god", "shining sky" are all interrelated" (Campbell-Dunn, 2009a: 149).

Iwn in Egyptian is also the word for "pillar, column" which is a by-form of the word *iwn* "length." A "column" is defined by its association with "height" and "length" and thus *iwn* "column" gets its name by metaphoric-extension which denotes its relative "height" to man's zero-point, the ground. We know this term is a result of metaphoric-extension (*up-down* schema) because it is also reflected in the word *iwn* "(a man is a) pillar (of his family)" in Egyptian (Mark Vygus, 2011: 1279). Now, one could argue that in this sense "pillar" could be a metaphor for "stability" or "groundedness." But I argue it has more to do with an individual being an "upright" or "standup" type of person. S/He is someone who "holds-up" the family, "one who holds high the values of his family." This can be seen in the phrase:

iwn mwt.f

(one of the names of Horus) "Pillar of his mother."

One could also argue that this term iwn could mean "the height of achievement, excellence." When we say that someone is the "pillar of the community," we mean to say that s/he is a representative of the best of what this community has to offer; that s/he personifies excellence. What you are saying is that this person has reached a "towering," or "exalted" status as a result

47 This root is also found in Proto-Semitic as **sm* "sky, heaven"

of their good deeds in the community; and it is their continued "support" (like a pillar) for the community that holds "up" (sustains) the society.

It's important to note that the Sumerian lexicon has many qualities in common with other African languages, and that includes its highly polesymous word base as a result of not being a very lexically rich language. Foxvog gives us some insight into why one sign would have so many meanings in the Sumerian language. The first out of the three given is:

> [in regards to Sumerian signs] It will usually have one or more logographic values, each with a different pronunciation. A single value may itself have more than one meaning, just as an English word may have more than one common meaning. Sumerian expresses the human experience with a relatively limited word stock; one must continually strive to develop a feeling for the basic meaning of any particular Sumerian word and how it can be used to convey a range of ideas for which English uses different individual words. (Foxvog, 2009: 15)

In other words, English has expanded over the years so much—this due to many borrowings and its inflectional nature—that it is able to convey many concepts without necessarily using the same word to convey every conceptual idea needed. In African languages, however, this isn't necessarily the case. This is probably why agglutination and tone became major features of many African languages. As noted by Stewart (1903), Niger-Congo words, for example, are formed from a very small number of roots. We see this in Sumerian.

The Sumerian and other African languages are *lexically* poor, but each lexical root is *conceptually* rich, as these languages build-up their vocabularies by a process of metaphoric-extension on common lexical roots. This is a feature of the ancient Egyptian language. James P. Allen (the author of a Middle Egyptian grammar and dictionary), in his book *The Ancient Egyptian Pyramid Texts* (2005) stated the following about the Egyptian language: "[The] Egyptian [language] is rich in allegory and metaphor but relatively poor in vocabulary" (2005: 13). In other words, the Egyptian language has relatively few actual words in the total lexicon, but these words have many uses because the Egyptians extend their meanings by way of metaphor and allegory. This has been demonstrated all throughout this essay and will be important to understand in this final leg of our discourse.

So great is this 'problem' of an accurate interpretation of certain words in Egyptian that Allen had to put out a disclaimer in regards to some Egyptian terms left untranslated. He goes on to state that, "In a few cases, our knowledge of the Egyptian language has not (yet) made it possible to know the meaning of a verb or noun; such words are represented in the translations by a transliteration of the Egyptian term" (Allen, ibid). This is why we turn to other related African languages to help us rediscover these obscure terms as we are currently doing at this moment.

An-Anki = ʾAḷah

In the chapter dealing with the religion of Afrabia, Muhammad dedicates much space to propose a linguistic, historic and conceptual connection between the Sumerian god *An/Enki* and the Arabic god of Islam *Allah*. In this section of *Black Arabia*, Muhammad makes the case that the Sumerian *An* is equivalent to the Semitic *ʾAḷah* (as a concept and linguistic term). Muhammad suggests that the god *Enki*'s name[48] is composed of two morphemes *En* "lord" + *ki* "earth."[49] *An* is just a variation of the -r-/-l- root spoken of throughout our discussion here. The Sumerian

48 *Enki* is *An* as a different manifestation of himself

49 We are reminded of the Nilo-Saharan speaking cattle herders of East Africa, the Maasai, whose name for God is *Enkai* or *Ngai*.

word for "earth" is also another Kongo-Saharan lexeme:

EARTH **Sumerian** *ki* "earth, place"

KI "earth"

PWS *g̱ì* "black", Ewe *yì* "black", Dahomey *wi* "black", Igbara *dži* "black"
PWN *CÍ* "country, ground"
PWN *KI, (KYI, CI)* "village, settlement"
Bantu *cí* "ground, country"
Kongo *nsi* "country", Swahili *inchi* "country"
Mande B *gere,* M *gete* "earth"
Mangbetu *giri* "on dry land"

***K = k** ***I = i**

However, this definition for the name *En-ki* may be folk-etymology as certain scholars are unsure of its etymology. I posit that it could easily be *En-ki* "Lord (on) High" as an alternate rendering of *lugal* "king, lord; master; owner; a quality designation" (l>n; g>k). We should note that *Enki* is also pronounced *Enkil*. As noted in Allan Bomhard's article "On the Origin of Sumerian" (2007: 3), final consonants, especially *t, d, k, g, m, n*, and *r* were often omitted. This makes it difficult to ascertain the form of the word.

The *ki* morpheme may derive from the same root as Sumerian *aga* "lord." The word *en* can also mean "lord, priest" in Sumerian. We may be dealing with a serial noun where essentially both terms mean the exact same thing (both referencing "high stature, what is above").

BIG **Sumerian** *gal* "big"

GA "big" **-l**

PWS gán *"big",* ka *"king, chief, ancestor"* ***Sumerian*** *daĝal* "large*"*

PWS gà *"hundred"* ***Sumerian*** *ár, ara* $_2$ *"*glorify*"*[50]
PWN *GÀ, (GÀNA)* "hundred"
Bantu *gana* "hundred"
"Bantu" (Johnston) *kañgi* "great" (237)
Mande *gyã* "big"
PCS **kpa* "big"

***G = g/ĝ** ***A = a** ***(L) = l** ***G = #**

GREAT **Sumerian** *gal* "to be great"

GA "great" **-l**

PWS *ka* "chief, king", *gán* "great, king"
PWS *gán* "big, king, topmost point"
PWN *KAKA* "grandfather or master"
Bantu *camba* "king"

---

50 The Sumerian *ár, ara* "glorify" fits well with our -r-/-l- root dealing with "above, height, exaltation." See Yorùbá *Olá* "elevated status, fame, honourable estate."

Mande *gyã, dyã* "great"
Mangbetu *ga* "the biggest tree"
PCS **kpa* "big"

[The *–l* is a definite, or PWS *li* "to be" (verbal adjective)].

***G = g** ***A = a**

<u>KING</u> **Sumerian** *lugal* "king"

LU "head"
GA "big" **-l**

PWS *lu* "head" *(du, ru)* + PWS *ka* "father, king" + *l* (article), PWS *lá* "the, he, agent nouns".
PWS *gán* "big, chief"
PWN *(GHIDU)* "head"
PWN *GÀ, (GÀNA)* "hundred" (big number).[51]
Mande *dugu-tigi* "chief of village".
Mangbetu *dru* "head," *dudu* "weak man"
ES Dongola, Kenuzi, Mahas, Gulfan *ur* "head"
CN Bertat *alu, kulu* "head"
PCS **d.u* "head"

***D = l** ***U = u** ***G = g** ***A = a**

In Egyptian we have *ḳꜣi* "tall, high, long, exalted, be raised on high, uplifted" (*ꜣ = l*); *ẖy* "high"; *ẖy* "the high one (sun god)"; *ẖy* to be high, be exalted, be loud (noise); *kꜣkꜣ* "god" (Mende *mahā* "king", Sumerian *maẖ* "great, exalted", PWS *gán* "big", *ka* "king, chief, ancestor").

The Sumerian name *Enki* is present in East Africa in its fuller form. Remember that the word for the 'sky' in many languages (or in cognate languages) is also the word for 'sun'. Among the Lang'o of Kenya the word for sun is *nikolonga*. On the West Bank of the Nile in the Sudan are a people called Bari and they call the Creator *Ngun lo ki*, "Ngun in the above/sky." The Maasai call the sun *E-ngolo-ng*. It is from this that the word *Enkai* (the sky) becomes its reduction. We see this root among the Kalenjiin for the epithet of *Asiis: Asiis Cheepo-Ngolo*, "Asiis the daughter of Ngolo." *Asiis*, as we know, is symbolized by the sun (*asiista*). So we have the following (with additional info for support):

Lang'o	*ni-kolo-nga*	"sun"	(k-l) [root]
Bari	*Ngun lo ki*	"Ngun of the above"	(k-; loss of *-l*)
Maasai	*E-ngolo-ng*	"sun"	(g-l)
Kalenjiin	*Asiis Cheepo-Ngolo*	"Asiis daughter of Ngolo"	(g-l)
ciLuba	*kuulu*	"sky, heavens"	(k-l)
ciLuba	*Nkole*(a)[52]	"God"	(k-l)
PWN	*GULU*	"sky"	(g-l)
PB	**gudu, *godo*	"sky"	(g-d) [l>d]
NC	*gui*[53]	*"sun"*	*(g-)*
Sumerian	*Enkil/Enki*	"God of the sky, rain"	(k-l; k-)

---

51 This is where we get the word for the country in Africa GHANA from. It means "king."
52 *Nkole*(a) can also mean "eminent or powerful"; *bankole* "spirits." We also have *cikala* "lieutenant, replacing the head"; Kiluba: *cìkalà* / *shìkalà* "replacing the chief, ruler."
53 See Campbell-Dunn "BASQUE AS NIGER-CONGO." Unpublished.

It is not likely that the *-kil* or *-ki* morpheme in the Sumerian name for God, *Enkil/Enki*, would mean "earth," but is associated with the "sky, heavens." However, in PWS we have **gi* "world, sky." Another word for "god" in Sumerian is *dingir/diĝir*. Cambpell-Dunn (2009b: 67) considers *dingir/diĝir* cognate with Bantu *dungu* "god" (intelligent) with loss of final consonant *–l*. I'm not convinced of this association. *Dungu* is a variation of *lunga* as in *Kalunga*, a popular name for the Divine in Central and East Africa.[54] I think his other assessment in (2009a) is more on the money.

> In Bantu however the accentuation is on the initial stem syllable, *dími*, "tongue", PWN *LÍMA*, *LÍAMI* "tongue". Sumerian *dumu* "son, daughter" is from the same root PWS *du* "head", with a different suffix, probably meaning "my". Sumerian *idim* "source, subterranean water" also has the same origin, again with an *m* suffix, but with *i* prefixed. Sumerian *im* "clouds, rain" come from the sky, the head of the world, but with loss of initial *d*. Related to "head" is "spirit", PWN *DIM*. Does *diĝir* "god" really mean "head of sky" or rather "spirit of sky" (*di* = "be", "being") . . .
>
> The Sumerian Determinatives used before certain classes of noun resemble the Niger-Congo prefix-classifiers preposed to nouns. Thus Determinative ^{d} is put before divine names (Sumerian *diĝir* "god", *ĝir* < PWS *gi* "sky" + *-r* "suffix"), and may be a reduction of Niger-Congo Prefix 5. An old demonstrative *di-* or *-di* occurs in some Niger-Congo and Nilo-Saharan languages (also in Meroitic). But this too must be from *di* "head". The classifiers were once full nouns. We have interpreted *diĝir* (*di-n-gi-r*) therefore as root + (nasal) + root (genitive) + suffix. (Campbell-Dunn, 2009a: 148-149)

It is the *-gir-* root that is cognate with *kil* which was reduced to *ki* in the word *Enki*. The *di-* is a prefix on the root.

Remember that *Enki* also represents the "stars" and is called "the bright light in the heaven" and "Great Light of the Apsu." All of his associations—conceptually and morphologically—can be found today in Africa, in-tact. For these reasons, and more, I interpret *Enkil* to mean "lord" (*en-*) of the "sky" (*-kil/-ki*). The more popular form of his name lost the consonant *-l*.

In Hebrew the word *Enki* is reflected in the word *nogah* "brilliant light," as in *nogah mim-ma-ro^{w}m* "the bright dawn from on high; the rising sun" (Luke 1:78). We see *Enki* reflected in the following:

Mende	*Ngwe*	"God"
	ngawu	"moon"
Birom	*Da gwi*	"God" (*da* "father"; < *ra*)
	gwi	"sun"
Fulbe	*nge*	"sun"
Ki-Kamba	*Ngai*	"God"
Ki-Kuyu	*Ngu*	"God"
Maasai	*Enkai*	"God"
PWS	**gui*	"sun" [Westermann's Index B (1927: 310 f)]

54 Proto-Bantu **-dung-* "to become fitting, straight, right"; Southern Kaskazi **-lungu* "God"; e.g., Nyanja *mlungu*, "god" pl. *achimlungu* "gods" *umlungo* "divinity"; Kikuyu n. *mũrungu*; Shambala *mulungu* "god"; Ngulu *mulungu* "god"; Zigula *mulungu* "god"; Kamba *mulungu* "god"; Itumba *mulungu*; god"; Kondoa/Solwe *mulungu* "god"; Yao *mulungu* "god"; Gindo *mulungu* "god"; Ganji *mulungu* "god"; Hehe *mulungu* "god"; Ziráha *mulungu* "god"; Nkwifiya *mulungu* "god"; Ndunda *mulungu* "god"; Kwenye *mulungu* "god"; Bena *mulungu* "god"; Sango/Lori *mulungu* "god"; Bunga *mulungu* "god"; Sukuma *mulungu* "god"; Turu *mulungu* "god." Ehret, *An African Classical Age*, 166–7; Nurse and Hinnebusch, *Swahili and Sabaki*, 620. The PB form **-dung-* (< -dOk-) also means "water, rain."

All these reflect God as *light*, and as we have stated, the word for "sky" is often the word for "sun." This explains, as stated before, why Sumerian *Enki(l)* is at once a "star" god and the god for "sky, rain."

Muhammad incorrectly suggested that *Enki* possibly had an earlier pre-Sumerian Semitic name. The Sumerians weren't a Semitic people and the terms used to describe their understanding of the Divine were all inherited by their Kongo-Saharan ancestors. They did not enter Arabia without any knowledge of *An* (*Alah*). Therefore *An* is not a 'Sumerianization' of a Semitic god. The similarities arise because 'Allah' is an inner African conceptualization of and a term for the Divine. It existed before Semitic and even Afro-Asiatic and spread out as a result of human migrations and natural language evolution.

As noted by Mbiti in *African Religions and Philosophy*, essentially all African terms for God relate to the heavens:

> As far as written sources available are concerned, all African peoples associate God with the sky or heaven, in one way or another. There are those who say that He reigns there; the majority think that He lives there; and some even identify Him with the sky, or consider it to be His chief manifestation. We have many peoples whose names for God mean sky, heaven, or the above. For example the Bari and Fajulu term for God is *Ngun lo ki* which means 'God in the sky (above)'; the Shona name *Nyadenga* means 'the Great One of the sky', and *Wokumusoro* means 'the One above'; the Tiv name, *Aondo*,[55] means "Heavens, sky'; and the Turkana word for God, *Akuj*, means '(of) Up, above'. Thus, God cannot be separated from heaven, and heaven cannot be separated from God; the object points to its Creator, and thoughts about the Creator point towards the heavens and the sky. (Mbiti, 1989: 52).

Hallet & Pelle, in their book *Pygmy Kitabu* (1973), reaffirms Mbiti's statements cited above. As told to the anthropologist Paul Schebesta by the Efé of the Ituri forest, as it regards the Creator, "God dwells on high, in the Frimament. God is the Lord above all things" (Hallet & Pelle, 1973: 62).

This equation of *God*, *heavens* and even *rain* is reaffirmed by historian and linguist Christopher Ehret in his essay, "Writing African History from Linguistic Evidence" in the text *Writing African History* (2005) edited by John E. Philips. In regards to these associations among Nilotic speakers, Ehret informs us that:

> Divinity is the source of good and evil; the bad happenings of life are the result of Divine retribution, visited upon people for the wrongs they or their parents before them have committed. In religious *metaphor*, **Divinity is identified with the sky and with rain and lightning**. (Philips, 2005: 98) (emphasis mine)

The association of the Sumerian *An* with "sky, heaven" is simply following in the ancient African tradition and the Arabic *Allah* is not a deviation from this ancient association. We get more insights from Muhammad in regards to the equation of *An* and *Allah* in his chapter on "The Religion of Afrabia." The following excerpt from Muhammad (2009) is worth quoting at length as it sets the precedence by which our ultimate argument is made. He goes on to note, in regards to the equation of *Enki* with *Allah*, that:

> The cuneiform 𒀭 is the Sumerian ideogram DINGIR indicating the god An and also the word 'god' in general and 'heaven/sky.' It has the phonetic value *an*. DINGIR often

55 I argue *Aondo* = *Ala*; n+l>nd.

> serves as a determinative for 'divinity' as well, affixed to a name to indicate that the name is that of a deity. As a determinative, DINGIR is not pronounced and it appears in transliterations as a superscript 'd' (e.g., ^{d}ENKI). DINGIR's Akkadian equivalent is 𒀭. It has the same properties as the Sumerian: it indicates the god *Anu*, means as well 'god' in general, and serves as an unpronounced determinative for 'deity/ divinity'. There is one critical difference, however: its phonetic value is *ʾḷ*, i.e. the Proto-Semitic *ʾAḷah*. In other words the Sumerian *An* is the same as the Akkadian *ʾḷ*, the Proto-Semitic *ʾAḷah*. It has been demonstrated through theophorous names (names of individuals which include divine names in them) that *Il* is the predominant name of God in the Early Dynastic period amongst the Mesopotamian Semites, indicating that this Proto-Semitic deity was the chief deity. There is therefore merit to Piotr Michalowski's suggestion that the divine pair that headed the early Mesopotamian pantheon, Enki and Ninhursag, are the same Il and Ashtar (read *ʾAḷah* and *ʾAḷat*) of Early Dynastic Period. Since 𒀭 = 𒀭 the Sumerian An-Enki is identical with the Akkadian (thus Proto-Semitic) *ʾḷ* or *ʾAḷah*. In other words, AN-ENKI IS ALLAH. The resident deity of the Barbar Temple Complex in Eastern Arabia was therefore Allah, the Black God. (Muhammad, 2009: 108-109). (emphasis that of Muhammad).

As we have discussed throughout this text, the root for *Allah* in Arabic is the same African root used for "sky, heavens." I argue in *Chapter 3* of this volume that the very word 'god' in English derives from this same root and simply is an ancient word for "sky, heavens, above." Muhammad cannot separate *Allah* from His "sky" context. The earlier branches of Afro-Asiatic provide more linguistic evidence of our hypothesis here as it regards '*Allah'* and his association with the sky. The TOB database also puts the sun and sky in the same category:

> Proto-Afro-Asiatic: **raʕ-*
> Meaning: sun, god
> Semitic: **rayʕ-* 'daylight'
> Egyptian: *rʕ* 'sun, Sun-god' (pyr) (?)
> Western Chadic: *(**ʔa-)riʔ-* 'sky' 1, 'cloud' 2
>
> > Proto-WChadic: *(**ʔa-)riʔ-*
> > Afroasiatic etymology:
> > Meaning: 'sky' 1, 'cloud' 2
> > Geji: *rii* [ ], *lii* [Cs]
> > Bokos: *riʔ* 2 [JgR]
> > Sha: *are* 1, 2 [JgR]
> > Daffo-Butura: *riʔ* 2 [JgR]
> > Notes: *-l-* < **-r-* in Geji is possible
>
> East Chadic: **raH-* 'god' 1, 'sky' 2
>
> > Proto-EChadic: **raH-*
> > Afroasiatic etymology:
> > Meaning: 'god' 1, 'sky' 2
> > Bidiya: *rāyà* 1 [JBid]
> > Mokilko: *rắ* 1, 2 [JMkk]
>
> Notes: Cf. Eg *rʕ* 'sun; god', rather <**lVʕ-*.

Above we have the associations of *r*ᶜ with "sun, cloud, sky and God." Chad and the Sudan are right below Egypt and it is common knowledge that the culture and people of Egypt primarily came from the South and West of Egypt (the Sahara). It makes more sense, if we are going to assume directionality, to suppose the direction of *Rᶜ* from the south where the Egyptians came from than from the Far East in Arabia where they did not. Also, the Chadic languages have every association for the name *rᶜ* in its native vocabulary, whereas the Semitic does not. It even has the **r-ḥ* form which we could equate with *'*ḷh* which would also account for the final *-h* in Semitic. So why these languages and cultures were ignored in one's analysis cannot be explained. As we will see in the next section, *Allah* is more specifically associated with rain and indirectly Muhammad's (2009) text supports this interpretation.

Almaqah a rain god?

In his chapter "Aḷḷāh: Black God of Pre-Qur'ānic Arabia," Muhammad discusses and showcases a few Arabian temples known today as Awwam Temple, a sun temple, in today's Republic of Yemen, and the Bar'ān temple complex located in the city of Ṣirwāh. These temples were centers of worship for the name of their deity *'Almaqah* who Muhammad equates with *Allah.* Throughout the entire text, Muhammad discusses an important feature of Arabian religion and that is that God is a "light" being "housed" in a place of "water." The temples represent the primordial waters that house the Divine. So strong are the connections of these places with modern Islam that Muhammad (also citing supporting scholars) believe that Islam is a continuation of the religion practiced at these southern Arabian temples.

The name of the god for whom these temples are dedicated is written in epigraphic southern Arabian as ʾLMQH; Ge'ez አለመቀሀ, *ʾLMQH*, Arabic المقة. This is conventionally vocalized as *ʾAlmaqah*, but this is considered a convention as they didn't write out their vowels. Muhammad contends, based on more recent research, that it should be vocalized as *ʾAḷah Muqah. ʾAḷah,* is of course, the god *Allah.* The second word *mqh* is argued to likely be the participle form, *muqah*, of *taqahwa* ("to drink"), and thus the full name meaning "The intensively watering one."[56]

The root of the word *mqh/qh*, is a common world root for "water" with an old Niger-Congo fossilized prefix *m-*: Niger-Congo *ma* "liquid" prefix; PWS *gi, gia* "water", Kpelle *ya* "water", Mampa *yi* "water", Mende *yia* "water" > *ye.* This is where we ultimately get our word in Latin for "water," *aqua.*

27 **ʔAQ'WA** 'water'[57]

Khoisan: Northern: !o !kung *kãũ* 'to rain,' !kung *k"ā* 'drink'; Central: Naron *k"ā* 'drink'; Southern: /kam-ka !ke *k"wã~ k"wẽ* 'drink,' *k'ãũ* 'to rain,'//ng !ke *k"ã~ k"ẽĩ* 'drink,' *kãũ* 'to rain,' Batwa *k"ã ~ k"ẽ* 'drink,' /auni *k"āa*'drink,' Masarwa *k"ã* 'drink,' /nu //en *k"ã* 'drink.' [KE 261]

Nilo-Saharan: Fur *kòí* 'rain'; East Sudanic: Nyimang *kwe* 'water,' So *kwèʔ,* Ik *čuè*; Central Sudanic: Mangbetu *'eguo*; Berta *kòì* 'rain, cloud'; Koman: Kwama *uuku* 'water,' Anej *agu-d* 'cloud.' [NSB, KER]

Afro-Asiatic: Proto-Afro-Asiatic (Illich-Svitych) **'q(w)* 'water,' (Ehret) **ak'w-*; Omotic: Proto-North Omotic **ak'-*, She *k'ai* 'wet,' Janjero *ak(k)a* 'water,' Kaffa *ačō,* Mocha *āč'o,* Gofa *haččā,* Shinasha *ač'č'o,* Badditu *wats'ē*; Cushitic: Proto-Cushitic (Ehret) **-k'w-* 'to be wet,' (Illich-Svitych) **'qw* 'water,' Agaw *aqw,* Bilin *'aqw,* Xamir *aqw¯a* 'drops of water,' Damot *agwo* 'water,' Proto-East Cushitic (Ehret) **k'oy-* 'wet,'

56 In a footnote Muhammad (2009: 131) also cites a source which argues this term is related to a root *k̲hw* meaning something like "fertility," related to Arabic *kahā* "flourish."

57 Bengtson and Ruhlen (2008: 327-328)

Hadiyya *wo'o* 'water,' Tambaro *waha,* Sidamo *waho,* Iraqw *¯aha* 'drink.' [N 139, EU, AM 87, CE 348]

Indo-European: Proto-Indo-European (Pokorny) **akwā-* 'water,' (Puhvel) **egw-*, (Bomhard) **ek'w-*; Anatolian: Hittite *eku-,* Luwian *aku-,* Palaic *ahuô-* 'drink'; Italic: Latin *aqua* 'water'; Germanic: Gothic *ahwa* 'river';

Tocharian: Tocharian A *yok-* 'drink.' [IE 23]

Uralic: Proto-Uralic (R΄edei) **yoka* 'river.' [R 99–100]
Japanese *aka* 'bilge water.' [JP 100]
Ainu *wakka* 'water,' *ku* 'drink.' [JP 100]

Caucasian: Proto-Caucasian *-*V̲qV* 'suck,' Proto-Lezghian **÷oχwa* 'drink,' Lezghian *χwa-l,* Agul *uχas,* Proto-Lezghian **ʔoqwa-* 'rain,' Lezghian *qwa-z,* Rutul *huΠwas,* Tsakhur *joΠwi*; Proto-Nax *-*aq-* 'suck(le),' Chechen *-aq-* 'suck'; Proto-Dargi *-*uq-* 'suck(le).' [C 3, 16]

?Burushaski *häy-um* 'wet.'
Sino-Tibetan: Proto-Sino-Tibetan **Ku* 'fluid, spill,' Newari *khwo* 'river,' Khaling *ku* 'water,' Kachin *khu.* [NSC 43]
Indo-Pacific: Awyu *okho* 'water, river,' Syiagha *okho* 'water,' Yareba *ogo,* Yonggom *oq,* Ninggirum *ok.* [FS 96, 134]
Australian: Proto-Australian **gugu* 'water.' [AC]

Amerind: Almosan-Keresiouan: Proto-Central Algonquian **akwā*'from water,'Kutenai *-qw* 'in water,' Quileute *kwāya'* 'water,' Snohomish *qwaʔ,* Caddo *koko*; Penutian: Nass *akj-s,* Takelma *ugw* 'drink,' Wintun *wak'ai* 'creek,' Zuni *k'a* 'water,' Atakapa *ak,* Yuki *uk',* Tetontepec *uuʔk* 'drink,' Yucatec *uk'* 'be thirsty'; Hokan: Chimariko *aqa* 'water,' Kashaya *ʔahqha* 'water,' *q'o* 'drink,' Seri *ʔax* 'water,' Diegueno *ʔaxā,* Quinigua *kwa,* Tonkawa *ʔāx,* Tequistlatec *l-axaʔ*; Central Amerind: Proto-Chinantec **gwa* 'stream, river'; Chibchan-Paezan: Shiriana *koa* 'drink,' Chimila *uk-,* Binticua *agu,* Allentiac *aka* 'water'; Andean: Iquito *aqua,* Quechua *yaku,* Yamana *aka* 'lake'; Macro-Tucanoan: Auake *ok˜oa* 'water, river,' Cubeo *oko* 'water,' Tucano *axko*; Equatorial: Amniape *¨ak¨u,* Quitemo *ako,* Uaraicu *uaka* 'wash,' Terena *oko* 'rain,' Chipaya *axw* 'wash'; Macro-Carib: Yagua *xa* 'water,' Witoto *joko* 'wash,' Macushi *u-wuku* 'my drink,' Waiwai *woku* 'drink,' Taulipang *ai'ku* 'wet'; Macro-Panoan: Lule *uk* 'drink,' ayoruna *uaka* 'water,' Culino *yaku* 'water,' *waka* 'river,' Huarayo *hakua* 'wash'; Macro-Ge: Koraveka *ako* 'drink,' Fulnio *waka* 'lake,' Kamakan k*wa* 'drink,' Chavante *k¯o* 'water,' Aponegicran *waiko* 'drink.' [AM 87,AMN]

As we can see here, this global root **ʔaqwa* "water" is used to mean "water, drink, rain, cloud (which gives rain), river, to be thirsty, stream, spill and to be wet." It is for this reason that I interpret the name *ʾAḷah Muqah* to mean "Lord of Water" or "Lord of Rain."

On January 13, 2012, Muhammad posted an image to his Facebook page which depicts the *nṯr* of Egypt *Wsr* (Washila, Osiris) on a thrown which stands on top of a pool of water. This iconographic writing is basically saying that *Wsr* is the "Lord of Waters." This scene was taken from a more expanded representation of the judgment scene of the Papyrus of Hunefer - *Prt m ḥrw* (Coming forth by day).

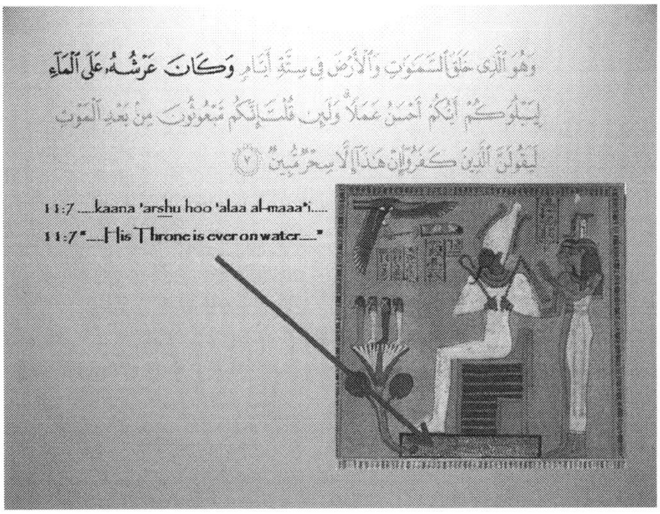

Inside of the image is a scripture from the Qur'an, which states:

> 11:7...kaana 'arshu hoo 'alaa al-maaa*i...
> 11:7...His throne is ever on water

Muhammad here is trying to make a connection between the imagery of Egypt and the scriptures of the Qur'an in regards to the two seemingly related concepts. His image supports my thesis that *Allah* is a god of "rain." In regards to *Wsr* being lord of the waters, I have discussed this in full in my work *Passion of the Christ or Passion of Osiris: The Kongo Origins of the Jesus Myth* (2011: 60-70). In this text I argue that the myth of *Yeshua* (Jesus) is inspired by *Wsr* (Osiris) of Egypt. Jesus is known in the Bible as the source of "living water" (see John 4:13-`4; John 7:38; and Rev. 21: 5-7). So is Osiris.

As I argue in Imhotep (2011), the throne is a symbol of power, rulership and command. *Wsr* (whose name, in part, means "water") has control over the dispensation of water. When the Egyptians have a water shortage, they call on the spirit behind the power of water (the sky) and ask it to send down, in this case "flow down,"[58] water from on high.

Wsr is a predynastic deity who came into prominence in the late fourth or mid fifth dynasty (there is still debate on precisely when he emerged). Robert Bauval and Thomas Brophy in their 2011 work *Black Genesis: The Prehistoric Origins of Ancient Egypt* lay out a very good synopsis of Osiris and his association with water in predynastic times. He was associated with the early monsoon rains that used to come as far north as the Sahara, but in predynastic times has since retreated and caused the desertification of North Africa. The "resurrection" of *Wsr* has everything to do with the rising of the star *Sirius B* which denotes that in predynastic times, rain was coming. *3st* represented the star Sirius B. The names for the goddess *3st* and the god *Wsr* are the same word (see *Chapter* 4 this volume): just two sides of the same coin. However, since the monsoons stopped as a result of the end of the last Ice Age, the one-time rain association of *Wsr* was transferred to the river Nile which flooded at the same time as when

---

58 Rainfall was rare in Egypt, so during dynastic times *Wsr* was not associated, primarily, with rain but with underground water sources and the river Nile. The Nile flows downstream from the highlands of Ethiopia and Uganda and empties into the Mediterranean Sea.

the rains used to come to Egypt.[59]

But at times *3st* retained her association with rain. L.V. Zabkar (1988: 51), citing an inscription in Room X (north wall) of the Temple of Isis at Philae in Upper Egypt, informs us about a hymn to *3st* hinting to her association with water. The hymn states, "Isis, giver of life... She is the one who **pours** out inundation that makes all people live and green plants grow" (emphasis mine). You can only "pour" something from an elevated position and thus this is referencing rain.

All of this to say that the temples dedicated to *ʾAḷah Muqah*, in association with "primordial waters," may actually also have a more down-to-earth interpretation. In practically all ancient traditions that see the primordial matter as "water," I argue that this was simply a reflection of a real world fact: the fact that water comes from the "sky" and is why in practically all human language families, the word for sky is the same for water. The sky is seen as a kind of ocean or lake. In Egyptian it is no different. The word for sky is *ḥrw* "sky, heaven" and a word for water is *ḥr* "a body of water." As we will see in the next section, not only does *rʿ* mean "sun" in African languages, it also means "water."

However, the Egyptians also thought of the heavens as a river, and more importantly the river Nile. In the *Great Hymn to Aten* written by Amenhotep IV, a.k.a. Akhenaten, during the New Kingdom period (found in the Tomb of Aye), Akhenaten informs us that that there is a "Nile in the sky," meaning there is a body of water in the heavens, and he equates this to *rain.* However, this isn't rain in Egypt, but rain in foreign lands. In giving deference to the Creator (*Itn*, Aten), Akhenaten discusses the nurturing and life giving aspects of the Divine.

ir.k ḥʿpy m dw3t
You generate the Nile underground
ini.k sw mri.k r sʿnḫ rhyt
and make it come at your will to give life to the peoples
mi ir.k sn n.k
As you created them for yourself
nb.sn r-3w wrd im.sn p3
You, Lord of them all, who take such care of them,
nb n t3 nb wbn n.sn p3
Lord of the universe entire, you who rise for it,
Itn n hrw ʿ3 šfyt
Sun disk of daytime, great in radiance
ḫ3swt nb w3t ir.k ʿnḫ.sn
To all foreign lands, however far, you give life.
rdi.n.k ḥʿpy m pt h3y.f n.sn
You have placed a Nile in the sky, to rain for them,
ir.f hnw ḥr ḏww mi W3ḏ-wr
forming currents of water on mountains as at sea,
r tḫb 3ḥwt.sn m dmiw.sn
watering their fields and towns:
smnḫ.wy sy sḫrw.k p3 nb nḥḥ
How manifest your plans are, Lord of Eternity
ḥʿpy m pt sw.k n ḫ3styw
A Nile in the sky: that is the gift you have given foreigners

59 *Wsr* was also associated with the fertile soil which gave rise to healthy crops in Egypt. This association, lexically, is reflected in the following Bantu terms: Proto-Bantu **-céd-* "clean"; proto-Northeast-Coastal Bantu (PNECB) "land readied for planting"; proto-Ruvu (PR) "prepared but unsown land"; e.g., Zigua ***uselu*** "a field under cultivation"; Tsonga *sela ku-* "to cover plants with soil." Hinnebusch, T., D. Nurse, and M. Mould, eds. *Studies in the Classification of Eastern Bantu Languages*. Hamburg: Helmut Buske Verlag, 1981. p.647.

> *n ʿwt ḏw nb šmw ḥr rdwy*
> And to every beast walking the mountains,
> *ḥʿpy ii.f m dwꜣt n Tꜣ–mrj*
> just like the Nile springing from below for the Beloved Land

The Egyptians were aware that foreign countries received their water directly from rain fall. The water for the Egyptians came as a result of underground water holes in the *dwꜣt*,[60] and from the rising of the Nile River. Akhenaten posited, because of his knowledge of rain in foreign lands, that they too must have a Nile (*ḥʿpy*) river of their own, only theirs is in the sky. We post this information here to reinforce the notion that the sky, for the ancients, is synonymous with a lake, river or ocean.

Muhammad seeks to associate *ʾAḷah Muqah* as a "sun-god" but given the name, and the fact that *ʾAḷah Muqah* is represented on monuments by a cluster of lightning bolts surrounding a curved, sickle-like weapon (also a club which in many traditions represents *thunder*), I believe his original attestation is that of a 'god' of storms. I've never heard of lightning bolts deriving from the sun. Lightning is a by-product of *black rain clouds*. We will see below why the gods were depicted black.

The association of *ʾAḷah Muqah* (*Almaqah*) with storms is explicitly stated in the *Encyclopedia of Spirits: The Ultimate Guide to the Magic of Fairies, Genies, Demons, Ghosts, Gods & Goddesses* (2009; HarperCollins Publishers). On page 160 it states (in regards to *Almaqah*): "He seems to have dominion over precipitation, controlling storms, rain and flooding. He is the guardian of irrigation, crucial to a desert nation." An entry on the following page turns our focus towards a type of spirit called *Alu* in Babylonia (Iraq). As we can see we are reintroduced to our -r-/-l- root. The entry goes on to tell us that:

> Alu are a type of Babylonian spirit. Their name may be translated as "Storm" or "Tempest" but is also sometimes considered a synonym for *demon*. In addition to destructive storms, they cause illness and nightmares, including night paralysis...Alu commonly manifest as black dogs, but they appear in half-human/half-animal form. (2009: 161)

As we can clearly see here, whether in Southern or Eastern Arabia, *ʾḷ* is associated with rain and thunderstorms. We argue here that this is the case because the root is used for the word "sky" which is often used to mean "rain."

It should be noted that in Egyptian we have *ḥrw ṯhn*  "Heru the Lightning" or "Heru the Sparkler" (Budge, 506a). In the Kalenjiin language this is *leetyen Iila. Leetyen* means "sparkle, flash" and *Iila*(t) "thunder" or "lightning." It is a name used for the Divine attributes of Asiis relating to the 'sky'. We should also note that the /h/ sound tends to be dropped in Kalenjiin in regards to compared words in Egyptian: *ṯhn* > *lee-tyen*; *ḥrw* > *Iila*. We also note in Egyptian *ḳri* "storm, storm cloud, thunder, thunderbolt." I argue *ḳri* is just another variation of *ḥr*(w) "sky, heavens." We also notice the Gardiner sign G7 determinative here as well: 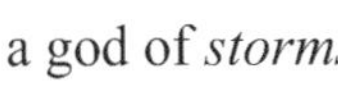 *ḳri* "thunderbolt." Notice the determinative of the god St (Seth)? He was also a god of *storms*.

Refocusing, if *ʾAḷah Muqah* was associated with the sun, I argue that this was probably a later association and not one historically based on his actual name. Some have associated *ʾAḷah*

60 In ciLuba *dwꜣt* is *Ndo* "nothingness, emptiness;" *nda* "inside" > *mu-nda* "in the inside;" *Ndondu/Ndondo* "well, depth;" *a-ndondu* "very deep;" *luTondu/kaTondo* "which has a depth or interiority" that can serve as a funnel. This gives rise to words like *ondol* "dig a hole deep, go deep" and *ondoka* "be deep, have a depth." Another way to say *dwꜣ.t* (tomb, grave) in ciLuba is *cidwaya, cilwaya, ciDwa*.

Muqah with the moon, while others now reject this association (or as a total association), but this may not be a far-fetched connection as the moon in ancient cultures was also associated with water: more so in relationship to tides. Since the moon was a vehicle by which to tell time, it could have also served as a basis for a lunar calendar which marked the upcoming *rainy* season. The sun association may relate to time as well.

Ra as a water god?

As Felix Chami (2006: 69-71) has noted, in African languages, especially in East and Central Africa, the name *r*(a,e,i,u) is not only associated with the sun, but also water. God, because of Its relationship to the sky/heavens, is in general associated with *rain* (see Imhotep 2011). As noted before, in African languages, often, the same name for sky/sun/rain/heavens is also the same name for God (by way of homonymy, homophone or cognation) and we argue here that the Semites are no different in this regards (in reference to *Allah*). Mbiti (1989: 53) further expounds on this African phenomenon as he notes:

> Rain is regarded by African peoples to be one of the greatest blessings of God. For that reason, He is commonly referred to as: 'the Rain Giver'. Some peoples, like the Elgeyo, Igbo, Suk, Tonga and others personify rain as a divinity, a supernatural being, or a son of God. **Others associate God with rain so closely that the same word (or its cognate) is used for both.** For example, the Didinga name for God is *Tamukujen* and for rain *tamu*; the Idoma use *Owo* for both; the Maasai word *En-Kai*[61] is used for both God and rain (or sky); and some of the Suk[62] have *Ilat* for both. The Ila and Nuer speak of God as 'falling in the rain', yet clearly distinguishing between Him and the rain. Others like the Akamba and Tiv, consider rain to be the saliva of God, this being a symbol of great blessing. (emphasis mine)

What's important to note here is that the Divine is associated with rain and this is common all throughout the world. In the same places where *ra* is the *sun*, *ra* is also associated with *water*. In the Chagga-Bantu language, *riwa/ruwa* is not only the name for "sun" but also the name of "water pools infested with gods/spirits" (Chami, 2006: 71). In Sumerian *ra* means "flood." In the Yorùbá language *ra* means "fall of rain" (Maori *rere* "fall of rain"). Even in the *Linear A* script of Greece, *ra* means "water" (Campbell-Dunn, 2006: 73).[63] Bender (2000: 66) gives us the following correspondences in Nilo-Saharan: **ar* "rain."

A Gao, Zerma	'water': *har-i*		Fc		'rainy season': *ar*(-*a*) (?)
B Zagawa	'river': *ɔr-ʊ-i*		G	Berta	(*r*)*rɔ*
K *Kuliak	*(*w*)*ar-*	H	Kunama, Ilit		(*ŋ*)*oo'r-a*
C Aiki	'lake': *ar-ɛ*	E			*ar*
D Fur	'river': *roo*	I	Twampa 'river': *wɔrr*		

In predynastic Egypt, *rˤ* may have had a greater association with water. Since *Wsr* was also associated with water, his role in this capacity may have overshadowed *Rˤ*'s connection with

61 As we have discussed previously, the Maasai god *En-Kai* is morphologically similar to Sumerian *Enki* and both are attributed to "god, sky, heavens and rain." I consider the Maasai *En-Kai* cognate with Sumerian name for God *Enki* (*Enkil*). Campbell-Dunn (2009a: 43) posits that the Sumerians left the Congo area prior to 3000 BCE. The Maasai currently live in Kenya and Tanzania which is in relative proximity to Central Africa.

62 An African group from Somalia living in Kenya. I argue that the Suk *Ilat* is cognate with Arabic *Allah*.

63 In Linear A, *ra* also means "snake"; Egyptian *r, rrw, wrw* "snake."

water and it was eventually forgotten. The term *ra*(u,e), however, was then dymotholized and simply remembered in common language. However, there still may be a clue to *R*ᶜ's former association with water as it is noted that *R*ᶜ created man (*rmṯ*) out of his own "tears" (*rmyt*). It's hard to imagine the sun releasing water (tears).

> *sḫpr.n.i nṯrw m fdt.i*
> I created the deities from my sweat,
> *rmṯ m rmyt n irit.i*
> and humans from my tears
> (*Coffin Texts*, Spell 1130: Four Great Deeds of Ra)

Here we clearly see that *R*ᶜ is creating the 'gods' and mankind out of his *liquid* essences which may point to an ancient association with water. In Kalenjiin we have *riir* "cry, cry out"; Egyptian/Coptic *rere*, *rim* "cry." We can see this -*r*- root reflected in the following terms:

Campbell-Dunn (2009b: 78)

INUNDATION — **Sumerian** *ra (-g/h)*

"inundation"

LA "water", "sky" — **-g/h**

PWN *BUDA* "rain"
Bantu *bú, da* "rain"
PWS *la, (da)* "day" (sky = rain)
PWS *gi* "firmament"
Gur **do* "sky"
Mande *la, (da)* "day"
Mangbetu *ro* "sky"
ES Afitti *araŋga* "rain", Tama *ar* "sky, rain", Dinka *uar* "river", Lotuko *(na)are* "water"
CN Berta *ro*: "rain",
CS Lendu *ra, arra* "sky"

***L = r** ***A = a** ***G = g/h**

Campbell-Dunn (2009b: 108):

RAIN — **Sumerian** *šèĝ* "rain"

DA, TA "sky" — **-ĝ**

PWS *la, (da)* "day", Mano *de̱* "day", Gio *de̱*"day"
PWS *ta* "sky, rain, clouds"
PWS *tu, tua* "water", Guang *n-tśu'* "water", Afema *a-su..-e* "water"
PWN *BUDA* "rain, raincloud"
PWN *TU* "cloud", *THU, THUA* "river, waterplace"
Bantu *dé* "sky, cloud"
Bantu *tu,* "cloud ", *du,nde* "clouds", *du,mb* "rain", *donga* "river", *to* "river"
Kele *use* "sky", Ngombe *buse* "sky"
Mande *sã* "rain"
Mangbetu *tu* "pool in the forest" ?

Mangbetu *ro* "sky"
Afro-Asiatic: Chad: Hausa (1) *ša:* "drink", Ngala (2) *še:* "drink", Logone (2) *se* "drink"

***T = š** ***A = e** ***G = g**

RIVER **Sumerian***id₂*, (*i₇*) "river, canal"

LI, DI "water" **[R]**

PWS *lì(d.i)* "to eat, to drink" (action of head) **Sumerian** *íd-a* "river, canal"
PWS *li, (di)* "head"
PWS *lim (dim)* "extinguish" (of rain from the sky, ie. the "top or head") ?
PWN *DI* "to eat", *DIM* "extinguish" **Sumerian** *idim* "spring, subterranean water"
PWN *DU* "drip, leak"
Bantu *dí* "to eat", *dí,m* "extinguish"
Nyanza (Johnston) 4 a-b *izi, di* "river", S. Rhodesia *izi* "river"
"Holoholo" *lil* "to weep"(weep rivers of tears)
Mande *du-mu* "to eat"
Mangbetu *ôdi* "to cook in water"
Afro-Asiatic : Cushitic : *dimena* "cloud" (under "rain") (Greenberg)

[The verb "to eat" was also used for drinking.]

***D = d** ***I = i**

POT **Sumerian** *utul₂*"pot"

TU "water" **[R]** **u-** **-l**

PWS *tu* "water", *tua* "water"
PWN *THU, THUA* "water place"
Bantu *to* "river"
Bantu *tu,ko* "water pot"
Swahili *mto* "river"
Mande *kulu-ntu* "winding river"
Mangbetu *tu* "pond in the forest"

***T = t** ***U = u**

Chami (2006: 68) notes that "ra/re/ri" and also "ru/lu" is associated with many names for *river* in Africa. To name a few: (Uganda/Rwanda/Burundi/Tanziania) *Rutunga, Ruembia, Chamburu, Rugaga, Eugwero, Ndurum, Ruvuvu, Ruiza*; (Mozambique) *Ruvu, Rufiji, Rutungu, Ruvuma, Ruikira*; (Central Africa) *Lualaba, Kalungu, Luangwa, Lubu, Luwumbu, Lufula, Luchinda, Lukulu, Bangwelu* and *Lufuko*. The *-r-* root is found in dozens of Egyptian words dealing with water.

wrw	"pond" [Wb I S 332]
pẖr wr	"river Euphrates"

km wr	"bitter lakes"
wꜣḏ wr	"the Great green, sea, ocean, Lake Moeris, Celestial ocean"
tꜣ wr	"larboard, portside"
nwn wr	"Nile, flood"
ḥtp wr	"excrement" (usually in the form of liquid waste)
šn wr	"ocean" (lit. "[large?] circle of water")
s-wr/sswr	"to drink, to water, to feed (corn to fowl)" [causative verb]
ỉš-rw	"water meadows"
ỉš-rw	"(crescent shaped) pond, pool, precinct of *Mw.t* at Karnak"
ỉs-rw	"rushes"
ỉšw	"spittle"
srm.t	"a body of water"
pẖ-rw	"a body of water"
h-r	"canal"
m-r	"canal, artificial lake"
ỉtrw	"canal, river, watercourse, basin, stream"
m-r.tyw	"a body of idle water near Heliopolis"
ꜥꜣ mw	"head of the water"
km wr	"a lake"

Remember that *ꜣ* = *l* which undergirds the following terms: *ꜥꜣꜥ* (*ala*) "water drain"; *ꜥꜣꜥ* "spit, splutter"; *ꜥꜣꜥ.t* "sperm, ejaculation." In these terms I see a mix of *-r-* as "water" and as "road, path" which gives us words for "river." It is the latter interpretation that is cognate with our *-r-* root dealing with "distance" as an underlying theme (Egyptian *ḥrt* "path, way, road"; Kalenjiin *oreet* "path"). We see it in the Egyptian words: *m-rr.t* "road"; *m-r* "water channel, canal"; *w-r.t* "canal"; *ỉtrw* "canal, river, water course, basin"; *h-r* "canal." In Coptic we also have *eiyero* "river, big canal"; Coptic *piour* (a.Egyptian *pair* "the river").

We get confirmation of this connection in Yorùbá and ciLuba as follows: Yorùbá *Ìbarà* "ford"; *afárá* "bridge" (ciLuba *Mwero/Mweru* "name of a lake" in Bukamain, Katanga (Kongo); *Malabale* = "extended water, wide-water" (*Mala-bale*) <*alabala*; *Ma*=*Mai* "Water" + *alabala* "extended"; *Mala* "*Ma-Ala*" Water area", "open extended location"; *Mai-Malabale* "sea, ocean, vast expanse of water." The Yorùbá term *Ibara* reminds us of *ebale* "great river" in Lingala. Rivers are literally WATER + ROADS (water highways) and in ancient times these were the fastest ways to travel long distance.

We must reiterate here that the word for "sky" is also the word "day, sun, rain." The sky becomes associated with its major features that are important for man: the *stars/sun* (in terms of seasons and telling time) and *rain* (for water, the source of all life). All of these terms get lumped together in one conceptual field. It is the association of "rain" with the *-r-* root (< sky < above) that people associate "water" in general. This leads to other sense meanings like *ꜥꜣꜥ* "spit, sputter" and *ꜥꜣꜥ* "water drain" in Egyptian. Over time the word for "road, path, and canal" became synonymous with "river" thus "water" in general.

Ra, Allah, and Blackness

Muhammad (2009) utilizes a lot of space in *Black Arabia* to highlight the *blackness* of not only pre-Islamic *Allah*, but of *Rꜥ* of Egypt and the Sumerian *An/Enki* in the form of "black-bulls." We noted before that another variation of the word *rꜥ* in Egyptian is *wr*, and we can see here again that the ancient Egyptians associated *rꜥ* with bulls because of the similarity of their names when verbalized:

wr	size	Wb I 330
wr	Large	Wb I 328
wr	big, be big	Wb I 326
wr	large quantity	Wb I 331
wr	highly	Wb I 330
wr	bull	Wb I 331
wr	[beef]	Wb I, S 331
wr	[animal]	Meeks: AL 781 029
wr	[God's name]	Meeks: AL 770 959
wrt	[Eye of Horus]	Wb I 332
sꜣ-wr	sun god	Wb III 415

Again, the Egyptian language is lexically poor and when they need new terms they often extend existing terms by way of allegory and metaphor. A bull is naturally "big" and "large" and the same word used to denote "size" became a general word for "bull" or any large animal. Since *rʕ/ḥrw,* on one level, deals with "height, length," there is an obvious agreement, conceptually, with the theme of "vastness, greatness."

Since the sun is the source of all life and gives birth to many forms on earth, the Egyptians saw some conceptual similarity between a single sun that generates and activates all life-forms on earth and the bull who can sire many cows in one night (thus giving birth to many generations of cattle). This concept of "generations" leads us right back to our *-r-* root which in Bantu is: *eela* "to make, express, to exit from the self (sound, idea, word, object, etc.)."

It is under this sense that the association between *rʕ/ḥr* as the sun and as the sky/heavens makes sense. Remember that *ḥr*(w) is just the word *rʕ* with a prefix (PWS **la, *da* "day, sun"; CS Kreish *kadda,* Bagirmi *kada* "sun, day", Mangbutu *kora* "day"; CN Didinga *kor* "sun", Dinka *akol* "sun", Bari *ko,lo,ŋ,* Turkana *ekoloŋ* "sun"; Gurage (Cushitic) *aher "sun,"* Oromo *haraa* "today"; ciLuba *lunKeLu* = "rising sun" (which signals the "day" is here). The Egyptian words *ḥr*(w) "sun, day" and *ḥr*(w) "sky, heavens" are homonyms. *Rʕ* and *ḥr*(w) "sun, day" are built off the same root. *Rʕ* and *ḥr*(w) "sky, heaven" are built on a totally different root. However, historically, these were treated as one and the same and the Egyptians weren't historical comparative linguists: they wouldn't have separated them if there were (seemingly) obvious associations that could be made.

In the Kalenjiin language the word *peet* means "today, day, day time, in daylight." But in its Egyptian form *pt* simply means "sky, heavens." But as we have stated before, the word for "sky, heaven" can also mean "sun, day" and there seems to be some conceptual overlap. In the case of Egyptian *pt* "sky, heavens," they already possessed numerous words for "sun" so it only retained its association with the sky.

The blackness of the bulls in ancient motifs is symbolic and is associated with rain clouds. Although Muhammad (2009: 86) cites Julian Baldick's *Black God: The Afroasiatic Roots of the Jewish, Christian and Muslim Religions,* he didn't discuss Baldick's premise as to why blackness is associated with the gods of the Afro-Asiatic speakers. Simply put, the gods are black to represent *black rain clouds.* Muhammad notes some critical observations of the Oromo, but this is done in passing.

For instance, he notes that among the Oromo of southern Ethiopia God is called *Waqa Quracca* meaning *Black* (Quracca) *God* (Waqa) (Muhammad, ibid.). This God rides the dark clouds, has red eyes representing his anger and is the Creator. The Oromo sacrifice black sheep to him hoping to procure rain. Baldick calls these type of gods among the Afro-Asiatic speakers "black-rain gods." This is the language of an outsider. An African would argue that one honors the spirit or power that allows rain to fall. The black clouds are simply the symbol of this Divine attribute (God's totem) and it provides a physical object to direct prayers and invocations too.

Baldick gives us some insight into the Egyptian association of blackness which essentially has the same connotations as that among the Oromo.

> Whereas elsewhere black was the colour of the violent but necessary storm-god, and red the colour of the brave young warrior-god who killed him and made fertilizing water flow, in Egypt black was usually a benign colour of fertility itself, and red was the colour of the generally useless and hated storm-god Seth. (Baldick, 1997: 8)[64]

The color black is used to symbolize fertility: whether in terms of women giving birth to children, economic prosperity in one's life or rain coming from the sky to nurture the earth. It has no racial connotations in African spiritual systems as it seems to be suggested in Muhammad (2009).

The reason that the gods are black (e.g., Isis, Osiris, Ptah and Hathor) is because they represent a productive quality present in the black soil, black heavens (outer space) and the black rain clouds. It is believed that because of their blackness, in part, they are able to create certain things that are essential to life here on earth. As a result of this understanding, man then seeks to align itself with the 'spirit' that allows those 'black' substances to create what they create.

This is the basis of ALL spiritual systems. I have coined the phrase *Spiritual Resonance*[65] to describe this phenomenon in human religious systems. By understanding the basics of the science of *resonance*, one is able to understand the inner logic of ancient rituals and iconic associations such as the "black bull" of the Nile Valley and Arabia. A living example will make this clear for us.

Continuing on this theme of black gods, black clouds and rain, we will look into the Kalenjiin people of central east Africa to give us some insight as to the purpose of these associations. Kipkoeech Sambu (2008: 222-223) discusses the practice of immersing black animals in river water as sacrifices to the "god" of rain among the Nilotic people of east Africa.

An early 20th century description of a purely symbolic offering to the god of Thunder (*Ileet*, the equivalent to the god of water, an aspect of *Asiis*) by the priests of Asiis (the *Supreme Being*; Asista "sun") is recorded among the Nandi by A.C. Hollis in his work *The Nandi: Their Language and Folklore* (1909: 48). When rains fail in Nandi-land, Hollis tells us that:

> The old men collect together and take a black sheep with them to a river. Having tied a fur cloak on the sheep's back, they push it into the water, and take beer and milk into their mouths, which they spit out in the direction of the rising sun. When the sheep scrambles out of the water and shakes itself, they sing the following prayer,

Asis! Kakisain	Asiis we pray to thee,
Konech rob	That thou may give us rain,
Irocho maiyo ak chei,	We have offered wine and milk
Mami chii nemaiio,	As we all have multiplied,
Tukwech tomono	Do protect the pregnant
nebo chi ak tany	of man and beast

Ileet (Thunder God) is associated with deep waters (Sambu, 2008: 222). The drama being played out here amounts to showing Thunder (*Ileet*) what he has forgotten to do, which is to

64 A cursory examination of this subject is conducted in Imhotep (2011), but a more detailed discussion takes place in a forth coming manuscript titled *Ogun, African Fire Philosophy and the Meaning of KMT*.

65 A deeper discussion of this will be conducted in the chapter on the *n<u>t</u>rw* in Vol. II.

come out of its water abode and shake the water off its wet feathers in heaven the way the sheep did when it emerged out of the water and attempted to shake itself dry (while in the process showering the people). This is an example of *Spiritual Resonance*. The people had yearned for rain for so long that when they saw the sheep shake itself dry, showering all those around him, and it rained not too long afterwards, the people got an idea on how to bring about rain in the future. The sheer force of the focused collective will (or wishful thinking), while viewing the sheep's actions, created a collective assumption that resonated with the idea that if they would imitate the sheep's actions, they would bring about rain from the spirit of *Ileet*.

This is the essence of resonance in a spiritual context. In physics, *resonance* is the tendency of a system to oscillate at a greater amplitude at some frequencies than at others. These are known as the system's resonance frequencies. Resonance occurs when a system is able to store and easily transfer energy between two or more different storage modes (such as kinetic energy and potential energy in the case of a pendulum). However, there are some losses from cycle to cycle, called damping. Our cell phones and our car radios exist because of resonance. All things vibrate and they vibrate at different speeds. In order to listen to *97.9 Tha Box* in Houston, TX, I have to turn my radio dial to the "frequency" of *97.9*. Once the frequency of my radio matches that of the satellite that is emitting the waves, then I am able to listen to what *97.9 Tha Box* is playing. All spiritual systems hold this paradigm as an inner logic.

All things vibrate and vibrate at a certain frequency. Things are able to do what they do because they exist on a vibratory level that allows them to do what they do. In our case, there is a certain "vibratory" frequency by which black storm clouds exists. If we want to communicate with the black storm cloud, we must ourselves (or our tools) vibrate on the same frequency as the black storm cloud so we can evoke it to do what it does best: bring down rain. So we as humans create rituals that will allow us to communicate with the spirit behind the rain cloud. Everything physical represents the vibratory frequency of a spirit that gives it substance and power. In other words, what we see manifested in the physical world represents an invisible reality that informs it how to *be*. The physical component is a representative of the invisible spirit that animates it. Since we can't necessarily see spirit, we must access spirit by going through, or imitating something physical that resonates with it on the same frequency. The logic is this: *like attracts like*. To do what spirit does, you "gotta do what spirit do!" And if a certain spirit manifests itself in blackness, then you must operate and communicate through blackness.

Remember, in physics, resonance occurs when a system is able to store and easily transfer energy between two or more different storage modes. This is where sacrifice comes in and this is why the sacrifice has to be black (in regards to rain).

The sacrificed animal transfers its energy to the realm of spirit that handles the making of rain. Again, the issue is resonance, so we must use an animal that best represents the spirit or vibratory frequency by which rain is induced. The energy of the slain animal is transferred back to the spirit realm. Since energy cannot be created nor destroyed, that energy must come back and since it is believed to already be vibrating on the level of the black rain clouds, it would come back to us in the form of a black rain cloud and bring about rain. This is rough a sketch, but most priestly traditions, that I am aware of that do sacrifices, operate under this premise in a similar way.

This is the spirit behind the usage of certain color schemes in African spiritual traditions. A black object for sacrifice had to be black without blemish, that is, no other visible colors emitting through it. Black was particularly associated with prayers for rain. We already mentioned this practice among the Oromo of Ethiopia. Among the Omotic neighbors of the Oromo, they also sacrifice *black animals* for rain. They also sacrifice 'white' animals to STOP rain. As we can see here, in order to bring about rain (among the Omotic speakers) one's ritual must resonate with *blackness* because storm clouds are *black*. But let's say it is raining too much (a flood situation). In order to stop the rains, we need more white clouds. We then sacrifice *white* animals to halt the coming of more black clouds (Cf. Baldick, 1997: 114, 117, 145). The Lutoko and the Bari communities of Sudan sacrifice a *black goat* for rain. The blood and fat content is smeared on a *black rain stone* (the pebbles obtained from the bottom of a river). The rainmaker later washes the same stones clean and puts them in pots for further ceremony activities (Sambu, 2008: 98).

This logic of resonance is not limited to Africa proper. In Virgil's *Aeneid* (19 BC Book III), he poetically discusses the practice of sacrificing a "milk-white ewe, the western winds to please, and one coal-black, to calm the stormy seas." Virgil was a court poet in Rome at the time of Augustus. Even in Europe, the colour black was associated with the storm (*water* and *thunder*).We note also that *Baal* of the Canaanites was the "Rider of Clouds; the Lord of Heavens; the Lord of the Storm. His voice was Thunder. He was the god who controlled the rain."[66] *Baal* (Kalenjiin *bool* "cloud")[67] is a dialectical variation of *Allah* and he is the 'son' of *El*. El, as noted by *The Oxford Interactive Encyclopedia* (1997) was "the supreme deity of Phoenician and Canaanite belief, the ***'god' of fertility, giver of rain, guarantor of rivers, and streams,*** and father of 'gods' and men" (emphasis mine). The relationship of *El* and *Baal* is similar to the relationship of *An* and *Enki* of Sumer, in that they are two manifestations of the same reality: different stages of a process. One cannot separate *El, Ilu, Allah, An, Enki* from its "sky" context and its "rain" manifestation.

Sacrifices to black 'storm-gods' are a part of Islamic history as well. As noted by Baldick, in Islam and pre-Islamic Arabia, a special type of animal sacrifice would be carried out by pilgrims on their way to Mecca called *Adha* at a special sunrise called *Tashriq* (11th, 12th and 13th of *Dhu'l-Hijjah*). Pre-Islamic legend regarded this special sunrise to be the moment that Light (the sun), in the form of a white bird, conquered Darkness who came in the form of a black cloud, and saved the children who had been left exposed as a sacrifice to the Black 'god' of rain. Interestingly, these children were sacrificed in the first place to the then much-desired black 'water-god' (who would come in the form of a black rain cloud) and collect his prize. In the process of collecting his offering, he filled the empty *wadi* with water and ended a long drought (Cf. Baldick, 1997: 30-31).

Conclusion

We note all of this to say that *Allah* is associated with the "sky" and "rain." His associations with the "primordial waters" and "black bulls" were because he was first and foremost a "rain" god; and to bring about rain required elaborate rituals involving black objects or black animals. The black stone inside the *Kaaba* is a remnant of this ancient practice.[68]

Allegedly, pre-Islamic Arabians 'worshipped' 360 'gods'. After the Prophet Muhammad's reform movement, these gods were reduced to one god, *Allah*. One wonders why *Allah* was saved, and not the other 'gods'? I argue this is the case, in part, because *Allah* (*'Aḷah Muqah*) represented the most important thing to a nomadic pastoralist group who lived in the desert: *water*. One can argue that you do not need any other 'gods' to make it here on earth, but one thing is for sure, you will not go far if you don't have water. Water is *life*; water is everything in a desert environment.

The pre-Islamic traditions are now forgotten—for the most part—among modern adherents of Islam outside of the academy. But a historical analysis of the name of their most cherished

66 *Catholic Encyclopedia*, McGrawhill Book Co. 1967.

67 The word *bool* could be a loan into the language.

68 The association of black stones and rain in Africa could shed light on the practice in Islam. Unfortunately, space will not allow us to explore this here. This may be the subject of a future essay.

surviving 'god' reveals the true historical nature of this being. Ultimately, this name derives from a very ancient Kongo-Saharan root *-r-/-l-* that meant, "remote, distant, high, above, and length" (e.g., PB **-dai* "far"; Sumerian *ri* "be distant").

As a result of many different processes of metaphoric-extension, this root created a *meaning-chain* of terms which included (but not limited to): "sky, heaven, rain, king, authority, measure, leader, generations, father, god, sun, head, master, chief, first, totality, truth, elder, old, ancient, history, ascend, stretch, give birth and produce."

The names for god—*El, Eloah, Illahu, Oluwa, MuKulu, Gulu, Mꜣ'ʿt, Elu, Ilu, Hrw, Tororrot, Obatala, Orishnla, Oludumare, Olodu, Enu, An, Anu*, etc.—are all 'catch-phrases' for basically all of attributes listed above. *Allah* is a *high god* because the name literally means "high, exalted" (sky). It is equivalent to the English phrase "The Most High." The phrase, "The Most High" is not a name in English. It is a phrase that denotes the position of the Divine relative to man and creation in terms of hierarchy. The word *Allah*, I argue, is in the same category. I render it *il* (the) + [most] + *ilāh* (high); or *il* (the) + *ilāh* (highest; *òrìṣà* "head").

After reviewing the data as presented by Wesley Muhammad (2009), I am not convinced that *Allah* (of Arabia) = *Ra* (the sun-god of Egypt) or that *Allah* was an import into Egypt from Arabia. As has been demonstrated in *Part I* and *Part II* of this series, all associations of *Allah*, including his very name, are indigenous to Egypt and Africa as a whole. The name 'Allah' is embedded in many names for the Divine, natively, across the continent. The root of *Allah* has gone through many sound changes in different areas of Africa and may not be recognized as *Allah* (*Ala*) to the non-specialist. With this said, the Arabs (Black or White) didn't introduce anything new or unique when they came into Africa in regards to concepts of spirituality and the Divine. The wide-spread nature of this name for the Divine in Africa informs us of how ancient this name is. And by this account, Dr. Yosef Ben Jochannan's statement in *The Black Man's North and East Africa* is vindicated:

> Should people of African origin have to continue compromising themselves to writings that profess a "SEMITIC JEHOVA" and/or "JESUS CHRIST," or even a "HAMITIC AL'LAH" as "...THE ONE AND ONLY TRUE GOD...?" No. Africans should be fully aware of the fact that "I AM" – the GOD RA.." of the Nile Valleys (Blue and White) and the Great Lakes regions of Alkebu-lan (Africa) predated all three of the other GODS mentioned before by thousands of years. (cited in Muhammad, 2009: 110)

Is Muhammad willing to argue that benevolent Semites came into Africa and introduced Ra (La) to the Africans before there was ever a "Semite?" Is he willing to claim that these benevolent Semites scoured Africa and 'loaned' this term to the Kongo-Saharan speakers during the proto-stages of their languages? Is he willing to claim that not only did the Semites introduce Ra (the sun-god) into Egypt, but also introduced Ra the sun-god to the Igbo of Nigeria? The Ashanti of Ghana? The Baluba of Congo? The Chagga of the great lakes? The Kalenjiin of Kenya? The Bidiya and Geji of Chad? Did these West and Central Africans "Niger-Congoize" the Semitic *ʾỊh*? Since *ḥr/ḥrw* is the expanded form of *Rʿ* in Egyptian, is he willing to argue that the Semites introduced the morphological form *ḥr* to the predynastic Egyptians in the Sudan as well; even though this word isn't Semitic? When the Egyptians talk about the nation being founded by *ḥrw* kings, were they talking about Semites?[69] What was the motivation and historical precedence that replaced the Egyptian's basic vocabulary terms for "sun, sky, heavens, water and god" with

69 More specifically the *sšw hr* or "people of Hrw" (Manethos *shemsu hor* "followers of Horus") discussed in the Temple of Edfu. Finch (1998: 34) discusses their metallurgical occupation in predynastic times. We should note that the word *sšw* can also mean "disk" (of metal). In other words, these were black-smiths.

Semitic ones?

When measured against the weight of the evidence, Wesley Muhammad's claim cannot be substantiated. How can you "introduce" something to a people who already had what you're trying to introduce? And not only do they possess it, but they possess different varieties of the same concept, all indigenously with certain aspects gaining more prominence at different periods of Egyptian history (*ḫpr, wr, rꜥ, ḥr, iwn, sꜣ*, etc.). This clearly shows its antiquity as there are multiple reflexes of the same term to reflect various time depths.

Why wasn't there first an examination of African languages to see if the claim that the 'gods' such as "[Ra], Amun, Ptah, Min, etc., are almost certainly Semitic" (Muhammad, 2009: 114)? All of these names for the 'deities', and the deities themselves, are indigenous creations of African people. Both, the meaning and form, can be reconstructed to proto-forms in Afro-Asiatic and Kongo-Saharan. There are many African nations that still honor the Divine by these names to this day (e.g., Setswana-Bantu *RaRa* "God.").

I don't discount influence and borrowing in both directions. In this case, as it regards *Ra* (Amun, Ptah, Min, etc.), the evidence doesn't support the premise.[70] One cannot give what one doesn't have; in this case *ḥrw/Rꜥ* = sun. The more likely correspondence between *Allah* and an ancient Egyptian 'god' would be that between *Allah* and *ḥrw/ḥr*. Their associations are more congruent and their phonemes are simply switched (*h-r* > *l-h*). But it is clear, from such evidence found in Cemetery L in Nubia,[71] that *ḥrw* is definitely not a Semitic conceptualization. *Allah* is simply *Heru* (*ḥr/ḥrw*) with the *ḥ-* prefix suffixed on the root. The word *Allah* is also cognate with Egyptian *wr*, but as we have seen in this essay, this is a native form of the word and couldn't have been introduced by Semites to the Egyptians and all of West and Central Africa in Proto-Niger-Congo times.

There is a tendency for practitioners of the Abrahamic traditions to try and claim the ultimate origins of spiritual concepts, or to hold a monopoly on concepts that existed in other human groups thousands of years before they came on the historical scene: e.g., monotheism, a savior, resurrection, etc. 'Allah', as a name and concept, did not originate in Arabia and it is not the sole product of the Semitic people. The Semitic branch of African languages (and therefore its culture) is the youngest of all the 3 major linguistic branches of Africa. There is very little, if anything unique and new that came out of Arabia (spiritually) that was not already conceived of in Africa proper or in some other part of the world. The traditions of the Abrahamic faiths are local adaptations to concepts and practices that already existed in Africa. One cannot hold a monopoly on a concept that one did not invent: in this case *Allah*.

The Arabs came into Africa thinking that they were 'introducing' *Allah* to the Africans when the Africans were already familiar with 'Him' in various different ways. *Rꜥ*, as the 'sun-god', has four primary linguistic forms in Egyptian: *rꜥ*, *ḥr*(w), *ḫpr*(r) and *iwn*. Each form derives from a word for "fire and light" which evolved into the word for "sun." The word for *fire,* that would have matched one of these forms, never evolved into the word for sun in Semitic. The Semitic etymology for *ʾAḷah* does not trace back to a word for "sun," (or "eye") but of an ancient root that denotes "above, height, length, distance" which extended to mean "sky, heavens, rain" and "sun" in other areas of Africa in association to "sky" and not "fire." There are African variations of the word *ra* that mean "sky," but it appears that *ra* alone, without

70 For example, the creator god *Ptḥ* (<*ptḥ* "create, to shape) and the sun-god *itn* are present among the Ibibio people as *O-bot* (<*bot* "create") and *utin* "sun" respectively. Did the Semites reach Nigeria and introduce *Obot* and *Utin* as well?

71 See for instance the book *Africa in Antiquity, The Arts of Ancient Nubia and the Sudan*, Steffen Wenig, The Brooklyn Museum, p. 177 (1978); *The A-Group Royal Cemetery at Qustal, Cemetery L* by Bruce Beyer Williams, The University of Chicago Oriental Institute Nubian Expedition, (1986) pp. 183, 185.

any affixation, doesn't exist in Egyptian to mean "sky, heavens."[72] During Pharaonic times *rʿ* (as *sky, water*) was bounded by other morphemes. *Allah* is an old Arabian 'rain-god' that was demytholized during the Muhammadian revolution as to hide His 'pagan' origins. The same was done with the rain/storm-god YHWH in the Bible (Cf. Imhotep, 2011).

(Table Footnotes)

1 Egyptian *ḫrpw* ultimately derives from a root cognate with ciLuba: *-kùlumpa* (*-kùlapa, -kùlaba*) "growing up, growing older, aging"; *-kùlakaja* "age"; *-kùlula* "use, wear, age"; *-kùlumpè*(à) "adult" ☛ Syn.: *-kolè*(à). Remember that elders were the leaders of traditional communities and their titles were just words that reflected an elder's "age."

2 It should be noted that within ciLuba, the /l/ is often interchangeable with /m/. The /l/ corresponds to Egyptian /m/ and /n/ as well.

72 The closet term would be *ꜣrt* "sky, heaven." But this may be a reduction of *ḥrt* "sky, heaven." One could also note the word *rw* "supports" (of sky, earth). But this may be a reduction of *rd/rwḏ* "strength." We must consider, however, the word *jʿrjt* "God's abode" [Wb I 42] in our analysis. We know that *ʿr* "to ascend, rise, go up" is the root with reflexes given as *jʿr* "move up" [Wb I 41]; *ʿrʿr* "climb" (of flooding) [Wb 210 I].

AFRICAN ORIGINS OF THE WORD GOD

The names of nearly all the gods came from Egypt. I know from the enquiries I have made, that they came from abroad and it is most likely that they came from Egypt, For the names of all the gods have been known in Egypt since the beginning of time.[1]

The sea made it natural for Greeks to turn to neighbouring maritime peoples rather than to the hill-dwellers who live on the European mainland. Egypt and Asia Minor were more interesting than Macedonia and Illyria. From these already ancient cultures the early Greeks learned many things: the names of exotic gods and goddesses such as Hera and Athena, who became fully naturalized . . .[2]

Introduction

In this essay we will take a look into the proposed etymology of a word that has come down to us in the English language as "God." It is this author's contention that the mainstream definitions given to this term, and its proposed origins, are the result of folk etymology. We then propose possible alternative etymologies for the word God from African languages. Historically, linguists have tried to separate the Indo-European languages from African languages, and as a result—when a dilemma arrives in the process of trying to ascertain a meaning for an obscure word in Indo-European—instead of looking into African languages (from which Indo-European languages derived), they instead make-up fanciful etymologies to try and make it fit an Indo-European reality.

Bengtson and Ruhlen, in their article "Global Etymologies" (Ruhlen, 1994: 278), note the following issue as it regards early linguistic attitudes:

> That we so seldom see mention of this corollary principle is largely because twentieth-century historical linguistics has been laboring under the delusion that language families like Indo-European share *no* cognates with other families, thus offering nothing to compare. At this level, it is alleged, similarities simply do not exist.

I argue that this is the case because the field in-and-of itself was created during a period of intense racism world-wide by Europeans. Making Indo-European an "isolated" world language family would fit into their now debunked theory known as the *poly-genetic thesis* in which it is believed that different "races" developed independently across the globe simultaneously. By asserting this conviction Europeans could claim no relationship to other human beings and could develop the attitude that they didn't receive any cultural artifacts from other groups in the surrounding areas. The works of Greenberg (2005), Obenga (1993), Bernal (2006) and Campbell-Dunn (2004), among others, have made it so that we no longer need to stop at Indo-European to find solutions for these linguistic conundrums within the Indo-European language family.

Many believe that a word, let's say, over a 6000 year span will lose its basic meaning and its shape will be unrecognizable. While this is probably true for most words, some lexical items have not fallen victim to such a fate. For instance, the Proto-Indo-European word for "nephew" **nepot-,* survives in Rumanian as *nepot*, virtually unchanged. One term that has come down to us in English, with virtually the same ancient pronunciation, is the very term "fly," which we can see in the following African languages:

Phylum	Family	Language	Attestation	Gloss	Source
NS	Maba	Mesalit	**fir**		Ed
NS	Berta	Berta	**hɔ'rɔŋ**		Bender (1989)
NS	ES	Gaam	**pərd-**	fly	Bender & Ayre (1980)
NS	ES	*PN	***pär**	fly, jump	D
NS	Songhay	Djenné Chiini	**firri**	fly	Heath (1998)
NS	Saharan	Kanuri	**fàr**	to jump, fly	Cy
NC	Dogon	Bunɔge	**pile**	to fly	RMB
NC	Ijoid	Nkoro	**fĩĩ**	fly	KW
NC		*PWS	***pi, pil̩-**	to fly, flutter	W
NC	Mande	Bamana	**pã**	fly, jump	VV
NC	Atlantic	Temne	**fal(ar)**	*voler*	GS
NC	Kordofanian	Moro	**abəro**	to fly	RMB
NC	EBC	Lokə	**fiilə́**	to fly	JS
AA	Beja	Beja	**biir**	fly	Hudson (p.c.)
AA	Agaw	Awngi	**pərr-**	jump	Applewyard (p.c.)
AA	Proto-East-Cushitic		***bar(ar)**	fly	Sasse (1982)
AA	East Cushitic	Burji	**burr-**	fly	HECD

The chart above is from Roger Blench's essay "The Problem of Pan-African Roots."[1] The Indo-European variants given by Blench (2008) are:

Phylum	Family	Language	Attestation	Gloss
Kartvelian		Georgian	**p'er**	
North Caucasian		Abkhaz	**pir**	
Indo-European	Iranian	Persian	**parr--**	
Indo-European		English	**fly**	
Uralic	Ugric	Khanty	**por**	
Dravidian		Tamil	**paRa**	fly, hover, flutter
Isolate		Gilyak	**parpar**	fly, hover about
Austroasiatic	Mon-Khmer	Khmer	**par**	
Sino-Tibetan	Sinitic	Chinese	**fei**	

Other examples can be found with other lexical items such as the word "man" in English.[2] The root of the term *man* is actually **ni* "soul, spirit, person." *Ma-* is an old Niger-Congo/Kongo-Saharan prefix (often used with mass nouns, liquids, pairs, etc.) which has been lexicalized in Indo-European languages. For instance, Latin *Ma-nes* (Etruscan *Mani*) "ancestral spirits", N-C *ni* "soul", *mani* "people", as in *Ma-n-d-e* (with intrusive *d*), Bamana, Djula, Sussu *ni* "soul", Gola *o-ngin, o-ngi:* "soul", Santrokofi *ku-ni* "soul" (singular prefix). In Indo-European: Oscan *niir* "man," Vedic Sanskrit *nar-* (often of gods); (PWS *ni, (ne)* "person," PWS *nu* "person, man") N-C *nir* "man", Kele *nir,* Dagomba *nire*, Gba *niri*, Konkomba *o-nir*,Yorùbá *e-ni*, Gbari *u-nu*, Ekoi *ni* "man," *ni* being (Campbell-Dunn, 2006b). We noted Niger-Congo *ni* means "soul." Thus Latin *a-ni-ma* "soul" (whence *animal*) can be further analysed as *a-* (prefix) *ni* ("soul") *ma* (suffix). The word has cognates not only in Latin *animus* "spirit, courage" but in

1 In: John D. Bengtson (Ed.). (2008). *In Hot Pursuit of Language in Prehistory*. Amsterdam / Philadelphia: John Benjamins. pp. 189-209.

2 See Ruhlen (1994: 310-312) for global attestations of the word "man" (Nostratic **mana*).

Greek *anemos* "wind," Sanskrit *anilas* "breath," Irish *anal* "breath." The Sanskrit and Irish forms share the *l* of animal. Basque has *arima* "soul" (with Akpafu n > r).

<u>MAN, WOMAN</u> **Sumerian** *mu,(mulu, munus)*

MU "person"
NU "person" **-s**
Sumerian *mu*$_{10}$ "woman"

PWS *nu, ni* "person"
PWN *NINTU (NITU)* "person, man"
"Bantu" (Johnston 1922: 343) *mui* "man"
"Bantu" (Johnston 1922: 418) *ωmuntu* "woman"
Mande M *musu* "woman"
Mande *mòg.ò,* M *moko* "man", *mu* "person"
Mangbetu *mu* "friend"
Afro-Asiatic : Chad : Musgu *muni* "woman"

As we can see here, fundamental concepts of life have been and are present in Indo-European languages from Africa. This is the case that will be made throughout this discourse as it regards the word God in English. Before we get into the meat of this discussion, we must first examine the mainstream definitions of the word God and its proposed history.

Current Definitions of the word God

The origins of the name God, the Divine creative force which fashioned and holds up the universe, has been elusive to researchers for many years. Although there is some consensus on its meaning, most texts assert that they are unsure of the word's etymology. This does not instill confidence in their proposals for its original meaning. Let us now examine these definitions given from various sources:

Webster's 1913 Dictionary: <u>http://www.hyperdictionary.com/dictionary/god</u>
\God\ (g[o^]d), n. [AS. *god*; akin to OS. & D. *god*, OHG. *got*, G. *gott*, Icel. *gu*[eth], *go*[eth], Sw. & Dan. *gud*, Goth. *gup*, prob. orig. a p. p. from a root appearing in Skr. *h*[=u], p. p. *h*[=u]*ta*, to call upon, invoke, implore. [root]30. Cf. {Goodbye}, {Gospel}, {Gossip}.]

Catholic Encyclopedia: <u>http://www.newadvent.org/cathen/06608x.htm</u>
(Anglo-Saxon *God*; German *Gott*; akin to Persian *khoda*; Hindu *khooda*). The root-meaning of the name (from Gothic root *gheu*; Sanskrit *hub* or *emu*, "to invoke or to sacrifice to") is either "the one invoked" or "the one sacrificed to." From different Indo-Germanic roots (div, "to shine" or "give light"; *thes* in *thessasthai* "to implore") come the Indo-Iranian *deva*, Sanskrit *dyaus* (gen. divas), Latin *deus*, Greek *theos*, Irish and Gaelic *dia*, all of which are generic names; also Greek Zeus (gen. *Dios*, Latin Jupiter (jovpater), Old Teutonic *Tiu* or *Tiw* (surviving in Tuesday), Latin *Janus*, *Diana*, and other proper names of pagan deities. The common name most widely used in Semitic occurs as *'el* in Hebrew, *'ilu* in Babylonian, *'ilah* in Arabic, etc.; and though scholars are not agreed on the point, the root-meaning most probably is "the strong or mighty one."

Oxford English Dictionary:
"god (gɒd). Also 3-4 *godd.* [Com. Teut.: OE. *god* (masc. in sing.; pl. *godu*, *godo* neut., *godas* masc.) corresponds to OFris., OS., Du. *god* masc., OHG. *got*, *cot* (MHG.

got, mod.Ger. *gott*) masc., ON. *goð, guð* neut. and masc., pl. *goð, guð* neut. (later Icel. pl. *guðir* masc.; Sw., Da. gud), Goth. *guÞ* (masc. in sing.; pl. *guÞa, guda* neut.). The Goth. and ON. words always follow the neuter declension, though when used in the Christian sense they are syntactically masc. The OTeut. type is therefore **guđom* neut., the adoption of the masculine concord being presumably due to the Christian use of the word. The neuter sb., in its original heathen use, would answer rather to L. *numen* than to L. *deus*. Another approximate equivalent of *deus* in OTeut. was **ansu-z* (Goth. in latinized pl. form *anses*, ON. *ǫss*, OE. *Ós-* in personal names, *ésa* genit. pl.); but this seems to have been applied only to the higher deities of the native pantheon, never to foreign gods; and it never came into Christian use.

The ulterior etymology is disputed. Apart from the unlikely hypothesis of adoption from some foreign tongue, the OTeut. **guÞom* implies as its pre-Teut. type either **ghudho-m* or **ghutó-m*. The former does not appear to admit of explanation; but the latter would represent the neut. of the passive pple. of a root **gheu-*. There are two Aryan roots of the required form (both **glheu*, with palatal aspirate): one meaning 'to invoke' (Skr. *hū*), the other 'to pour, to offer sacrifice' (Skr. *hu*, Gr. χέειν, OE. yéotan YETE v.). Hence **glhutó-m* has been variously interpreted as 'what is invoked' (cf. Skr. *puru-hūta* 'much-invoked', an epithet of Indra) and as 'what is worshipped by sacrifice' (cf. Skr. *hutá*, which occurs in the sense 'sacrificed to' as well as in that of 'offered in sacrifice'). Either of these conjectures is fairly plausible, as they both yield a sense practically coincident with the most obvious definition deducible from the actual use of the word, 'an object of worship'. Some scholars, accepting the derivation from the root **glheu-* to pour, have supposed the etymological sense to be 'molten image' (= Gr. χυγόν), but the assumed development of meaning seems very unlikely.

American Heritage Dictionary: http://www.bartleby.com/61/21/G0172100.html
ETYMOLOGY: Middle English, from Old English. See *gheu*(): in APPENDIX I
DEFINITION: To call, invoke. Oldest form **heu*()-, becoming **gheu*()- in centum languages. Suffixed zero-grade form **ghu-to-*, "the invoked," god. a. god, from Old English *god, god*; b. *giddy*, from Old English *gydig, gidig*, possessed, insane, from Germanic **gud-iga-*, possessed by a god; c. *götterdämmerung*, from Old High German *got, god*. a–c all from Germanic **gudam, god*. (Pokorny hau- 413.)

Thus from the above we have the following:

	Webster	**Catholic Enc.**	**Oxford**	**American Heritage**
Anglo-Saxon	*g[o^]d*	*god*		
Old English			*god: (godu, godo neut., godas masc.)*	*god, giddy*
Old High German			*got*	
German	*gott*	*gott*	*gott*	*got, god*
Icelandic	*gu[eth], go[eth],*			
Swedish, Danish	*gud*		*gud*	
Old Norse			*goð, guð*	
Gothic	*gup*	*gheu*	*guÞ*	

Old Teutonic			*guđom: *ghudho-m or *ghutó-m.	*gud-iga-, *gudam
Proposed Indo-European root:			*glheu,	*heu()- > *gheu()- :*ghu-to

Mallory and Adams, *The Oxford Introduction to Proto-Indo-European and the Proto-Indo-European World* (2006: 354), offers the following analysis:

> The connotation of 'invoke' **seems to** lie behind some of the cognates derived from *g'heu(h_x)- (e.g. OIr *guth* 'voice', OCS *zovo̧* 'call', Av *zavaiti* 'calls', Skt *ha'vate* 'calls, invokes', Toch B *kuwā* - 'call, invite'); it supplies the Germanic word for 'god' as 'what is invoked' (**ghuto'm*) and **probably also** in Tocharian (e.g. Toch B *nakte* 'god' < **nı'-ghuto-* i.e. 'the one invoked downward') and, as we have seen, it may carry the meaning 'invoke' also in Indic. (bolded emphasis mine)

The bolded terms above highlight the uncertainty of the proposed etymologies. The same analysis is virtually repeated in Don Ringe's work *From Proto-Indo-European to Proto-Germanic: A Linguistic History of English Vol.I.* (2006). The same can be said for the Wikipedia entries for the word God.[3] The following chart summarizes these sources:

Language	Reconstruction	Meaning	Source
PIE	*g^heu̯-	"to pour, libate" (Sanskrit *huta*, see *hotr*),	Wiki
PIE	*g^hau̯- (*$ǵ^h$eu̯h_2-)	"to call, to invoke" (Sanskrit *hūta*). Sanskrit *hutá* = "having been sacrificed", from the verb root *hu* = "sacrifice."	Wiki
PIE	*ĝheu(hx)	(e.g. OIr *guth* 'voice', OCS *zovo̧* 'call', Av *zavaiti* 'calls', Skt *ha'vate* 'calls, invokes', Toch B *kuwā* - 'call, invite');	Mallor & Adams (2006: 354)
PIE	*ĝhuto'm		Mallor & Adams (2006: 409)
Germanic	*ĝhuto'm	'what is invoked' ***probably*** also in Tocharian (e.g. Toch B *nakte* 'god' < **nı'-ghuto-* i.e. 'the one invoked downward')	Mallor & Adams (2006)
Ger. (Gothic)	*guda̧	god	Ringe (2006:293)
	*gudjo	'priest'	Ringe (2006:293)
Toch. A	(*nkät*)	from (see below)	Mallor & Adams (2006: 409)
PIE	*nı'-ĝhutos	'he who is invoked downwards (i.e. from the sky)'.	Mallor & Adams (2006: 409-10)

Many modern Christian theologians are shunning away from the word God for its alleged "pagan" origins. One such online publication has the following to say on this topic:

3 "God" (word): http://en.wikipedia.org/wiki/God_(word) (retrieved June 22, 2013).

Word origin: God - Our word god goes back via Germanic to Indo-European, in which a corresponding ancestor form meant "invoked one." The word's only surviving non-Germanic relative is Sanskrit *hu*, invoke the gods, a form which appears in the Rig Veda, most ancient of Hindu scriptures: *puru-hutas*, "much invoked," epithet of the rain-and-thunder god Indra. (From READER'S DIGEST, Family Word Finder, page 351) (Originally published by The Reader's Digest Association, Inc., Pleasantville New York, Montreal; Copyright 1975)

Now if the sources noted above are accurate, then the word that we use for the Supreme Being, God, comes from a very pagan origin. Thus the word god is used generically by many different religions to refer to their deity or "invoked one."

Some may laugh at the notion, the very idea that the word "God" has any origin or association with Hindu Sanskrit. To illustrate how this is possible, we again quote from 'Family Word Finder' on the historical development of our Modern English language:

Page 7, 'Word Origins' - "English belongs to the Indo-European family of languages, which consists of about 100 related tongues, all descended from prehistoric language of a pastoral, bronze working, horse breeding people, the Aryans, who inhabited the steppes of Central Asia about 4500 B.C. Scholars refer to their language at this stage as proto-Indo-European, or simply Indo-European.[4]

Other Biblical scholars derive the word God from Babylonian *gad* (pronounced *ga*^{w}*d*) which was their "god" of *fortune*. One such discussion from Wade Cox[5] is as follows:

Objections to the use of the word *God,* stem from the understanding that the Babylonian deity of fortune was *Baal-Gad* (pronounced *gawd*). It is then assumed that the term is pagan if the word *God* is used.

The term *God* in the ancient Anglo-Saxon comes from the word *Goode*, or *Goot* as in the Dutch and German. The word is actually a Hebrew word from which *gad* itself in the sense of SHD 1410 is derived. The word is SHD 1464 *Guwd* (pronounced *goode*). The tribes of Israel, when taken into captivity, took with them this name. It was used also by the Assyrians who captured them. It is a prime root meaning *to crowd upon* or *attack* and this means *to invade* or *to overcome*. It is this sense of overcoming, as God is the centre of power, that the term is used. *Guwd* or *Goode* is not the same as *gad* or *Baal-Gad* worshipped by the Babylonians. One is a perversion of the concepts of the other.

The word *God* is derived from the old Teutonic form *gudo* which means *that which is invoked (or worshipped) by sacrifice* (cf. *Oxford English Universal Dictionary*, art. *God*, p. 808). This was adapted among the Teutonic tribes in the variant forms.

The representation of the loyal heavenly Host as bulls representing God is ancient, even being found in pre-Hebrew culture. The Babylonian system in its mystery cults adopted the bull-slaying typology, which carried into Mithraism. The bull-slaying typology is a representation of the wars in the heavens (see David Ulansey *The Origins*

4 "The Origin of the English Word for God," by Craig Bluemel: http://www.bibleanswerstand.org/God.htm.

5 "The Etymology of the name God," by Christian Churches of God: http://www.ccg.org/english/s/p220.html.

> *of the Mithraic Mysteries*, Oxford, 1989 for the cosmology; Perseus is the bull-slayer for the Mysteries). This symbolism is carried on in the association with the mighty one and the centrality of goodness or *Gott* or *Goode*.
>
> The English word *God*, via the Teutonic *Gudo* and the earlier forms, is associated with the ancient Semitic and Hebrew as we see above. Thus, the bull was both symbol of reverence and the significant sacrifice. Hence, the name came to be associated with the bull. This pointed towards the sacrifice of Messiah as the Bull of Atonement. This understanding was long held among the Semites from Shem as high priest from the post-flood epoch. From recent finds, it seems this was further distorted in the system at Ur.[6]

The book of Isaiah is where the word *gad* is defined.

> **Isaiah 65:11-12,** But you who forsake the Lord, who forget and ignore My holy Mount Zion, who prepare a table for **Gad the Babylonian god of fortune** and who furnish mixed drinks for Meni the god of destiny. I will destine you says the Lord for the sword, and you shall all bow down to the slaughter, because when I called, you did not answer; when I spoke, you did not listen or obey. But you did what was evil in my eyes, and you chose that in, which I did not delight. -AMP

All of the confusion over this term arises as a result of not consulting African languages. Each of these resources gives us clues on how to properly interpret this term. It is only the historical bias of thinking that Africans, let alone African languages, had no influence on the development of ideas in Europe and its languages that prevent us from gaining more plausible meanings for obscure words in Indo-European. We hope to reverse this train of thought in this essay.

Quandaries in Analysis

Linguists assert that the word God derives from a Proto-Indo-European (PIE) root **ǵ^{h}eu̯-* "to pour, libate" (Sanskrit *huta*, see hotr), or from a root **ǵ^{h}au̯-* (**ǵ^{h}eu̯h$_{2}$-*) "to call, to invoke" (Sanskrit *hūta*); or from a root cognate with Sanskrit *hutá* = "having been sacrificed", from the verb root *hu* = "sacrifice." The fact that there are three possible roots, with totally different meanings, gives us reason to question and reconsider the proposed etymologies currently accepted for this term.

Although Wikipedia is not always considered a credible source, in this case it accurately conveys the sentiments in other source materials I have examined. It is believed our current pronunciation of God derives from proto-Germanic **gudan*, which many believe derives from a Proto-Indo-European neuter passive perfect participle **ǵ^{h}u-tó-m*. As Wiki notes, "The Proto-Germanic meaning of **guđán* and its etymology is uncertain." Everywhere we look for the meaning of this word, the ultimate etymology is "uncertain" and it is this uncertainty that guides the folk-etymology. The nature of the uncertainty is clear in the language of the following passage from Wiki:

> Depending on which possibility is preferred, the pre-Christian meaning of the Germanic term may either have been (in the "pouring" case) "libation" or "that which is libated upon, idol" — or, as Watkin opines in the light of Greek χυτη γαια "poured earth" meaning "tumulus", "the Germanic **form may have referred** in the first instance to the spirit immanent in a burial mound" — or (in the "invoke" case) "invocation, prayer" (compare the meanings of Sanskrit *brahman) or "that which is invoked"*.

6 http://www.logon.org and http://www.ccg.org. (1997).

The reason why there is uncertainty here is because there is no evidence of how the ancient term was applied. Therefore, it states that it "may" have applied to "pouring" libations, for example.

Another problem here is that linguists have no explanation as to how a verb "to invoke, call, libate, pour, sacrifice, etc.," somehow became a noun and applied to a Supreme Being. They speculate that "with a slight change in meaning, it (*hu/huta*) *could* mean "that which is invoked," but supply no linguistic grounds for the change (e.g., by inflection or agglutination of morphemes). Such a process can be seen in Ringe (2006). In discussing the deverbative suffixes in PIE, Ringe (2006: 293) notes that a PIE agent noun suffix *-ter- scarcely survives in Germanic. It seems to have been replaced, in the first instance, by *-(i)ja-, of which a few examples survive in Gothic (e.g., *fauramaþleis* "chief, leader," derived from *maþljan* "to speak"). However, it was the extended *n*-stem form *-(i)jan- that became productive in P.Gmc. Ringe argues that most seem to have been formed from nouns (e.g., **murþrijo* "murderer" to **murþra* "murder"; **fiskijo* "fisherman" to **fiskaz* "fish"; *gudjo* "priest" to **guda* "god," etc.). For Ringe, "God" derives from a word meaning "priest" by way of the loss of the inflectional suffix *-jo*. If so, this would provide evidence for the *-gud-* root being a verb. But it is also possible that this word was reanalyzed because it sounded like a term in its inventory (assuming a possible loan).

Through my limited research, I have not been able to find sufficient evidence in the Germanic languages, nor in Sanskrit, of this alleged root being used as a name or title for the Creator or group of "divine beings." Pouring, invoking and sacrificing are distinct conceptualizations. It is safe to assume that the ancient users of this term knew the difference between *pouring* libations and *that which* the libations are being poured for, for example. The real question is, "What were the ancients calling 'God' before **hu*/*g^h*ua/huta*, etc., became the substitute for that term?" What was the general term used for what we call God or gods in PIE, Sanskrit and Germanic? The dominant form of God in Indo-European is some variation of Latin *dues* (Greek *theos*). Germanic had the forms *dia*, *tia* or *tiw*.[7] How did the verb "to invoke" come to overshadow the actual name for the Creator *tiw* in Germanic?

We notice from all of the examples given above for the word God, the sources only site two lines of entry in the Indo-European languages: Germanic and Sanskrit. If this term was used since Proto-Indo-European times, what caused its disuse in the other branches?

Reinterpretations

It is our contention here that the word for God derives from an ancient African root with a derived meaning of "sky" or "heavens" (*lu, ru, du*). There are several reasons why we are going along this path. The first is that what we call "God" in modern languages, in ancient times, was almost always associated with the *heavens* and *rain*. This is a universal association and not restricted to Africa. The concept of **ghua* betrays this association in Indo-European languages. The Supreme deity among Indo-Europeans is associated with a *sky-father*. This is a concept inherited from their African ancestors who also viewed God as a remote (yet all encompassing) entity that supports life from a distance (from the sky). The sky is almost always assigned the gender of male, as the rain (a fructifying agent) is analygous to sperm that "impregnates" mother earth who gives birth to life as we know it.[8]

---

7 The variant *tiw* is the root in the word *Tue*sday "God's day."

8 There is an exception in Ancient Egypt. The sky is feminine and known as *nwt*. In North-America, there is a Sky Woman among the Abanaki in Vermont, and Manitou among the Great Lakes tribes.

As noted by Mallory & Adams (2006: 344):

> The basic word for 'god' in Proto-Indo-European appears to have been **deiwo´s*, itself an o-stem derivative of **dyeu-* 'sky, day' < **dei-* 'shine, be bright' and it is widely attested across the Indo-European groups, e.g. OIr *dīa*, Lat *deus*, Lith *diẽvas*, Hit *sius*, Skt *deva´-*, all 'god' in turn; in both Slavic and Iranian, e.g. Av *daeva-*, the word means 'demon', a result of a religious reformation that degraded prior deities to demons to make way for the new religion preached by Zarathustra. (The change, which began in Iranian, presumably spread to Slavic during the long period of prehistoric cultural exchange, centered on the south Russian steppes, between Iranian and Slavic.) In Germanic, the word for 'god' survives as the name of the god *Tyr*, a Germanic war god, e.g. OE *Tīw* and NE *Tue*sday, a specific deity whose name is built on the same word was **dyḗus ph*$_{a}$*tḗr* 'sky father'. There are both exact cognates of this form, e.g. Lat *Jūpiter*, Illyr *Dei-pátrous*, Grk *Zeús patḗr*, Skt *dyáuṣ pitā́*, and modified reworkings employing other words for 'father', e.g. Pal *tiyaz . . . pāpaz*. A derived adjective, **diwyós* 'divine', is attested in Lat *dīus*, Grk *dîuos*, and Skt *divyá-*.

Mallory & Adams further notes:

> The celestial nature of the Proto-Indo-European gods is also supported by the two etymologically unrelated words for 'god' in Germanic and Tocharian. NE *god* and its congeners (e.g. NHG *Gott*) is from Proto-Indo-European **ĝhuto´m* 'that which is called/invoked' while in Toch B we have *nakte* (Toch A *nkät*) from Proto-Indo-European **nı´-ĝhutos* 'he who is invoked downwards (i.e. from the sky)'. (2006: 409-410)

It is clear that the Creator is associated with the "sky" and we now turn to see examples of this sky association across the world.

The Sky-Father

We mentioned previously that the dominate conceptualization of God is that of a "Sky-Father." This notion is ubiquitous around the world. What we want to do here is establish a framework for which we can interpret the name God in a global context. We will do this by examining a few examples from each corner of the world.

A book titled *Indigenous Religions: A Companion (2000),* edited by Graham Harvey, provides us with a wealth of information pertaining to God as a sky-father in many indigenous cultures around the world. In discussing the connection between mythos and animism among North American Apache creation stories, M.A. Jaimes Guerrero,[9] in relation to the Jicarilla in northeastern New Mexico, informs us of their thoughts whose:

> emergence myth, with *creation from chaos* and animistic characteristics, gives a prominent role to kachina-like personifications of the basic natural powers ... These beings, called Hactin, existed before creation, when there was only dark, wet, chaos - the world womb, as it were. Being lonely, Hactin created the essential elements of the universe and also created Earth Mother and Sky Father ... Once there was only the Great Spirit. He created the world in four days. He made Father Sun, Mother Earth, Old man Thunder, Boy Lightning, and the animals. Then on the fourth day he made the People, the Tinde. (Harvey, 2000: 40)

9 Citing D. Leeming & M. Leeming (1994), *A Dictionary of Creation Myths.* Oxford University Pres. Oxford. pp 8-10.

Harvey (2000: 162) also recognizes a "Sky-Father" (Ranginui) among the Maori in his essay "Art Works In Aotearoa." *In the essay "Gifts for the Sky People," Mark Woodward notes among groups in Southeast Asia that:*

> With respect to the human realm, the sky is a superior exchange power and the source of spiritual potency. The Ao Naga of Assam refer to this potency as *aren*[10], the literal meaning of which is 'to increase' (Clark 1911). *Aren* is understood to be a nonmaterial substance possessed by the ancestors, sky people and wealthy and powerful humans. It is believed to be responsible for the fertility of crops, animals and humans. Mills reports that the primary purpose of sacrifice is to acquire *aren* and that it is conveyed to the fields in agricultural ceremonies (Mills 1922, 380-1).

This reminds us of the Babylonian god Baal-Gad/Ga^{w}d "fortune" as mentioned in the Biblical text of Isaiah. The idea is that one's blessings and increases are a direct result of the rains which support a civilization. One is only able to raise a family, conduct business, grow crops, etc., in an area that has rain (water). For this reason water/rain/the sky is associated with "good fortune." Compare Babylonian ga^{w}d "fortune," to Egyptian *kꜣ* 𓂓 "fortune, will (of king), kingship, goodwill"; *wḏꜣ* "prosperous" (Afro-Asiatic g > *ḏ*). In Babylonian we would assume a sound change of ꜣ (=l) > d.

As it regards a common praxis among Indo-European worshipers, Keith (1989: 37) informs us that, "There are a few cases where the parallelism existing among the words used by the different Indo-European peoples gives us the right to conclude the existence of common worship." The reason for this statement is that one observes that the primary word for God in Indo-European languages is associated with the sky: **dyeus ph$_{a}$tēr* (lit. "sky father"; > Ancient Greek *Ζευς (πατηρ) / Zeus (patēr)*; **dieu-ph$_{a}$tēr* > Latin *Jupiter*).

Linguistic evidence links the root words for "day", "sky" and "god" in all classical Indo-European languages and the name for the God of the Sky descends from the Proto-Indo-European word **deiuo'* or **deiwo'* meaning "clear sky" or "day light or day sky" (Winn, 1995: 20-23). We see this association with the Roman God *Jupiter* who was worshiped as a god of rain, thunder and lightning, whose center was the temple on the Capitoline Hill. "Dyaus has the honour of being the only Indo-European god who is certainly to be recognized as having existed in the earliest period, and he has been claimed for that time as a real sovereign of the gods, much as Zeus among the Greeks" (Keith, 1989: 95).

In Africa "God" is often identified with the "sky, the heavens" (Johnston 1919: 30, paragraph 3). Jan G. Platvoet (Harvey, 2000: 92) in his article "Spirit Possession among the Bono of West Africa," reminds us that:

> In Akan traditional religion Nyame is the (unseen) creator-god as well as the visible sky, and descends on earth as rain to become rivers and lakes. *Tano*, likewise, is both his 'eldest son', the greatest of the Akan *atano* gods, and *obomuhene*, 'king inside the rock', as well as that rock, the source of the River Tano, and the River Tano (Rattray 1923, 183-6, 191-2; Platvoet 1983,208-11).

God is the distant cause of fructification. Oduyoye in Saakana (1991: 80-81) notes that the concept of God as father in heaven fits more into the situation of matrilineal societies where the father does not reside with the child but is seen only now and then. The mother of the child is traceable; she is a body, thus the association with the earth which is visible and tangible.

10 The word *aren* "increase" (from heaven) sounds much like the Yorùbá word for "heaven" *orun* for which it is believed all blessings derive. There may be a connection here after further investigation.

The father of the child is elusive but as influential as a spirit. These ideas produce a situation where “Father is a spirit far away; Mother is a body near at hand.” We do not “see” spirits, but understand them to be working on our behalf from a distance. These ideas are thus associated with rain which comes from the distant sky, an “invisible” source who none-the-less supports creation (the earth-mother) by implanting its seed, the causal agent (of life).

Rain is a symbol of purity and fructification. This association of purity as symbolized by rain (water) is at the heart of one of the ancient Egyptian terms for the divine: *nṯr*. Among the Azande of central Africa we have (see Imhotep, 2011: 35-38):

	toro	is “rain” (cleansing agent, fructifying agent)
	Ma-toro	is “God”
cf. Hebrew	*ma-tar*	“rain” (cf. Hebrew *thr* “be pure”)
	tal	“dew” (uncontaminated water)

The ancient Egyptians, and other African nations, associated their gods with the purity and the life causing essence of water.

Egyptian	*ntr*	“natron” (cleansing agent)
	ntr	“God” (unseen fructifying agent) (Coptic *noute*)
Twi	*ntoro*	“spirit of patrilineage”
Yorùbá	*ntori*	“because”
Lugbara	*adro*	“guardian spirit”
	Adro	“God” (also the whirlwind found in rivers)[11]
Mbuti	*Ndura*	“God” (<of the rainforest)
ciLuba	*Ndele*	“divine, begetter, Ancestor”
Gurma	*Unteru*	“God”
Gurmantche	*Untenu*	“God”
Fulani	*Ntori*	“God”
Masai	*Naiteru*	“God”
Kwasio	*Nture*	“sacred”
Mombutu	*Noro*	“God”
Ewe	*Tre*	“clan spirit, fetish”
Ijo	*Toru*	“river” (Egyptian *i-trw* “river”)[12]
Tonga	*Tilo*	“blue sky, God” (from which the rains fall)
Amarigna[13]	*AnäTära*	“pure”
Wolof	*Twr*	“protecting god, totem”
	Twr	“libation” (Egyptian *twr* “libation”)

In the vast majority of African spiritual systems, the sky is symbolic of the infinite vastness of the Creator and is used as a symbol of *distance*. Since the sky, its height, and rain are related concepts, the same word is used for all three, often with slight changes in vowels. We noted earlier that African terms followed Africans as they migrated out of Africa and are still recognizable in European languages. The following chart will demonstrate a few of these terms

11 See Patricia Ann Lynch (2004). *African Mythology from A-Z*. Facts on File

12 Note that Budge (1008a) has a rendering of *nṯr* “temple of Isis” with the water canal glyph as a determinative.

13 This word *ntr* is reflected in Amarigna in the following terms: *NiTir* - adj refined, *Tnte nTr* - n. Element (chemical), *NTr qbe* - refined butter, *Ntr werq* - n. refined gold, *teneTere* v.i. was refined, *AneTere* v.t. refined; bounced, *AnTari* - n. refiner, *werq anTari* - n. goldsmith, *AnT'renya* – silversmith, *ManTeriya* - refining flux, *AnaTere* - v.i. acted flamboyantly, *AsneTere* v.t. had refined, *AnaTara* - pure

which should be recognizable given the nature of this discussion.[14]

Connections proposed by Karst		**Proto-Bantu**		**Remarks**
Mediterranean	**Bantu**	**Guthrie, w/ Guthrie number**	**Meeussen, w/ noun classes**	
Canaanitic *El / Bel*, cf. Sardinian / Aegean *Julus, Jolos, Jolaos* (j-l)	*y-ulu, e-ulu, wilu* 'God, Heaven'	-**gòdò* 5-, top; sky, 880, [>-ilu- in S.C.	-**gudu* 5 L LH, sky, above, 6.3.,	Proto-Bantu **d* often changes into *-l-* in historic attestations.
Phoenician/Punic *Moloḫ*	*muluku/m-luko, mlungu, mulungu,* 'God, Heaven'	-*dÓk-*, to rain, 650, > ? *Mu-lungu*, 'God'	-*dók-*, rain, drip, 5.4., [> S.C. & S.	***Borean** (approx.) : **TVKV* 'to pour, drop' (> **Eurasiatic**: **tUKV ;* **Sino-Caucasian**: **[.t]Hän.kó;* **Austric**: **Proto-Austronesia**n **itik*, **Proto-AustroAsiatic** **tVk* 'drop'; **Amerind** (misc.) : *tok ʷ 'saliva; spit
Loḫios (Apollo), *Meiliḫios* (Zeus), *molo*, magical herb in Homer	Bantu *mlogi, mlozi, moloki, m-rogi*, 'magician, sorcerer',	-**dÒg-*, to bewitch, 644, [> -roθ – in S.C. & S. Bantu] / **dÒgì* 14, witchcraft, 646, [> S.C. & S. Bantu	-**dog-* L, bewitch, 5.4., / -**dog*-L 1, witch, 5.4.,	
Minos, *Menuas* [Urartean king]	Bantu *m-ngu, muungu, mu-ingu*, 'God',	? -**nÉnÈ* DP, big, 1350; ? -**dÓk-*, to rain, 650, [> S.C. & S. Bantu *mulungu*, God]	-**néne*, big, 3.3.; -*dók-*, rain, drip, 5.4., [> S.C. & S. Bantu *mulungu*, god	

14 Chart from Wim van Binsbergen, "The continued relevance of Martin Bernal's Black Athena thesis: Yes and No," 2009. pp. 26-28. See also, J. Karst (1931). *Origines Mediterraneae: Die vorgeschichtlichen Mittelmeervölker nach Ursprung, Schichtung und Verwandtschaft: Ethnologisch-linguistische Forschungen über Euskaldenak (Urbasken), Alarodier und Proto-Phrygen, Pyrenaeo-Kaukasier und Atlanto-Ligurer, West- und Ostiberer, Liguro-Leleger, Etrusker und Pelasger, Tyrrhener, Lyder und Hetiter*, Heidelberg: Winters, pp. 245f.

Basque. *yinko* 'God'	Bantu-Zulu *Nkulu*, God; Massai *ngai, engai.*'	-**yiNk-*, to give, 2085, ? ; -**kódò* DP, old, 1197, /- **kódò* 1/2/14, old person/old age, 1197, [> -*kulu*, in S.C. & S.	-**nink-*, give, 2.3.; - **kúdú* 1, big, senior, adult, 6.3. [> -*kulu*, in S.C. & S. Bantu]	Not necessarily Bantu-related, cf.: *Borean **(approx.) :** **KVRV* 'old' (> **Eurasiatic :** **gwVrV* 'old'; **Afroasiatic :** **gVrʕ* - 'old' (Cushitic, Chadic and Berber **gVr-* 'be bigger, older'); **Sino-Caucasian :** **xq̇(w)VrV* 'old'; **African (misc.) :** Bantu *-*kúdù* 'old'; Ijo *kUrai* 'year'. (?); San. *ḳarē* 'full grown person'.

The German linguist and Africanist Wim M.J. van Binsbergen, the one who created the chart above, is also suspicious of the common proposed etymology of the word "god." As he notes:

> Cf. Germanic *god*, whose etymology is unclear – both semantically and phonologically the Bantu connection is more convincing than Old Indian *huta*, 'the one who is invoked'. No obvious long-range etymology available. (2009: 27)

The proto-Bantu forms **godo, *kodo* and **gudu* are inverses of the proto-Bantu form *-*dOk*. In early Niger-Kongo there is evidence of free-word-order (see Campbell-Dunn, 2009a, 2009b). As we can see, **godo* becomes *julus, jolos, jolaos* in Sardinian/Aegean. In the Phoenician/Punic languages, Bantu *mu-luku, mulungu* becomes *Moloẖ*.

The Nilo-Saharan, Niger-Congo consonantal root for sky/heavens/God is *-l-, -n-,* and *-d-*[15], *often with k-* or *g-* prefixes which gives us the *g-d* (god) root. It is our contention that the Germanic word God derives from the African word *Godo/Gudu* where *g-* is a prefix and the root is *du/do*. It is this root from which we get Yorùbá *Olu, Elu, El* "God," *Oluwa* "lord"; Hebrew *Eloah* "God," *Eloh'iym* "Gods"; Canaanite *El* "God"; Babylonian *Ilu* "God"; Arabic *il'ilah* (Allah) "God." In Bantu this term is rendered *G-udu, G-ulu, K-ulu, (n)K-ale, K-ule, P-ala/H-ala, Z-ulu, Z-eru, Bw-ena, Mw-ene*. Specific examples of the name God in Africa can be seen in the name *Guéno* (the Eternal) among the Fulani (l>n); *Gulu* among the Chagga-Bantu of East Africa (d>l); Bambara *san* "rain, sky, buy, year;" *san-kolo* is "heaven"; *Kulu* among the Bakongo; *Unkulunkulu* (the oldest of the old) among the Amazulu; *kuru* "God point" in Bambara (center of cross).

In Ancient Egyptian this term became *Hrw* "sky, sun, God." The root of *Hrw* is *wr/ulu* (Yorùbá *Olu* "great, lord, God"; *enu* "top, high"; Igbo *enu* "top of, up"). These terms evoke a sense of "eldership, distance, height, an apex, exaltation, the peak of something, etc." For this reason, anything that is tall or reaches the heavens can be an *ulu* (sun, moon, stars, mountains, etc.). A related Yorùbá word *Olá* means "elevated status, fame, honourable estate." It can be seen in such names as *Oláseni* "fame is not unachievable," *Oládŭnní* "high status is sweet to have," *Olánrewájú* "status is progressing forward," *Oláitán* "honour never gets used up." It is from this variation I believe that the word *Allah* (*'l*) ultimately has its origin.

15 These sounds are known throughout world languages to mutate and interchange with each other. So in one language, for instance, the /l/ root (*ilu*) in another language will be a /d/, /r/ or an /n/. Often the *k-* or *g-* prefix will go through a process of palatalization and it will become an /s/ (e.g., Akan *O-s-oro* "sky, god") or a /z/ (Amazulu *Z-ulu* "heavens, sky"; as in the famous Tshaka Zulu).

The sky is only used as a metaphor to denote the highest example of excellence; the summit of achievement (what a priest represents); the most honourable; the head honcho; the eldest (the oldest thing in existence); the grandest/biggest; the distance (in ability, consciousness and wisdom) between man and the Creator; the possessor of all things (as the sky encompasses all things in the universe) and general absence from. [16] Campbell-Dunn (2009b) demonstrates this with the following terms which support our thesis above:

<u>**DISTANT, REMOTE**</u> **Sumerian** *ul* "be distant, remote"

KU "big" -l
PWS *ku, kul* "old"
PWS *kua* "road"
PWN *KUA* "go" (from **kula*)
PWN *KWUL* "be big"
Bantu *kúdú* "adult"
Bantu (Meinhof) *kulu* "big"
Bantu *buk* "go away"
Mande <u>*ku*</u> "return"
Mangbetu *eku* "to return"
ES Dilling *okul,* Kondugr *oŋgul* "road"
CS Bulala *kori, gõri* "road"
Khoisan /Nusan (S) *!nu* "foot"

[Sumerian has lost initial *k* and final *a*]

***K = #** ***U = u** ***L = l** **or** ***B = #**

The underlying essence of this theme is "distance" which is symbolized by "height" and "age." This can be seen in the *Linear A* script of Crete: *da* "old man" (with walking stick). Niger-Congo explains the association: **da* "old," I Tschi *dadaw* "old," Agni *lala* "old," Guang, Ga, Grebo *da* "old," III Animere *da* "to grow, be grown," II Bantu (Meeussen) *dada* "old," PWN *DADA* "old." Here the *d/l* root is signifying distance through age. In the ancient Egyptian language *Hrw* derives from *hr* "distant."[17]

As we mentioned previously, the sky, rain, day and God share the same root in African and Indo-European languages. We see this reflected in various African terms, which in many respects may be homonyms. From Campbell-Dunn (2009b):

<u>**GOD**</u> **Sumerian** *diĝir* "god"

LI, DI "head, spirit, hand"
GI "sky" **n-** **-r**

PWS *li (di)* "head", PWS *ti* "head", "roofing straw" **Sumerian** *rín* "to shine" ?
PWS *ni* "world", PWS *g̱i* "world, sky"
PWS *ti* "black"
PWN *DIM, TIM* "darkness"
PWN *DIM, (DIUM)* "spirit"
PWN *THITHUKA* "night"
Bantu *dim* "masculine"

16 The vast majority of African traditions do not view the Creator as intervening directly into the lives of humans, thus why Africans call on his agents: *abosom, òrìṣà, niombo, ntrw, angels*, etc.
17 Schenkel (1980, col. 14).

Bantu *tiku* "night'
Bantu *dungu* "god" (intelligent)
Bantu *gudu* "sky"
Mande *sì* "night"
Mangbetu *kini* "night"
Mangbetu *kudukudu* "soul"
Mangbetu *kudili* "respect" (noun)
PCS **di, *dib* "person, man"

[The word refers to "head", "spirit", "sky", "rain", "darkness", "masculine" etc. Cf L. Juppiter Pluvius, the Sky Father who rains.]

[The *–n-* indicates "person", the *–r* is demonstrative or plural, or "shine"].

***D = d** ***I = i** ***NG = ĝ** ***I = i**

HEAVEN

Sumerian *u-na* "heaven" (Wanger) "time, night" (Delitzsch)

TU "fire" **u-**
NA "above"

Sumerian *an* "heaven"

PWS *tùà, (tọ̀)* "to roast" (of the sun)
PWS *na* "above"
Or PWS *tu, tua* "water" (rain from sky) ?
PWN *THU, THUA* "water place"
Bantu *tu,mb* "to roast" (compare *utu* "the sun")
"Bantu" *tuna* (273), *tuwana* (256), "sky"
Bantu *to* "river"
Mande *Nala* "God" ?
Mangbetu *anana* "climb tree" (to sky ?)
Khoisan : Naron (C) */am, /gam* "on" ?
Afro-Asiatic : Chad : Hausa (1) *sama* "above", Logone (2) *sama* "rain", Mandara (6) *samaya* "sky" (Greenberg)

***T = #** ***U = u** ***N = n** ***A = a**

RAIN

Sumerian *šèĝ* "rain"

DA, TA "sky" **-ĝ**

PWS *la, (da)* "day", Mano *dẹ* "day", Gio *dẹ* "day"
PWS *ta* "sky, rain, clouds"
PWS *tu, tua* "water", Guang *n-tśu'* "water", Afema *a-su..-e* "water"
PWN *BUDA* "rain, raincloud"
PWN *TU* "cloud", *THU, THUA* "river, waterplace"
Bantu *dé* "sky, cloud"
Bantu *tu,* "cloud ", *du,nde* "clouds", *du,mb* "rain", *donga* "river", *to* "river"
Kele *use* "sky", Ngombe *buse* "sky"
Mande *sã* "rain"
Mangbetu *tu* "pool in the forest" ?
Mangbetu *ro* "sky"
Afro-Asiatic: Chad: Hausa (1) *ša:* "drink", Ngala (2) *še:* "drink", Logone (2) *se* "drink"

***T = š** ***A = e** ***G = g**

SKY **Sumerian** *an* "sky, heaven"

NA "above" **[R]**

PWS *la* "day", Ga *d.ā* "day", *d.á* "always"
PWS *na* "above"
PWN *MUAL* "to shine"
PWN *GULU* "sky"
Bantu *mue* "splendour"
North Guinea (Johnston) *dana* "sky" [*a* + *a* > *ā*]
Mande (Delafosse 1929) *tele-ra* "sun", *lā, dā* "day"
Mangbetu *anana* "climb"
Mangbetu *ro* "sky"

[But see also PWS *man, mal* "flaming", Bamana *mana* "flame, light" (of sky)]

Afro-Asiatic : Chad : Hausa (1) *sama* "above", Logone (2) *sama* "rain" ?

[Initial retroflex *d.* is lost in Sumerian.]

[Greek *ana* "up, on" is probably related].

***D/M = # ?** ***A = a** ***N = n** ***A = a**

WATER **Sumerian** *ra* "deluge"

LA, DA, RA "water"

PWS *la, (dā)* "day" (sky, rain)
Eastern Sudanic: Afitti *araŋga* "rain", Tama *ar* "sky, rain", Dinka *uar* "river", Lotuko *(na)are* "water", Bari *kare* "river"
Central Sudanic: Lendu *ra, arra* "sky"
Mande *la, da* "day"
Mangbetu *zoro* "rain", *ro* "sky"
Nilo-Saharan: Fur *ara* "rain".

[Linear A has RA_2 "water"].

****R = r** ***A = a**

PWS *lu,* *(* *du)* "head"
PWS *lé,(dé, dó)* "one'" (total), with *dó* as common reflex **Sumerian** *dù* "totality"
PCS **d.u* "head" PCS **d.u* "head"
ES Dongola, Kenuzi, Mahas, Gulfan *ur* "head"
CS Madi *oru* "up", Moru *kuru* "up", Lendu *ru(na)* "up"
PWS *lu* "head" *(du, ru);* Yorùbá *o-ri, o-li* "head" (one head)
PWN *TÚI* "head"

YOUNG BULL **Sumerian** *amar* "young bull"

GA "horn"
MA "head", "animal", "mass", "meat"
LU, RU "head"

PWS *lu, (ru, du)* "head"
PWS *lu (du)* "tower"
Gur **dun* "animal" [*r* = *d*]
Yorùbá *maluu* "bull"

See previous example.

[Sumerian has a preprefix *a-* + prefix *ma-* + root *ru, lu* "head, cow" etc.]

***A = a**	***M = m**	***A = a**	***L = r**

<u>CITY [Ur]</u> **Sumerian** *uru* "city"

DU "head" **[R]**
LU "head"

PWS *li, lu* "head", Grebo *lu* "head", Dewoi *du-ru* "head", Gbe *du-ru* "head"
PWN *TÚI* "head"
Bantu *túe* "head"
Ngombe *molu* "head"
Mande *dugu,* M *duhu, dū* "village"
Mangbetu *dru* "head"
PCS **d.u* "head"
ES Dongola, Kenuzi, Mahas, Gulfan *ur* "head"
CN *kuru* "head"

["City" comes from "head", ie "capital".]

***L = r**	***U = u**	***D = #**	***U = u**

<u>CLOUD</u> **Sumerian** *muru*$_9$ "cloud"

BU "abundant"
LU "head"

PWS *lu* "head", Gbe *du-ru* "head" ("top, summit")
PWN *LUND* "clouds"
Bantu *du,nde* "clouds"
Mande (Delafosse) *munda, muna, mūrā* "cloud"
Mangbetu *mundukuba* "cloud"
PCS **bu* "cloud"

[The root is *lu, ru, du* "head"]

***L = r**	***U = u**	***M = m**	***U = u ?**

Tying it all together

The evidence for an African origins thus far provides a better case for the word God than the

PIE *g^hue* "libations, pour" or *$\acute{g}^ha\underset{\frown}{u}$-* "to call, to invoke." However, the libations etymology may be redeemable as will be shown towards the end of this essay. In the meantime we examine our African terms side-by-side with the Indo-European and find interesting commonalities as it regards their form and function.

Indo-European	**African**
Teutonic *Gudo* (Oxford dic.)	PB **gudu, *godo* (PWN *GULU* "sky")
P-Tuet. **ghudho-m* or **ghutó-m.*	*lu/ru/du* "head, sky, up"
P-Germanic **gud-iga-,* (American Heritage dic.);	
PGmc. **guthan*	
OE. *godu*, *godo* neut., *godas*	
**ghu-to* "that which is invoked?"	
Tuetonic *tia, tiw*	PWS *la, (dā)* "day" (sky, rain)
Irish/Gaelic *dia*	*lu/ru/du* "head, sky, up"

We see here that the earliest reconstructed forms of the word in the Germanic branch of IE match (for the most part) the renderings found in the reconstructions for Africa. We mentioned earlier that it is believed that there are no other attestations of *God* outside of Germanic and Sanskrit. This may not be the case. As the *Catholic Encyclopedia* mentioned earlier, in Persian we have ***khoda/khuda*** (خدا); Hindu ***khooda*** (a loan word) meaning "lord, master, king." Knowing the African origin of this term we know why it means "lord" because of the *lu, ru, du* root meaning "head" (Yorùbá *olu, Olori* "lord", Egyptian *wr* "lord", Bantu *kulu* "ancestor, lord, elder, chief"). The form and usage of *khoda* conforms to how it is used in Africa: Proto-Bantu **kodo* "old." Per Wiki:

> The term derives from Middle Iranian *xvatay, xwadag* meaning "lord", "ruler", "master" (written as Parthian *kwdy*, Middle Persian *kwdy*, Sogdian *kwdy*, etc.). It is the Middle Iranian reflex of Avestan *x^va-dhata-* "self-defined; autocrat", an epithet of Ahura Mazda.. The Pashto cognate is *Khwdai* (خدای). Prosaic usage is found for example in the Sassanid title *katak-xvatay* to denote the head of a clan or extended household, or in the title of the 6th century *Khwaday Namag* "Book of lords", from which the tales of Kayanian kings as found in the *Shahnameh* ("Book of kings") derive.

In Persian we have a *k-d* root with subsequent suffixes. We noted earlier that the root of the term deals with "distance" which included "age" and any form of exaltation or elevation: "elder, king, lord, someone who owns, a possessor." We see the same thing play out in the Persian language. The Babylonian word *Gad* (pronounced *Ga^wd*) would also fall under this rubric. *Baal-Ga^wd* was used in the sense of "Lord God."

In actuality, all forms of the African words for God can be found in Indo-European languages, as well as in some Asian languages. Campbell-Dunn (2007: 129) argues that the Maori language derived from the earliest formation of Niger-Congo. It should be of no surprise to find the following as noted by Campbell-Dunn:

> **GOD** Maori *Io* is the Maori Supreme God. In Africa "God" is often identified with the "sky, the heavens" (Johnston 1919- : 30, paragraph 3). PWS has *gi* "air, atmosphere, firmament". We compare Maori *Io* with Lolo *jiko* "sky", which, with consonant loss (as in *io* "flesh") would give *Io*. Comparable examples: Bangi, Ngala, Poto *likolo* "sky". The word is probably also related to the word for "he", PWS *gi* "this", PWS *gu(a)* [*ghwya] > *wo, o, yo,* "he" .In early languages people say "He, the sky rains" etc. Greek *Zeus huei* "Zeus rains".
> ***GHWY = I/Y, *WA = O (*J = Y, *UA = O)**

On page 26 concerning the *ai-* prefix in Maori, Campbell-Dunn notes the following:

> The prefix *ai-* in Maori is found on *aituā* "accident, calamity", *aitu* "sickness, demon", which must be related; (it is also related to *atua* "god, supernatural etc"). Also found on *aitanga* "progeny". Compare Rarotongan *ai-,* "a sign of the plural used with certain classes of nouns" (Savage) : *ai-metua* "the elders", *ai-tupuna* "the ancestors", *ai-tuakana* "the elder brothers", *ai-tuaine* "the elder sisters", *ai-tungane* "male members of woman's family" (used by women)

The root we are concerned with is *a-tua* "god, supernatural." This *tua* is related to our African *lu, ru, du* roots meaning "head, top, apex" (PWN *TÚI* "head"; PWN *TU* "cloud", *THU, THUA* "river, waterplace"). This root is found in the Rarotongan words *ai-tu-puna* "the ancestors," *ai-tua-kana* "the elder brothers," *ai-tua-ine* "the elder sisters," *ai-tu-ngane* "male members of woman's family." Again, we are seeing a pattern with an underlying sense of "distance" and in this case by "age." The head is the upper most part of the body. It is the highest point of the physical body. This metaphor is used time and time again to denote distance in terms of age, societal rank and skill. The highest form of excellence in all things is always attributed to *G-od*: "the Most High."

> The Maori third singular personal pronoun *ia* is from PWS *gi* "this", with added *a,* an article (giving *gia* = **ghwia*). The Polynesian *Io* "Supreme God" (also Rarotongan) is from PWS *gu* "he" + *a* (giving *gua* = **ghwua*). This gives *o, wo, yo* (Ngala), *iyo* etc in various Niger-Congo languages, meaning "he" (also "flesh"). The male Supreme Being was originally African. Compare the biblical expression "The word was made flesh". The possessives *āna, ōna* "of him", "of her" incorporate PWS *na* "this". (ibid, 41).

What Campbell-Dunn is suggesting is that the Polynesian name for God, *Io* "Supreme Being," derived from a PWS root *gua* (see also PWS *gi* "air, atmosphere, firmament".). What's interesting here is the African reconstruction, **ghwua*, which closely matches the PIE **ghua*. What happened is that there was a consonant loss of *g-* in the Polynesian term which left the vowels. I'm not too enthused about this correspondence. I think, that if there is a connection, a connection through rain, sky, day, or the heavens would be stronger: e.g., PWN *KWUL* "be big."

The African roots for *sky* and *clouds* (and even *spirit*) can be found in Indo-European as can be seen in Allan Bomhard's article "The Glottalic Theory of Proto-Indo-European: Consonantism and Its Implications for Nostratic Sound Correspondences."

> Basque **_*ħodai_** > (BN, Z) **_hodei,_** (AN, B, G, R) **_odei,_** (B, G) **_odai,_** (B, R) **_odoi_** 'cloud' (also 'thunder' in B, G, AN, BN, R) ~ Dargwa (Akushi) **_da__** 'wind', Archi **_di_** 'odor, scent' < PEC **_*dwiHV_** 'wind' (NCED _0_).
>
> Basque **_*sohar_** > (c) **_zo(h)ar_** 'clear (sky, weather), to clear' ~ PEC **_*HuIV-n_** 'to clear up (of weather)' > Udi **_muč:ur_** 'clear sky', etc. (NCED 6__) ~ Burushaski **_*_āŋ_** 'to clear (of sky)', **_*_ān_** 'to half-clear (of sky), **_*_āŋ_** 'to stop (raining)' ~ PST **Ć$j* > Burmese 'to stop (rain or sound), to clear (weather)', etc. (ST IV: __) ~ PY **ʔēč-(*ʔēǯ-)* 'clear (of weather)' (SSEJ _89)
>
> PNC **_*h[ă]_ʔa_** > Andi **_hal_** 'steam', Udi **_el-mu_** 'soul, spirit', etc. (NCED_85) ~ PST **_*lă_** 'spirit' > Tibetan **_lha_** 'the gods', etc. (ST III: 2) ~ Na-Dene: Haida (S, M) **__oał_** 'steam'

Compare the above with a few entries from S. A. Starostin's "A concise glossary of Sino-Caucasian" [*Appendix to "Sino-Caucasian"*]:

> PY **xu-r* 'rain' > Ket. uleś5,6, Yug. ures5,6; Kott. *ur*, *ūr*, Koib. *uraš*; Ar. kur (M., Сл., Срсл., Кл.) "rain"; kuraasa (Лоск.) id.; Pump. *ur-ait* (Сл., Срсл., Кл.) "rain". See CCE 297, Werner 2, 338. All languages, besides the simple form **xur,* reflect also the compound **xur-ʔes* 'rain-sky'. The same root is evidently reflected in PY **xura* 'wet, rainy' (see CCE 298, Werner 2, 345). Bur. **qhuró-* 'cloud' > Yas. *xoróŋ,* Hun., Nag. *qhurón.*

Observing these forms for "cloud, sky, day, soul, spirit, wind, and rain," they all conform to the following basic consonant structures found in Africa: *k^h-r*, *q-r*, *h-l*, *h-d*; or without the *k-/h-* prefix giving us: *d*, *l* or *n*. What this exercise is showing us is that there are many formations to the word God. God is just one form of many. There are so many variations of the word because this is a very ancient term that has travelled out of Africa with the many migrations of people that populated the earth over a period of millennia. Because its meanings are so essential to human *beingness*, it has remained with us just like the very words *man* and *fly* spoken of at the beginning of this discussion. Not only does the Germanic form derive from Africa (we argue), so does the Latin and Greek forms for God.

Wiki has been consistent with various interpretations I've read in other literature concerning the word God. They state, in regards to the usage of God in the Bible, that:

> The name God was used to represent Greek Theos, Latin Deus in Bible translations, first in the Gothic translation of the New Testament by Ulfilas. For the etymology of deus, see *dyēus. Greek "θεός" (theos) is unrelated to god, and of uncertain origin. It is often connected with Greek "θέω" (theō), "run", and "θεωρέω" (theoreō), "to look at, to see, to observe", Latin feriae "holidays", fanum "temple", and also Armenian di-k` "gods". Alternative suggestions (e.g. by De Saussure) connect *dhu̯es- "smoke, spirit", attested in Baltic and Germanic words for "spook," and ultimately cognate with Latin fumus "smoke." The earliest attested form of the word is the Mycenaean Greek te-o (plural te-o-i), written in Linear B syllabic script.

If the word "god" was used to replace *Theos* (Greek) and *Deus* (Latin), this would generally mean that more than likely these words had the same or similar meanings. If this is the case here, then this would indicate that the word "god" was synonymous with "sky" and its underlying connotations.

The claim that Greek *Theos* is not related to *God* is, I think, unfounded and an expected result of not looking into African languages.[18] It should be noted that the *-s* ending is a suffix and not a part of the root. Thus, the root of *Theos* is *The*o, *Thea* (goddess) from PIE **dhes-*.[19] However, there is no meaning provided for this root. Mallory & Adams (2006: 410) and many other sources I've consulted do not provide a meaning for this root either. I think further investigation into African languages may provide the answers we are looking for. *Theos* and *Deus*, we argue, derives from the *lu, ru, du* roots in Africa.

We mentioned earlier that the inverse of **gudu, *kodo* is **dOk* for which we get in Bantu *mu-luku, mu-lungu* "God" (Tshiluba *lok-a* "rain"; *luka* "vomit"). This root is comparable to Arabic *Al-Malik* "king, lord, master." Again, we reiterate, that the underlying theme is "distance" and the root (*lu, ru, du*) denotes distance, vastness, height in all planes of existence.

18 The Sanskrit form *dyaus* may be a loan from Greek as the Greeks invaded India starting in 327 BCE.

19 www.etymonline.com

In Ancient Egyptian our root takes on the following familiar form:

> *wr* "great one, great man, **god**, chief, elder" (Budge 170b); *wr* "master"; *wr* "great one"; *wr* "great one, great man, god, chief, elder"; *wr* "great one, title of Osiris" (Faulkner pg. 64); *wr.t* "great one" (of uraeus, of goddess); *wrr.t* "crown"

The Egyptian word *wr* is built off an ancient ***l*** root meaning "to have, to own, the owner of..." which is translated as "lord, master, God" (someone of "high" rank who has the power to command; has power over life and death; someone of great skill). This *l* root in Yorùbá is realized as an *n* when the initial vowel of the noun is /i-/. When this happens the vowel prefix /o-/ is used: e.g., *Ifá* (the Yorùbá divination system) > *Onifá* (the diviner: *olu+ifa* : l>n); *Iyì* (dignity) > *oníyì* (the man of dignity). In Bantu the word *ini* means "master, owner" (Bantu (Meinhof) *γini* "owner") and is at the heart of Kiswahili *bwana* "master" (Egyptian *nb* "lord, master" by way of metathesis). In Yorùbá *Olú* is at the heart of *Olúwa* "lord, master," *Olúwo* "head of the Osugbo, the council of chiefs, head priest of Orúnmilá," *Orúwo*[20] "head" (Ijebu dialect). *Oluwo* and *Oruwo* is Egyptian *wr* by way of metathesis. *Wr* is reflected in the Tigrigna language as *wärä "famous."* In Kiswahili-Bantu we have *waria* "a skilled person, an expert, a capable person, a champion, a master at his work, a blacksmith, metal worker, smithing."

This underlying sense of "distance" can be seen in the following African words that have the same shape of the word God.

> Northwest Zambezi *suku, kucu, sika** "long", Cameroons-Cross River *kuri**, Wu-Nyamwezi *gulu** "long", South Sierra Leone *şul* "long" [Alternation of *l/r/d*]. Mande *kunu* "long" (garment)
> Afro-Asiatic: Chad: Podokwo (3) *guda,* Cushitic: Galla (E) *guda* "many"

Over and over again we are seeing the same themes being expressed with the same cluster of consonants. These consonant clusters belong to an associative field of meaning where each concept is associated with a similar concept under an overall "theme." For example, the *sky* is where *rain* comes from. Thus *rain* and *sky* are synonymous. Because the sky is at a far *distance* from the human being on the ground, the sky is associated with "height, tallness, length, remoteness." Because we use the same word for the concepts of *sky* and *top*, we also use it to represent our *heads* as it is the *upper most part* of our body. Thus, the same word for *head* is the same word for "sky, upper, top." After a period of time, there has to be some differentiation between these lexical items to distinguish their different contexts. Therefore, naturally, the vowels begin to change to discriminate one context from another.

Words belong to never-ending chain sequences, to phrases, sentences, contexts to the fabric of the entire language (Lord 1966: 241). Words have no meaning until they become joined together in a linguistic whole. As long as there is no clash of context, this range of associations can coexist (like in the case of homophones). Whenever homophones exist, the homophones will acquire different spellings wherever possible (i.e., person—parson; soul—sole; maze—maize; bell—belle). When homonyms threaten to arise, the two forms will diverge phonetically or morphologically (i.e., cloth—clothe; brothers—brethren; shade—shadow). A word will either adjust itself dynamically in a field or be rejected. Meanings build up composite meanings in a larger "field of tension." This is exactly the case with our term that has come down to us as God. The reason why Indo-Europeanists only recognize one line of retention in Germanic

20 Is cognate with Middle Egyptian *hrw* "upper part, top." Also cognate with Bantu *kulu* "top, upper part, high, sky, heaven."

(maybe two if you count Sanskrit) is because God is only one form of many that survived in Indo-European: they do not know the other related forms. There are other variations:

Greek:	*the-os*	"god"
Greek:	*zeus*	"a god who shoots thunderbolts"
Latin:	*deu-s*	"god"
Armenian:	*di-k*	"gods"
Persian:	*khooda/khudu*	"lord"
Teutonic:	*gudo*	"god"
Old English:	*gudo, godo*	"god"
German:	*gott*	"god"
P.Gmc:	**guth-an/*guđán*	"god"
Basque:	*yinko*	"god"
Eurasiatic:	**gwVrV*	"god"
Sardinian	*julus, jolos*	"god"

As we saw earlier, these forms and their variations are present for the words "day, rain, clouds and sky." These are all consistent with their African counterparts for which we argue they ultimately derived. It is based on this evidence (linguistic and anthropological) that I cannot accept the common meaning of God to mean "that which is invoked." I would, however, like to propose a compromise to the proposal of God = libations, which I think is on more solid grounds.

God = Libations = Water

We have already connected the word God (*g-d* root) and words for god with "the sky" and "rain." It is because of this association that I find the connection between *God* and *libations* tenable. The concept of libations (**g^{h}ue, hu*) may have been a tertiary meaning that originally derived from *rain*. In the Egyptian language, we again, have the *k-r* root in regards to pouring: *ḫr* "to pour out, to eject fluid." Compare with *ẖd* "stream," *ẖdw* "a liquid." A related and alternate term in Egyptian is *gr* "stream": *r/l/d* alternation.

Libations in African traditions act as a fructifying agent for ancestors on the other side: the underworld (ancestral realm). Just as the Creator "pours libations" (rain) onto the earth to sustain the living, human beings pour libations on the ground to sustain the doubles of the ancestors who are dead in this realm, but living in the spiritual community *underground*. The spirit double (*ena*) is not eternal and must be nourished with water and animal sacrifices in order to live (Mutwa 1964, Kajangu 2005, Imhotep 2011b).

Suffice it to say that there is a stronger connection between the word *God* and *libations* through "the sky" and "rain" more so than "sacrifice" and "to invoke/to call." If these concepts are connected, I argue that the idea of "pouring" is not the sense being evoked by this term, but the actual liquid (water) being poured. When we consult Africa in times like this, there is no need for fanciful etymologies. No matter where we turn, water is closely related to the term God and gods.

Water is a clear, pure, shapeless, odorless entity that sustains life and from which all life emerged. These are the ideas that the ancient Africans probably had in mind when they associated these words with the r/l/d roots and their variations with what we know as God. The ancient Africans believed God to be an entity that has always *been* and will always *be*. No matter the challenge to water's beingness, it will only change form (liquid, solid or gas) and maintain its essential character (H_2O). The ancient Africans believed the Creator to operate in this manner: it is an infinite sea of matter perpetually evolving within itself, but still keeping its essential character (Yorùbá *ìwà* "character, existence, life, manner of being, manner of existence").

In practically all African traditions, the Creator is seen as existing in a boundless void of matter characteristic of liquid. This is seen in ancient Egypt as the *Nwn* and in the Bible as "waters of the void" in Genesis. It is this far remote, infinite, vast, boundless substance that gave birth to all life in the universe and that is what the ancients equated as what we know now as God. It is my argument that to understand God, we must understand water (from the sky) and I think that has been demonstrated in this work.

Conclusion

In summary, the word God deals with two primary conceptualizations: *distance* and *water*. The r/l/d root has a primary meaning of "sky, heavens, rain, top, upper, height, age." These forms give way to secondary meanings of "ownership, lordship, chiefs, kings, elders, and ancestors" (those in relatively high social positions). God is a title of "rank" and is why the kings of Africa are "divine" kings. Kings are believed to be intermediaries between the ancestors and the community at large. They are also the incarnation of an earlier king (or founding father) for which he shares a royal bloodline. The Christian notion that African kings are "gods," as in super-human beings, is false and is based on an ignorance of African languages and customs.

A king is a "god" (*mukulu*) because he is the *highest ranked* person in the society. Africans have many "gods" because a god is an "ancestor or elder." Every community has thousands of "gods" who lived "before" those currently living now. Because they lived before us in the community, and it is their discoveries that allow the community to thrive currently, they are "ranked higher" (given high accolades) than those in the community living now (in wisdom and in age). Since all living human beings trace their lineage all the way back to God, God is our *primary* "ancestor." Elders in the community are also "gods" (*kulu*). Their "age" and wisdom provides them with a special status in African societies. They have a proven track record of service and have made major contributions to the expansion and sustaining of the community. For this they are given a *high* status and title. Without understanding why God is God, one will never get to the more meaningful understanding the ancient Africans were conveying by the usage of this term.

Allah and *El* are only the high gods of Islam and Christianity, respectively, because the meanings literally mean "most high." There is nothing spectacular about these names. The ongoing dispute between Christians and Muslims to whether *Eloh* or *Allah* is the "one" and only true god is based on an ignorance of Africa, its customs and philosophy: they are the same god, same word from the same origins in Africa. All of the Biblical names for God are indigenous to West Africa.

Hebrew		**Yorùbá**	
'el	Divine being	*Elu/Olu*	God
'eloah	God	*Oluwa* (-l-w)	Lord, master
'el šadday	God Almighty	**Jukun** *Tsido*	God

‘el ‘el^{e}*y-o*^{w}*n*	God Most High	**Ibibio** *Abasi Enyon*	The Supreme God
‘el^{e}*-yo*^{w}*n*	Topmost	*enyon*	“peak”
		Fon *Yehwe*	“spirit, the power in lightning and thunder”
Yahweh	God	**Ewe** *Yeve* “spirit” and **Gun** *Yihwe, Yehwe*	“God.”

The cultures of the Abrahamic traditions used a “title,” a “description” and made it a *proper name*. Because they made it a proper name, the essence of its “meaning” was lost among practitioners and it has caused much confusion, even to this day.

(Table Footnotes)

1 Herodotos 2: 50. See the discussion in Martin Bernal, *Black Athena* Vol. 1, 1987, 98–101.

2 Griffin (1986, 4).

ADDENDUM: African Origins of the Word God

Since the original writing of this essay, I have come across some additional information that might aid in moving this discussion forward. The previous hypothesis in *Chapter 3.1* is that the word "God" derives from a root that came to mean "sky, above, top, head" with a possible derived meaning of "rain." In this addendum, I would like to suggest a different etymology, but one that ultimately derives from the same African root as suggested in *Chapter 3.1.*

The Name of God in Gothic

Scholars believe that the popularity of the word "god" in the Western world is the result of the Bible entries for "god" given by Ulfilas (bishop, missionary and bible translator; 311—382 C.E., Constantinople) who invented the Gothic alphabet. During the third century, the Goths lived on the northeast border of the Roman Empire, in what is now Ukraine, Bulgaria and Romania. At the age of 30 Ulfilas was supposedly sent on an embassy to the Roman emperor and was consecrated (341) bishop of the Gothic Christians by Eusebius of Nicomedia, bishop of Constantinople, an Arian (i.e., a follower of the heretical doctrine that the Son was neither equal with God the Father nor eternal). Because of persecution by the Gothic ruler, Ulfilas and his converts —after working for seven years among the Goths north of the Danube—migrated to Moesia and settled near *Nicopolis ad Istrum* in modern northern Bulgaria. There, Ulfilas translated the Bible from Greek into the Gothic language spoken by the Eastern Germanic, or Gothic Tribes.

The word for "god" in the Gothic text is *gþ* (also *goþ*[1]), *gþs,* and *gþa* (Hatto, 1944: 248). The [þ] sound is that of /θ/ in Greek (/θ/ = /th/ as in "through"). Because of the monotheistic nature of Christian doctrine, the label "god" had two applications: the "true" *god* and the "false" *gods*. The "false" gods occur in the text as *-guda, -gude* or *-gudam* (Hatto, ibid.). The etymology given for this term is the same as those argued by the sources in *Chapter 3.1* (i.e., "to pour"). However, I reject this suggestion given the fact that in the Gothic language, the word for "to pour" is *giutan* (from P.Ger. **ghud*) and this is not the term used in the Gothic Bible for "god." As noted in the previous chapter, the idea of "to invoke" was also suggested by many sources and this I reject also. The word for "to call" in Gothic is *haitan*. Again, this in no way resembles *gþ* or *gþa.*

1 The word *goþ* is the neuter form and used pre-eminently for 'heathen god', and the masculine *guþ* is used mostly for 'God'.

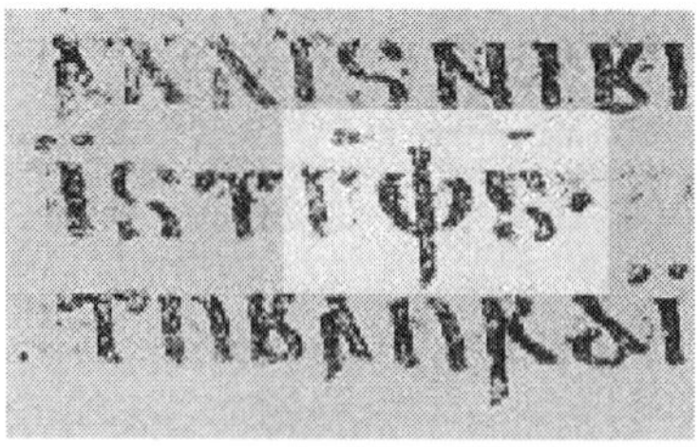

Earliest attestation of the Germanic word in the 6th century Codex Argenteus (Mt 5:34)

In this addendum, we posit that the word "god" derives from the same root as the word "good" in modern English. The word "good" in Gothic is *gōþs*. The entry in Rajki (2004) is:

> *goths* (god-) [akin to Eng *good*]: well. Deriv. *godei* nicety. Comp. *gastigodei* hospitality, *gastigoths* hospitable, *godakunds* of noble birth.

The Gothic *gōþs* is similar in shape to Gothic *guþs* "god." Given that in many of the transliterations for "god" in the Gothic Bible only had the *gþ* form (with no vowel) and *goþ*, it leaves room for speculation on what were the actual idea(s) that the author had in mind for these consonant clusters. If the Goths, prior to Christianity, were 'polytheistic' and used the word *goþ* to refer to the 'heathen god', then this form would be the original by which they articulated their conceptualization of "God." What is interesting is that in Balg's dictionary (1887: 144) it states that the phrase "good-bye" is a contraction of "God be by you." The *Online Etymological Dictionary* (OED) reaffirms this meaning but gives "God be with ye" for which Balg also suggests, but feels that the evidence for "God be by you" is stronger. This would hint that "god" is a variant of "good." The following section provides the proposed etymologies for the word "good" in Indo-European languages. We will then follow-up with our own proposed etymologies rooted in African languages.

Etymology of "good"

Practically all dictionaries reject the notion that the word ***god*** derives from the same root as ***good***. I think, however, that this position should be reconsidered given the African evidence that is to follow. The *Online Etymological Dictionary* (OED) provides the following etymology for "good":

> **Good** (adj.): Old English *god* (with a long "o") "virtuous; desirable; valid; considerable," probably originally "having the right or desirable quality," from Proto-Germanic **gothaz* (cf. Old Norse *goðr*, Dutch *goed*, Old High German *guot*, German *gut*, Gothic *goþs*), originally "fit, adequate, belonging together," from PIE root **ghedh-* "to unite, be associated, suitable" (cf. Old Church Slavonic *godu* "pleasing time," Russian *godnyi* "fit, suitable," Old English *gædrian* "to gather, to take up together"). As an expression of satisfaction, from early 15c.; of children, "well-behaved," by 1690s.

The phonemes are a definite match and the notion that God is "virtuous, desirable, valid, etc.," is not far-reaching. However, I do not posit the etymology here based on that definition, but the proposed Proto-Germanic meanings of "fit, adequate, belonging together (< PIE **ghedh* "to unite, be associated, suitable"). The TOB database paints a more detailed picture and has the following reconstructions:

> Proto-IE: **ghādh-*

Meaning: **good, to be good, to fit**
Slavic: * *god iti* * *god ъ*, * *gādātī*
Baltic:**gõd-a- c.*, **gõd-â- vb.*; **gãd-, gãd-â- vb.*, **gãd-a- c*[2]
Germanic:**gōd-a-* adj., **gad-a-* vb., *-ō-* vb.

Proto-Germanic: **gōda-*, **gadan-*, *-ōn-* vb. "good"; Gothic: *gōɵ*-s, *gōd*-s (a) `good, kind, beautiful'; {*gadiliŋgs* 'Vetter'; Old Norse: *gōδ-r* `gut'; Run. Norw *godagas;* Norwegian: *god;* Swedish: *god;* Danish: *god;* Old English: *gōd;* English: *good;* Old Frisian: *gōd* 'good'; *gada* 'unite', *gadia* 'dass.; make them fit, pacify, confirm'; Old Saxon: *gōd* 'good'; gegada 'comrade, husband'; *gaduling* 'relative'; Middle Dutch: *goet;* Dutch: *goed;* Old Franconian: *guot;* Old High German: *guot* (8th century); Middle High German: *guot* 'proficient, well, good, etc.'; German: *gut*

Russ. meaning: добрый, добро, годиться "kind, good, fit, suitable"
References: WP I 531 f

Number: 628
Root: *ghedh-* , *ghodh-*
English meaning: to join, make a bond
German meaning: `unite, be closely linked, matching '**; älter **'embrace`, fixed or stick together'
Material: Ai. *gadhya* - H `hold '; *gadhita-ā-h* `clipped ', *pari-gadhita-h* `clasps' (of sexual union);

afries. *gadia* `unite', mnd. *gaden* (*\*gadōn*) `fit, fallen, spouses', ahd. *bigatōn*, mhd. *gaten*, *gegaten* intr. `come together, so that it matches', trans. `same, joined, alike, bring together', refl. `to fit', ahd. *gi-gat* `fit', as. *gi-gado* `peer', ags. (ge)*gada* `mate, husband', nhd. Gatte; *got. gadiliggs* `cousin', as. *gaduling* `relative', ags. *gædeling* `comrad', ahd. *gatulinc*, *gatilinc* `relative, cousin, friend'; ags. *geador*, *tō gædere* (engl. together) `zusammen', afries. *gadur*, mnd. *gader,* mhd.*gater* ds., ags. *gadrian*, *gæd*(e)*rian* (engl. gather) `collect', afries. *gaderia*, mnd. *gad*(d)*eren* ds., mhd. *vergatern* `unite', nhd. *vergattern* ds.; dazu vermutlich auch ahd. *gataro*, nhd. *Gatter* (umgelautet mhd. *geter*, nhd. *Gitter*), aschwed. *gadder*, mnd. *gaddere* `grid/ mesh'; with lengthened grade: goth. *gōþs*, aisl *gōðr*, OE *god* , OHG *guot* , NHG *good* (Germanic **gōða-* `match '); aisl. *gōða* `make good ', etc.

OCS. *godъ* `time, right time ', *godina* `ὥρα ' godьnъ `complacent ', russ. *godnyj* `fit ', OCS. *goditi* u `like ', Russian-ksl. *goditi* ds., ksl. *ugoda* `pleasure ' russ. *výgoda* `advantage ', OCS. *negodovati* be 'unwilling', iter. OCS. *ugoždo* , *ugožditi* `make it, fairly pleased '(etc. Berneker 317 f, where also lit the poln loanwords. *gãdas* `union ', *gãdytis* `occur, make ', etc.).

This perhaps lit. dial. *guodas* , lett *guods* `honor, glory, dignity, courtesy, festivity, feast '; however, lett *Gad* , *sagāds* 'stock, I purchased', *gādāt* `make', probably borrowed from Russ. here (see Van Windekens Lexique 32) toch. AB *-katk*, softened A *kāck-*, B *kācc-*`enjoy '(mnd see above *gaden* `like '); otherwise Pedersen Toch. 172.

References: WP. I, 531 ff, Trautmann, 74, 218 Feist
See also: p under *-ghend* .
Pages: 423-424

As we can see here, the **g-d* root has the following connotations: "unite, together, join, make

2 Proto-Baltic: **gõd-a-* c., **gõd-â-* vb.; **gãd-, gãd-â-* vb., **gãd-a-* c. "respect, care"; Lithuanian: *gōdṓti* (žem.) 'honor', *gōdà* 'worry, grief, sorrow', *gōdṓti* ''(to) think, consider, considerate, beautiful, have compassion', dial. *gõsti*-s, at=si=*gõsti* ''remember to come back to him, come on something'; *guõda-s* 'honor, worship, entertainment', *guodṓti* 'honor', *gúosti* 'comfort, care about sth, care, can be set to be sth; Lettish: *gùods* 'honor, glory/fame', *gùodât* (-ãju), *guodêt* (-ẽju), *guodît* (-īju) 'protect, honor, cherish', *gãdât*, *gâdât* ' thinking, to come to terms search; ensure , endeavor, try'; *gàds* 'the Anxious, stock'

a bond, mate/husband (marriage *union*), relative, cousin (from uniting sexually, family ties), friend (close *bond*), collect, clasp, embrace, stand or stick together, fix(ed), honor, glory, dignity, same, match, (a)like, festivity, time, right, think, care, cherish, protect and hold." These meanings have an underlying sense of "order, alignment, arrangement, collecting and unifying." When things are in "order," then all things are "good." When all the pieces are put "together"; when there is relative "unity"; when "family" and "friends" come "together" (ideally), then all things are "good."

God, Tying Things Together and Putting Things in Order

Chapter 8 of this volume goes into more details about the linguistic connections to this *g-d* root as it regards *ropes*, but it can be said here that these terms are present in the African languages and are also associated with "God." The underlying theme is "uniting, order" and reflexes in Proto-Bantu (PB) are:

> **PB **túng*** "put through; thread on string; plait; sew; tie up; build; close (in)
> **túngo* "twig used for strimping fish"
> **túngudu* "lead"
> **túngudu/*kúngudu* "walk in single file"
> **túung* "build"
> **tunga* "country, village"
>
> **PB **túng*** "tie up"
> **túnged* "untie"
> **túngé* "prisoner, hostage"
> **kúng* "gather up, assemble, tie up"
>
> **PB **kúnd*** "tie knot"
> **kúndò* "knot"
> **kúndò* "fist, knock" (Zone J)
> **púnd* "fold, tie knot"
> **pínd* "tie knot"

Here we have the root with skeletal variations: **t-g*, **k-g* and **k-d*. Another variation is introduced as **p-d*. The underlying theme is just like in our IE examples with the **g-d* (PB **k-d*) root. This root is reflected in the following Proto-Bantu terms from the BLR3 (Bantu Language Reconstruction) database:

> **dùng* "join by tying"; **dùng* "season food"; **dùngò* "joint, genou"; **dùngé* "seasoning; seasoned food"[3]; **dùngò* "knee" (from the concept of bending); **jùng* "cure fracture" (in other words, join fracture together); **dùng* "be straight, right, put straight, fitting, adjust"

This root is cognate with PIE **ghedh,* but as we can see the phonemes are reversed. This reversal can be seen in PIE **yug* "to join, union, yoke," PIE **leg-* "to pick together, gather, collect"; Egyptian *ʿrḳ* 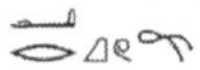 "bind," *ȝk* "bind" (*r* = *ȝ*). The /l/ and /d/ sounds appear to interchange in PIE. We can observe another word for "good" in IE from the TOB database to confirm:

---

3 The word for "seasoning" may come from the notion of "combining" or "mixing" spices. I am not quite sure the reference in this case.

PIE	**bhil-*	"good, descent"	(b-l)
PIE	**dhAbh-*	"appropriate, good"	(d-b)
PIE	**bhAd-*	"good"	(b-d)
PIE	**bher-*	"good, valiant"	(b-r)
PIE	**b(h)Alg(h)-*	"honorable, good"	(b-l-g)
PIE	**noib(h)-*	"good, holy"	(n-b)
PIE	**lep-, *lēp-*	"nice, good"	(l-p)
PIE	**wel-*	"good, best"	(w-l)

As we can see, there is metathesis going on here and the /l/, /d/ and /n/ interchange as well. We also have a sound change of the labials: p > b > w. Therefore, as it regards **g-d* "god," a *d-g* form of the word from Africa is within historical plausibility.[4]

As it regards this notion of "tying, binding," see also in Egyptian *krj*  "to be restrained, caged"; *krj*  "prison." Compare to Sumerian *kad* "tie, gather"; PB **kand* "bind." The Proto-Bantu /l/ is realized as /d/. This kind of reversal is quite common. We can take for instance PCS **nanga* "ground"; PCS **ngala* "ground." The /l/ in the final position of example 2 becomes /n/ in initial position of example 1. This provides evidence of free-word-order spoken of in Campbell-Dunn (2009a, 2009b) for early Kongo-Saharan languages. Lord (1966: 92) also notes that the consonants [l] and [r] are the most frequently 'metathesised' consonants. Metathesis, says Lord, is a primitive feature belonging very much to the infancy of language, a time when the position of vowels and consonants were not fixed. I believe metathesis and free-word-order are both at play in many of these examples as we posit a monosyllabic root with an accompanying affix.

In ciLuba we have *lunga* "bind, connect"; "something folding on itself, join, make ends meet"; "weaving, making chains" (*diLunga, llunga, lungakaja; ndungabilema* "person who repairs, a mender, repairer, doctor, shoemaker, therapist, mechanic"). Other forms in ciLuba-Bantu are reflected as: *-luka* "braiding, weaving" (der. *-lukila*); *banda* "braid"; *ciluka* "network"; *joba* "braid"; *lukakaja* "form projects, plan"; *-lukakanangana* "be interspersed, be complex"; *-lukulula* "repair" (e.g., "a thread"); *nunga* "braid."[5] Note also PB **-dùk-* "plait, braid." Compare that with ciLuba *-tenga* "tie, bind"; *ntèngelu* "way or means of linking the chevrons on the rooftop"; *-tènga* "attach by tightening." All of these terms have to deal with "union" or "collecting" of some sort.

The terms above are variants of the very title of this book, *aaluja* (Egyptian *rwḏ* ), which expands our understanding of the attributes of the divine. In ciLuba we have: *aaluja/ aalwija* "restore, replace what had been removed or deleted"; *aaluka* "return, retrace (one's steps)"; *aaluja* "make, provide, to retrace one's steps, refer to the place of origin"; *-aalukija* "to think, reflect, consider, to render, to make"; *dyalukija* "reference, reaction, feedback"; *Aaluja* is related to the term *-aalabula* "change, modify, alter, return, extend, open"; *-aalabuka* "changed, alter, be modified, turn back, withdraw"; *aalula* "change (of place, position, shape), transformation, metamorphosis"; *-longolola* "repair, store with care, arrange methodically";

4 I am in agreement with Campbell-Dunn (2006b)—*Comparative Linguistics: Indo-European and Niger-Congo*—that Indo-European derives from Kongo-Saharan languages. Many Nostratocists argue that IE derives from Afro-Asiatic or comes from a common ancestor. See for instance, Allan R. Bomhard, (1984), *Toward Proto-Nostratic: A new approach to the comparison of Proto-Indo-European and Proto-Afroasiatic* (Amsterdam: John Benjamins Publishing Company). Either way it goes, the evidence points to an African origin, which would explain the doublets in Indo-European and Kongo-Saharan for example.

5 CiLuba suffixes include the following: -ij, -ik, -am, -at, -in, -ibu, -ish, -ulul, -il, -angan, -akaj, -akan, -akanangan.

-longa "reward, give tip; *-longa* "arrange, put in order"; *bulongolodi* "administration, management"; *cilongolwelu* "garage"; *dilongolola* "preparation, preparing"; *ndongolwelu* "how to govern, how to arrange, arrangement, organization." Here we get a sense that the root not only deals with "repairing, restoring," but also with "organizing, putting something in its proper order and place."

The PIE root meaning "fit" also holds the meaning of "to be in harmony, to agree." In order to agree, things must be put in "order"; all parts must be properly "linked" in a logical way. This is at the heart of the root of this term. The primary root—like our "sky, head, top" examples given previously in essay 3.1—derives from an *-l-* or *-r-* root. This root is reflected in ciLuba-Bantu as ***eela*** "introduce, put/set/make, push"; "dispose, arrange, lay, apply, put out, place." This root is reflected in the following PB forms:

> PB **dòng* "heap up; arrange; pack up"; **dòngid* "pack carefully"; *dòngici* "teach"; **dòng* "speak, teach"; **dòngò* "line, row"; **dòngò* "lineage, kingship, clan, tribe, brother"; **dòngùd* "go ahead, preceded, guide"; **dòngùdi* "leader, guide"; **dòngò* "twin"; **dòng* "arrange"; **dòòngò* "line of objects"; **dùng* "be straight, put straight, right, be fitting, adjust"; **jòng* "add to."

The **d-g* root here has all of the connotations given for the PIE **g-d* roots given above with added derivations which include "kingship, speech, addition, guiding, teaching, packing[6] and arranging." The "lineage" aspect gives us the sense of "family," also present in the IE reconstructions. This sense of family is reflected in PB **túngá* "country, village" (ciLuba *musoko, diTunga* "village"; *ciMenga, ciHunda* "large collection of, metropolis"). Remember that our initial Bantu reflexes had to deal with "tying knots" and "ropes."

Christopher Ehret, in his book *The Civilizations of Africa* (2002), provides insights into how the concepts above are related. In describing the Bantu conceptualization of community, Ehret notes that:

> The people in such a village saw themselves as part of a mutually recognized wider grouping of many villages, which they called **-lungu*. This word derives from a proto-Bantu verb, **-lung-*, meaning "to join by tying." The metaphor encoded in the word shows that even though the earliest Bantu people based their rights in the local village community on kinship, they saw their wider society or ethnicity as a joining together of separate kin groups—as something mutually entered rather than imposed by birth. (Ehret, 2002: 111-112)

We find the same associations in the ancient Egyptian language with the word *mr* "to tie, to bind, fasten, be bound, join, collect, connect, bundle." It has a by-form: *mꜣꜥ* "rope" (at front of ship), *mꜣꜥ.t* "towing rope" (r>ꜣ). The same root is used for the word "*mꜣꜥ* "village." These things are important to keep in mind because in Bantu the same root is used in the name for "God."

> **Note 5**: CS 711; Proto-Bantu **-dung-* "to become fitting, straight, right"; Southern Kaskazi **-lungu* "God"; e.g., Nyanja *mlungu*, "god" pl. *achimlungu* "gods" *umlungo* "divinity"; Kikuyu n. *mũrungu*; Shambala *mulungu* "god"; Ngulu *mulungu* "god"; Zigula *mulungu* "god"; Kamba *mulungu* "god"; Itumba *mulungu*; god"; Kondoa/Solwe *mulungu* "god"; Yao *mulungu* "god"; Gindo *mulungu* "god"; Ganji *mulungu* "god"; Hehe *mulungu* "god"; Ziráha *mulungu* "god"; Nkwifiya *mulungu* "god"; Ndunda *mulungu* "god"; Kwenye *mulungu* "god"; Bena *mulungu* "god"; Sango/Lori *mulungu* "god"; Bunga *mulungu* "god"; Sukuma *mulungu* "god"; Turu *mulungu* "god." Ehret,

6 Compare with ChiShona *-rong-a* "arrange"; Efik *döny* "pack, load."

An African Classical Age, 166–7; Nurse and Hinnebusch, *Swahili and Sabaki*, 620.

Note that these words above have the same consonant cluster as the word "good" in Indo-European: IE **ghedh* (g-d), PB **-dung-* (d-g), just deaspirated and metathesised. The note above is from *Chapter 3* of Rhonda Gonzales' work *Societies, Religion and History: Central East Tanzanians and the World They Created, c200 BCE – 1800 CE* (2008).[7] The work focuses on the Ruvu-Bantu people of Tanzania. For Gonzales, "God", as expressed by the root *-lungu-*, means "the one who makes things straight, right and fitting." As it concerns the root she adds that, "Such an underlying verb intimates that **Mulungu* conveyed the idea of a force responsible for ordering things in a "right or good way" (Gonzales, 2008: 8, Ch.3). Here we are reintroduced to the term "good." These are the same connotations that we posit for the name God. The word *Mulungu* is reflected in the Arabic language in one of its epithets for God: *Al-Malik* "king, lord, master."[8] Therefore, **God** is a polysemous term that means:

> GOD = "the one who arranges, who makes things straight, right and fitting, the architect, the designer, the spirit that holds/binds all things together, the one who establishes order, our teacher, our guide; the one who is ONE, alike, matches; the one worthy of honor, dignity and glory; our comforter (friend, companion), the one who treats you like family, our father; our mender, repairer; our doctor and healer (the one who redresses wounds, sews on stitches); the cosmic weaver who connects all things; the infinite one; king, lord and master."

These variations for God make more sense than the forced definition of "to pour libations" or "the one invoked."[9] In this definition we do not have much, if any, phonological difficulties and we don't have to assume a loan into IE. Ironically, this root is the same root that would give us the previous suggestions in the original paper: ***eela*** "introduce, put/set/make, push"; "dispose, arrange, lay, apply, put out, place"; ***eela*** (*-le-*) "send away, or exit from the self (a sound, an idea, word, object...), transmit, show, express, speak." With the root *eela* also meaning "make" and "express," the word "God" (Mulungu, MuTúngo, Itongo, MuKúndò, MuTúngudu, ciTanga(mane), Al-Malik, God, Godo, Gudu, Gueno, Kulu, Nkulu, nGole) is simply a word for "Creator" (one who makes, produces, arranges). Interestingly, the PIE has the *k-r* variations dealing with "make" and "productions."

> Proto-IE: **k(ʷ)Ar(ə)-*
> Nostratic etymology: **Meaning: to make**
> Old Indian: *karóti*, imp. *kuru*, *kr̥ṇóti* \`to do, make', ptc. *kr̥tá-*; *kará-* \`doing, making', m. \`hand; elephant's trunk'; *kāra-* \`making, doing', m. \`act, action'; *kárman-* n. \`act, action, performance'
> Avestan: *kərənaoiti* \`makes, executes, preparing, doing'; *čarā* \`resources, tools', *čāra* \`resources, help, list'
> Other Iranian: NPers *čār* \`Mittel'
> Slavic: **kъrčь(jь)*

---

7 The full book can be read online here: http://www.gutenberg-e.org/gonzales/ (retrieved October 29, 2012).

8 See discuss in *Chapter 3.1* on this point.

9 However, in ciLuba-Bantu we have the *mutèndu* <*-tènda* "scream her pain, cry, whine; make noise, shout, sing, **INVOKE**"; *mitèndu* > *kudìila mitèndu* "make a meal in honor of the spirits for a favor received"; -à/-a *mitèndu* "given as an offering to the spirits"; *kwimbila muntu mitèndu* "exalt someone by citing their names of the spirit"; *mutèndù* "small gourd in which hemp is smoked"; *cilèwu* ≈ *cilòwa* "calabash" (to pour libations out?). We will see below how the *g-d* root becomes *d̲-d* > *t-d*, thus corresponding to *-tènda* (t-d) above. This may lend credence to the "invoke" or "libations" argument. However, I think the evidence for "good" is stronger.

Baltic: *kur̂- vb. tr.
Celtic: OIr *cruth* `shape, form, build', MIr *creth* `seal'; Cymr *paraf* `effecting, procure', inf. *peri*, 3 sg. prt. peris; *pybyr* `active'; *prydu* `tight', *prydydd* `poet'; *pryd* `appearance', Corn *pery* `you will make'
Russ. meaning: делать, творить "to do, to make"
References: WP I 517 f

These connections cannot be the result of chance. The *k-r* root for "God" is found in the Egyptian language: *k3k3*  "God"; Luvale Bantu: *kaka* "ancestor, elder, God"; Luvale-Bantu: *kaka* (*yetu*) "our god" (*yetu* = our); Kiswahili: *kaka* "an elder relative, elder brother, brother"; IsiZulu: *NkuluNkulu* "God." The word *ʿnẖ* may be a variation of this root: *ʿnẖ*  (Bantu *nganga*) "life personified, the name of a god" (Budge 125A).

God, Wholeness and Perfection

Fu-Kiau (2001) informs us of a name for God among the Bakongo of Central Africa whose name is *Kalûnga* "the completely complete being all by himself." The root of this name is *-lunga-* "complete, perfect."[10] It is meant, in part, that *Kalûnga* is "everything and all things at once"; the totality of existence. A reflex exists in Egyptian as:

	*ʿrḳ* to complete
	*ʿrḳ* the end, limit

One can argue then that God can also mean "the complete one; the perfect one, the completely complete being all by Himself, the Alpha and the Omega (the end)." This root is also reflected in the word *3ẖ*(t)  "spirit, glory, splendor." Remember that our PIE root **g-d* also means "glory, honor" [*guodas*, lett *guods* `honor, glory, dignity, courtesy, festivity, feast'[11]]. We also note in Egyptian  *3ẖw* "benefactions, **good**, excellent things, **glorifications**, ability, mastery"; *3ẖw* "power (of god/spirit) [Wb I 15], magic, magical words, useful knowledge, master"; *3ẖ* "spirit, successful, **right**, be beneficial, useful, profitable, **glorious one**, **good**, beneficial, advantageous, **fame**, worthy of, devoted to, to please." Compare to Greek *koîlu* "good" (Mallory & Adams, 2006: 195)

All of these terms are appropriate and in alignment with the common understandings of this notion of "God." Notice in Egyptian: *3ẖ* "good" and "devoted to." This is in combination with the meanings of "spirit, glorious one, right, beneficial." Compare to ciLuba *-lenga* "beautiful, good, to improve, be good, be beautiful, be advantageous, be at peace, be sure" (PB *-dɔ̄ng- "good, beautiful"; Sumerian *dug* "be good" [verb])[12]; *-lengele* "good, nice, pleasant, beautiful,

---

10 See my article "Egypt in its African Context: Note 2" (2012) for the full range of meanings for the name *Kalûnga*. The Bantu-Kongo, in association with this name, are utilizing *paronymy* and *homonymy* to expand the range of meanings associated with *Kalûnga*. Each meaning actually derives from a root *-*lung*-, which may have different etymological origins. This is a typical practice of African wisdom traditions as it regards the conceptualization of deities.

11 Compare *guods* "festivity, feast" to Egyptian *ḏt* "a festival."

12 See Hermstein (2012: 79) on the discussion of PB *-*dɔng*- meaning "speak" and "pot," and Sumerian *dug* meaning both "(clay) pot" and "speak." For him, these all belong to the same root as PB *- *dɔ̄ngI*- "good" (adj.). It would make sense given the data above, for the same root *-eela-* also means to "speak" and to "express, make" (e.g., a pot). It is also used to mean, "arrange, and put in order."

useful, advantageous, course." Therefore, **God** literally is "what's good and beautiful."[13] Compare also with Omotic **log* "good, sweet."

> Om. **lak'-* > (N) Ometo **lo[k']-* > Wolaita-Kullo *lo'-uwa*, Gofa, Zala, etc. *lo'o*, Gidicho *lQ:kP* || (S) Ari *laγa-mi*, Ubamer *laγ-mi* id. (E 397, #806: NOm. **lo'-*) ||| Berb.: (S) Ghat *iulaγ-ən* id., Ahaggar *aləγ* "to be good" < **w-l-γ* (Militarev 1991, 262).[14]

The word *ꜣḫw* is one word for "God" or "Good" in Egyptian and Bantu with the consonants reversed: *g-d* > *d-g*. There is no semantic difficulty here. The word "god" (**ghedh, *ghādh-*) simply was transposed into the word "good" with all of these connotations embedded.

God: The Power That Makes Things Stand

There is another term in the Egyptian language that would directly correspond to the meanings of *good* "fit, fixed or stick together": *ḏd*  "stable, enduring, to be stable, endure, to abide"; *ḏd*  "to be established"; *ḏd*  "self, also" (*ḏt* "self, person, body image"; *ḥꜥt* "body, self"); *ḏd*  "the djed column"; *ḏdw*  "Busiris" (place of Osiris). We should note that historically the /*ḏ*/ sound in Egyptian derives from a /g/ sound (Loprieno 1995: 31, Anselin 2001, Bernal 2006: 194).[15] Therefore, historically *ḏd* was **gd* or **gl* "stable, enduring, to be stable, to abide." We can confirm this with a variant of this word in Egyptian: *wḫꜣ* "column, tent pole" (ciLuba *dikunji* "column, pillar, pier, stake"); "hall of columns, colonnade"; "pillar, support" (*ḏ* < *ḫ*; *d* < *ꜣ*); *ḏri*  "harsh, firm, solid, hard, arduous"; *ḏri*  "be hard, solid." Compare to PIE **deru* "be firm, solid."[16] The word *ḏd* < *ḏr* is also given with the phonemes reversed in Egyptian as the word *rwḏ*  (Coptic *rōt* (SBA) or *rot* or *lot* (F)) "hard, firm, strong, enduring, permanent, effective, persistent"; "to persevere, to inspect, to grow, to become firmer, shoot of a tree"; "strength, firmness"; "prosper, grow, flourish, prosperous, effective, successful, prevail (over), health in bones and limbs." This further

---

13 See discussion in the companion book to this volume on the Egyptian concept of *nṯr*. It will be demonstrated how *nṯr* derives from this root *eela* and how "extending, stretching, etc.," has come to mean "goodness" from the action of "extending one's self or hand for someone in need." A reflex in Egyptian of this term is *nfr* "goodness, beautiful."

14 Vaclev Blazek, "A lexicostatical comparison of Omotic languages." In *In Hot Pursuit of Language in Prehistory: Essays in the four fields of anthropology*, ed. John D. Bengtson, John Benjamins Publishing Company, Amsterdamn, 2008, p.108.

15 For example, Egyptian *nḏs* < **ngs* /n-/, cad : *n* + **gs*, C.Chadic: Proto-Higi : ***gwus-*** "short"; Higi-Gali: ***gusi***, Fali-Kiria: ***gusu***, Fali-Jilbu, Gude: ***gwus***, Nzangi: ***gus***, "short"; E.Cushitic: Gidole: ***guusi*** "small." Compare to Egyptian *kt* "short (moment), childhood, pettiness, little one" (**gs* < *kt*); Haddiaya: ***k'aass-***, Bayso: ***kiçere***. Omotic vocabulary developed a root ***k'ut'-***, ***-k'uç***: Dache: ***guç*** "small", Dokko: ***guçee***, Dorze: ***guuç***, Gofa: ***guuçço***, Kulla: ***guuça***, Sheko: Koota, Wolamo: ***guttaa***, Gidicho: ***gussi*** "small." Aaron Dolgopolsky (1973: 83) has come to similar conclusions but adds to the data the Semitic tri-consonantal form where the prefix is suffixed: ***ktn*** "small" (<*kt + n). In ciLuba-Bantu we have ***-nci*** "small, insignificant," (*banci, binci, bunci, cinci, dinci, kanci, lunci, manci, munci, ncidi*; *-ncinci* "minuscule, infinitesimal"; *panci, tunci*), ***-nte*** "small, menu"; ***-kesè***(à) "small"; ***bikesè***(à) "bit by bit". This demonstrates that in the word *nḏs* (<**ngs*), the *-s-* is the root; *-t-* in other attestations with possible g-/k- diminutive prefix.

16 *Online Etymological Dictionary* (OED): http://www.etymonline.com (retrieved June 6, 2013). See the word ***endure***: early 14c., "to undergo or suffer" (especially without breaking); late 14c. "to continue in existence," from Old French *endurer* (12c.) "make hard, harden; bear, tolerate; keep up, maintain," from Latin *indurare* "make hard," in Late Latin "harden (the heart) against," from *in-* (see *in-* (2)) + *durare* "to harden," from *durus* "hard," from PIE **deru-* "be firm, solid."

demonstrates the *r-k/k-r* variations we have been observing throughout this essay.

We are reminded of the entries from the TOB database that gives us in IE: *ghedh-* , *ghodh-*; English meaning: "to join, make a bond": German meaning: "unite, be closely linked, and matching; embrace, **fixed** or **stick together**." To be "fixed" is to be "stable" and "enduring." The definition of *fix* in the OED is as follows:

> late 14c., "set (one's eyes or mind) on something," probably from Old French **fixer*, from *fixe* "fixed," from Latin *fixus* "fixed, fast, immovable, established, settled," past participle of *figere* "to fix, fasten," from PIE root **dhigw-* "to stick, to fix."

Notice the root: PIE **dhigw-* (d-g) "to stick, to fix." The words stable and fixed are synonyms. In a philosophical sense, to be "fixed" and "stable" is to be "imperishable, everlasting, constant, immovable and eternal" (*jmn*). These are attributes associated with the Divine and symbolically represented by *ḏd* 𓊽𓊽, which are large poles that are fixed, set and established deep into the ground. This root (d-g) is just the reversal of Proto-IE: **ghādh-* (g-d).

Many scholars have suggested that originally, in the predynastic Period, the *ḏd* 𓊽𓊽 symbol depicted a pillar around which sheaves of corn were tied. If so then it would be in alignment with the concept of "gathering, uniting" or "collecting." Others have proposed that it represented a leafless tree, a pole with notches, made up of reeds or sheaves of corn. A deeper look into the subject definitely reveals the practice of paronymy with similar sounding words. For example, we have *ḏꜣḏꜣ* 𓂋𓈖𓂋𓈖𓏏𓏏𓏏 "a tree, a wood"; *ḏd.tw/ḏdw* "olive tree," *ḏdw* "olives, olive trees, olive oil." The association with "trees," linguistically, derives from:

> PWS *gí, gíl, (git)* "tree", PWS *ti* "tree"
> PWS *gi* "root, vein"
> PWN *GHI, (GHIM)* "be alive"
> Mangbetu *ga* "the biggest tree"
> Mangbetu *ki* "wood for heating", *aki* "to break"
> Mangbetu *gi* "kind of tree" (protection)
> Afro-Asiatic: Chad: Njei *kadi* "tree": Egyptian *ḫt* "tree"[17]

The association of *ḏd* with "stability, enduring," is a reflex of the word *ḏt* 𓆓𓏏 "everlastingness, eternity." In fact, the word *ḏt* may simply be a variation of *ḏd* where /d/ interchanges with /t/. A variant of *ḏd* might also be *tks* 𓏏𓎡𓋴𓏛 "to be fixed, settled, to be stigmatized" with a possible -*s* suffix (*t* > *d*; *k* > *ḏ*). However, the root in this term may be *ks* "strong, strength" with reflexes such as *ks* "bone, frame." It is probably the latter given that we see this feature in Egyptian with the word *ꜣḫ* "fire, flame," and *tꜣḫ* "flame, light, torch, wick, taper, illumine, burn, illumination." This demonstrates that the *t*- prefix is grammatical.

ciLuba has all of the variant sounds. We are reminded of in ciLuba of -*iikala* (k-l) "rest, remain, dwell, abide, stick on; to be"; *ndààdìlà* (d-d) "reason for which one remains in a place";

17   We are keeping in mind that Egyptian /ḏ/ derives from and/or corresponds with Afro-Asiatic/ Kongo-Saharan /g/ and /k/; thus Egyptian *ḏꜣḏꜣ* < PWS **gil* "tree"; Yorùbá *igi* "tree." This is verified with the Egyptian variants: *kꜣꜣ* 𓈎𓄿𓄿𓏏𓏥 (part of a tree); *kꜣꜣ* 𓈎𓄿𓄿𓆰 (a type of plant); *kꜣkꜣ* 𓈎𓄿𓈎𓄿𓆭 (a tree); *ḫt* 𓐍𓏏 "wood, timber, tree, woodland, mast, stick, pole"; 𓎡𓂧𓏏𓏥 *kdt / kdy* (a tree, wood). It would appear that the *ḏd* pillar was indeed inspired by the trunk of "trees" and it may turn out that the Egyptians were aware that it is the trees that create the oxygen in the atmosphere, as the *ḏdw* 𓊽𓊽𓏥 were believed to be holding up the "sky" and separating outer space from the earth. As we can see this variation of *ḏdw* has the *ḫt* "tree" determinative. We should note as well that the *ḏd* columns were used in temple constructions and were meant to look like the forests, which I think were located in central Africa (the original home of initiations).

ndààdilu (d-d) "manner in which one remains or is settled." In the (t-g) root-form we have *-tunga* "establish, train; institute, set"; *kantùnga* "in line." To be settled is to be *fixed* in a place. Compare to Omotic: Bench *yit'* "stand"; Gonga **(y)eed'* "stand"; Cushitic: E.Somali *heed'* "to remain over"; Sidamo *heed'*- "Hadiyya *hee'*-, Burji *yed'*- "to live, be in a place" (Bengtson, 2008: 128). We posit: *g > y, g > h; d <> t.*

The *k-l* root would also be *ḏ-r* in Egyptian (*k > ḏ*). We have in ciKam, as it regards our PIE **g^h-d^h* root: *ḏr* "walls" (= *dr* "to delimit, to demarcate"); *ḏr/ḏrjw* "relatives, kin"; *ḏr* "area, district, limit" (*ḵd* "area"); *r ḏr* "whole, entire, all"; *ḏꜣ* "head, skull." Note that "good" in IE deals with "relatives, kin, stability (walls), kingship (head, skull)." I think we can add to that list "whole, entire, all," for "God" is considered "omnipresent" and "infinite." In African languages, "wholeness" is associated with "fullness" and connotes "perfection."

Thus Egyptian *ḏd/ḏr* becomes ciLuba: *-tenta* "be full, be filled"; *tentàà* (ideophone) "abundance, fullness"; *-tentama* "be filled, being full"; *tèntè*(à) "right, open; filled with." This notion of "perfection" is captured in ciLuba by a *k-t* root as well: *-kète*(a) "perfect, in perfect condition"; *-kèta* "do it perfectly, make perfect"; *katàpùle*(a) *katèèke*(a) [-à/-a *katàpùle*(a) *katèèke*(a)] "authentique, perfect"; *cishikì* > <-à/-a *cishikì*> "authentic, true; perfect."

The *ḏd* 𓊽 pillar is a column that "holds" things up and I equate this term with *ḏr* "walls." It is a building's "support system." The root of this word is reflected in ciLuba as *lela* "birth, produce, cause, a family, a home, adopt, educate, ***raise***, subject, submit" (< *eela*). It is this notion of "raising" (lifting, projecting up) that underlies the definition of *ḏd*; it's the verticality that is being conveyed here.

Remember that the Germanic words *ghedh-* and *ghodh-* mean, "**fixed**, to **stand/stick** together." This is exactly what a *ḏd* 𓊽 is and does. This is reflected in ciLuba as *tèndee* (t-d) "standing, straight ahead"; *tèndu* "vertically." In the *t-g* root-form we have *-tàngama* "be high"; *-tàngamaja* "raising, at the top, exhibit, highlight"; *-tàngamana* "rise, explain, to show, highlight"; *-tàngamika* "show, demonstrate, stand, make straight." Note that the *t-* sound often corresponds with *k-*, and thus a variant in ciLuba is *kuulu* "above, in the air, standing, time (atmospheric situation); <*-iimana kuulu*> "stand"; <*Mwena-kuulu*> "God." That which is "above" comes to denote that which "covers" you and "protects" you. This is reflected in the ciLuba words, *ciTanda* "shed, hangar, air-shed"; *kaTanda* "canopy, small overhanging roof"; *diTanda* "workshop, factory, manufacturing, shed, place of worship" (Egyptian *itr.t* / *itꜣ.t* "temple, chapel, niche"); *cyandà* "trap" (a closed-in space). Compare the above to the following in ciLuba (*k-d* root):

> *ngandà* "courtyard"; *-kanda* "complete, whole"; *-kànda* "prevent, prohibit, refused permission" (in alignment with "fixed" in the sense of "stubborn, firm." (see Egyptian *kt* "adversity, hardships"); *-kàndika* "defend, ban, prevent, censor"; *-kànda* "binding, retain"; *-kàndama* "be prevented, held"; *-kàndamana* "establish, maintain, be blocked, be retained, hang"; *-kànda* "separate (Egyptian *ḏr* "walls").

God, therefore, is that energy force that "holds up the universe"; "the one who holds firm the universe" (keeps it a unity, whole and complete). This last connotation is present among the Bantu-Kongo of central Africa. Fu-Kiau, in his work *Simba Simbi: Hold Up That Which Holds You Up* (2006), discusses the underlying theme behind the Kikongo word *simbi*, which for Fu-Kiau means "that which holds things up" (< *simba* "to hold up, to keep something, to bless, to treasure, to touch, to retain"). Compare with the following ciLuba reflexes: *ciTamba* "platform, podium, stage"; *ciTapa* "shelf, grill on which you place meat on or put cassava leaves to dry out." When referred to God, *simbi* is simply "The living energy force that holds things up." *Simbi* is the power behind all life; it is life itself. *Simbi* is the God-principle; it the principle that makes "things" the way they are. The phrase *Simba Simbi* means, "To hold up that which holds you up." To *simba simbi* is to be boldly "standing" in the posture of a true master (see Fu-Kiau 2001). *Simbi* is the "life-*holding* power, God." Although it cannot be seen, it is a living presence that holds up all things seen. This is more than likely the idea behind the name *Nzambi* "God"[18] in many Bantu and West African languages. It is associated with "power" and the power to make things "rise" or "stand up." This is ultimately the conceptualization behind the modern vilification of the term *zombie* in modern cinema. It refers to a dead person who has *risen* from the dead: the dead made to "stand up." One could argue that Yeshua (Jesus) was in fact a *zombie/nsambi* in a literal sense according to the Biblical myth.

These are the attributes found in the word and application of *ḏd*  in Egypt (<**g-d*). The *ḏd* pillar is associated with *Wsr*  (Osiris) and *Wsr* is seen as the "life principle" that holds things up in Egyptian ontology. It was first associated with Ptah and later Sokar (an aspect of Osiris). Ptah was known as "the noble *ḏd*." One will notice the following glyph in Egyptian that refers to the *nṯrw*:  *i3t.*[19] Often this sign has the hawk  symbol above it [], reaffirming its association with "elevation" and "holding up/support." I argue that this term *i3t* [>*it3*] is ciLuba *tèndee* (t-d) "standing, straight ahead"; *tèndu* "vertically" [n+l>nd].

This sense of verticality is what makes human beings "human" (*muntu*, *luntu*, *rmṯ*) and what makes a human being "god-like." Fu-Kiau (2001) describes this philosophy within the Bantu-Kongo context. In contrast to other beings on earth that walk horizontally (*kilukongolo*), the *muntu* is fundamentally a "vertical being" (*kintombayalu-kadi*). He thinks and he is spiritual: he is a thinking-acting-being [*kadi-biyindulanga-mu-vanga*]. The *muntu* thinks, reasons, and ponders before he walks [upright] and acts to meet, horizontally, the challenges of the instinctive world. The horizontal being (e.g., beasts, reptiles) acts "instinctively". These are dimensional concepts in relation to the Bantu cosmological wheel of time [*ntangu*] and processes [*dingo-dingo*] (see Fu-Kiau, 2001: 35, 43). The cosmography represents the four fundamental stages of the life cycle symbolized by the sun's apparent movement around the earth. When the sun is positioned at "noon" time [Vanga, V3], this represents the most powerful stage of development; the stage of creativity and great deeds (*tukula* of the root verb *kula* "to mature, to master").

This is the stage of the *nganga* (masters) [*ꜥnḫ* ]. A *muntu* is expected to be a "doer" (a specialist) in a community of doers. The *Vanga* function is accomplished by the *kula*, grow action, i.e., learning to stand "vertically" [*telama lwimba-nganga*] inside one's "V" (Fu-Kiau, 2001: 140). To "stand" well inside this scaling *Vee* is to be able not only to master our lives, but also to better know ourselves and our relationship positions with the rest of the universe as a whole. The Kikongo word *kula* "grow, mature" is cognate with the root in the Egyptian words *sḳ3i*  "make high (a building), set up, raise, set upright (a person), exalt (a god, king), extol"; *sḳ3*  "to magnify"; *sḳ3*  "to set up, exalt, prolong, to make high." The overall theme is "increase" and "rising up."

This idea is confirmed by the glyph of a man raising his arms (*ḳ3i*) 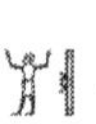 with the meanings "tall, high, long, exalted, be raised on high, uplifted" and as we have asserted, this is a variant

18 PB **jàmbé* "god"; **jàmbí* "belief"; **nyàmbé* "god, spirit" (j>y). Christopher Ehret, however, argues that the word *nyambe* derives from a root *-amb-*, an *-e* suffix needed in order to make the verb into a noun, and the *ny-* prefix which signified a category for animals and things that don't fit into any category. So we have, according to Ehret, "the beginner of all things": literally, "The origin of all things." Given the application of *zombie*, I would argue that this definition should be revisited. See "A Conversation with Christopher Ehret": http://www.scribd.com/doc/91975268/A-Conversation-With-Christopher-Ehret (retrieved June 6, 2013).

19 See expanded discussion in the companion book to this volume on this symbol in relation to the word *nṯr*.

of the word *ḏd,* which derives from a *g-l* or *k-l* root. A reflex of this word is given in Egyptian as *grg*  "provide (for), set in order, furnish, settle (crown on king); found (a land), establish (a house), people (a place), to make ready; settlement; to arrange, to furnish, to prepare, to set, to put in order." This is a partially reduplicated term: *gr-g(r)*. These are the same connotations given for the PIE **ghedh* > *good.* As mentioned earlier, this *g-l/k-l* root is reflected in Egyptian as *rwḏ* 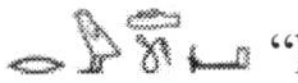 "hard, firm, strong, enduring, permanent, effective, persistent"; "to persevere, to inspect, to grow, to become firmer"; "strength, firmness"; "prosper, grow, flourish, prosperous, effective, successful, prevail (over)." As we can see, we are dealing with numerous variations of the same root-term (many derived forms). In Indo-European, Egyptian *rwḏ* comes to us in English as the word "ready" (r-d).

> PIE ***reidh-*** "to put in order, to make comfortable"; Tokharian: A *ritk-* 'raise, produce', B *rätk-* 'heal' (Adams 531); Baltic: **raid-u-* adj.; **reid-ī̂-* vb.; **rid-ā̂-* f. "ready"; Lithuanian: *raidù-* 'bereit, fertig, usw.; Lettish: *riedît* (-u, -ĩju) 'order, have'; *raids* 'ready, to finish'; *rida* 'device, stuff'; Germanic: **raid-a-*, **raid-i-* adj., **raid-ia* vb.- etc. "ready"; Gothic: **ga-raio-s* (-d-) (a) `arranged, commanded'; *\*raidjan* wk. `establish, correctly determine, interpret'; Old Frisian: *rēde* ` finished, lightweight, clear, simple'; Old English: *gerǣde, rǣde* `finished, readily, clear, easy', *gerǣde* n. `eschirr, armor'; (ge)*rǣdan* `organize, help'; Celtic: **reidi-* > Ir *rēid* `flat, easy', gently *rēidi* `navigable fields'; OCymr *ruid* `successful, unencumbered, not impeded', Cymr *rhwydd* ` successful, unencumbered, not impeded'

In the Yorùbá tradition, the god *Èṣù* is often depicted with an erect phallus. This symbolizes that he is "ready" and most of all "potent," meaning "able to deliver and expand." We see the same connotations in ancient Egypt with the gods *Mn*  and *Wsr*  who are both depicted often with erect phalli (*ḏt*  "phallus"). Both represent the regenerative energy in life-cycles and vegetation.

Man as God(s)

Another Bantu group, the Amazulu of South Africa, also associates the human being's uniqueness with his ability to walk upright. Jordan Ngubane, in his work *Conflict of Minds* (1979: 86), discusses a conversation the author had with his grandmother who told him that when someone gives you something, you shouldn't say "thank you," but should reply with, "Ume Njalo" (may you *stand* forever). A bit curious as to why he should say these words instead of thank you, Ngubane then asked her why he should say, "stand forever" and she replied:

> …in the mists of antiquity, when stones cried if pinched, early Man walked upright and sometimes on all fours. Then, one day, he found a formula in his mind for walking upright. He shared it with his neighbours and from that day each human being was so grateful they all thanked or blessed each other by wishing each should forever walk upright.

We as human beings (*Bantu*) are able to walk upright because of the verticality of our spine. The spine is an ancient symbol of humanness as well as good character and heart. The god *Wsr*/ Osiris was associated with the *ḏd*  pillar, which is symbolic of the spine of *Wsr*. The *ḏd* came to represent *Wsr* himself, often combined with a pair of eyes between the crossbars and holding the crook and flail. *Wsr* was the spirit behind the concept of renewal; what Westerners would call "resurrection." The *ḏd* pillar design was made into an amulet or charm that was often placed on the spine of the deceased so that the ancestor could "rise" like the living in the spirit world. Chapter 155 of the *rʿw nw prt m ḥrw* (The words for coming forth by day), possesses a spell that promises that the dead person will get back the use of his or her spine and be able to sit up again like Osiris.

> Raise yourself, O Osiris, place yourself on your side, that I may put water beneath you and that I may bring you a *ḏd* of gold so that you may rejoice at it. To be said over a golden *ḏd* embellished with sycamore-bast, to be placed on the throat[20] of the deceased on the day of interment. As for him on whose throat this amulet has been placed, he will be a worthy spirit who will be in the realm of the dead on New Year's Day like those who are in the suite of Osiris. A matter a million times true.

This symbol is also associated with *Ptḥ* who was the patron spirit of all architects and engineers and is credited with the invention of the crafts. It is he who laid the foundations for creation as the first creative principle that arose from the primordial hill (*t3 ṯnn* "risen land, Memphis earth god"; Kalenjiin *yeto tonoon, ol-ta tonoon* "risen earth, high land").[21] *Ptḥ* carried a staff with an *ʿnḫ* symbol superimposed on a *ḏd* pillar. The most famous of his devotees was Imhotep, the designer of the first step-pyramid during the 3rd Dynasty under king Zoser (2700 BCE). Imhotep was also known as the "Son of Ptah." The high priests of *Ptḥ* were known as "Lord(s) of the Master Craftsmen" (*wr ḫrp ḥmwt*). As the name *Ptḥ* is a paronym of the word *ptḥ* "to create, to shape," we argue that his fundamental attributes are linked to the ability to make things "rise," "to erect and build" (structures, systems, etc.); "make and fashion." *Wsr* would represent the energy, spirit and power (*àṣẹ*) needed to erect (resurrect) phenomena and initiate cycles: to give primordial matter form.

We mentioned one of the symbols that helps to define a *nṯr*, and that is the *i3t* 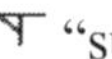 "support bar, platform, standard (for cult objects)." The word *i3t/3t* is also the same word used for "spine (of man), back (of animal), backbone, middle (of lake, river)" (also *3dt*). To demonstrate that the spine is also associated with "lifting up" conceptually in the minds of the Egyptian, we also have *ṯs* "spine, vertebra," *ṯs* "neck"[22] and *ṯs* "to raise up, to go up, to climb." In addition, we have *i3t* "mound," "office, function, rank, kingship, post, profession, job, work"; "building,

20 Remember that the spine goes through the neck. As concerns our *k-d* root, compare to the following in Bengtson (2008: 118) for Afro-Asiatic: **58-Neck**: Om.: (N) Ometo **k'od'-* id., cf. Mocha *qo:t'-* "to swallow" (E 249, #452; Lamberti & Sottile 1997, 436), but cf. Hamer-Banna *k'orči* "neck" ||| Cush.: (N) Beja *kwod'ad'~ kad'ad'* "base of skull, foot of mount" (R. Hudson) = *kad'at* "scruff of neck" (Roper) || (E) **k'uc'-(t-)* > Jiddu *quj'* "neck" (Lamberti); Oromo *quc'-e* "back of the neck" (> Gedeo *k'uc'-e*), Kambatta *k'utta-ta*, Burji *k'uc'-oo* "nape of neck" (Hudson 1989, 104).

21 Compare with the Gikuyu word *tene* "ancient." Ptah is believed to be one of the most ancient deities and his name, in part, may reflect this attribute. Compare *Ptḥ* with Kalenjiin *aap-taa* or *po-taa* "of the beginning." The /h/ sound is rendered zero in Kalenjiin. It should be noted that the deity *t3 ṯnn* also embodied a chthonic aspect in which he was viewed as a protector of the deceased king in the netherworld (Wilkinson, 2001: 130). In the New Kingdom *Litany of Ra* he is cited as the personification of the phallus of the dead king. This could be due to two reasons. The first is that a word for phallus, *ḥnn*, sounds 'somewhat' similar to *ṯnn* "risen" and has a similar underlying connotation. It could be related to the word *wn/wnn*  "to be, to exist, to live." Verticality signals "life" and horizontal signals "death." To be, to be alive is to stand vertically and move about. Or secondly, since the dead king was associated with *Wsr*, the god of resurrection, the concept of "risen" would also be associated with that divine principle: Osiris. *Wsr* also was a chthonic and phallic deity as well. An erect phallus and a mound/hill both convey the notion of "verticality" discussed above. See also in Egyptian *ḏt*  "phallus" which is a reflex of *ḏd* "pillar."

22 It is the neck that *holds up* the head.

place, site, ruin." All of these terms have to deal with the underlying theme of "verticality/ erection (e.g., "a building")," "high ranking," or "fixed" (like a building, place, mound, ruin into the ground). These same attributes are associated with the *ḏd* pillar, which historically is pronounced **gVd* (god) and this further confirms that a "god" is a spirit, force or person of "high rank," "one who holds things up or together," "who erects things (e.g., monuments, life)," "one who makes or provides," or "something of high value and integrity."

God and Stacking Power

Another meaning of "good" in the Indo-European languages given by the TOB database is:

> Latvia *gāds, sagāds* 'stock/supply, I purchased/bought', *gādāt* `make, provide, ensure, care for ' probably borrowed from Russ.

Again, ciLuba has this term as well and the PIE **g-d* order is reversed in ciLuba: *ntungù* (t-g) "gratuity, benefit, bonus, advantage, reward, compensation, payment"; *tùngà* "how much" (interrogative pronoun). There appears to be an underlying theme of commerce here. The Latvia term for "stock/supply" seems to derive from this notion of "row," as in to put something into rows (like stocking a shelf). It reminds me of the ancient Egyptian word *ꜣḫt*  "horizon." This word in ciLuba is *lukèndù* "row, horizon, stacked rows, superimposed rows" (PB **déng* "go beyond, fade from the horizon"). The consonant forms are as follows: Latvia (*g-d-s*) [< *d-g-s* → Egyptian (*ꜣ-ḫ-t*); ciLuba (*l-k-d*)]. The notion of "stock, supply" can also be seen in ciLuba *-tènga* (t-g) "to order, store, cram." The idea of purchase "goods" in English derives from the notion of items "stacked" and "stocked" and are "ready" for purchase.

God as a Builder and Architect

We, thus far, have been building a case that the word "god" (=good) derives from a root with an underlying theme of "verticality" and "dimensionality" with numerous derived forms and extended meanings. Within this collective framework exist the idea of "holding up" and "raising up" ideas, people, and things. The ancients understood the Supreme Creator as an energy force that sustains and holds up creation. It is also the force responsible for the "rising" of phenomena out of the eternal ocean of unformed matter. Therefore, God is seen as a "builder" or "stacker" of some sort. The Creator is also a type of "molder" or "potter" who takes the unformed "clay" of matter and "erects" living monuments. The mold receives the *breath of life* from the Creator and activates the life form.

In the Egyptian language these ideas are reflected in the following terms: *ḳd*  "builder, method of building"; *ḳdw / i̓ḳdw* Bricklayer, Potter"; *ḳd*  "build, fashion (men)"; *ḳd*  "build"; *ḳdw / i̓ḳdw*  "Bricklayer, Potter"; *ḳd*  "use the potter's wheel, build, fashion (men)"; *ḳd* 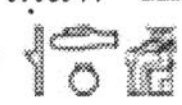 "potter" (epithet of Khnum). As we can see, this term also has the *k-d* (<*k-l*) root. The primary sign is that of an erected wall , which is used in the word *ḳd* "Potter, Creator."

We argue that "good" and "*ḳd*" are cognates. We observe in Egyptian: *ḳd*  "like" (Germanic **gōða-* `match '; mhd. *gaten*, *gegaten* intr. `come together, so that it matches', trans. `same, joined, alike, bring together'; Toch B. *gaden* 'like'; OCS. *goditi* u `like '); *m ḳd* 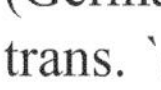 "together" (*ghedh-* , *ghodh-* German meaning: "unite, be closely linked, matching";

älter "embrace, fixed or stick together"; English meaning: "to join, make a bond"; Old Frisian: *gōd* "good"; *gada* "unite"). See also in Egyptian *m-ḫ3* "to balance, be straight, level, match, equal, make even"; ciLuba *mulongo*(u) "range, rank, file, row"; "line, series, many"; *mwena mulongu* "equal, match; of the same age group" [metathesis].

One of the manifestations of the Creator in Egyptian cosmology is that of the *nṯr* Khnum (*ḫnmw* ), who is often shown creating man on his potter's wheel. As we can see above, *ḳd* ("god") is used as an epithet for *ḫnmw*. Khnum is the one who builds and fashions creation (*ḳd*  "figure, form, shape"). This epithet is also used for the *nṯr* Ptah (*ptḥ*) in his name *ptḥ ḳd*. To further demonstrate that *ḳd* = "god," the Egyptian language explicitly states so: *nḳdḳd* 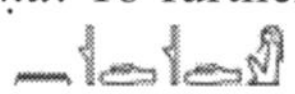 "name of god, God" [Wb II 345, Budge 396a[23]] (see also *3ḳdḳd*  [Wb I 22]), for which I argue is cognate with Isizulu *nKulunkulu* "God" (Egyptian *k3k3*  "a God" (Budge 791a); ciLuba *nGole* "God"). We find also this root in association with the *nṯr* Osiris (Wsr): *ḳd-n* "Patron god Osiris" [Wb V 80]. Remember that Osiris is the generative power that makes things "be" and "rise."

The Creator is the ultimate architect and builder. This type of conceptualization exists in modern Freemasonry where "G" is the "Great Architect of the Universe." Freemasonry took this concept directly out of Africa from the original "gods" who were stonemasons in Egypt: *ḳdw / iḳdw*  "Bricklayer, Potter, Builder." This can extend into other crafts as reflected in *sḳd* "sailor, traveler" (< *ḳd* "move around").[24] These are the people responsible for expanding trade, so keeping secret the sources of trade goods and trade routes was tantamount.

To be a "god" is to be a *builder* or *creator* (to erect things from unformed matter) and it is this notion that the Hebrews in the Old Testament detested (as they were shepherds). The story of the Tower of Babel demonstrates this conviction.

> Come, let us build ourselves a city, and a watchtower with its top in the skies, and let us make a name for ourselves lest we be scattered over the face of the earth [Gen. 11:4].

The Old Testament indirectly attests to what a god is. Human beings were trying to be like gods and as a result, the tower fell. In other words, gods "build" and "create." Those who exalt the pastoral lifestyle shun these activities. This is reaffirmed through the vilification of Qayin (Cain) who represented agriculture ("he was a worker of the soil") and urbanization (he was a city builder," Gen. 4: 17). The Bible accuses Qayin of killing the pastoral lifestyle (personified by Hebel/Abel) in the book of Genesis, which cursed him forever to till the soil and be a vagabond around the earth.

In Egypt, as in the rest of Black Africa, all the major guilds were itself a priesthood. To gain entry into the priesthood, one had to have demonstrated to the elders that one was of good character and that one could be trusted with the secrets of the craft. This is, in part, reflected in our very *ḳ-d* root: Egyptian *ḳd*  "nature, reputation, character, disposition, extent." The community expects the priest to be a person of high moral character. A word for *priest* in

23 Hh 101: Text of Her-hetep. A transcript of this text is given by Maspero, *Trois Annees de Fouilles, in Memoires de la Mission Archeologique Franfaise au Caire*, 1881-84. Paris, 1884. Folio, p. 137 ff.

24 This term is more than likely a homograph. But note that modern Freemasonry is heavy on this notion of being a "travelling man."

Egyptian is *ḳd wr* "a priest" (a great builder; craftsman?)[25]; ciLuba *mwakwidi* "priest" (<-*aakwila* "advocate, defend [a person or cause], intercede for; rule, to govern); *mukulu* "senior, old, grandfather, Chief, Director, Chairman, chief of a polygamous household"; "ancient, primordial, primary, Supreme"; *Mvìdi-Mukùlù* "God, Supreme Spirit"; *Nkole*(a) "God"; *Kuulu* "God; above, in the air, standing, stand, be healthy." This is interesting because the very word *priest* (< Latin *presbyter* < Greek) means "elder." The priests are elders and the leaders of the nation.[26] In Zimbabwe, male leaders are called ***Mugudo***.

We should note that in Icelandic we have *goði* "heathen priest" and in Gothic, *gudja* "priest."[27] As noted in *Chapter 3.1*, Ringe (2006: 293) seems to suggest that the word "god" (P.Gm **guda*) derives from **gudjō̃* "priest." If this is the case, then this is in alignment with what we see in Egyptian where the same word for "builder, potter, creator" (*ḳd*) is used for "priest" and *nḳdḳd* "God." If this is indeed the case, then the concepts of "pouring (libations), sacrifice and invoking" are all activities of the priest and we can see where the confusion begins with Indo-European linguists.

God, Kudos, and Leadership

Because of the priests' social standing within society, they are often viewed as people to be honored, and in an extreme sense "worshipped" (*worship* (< *worthy*) simply means, "To honor, conditioned of being renowned"). The African community deems a person *worthy* based on one's character and proven ability to master a thing and be prolific in one's endeavors. These are the kinds of characteristics that gets one moved "up" in "rank" and again we are immersed in the "up-down schema" of semantics. When one reaches a "high" status due to one's consistent demonstration of skill and integrity, then the people give *kudos* for one's accomplishments. I argue here that the word *kudos* contains our *ḳ-d* root associated with an artisan or builder.

Kudos (from the Ancient Greek: κῦδος) is "acclaim" or "praise" for exceptional achievement. Bernal (1987: 60) renders *kudos* "divine glory" from a Semitic root √qds "sacred." In Hebrew this word is *qōdeš* "holy" (*u*-class segholate) and has been reconstructed as **quds* (Bernal, 2006: 336). As noted by Bernal, the word *kudos* and *kudros* is used in both a positive and negative sense: "divine glory" and "vile" respectively. Another negative form in Greek is *kûdos* "insult." It could be argued that this dichotomy stems from the Semitic √qds root (a loan into Greek) that also means "apart, unclean, vile." If the terms used in the Gothic Bible derive from this root, it would explain why *gþ*, *gþs,* and *gþa* was used for the "Good God" and why *-guda*, *-gude* or *-gudam* was used for the "false gods" according to Hatto (1944: 248). For them the "false gods" would be "unclean, vile" and "apart" from the one and only "true" God that Christianity professes.

As noted in Bernal (2006: 336), the √qds triconsonantal root is actually *q-d* with an *-s* suffix.[28] If so, then I would equate Semitic √qds "sacred" with ciLuba *cijila* "abstinence, fasting"; *-à/-a cijila* "sacred, religious" (*-jila* "fast, abstain from (food), avoid, quarantine, refuse to talk to"). The Semitic root √qds may be a loan and derive from Egyptian *sḳd*

25 The word *wr* in Egyptian is cognate with Yorùbá *olu* "lord, master, owner" and Bantu *mw-ena* "lord, master, owner, one who, the quality of"; Tigrigna *wärä* "famous." When *wr* is attached to another word (X), we should read it like "one who is" or "the quality of being" -X.

26 The priests (the skilled ones) are the life-blood of any nation and its economy and if they are of bad character, the whole economy could suffer. This is the reason for industry regulations to keep businesspersons honest and protect the consumer in the modern world.

27 See in the Gothic Bible John xviii, 22 for an example of *gudja* "priest."

28 Bernal (2006) argues that the early Canaanite final *-s* was taken into Greek as the marker of a type of neuter noun, in which all cases of the singular, except the dative, end in *-s*.

"walk around, avoid, evade, shun" [Meeks: AL 783 877]. Note also *sḳd* "to build." The extended form could derive from the notion of building a wall  that automatically separates one area from another; it blocks access to something treasured. Note that virtually all "holy" items are kept separate and distinct from other items and areas; whether we are talking about holy land, holy parts of temples, an area where an ancestral shrine is located, or people. For instance, the Hebrews—alleged to be a holy people—were to be "of" the world but not "in" the world; they were to remain something unique and separate from all other human groups.

The Egyptian term *ḏsr* "holy, sacred, glorious, sanctity, splendid, costly" may also be cognate with *sḳd* and be the product of metathesis (*ḏrs* > *ḏsr*). As the ciLuba *cijila* informs us, it is this notion of "separation" or "abstaining" from—that which is undesirable—that makes something sacred. As we can see in Egyptian, the word *ḏsr* also means "consecrated, set apart, separate" (ciLuba *kanda* (k-d) "separate").[29] I argue this is so because the root is actually *ḏr* "wall, flank, area, distinct, limit, side; end (hunger), end up as, hinder, obstruct" which would also confirm its metathesis on the *s* and *r* graphemes. The underlying theme is "separation," and in a sense, "blocking."

To test that *q-d* is indeed the root, we note that Semitic √qds is also used to refer to *cedars* (an evergreen tree with needles and cones). In Egyptian, we have *ḳdtt*  "a conifer (from Syria)." Conifers are also evergreen trees with needles and cones. We also have in Egyptian *ḳdt* / *ḳdy*  (a tree, wood).

A priest is "distinguished" from the "ordinary" person as he is the one who quarantines himself from the common activities of the uninitiated. Even during initiations, the elders separate African initiates from the larger society to complete their training. They are the disciplined members of society who the people hold to a higher standard of conduct due to their position and assumed knowledge. The Egyptians created special sections of the temples, called the Holy of Holies, for the priests only. The most famous in Egypt is *ḏsr ḏsrw* "Holy of Holies" (Temple of Deir el Bahri).

Remember that our Greek term *kudos* (k-d-s), on one level, means "acclaim, praise" for exceptional achievement. As it regards our term "good," we have in Proto-Baltic: **gõd-a-c*.; Lithuanian *guõda-s* 'honor, worship, entertainment'; Lettish: *gùods* 'honor, glory/fame', *gùodât* (-ãju), *guodêt* (-ẽju), *guodît* (-īju) 'protect, honor, cherish'. In Egyptian the IE /d/ is primarily an /l/ and in Egyptian /l/ interchanges with /n/. This gives us the following reflexes in Egyptian (without -*s* suffix):  *hny* praise (of god or king) (< *hnw* "rejoice, exult, acclaim, jubilation, praise"). This initial /h/ more than likely derived from a /s/ sound, thus we have: *snsn* 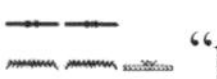 "praise, worship"; *smsm*  "praise, worship, homage to" (n>m). We also have *ḥst* 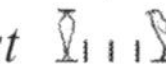 "favour, praise, blessings" (*kudos* < *ḥst*; metathesis?) that may be relevant. Worthy of noting is Egyptian *kwt* / *kjt* / *kiw* "acclaim, respect, shout of acclaim."

The sound change *g* > *ḏ* > *d* in Egyptian could have happened very early in the proto-language, thus giving us a number of doublets either natively or reintroduced by neighboring dialects and related languages. What became *kudos* in Greek, I argue, became *dw3* 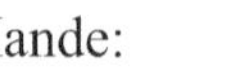 "praise, worship, to adore" in Egyptian. Observe the sound correspondences with Mande:

Egyptian	**Mande**
d3t, dw3t "the underground world"	*do, du* "hole, hollow, depth, etc."
dw3 (doua) morning of	*duhu* "daylight, day"
dw3 (endowed) to adore	*duwa* "invocation" (God)

29 Bernal (2006) argues that the early Canaanite final -*s* was taken into Greek as the marker of a type of neuter noun, in which all cases of the singular, except the dative, end in -*s*.

The Mande lost the final *-l* in *dwꜣ*. It is, however, maintained in ciLuba with a conditioned sound change: *-tènda* "invoke" (n+l>nd); *-tèndelela* "ask forgiveness and to praise somebody, congratulate, ease with praise, thank"; *-tèndeleela* "pray"; *katèndakanyi* "praise, commendation speech, thank, pray humbly, beg".

The *kꜣ* sign is a sign of adoration and praise with an underlying connotation of "lifting and raising," as in to "exalt." We can see this determinative in the word *wꜣš* "be pleased, be glad, be distinguished, be honoured, be strong, honour (due to god or king), prestige." A variant of this sign is in the word *dwꜣ* "praise, worship, to adore." The word *dwꜣ* also means "morning" and derives from *dwꜣ* "to *rise* at dawn." Again, the focus is "exaltation." This is the result of the *-r-* root's underlying theme of "rising, verticality, distance and expanse." This underlying theme is reflected in the Egyptian word *rw* "part of the sky [Wb II 403], sky" (> *ḥrw*) which denotes "height, length, above." Reflexes exist in PAA:

> PAA: **raw-* "sky"; Egyptian *rw* "sky" (pyr); W.Chadic **ruw* "sky" (Proto-WChadic: **ruw-* (var. *ray*) "sky"; Karekare: *rəwì* [Kr N 116]; Fyer: *rúrùwê* [JgR]; Sha: *ʔarè* [JgR]); S.Cushitic **raw-* "sky" (Burunge (Mbulungi): *raw*)

It is this sense of "rising" that is part of the root *rwḏ* "prosper, succeed, prevail (over), be strong, be firm, flourish"; "hard, firm, strong, enduring, permanent, persistent, effective." *Flourishing* is connected to "growth," which itself is connected to "height." This focus on "height" and "above" extends to *mastery* and *authority*. Someone who has authority to do something is seen as someone in a position of power. In the Egyptian language we see the *-rw-* root reflected in *jrw* "maker of" (job title) [Wb I 113]; *rwjt* "Authority, elder" [Wb II S 407]. Compare to Yorùbá *asalu* "a title of honor among the *Ogboni* people" (Egyptian *sʕr* "elevated, prominent"; *sʕꜣ* "to make great, to enlarge, enlargement, to increase, to aggrandize, to magnify, be rich, be great, to exalt, enrich, honour, glorify, ennoble."); Tigrigna *asäri* "employer" (Egyptian *wsr* "strong, rich one, powerful"; *swr* "promote (an official), increase (herds), extol, to augment, to multiply"), *əsari* "jailer" (Egyptian *wsr* "strong one, oppressor").

The *-rw-* root is then reflected in *rwḏ* "manage, supervise, Controller, Administrator, Guardian." The Egyptian language maximizes its terms by switching its phonemes. The word *rwḏ* is just a variation of the word *wḏꜣ* "salvation, prosperity, welfare, uninjured, sound, healthy, hale" (=ciLuba *kuulu* "be healthy");[30] *wḏꜣ* "attain (a rank)." We should note that in Egyptian the word *kꜣ* (=*wḏꜣ*) also means "kingship," an institute for which we would argue is the ultimate living *authority* in a kingdom. Therefore, *k̠d* = *kꜣ* = *wḏꜣ* = *rwḏ* = "god."

God as Scholar

Because the concept of god is associated with "skills, mastery and knowledge (that comes with age)," this term extends itself and is associated with *scholars*. This notion is best expressed in the ciLuba-Bantu term *shushukulu*, which is also built off of the *k-l* root spoken of throughout this essay.

Shushukula is an archaic term in ciLuba and exist only as a title in the lodge of *Buloshi-bwa-Ditanga* "High-Science of the Kingdom," a sort of Supreme Council and secret for the promotion and defense of *life* or *welfare* in the kingdom (Kalamba and Bilolo, 2009: 13). *Shu-Shukulu* comes from *-shukula/-shukula/-zikula* "reveal, explain, go up the taproot, enlighten."

30 The *Law of Belova* would render this term *ḏwꜣ* (<*gwl* ?).

The title *Shu-Shukulu* means "Luminous spirit that illuminates the roots,[31] brings up-to-date what is hidden, which unveils what is covered." Instead of using *shu* "spirit" = *Eshi* > *MeEshi*, we read also *Shua*/*Shuwa-nShukulu* "Revelator of Truth" = "One who reveals, is enlightened, who shows *BuShuwa* ("the truth")." A *Shu-shukulu* is a *Mujikwidi* (<-*jìkwila* "tell the truth").

The *shushukulu* is a superior-spirit, but with a more scientific connotation of "Savant", "Scout", "Doctor highlighting the source, the root of things and phenomena." *Shushukulu* is related to the word *Bushukudi* [l+i>di] (kulu>kudi) whose variants are *bujukudi* and *dijikula*. These come from the verb *kushukula* or *kujukula*, which means, "to show the bottom or base of something"; "explicit what is implicit"; "clarify what is unclear"; "expose." *Bushukudi*/*kushukula* is essentially an intellectual activity which is realized in the language from the verb *ku-shuku-la* from which two words derived: first, the abstract word *bushu-kudi* or *bu-di-juku* which means "clarification," laid bare," "elucidation," "enlightenment" and so on. The second word *shushukulu* (var. *mujukudi*) denotes "one who knows the foundations of something," "one that can release 'tap root' of a fact or a problem."

Shushukulu is not simply a "steward" but is a "scholar, a scientist," or in the Greek conceptualization, a "sophos." In a strict sense, he is the Divine (God) itself. *Shushukulu* (as God) is regarded as *cibitoke wa mmona kubidi* "Door that sees both sides, a being who has eyes in the physical world as well as in the spiritual world; neither the inside or outside has a secret. He is everywhere present. When applied to man, it simply means wise or one who is a scholar. Therefore, the one who the Greeks called a *philosophos,* is called in Luba *shushukulu*.

In this category of *shushukulu*, there is a singular class, namely, that of *Nkindi*. To the question: what is *Nkindi*? The Luba answer: *udi Nkindi shushukulu ngelelu wa mu ngenyi*, "Nkindi is a specialist or a scholar in the art / way of thinking" (Bilolo, 2003: 77). By combining the different variants of "thinking" or "to think", we get the following definition: "*nkindi udi shu-shukulu mu diela, diluka, dilunga, dinana ne difuka dia Ngenyi*," that is to say "The *Nkindi* is a *Shushukulu* in the art or manner of 'making, building, developing, weaving, stretching, extending, expanding, creating and inventing' thoughts or ideas." And insofar as the mastery of the art of building, to develop and create thoughts are revealed in language, the word *nkindi* can also have a very pejorative sense.[32]

The word *Nkindi* refers to both *subject* and *object*. Applied to the subject, it means *shushukulu* or specialist in the creation and development of deep *lungenyi*, "thought" or "idea". The ciLuba word *lungenyi* I equate with Egyptian *rḫ* "to copulate, to know a woman sexually, wise man, scholar, to learn, to find out, to know, be aware of, diagnose, inquire, wisdom, experience, opinion, to be able, to list").[33] The *Nkindi* is characterized by its perspicacity and depth in the approach of major problems that mortals face during their earthly pilgrimage. Applied to the object, it denotes the art of getting to the bottom of things, to penetrate into the abysmal depth of the problems relating to man, the world and God; and

---

31 One must consider that the roots of a tree or plant are hidden under the ground. Therefore, this notion of illuminating the roots means, essentially, to uproot something, to penetrate the depths below to reveal the roots or the source of that which appears on the surface (above ground).

32 Among the Bakongo people, the ciLuba *nkindi* concept is personified in the spiritual object called *nkondi* in the KiKongo language. The *Nkondi* object is like a diploma given to an *nganga*, a specialist who deals with social issues. He can be seen as a therapist who is invited in a village, in the community circle to deal with any issue that is a problem. Before the *Nganga* starts discussing the matter at hand, he has to show his *nkondi* to assure the villagers that he is qualified to discuss the *mambu* (the matter, problem). The word *mambu* is what became "mumbo jumbo" in the United States. Without this object, the community will not accept him as trained or qualified. See Fu-Kiau (2007) for more information. Also Robert F. Thompson "Faces of the Gods: the Artists and their Altars" in *African Arts*, Vol. 28, No. 1, (Winter, 1995), pp. 50-61.

33 A case can be made that the word *rḫ* is the reverse of nkindi by way of metathesis.

also profound ideas or answers obtained during this investigation. These responses are often concise, brief, but of great perspicacity.

Nkindi is a lifestyle; a way of being that reveals itself even in the most trivial of acts. *Nkindi* is a title equivalent to a Nobel Prize of Philosophy. To have it, one must have demonstrated a certain amount of intellectual and moral qualities, an extraordinary acumen in the approach of facts and problems and the promotion of human values: i.e., goodness, the spirit of unity, love of truth, justice, peace and humanity. In this sense, the *Nkindi* person is worthy of the name.

So not only is a *Shushukulu* and *Nkindi* a wise person and scholar, s/he is also a creator, a builder, and a generator of ideas. These qualities are guided by values (virtues) that seek to ensure the integrity of the creative work and the harmony of the system for which it belongs. *Shushukulu* is an epithet of the Supreme Being, again, because it is the eldest and most wise sage and creator; It is a being that can get to the root of problems and reveal solutions that are hidden below the surface. This reminds us of our interpretation of the god *Rꜥ* in *Chapter 1* of this volume. We argued that *Rꜥ* is symbolized by the sun to represent, in part, that aspect of the Creator which reveals, through light, that which has been hidden. These are the qualities of a scholar and a builder.

God and Time

In the TOB database, as it regards our word "good," one of the entries provided was given as OCS (Old Church Slavonic) *godъ* "time, right time." The OED has OCS *godu* "pleasing time." It is interesting to note that Bantu also has this word for "time." Fu-Kiau in his essay "Ntangu-Tandu-Kolo: The Bantu-Kongo Concept of Time" (Adjaye, 1994: 17-34) provides us with the three major concepts of time in the Kikongo language. The first and most commonly used term is *ntangu*, which derives the word *tanga* "to count, put in order, accumulate, go into steps, go back and forth" (Egyptian *ḫ3ꜥ* "to throw, to cast, measure, examine, treat"; *metathesis*).[34] The second key word is *tandu*, from the verb *tanda* "to mark or to set on line, to cast." The third keyword is *kolo*, which is linked to the verb *kola*. This term expresses a state of being (ciLuba *iikala* "to be"); a level of strength at a given period of time. An additional key concept is *dunga* "events," which are understood as "dams of time" (*n'kama mia ntangu*). Each "dam" (event) is a division of time.

"Cosmic time" is called *tandu kiayalangana* or *tandu kia luyalungunu*, "the unlimited and ongoing formation process of *dungu* (events) throughout the universe (*luyalungunu*) through the power and energy of *Kalunga* (God, the completely complete being all by himself)" (Adjyaye, 1994: 23). That is to say that cosmic time represents the actual, ongoing, active time line of *Kalunga* energy and its "dams" (*n'kama*). Another way of saying this is that new creations throughout the universe come into being through the instrumentality of Kalunga's power, the agent of change and creation. This is very important to note as the concept of time (*ntangu*) is seen as an "unfolding" of time which is the Creator itself (God = change). Existence and time *is* the Creator and all events (*dungu*) are simply snap-shots of an unfolding process.

Notice that each term has the consonants we have associated with "god" throughout this text: *ntangu* (t-g), *tandu* (t-d), *kolo* (k-l), and *dunga* (d-g). All of these terms derive from the same root (*eela*) which lends itself to the concept of "time": measurable segments of ongoing change.

---

34 This same verb translates as *read* or to *dance*, as with one's own *ntanga* "feet, legs." From this root we get the term *matanga* (sing. *tanga*), which is an exuberant dance ceremony held in connection with the final funeral rites of a community leader. It is ultimately where we get the word "Tango" (the dance) from.

God the Father

Lastly, the word "good" deals with lineage in terms of "family, kin." We argue here that this could possibly extend into the notion of "father" (or mother) which is a common association for "God" as the primordial parent of all things (the beginning). This is expressed in our root *eela*: "to express, to make, to exit from self (a zero-point)." The root not only deals with *distance* and *generations*, but also deals with that which *causes* the perpetuation (to exit from the self). We see this reflected in the following terms in ciLuba:

> ***Lela*** "birth, give birth, produce"; "cause, source, generate"; "a family, a home"; "adopt, educate, raise"; "subject, submit." : ***baledi*** "parents" : ***buledi*** "to engender, maternity, paternity" : ***bulelà*** "relationship"; "relationship characterizing those who cannot marry them; "charity, kindness, generosity" : ***ciledi*** "cause, origin, source" : ***cileledi*** "matrix" : ***cilelelu*** "Time of Birth, date of birth" : ***cilelelu*** "placenta" (Syn.: *ndanga, nkìshyabendè*) : ***dilediibwa*** "birth, Christmas (birth of Jesus)" : ***dilela*** "birth, childbirth, labor, complicated thing, to be tricky" : ***Lelela*** [n + l> n, l + i> di] ⇒***-Badila*** > ***Lelesha***- "facilitate childbirth, attend a woman in childbirth" : ***Lelulula*** "be born again, to revive" : ***lulelu*** "childbirth, fertility, generation" : ***Mulelu*** > ***muledi*** "parent, mother, father" : ***mulelà*** "member of the extended family, parent" : ***mulelu*** "human fertility, fertility" : ***Ndedi*** "cause" (syn.: *ciLedi*) : ***ndela*** "prolific person, with many children" : ***ndelàngànyì*** "offspring, descendants, generations" : ***ndelelu*** "descendants, generation"; ***ndelelu Mulenga*** "family planning" : ***ndelu*** "generations, offspring, progeny" : ***Tanda*** " bring into the world, give birth, born/rise ☛ App.: ***Lela-> a-TEETA*** : ***lela***- "be abundant, abound, overflow" [☛ Syn.: ***Tèngeka***-> Akan, akanangan [n + l> n, l + i> di] ⇒-SELA] : ***Tèngeka***- ≋ ***Tenka***- "be abundant, abound" : ***Lèlakana***- ≋***-lèlakanangana*** "be found in large quantities, abound on all sides."[35]

Important to this discussion are the words *-tanda* "give birth to, bring forth, give birth" (<*lela* "birth, produce, cause, a family, a home, adopt, educate, raise, subject, submit); *-tanda* "original, native." We have another term worth mentioning: *ntungààmùlòngò*(ù) ≋ *ntùngu wa mulongo*(u), *ntùngaamulongo*(u) "first in the queue, leading." The underlying sense is "primary, primordial, first cause, leader, head, that which is before." Also embedded in this root is the concept of "generations, descendants, offspring, bringing into being," and these are all attributes given to "God" as our primary ancestor.

The concept of "order" is associated with "rank" or "row." A synonym for "order is "arrange" and "organize." These terms define "good" in English. These definitions would coincide with ciLuba *-longo,* in the word *mulongo*(u) "numbers"; *mulongo*(u) "row, rank, file, line, series, many, amount, of the same age, rival, to line, queuing, genealogy." These are essentially all of the concepts related to our Germanic: **gōd-a-* adj., **gad-a-* vb., *-ō-* vb "unite, be closely linked, matching; embrace, fixed and stick together." To be at the beginning of the ranking order is to be the "head." If you are the "source" of a line, a "lineage," then you are the mother or father of that "series" of lives thereafter. This notion of "beginnings" is captured in IE with the root *r-d*:

> Proto-IE: **ōrəd*- "to put the warp"; Old Greek: *ordéō* `laying a fabric on', *órdēma* = hē tolüpḕ tỗn eríōn (Hsch.), *órdikon* = tòn khthonískon (Parian word) Hsch.; Latin: *ōrdior, -īrī, ōrsus sum* `**instigate**, be stringed, **start**; sewn to a fabric; **begin**', *redōrdior* `hasple ab', pl. *ōrsa*, -um n. `**beginning**, investigation, speech', *ōrsus, -ūs* m. `beginning'; *ōrdō, -inis* m. `Series (originally `of the threads in the fabric'); **order**; **ranking**; status/

35 See PB **dèd* "bring up; caress, hold on knees; bear (child)."

stand; battle order' ; Other Italic: Umbr pl. abl. urnasier, gen. urnasiaru *`ōrdinariīs*, -ārum'; Russ. meaning: накладывать основу ткани

When discussing attributes of the Creator, not only is s/he the "beginning," the mother/father of all things, but this being is seen as the "biggest" or the "greatest" of all things. The languages reflect this and this is present in the *g-d* root. The following list of terms comes from Vaclav Blazek (2008), "A lexicostatistical comparison of Omotic languages."

5. **BIG**
5.1. Om.: (N) Ometo **dar-* id.; cf. Bench *dorg* "fat, stout" ||| Cush.: (E) Afar-Saho *adar-* "be big" || ?(S) **dir* "big" (Kiessling & Mous 2003, 96) ||| Sem.: Sabaic *drr* "plenty" > "harvest" (Biella 1982, 86), Arab. *darra* "to abound, yield in abundance" (E 135, #150: Ometo & Bench. + Arab.).
5.2 Om.: (S) Dime F *gad* "big" || (N) Zergulla *gudɛsa* "all" ||| Cush.: Beja *gwud* "many" || (C) Awngi *gud* "good" (Hetzron), cf. also Amhara *gud* "wonderful, marvelous" (CDA 76) || (E) **gud-/*gad-* "big" > Elmolo *guuta/guuda* "many", Arbore *gouda* id., *gudd'á* "big", Dasanech *guddu*, Oromo *guddaa*, Konso-Dirayta *kutt-* id. ||| Berb.: (N) Central Morocco *gudy* "être nombreux, en grand nombre, beaucoup" (NZ III, 737) ||| Chad. **gudV* "many": (W) Bolewa *gfdfŋ* "many" || (C) Padukwo *guda* "many" (Newman & Ma 1966, 237) ||| Sem.: Sabaic *gdd* "(the) great, great ones" (Biella 1982, 65), Arab. *ğadda* "to be great", Tigre *gäddä* "être plus grand" (Cohen 1970f, 99; Greenberg 1963, 59, #48: Bolewa+Padukwo+Wandala *kwottya* id. + Beja + Oromo; E 180, #265: Dime + Cush. + Chad. **g-d-* + Arab.) 5.3. Om.: (N) Ometo **git-* id. (E 183, #275) ||| Cush.: (E) Oromo Harar *guutuu*, Borana *gutu* "full" ||| Berb.: (E) Sokna *uggut* "abondamment; beaucoup; très" | (N) Djerba *egget* "beaucoup; très"; Shawiya *igit* "être nombreux", Kabyle *ggwet* "abonde", Shilha *igut* "abonder; être abondant, nombreux, en grande quantité, *tugut* "multitude; nombre; abondance" | (S) Ahaggar *iğat* "être nombreux, abondant", *ăğut* "grande quantité; la plupart" (NZ III, 908–09) ||| ?Chad.: (C) Wandala *kwottya* "many". (Bengtson, 2008: 95-96)

As we have stated throughout, the African root is *-r-* (ciLuba *eela*) that has a velar prefix fossilized in Indo-European. This root is reflected in Central-Sudanic: CS **oro* -r- "be big, tall, wide"; **ale* -l- "grow tall, grow, big."[36] The TOB database has the following supportive entries to go with Bengtson (2008):

Proto-Afro-Asiatic: **gad-* "old age group; elder"; Semitic: **gadd-* 'grandfather, ancestor'; East Chadic: **gaḍ-* (<**gaHad-*) 'old'; High East Cushitic: **gad-* 'age group, generation'; South Cushitic: **gad-* 'old man'; Notes: Cf. 1287 **gi/ud-* 'to be big, many'

Proto-Afro-Asiatic: **gVdVl-* 'be big'; Semitic: **gVdVl-* 'big' 1, 'be big' 2, 'become big, strong' 3; Central Chadic: **digwal-* 'big'; Notes: Derived from **gid-/*gud-* 'be big, be many'?

Proto-Semitic: **gVdVl-* 'big' 1, 'be big' 2 'become big, strong' 3; Ugaritic: *gdl* 1; Hebrew: *gdl* 2, *gādōl* 1; Aramaic: *gədal* 2; Arabic: *ǯădil-* 1, ǯdl 3; Notes: Cf. Har g(i)*dīr* 'big'.

Proto-CChadic: **digwal-* 'big'; Kilba: *dùgōlù* [Kr N 281]; Margi: *digàl*

36 Proto-SBB (P. Boyeldieu, P. Nougayrol & P. Palayer 2004) La liste de Swadesh pour le proto-SBB (Sara-Bongo-Bagirmi, branche Soudan Central des langues Nilo-Sahariennes) http://sumale.vjf.cnrs.fr/NC/Public/pdf/swadesh_SBB.pdf (retrieved June 1, 2013). See also PWS **la* "old"

[Kr]; Wamdiu: *digàlu* [Kr]; Hildi=Margi Mbazuwa: *dīgalu* [Kr]; Notes: it cannot be excluded that *-l* is a suffix.[37]

Proto-Afro-Asiatic: **gi/ud-* 'be big, be many'; Semitic: **gidd-* 'many, much'; Berber: **gud-* 'many' 1, 'be numerous' 2; Western Chadic: **gVd-* 'increase' 1, 'many' 2; Central Chadic: **gVḍ-* <**gVHad-* 'many'; Saho-Afar: Af *gide* 'amount, quantity', *gidiidin* 'the entire, complete' PH 113; Low East Cushitic: **gud*(d)- 'big, large'; Omotic: **gVd-* 'big'; Notes: Cf. 66 **gVd-* 'old age'[38]

It is this notion of "big," "old," "many," "grandfather," "ancestors" that gives way to the *g-d* root meaning "leader, guide, chief person; summit; capital city"; "highest in rank or power; most important or prominent; supreme, best,"; "chief, principal, first." These are the ideas we argue are meant behind the term "God" which comes from the same root as "good" (< PIE **ghedh* "to unite, be associated, suitable"; "good, to be good, to fit"; "unite, be closely linked, matching"; "embrace`, fixed or stick/stand together"; "relative, same/alike, hold, time, advantage, honor, glory, festival, feast, make, think, order, arrange").

An interesting development in the discussion of the word "god" via Wiki posits that the very name *Goth* derives from the same root as the word for "god" in the Proto-Germanic language. As it regards the Gothic tribal names, the entry states:

> A significant number of scholars have connected this root with the names of three related Germanic tribes: the *Geats*, the *Goths* and the *Gutar*. These names may be derived from an eponymous chieftain Gaut, who was subsequently deified. He also sometimes appears in early Medieval sagas as a name of Odin or one of his descendants, a former king of the Geats (Gaut(i)), an ancestor of the Gutar (Guti), of the Goths (Gothus) and of the royal line of Wessex (Geats) and as a previous hero of the Goths (Gapt). Some variant forms of the name Odin such as the Lombardic Godan may point in the direction that the Lombardic form actually comes from Proto-Germanic **guđánaz*. *Wōdanaz* or *Wōđinaz* is the reconstructed Proto-Germanic name of a god of Germanic paganism, known as Odin in Norse mythology, *Wōden* in Old English, *Wodan* or *Wotan* in Old High German and *Godan* in the Lombardic language. Godan was shortened to God over time and was adopted/retained by the Germanic peoples of the British isles as the name of their deity, in lieu of the Latin word Deus used by the Latin speaking Christian church, after conversion to Christianity.
>
> During the complex christianization of the Germanic tribes of Europe, there were many linguistic influences upon the Christian missionaries. One example post downfall of the western Roman Empire are the missionaries from Rome led by Augustine of Canterbury. Augustine's mission to the Saxons in southern Britain was conducted at a time when the city of Rome was a part of a Lombardic kingdom. The translated bibles which they brought on their mission were greatly influenced by the Germanic tribes they were in contact with, chief among them being the Lombards and Franks. The translation for the word deus of the Latin bible was influenced by the then current usage by the tribes for their highest deity, namely Wodan by Angles, Saxons and Franks of north-central and western Europe and Godan by the Lombards of south-central Europe around Rome. There are many instances where the name Godan and Wodan are contracted to God and Wod.[4] One instance is the wild hunt (a.k.a. Wodan's wild

---

37 Compare Proto-CChadic **digwal-* 'big' (d-g-l) to Sumerian *diĝir* "God" (d-g-r).

38 We are reminded of a proposal mentioned in *Chapter 3.1* of the word "god" deriving from the Babylonian word $ga^{w}d$ meaning "fortune." This would derive from the same AA root **gi/ud-* 'be big, be many' which denotes "increase, flourish" and thus "fortune."

hunt) where Wod is used.[5[39]][6[40]]

The sources assert that the name for the founding chieftain *Gaut* derives from the Proto-Germanic root **guđ-* "to pour."[41] The reasoning is unconvincing to me and requires some conceptual and linguistic acrobatics to make it work. My suggestion is that the name *Gaut* was an ethnic name for the Proto-Goths. With "good" having derived forms of "kinship, family, cousin, etc.," the term could have been used simply as a term to denote the first royal "family." In ancient times people would often take as their ethnic name the name of a king. For example, Credo Mutwa in his book *Indaba My Children* (1964: 656) provides some comparative commentary on such a practice among the Amazulu of South Africa. He goes on to state that:

> The Black man has a strong parent, or fetish complex, dating from the days when a community could produce only one brave man at a time, who could challenge a savage beast with a bone-tipped spear. The whole community then looked upon such a hero for its protection. Even today we still choose that one man or woman who will be our living totem pole, our god-on-earth, our parent symbol; who is the embodiment of all our aspirations and our unity, and to whom we shall give all our love and loyalty and around whom we shall rally in times of evil. This person will be our nation, the symbol of all our ideals and our dreams. He or she shall be part of us and we shall be part of him or her. Thus a Barotse from the west of Zambia never says 'I am a subject of Paramount Chief Mwanawina'. He will always say 'I am a Mwanawina'. At the time of the Zulu King Cetshwayo his subjects called themselves 'the Cetshwayo'. This is how most tribes got their names.

The king is the living totem, the parent symbol, the embodiment of all of the community's aspirations and is the symbol of their national unity to which all gives their love and loyalty. It is under this symbol, the king, who the community rallies behind in times of evil. If "god" is named after the king, then PIE * *ghādh-* could be the origin either relating to "linked together, family" (as it regards an ethnic group), or as it regards someone in authority, a "big man" (PIE * *ghādh-* "fixed, firm, strong"), Proto-Afro-Asiatic **gi/ud-* 'be big, be many'; **gad-* "old, age group; elder." The proposed eponymous founder may in fact be legendary or the name could have been just a general word for someone who was "big, strong." Compare PIE **gʷrandh-/-e-* 'strong, big, tall' (g-r-d) to PAA **gVdVl-* 'be big' (g-d-l); P.Chadic. **digwal-* 'big' (d-g-l). It can be postulated that metathesis occurred between the /d/ and the /l/ sounds in PAA **gVdVl-* 'be big,' giving us PIE **g-r-d* (with nasalization of /d/). Note the commentary on the very word

39 See the chant in the Medieval and Early Modern folklore section of the Wikipedia entry for Wōden.

40 Edward Lumley. (1852). *Northern Mythology, Comprising the Principal Popular Traditions and Superstitions of Scandinavia, North Germany and the Netherlands: Compiled from Original and Other Sources*. In Three Volumes. *North German and Netherlandish Popular Traditions and Superstitions, Volume 3*. London.

41 [Moreover, the names *Geats*, *Goths* and *Gutes* are closely related tribal names. *Geat* was originally Proto-Germanic **Gautoz*, and *Goths* and *Gutes* were **Gutaniz*. According to Andersson (1996), **Gautoz* and **Gutaniz* are two ablaut grades of a Proto-Germanic word with the meaning "to pour" (modern Swedish *gjuta*, modern Danish *gyde*, modern German *giessen*; English *in-got*, *gushing*) designating the tribes as "pourers of metal" or "forgers of men"]. In other words, it is proposed here that "god" derives from *pouring* as in previous claims, except this time it refers to the blacksmiths who poured liquid-metal to be shaped. Given our commentary, I would go with the term actually referring to the smith itself in alignment with *ḳd* "craftsman, builder, potter, bricklayer" with any other associations being derived meanings. As noted in Diop (1991), Barnes (1997) and Finch (1998), many kings in Africa were associated with the craft of metallurgy and were credited with supernatural attributes (god-like powers). This may have been the case in early Europe.

"king" from the OED:

> **King**: Old English *cyning* "king, ruler," from Proto-Germanic **kuninggaz* (cf. Dutch *koning*, Old Norse *konungr*, Danish *konge*, Old Saxon and Old High German *kuning*, Middle High German *künic*, German *König*). **Possibly related to Old English *cynn* "family, race"** (see ***kin***),[42] making a *king* originally a "leader of the people;" or from a related root suggesting "noble birth," making a *king* originally "one who descended from noble birth." The sociological and ideological implications render this a topic of much debate... In Old English, used for names of chiefs of Anglian and Saxon tribes or clans, then of the states they founded. Also extended to British and Danish chiefs they fought. The chess piece so called from early 15c.; the playing card from 1560s; use in checkers/draughts first recorded 1820. Applied in nature to species deemed remarkably big or dominant (e.g.*king crab*, 1690s). In marketing, *king-size* is from 1939, originally of cigarettes. (bolded emphasis mine)

As we can see here, a king was simply the "head of a family" (head of household) and this archaic term extended to encompass the leader of a community, village or kingdom. We argue these same connotations extended to the Creator who is the original "head of household" which is the Universe itself. The Divine is also the "big (wo)man," the one who gave birth to us all.

Conclusion

We posit that these are the ideas that the Indo-Europeans had in mind when conceptualizing the attributes of the Supreme-Force of Heaven. They called on He who is primordial; the one who arranges things and puts them in their proper order; the infinite unity; the best; Supreme Being; the Old Man; the one who guides us; our Primary Ancestor; the highest in rank and power; the Head; the "Unmoved Mover," the one who is fixed and permanent; the one who endures forever; the one who causes things to "rise" and "be"; the power that holds things up; the standing ground from which things arise; the Architect and Builder; the Divine Potter; the one worthy of honor and glory; the one in whose honor we hold festivals and feasts; the maker of all that exist; the one whom all things are GOOD (in order); the everlasting, established and imperishable one: *ḏd* 𓊽𓊽 = "God."

A god is someone who understands, creates and maintains systems. As Fu-Kiau (2001: 70) notes, man is a "system-of-systems" [*Muntu i kimpa kia bimpa*][43] and it is our ability to create systems that gives the *muntu* "god-like" powers. God is "god" because it created the ultimate system, the Universe. God is a master who created a system that *adds life to life* and if we are to emulate its genius, we must understand that fundamental principle: i.e., the principle of *life*.

---

42 Kin: c.1200, from Old English *cynn* **"family; race; kind, sort, rank; nature; gender, sex,"** from Proto-Germanic **kunjam* "family" (cf. Old Frisian *kenn,* Old Saxon *kunni,* Old Norse *kyn,* Old High German *chunni* "kin, race;" Danish and Swedish *kön,* Middle Dutch, Dutch *kunne* "sex, gender;" Gothic *kuni* "family, race," Old Norse *kundr* "son," German Kind "child"), from PIE **gen(e)-* "to produce" (see *genus*). Compare to Proto-Bantu **kodo* "grandparent, female ancestor, family"; **kódò* "kinship"; **kodi* "resemble"; **kódò* "base of tree trunk, big root"; **kodan* "resemble each other."

43 Alternatively man is also called *n'kingu a n'kingu* "a principle of principles," i.e., a pattern of patterns. The human being is a microcosm of the greater macro-universe and thus the saying, "Know thyself and thou will know the gods and their functions." The gods are nothing more than the creative agents responsible for perpetuating the life-systems of the universe.

Not only is God the creator of the system, it is the system itself.[44]

I would argue that if African/African-American people are going return to being the "gods" that we were, we have to understand systems (biological, political, economic and social). This is why African priests studied nature so they could understand the nature of "systems" and how to recreate these systems in the social sphere. As the African-American proverb states, "You can't lead the people unless you feed the people." In order for us to be "gods," we have to create (wisely) a system by which the community can comfortably take care of its basic needs. In order to this, we must create a social system among ourselves that will allow African/African-Americans (BaMelela/Nkale) to better relate to each other and our respective environment(s). Dr. Amos Wilson (*Blueprint for Black Power*, 1998) and Dr. Cheikh Anta Diop (*Black Africa: The Economic and Cultural Basis for a Federated State*, 1987) understood these principles with the utmost perspicaciousness. With a better understanding of what a *god* is, we better understand the missions of these warrior scholars and the charges they left for us—the future leaders of our people—to carry out. For those of us who are gods (*ḳd, d̲d, kȝ, bakulu*) in training, the following excerpt is our current mission, if we choose to accept it.

> We're suffering from the absence of an economic system. Money is not a system; money is what it is. A system involves the systematic and organized utilization of money; a systematized utilization and distribution of money. Without the pattern, without the system, without the organization, one does not have an economy. An economy exists prior to money. There were economies in the world before money was invented. We don't even have to have money to have an economized system. So ultimately, when we study an economic system, we recognize that an economic system at its base refers to the nature of the relationship between people. It's the systematic way people choose to relate one to the other that makes an economic system - not money. When we lack a systematic way of relating to each other then we can have money and still be poor, have money and be robbed - which is what we are. (1993: 45)
>
> *The Falsification of Afrikan Consciousness: Eurocentric History, Psychiatry and the Politics of White Supremacy* –Amos N. Wilson

---

44 We are reminded of the conclusion derived at by the physicist Dr. Gabriel Oyibo in his *Highlights of the Grand Unified theorem: Formulation of the Unified Field Theory or the Theory of Everything* (2001). In this text Oyibo argues that God is essentially an infinite unified force field of energy in motion that can be described by the formula $G_{ij},j=0$ for which matter is just a concentration of this field. Oyibo posits, mathematically, that as time (t) approaches infinity, G approaches a wave function. Oyibo's GOD Almighty's Grand Unified Theorem (GAGUT), which is represented by an absolute exact mathematical equation $G_{ij},j=0$, can be interpreted as GOD (G_{ij}), in GOD's Material (i) and Space Time (j) Dimensions, does not change, where the comma symbolizes change in tensor notation. In a simple language, GAGUT states that GOD or everything including the Unified Force Field or any fundamental force or particle interactions, is conserved within a transformation process over space and time, which cannot be disputed by any logical process (Oyibo, 2001:96). This formula is rooted in a number of Maxwell conservation equations. Creation therefore becomes a transformation *of* God, the only *entity* that was in existence at the beginning of creation (if there ever was a beginning). That is to say that nothing can exist outside of infinity, so all that exist exists as a component of the infinity. Since part of God transformed into the material universe during creation, we understand that God existed in non-material form before creation. One version of that Non-material form is Waves, what the ancients called *Spirit*. The Egyptians called this "spirit" *Nwn*, "the primordial water waves of pre-creation." The wave component of the Force Field in Oyibo's formula is given by the equation $F(\eta_0)$.

UNDERSTANDING ÀṢẸ AND ITS RELATION TO ÈṢÚ AMONG THE YORÙBÁ AND ASET IN ANCIENT EGYPT

Introduction

This is a preliminary essay to discuss the possible origins, meaning(s) and applications for the concept in the Yorùbá *Ifá* tradition called *àṣẹ*. We also take a look at the possible connections between the Yorùbá deity *èṣú*, and the goddess of *ciKam-ciKulu* (ancient Egypt) *ꜣs.t* (Isis). Throughout this discourse we hope to expand our understanding of this term and its earliest conceptualizations using the analytic tool of comparative linguistics. This essay is concerned with defining *àṣẹ* and its relationship to other African deities. We argue that the word *àṣẹ* derives from an old Kongo-Saharan word for "head" and it is the action of the head by which *àṣẹ* derives its popular meanings. There are other connotations associated with this term that might be the result of a creative synthesis of other terms that have a similar pronunciation, that might appear to have a conceptual relationship with the primary term (*àṣẹ*).

Definition

John Pemberton, III in his article "The Dreadful God and the Divine King" (in Barnes 1997: 123), notes that the "meaning of *àṣẹ* is extraordinarily complex." I argue that this is the case because the word is very old and has taken on various extended meanings over the millennia by way of metaphoric extension—thus expanding the term and its possible applications within the language. One dictionary entry defines *àṣẹ* as:

> ***Àṣẹ:*** a coming to pass; law; command; authority; commandment; enjoinment; imposition; power; precept; discipline; instruction; cannon; biding; document; virtue; effect; consequence; imprecation.[1]

This term is comparable to Egyptian *šꜣ* "to read, to authorize, to determine, to decree, to allot, to design, to ordain, to commission;" *šꜣ.t* "something decreed, ordained by God; dues, revenues, taxes, impost."

Pemberton (Barnes 1997: 123) notes that one of the contexts for *àṣẹ* is "kingship." As we can see from the dictionary entry above, this association is derived from the meanings

1 *Dictionary of Yorùbá Language*.(1913). Church Missionary Society Bookshop. Lagos, Nigeria.

"law, command, authority and power." Verger (1966:35) defines *àṣẹ* as "the vital power, the energy, the great strength of all things." It is also the "divine energy manifest in the process of procreation" (Egyptian *sꜥꜣ* "the source of life, to begin;" *šꜣ.t*  "the goddess of primeval matter—a form of Hathor" (Budge 723a)).

As noted by Pemberton, *àṣẹ* does not signify anything particular, yet it invests all things, exists everywhere and as the warrant for all creative activity, opposes chaos and the loss of meaning in human experience (Barnes, 1997:124). Kamalu (1998: 142) recognizes *àṣẹ* as "vital force." This vital force is known as *se* among the Fon of Benin. This *se* is a part of *Mawu* (the feminine aspect of the Divine *Mawu-Lisa*) that permeates through each person and the divine *word.*

The linguistic consonant root of this term in African languages is *-r-* and can refer to the "head, the beginning, to express."[2] It is possible that the evolution of the root *-r-* is as follows: r > d > t > s. The root is best explained by ciLuba-Bantu: ***eela*** "remove, send away, clear out, dismiss"[3] or "to exit from the self (sound, idea, word, object...) make, express, speak." We have: PWS *LI, DI* "head, spirit, hand"; PWS *ti* "head"; PWS *lu*, (*du*) "head"; PCS **d.u* "head"; PWN *TÚI* "head" (Campbell-Dunn, 2009b). Because the word for "head" is associated with "leadership," the term extended itself to mean "power" in general (biological and social). The same root also means "to express" and therefore is associated with "speech" (the action of the head). The verb "to make" may come from PWS *LI/DI* "head" (as in command to make things happen), or it can come from PWS *LI/DI* "hand" and the "action of the hand" that "makes, manufactures" things. I am not sure what came first in the latter. Did the verb "express" come first and then was associated with the noun "hand," or is it the reverse?

However, there is an alternative theory which is just as plausible and that is the original *-r-* root tacked on an affix like we saw in *Chapter 2*: e.g., **k-l* "head" > *s-l* "head." The *s-l* or *t-l* forms could have lost the final *-r/-l* leaving only *-s-/-t-* as the root. We will see why this may be the case when we start including the ancient Egyptian data. If both of these processes did indeed occur at different periods, then what we may be witnessing are doublets in the language (Yorùbá has many doublets in its language).

We can see all of this culminate in the following: Tshiluba *asa* "to begin"; Hebrew *swh* and Yorùbá *se* "to come to pass"; Yorùbá *àṣẹ* and Tiv *tsav* "the power to cause to happen;" Hebrew *siwwah*, Amarigna *ez*, Yorùbá *se* "to command," Egyptian *sꜣ* "ordain, order." We also have Yorùbá *ṣe* "do"; *isé* "work" and Hebrew *asah* "to do, to make" (Yorùbá *sëse*). Compare to the Afro-Asiatic data for the word "stand":

> 80-STAND: 80.3. Om.: (N) Chara *aš-ne*; Dizoid **aš-* id. ||| ?Cush.: **'əs-* "to do, make" (CDA 55–56) || (E) **'as-/*'is-* > Saho *is-* ~ *iš-* "to do, make"; Boni *as-* "to prepare, make"; Sidamo *ass-*, Kambatta *ass-*, Hadiyya *iss-*, Burji *iss-* "to do, act, make" (Sasse 1982, 107; D 151). (Bengtson, 2008: 128)

In Tshiluba we also have *esa/enza* "to make, act, behave, take the appearance of"; *dy-enza* "action, treatment"; *enji* "legislative" (*bukalenga bw-enji* (*j<>z/s*) "legislative power"); *enze-ka* "cause, happen, occur;" *Ngenzi* (*<enza*) "officer, manufacturer." The underlying spirit of this root is "the power to cause to happen, the authority to make changes." People in legislative

---

2 See *Chapter 2* for an expanded discussion on how "head" became a word for "authority."

3 This root is present in the Egyptian word *srw* "remove" where *s-* is a causative prefix.

office (the *heads* of state) are the ones with the authority to make things happen in the nation.[4] This is reflected in the personification of *wsr* (Osiris) and *ꜣs.t/js.t* (Isis): for not only are they officers/administrators of the state (the first king and queen), they are also progenitors of man and creation according to the ancient Egyptian myths.

The underlying theme for *àṣẹ* is "power" and this power is manifested in two primary forms: 1) **biological power** which shapes one's physical existence for good or ill, and 2) **political power** which shapes people as moral and social beings (Barnes, 1997:124).

It is in its latter branch of meaning by which "kingship" becomes synonymous with *àṣẹ*. In the Igbo language, this root is reflected as *ọzō* "title of high degree conferring on the owner privileges and honour as a sacrosanct (sacred, holy, revered, untouchable) being" (s > z). The Igbo word *Ezè* means "king." *Eze* can also mean "to honor, to participate, and to assume a role of privilege."[5] A variant of this form is *isi* "head, chief."[6]

Antonio Loprieno, in his book *Ancient Egyptian: A Linguistic Introduction* (1995: 246, n26), informs us of a possible sound feature in the ancient Egyptian language that is meaningful for our current discussion.

> W. Schenkel, "Das Wort fur Konig (von Oberagypten)'," GM 94 (1986), 57-73 suggests the interpretation of /z/ as affricative [ts], among other reasons because it stands for /t/ + /s/ in the word /nzw/ "king," whose more traditional writing is /ntsw/. Whether an affricate (as suggested by Schenkel and by the equation with Afroas. **s*) or an ejective (as suggested here on the basis of the historical evolution to a voiceless counterpart which it shares with voiced plosives), it is not surprising that this phoneme should be used to indicate a sibilant immediately following a nasal, a phonetic surrounding which often tends to generate affrication: /ns/ < or = [vnts] (Schenkel) or else = [vns'] >= /ns/ [vnts]) see Hock, Principles of Historical Linguistics, 117 ff.

The Egyptian word *nsw* "king" is cognate with Yorùbá *àṣẹ*. Loprieno informs us that it is more likely pronounced *ntsw* "king" (with *n-* prefix denoting "one who is" or "possessor of"; "the quality of" [being]). The *-sw-* root is a by-form of the word *šw* "to win power, to gain power." So an *ntsw* "king" is in reality a "possessor/owner of power." In the Nupe language of Nigeria we have the word *Etsu* "king." The Egyptian *ntsw/nsw* may be a reflex of *nḫt* "victory, strong, might, victorious, stiff (of joints), to protect; Giant (name of a constellation); a strong arm, adult, a champion, hero, heroic, powerful, obdurate." The underlying theme is "bigness, increase" which equates to "power."[7] A reflex is *ḫꜣ* "numerous, 1000."

The Yorùbá deity *Ẹ̀ṣú* is also known as the "King of Ketu" and we know his name is a by-form of *àṣẹ* which is connected to *kingship*. In Bantu you may not see the *ntsw* or *etsu* variant. However, its root is present in the following forms: Proto-Bantu **koci* "lion, chief"; **gocal* "husband, man"; **kodi* "be strong, be difficult, be hard"; **koda* "strength"; **kodi* "hawk, bird or prey" (Egyptian /*ḥrw*/); **kodi* "crocodile." This is reflected in Ngala *nkasu* "strong"; Mande bar' *ka-le* "strong"; Mangbetu *kwakwara* "strong"; Sumerian *kalag* (*kala*) "be mighty"; Nguni-Bantu *nkosi* "king, master, chief, lord"; Sepedi-Bantu *kgosi* "king."

---

4 In a modern sense this *-s-r-* root would signify, for example, someone like a manager at a retail store. For if you have a dispute with a product or service, one usually ask to speak to a "manager" because it is she who has the authority to make changes to the normal milieu to rectify the situation.

5 Kay Williamson. (1972). *Dictionary of Onitcha Igbo*, 2nd Edition. Ethiope press.

6 It would appear that *ꜣs.t* 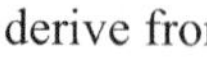 is a feminine form of this root.

7 All of these concepts derive from a root that means "height, tall, big." See *Chapter 2* of this volume.

The /ḫ/ sound in Egyptian interchanges with /š/ and /s/.[8] With that said, the following are of importance to this discussion: *ꜣḫw* [*r-ḫ*] "power (of God), mastery (over work)," *nḫt/nḫtw* "strength, force, power, victory, victorious, mighty, stiff, hard, stiffen, become hard, successful, champion."[9] We find a variation of this root as *šꜣ* "ordain, order, predestine, assign, settle, determine, decide, foretell"; *sr* official, nobleman, magistrate > *wsr* "power, part of the head" (Yorùbá *Òrìṣà* "head, authority, power"). In ciLuba *n-ḫt* is reflected as *ciNtu* "man of authority, considerable; person of disproportionate size"; *-kìtù* "valiant, valorous"; *-kìta* "dare, daring, show/audacity" (boldness, courage)."[10] Since the underlying theme is "bigness, expansion—and one can add to this list "potency—we see this root reflected in ciLuba *bi-ntu/ka-ntu* "wealth, possessions" (Egyptian *ḫ-t* "things, possessions, offerings"; ciLuba *ci-Ntu* "object, thing"); *citoto, citota, citotu* "100" (Luba-Katanga), "1000"·(Luba-Kasayi) (Egyptian *ḫꜣ* "1000"; *ḫt* "rod"[100 cubits]).[11]

This association of kingship with *àṣẹ* is also reflected in another meaning for *àṣẹ* as given by E. Bọ́lájí Ìdòwú in his classic work *Olódùmarè* (1994: 72): *àṣẹ* "scepter." A scepter is a classical African emblem of power. The word *àṣẹ* "scepter" in Yorùbá I equate with *wꜣs* [𓌀] "scepter, staff, rod" in ancient Egyptian.[12] Words that begin with an *h-* or a *w-* in ancient

8 The /ḫ/ interchanges with /š/. In Egyptian the [M8 - 𓆸] glyph can be rendered both as *ꜣḫ.t* and *šꜣ*. For example we have *ꜣḫ* "orchard, field, arable land, meadow, tilled land" and *šꜣj* "estate, garden, orchard, grove" (Budge 723a) (metathesis). We see this interchange in ciLuba as well. In Egyptian we have *ꜥšꜣ* "many, numerous, much, plentiful, ordinary, quantity, multitude, multiply"; *ꜥšꜣ.t* "the many, the masses, many, abound, rich, numerous, much." In ciLuba: *oso, osu, onso*; *onsu*; *-ònso*(u) "all, whole, entire, each, every"; *bwônso*(u) "totality, ensemble"; *mwonso, mooso, monsu, munso*; *lonso/loso* (*sasa*) "extend, become many"; *kwônso*(u) "everywhere"; *ponso* "everywhere"; *yônso*(u) "whole, each" (see Bilolo, 2011: 141). Here we can see that the Egyptian variation (*ꜥšꜣ*) in *lonso/loso* where Egyptian /*ꜣ*/ = /l/ and the phoneme order has been reversed (metathesis). Egyptian *ꜥšꜣ.t* becomes ciLuba *shiya* > *di-shiya* (*t.ꜥšꜣ*) "multiply, many, crowd, multitude." With that said, we also have in ciLuba this progression: *-angi/-ungi*; *sadika* "increase, to grow, to multiply, to expand." Other variations in ciLuba are: *-ingi-*, *-angi-*, *ungi* > *abungi, a-wungi*; *-anga* > *-bangi, a-bangi, mangi*; *cyanga* > *ambula cyanga*; *bingi*. This phenomenon allows us to read *šꜣ* as "*nga/ngi/ngo*" in the words *Cyanga* or *CaNga, bwaNga* ("manufacture, produce"; also "medicine"), *biNgi, Cyenga, mweNga*. To verify that /*ḫ*/ and /*š*/ interchange in Egyptian as well, note: *ꜥšꜣ* "numerous" and *ḫꜣ* "numerous, 1000" [M12]; *ḳnw* "plenty, numerous" (*ꜣ* = *l* > *n*); *swr* "to multiply."

9 The following Egyptian terms may be of importance: *mnḫ* "potent" (of king); "to be excellent, efficient, potent, well established, beneficent, efficacious"; *mnḫw* "excellence, virtues (of someone), benefactions, acts of grace." Compare to Mandika *mansa/masa* "King, Emperor."

10 To cross-check the sound correspondences, we observe Egyptian *ḫt* "wood, timber, tree, woodland, mast, stick, pole," ciLuba *mu-ci, ka-ci, tu-ci* "tree, plant"; Egyptian *ḫtꜥ* "a weapon," ciLuba *citota* "hammer"; Egyptian *ḫtꜥ* "a drug" (medicine), kiKongo *nkisi* "medicine" (but ciLuba *muci* "plant, tree" would be cognate here; medicine from plants); *nḫt* "youth," ciLuba *bu-nsongè*(à) "youth, adolescence" (<*nsonga* "young girl or boy"; Egyptian *nḫ.t* > *t.nḫ*? : *kt.t* "small, the young"); *-tekète*(a) "young, tender, delicate," *cijila* "young, youth" (Egyptian *ḫꜣ* "be young, be little"; *nḫn* "infant, baby, young, youthful, the younger"; ciLuba *-akùnyì* "young, younger").

11 These are considered "big" numbers.

12 The word *àṣẹ* "power" and *àṣẹ* "scepter" have two different etymologies. The *àṣẹ* of power derives from "head" while "scepter" derives from "wood, stick." This is confirmed in Egyptian with *wꜣs* "scepter, staff, rod." Compare with *ḫt* "wood, timber, tree, woodland, mast, stick, pole" (*ḫ* > *s?*). Note also *wḫꜣ* "column, tent pole"; *šbd / šꜣb / šti* "staff, rod, cudgel"; *twrit* "wand, stick, staff, rod"; *nṯryt* "pole, cult flag" Compare the *š-r* to *k-r* in *mkr/mꜣkr* "staff."

Egyptian and Semitic often yield zero for cognate terms in Yorùbá.[13] *Table 1* below provides further evidence for this correspondence.

Table 1:

Egyptian	**Yorùbá**
w3s "scepter" 	*àṣẹ* "scepter"
w3s "dominion, have dominion, power"	*àṣẹ* "authority, power, law, command"
w3s "honor (due to a god or king), prestige"	*ọ̀ṣọ́* "elegance, finery, neatness, jewels" *ọzō* (**Igbo**) "honor, title of high degree" [Pulaar *wasu* "glorification" (Lam, 1994: 44)]
w3s "fortunate, prosperous, well-being, prosperity"	*ajé* "money, the goddess of money"[1] (s>j) *àṣẹ* "the force to make all things happen and multiply" (Thompson, 1984:18) [Pulaar *waas* "riches" (Lam,ibid.)]
w3s "to batter, to strike, to break, to bruise, to lay" *w3s* "ruin" *wsi* "to saw, cut up, trim"	*ọṣẹ́* "hurt, injury"; *ẹṣẹ́* "blow with the fist"; *ṣá* (*ṣalogbe*) "to cut, to wound with a knife"; *aṣá* "a heavy spear or javelin used to kill elephants"(with noun forming prefix *a-*); *oṣe* "club of god of thunder [*Ṣango*]" (a striking instrument);

The *w3s* ("power, dominion") scepter [𓌀] is a symbol that appeared often in relics, art and hieroglyphics associated with the ancient Egyptian religion. They appear as long, straight staves, with a stylized animal head on top and a forked end. These are old pastoral emblems that came to symbolize royalty in the Egyptian culture. It may be a predynastic symbol, but it is definitely attested in the first dynasty (Wilkinson, 2001: 189). It was associated with the *nsw bjty* "king," as well as the deities (e.g., Set and Anpu). In later times it became a symbol of control over the forces of chaos. It also took the place of, in many reliefs, the *ḏd* 𓊽 pillars which are depicted holding up the sky.[14]

The term *w3s* is also present in the name for the New Kingdom capital of Upper Egypt *w3s.t*, later known as Thebes. There was also a goddess (pictured below) by the name of *w3s.t* (often written as *wosret*), which Wilkinson (2003: 169) defines as "the powerful female one." Wilkinson (2003) speculates that *w3s.t* was probably an early form of *hwt ḥrw* (Hathor). I would argue for an early form of *3s.t* (Isis) based on the root of their names respectively (*w3st* > *3st*).

13 For example: Eg. *wꜥb* "cleanse," Yorùbá *bọ́* "wash"; Arabic *wady* "lowland," Yorùbá *òdo* "lowland, river valley, valley"; Eg. *wꜥb* "priest," Yorùbá *oba* "king, priest"; Eg. *wꜥb* "free woman," Yorùbá *obí* "the female of cattle"; *òbò*/*abẹ* "vagina"; Eg. *wḏ.t* "eye of Ra"; Yorùbá *oju* "eye"; Egyptian *ḥḏ.t* "white crown," Yorùbá *ade* "crown"; Egyptian *w3b* "be distinguished, be honored, be strong" (<*b3* "power, might"); Yorùbá *oba* "king"?.

14 This is reminiscent of the Bakongo concept of *simbi*: an energy force, the God power that "holds up" the universe. See K. Bunseki Fu-Kiau (2006). *Simba Simbi: Hold up that which holds you up*. Dorrance Publishing Co. Inc.

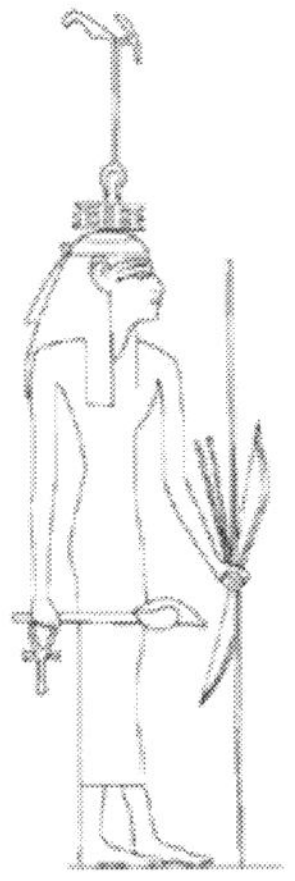

The goddess *w3s.t*

The *w3s* (*àṣẹ*) scepter was not only found in Egypt, but among many pastoral societies across Africa with varying names. **Table 2** below shows a few of these staves and their locations across Africa.

Table 2: *w3s* staves in Africa[15]

Hangool Staff – Afar	Woko Staff – Hamar, Ethiopia	A = Egyptian staff (Cairo Museum) B = Peul of Sengal (A. M. Lam) C = Nanakana of Ghana (I'Fan Museum Dakar)
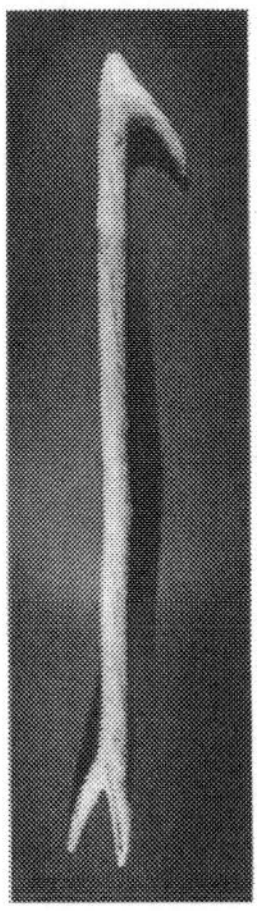		

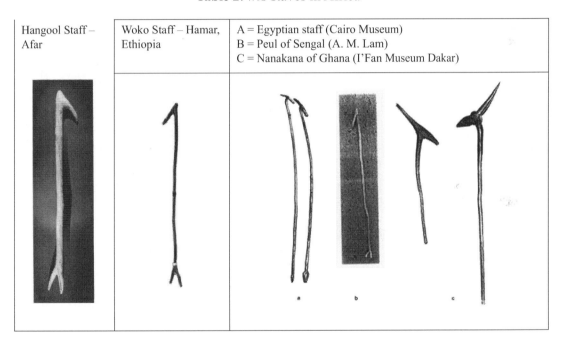

Alain Anselin, *i-Medjat Journal* (Num. 4, February 2010, pg. 17), in his brief article entry titled "Note sur le w3s égyptien et le woko hamar" (Note on the Egyptian *w3s* [scepter] and the Hamar *woko* [staff]), provides us with an example from Ethiopia on the possible meaning of the Egyptian *w3s* scepter as inspired by its shape in the Egyptian tradition. The emblem is the symbol for the *South Omo Research Center* and the staff is called *shonkor* in Arbore and *woko* in Hamar (Ethiopia). Dr. Hisada, during a dedication ceremony for the center, explained that:

> *...a hook at one end and a fork at the other end was already known in Ancient Egypt and today is still used in South Omo by the Arbore, the Hamar and others"*

15 For third colum images, see Lam (1994: 58)

> In Hamar, the *woko* "*is also extended to the realm of ritual where the fork of the staff is used to ward off what is unwanted (disease, drought, war) and the hook is used to draw close what is wanted (health, abundance, peace). Hisada should use the hooked end of the staff, Ivo said, to attract large funds and many scholars to the center, and with the forked side he should keep away poverty, thieves and liars.*"

The meaning of the *woko* staff falls in alignment with the meaning of the *àṣẹ* staff among the Yorùbá as we will see later on in our discourse when we discuss the relationship between *èṣú* and *àṣẹ*. Both emblems are a symbol for *abundance* and *prosperity*, which is why *wꜣs* is also associated with *prosperity* in the Egyptian language. I've come to know personally that in Tanzania, these staves are present and that these scepters indicate that the holder is a *leader* of a kraal. But notice also that Dr. Hisada mentioned that the "head" of the object is used to draw in "prosperity," and that it is symbolized by the pulling action. This connection between the "head" and "wealth, prestige" will be made apparent throughout this discourse.

In summary, *àṣẹ* among the Yorùbá is associated with the very force that is *life* and brings things into being in the universe. It is also associated with the power of *speech* as can be seen in its meanings of "command, ordain, and law" (from *a-* "noun-forming prefix" + *ṣẹ* "message"). We also note that there are two primary themes for *àṣẹ: power* and *speech*. We will now demonstrate how *àṣẹ* is related to the Yorùbá deity *Èṣú* and the ancient Egyptian *nṯrw* [ciLuba *ndele*(a,u)] *Wsr* and *ꜣs.t*.

Èṣú, Isis and Osiris: Personifications of *àṣẹ*

In Imhotep (2011), I went through painstaken efforts to demonstrate the conceptual and linguistic cognate relationship between *Yeshua* (Jesus) of the Hebrews, *Wsr/Jsr* (Osiris) of the ancient Egyptians and *Èṣú* among the Yorùbá. As it turns out, all three of these names are derived from the same linguistic roots. As we discovered in that publication, African people tend to develop a central character or deity for their myths that represent an array of themes simultaneously. These deities do not represent one single concept, but come to embody the crystalization of multiple themes. As Durkheim & Mass (1963: 78) insists, a deity collects and classifies information. These characters over time pick-up various attributes that become staples to the identity of the deity, and thus the overall principle that the deity represents. The deities are in reality classifitory principles that are more inclusive than exclusive regarding its defining principles. Barnes (1997: 12) calls this phenomenon a *polythetic system*. In a polythetic system of classification, no one feature gives definition to a domain. What I add to this analysis is that many of these attributes associated with these deities are derived from lexical items that share the same consonant root structure as the word that has come to initially define the deity itself. This is the phenomenon of *paronymy* spoken of throughout this larger work.

Ludwig Wittgenstein proposes a useful way to classify polythetic themes as a chain of "family resemblances" where the defining attributes changes from one link to another (Needham 1975: 350). An example by Barnes (1997: 13) is given by the following sets:

ABCD
AB DE
A CDE
 BC EF

We see here that there is no one monotypic feature that gives definition to all of the sets. However, there is sufficient overlap to establish a family or chain of resemblances. In polythetic classifications, stress is laid on each set's having a simple majority of the defining features and not on assigning decisive weight to any one of them. By thinking in a polythetic way, we shift the discussion from meaning in the *singular* to meaning in the *plural*. We argue that this method of identifying plural meanings can be used in this debate on the meaning(s) of spiritual concepts in African languages. The concepts of *associative field theory* or *lexical fields* in linguistics allow us to move along these lines. The key feature in this comparative process is *redundancy*.

Finding redundant themes allows us, analytically, to delineate domains. It is in the redundant clusters of meaning—not the singular clusters—that allow us to gain understanding of the domain that have been deified in African traditions. Erwin Goodenough has created a 12 volume work that examines religious symbols common to the Mediterranean world in Greco-Roman times that derived from the Old and New Testaments that stresses the search for redundancy in symbolic literature.[16] In this series of texts, Goodenough suggests that by accumulating scores of repeated cases, we establish a probability, a hypothesis, for assigning meanings, in his case, to symbolic representations (Goodenough 1953, V.1: 31). I argue that—in the African case—it is best to understand the principles of paronymy, as well as the rebus principle, to better understand the complexity involved in defining African spiritual concepts.

This is very important to understand throughout this discourse because *Èṣú* is a prime example of this ancient African practice among the Yorùbá people in regards to the merging of concepts (due to paronymy and homonymy).

Who is *Èṣú*?

Èṣú is a spiritual force that represents the "owner of the crossroads, the trickster, the divine messenger, the one who carries the staff of god." He is the force that "activates" or causes things to happen. *Èṣú* rules through the *ajogun*. The good *ajogun* control wealth, children, wives/husbands, success, love, and so on. The evil *ajogun* control death, illness, loss, mental unrest and similar forces (Neimark, 1995: 73). *Èṣú*, through sacrifice, serves as a messenger between humans and the other *òrìṣà* and between humans and God. The goddess *Oṣun* is *Èṣú's* mother. She is the personification of beauty and sexuality. She represents the generative life-force in the universe, love, harmony and rivers.[17] *Èṣú* and *Oṣun* are different aspects of the same conceptual idea and it will become evident later on in our discourse.

Funso Aiyejinain, in his essay "Esu Elegbara: A Source of an Alter/Native Theory of African Literature and Criticism," provides us with an indepth articulation of the dynamics of *Èṣú*. On pg. 6 (no date given) he informs us that:

> In Yorùbá philosophy, Esu emerges as a divine trickster, a disguise-artist, a mischief-maker, a rebel, a challenger of orthodoxy, a shape-shifter, and an enforcer deity. Esu is the keeper of the divine *ase* with which Olodumare created the universe; a neutral force who controls both the benevolent and the malevolent supernatural powers; he

16 Erwin R. Goodenough (1953). *Jewish Symbols in the Greco-Roman Period, 12 Vols.* Pantheon Publishing. New York, NY.

17 We note the following from the TOB database: Proto-Afro-Asiatic: **sunVʔ-*, "peace, love"; Semitic: **sVʔVn-* ~ **šVnVʔ-* 'be at peace with smb., agree'; Omotic: **šun-* 'love'; [OMOTIC]: Proto-Omotic: **šun-* 'love'; Janjero (Yamma, Yemsa): *šun-*; Kafa (Kaficho): *šun-*; Mocha: *šunn-*; Anfillo (Southern Mao): *šun-;* Bworo (Shinasha): *šun-*; Gimirra (Benesho, She): *šun-*. The *-n* appears to be a suffix attached to the root: Proto-Afro-Asiatic: **ŝaʔ-*/**ŝaw-*; "wish, like"; Semitic: **ŝVyaʔ-* 'wish'; South Cushitic: **ŝaʔ-* 'like'; Dahalo (Sanye): *hlaw-* 'love, like'.

> is the guardian of Orunmila's oracular utterances. Without Esu to open the portals to the past and the future, Orunmila, the divination deity would be blind. As a neutral force, he straddles all realms and acts as an essential factor in any attempt to resolve the conflicts between contrasting but coterminous forces in the world. Although he is sometimes portrayed as whimsical, Esu is actually devoid of all emotions. He supports only those who perform prescribed sacrifices and act in conformity with the moral laws of the universe as laid down by Olodumare. As the deity of the "orita"—often defined as the crossroads but really a complex term that also refers to the front yard of a house, or the gateway to the various bodily orifices—it is Esu's duty to take sacrifices to target-deities. Without his intervention, the Yorùbá people believe, no sacrifice, no matter how sumptuous, will be efficacious. Philosophically speaking, Esu is the deity of choice and free will. So, while Ogun may be the deity of war and creativity and Orunmila the deity of wisdom, Esu is the deity of prescience, imagination, and criticism—literary or otherwise.

We are introduced to some very important associations in this citation. The most important for us here, however, is his attribute as the "keeper of *àṣẹ*." We mentioned earlier that *àṣẹ* represents two major themes: *power* and *speech*. We will see how both of them play out in the meaning of *Èṣú*. One way to know the attributes of *Èṣú* is to examine the praise titles given to *Èṣú* or poems dedicated to him:

> Esu is the Divine Messenger between God and Man.
> Esu sits at the Crossroad.
> Esu is the Orisa that offers choices and possibility.
> Esu is the gatekeeper, the guardian of the door.
> Esu safeguards the principle of freewill.
> Esu is the keeper of Ase.
> Esu is called the divine trickster that lures man's emotions creating variety which spices life.
> Esu brings out the fool in man.
> Esu brings out the symbolic child in man.
> Esu's mischief serves to wake a person up and teach them a lesson.
> Esu represents the balance of nature.
> Day and night, white and black, construction and destruction. Esu is an old man and a child. Absolute balance of nature.
> Esu has a voracious appetite.
> Esu has a constant drive and is always ready (erect penis).
> Esu counterbalances aspects of our reality.
> Esu is the patron of the "underworld" and their way of survival.
> Esu---The means justify the end!
> Esu must always be appeased first.
> Ase O!

Èṣú and *Legba* (a title of *Èṣú*) are "keepers of the *word*" (which is also the life-force) and are masters of language (Kamalu, 1998: 141). In Yorùbá, one of the paths of *Èṣú* is known as *Elegbara*. This term consists of two words *El* "God"+ *agbara* "power"(Hebrew *Gebuwr-ah* "power," Igbo *agbara* "powerful oracle," *Ebira 'Ne Gba'* "spirit"). *Elegbara* among the Yorùbá became in the Biblical literature the angel *Gabri-El* (word reversal). El/Olu/Ala all mean GOD (proto-bantu **y-ulu*). This is important here because when the Arabs say *Allahu Akbar* (*el* + *agbara; k > g*)—which means "Allah is the Greatest, most powerful"—they are invoking an old African god: *Èṣú* (the owner of power).

Gabriel is also known as the messenger of God: *Gaber-iy-el* "the gaber of God." In Amharic *gebre* means "servant." This *g-b-r* root in Hebrew lets us know that he is not only a messenger of God, but a *geber* "valiant man," and a *gibbowr* "powerful man." In Yorùbá we have *egbere* "gnome" and *al-agbara* "a powerful man."[18]

Yorùbá:	*Elegbara, El-egba*
Fon:	*Legba*
Ebira:	*Ne gba* (spirit), *obi-negba* "great spirit" is God)
Owerri Igbo:	*Agbara*
Onitsha Igbo:	*Agbala*

What's interesting about this correlation is that according to SalmanSpiritual.com, a website dedicated to the study of Islam:[19]

> The phrase 'Allahu Akbar' is the opening declaration of every Islamic prayer and is a slogan which was prescribed by the Holy Prophet Muhammad (upon whom be peace) to the mujahids of Islam.

All prayers among *Ifá* practitioners open with an invocation to *Eṣu-Elegbara* first before proceeding with any aspects of the prayer (or ritual). The Muslims kept this ancestral practice while de-emphasizing and de-mythicizing the deity aspect of the invocation as to appear to be monotheistic.

This association of *Èṣú* being the "messenger" is important for the aspect of *àṣẹ* which deals with "speech." *Èṣú* is the keeper of the *àṣẹ* authority scepter. *Èṣú* is associated with a "messenger" because of the close association with the word *ṣẹ́* "message" (Egyptian *šʿ.t* "message"); from Yorùbá *ṣe* "do"; *isé* "work" seen in the word *ìránṣẹ́* "messenger". As we have stated previously, the Yorùbá *àṣẹ* scepter is the Egyptian *w3s* [ ] scepter and has the same connotations. The name *Èṣú* is a by-form of the word *àṣẹ*. Both *àṣẹ* and *Èṣú* are built off an old Kongo-Saharan *-s-*root (*s-r*):

Table 3: The Kongo-Saharan *-s-* root[20]

	Hebrew	Yorùbá	Mende	Tiv	Nupe	Chu-chewa
To come to pass	*swh*	*ṣẹ*				
To command	*siwwah*	*ṣẹ́ (ékpè)*				
To cause to come to pass	*Saw (imp.s)*					
A command, authority	*mi-sewah*	*àṣẹ*				
The power to cause to happen		*àṣẹ*		*tsav*		
magic			*sawa*	*tsav*		
witchcraft				*tsav*		*Ma-sawe*
Ruler					*Etsu*	

18 I equate the root *g-b-r* with Egyptian *ḫpr* "be effective, take place, occur, happen, come to pass, bring about, entity, being (god)." A "powerful, valiant man" or "being" (god) is someone with the "power" to bring about "change" (*ḫpr*) and "effect" their environment in significant ways.

19 http://salmanspiritual.com/akbar.html. Retreived January 2011.

20 See Oduyoye in (Saakana, 1991: 75)

The angel who holds God's staff of authority		*Èṣú*				

The authority scepter is a symbol of *Èṣú*'s possession of *àṣẹ*: both the potent word or incantation and the power of *Olódùmarè* (the Supreme Being) (Kamalu, 1998: 141). In traditional African societies, the king would speak to the people through a messenger. You'd know who this messenger was because he carried the king's staff of authority. In places like China the messenger would have a special seal on a document. What the messenger stated was in fact the *law* as spoken by the king as if the king was stating it before the people himself. The king is the "head" and/or "mouthpiece" of the people.

The king, however, represents the messenger of the Divine and the ancestors; so he too is associated with *Èṣú* as the divine messenger of the society at large. In fact, *Èṣú* is known as a "royal child, a prince, a monarch" (Thompson, 1984: 19). It is out of this tradition for which *Yeshua* takes his characteristics in the Jesus myth of the Hebrews as "king of kings," but at the same time being the messenger of the Divine (God's son). This explains why all prayers must go through Jesus: it is rooted in ancient African kingship customs of speaking to the public through the royal messenger. Like *Yeshua*, *Èṣú* takes the prayers (and sacrifices) to the appropriate deities and corresponds directly with *Olódùmarè*. *Wsr* is also the bringer of sacrifices. We contend that the *s-r* root is at play here and is reflected in Egyptian *šʿr* "bring, present, to sacrifice, send up, to make rise" by way of paronymy.

Èṣú represents a moral power—the power to save and kill;[21] the knowledge of good and evil, the efficacy of medicine and poison, the usefulness and destructive potential of fire, water or atomic energy—and this is why *Èṣú* is associated with good and bad qualities and deemed "a trickster." One's ignorance of how to handle power can blind one to reality and ultimately cause conflict in one's life. All of these attributes are represented by the power of *àṣẹ*.

A similar association with the potent word and the staff of authority can be seen among the cousins of the Yorùbá: the Igbo of Nigeria. The term for "upright speech" in Igbo is known as *Ofo* "the power/god of truth, justice and righteousness" (Kamalu, 1998: 142). Among the Yorùbá, *ofo* is "potent speech and authoritative utterance" (short form of *afọṣẹ* "authority of sanction through utterance, the power to cause to happen through verbal command" in Yorùbá). Among the Igbo *ofo* is also a *staff* or *stick* held by an elder with the *ozo* title. Whatever is said by the elder whilst striking the lineage *ofo* on the ground is deemed authoritative (because the elder personifies truth). In other words, what he/she says at that moment is law (*àṣẹ* "law, command, authority").

Èṣú and Wsr

What I want to highlight in this section is the *s/ṣ-r* linguistic root which gives *Èṣú* and *Wsr* (as a concept) their thrust and potency in their respected African traditions. As we know, *Èṣú* is built off the same root as the word *àṣẹ* "power" which makes *Èṣú* the personification of power (holder of *àṣẹ*). I argued in Imhotep (2011a) that the full linguistic root is *s-r*. The *-r* as a final consonant is highly amissable in African languages and is dropped in Yorùbá quite often in relation to compared cognates in Egyptian. The god *Wsr*, as the primordial king of ancient Egypt, derives his authoritative attribute from the *w-s-r* root meaning "power" (head) in ancient Egyptian.

21 One is reminded of the scene in the movie *Shaka Zulu* (1987) where Shaka had to remind the doctors from Europe that it was he (Tshaka) that had the power of life or death in his kingdom when two doctors allegedly brought a woman back from the dead in a previous scene. This is a common feature in African kingship and is personified in *Èṣú*.

wsr "make strong, powerful, wealthy, influential"

Richard Wilkinson (2003: 118) speculates that the etymology of the name *Wsr* derives from *wsr* which means "power," therefore making *Wsr* to mean "mighty one." I agree with his hypothesis based on the comparative data, but as I discuss in Imhotep (2011a), the name *wsr* is a synthesis of various different roots which have been crystallized into a 'mythicalized' anthropomorphic figure (Osiris). The *wꜣs* lexeme meaning "fortunate, prosperous, well-being, prosperity"; "honor (due to a god or king), prestige" is just a variant form of the word *wsr*. The *-r* has been inverted as *ꜣ* (= *l/r*). We can confirm this by examining the following: *wꜣs* <= *sꜣt* "rich" [Wb IV 15]; *sꜣwtj* "treasure" [Wb III 418]; *sꜥšꜣt* "increase, multiply"; *sꜥšꜣt* to make abundant, increase, multiply; *ꜥšꜣ* "many, numerous, much, plentiful, ordinary, quantity, multitude"; *ꜥšꜣt* "the many, the masses, many, abound, rich, numerous, much"; *ꜥšꜣt* "the many, the masses, many, abound, rich, numerous, much." The ideal of "wealth," in this sense, is organized around the concept of "increase, multiplication, expansion, bigness" and it is this concept of "bigness" (wealth, prestige) that one becomes "powerful, influential." Osiris and *Èṣú* are connected to the concept of "potency" and the ability to bring-forth/be prosperous, make flourish, expand and make things happen.

To provide an Egyptian example, the king Senusret III, the 5th king of the XII Dynasty, managed to expand Egypt's borders further south than any ruler before him, of which he was proud. This was a period after the Hyksos invasion. A stele at Semna, with a duplicate at Uronarti, records:

jrt ḥm=f tꜣš rs r ḥḥ
His Majesty established the southern border at Heh.
jw jr.n=j tꜣš=j ḫnt=j jtw=j
established my border further south than my forefathers.
jw rḏj.n=j ḥꜣw-ḥr swḏt n=j jnk nsw ḏdw jrrw
I added to what was bequeathed to me. **I am a king who speaks and acts.**
kꜣꜣt jb=j pw ḫprt m-ꜥ=j ꜣdw r jṯt
I make happen what I conceive, eager to seize,
sẖmw r mꜥr tm sḏr mdt m jb=f
hasty to succeed, in whose heart a matter doesn't slumber
ḫmt twꜣw ꜥḥꜥ ḥr sf tm sfnw n ḫrwy pḥ sw
anticipating inferiors, suppressing mercy, merciless to the enemy who attacks him,
pḥw pḥ.tj=fj grw gr.tw
who attacks one who would attack, who is silent when one is silent,[22]

Here we can see that the king is expected to be a fierce warrior and one who can get the job done. Whatever the king's heart conceives is made manifest. Whatever the king utters comes into existence because he acts on that which he speaks. This is why these terms are associated with kingship. A matter of fact, the word *wsr* is in the name of *Ś-n-Wsrt* 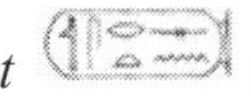 (associated with the goddess *Wsrt*). So according to his declarations in the text cited, he apparently lived up to his name. Because Osiris was a king, we see our term *wꜣs* given as one of his titles:

22 Transcription for "Second Semneh stela of Sesostris III," Berlin 1157. Following K. Lepsius (1849-1859; 12 volumes of plates), *Denkmäler aus Ägypten und Äthiopien*, p. 136.

wꜣsry "a title of Osiris" (Budge 149a)

It is reaffirmed here that Osiris is the personification of prosperity, growth and flourishing and this is why he is associated with agriculture and resurrection. As the spokesperson for the living community among the ancestors, the king is also expected to be the pipeline through which order and prosperity are to enter into the kingdom. If he is on good terms with the spirit world, then they will in turn ensure that the living community has what it needs in order to flourish. The kingdom's level of prosperity is directly proportional to the degree that the king maintains positive relationships with the ancestors and spirit forces through which he inherits their *àṣẹ*.

Wsr was (according to one myth) Egypt's first king or head of state and the root of his name (*s-r*) is a word associated with administrative positions in the Egyptian language. The terms with the *s-r* root are the same terms with the *-s-* root in Yorùbá as we will see below:

Table 4:

Egyptian	**Yorùbá**
sr "nobleman, magistrate" (a judge, in other words a law maker and enforcer)	***Àṣẹ***: law; command; authority; commandment; enjoinment; imposition; power; precept; discipline; instruction; cannon; biding; document; virtue; effect; consequence; imprecation
sr "official, great one, chief"	*ọzō* (**Igbo**) "title of high degree conferring on the owner privileges and honour as a sacrosanct being"; *eze* "to honor, to participate to assume a role of privilege"
sr "foretell, make known, to promise, to reveal, to announce, to spread abroad, to challenge" *šʿ.t* "message"	*oṣò* "wizard" (seer, diviner <*ṣẹ́* "to see") [Arabic *haza* "to divine," *hazin* "astrologer"; Aramaic *hazah* "to see"] *àṣẹ* "command, effect, precept, instruction" *se* "to command," *ṣẹ́* "message" *ìránṣẹ́* "messenger".
sr "prophetize, to prophesy"	*àṣẹ* "a coming to pass"
sr.t "proclamation"	

The term *sr* (s-r) "official, great one, chief" is reflected in Yorùbá: *asalu* (s-l) "a title of honor among the *Ogboni* people" (Egyptian *sʿr* "elevated, prominent"). The *ogboni* are the wise elders (leaders) in Yorùbá traditional society. As we can see the Egyptian term *wꜣs* "dominion, honor" is just an alternate form of *sr/wsr* (Yorùbá *asalu, àṣẹ*) with loss of final consonant *-r* (or is inversed to become *ꜣ*). As noted in *Chapter 2*, the -r- root deals with "expansion, rising, height, length, greatness, etc." and it is present in the Egyptian word *sʿꜣ* "to make great, to enlarge, enlargement, to increase, to aggrandize, to magnify, be rich, be great, to exalt, enrich, honour, glorify, ennoble." This word *wꜣs* is just an inverse of *sʿꜣ* and it is this theme of "expansion" (built off of the *-r-* root) that we get the derived meanings for *wꜣs* "dominion, have dominion, power, honor (due to a god or king), prestige, fortunate, prosperous, well-being, prosperity" and *wsr* "wealthy, powerful, strong, influential, wealthy man, rich (in years)."

There is another variation of the *wꜣs* root in African languages that deals with authority and kingship. As demonstrated throughout this larger text, the *ꜣ* sound in Egyptian fluctuated between an /a/ and an /l/ sound in certain dialects. This /l/ would be an /r/ in other African languages. Alain Anselin (2010: 17, ft.1) demonstrates this sound alternation in other African languages:

> *wꜣsj/wꜣs* <***rus** "crumble, fall to pieces, ruin" (*w* governed by the law of Belova,[23]and *ꜣ* = /r/) Western Chadic: ***rus**, "destroy"; Hausa: *rúúsā* "thrash"; Kuler: *ryaas* "break into pieces," bol: *ruuš* "destroy"; ngizim: *ràasú* "act violently on purpose (Takacs, 1999: 396).[24]Fulfulde: *ruus*, "collapse"(Seydoni, 1998: 578).Wolof: *Ruus*, "crumble, is defoliates" (Diouf, 2003: 294)

This is very informative as we have the linguistic grounds to speculate another variation of *wꜣs* ("dominion, scepter") as reflected in African languages with the terms *ras* and *òrìsà*. The word *òrìsà* in the Yorùbá language is defined as "head" in common dictionaries. Henry John Drewal and John Mason in their article, "Ogun and Body/Mind Potentiality: Yorùbá Scarification and Painting Traditions in Africa and the Americas" (Barnes, 1997: 337), defines *òrìṣà* as "anciently selected head." Neimark (1993: 14) informs us that the *òrìṣà* are "energy" (powers) that, for the most part, represent aspects of nature. This liturgical association between *power* and *òrìṣà* finds synergy with the concept of *àṣẹ* "power, energy."

In Barnes (1995: 143, n38) we are informed that the word "*òrìṣà* is employed as a simile for the power of the king. *Ekeji* may also be translated as 'next to' or 'second to', suggesting that the king's power is not simply like, but is of the same substance or nature as that of the gods, although of a diminished order." When the king is crowned, the chiefs affirm it in their salutation to the king: *ọba aláàṣẹ èkeji òrìṣà*! (The king's power is like that of the gods).

The *òrìṣà*, as conceived by the devotees of Ifá, are the primordial energy forces that give rise to phenomena in nature (i.e., "the head, the beginning"). There are two primary reflexes for *òrìṣà* in the Yorùbá language. The first deals with "head, first, and leadership"; the second with "patron saints, divine ancestors, divinities" (Oduyoye, 1984: 19).

Ìdòwú (1994: 60) defines *òrìṣà* as a corruption of the original term *orísẹ̀* "head-source." He goes on to further explain that:

> *Orí* is "head." It is the name for man's physical head. It means also, however (and, I think, primarily) the essence of personality, the ego. *Ṣẹ̀* in Yorùbá is a verb meaning "to originate," "to begin," "to derive or spring (from)." The name *Orí-ṣẹ̀* then would be an ellipsis of *Ibiti-orí-ti-ṣẹ̀* "The origin or Source of *Orí*." Now, what is this Origin, or "Head-Source?" It is the Deity himself, the Great *Orí* from whom all *orí* derive, inasmuch as He is the Source and Giver of each of them. I am strengthened in this view of the derivation of the name by the analogy of the Igbo *Chi*. In a general sense, *chi* is the essence of personality, or the personality-soul. The generic name for the divinities is also *chi*. All *chi*, man's or the chi which is the divinity, derive from *Chi-Uku*, the Great *Chi* which is the Deity. So that either the Yorùbá *orí* or the Igbo *chi* means, in the general sense, that essence which derive from the Head-Source, the Great Source of all life and being, the Source from which all take their origin. (ibid.)

However, this is folk-etymology. You cannot split up *òrìṣà* into two words in Yorùbá (see *Chapter 2*). Nevertheless, it does speak to the nature of the "head" being the "source" and with

23 "According to this rule, the first *w*- and *j*- in Eg.triconsonantal roots cannot be always treated as morphological prefixes, but in many cases rather reflect the original PAA [Proto-Afro-Asiatic] internal root vocalism *-u-, *-i- (i.e. Eg. wC_1C_2 and jC_1C_2< AA $*C_1uC_2$- and $*C_1iC_2$- respectively). As for PAA (C_1aC_2, it may eventually yield Eg. jC_1C_2, but $ꜣC_1C_2$ as well though the examples for it are of very limited number."Takacs in (Rocznik, 1998: 115)

24 A reflex of this term in Egyptian is *šr/šʿr* "threaten" (r-s metathesis).

this I agree. But the concepts are explained by the same word, not two separate words.

In Egyptian *wꜣs* and *wsr* are both titles for *Wsr* (Osiris). It is our contention that *wsr* = *òrìṣà* in the inverse. *Òrìṣà* worship is all across Africa. The *-r-* shows an interchange of liquid consonants (r/l) and the *-s-* shows a *shibboleth/siboleth* dialect interchange (sh/s) in the roots *-r-ṣ-* and *-l-s-* (Oduyoye, 1996: 30).[25]

From the concept of "head, source and beginnings" derive the meanings in association with "ancestors" (the ones who came and went before us: first in rank). The Hebrews of the Bible also venerated the *òrìṣà* but they knew them as *He-**ri'sh**-on-iym* "the ancestors" (Psalms 79:8). The following *ri'sh-on-iym* (*òrìṣà*) are mentioned in Genesis 5:

'adam	(Yorùbá *Àdàmú Òrìṣà*)
Šet	
^{e}*no*^{w}*š*	(Yorùbá *eniyan*)
Qeynan	
Ma-halal'el	
Yered	
Ḥano^{w}*k*	(*Nok* of Nigeria)
M^{e}*tu-Šelah*	(Kiswahili *watu m-šale*)
Lamek	
Noah	(Shona *mu-nhu* "a person of good character")

All of these were the divine spirits or human chiefs of the Hebrews for which they trace their ancestry. *'Adam* (man and woman made he *them*) are the progenitors from which all derive according to the myth which makes Adam the primary *òrìṣà* (*ri'š-on'adam*). Adam is the principle behind all life—the self-reproducing force (Oduyoye, 1984: 19; Imhotep 2012).

Comparatively, it is with this understanding for which we gain clarity on the names *Wsr* and *ꜣst* and their correct meanings. The word for Asar/Osiris in Tshiluba can be rendered *Ashil, Asha, Ajil, Wa-Shil, Wa-Shal, Mu-jilu, and Mushilu.*[26] *Mujilu* means "sacred one." *Ashil* means "to build for;" derived from *asa* "to begin" (Egyptian *šꜥꜣ* "the source of life, to begin"; *šꜣ.t*  "the goddess of primeval matter—a form of Hathor" (Budge 723a)). *Wsr* was the first king because he literally represents the "primordial" ancestral spirit that gave rise to the kingdom of ciKam (Egypt). In Imhotep (2011a: 131) I demonstrate, using a modern example in the Congo, how *Washil* is still considered to be the progenitor of a particular ethnic group which is identified by his name (*Luba-Mushianga*; *Bashilanga*; Egyptian *Wsr-ꜥnḫ*). It is from this ethnic group for which the renowned Egyptologist Dr. Mubabinge Bilolo of Congo was born and is a living prince of his lineage.

What these people of the Congo state is that *Washil* is their "primary ancestor." When they invoke their "totem" they say: *Bashila/Washila/Bajil*–X (-x being whatever their personal name is). For example, if I was of the Baluba of Congo, I would say I am *Bashila-Imhotep* (Imhotep of the *Bashila* people). Here I am acknowledging my ancestry and my progenitor (my "god"). The exact same practice went on in ancient Egypt with this life-force, progenitor and primary-ancestor: *Wsr/Èṣù/Washil/Òrìṣà*. This is why all of the deceased took on the name of *Wsr* (Osiris) as living initiates, and after death, which is evident in all of the *Prt-m-Hrw* (Books of the Dead) (see Ashby 1996, 2001).

Space will not allow us to get into any detail here, but in Africa the concept of "God" is totally different than how we understand this concept in the West.[27] But for now, God is the

25 Again, see the expanded discourse in *Chapter 2* for the variations of *òrìṣà* in the African languages.

26 See Mubabinge Bilolo (2011: 208); also Bilolo (2009: 143-148)

27 Chapters 3.1 and 3.2 are dedicated to the topic of the African concept of God.

source from which everything derives. It is the primordial causal agent of all things (the LAW). When one traces one's lineage, one goes from the self, to one's parents, on to one's grandparents and then continues to the first human being that ever lived. From there one continues into the animal world, then the plant world…all the way down to the earthly elements (*òrìṣà*) which come together to create all life on earth. These elements are further broken-down into chemical agents found in the universe (birthed from stars) who all derive from the **Source** of all things (*ṣẹ, àṣẹ, Ori, Orìṣẹ*). **God is our primary ancestor**. So when the Congo-Baluba say they descend from *Mushilanga*, they are saying they descend from "The Source of All Life" (*Wsr-ʿnḫ* "*Wsr*-life").[28] Here are a few representations of the name of *Washil/Wsr* in the Egyptian hieroglyphs:

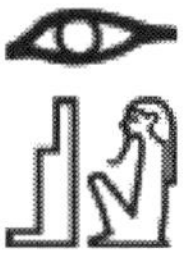

Ancient Egyptian **wsr** = Osiris (*òrìṣà*)

Wsr **with** *W3s***Scepter** = 		**Wasri (title of Osiris)**	
		 Budge 149a	
Eye in Front	**With Seat in Front of Eye**	**Alternative Variations**	**Alternative Variations**
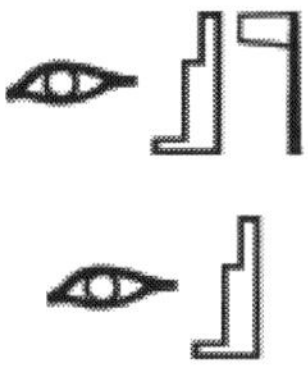	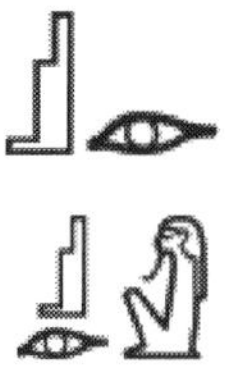	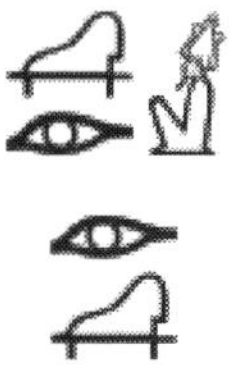	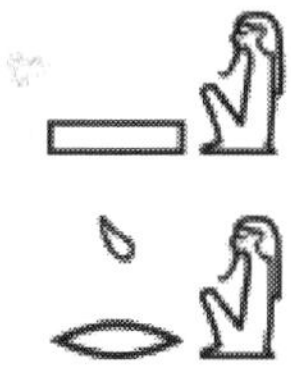
Later Forms of Wsir			

28 Compare *wsr* > *wa-shil* with: *šʿ3* "the source of life, to begin"; *š3ʿ* "begin, start, be the first, spring, originate, to elapse"; *š3.t* "the goddess of primeval matter-a form of Hathor" (Budge 723a).

It is my contention (Imhotep, 2012, 2011a) that the name *Wsr* can be rendered as: *wsr, jsr, sr* and *rs*. I further contend that the switching of the eye 𓁹 /*r*/ and thrown 𓌙 /*ȝs*/ glyphs in some of the depictions were not done by accident or style. With each switch of the glyphs derives a different name which essentially belongs to the same theme. In other words, the phonemes were switched on purpose.

There is evidence to suggest that the ancient Egyptians played around with the reversal of syllables and with reading them forwards and backwards. This is a typical African practice in regards to liturgical vocabulary. As Campbell-Dunn (2006: 144) explains:

> Homburger asserts that "Among the Fulbe [Fulani]...the syllables of words are inverted to allow speaking before women and commoners not trained to understand" (Homburger 1949: 36). *Fulbe ngari* "Fulbe came" becomes *beful riga*. It follows that these mobile elements were once independent full words. They correspond to Westermann's reconstructed PWS monosyllables. **The African secret languages exploit this mobility**. See Westermann (1930: 187) on Ewe. (emphasis mine)

The Egyptian language is definitely a priestly language and one of the clues is that it is not very rich in vocabulary. James P. Allen in his book *The Ancient Egyptian Pyramid Texts* (2005: 13) reaffirms this notion when he states that, "Egyptian [the language] is rich in allegory and metaphor, but relatively poor in vocabulary." This is compounded by the fact that many of the words are just dialectical variations of each other.

Credo Mutwa (an Amazulu shaman) in his work *Indaba My Children* (1964: 558) informs us of the oral traditions which assert that the great Bantu tribes originated in the Cameroon/Kongo area in ancient times. He states that the tribes are so old in this area that:

> [T]hese tribesmen still speak the language their witchdoctors call 'spirit talk', which came down to us through the Ba-Kongo and the Ba-Mbara. We use this language when communicating with the very old spirits of the 'Ancient Ones'. This language is actually the language of the Stone Age – the first efforts by Man to speak. It consists largely of grunts and guttural animal sounds in which the words we use today are faintly distinguishable. (ibid.)

This reaffirms that African communities of memory have secret priestly languages: vocabularies with meanings and pronunciations not privy to the commoner of a society. Another famous African group also has a priestly language and it too has a limited vocabulary.

Laird Scranton discusses this phenomenon among the Dogon of Mali in his book *Sacred Symbols of the Dogon: The key to advanced science in the ancient Egyptian hieroglyphs* (2007: 13). He reminds us that the Dogon possess a secret priestly language called *Sigi so*, the language of the *Sigui* ceremony, which includes far fewer words than *Dogo so* (the common Dogon word language). As he also notes, citing notes from Calame-Griaule's *Dictionnaire Dogon*, that the Dogon priests define relationships between their words purely on **similarities of pronunciation** (Scranton, ibid.). As we have discussed previously, this is a staple in the Egyptian language (paronymy) and these similarly sounding words are amalgamated into a single anthropomorphic entity known as a "deity" (*nṯr*).[29] This is the dominant praxis among

29 See also Serge Sauneron in his work *The Priest of Ancient Egypt* (2000: 125-127) as he reaffirms this practice of finding connections and synthesizing words based on similarities in pronunciation in the Egyptian language.

traditional African centers of wisdom (misnomered "secret societies").[30]

All of this to say that in order to get to the crux of the terminologies and their associated iconography, one has to start thinking like an African priest. African priesthoods play on words and even reverse phonemes to expand a common theme (kind of like *5 Percenters* do in the United States). The following table demonstrates this in action, although we could also simply argue metathesis as the *r/l* sounds are most subject to this phenomenon.

Table 5: A few examples of reversals

Yorùbá	**Egyptian**
ọṣò "a seer, wizard (priest), diviner" (<*ṣẹ́* "to see")	*sꜣꜣ* "wise man, sage";[2](*ꜣ* = r/l) *sꜣr* "be wise, be smart" *sr* "official, great one, chief" *sr* "prophetize, to prophesy" *šꜣw* "fate, destiny" *sꜣw* "magician, amulet maker"
	sr "foretell, make known, to promise, to reveal, to announce, to spread abroad, to challenge" *sr* "to show" (to make known, make someone aware; to make someone see something) *sꜣw* "to be aware of" (*ꜣ* = r/l)
ji, jiji "to awake, rouse, enliven" *ẹṣọ, iṣọ, ṣọ* "watch"; *ṣẹ́* "to see"	*rs* "to be awake, to watch, wake" (conscious) *rsw* "watcher, keeper"
àṣẹ "instruction, discipline, document" [processes and items for gaining knowledge]	*siꜣ* "recognize, to know, perception, knowledge, " *siꜣ* "to notice, be aware of, insight, reason" (*ꜣ* = r/l) (reverse for *rs*) *ʿš* "to read, to read aloud"
asalu "a title of honor among the *Ogbóni* people." (*ogbón* means "wisdom"); *eze* (**Igbo**) "to honor, to participate to assume a role of privilege"	*tr* "respect, worship (god), show respect, to revere" (t<>s) *tꜣr/tꜣ.t* "influence" (of the dead) (*ꜣ* = r/l)
àṣẹ "the power to multiply" *ọṣun* "goddess of love and prosperity" *ajé* "money, the goddess of money"	*šꜣw* "the god of prosperity, good luck and good fortune" *wꜣs* "fortunate, prosperous, well-being, prosperity"
ọzō (**Igbo**) "honor, title of high degree" [Pulaar *wasu* "glorification" (Lam, 1994: 44)]	*wꜣs* "honor (due to a god or king), prestige"
àṣẹ "scepter"	*wꜣs* "scepter" *šʿw* "a rod, a stick" *š rsi* "staff, rod"
àṣẹ "power" *Oni-iṣe* a Yorùbá term meaning "a man of work" *onìṣẹ, onṣẹ* "messenger, postman, herald, ambassador, forerunner" (see section on *Èṣù*) [from the root *ṣẹ* "to do, work"]	*šw* "to win power, to gain power"[3] *nsw* "king" (with *n-* prefix denoting "one who is" or "possessor of." So a *nsw* "king" is a "possessor of power"; *àṣẹ*). The king was also the messenger of the ancestors and the Divine: Egyptian *šʿ.t* "message"

30 Dr. Mubabinge Bilolo demonstrates this practice in essentially all of his works as it pertains to the Tshiluba language. See bibliography.

ọṣẹ́ "hurt, injury"; *ẹṣẹ́* "blow with the fist"; *ṣá* (*ṣalogbe*) "to cut, to wound with a knife"; *aṣá* "a heavy spear or javelin used to kill elephants" *oṣe* "club of god of thunder [*Ṣango*]" (a striking instrument);	*sw* "kill, booty, quarry" *sꜣw* "to break off, be broken, be tired" *wꜣs* "to batter, to strike, to break, to bruise, to lay" *wꜣs* "ruin" *tp sw* "ruin, neglect, decay" *wsi* "to saw, cut up, trim"
*àṣẹ*law; command; authority; commandment; (oath)	*ʿš* "summon, call"

It is with this evidence that it becomes clear that the god *Wsr* and the goddess *ꜣs.t* are literally inverses of each other and essentially have the same meanings: they are conceptually and linguistically two-sides of the same coin.

Osiris **Isis**

jsr > *rs* →→→→→ ←←←←←*ꜣs.t* = *rs.t* (Coptic *Ese*)

As noted in Imhotep (2011a: 110-111):

> When examining the glyphs for names *ꜣs.t* and *Wsr*, we notice that they both utilize the throne glyph with the *js/ꜣs* sound value. Egyptologists simply render the word *ꜣs* as "throne" but this is not an accurate reading. The throne is a symbol for the "seat" of authority where the queen and king make their commands for the kingdom. [the focus is authority]

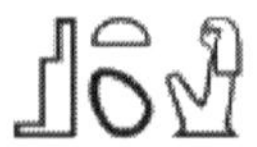

Aset (*js.t/ꜣs.t*)

Aset (*js.t/ꜣs.t*)

Asr

> Examining Aset's name provides additional insight. The first variation of Aset's written name consists of a throne with the phonetic value of *ꜣs/js* ; the feminine suffix *-t* represented by a loaf of bread; and the determinative of an egg which is the symbol for motherhood (child in the womb) which carries the *swḥ.t* pronunciation matching our *swh* Afro-Asiatic root [mentioned earlier]. Here we have the visual representations of the two types of *àṣẹ* mentioned previously. The throne represents the *àṣẹ* of *political* power. The egg represents the *biological*, procreative power (*àṣẹ*); the egg is a symbol of new life to be (Egyptian *šʿꜣ* "to begin, the source of life;" *šꜣʿ* "to begin, be the first, spring, originate"). *Eṣu* also represents this principle of *life* (being a causal agent). As Thompson notes, "*Eṣu* represents the principle of life and individuality who combines male and female valences (Thompson, 1984: 28).[31] We should note that in Kiswahili the name *Eshe* means "life" as well. I think this strengthens our case for the non-mytholized Yorùbá concept of *àṣẹ* as being the linguistic and conceptual equivalent to the Egyptian goddess *ꜣs.t* (Coptic *Ese*, Somali *AySitu,* ciLuba *DiSwa/*

31 The feminine aspect of *Eṣu* is *Oshun*.

> *CyAsa*[32]). It should be noted that there is an ancient Egyptian god by the name of *šꜣw* "the god of prosperity, good luck and good fortune" that may be relevant to our discussion and related to Yorùbá *àjé*. *Ọṣun* among the Yorùbá is also the goddess of ood fortune and prosperity; which we equate with Hebrew *shuwa'* "riches, wealth." Underlying all of these different renderings for this *-s-* root is the "ability to make things happen": to "cause" something to be, to initiate something.

It should be noted that the throne symbol in the names for *Wsr* and *ꜣs.t* is a sign of *political power* and in this case doesn't mean "throne" in a physical sense. It is a derived form of "head" which denotes "leadership, ruler, top, upper, administrator, etc." Osiris' connection to Isis and *àṣẹ* is solidified when we examine a late rendering of his name which incorporates the egg (*swḥ.t*) symbol which represents the new life potential and new beginnings.

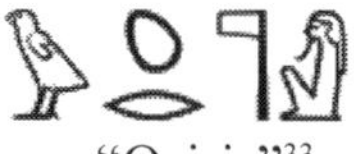

wsr "Osiris"[33]

We have mentioned in Imhotep (2011a: 136) that *Èṣù* and *Wsr* are associated with plant life and this is based on the connection between these deities and the "life-force" found in all living things. *ꜣs.t* is also connected with plant life, and can be seen in the following term:

sꜣ ꜣs.t "a plant"[34]

Everywhere we look, in association with this *-s-* root, we find associations dealing with "life, production, coming into being, and the power to create." Based on our new found knowledge of the practice of reversing phonemes in the Egyptian language, we can also equate *ꜣs.t* with another goddess of ancient Egypt: *šꜣ.t* "the goddess of primeval matter"(<*sꜥꜣ* "the source of life, to begin"; i.e., "the head"). As we noted earlier in our discussion, *ꜣs.t* is another form of the goddess *wꜣs.t* for which the city of *waset* was named after (ciLuba *ciBanza* "capital" [w>b, s>z]; *wꜣs.t* was the capital of the new kingdom).[35] As we can see here—like with the examples between *wsr* and *ꜣs.t*—*wꜣs.t* and *ꜣs.t* are different forms of the same name; just with the loss of the *w-* prefix in the name *ꜣs.t*.

As noted by Wilkinson (2003), *wꜣs.t* is another form of the goddess *hwt ḥrw*. *Ḥwt Ḥrw* (Hathor) is also a form of *ꜣs.t*. The reason for all of these different depictions for the same concept is that each "deity" represents a slight distinction on the main theme. It allows the story teller or teacher to highlight a particular effect of that energy. A close examination of the iconography associated with *ꜣs.t* and *wꜣs.t* will reveal their close associations.

---

32 *Ast* is also known as the goddess of divine love. Our ciLuba rendering of *diswa* means "love, will, desire" (<*swa* "love, want"). *DiSwa* also means "love yourself, be proud, be self-satisfied." We've already connected *Ast* with the Yorùbá concept of *Àṣẹ*. This homophonic root is in the god Eṣu and Eṣu's mother is **Osh**un. Oshun is the goddess of "love" among the Yorùbá.

33 The word for "egg" in Egyptian is *swḥt*. Therefore the egg symbol was used strictly for the /s/ sound. For an example of the cryptic or acrophonic principle, see Loprieno *Ancient Egyptian: A Linguistic Introduction* (1995: 24).

34 I would argue that this is an herb used in medicines (protection against illness). Thus, the *ꜣs* plays on its inverse *sꜣ* "to repel, drive back" in terms of illness.

35 The word "capital" means "head." *Òrìṣà* (*wꜣs*) means "head"

Table 6: Different forms of the same goddess

A) *wꜣs.t*	**B)** *ꜣs.t*	**C)** *hwt hrw*
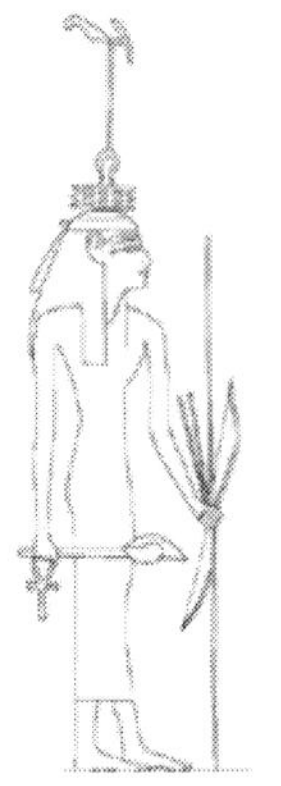	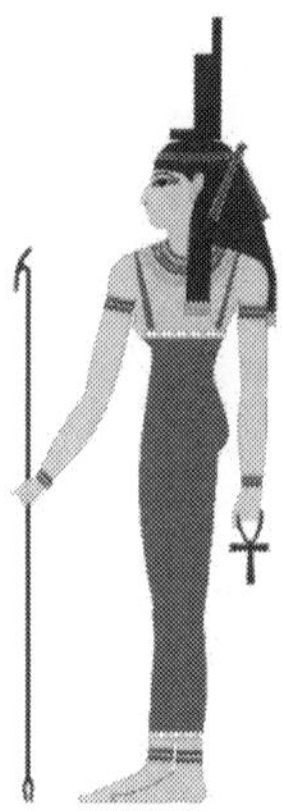	

Take note that each figure is associated with the *wꜣs* "scepter" of authority. The goddess *wꜣs.t* has the scepter placed on her head. The goddess *ꜣs.t* and *hwt ḥrw* are holding the scepters in their hands respectively. Whenever you see a figure "holding" an emblem in their hand(s), it is a sign that the holder of the object "possesses" that quality or has mastery over the object or idea for which the object symbolizes.

We mentioned at the beginning of our discussion that the god *Ẹ̀ṣú* in the Yorùbá tradition is equivalent to the goddess *wꜣs.t* in the Egyptian tradition. We also noted that *Ẹ̀ṣú* is the power that controls "life and death" (through the *ajogun*). If we look at the image of *wꜣs.t* in **Table 6** above, we note that in her hands are three emblems: the *ꜥnḫ* "life," the *ꜣms/jms* "club, sceptre" (and long staff) of authority and the bow (*sti*) and arrow (*ꜥḥꜣ* "arrow, weapon"). What this image is telling us is that *wꜣs.t* is the force (*ꜣms* power) that controls "life and death" as symbolized by the *ꜥnḫ* and weapons in each hand.

The word *ꜣms* can also mean "falsehood" which would indicate a play on words here as *wꜣs.t* uses the "club" and wisdom to battle "falsehood." This is reinforced by the *wꜣs* "scepter" emblem placed on the top of her head. The icon placed on the "top" of the head in African iconography suggests that the "person" or "deity," whose head is under the emblem, possesses a certain kind of "consciousness" or frame of thought that allows them to use the symbolic emblems effectively (the concept behind the symbol).

In the Yorùbá Ifá tradition, the *Orì/Òrìṣà* "head" (*wꜣs*) is associated with "consciousness and destiny." The goddess *wꜣs.t* possesses the kind of consciousness and insight to rule effectively. The aspect on "insight" is demonstrated by the addition of the ostrich feather alongside the *wꜣs* emblem on her head. From personal experience with traditions in Ethiopia, the ostrich feather represents "total vision." This is so because an ostrich can (appear to) turn its head completely 360 degrees thus being able to "see" all around them. As noted earlier, a priest in African traditions is believed to have the ability to "see" not only the affairs of this world, but the changing landscape in the "other world" as well (what we call in Ifá *orun*). This association between the ostrich feather and "sight" is confirmed in the Egyptian hieroglyphs as can be seen in the depictions of the goddess *mꜣ'ꜥ.t* whose name, in part, derives from *mꜣꜣ* "to see, inspect, observe."

mꜣꜥ.t "Goddess of truth, justice, righteousness, reciprocity, balance and harmony"

As we can see from the glyphs, the determinative is of the goddess with the ostrich feather on her head. The root is present in a by-form of the word *mꜣꜥ.ty* which means "judgment." One cannot judge a thing unless one is able to "see" (or "perceive") a thing with clarity (*mꜣꜣ* "to see, inspect, scrutinize, observe, look, regard"). One cannot discern truth from falsehood unless one can "see" the "evidence" in support of one or the other. In the book of Coming Forth by Day, one can see various depictions of *mꜣ'ꜥ.t* with a blindfold around her eyes. Some have interpreted this to mean "blind judgment" (objectivity). I would add that it signals the ability to judge based on the totality of evidence. One does this by not only seeing in the world, but having eyes open in the spirit world as well (see Imhotep 2011a, Kajangu 2006, Somé 1994).

In order to be a good "judge" of anything (e.g., of character), one must have exceptional *insight* into the matter. And as fate would have it, the word for insight in Egyptian is *siꜣ* (*s-r*) "perception, to understand, recognize, perceive, know, be aware of, knowledge, to notice, wisdom, shrewdness, prognostication" (an action of the *head*).

This word consists of the *s-r* (*ꜣ* = l) root spoken of throughout this essay. This word is reflected in ciLuba: *kala* "to seek, probe"; *kela* "develop by repeated practice, to train, educate"; *lukèlà* "training"; *mukela* "educated man, educated, trained"; *-sòòlakaja* "clarify, space, separate, determine, analyze" (<-*sòòla* [s-r] "clear, clear out, prune"); *nsòòlelu* "format" (plan, arrange, organize, layout); Kikongo *zayi* "intelligence," *a-zayi* "intelligent." The /s/ in Egyptian derives from /k/ (see *essay two*). We note also that the ostrich feather by itself is associated with *mꜣꜥ.t*.

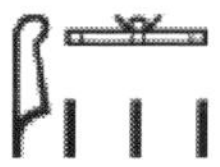

mꜣꜥ.t "truth, righteousness, justice"

We still witness the ostrich feather being used in places like Uganda and Ethiopia after a person has gone through initiation. One of the aims of initiation is to help the initiate to learn how to "see" the hidden workings of our world: the not so obvious patterns of existence. This concept is reinforced among the Dagara people of Burkina Faso. Dr. Malidoma Somé (a Dagara shaman) in his work *Of Water and the Spirit* provides the best explanation, in my opinion, as to the purpose of initiation (education) in the African schools of wisdom which reinforces this notion of "insight."

> Traditional education consists of three parts: **enlargement of one's ability to see**, destabilization of the body's habit of being bound to one plane of being, and the ability to voyage transdimentionally and return. Enlarging one's vision and abilities has nothing supernatural about it; rather, it is "natural" to be part of nature and to participate in a wider understanding of reality (Somé 1994: 226). (emphasis mine)

African wisdom centers develop sages through a process of initiation. For instance, in his book *The Religion, Spirituality, and Thought of Traditional Africa*, Dominique Zahan says:

> Initiation in Africa must be viewed as a slow transformation of the individual, as a progressive passage from exteriority to interiority. It allows the human being to gain **consciousness** of his humanity (Zahan 1979: 54). (emphasis mine)

The development of the person will take place at the rhythm established by the great periods of bodily development, each of which corresponds to a degree of initiation. As Amadou Hampate

Bá (1972) notes:

> The purpose of initiation is to give the psychological person a moral and mental power which conditions and aids the perfect and total realization of the individual.[36]

We go through all of this in-depth to make clear that initiation is about gaining "sight" or "consciousness" (*Orì/Òrìṣà/w3s/àṣẹ*) and as the saying goes, "knowledge is power" (*àṣẹ*). With this said we can see a living example among the Karamojong of Uganda. The *Randa African Art* website provides us insight into the Karamojong headdresses which displays the ostrich feather:

> "Karimojo men are divided socially into age groups, which are associated with warrior status. When a boy or man is initiated into a new age set he shaves his head. When his hair has grown long again it is plastered with mud, which is painted and set with ostrich feathers. The mud cap and ostrich feathers are symbols of bravery and display his new status."[37]

We show below the headdress of the people and warriors who have undergone various initiations (education) among the Karamojong with another example from the Bumi people of Omo Ethiopia.

Table 7: Karamojong of Uganda headdress

A beautiful Karamajong young man's headdress.
Human hair, ostrich feathers, clay, pigment, metal

Bumi man with elaborate mudpack.
Lower Omo River, southwestern Ethiopia

36 Amadou Hampâté Bâ. *Aspects of African Civilization (Person, Culture, Religion).* Translated by Susan B. Hunt. Originally published in French as *Aspects de la civilisation africaine: personne, culture, religion* Paris: Présence africaine, 1972.

37 Images and text taken from this website: http://www.randafricanart.com/Karamojong_headdress.html. Retrieved Wednesday January 4, 2012.

Getting back to our description of the *wꜣs* staff on the head of goddess *wꜣs.t* with the ostrich feather on top, we are given an example that this depiction of the goddess is a reflection of real life practices in Africa. As the *Randa African Art* website (op. cited) informs us, in regards to the Latuka people of Uganda/Southern Sudan and their headdresses:

> At the beginning of the XXth century, a long, thin staff adorned with weaverbird feathers was fixed to the top of these helmets in order to increase their magnificence still further.

This is exactly what is depicted by the goddess *wꜣs.t* in ancient Egypt. We further support our association between *wꜣs* ("scepter, power, dominion") with having the right consciousness and insight to lead, by examining the goddess Hathor in Column **C)** of **Table 6**. On her "head" is the sun (*hrw*) and the sun in African traditions are associated with "light, enlightenment, revelation, intelligence, etc." (see Bilolo 2010, Imhotep 2012). The cattle horns  symbolize a person's "generative" ability (power to make things happen) as cows/bulls were symbols of fertility in ancient times across the world. In other words, it symbolizes someone's ability to get something done; to produce something; their ability to take ideas and make them manifest (they are not idle talkers). The same meaning is associated with the throne  sign on the head of *ꜣs.t* in **Table 6** Column B): the seat where commands are made and work gets done.

Snakes generally were a sign of wisdom in the ancient world (see Scranton 2006: 178-187). We are reminded of the old adage, "Be wise as serpents" (Matthew 10:16). This, we assert, is the meaning and association of the snake depicted on the head of *ḥwt ḥrw* (Hathor) in Column C) in **Table 6** above.

We suggest here that the Egyptians did not depict snakes on their heads because they "worshiped" snakes. We posit that it symbolized "consciousness, wisdom, insight" and they used a variety of emblems to represent these concepts (e.g., *wꜣs* scepter, sun-disk, ostrich feather, etc.). One must possess all of those qualities if one is to be a great leader and these icons are reminders of this fact. The depictions of the "deities" are communicating to us that if you want to be a leader, these are the qualities you must possess in order to be an effective leader. Deities in African myths are just symbolic representations of the many characteristics of the human being. The myths are creative stories to teach a community about what can happen when you use your *àṣẹ* (*wꜣs*) for good or evil and the kinds of relationships that are created when we righteously, or unrighteously, handle power.

The god Set in Egyptian lore is also built off this *-s-* root and he represents the negative use of power (*àṣẹ*). These icons are for initiates and initiation (education) is developed by societies to train/educate (*siꜣ*, *kale*, *lukela*, *mꜣꜣ*, etc.) the next generation of leaders (the soon to be elders) on how to properly *obtain*, *control* and *maintain* power (*àṣẹ*).[38] It's a simple equation: if you want to be a leader, you have to be intelligent and have good character. There is no way around it.

Conclusion

As we have discovered here, *àṣẹ* is the vital power or energy that animates and brings forth phenomena in the universe. Africans in various wisdom traditions have sought, since time immemorial, ways in which they can harness this energy for their physical, spiritual and political needs. The aim has always been to discover strategies and resources for which one can tower over the one thousand and one challenges of life. The ancient Africans noted that

38 See Dr. Amos Wilson's book *Blueprint for Black Power* (1998) for an excellent discourse on this topic in the modern world.

with great power comes great responsibility. To reinforce this adage, and to keep this truth in the public memory, the great and creative sages developed myths and anthropomorphized the different aspects and dimensions of this energy source. The aim was to demonstrate how energy moves in the universe and the kinds of relationships that ensue when different types of energy or personalities meet.

Part of the ancient method of teaching was to divide these concepts into "masculine" and "feminine" personages. This makes it easier to understand the *relationship* between interacting forces. It is to be understood that many of these forces derive from the same conceptual theme and each culture has provided a method to demonstrate that relationship between concepts. In Yorùbá-land and in Ancient Egypt, the method most often used was to give the deities a "family" relationship. In the Egyptian myth *Wsr, ꜣs.t,* and *st* are "brothers and sister." This is to say that they come from the same source and often this is based on a linguistic relationship as well. This family relationship in Yorùbá-land is given by *Ọṣun* and *Èṣú*, but the relationship is mother and son respectively. All of these "deities" represent, on some level, "the power to make manifest" or "the source of change or being." Anyone who has this power is considered a *Big Willy* in any human society. This is why these terms are associated with royalty, administration, leadership and the Creator itself (i.e., "the *heads* of state").

In ancient Egypt the myths reflected the living culture of the people. When the Egyptian royal couple acknowledged each other as "brother and sister," they weren't literally immediate kin; they are stating we share the same "ancestor." In Africa the ancestors not only include former living human relatives, they include all of the natural elements that are anterior to them that came together to form the human relatives. It is within this framework that we are to understand why Africans acknowledge rocks, trees, minerals, sky, air, water, animals, stars, fire, etc., as ancestors because all of these entities, forces or powers came together to create the human being. All of these elements are endowed with energy and consciousness. This is not mythology but a scientific fact (see Imhotep 2012, 2009). All of these elements, including the composite which is the human being, traces its ancestry to the Source of all things, making God our greatest and oldest Ancestor.[39]

Part of the goal of this essay was to help the reader better understand and provide the intellectual tools necessary to properly understand African myths. When one is empowered by the tools of insight, of knowing languages and cultures intimately, one can unlock the secrets of these age old traditions. But the more one digs, the more one understands that these aren't secrets at all. These are just time tested insights and wisdom developed by wise sages who just wanted to remind us about how we are supposed to act and treat each other. When we learn how to do that, then we increase our self-healing power: our *àṣẹ*.

Aṣẹ, as a term, has come down to us in many forms throughout history and a few of them have been revealed to us throughout this discourse. Some of its forms have come to us in the form of characters in myths; others in the titles of living human beings. The ancient Egyptians were the first to record the science of *Aṣẹ* and personified this force as Isis and Osiris: both the masculine and feminine qualities of the force. If we are to vocalize Osiris in modern African languages, it would be pronounced: [in full] *Washil* (w-s-l <*wsr*) (Tshiluba); [in reverse] *Òrìṣà*/ *Orìṣẹ* (Yorùbá), *Ras* (Ethiopic); [reduced] *Èṣú* (Yorùbá). The goddess Aset/Isis would simply be vocalized as: [in full] *Ras* (Ethiopic), *Olísà* (Yorùbá); [reduced] *Ese* (Coptic), *Aṣẹ* (Yorùbá), *Eshe* (Kiswahili). May the Creator continue to grant you *peace*, *victory*, and *satisfaction* (*ḥtp*), and may the ancestors (in all their forms) open the channels for increased *health*, *wealth* and *knowledge of self* (*Aṣẹ*)!

---

39 Which is why the same word for God is often the same word for man in African languages.

(Table Footnotes)

1 There is also ***àjé*** "the spirit of a bird" used by women (*Ìyáàmi*) to invoke powers used for **abundance** and justice.

2 In Africa, wisdom is associated with being able to "see": not only physically in this world, but the "unseen" in the spiritual world. Those who can see on both plains are considered priests.

3 I argue that this *sw* derives as a palatalized form of *3ḫw* "power (of God), mastery (over work)" which would further validate its relation to Yorùbá *ṣẹ* "to do, work, to create"; *àṣẹ* "power, to power to make things happen"; Egyptian *š* "work," *sw.ti* "be great, be powerful," *sw.t* "force (of wind), gust."

REINTERPRETATION OF THE ANKH SYMBOL: Emblem of a Master Teacher

In this essay we will look at possible alternative interpretations of the ancient Nile Valley symbol known in modern Egyptological literature as the *ʿnḫ* 𓋹 (Coptic *onkh*). The popular definitions of *ʿnḫ* are as follows: 𓋹 *ʿnḫ* → "life"; 𓋹𓈖𓐍 *ʿnḫ* → "live, life, be alive"; 𓋹𓅱𓏥 *ʿnḫw* → "the living"; 𓋹𓈖𓐍𓀀 *ʿnḫ* → "person, inhabitant, citizen, living one"; 𓋹𓈖𓐍𓀀𓁐𓏥 *ʿnḫ* → "person, citizen, living one."

Although some of the definitions are clear, the inspiration behind the symbol of the *ʿnḫ* has eluded historians for decades. Some of the more popular interpretations of the symbol used to represent life are 1) that it is a combination of a womb and phallus together to represent the union of masculine and feminine energy, 2) it is an early representation of the cross most popular in the religion of Christianity known as the *Crux Ansata* (handled cross), and 3) that it is a representation of a *messob* table used to serve food in Ethiopia.

That latter is an interpretation espoused by Legesse Allyn who wrote a book titled *Amarigna & Tigrigna Qal Hieroglyphs for Beginners: Perfect for Travelers To Egypt and Students of Ancient Gebts* (2009) for which he claims that the ancient Egyptian language is in fact the Amarigna and Tigrigna languages.[1] In a great number of African cosmological myths, all life comes from an egg (e.g., among the Dogon and Ancient Egyptians). In the Amarigna and Tigrigna languages of Eritrea and Ethiopia, the word *enqalal* means "egg." The hieroglyph used to represent the phonetic sound of [*ḫ*] 𓐍 can also represent the *k, q* and *g* sounds in corresponding words in Amarigna.[2] As we can see the *ʿnḫ* and *enq-* are phonetically similar. With that said, the verb meaning *to motivate* or *to give life* in Amarigna is *anäqaqa*. Allyn claims that the *ʿnḫ* (*anäqaqa*) in the Eritrean tradition is really a *messob* table with an egg (*enqalal*) on top of it (p.c.). Here are a few pictures of a *messob* table:

1 Although Egyptian is currently classified under the Afro-Asiatic super language family, it is demonstrated that Egyptian is not a Semitic language which Amarigna and Tigrigna are.

2 This is according to Legasse Allyn. See http://hieroglyphalphabet.com/ (retrieved April 26, 2013)

Messob tables[3]

For the Amharic speakers, asserts Allyn, the *ʿnḫ* ☥ symbol is possibly a *messob* table with its top off and an egg on top of it (personal communication). It is kind of like the *hotep* 𓊵 (Kalenjiin *ketepi*; Yoruba *adaba*) symbol that has a cake on top of a floor mat. As Ethiopia in ancient times was a major trading station for central east Africa and the upper Nile Valley, their symbolic associations often deal with commercial interests. At the same time we can assume they are used metaphysically as well. Just as an egg incubates/produces life, life is maintained by the consumption of food (as an egg is a food staple).

Messob table with top off displaying food items,
the source of life

This is just one interpretation. However, given the evidence that is to be presented below, I am not convinced that we can look into the Amarigna language for the ultimate etymology of this term or for the origins of the *ʿnḫ* symbol.

The *ʿnḫ* symbol may be predynastic and Mutwa (2003) argues that the symbol is native to the Amazulu of South Africa.[4] For the West and Central Africans, the *ʿnḫ* symbol is more in alignment with the common interpretations of *life* and *man* (humanity) attested to in mainstream Egyptology material. What I want to add to this discourse is the notion that the *ʿnḫ* symbol is

3 Images courtesy of http://aradarestaurant.com/.

4 See discussion "The ZULU History of the Cross" in this excerpt from an interview: http://www.esotericonline.net/profiles/blog/show?id=3204576%3ABlogPost%3A502791&commentId=3204576%3AComment%3A503120&xg_source=activity. (retrieved April 28, 2013)

not only a symbol for *man* and *life*, but is also a symbol for an initiated *master* or *priest*.

To understand the connection between the *ʿnẖ* symbol and a master teacher, one has to be familiar with the African concept of the *Four Moments of the Sun*. I take this name from Robert F. Thompson's book *The Four Moments of the Sun,* as the original concept is known by many names across the continent of Africa.

In short, African people are generally not of the belief that our existence ends when we die. The overwhelming consensus is that the soul has a pre-human existence. The soul descends to earth to have experiences; the body then dies and the spirit continues to have an experience in another realm before coming back to earth to have more human experiences. In essence they speak of life being a cycle of change: of living-dying-living. African people have encapsulated this philosophy within a diagram that we call the "four moments of the sun." It is called this because African people symbolically associate the human being as a living packet of energy—a miniature sun—going through a cycle of birth, maturity, death and rebirth symbolically represented by four main positions of the sun (east, north, west and south).

The birth of a child is seen as the rising of a living sun and death as the setting of a living sun. We may have in the Egyptian this same conceptualization in the *mdw nṯr* script:

ẖi – "babe" *i.e.*, "the rising sun"
Budge 525a

The sun apparently travels around the earth in a 360 degree circular path. The Bantu marks the four cardinal points of interest in a diagram: one sun at each cardinal direction (north, south, east and west), with each position of the sun representing a certain key stage of development. These stages of development are not relegated to human beings and represent the life-cycle of all living or created things. The most complete work on this subject is Dr. Kimbwandende kia Bunseki Fu-Kiau's 2001 book titled *African Cosmology of the Bantu Kongo*. An in depth treatment of this aspect of the subject is beyond the scope of this essay and I leave it up to the reader to read the source material in their own time. For now please observe the following graph called the *Dikenga* among the Bakongo of Central Africa[5] that represents perpetual change [*dingo-dingo*] among the Ba-Ntu people:

5 Author's rendition of the Dikenga diagram in association with the cosmology of African-Americans. See *The Bakala of North America: The Living Suns of Vitality* (2009), MOCHA-Versity Press.

<Author's rendition of the sun's four primary positions. See Fu-Kiau (2003:9) and (2001:33)>

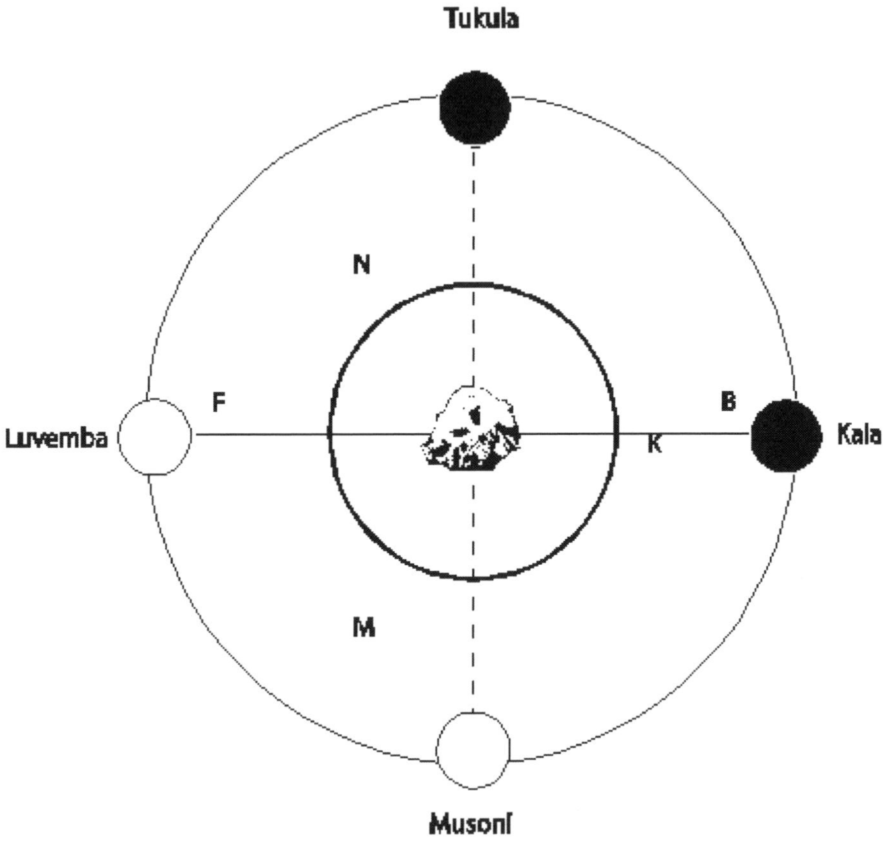

A human being is a rising and setting sun around the world.

B – The birth (butuka) of a child is the rising of a living sun in the community
F – The death (fwa) of a human being is the setting of a living sun in the community
N – The upper world (ku nseke) or the physical world
M – The lower world or spiritual world (ku mpemba)
K – Kalunga, the invisible wall between the physical and spiritual world

< Living Sun (human being) < Burning Coal of Community (BAKAYA)

In the Kongo each demarcation is called a "V." A more elaborate graphical interpretation of the Kongo *Dikenga dia Dingo-Dingo* is provided below:

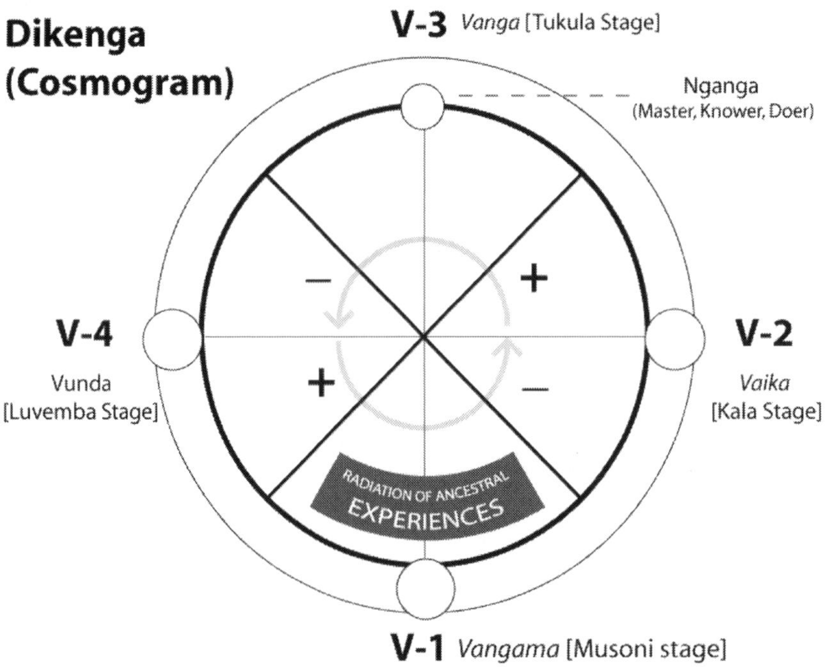

The most important stage that concerns us here is V-3 (Vanga) which represents the Tukula (red colored) sun of maturity, leadership and creativity. The word *Vanga* derives from an archaic Bantu verb *ghanga* which means *to do, to perform*. It is where we get the term *nganga* (in part) which means a master, a knower, a doer, a specialist, etc. In Bantu languages one can often turn a verb into a noun by means of affixation (often called *deverbalization*). In this case the letter *-n-* is a contraction of the word *enie* or *enyie* which means "one who, a possessor, that which." In the case of the Kikongo term *n-ganga,* it is a statement simply saying "one who does" or "one who performs." This *Vee* is the most critical in life as it represents the stage of creativity and great deeds or *tukula* stage of the root verb *kula,* which means *to mature* or *master*.

What is implied by this term is that an *nganga* is someone who is highly knowledgeable, highly respected and also a community leader who has put in the necessary work to enhance the lives of the community and maintain the balance of village life (to make sure the community waves aren't shaken). An *nganga* is a master, a doer and a specialist in a community of *doers*. Dr. Fu-Kiau (2001) expounds on this subject and stage of development. He informs us that:

> This Vee, the third, is a reversed pyramid. It occupies the position of verticality [kitombayulu], the direction of **gods, power and leadership**. People, institutions, societies and nations as well, enter and exist in this zone successfully, only if they stand on their own feet. One enters and stands up inside this Vee to become a doer/ master [nganga], to oneself first before becoming an nganga to the community (…) To stand "well" inside this scaling Vee is to be able not only to master our lives, but to better know ourselves and our relationship positions with the rest of the universe as a whole. (Fu-Kiau, 2001:140-1)(emphasis mine)

An *nganga* is an initiated master. The word for initiation and the word *nganga* are similar in morphology. The word *ghanda* means "initiation." It is similar to the word *ghanga* which means "to perform" or "to do" which becomes *nganga*: a master, a doer, specialist, community leader. This directly informs our discussion in many ways. The first is linguistically which we will discuss further below. The second is iconographically as Dr. Fu-Kiau plainly informs us that:

> This power figure, the leader/priest [nganga], who stands powerfully at the center of the community issues [mambu], **became the Egyptian ankh or symbol for life**. Of course, among Bantu people, an nganga stands "vertically," and powerfully inside the community "Vee" [telama lwimbanganga mu kanda], **as the symbol of active life in the community**. (Fu-Kiau, 2001:131-2) (emphasis mine)

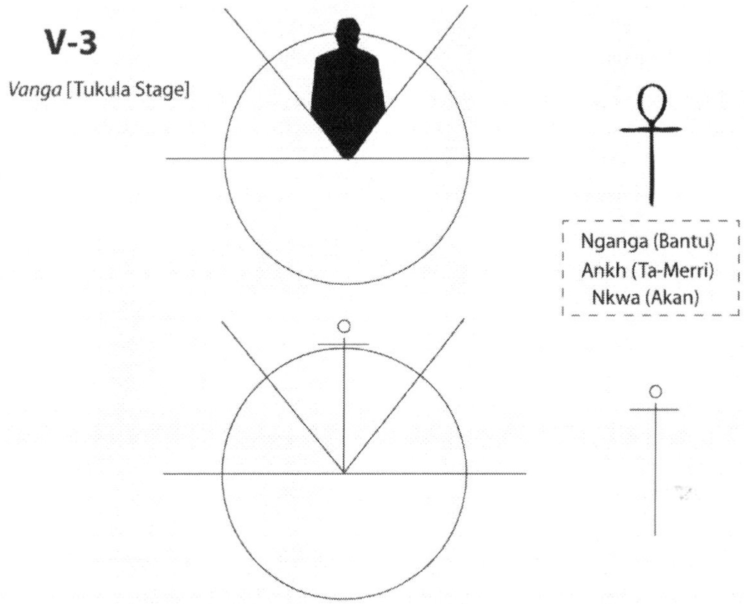

As we can see in the account given by Fu-Kiau, the *ˁnḫ* symbol—in the Kongo context—means more than simply *life*: it represents an **active life of a master,** thus *ghanga* (to do, to perform). It is my contention that the actual pronunciation of the word *ˁnḫ* is closer to the pronunciation of the word for *life* and *man* in the Niger-Congo languages: *nkwa*. At the heart of the word *nkwa* or *ˁnḫ* is the word *ka*(*a*) which in the Egyptian and Niger-Congo languages mean *fuel, power, life, to have life, be, have being, spirit, energy, be burning* and more. In my publication *The Bakala of North America: The Living Suns of Vitality,* I argue that the word *nkwa* is associated, symbolically, to an internal fire which represents the life-force:[6]

> Fire in African philosophy represents not only life, but the soul of a human being. This is why *kaa* or *kala* also means "man" or "living person." *Kaa* is a variation of *kwa* which in the Niger-Congo languages means "man, person, life." When the prefix *n-* is added to *kwa* you have *nkwa* meaning "life" in the Niger-Congo languages. The *n-* prefix is a Bantu formative morpheme, interchangeable with the *mu-* morpheme, that means "that which" or "he who." It denotes "something pertaining to." It may derive from a word that is present in Kiswahili *enyi* or *enie* which means 'possessing' or 'having' or "being in a state or condition." There is a similar adjective in Kiswahili *enyewe* or *eniewe* and it is used to express identity or uniqueness and used to express the personality of a person. The *n-* prefix may simply be a contraction of *enyi/enie*.
>
> *Wa* is a passive suffix which indicates that the subject is being acted upon by an agent. It can also be rendered as *ua* or *we* and expresses identity or distinctiveness. A major feature of Bantu is its ability to turn verbs into nouns by way of affixation. So ***kaa***

6 I have since modified the excerpt from the original publication.

would be in this sense a verb meaning "to live." ***Kaa*** + ***wa*** → ***kwa*** would mean "to be alive." The variation ***n-*** (*enyi*) + ***kaa*** + **wa** → ***nkwa*** would mean "he who has life" (fire) or the "possessor of life." *Nkwa* is more than likely the correct way to say the ancient Egyptian word *ʿnẖ* (*onkh* in Coptic, *-ong-* in Duala-Bantu) which means *life, living* or *person* (see below). We have a similar rendering of the term in *Igbo* but it does not have the intrusive [*k*] sound. Our term in Igbo is *onwe* (the self) which is a contraction of two words *onye nwe* which means *the possessor*, or *own lordship*. The Igbo sees a given human being as *onwe ya*: *a lord unto himself*.

NKWA

Ancient Egyptian *ankhu* = man
Budge 124B

As mentioned earlier, the *ẖ* sound corresponds to *k, q* or *g* in related languages, and sometimes in dialectical variations of Egyptian. It is my contention that the heart of *ʿnẖ* is really *ka*. [k] and [g] are often interchangeable (at least dialectically). Thus the /k/ in the Egyptian could also be rendered /g/ which would render our term *nk* → *ng* (by the weakening of the /k/ due to the preceding nasal) in Niger-Congo.[7] What we would have in the Bantu languages is a case of reduplication. *Nganga* is really *nga-nga*. It is sometimes found in the form *ngaa* or *ga*.[8] Often words are reduplicated to add a change in emphasis. For example, in Yoruba (Niger-Congo in general) the word *ba* means *expansive power* or *male energy*. From this root we get *baba* (father), *babagba* or *baba baba* (grandfather). Another example is *da* which means to create. *Dada* is the *Spirit of Vegetation* in liturgical *Ifa* (Yoruba spiritual system). Repeating the word *da* (create) suggests recreation or the power of vegetation to continuously go through the process of birth, growth, death and rebirth. So in the case of *nganga*, the root is *ga* which is reduplicated to refer to someone one who does the work. Remember *k* and *g* are variants of each other. So it is no surprise that we find in the Egyptian:

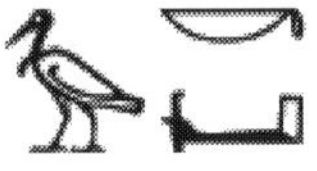

bʿk "to work, to labor, to toil, to *serve*, to do *service*, to pay tribute"
Budge 206b

kꜣ.t "work, labor, toil"
Budge 784a

The word *ka* is found in the Hausa root (t-r-k-) *tiraka*, and the Yoruba *talaka* (t-l-k-) which means "poor, working class." These are variations on the same theme. The root is found in Semitic *l'k* "to work, to labor" (see Hebrew *mala'kah* "occupation, work") and *l'k* "send" (see Hebrew *mal'ak* "messenger – hence angel). This initial *l-* is lost in Hausa *aiki* "work" and *aika*

7 See *Appendix B* this volume.
8 Modupe Oduyoye, *Words and Meaning in Yoruba Religion: Linguistic Connections in Yoruba, Ancient Egyptian and Semitic* (1996:134, endnote 18). Karnak House Publishing, London.

"to send."

The word *ka* (probably a homonym) is also a term for authority which also adds credence to our interpretation. Observe the following (Imhotep 2009):

k3k3 →	"God" – Egyptian (Amazulu *nkulunkulu* "God")
Kaka Yetu →	"description of God as primary ancestor" – Luvale-Bantu
nkaka →	"family head" – Kikongo
ka →	"greater, superior" – Igbo
kaananke →	"leader, leadership" – Soninke
nkwa mavanga →	"mature leadership" – Kikongo
nkwiki →	"coal fighter, metaphor for leader"[9] – Kikongo
nkani →	"a judge" – Kongo, Loango and Tio (see Kleiman 2003:155)
kumu-a-mbuku →	"owner of the village" – Mitsogho
tunka →	"chief, leader" – Soninke
tunke →	"master, chief" – Soninke

As we can see in the Egyptian, by reduplicating the term *ka* we get a term that represents God. The word *ka*, again, means power, energy, spirit, man and life and by doubling the term we add greater emphasis on these concepts to reflect the magnitude of the Supreme Being. Here is our term *ka* reduplicated in the *mdw nṯr* script:

k3k3

Ancient Egyptian = God
Luvale Bantu: *kaka* "ancestor, elder, God"
Luvale-Bantu: *kaka* (*yetu*) "our god" (*yetu* = our)
Kiswahili: *kaka* = "an elder relative, elder brother, brother"

The ancestral pronunciation is something more like *kulu* with the *3* approximating an *l*, thus Egyptian *k3k3* is *Nkulunkulu* "God" in Isizulu. In the ciLuba-Bantu language this word is given as *MuKulu* "God," *Nkole*(a) "God"; Kalenjiin *Nkoolo* "God." It should be noted that the determinative in the word *k3k3* , of the seated man with beard, is often rendered solely as a sign of a deity. In actuality, it represents any person of authority or of high rank including ancestors. Oduyoye (1996:73) provides a parallel among the Yoruba, "The idea of the wisdom of the elders is *igbon* "chin," where the beard grows, the beard being a sign of age and of mature wisdom. Hence Hebrew *zaken* is 'old' and *zakan* is 'beard' and 'chin'." We find conceptual support in the following Yoruba sayings:

Ewú l ogbó	"Grey hairs signify age"
Irungbòn l'àgbà	"Beards signify elderliness"

Here we have a possible frame for which to interpret the meaning behind the sacred beards in the "deity" determinatives in the ancient Egyptian writing script. It is clear that it is a sign of a *wise man* or *master*. We will discover that the Western practice of trying to interpret everything when it comes to Africa "religiously" leads to gross misinterpretations of the data.

Our interpretation of *ʿnḫ* to mean *nganga*, in relation to master teachers, elders, etc., is supported by the Bantu cognates mentioned above, which extend the term *k3k3* to elders and

9 See Fu-Kiau (2001:27)

ancestors. Therefore, given what has been discussed so far, we can reinterpret the Egyptian symbol for *life,* given as *ʿnẖ,* to be *nkwa* or *nganga*:

NGANGA

ʿnẖ "life personified, the name of a god" (Budge 125A)
reinterpretation: "a master, doer, a true knower, a specialist, teacher, priest, healer, a power figure"

The Bantu cosmology, symbolized in the Dikenga cosmogram above is going to be key in interpreting some other concepts below. It is this cosmogram, and its corresponding symbolisms, that may help us to accurately interpret certain poses in Egyptian reliefs. The following is an excerpt from an online article I wrote titled "Posture and Meaning: Interpreting Egyptian Art Through a Kongo Cultural Lens."[10] In this article we analyze certain poses and their meanings in the culture of the Kongo and compare them to Egyptian motifs in hopes to better understand the meaning behind the Egyptian postures. A key pose of the Kongo that is important to the topic of the current article under examination is the *Crossroads Pose*:

> The crossroads pose, with right hand up to heaven and left hand parallel to the horizon line, characterizes the *niombo* figure. The *niombo* of the Kongo would be equivalent to the *orisha* of the Yoruba, or the *neters* of the Egyptians. This gesture is found in Kongo, Cameroon and Nigeria and has made its way to Haiti via *vodun*. The right hand up and left hand down recalls the anthropomorphic reading of the hand-guards of the *mbele a lulendo* (knife of authority), the royal swords of execution in ancient Kongo. In Kongo this gesture, on swords and *niombo*, marked the boundaries between two worlds (upper and lower worlds).

> We see this pose on another version of the *nkondi* figure below.

10 http://asarimhotep.com

Nkondi (Kongo) with *crossroads* pose[11]

Egyptian Bes with the *crossroads* pose

This pose relates to the cosmogram mentioned earlier and could signify in the Egyptian the meeting place between the ancestral realm and the manifest realm. Remember that an *nganga* has the insight to 'see' what goes on in the community. That is another way of saying that he has the eyes of the ancestors. The *nganga* is the link between the living and the dead and this pose informs the wisdom seeker that this person in fact

11 Unknown Kongo artist and ritual expert, Democratic Republic of the Congo or Angola, *Nkisi nkondi* power figure, about 1890, wood and mixed media. Purchased through the Mrs. Harvey P. Hood W'18 Fund, the William B. Jaffe and Evelyn A. Jaffe Hall Fund, the William B. Jaffe Memorial Fund, the William S. Rubin Fund, the Julia L. Whittier Fund and through gifts by exchange; 996.22.30233. On view in the exhibition Art That Lives?

has the wisdom, insight, ability and authority to operate in both the realm of the living and the dead: that he is indeed the link between the realms.

Now examine the following predynastic Egyptian image with the same pose:

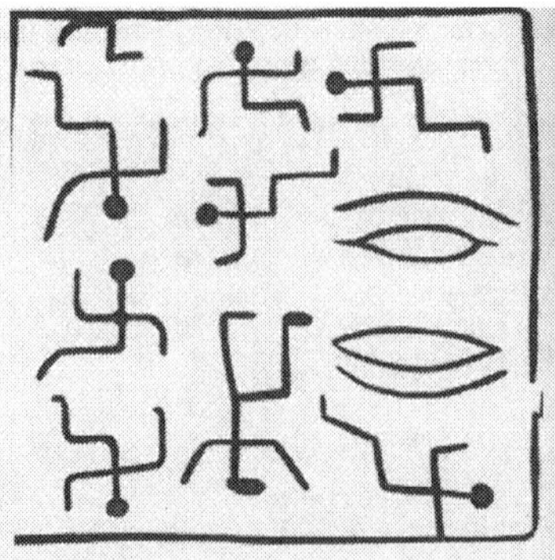

Humans in Crooked Cross/Swastika Shape, Early Egyptian Cylinder Seal from Negada. (*Proceedings of the Society for Biblical Archaeology*, XXII, 278, 28[illegible])

To further substantiate our interpretation of *ʿnḫ* to mean a master, priest, etc., we will have to side track a moment to another Egyptian term that is often not accurately translated: *pr* (*per* = house). This particular excerpt discusses the term pharaoh, which derives from the Egyptian *pr-ʿꜣ* which means *great house*, and its spread across Africa. We note the following:

Egyptian	Walaf
Per-aa = Pharoah	Fari = Supreme King Fara = officer in charge Fara leku = keeper of harem
Paour = the Chief P-our = the King P-ouro = king (Coptic)	Bur = king (b > p)

In the ciKam language, the term *pr-ʿꜣ* not only referred to the Supreme King, but to administrators as well. In the Mande language of Mali and Upper Guinea, we find the same terms as we do in Wolof: *Fari, Farima, Farma* all designating political functions. In Songhai we have *Faran* and in Hausa we have *Fara* (Diop 1991:168-9). Among the Amarigna speakers of Eritrea and Ethiopia the term is *Biro* which is usually interpreted as *office*. In ciLuba-Bantu this term is reflected in *-bedi* "first, primary"; *cipàla* "public"; *kumpàla* "before, previously"; *-à/-a kumpàla* "first, initial"; *mwènàmpalà* "ambassador, replacement, substitute, person commissioned, lieutenant"; *mpala-ne-nyima* "before and behind = well, completely, to perfection"; *mumpela* "master of good advice, wise-perfect"; *mwimpila* > *mwimpe* [Egyptian *nfr*] "good-nice-just-perfect, what is good, to be perfect, good-man (*mu-Mpela*> *mumpele, mwimpe, mpwila, Mpela, mpelu*)." This term means the same thing from West to East to South East Africa as demonstrated above. So we have a direct correlation in name and in function in ancient Egyptian and the rest of Black African societies.

Ancient Egyptian *pr-ꜥꜣ* "house, seat of government, pharaoh, palace"

It must be said, however, that the term *fara, fari, faro*, etc., is not just a title of political office: it represents a secret society. In other words, the secret society is the political office. In many cultures of Africa, a king is an initiated high priest. You cannot hold "office" in traditional African societies unless you have been initiated into the customs and spirituality of the community. This practice is no different in ancient Egypt. The *fari* represent those initiated persons who belong to the society of initiated priests. Evidence of this is still kept alive in West Africa in Liberia among many ethnic groups. Observe the following:

> **Pora** → *the great secret society of men* (Mande, Vai, Gola, De, Kpelle, Kissi, Gbande, Belle, Loma, Mano, Gio Ge, Bassa, Kru, Mende, Kono, Temne, Lokko, Krim, Limba)
> **Beri** (in Sierra Leone) → *ibid*, sometimes called **poro**.[12]

These organizations operate from a very Afrocentric perspective. They understand that you cannot govern this society without first being initiated into its history, philosophy, spiritual nuances and social norms. Dr. Fu-Kiau informs us that in the Kongo this concept is called being able to "tie and untie knotty ropes" (Fu-Kiau 2001, 2007). You can't begin to interpret and understand why we do what we do unless you have been initiated into this organization/ wisdom-center which was created to maintain the integrity of a body of knowledge on how to effectively govern our society and handle power without abusing it (Imhotep 2008:87-95).

This same organization made its way into the United States as a result of slavery. Among the Gullah of South Carolina the secret society became known as *beri, berimo* and *poro,* all meaning "the great secret society of men." In essence, we literally had 'pharaohs' who became enslaved in the United States. Due to the restrictions of slavery and segregation, these societies were reorganized into burial societies and insurance companies to take care of the sick and dying and to cover the cost of funerals (Halloway 2005: 204, 216).

Here we posit that the *pr-ꜥꜣ* was not simply a political office, but a wisdom center (misnomered secret society) or an organization of leaders in African societies. It was/is a society that trains and initiates leaders. We mentioned earlier in our discussion that an *nganga* is an initiated master and community leader. We see that in the ancient Nile Valley the *ꜥnẖ* (*nganga*) followed the same milieu.

BIRO/FARI/PORO NGANGA

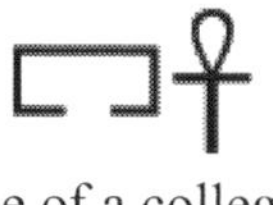

pr ꜥnẖ "house of life (the name of a college of priests)" (Budge 124B)
reinterpretation = (secret) society of [wisdom-center for] masters (priests)

It is becoming clear that there is more to *life* in the ancient Egyptian framework. But what does it mean to *live* fully in the African context? Fu-Kiau has already informed us that the

12 See Margaret Washington "Gullah Attitudes toward Life and Death," in *Africanisms in American Culture, 2nd Edition*, edited by Joseph Calloway. Indiana University Press. Bloomington and Indianapolis. 2005, p.152.

ꜥ*nḫ* symbol in the Kongo represents the active *life* of a specialist in the community. We find a similar connotation among the Akan of Ghana, where the term ꜥ*nḫ* is pronounced *nkwa. Nkwa* is commonly referred to as the abundance and fullness of life. Beyond mere existence, the full manifestation of *nkwa* includes long life, fertility, vigor, health, wealth, happiness, felicity, and peace (Asante & Mazama, 2009: 453-454). *Nkwa* is connected to the Akan concept of the supreme manifestation of the abundant and joyous life. The Twi term *nkwagye* refers to *nkwa* (life in all its fullness) and *gye* (rescue, retake, recapture). In this context, *nkwagye* represents the preservation, protection, and sustaining of life.

Rev. Dr. Emmanuel Kingsley Larbi in his essay *The Nature of Continuity and Discontinuity of Ghanaian Pentecostal Concept of Salvation in African Cosmology*[13] supports this expanded African concept of *living* in the Akan tradition. He states:

> As one critically examines the prayers of the Akan in the traditional religious setting, one cannot help but come to the conclusion that the overriding concern is the enjoyment of *nkwa* (life). This is not life in abstraction but rather life in its concrete and fullest manifestations. It means the enjoyment of long ***life, vitality, vigour, and health***; it means life of happiness and felicity. *Nkwa* also includes the enjoyment of *ahonyade*, (possessions; prosperity), that is, wealth, riches, and substance, including children. *Nkwa* also embodies *asomdwei*, that is, a life of peace and tranquility, and life free from perturbation. (bolded emphasis mine)

For those familiar with ancient Egyptian texts, one will immediately recognize the bolded text in the cited passage above as it is very similar to the following salutation given to the king in ancient times:

NKWA, WAJU, SIMBA

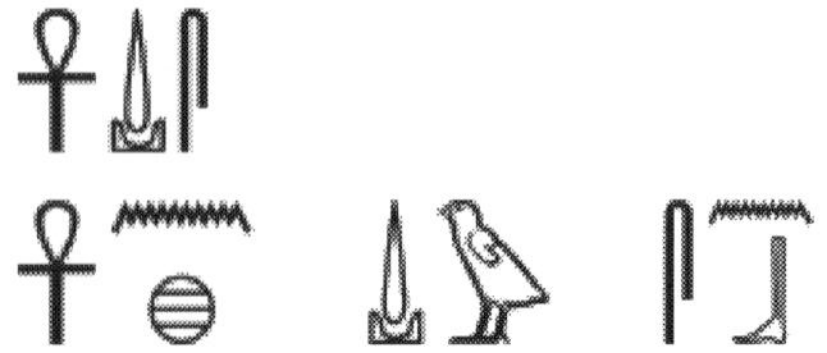

Ancient Egyptian ꜥ*nḫ, wḏ*ꜥ*, snb* = life, prosperity and health
reinterpretation = life, vitality and blessings
Budge 124B

These are the wishes appended to the name of the king and bestowed upon honored persons by the Netchers.[14] I think that a few of the words above are in need of a reinterpretation. We have already discussed the word ꜥ*nḫ*. The next word up for revision is the word *wḏꜣ* which is commonly rendered to mean *prosperity*. I think that this term does, on one level mean prosperity, but that this definition is in fact an extended definition. The clue is the glyph that makes up the term: an active flame on raised earth or a heap of coals. It is argued that Egyptian belongs to the Afro-Asiatic languages in which the Semitic is one of its branches. When we look at the term *waju* or *wajo* in a few of these languages, then the term becomes clearer. In Ethiopic the term *waju* or *wajo* means to *heal* or *recover health*. *Wajo* also refers to a person who *roasts* and distributes meat at ceremonial meals. A dialectical variant is pronounced *waya*

13 Retrieved from the following website 11/8/2009: http://www.pctii.org/cyberj/cyberj10/larbi.html

14 *Let the Ancestors Speak: Removing the Veil of Mysticism from Medu Netcher* (1995:68). JOM International INC., by Ankh Mi Ra

which means heat, warmth; *wayyaa*, recovering from illness. *Wayu* means "fire-brand." In the Yindin language the word *waju* means to *burn* or *cook*.[15] Among the Kuku Yalanji of Australia *waju* also means *to burn.*[16]

The word *snb* corresponds to the Bantu word *simba*. In the Egyptian, the water sign used to represent the [n] sound may have assimilated under certain phonic conditions to become [m].[17] The word *snb* is defined to mean *be healthy*. In the Shona-Bantu language, the word *simba* means a *force, be healthy, be strong*, and *powerful*. Dr. Fu-Kiau however gives us other reflexes for this term. *Simba,* in Kikongo, also means *to hold up, to keep, to bless, to treasure, to touch* and *to retain*.[18] In the context of the salutations given above, it is my belief that the word *wḏꜣ* (*waja*) is a word also referring to being healthy as *wḏꜣ* deals with healing and vitality (thus the use of the flame symbol). The word *snb* (simba), by extension, should also refer to being *blessed* and having *prosperity*. Although this phrase is written with separate glyphs, Budge (124B) in one rendering only uses the word *ꜥnḫ* to mean life, strength and health. This would correlate with the Akan *nkwa* which means *life, vigour, health* and *vitality*. Essentially, all three terms belong to the same theme.[19]

All of this to say that for the African *life* is simply not reduced to simply having a heartbeat. It is an *active life* full of *vigor*, *great health*, *vitality* and *service* to the community. An *nkwa* (*ꜥnḫ, ong, onkh, nganga, kaka*) is a human being who is initiated into the secrets of vitality, that uses their wisdom for the betterment of the community by means of service. Kykosa Kajangu, in his unpublished PhD dissertation titled *Beyond the Colonial Gaze: Reconstructing African Wisdom Traditions* (2005), provides us insight into the character of an elder; who in our case would be the *nganga* (*ꜥnḫ*), sometimes called in the Bantu the *Bakoles* or *Bakulu*. The elders, the living libraries in a community of memory, are people who are:

> … [M]otivated actors who construct symbolic worlds in which people live and die in Africa. These builders of symbolic worlds manage the destinies of African wisdom traditions. These sages exhibit the following characteristics. **First, they have learned to the highest degree the secrets for knowing life and the strategies for stemming the tide of its challenges.** It is this reservoir of knowledge that enables elders to be effective teachers. Second, they embody the teachings of centers of wisdom. They have developed countless strategies or teachable viewpoints to take people to places where they have never dared to go. Third, they have proven track records of success in taking direct responsibility for the development of the youth in their community of memory. (emphasis mine)

Dr. Kajangu adds an important element to this discussion that I think we can add to our expanding definition of *ꜥnḫ*: that is *ꜥnḫ* just isn't life itself, but the obtainment of the highest degree of knowledge as it pertains to life. The secrets of life that are discovered by the *Bakoles* are the strategies necessary to tower over the one thousand and one challenges of life. Fu-Kiau wouldn't find any disagreement with Kajangu's assessment of the role and characteristics of an elder (the *nganga*). It is these characteristics that make the living worthy of deification after death by the community. Remember that the term "god" commonly rendered in the Egyptological

15 See *Ergativity* (1994:120 fn 11) by Robert M. W. Dixon. Cambridge University Press.

16 This language is not Afro-Asiatic and this can be a chance coincidence, or a global term. More investigation needed here.

17 Note that in Egyptian *nw* 𓈗 can also be pronounced *mw* "water, semen, rain, bodily fluids." We also have the m<>n interchange in *mgg/ngg* "cluck" (of bird); *mkt* "protection, defense"; *nḫt* "protection"; *nḫ* "protection"; *nhw* "protection" (of king's arm); (<*ḫw* "protection"). See also Allyn (2010) for correspondences in Amarigna.

18 *Simba Simbi: Hold up that which holds you up*. (2006:1) Dorrance Publishing, Inc.

19 This is explored further in the second essay of this series.

literature actually refers to initiated priests, elders, ancestors and the divine aspects of nature. In regards to the *nganga,* Fu-Kiau (2001:78) instructs us about responsible leadership:

> Political and diplomatic missions were akin to deification for those who knew how to handle the people's responsibility. Coming back from an important and successful mission for my community, a *simbi kia nsi*, literally, holder of the country's equilibrium, a wise man took my hands, spit on them, and said: "If you season the policy of people and the community correctly, you are deified" [*Watwisa mungwa ye nungu mu kinzozi kia n'kangu ye kanda, zambusu*]. This Kongo proverb shows us that only obedience to the people's will makes people heroes and gods and not otherwise for the red carpet is not requested, it is earned [*nkwal'a luzitu ka yilom**bwanga** ko*].

If a community member was in fact a doer (*nganga*, a performer of service to the community) then s/he would be deified among the people. It is the learned and skilled sage who can bring balance to the country, who knows life to the highest degree and how to successfully meet its challenges that are worthy of the name *nganga* and can truly say that they have in fact ***lived*** in every sense of the word.

Mutwa (1964) made the bold claim that the elders are the most suited to solve the African crises that was brought about by colonialism, and in many ways reaffirms the sentiments expressed by Fu-Kiau (2001):

> The fate of Africa lies in the hands of its witchdoctors. One single witchdoctor in a position of authority can do more to repair the damage done in a strife-torn country in Africa, like the Congo, than can the whole of the United Nations. The ordinary Bantu, no matter how educated or "civilized," are still firmly rooted to the beliefs of their forefathers. No matter how they have been subjected to Christian influences, they still have greater confidence in their local *nganga* (or witchdoctor) than the host of Catholic saints who were fed to the lions in the Coliseum in Rome (Mutwa 1964: 469).

It should be noted that the *ꜥnḫ* ☥ symbol is not exclusive to the Nile Valley and the Kongo. It is a sign that means *life* all over Africa, especially in South Africa among the Zulu and the Khoi Khoi. Among the Zulu, according to Credo Mutwa,[20] this symbol is known as "the knot of eternal life" or "the knot of eternity." It should also be noted that the sign in ancient Egyptian symbolism is represented by a knotted rope, which modern Egyptologists mistakenly refer to as a "sandal." The *ꜥnḫ* symbol is used among the Khoisan as an amulet for *healing*. It also represents for the Khoi Khoi a symbol for the supreme Creator which they call *Heitsie-Ibib*. Among the Zulu, the symbol is associated with a story that states the Supreme Being's son lost his leg in a battle with a dragon (some say a crocodile) and they call the sign ☥ *Mlenze-munye* which means "the one legged one." When Christian missionaries came into South Africa wearing the cross on their necks, the natives thought that the Christians were wearing the Zulu sign for their God the "one legged one" that dies and is born again forever and ever.

The Dogon of Mali represents the universe with an image called *aduno kine,* which means, "The life of the world." As we can see below, it resembles the *ꜥnḫ* symbol with minor variations. This sign is given two meanings that are in line with our definitions for *nkwa* or *ꜥnḫ*. The first meaning is 'humanity' and the celestial placenta (the upper ellipse). The second meaning is the earthly placenta (the open ellipse). The cross in the center represents the four cardinal points.[21]

---

20 See his Biography at: http://www.bibliotecapleyades.net/esp_credo_mutwa04.htm (retrieved 7/29/2013).

21 See Marcel Griaule, "*L'Image du monde au Soudan*," in *Journal de la Societe des Africanistes*, Volume XIX, Paris. pp. 81-88.

Aduno Kine

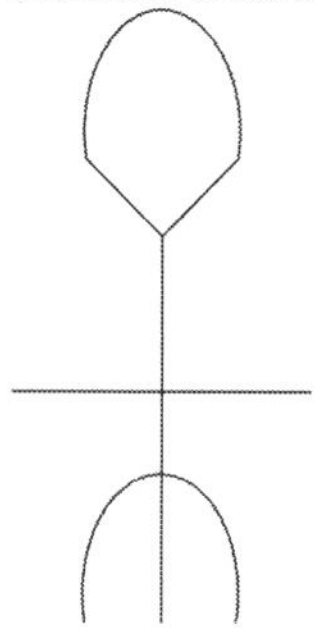

Dogon symbol for the "life of the world"

Among the Akan of Ghana, the *ꜥnḫ* symbol has gone through a unique transformation that many people would look over if they are not symbolically literate in African iconography. The *ꜥnḫ* symbol has morphed into a figure known as the *akuaba* fertility "doll."

Asante akua'ba doll

Ghana 1936

> The legend of the origination of the Akua'ba doll comes from the story of a woman named "Akua" (many variations of the name are found as there are many variations of the spelling of "akua'ba") who could not get pregnant and went to a local diviner or priest and commissioned the carving of a small wooden doll. She carried and cared for the doll as if it were her own child, feeding it, bathing it and so on. Soon the people in the village started calling it "Akua" "ba" - meaning "Akua's child", since "ba" meant child. She soon became pregnant and her daughter grew up with the doll.
>
> *The legend and tradition still live on today...*
>
> If an Akan/Asante woman had difficulty conceiving she would be encouraged to visit a local shrine accompanied by a senior woman in her family. There she might purchase a figure such as this, which would be placed for a period on the altar, later to be reclaimed by the woman along with certain medicines. The sculpture was then carried, fed, bathed, and otherwise cared for by the woman as if it was a living baby. It was thought that in doing this the woman would have a better chance to have a healthy and beautiful baby. Once the woman conceived and had a successful delivery, she would return the figure to the shrine as a form of offering. If the child died, the akua'ba might be kept by the woman as a memorial.[22]

The *Akuaba* "dolls" are fertility figures and we know that these motifs are used to bring forth ***life*** as the story attests above. One will notice the phonetic similarity to the word *ʿnẖ /nkwa* (*akua*). The /w/ and /u/ are interchangeable so *nkwa* can be rendered *nkua*. When the Akan say *akua'ba,* they are saying, "to bring forth the life of a child." One will also recognize the similarity in shape with the Egyptian *ʿnẖ* symbol.

There is another version of the Egyptian *ʿnẖ* that is actually three symbols super imposed on each other: the *ʿnẖ*, *wʿs* scepter and the *ḏd* pillar. What's important for us in this segment is the association of the *ḏd* pillar with the *ʿnẖ*. It is believed that the *djed* pillar represents the vertebrae of *Wsr* (Asar) and that when it is super imposed on the *ʿnẖ,* that it reinforces the notion that the *ʿnẖ* is a human being and the *djed* is the spinal column of man.

22 Retrieved from the following website 3/8/2010 http://www.randafricanart.com/Asante_akuaba_doll_3.html

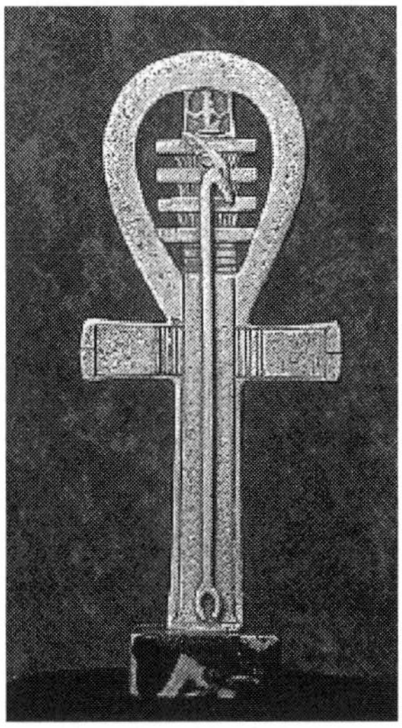

ʿnḫ, ḏd, wʿs scepter super imposed

Compare the super composition *ʿnḫ* with the back of the *akua'ba* figure from Ghana. Notice the "djed" pillar super imposed on the figure from Ghana. Coincidence?

It should be noted that several authors have demonstrated that Black African people were in Greece before and during the formative stages of, and contributed to, important concepts in the development of Greek civilization [Obenga (1992), Campbell-Dunn (2008, 2006), Bernal (1987, 2006), Diop (1991), Van Sertima (1983)]. So it is no surprise when we find images like these in the ancient Mediterranean on the island of Cyprus[23]:

23 Retrieved from the following website 3/8/2010 www.cyprus-archaeology.org.uk/

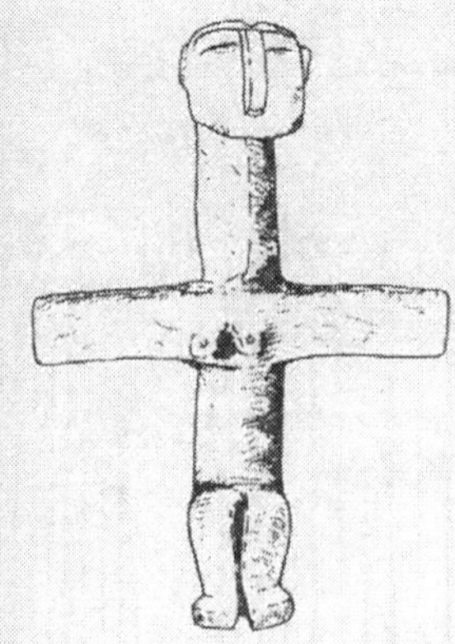

[illegible] statuette from Lemba-Lakkous, Cyprus, c. 2500 BCE. (Biedermann, 82)

ADDENDUM:

After writing my initial findings in regards to the ʿnḫ symbol and its reinterpretations, I later spoke with Dr. Mubabinge Bilolo (linguist and Egyptologist) and he led me to a book he had edited with Nsapo Kalamba titled *Renaissance of the Negro-African Theology: Essays in Honor of Professor Bimwenyi-Kweshi* (2009). In this work—utilizing the Tshiluba-Bantu (or ciLuba) language as support—he confirmed everything in my original thesis and expanded its discourse.

In the ciLuba language *Bw-Anga* means "medicine" which is used for the protection of "life" and for the increase of "health" [*BuKole-bwa-Moyo*]. We've already mentioned that *nganga* refers to a healer in Kikongo. In the book *Biblical Revelation and African Beliefs* (1969: 57) by Kwesi A. Dickson & Paul Ellingworth, R. Buana Kibongi—in his article titled "Priesthood"—notes that "[T]he *nganga*, by fighting against illness, contributed to the development of **medicine**." We see this *-g-n-/n-g-* root (by way of metathesis?) in Yoruba as *oogun* "medicine, juju." It is reflected in Hausa as *magani* (ma-gani) "medicine."

Therefore, in ciLuba the *power of life* is a title of one who cures, who calms the suffering [*mw-anga, Nga-Nga, CyAnga, Sangula, Sangala, Sangalasha, Sangaja, Sungila*]. All of these terms have the *-ng-* root, which is really *-g-*. It is the same root in the word *Sangoma* "healer, priest" among the Zulu.

We add to this revised essay the ciLuba language equivalents to better understand the varying connotations of the ancient Egyptian word *ʿnḫ* that backs-up our initial investigation (Kalamba & Bilolo, 2009).

-Sanga	to cross, join together, gather, mix
Ø *di-/ma-Sanga*	crossroads, confluence, junction, joint, node
Ø *ma-Sang(u,o)*	interval between the shoulders; junction point of two shoulders or two arms = *nTangani/diTung* (u,a) - *a-mapa/makaya/mapwapwa*
Ø *mu-/mi-Sangu*	time, period
Ø *muSangu*	congenital defect, pathology of birth
Ø *sangisha*	to make gather, join together, mix
Ø *Sangila, diSangila, Cisangilu*	gathering, reunion, meet, communion, community
Ø *sangala*	to be delighted, to be happy, to be in good health
Ø *sangala*	to recover (health, vitality/strength joy, the calm one)
-sàngalala	to be full with joy, good fortune, to be completely happy
-sàngaja	to cure
-sàngalaja	to cure, return health
Sangasanga	joy
Sangesha	to welcome
Ø *Mu-Sangelo*	good fortune, success, happiness, joy

The *s-ng-* root also corresponds to *ś-h-* and the words can also mean:

Shinga/Singa/Jinga	to bind, thread, roll up, knot, encircle, tie with a wire; to braid/weave
Ø *MuShinga/ka-Nzinga*	newborn with the umbilical cord rolled up
Ø *muJinga*	cord, reel; braided rope
muJinga	invocation ritual
Nshinga	neck
Zinga/Shinga	to wish, desire, prefer
Ø *MuShinga/Ka-Zinga*	child's desire, wishes, expected
Ø *MuShinga*	price, value, dignity = *bunema*

Sanga is a synonym or variant of:

Sanka	be happy, rejoice, have joy, to be delighted
Disanka	happiness, joy, pleasure
Sankila	to be delighted for
Sankisha	to please, make happy, rejoice
tunka	be happy, happy, joyful, dance of joy, rejoice, merry, exalter

But *s-ng-* < *ś-h-* is also the opposite of *Sanga* or *Sangala.*

Sunga	to hang; to strangle by tightening the throat or the neck (*nshingu*)
Ø *diSunga*	to hang one's self
Sunga	to separate (combatants), appeaser, to reconcile, pacify
Sunga	to choose, elect
Ø *kansunga-nsunga*	partiality, bias
Sungula	to choose, select; to prefer; elected
-sungila	to deliver, protect from; to save
sungidila	to separate, deliver, defend against, to help

This is very instructive. Apart from the connotation of *health* or *life force*, there is a predominance of the concepts of "joy, happiness, rejoicing, etc." This correlates perfectly with the Akan and ancient Egyptian notions of *nkwa* (*nkwa, waju, simba*).

You will also recall our assertion that the *ʿnḫ* ☥ symbol is a simplified human body with the base as the spinal cord, and the bar as the shoulders or arms spread out.[24] So it is no surprise that our *-ng-* root is in the word *muSangu(o)* "interval between the shoulders; junction point of two shoulders or two arms." *Nshinga* means "neck." The *ʿnḫ* symbol is often represented as a tied/knotted rope (especially in the Old Kingdom). In ciLuba we have *Shinga* "to bind, thread, roll up, knot, encircle, tie with a wire; to braid/weave." A variant of this term is *muJinga* which means "cord, reel; braided rope."

There are varying terms that correlate with the many meanings of the *-g-/-ng-* root: *Nanga* "has love, charity, solidarity." *Nenga* "at the duration, with durable movement, without end [in other words, eternal, stamina]; *BwAnga* "medicine, means of protection, support of health"; *NgaNga* "doctor"; *Mungi* "heart"; *Nke/Nko* "solid, fort" [in other words, protection].

I argue elsewhere[25] that the cross symbol typically associated with the Christian crucified savior is none other than the *ʿnḫ* symbol and it is a sign of Yeshua (Jesus) who essentially is a deified ancestor who was a master teacher: an *nganga*. So it is no surprise that in ciLuba we find *Sungula* "to choose, select; to prefer, elected" as Yeshua was the "choosen one" of God to bear the sins of mankind according to the Hebrews. From that word we get *Sungila* which means "to deliver, protect from, to save." Is not Yeshua the "savior" of mankind? The deliverer? From there we have *Sungidila* "to separate, deliver, defend against, to help." Could Yeshua have been originally from the Kongo? Nigeria/Cameroon?[26]

---

24 In part II of this article we actually make the case that the inspiration behind the design came from the thoracic complex of the human body. Andrew Hunt Gordon and Calvin W. Schwabe—in their book *The Quick and the Dead* (2004)—speculated that the ankh, symbol of life, was that of the *thoracic vertebra* of a bull (seen in cross section). I came to a similar conclusion independently (Imhotep, 2011), but I argue for the thoracic vertebrae of the human body, not a bull's. This will be the focus of Part II of this series concerning the *ʿnḫ*.

25 Asar Imhotep, *The Ena, The Ancestors and the Papyrus of Ani: Towards a Greater Understanding of the African Concept of Spirit*. MOCHA-Versity Press. Houston, TX (forthcoming).

26 Keep in mind that this article, initially, was written in 2009 and revised in 2010. In 2011 I expanded this argument and it became the book *Passion of the Christ or Passion of Osiris: The Kongo Origins of the Jesus Myth*.

Black Jesus[27]

I also argue that Yeshua (Jesus) is none other than a local variation of the Egyptian deity *Šw* (as well as *Wsr*) and the Yoruba deity *Ẹ̀ṣú* (pronounced *eshu*). *Ẹ̀ṣú* of the Yoruba system of Ifa is the "bridge" between heaven and earth. *Šw* of Egypt is also the bridge between heaven and earth as air (*šw*) separates the earth (*gb*) and outer-space (*nw.t*). All prayers and sacrifices MUST go through *Ẹ̀ṣú* or they will not reach the Creator. In order to get to outer space you have to go through *Šw*. Doesn't this sound familiar? *Ẹ̀ṣú*'s symbol is the "crossroads" and this is very important in regards to this discussion.

We've mentioned previously about the significance of the "crossroads" pose in the Kongo and its relation to the ancient Egyptian motifs. What I'd like to make known is another pose from the Kongo that is related to the crossroads pose. This pose is called *Tuluwa Lwa Luumbu*. In the book *Africanisms in American Culture* edited by Joseph Holloway, Kongo scholar Robert Farris Thompson (2005:295) describes the pose as such:

> A second gesture, *tuluwa lwa luumbu*, **arms crossed on the chest to symbolize self-encirclement in silence, retains its strong symbolic wordlessness** in some North American black communities. In 1980 I saw a black man on the New Haven city green cross his arms before his chest to end a conversation. This sign signaled that he had no more to say. Stewart has seen the same emblem of negation among the Gullah of South Caroline, "used in slightly combative situations, where a person, crossing arms on chest, is not arguing, per se, but wishes to communicate that he definitely does not like what is being laid on him." The *luumbu* gesture survives, clearly and distinctly, among certain African Cuban populations in the Caribbean. Lydia Cabrera has seen a Kongo ritual expert (*nganga*) in Havana **cross his arms thus, signaling hauteur and reserve**. The same gesture, with contrasting Yoruba and Kongo meanings, appears in a strongly Kongo-Flavored folk dance, *rumba yambu*. Once again, an aspect of the culture of the Bakongo is echoed by patterns of dance and music in the black New World. [emphasis mine]

It is important to note that the pose signifies having reserve and the act of being silenct. These

27 Image courtesy of http://old.rejesus.co.uk/expressions/faces_jesus/gallery/black.html

are both characteristics of a wise person. This appears to be a wide spread African concept. Among the Amazulu, the sign used for *silence* (a finger over an open mouth, think of how you say *shhh* in a library), is the same symbol for the word *wisdom* (see all, say little).[28]

We find the *luumbu* pose among the deceased Egyptian priests and "deities" which I interpret as *ancestors*. When we see an Egyptian statue or relief with the person's arms crossed, that means at the time this motif was created, the person was deceased. Observe the following image.

Muntu Katapa (Nebhepetre Mentuhotep II, 2055-2004 BCE) with arms crossed.[29]

> (He is the one) whose heart is informed about these things which would be otherwise ignored, the one who is clear-sighted when he is deep into a problem, ...who penetrates ancient writings...who is sensible enough to unravel complications, who is really wise...(from the inscription of Antef, 12th Dynasty; Middle Kingdom, 11th and 12th dynasties 2052-1778 BCE).

As we can see, Muntu Katapa is a Master Teacher, an *nganga* sitting in the pose of a worshipful Master. By this pose he is reminding us to use reserve, that the teachings of this temple are to remain hidden and to keep quiet. Talking less and observing more is a prerequisite for self-mastery.

We also see this pose associated with *awujale* (*Wsr*, Osiris) "supreme king" (Yoruba). Often the arms crossed are symbolized by an "X" on the chest of Osiris. All of this is symbolic of a person who has completed his journey around the *dingo-dingo* wheel of "life."

---

28 See Credo Mutwa's *Indaba My Children*. Grove Press. New York, NY. 1964. p. 675

29 Limestone *k3* statue; Found in his burial tomb at Deir El Bahri. (tomb built within the cliffs); face & body painted black, arms crossed referencing Osiris. When sun hits the black statue, it looks green – also a reference to Osiris. (Like the *k3* statue of Kaphre made of dyrite); wearing the Red Crown of Lower Egypt, seated, enthroned; Mentuhotep is significant because he reunited Upper & Lower Egypt after the collapse of the Old Kingdom. Later Pharaohs will refer back to him.

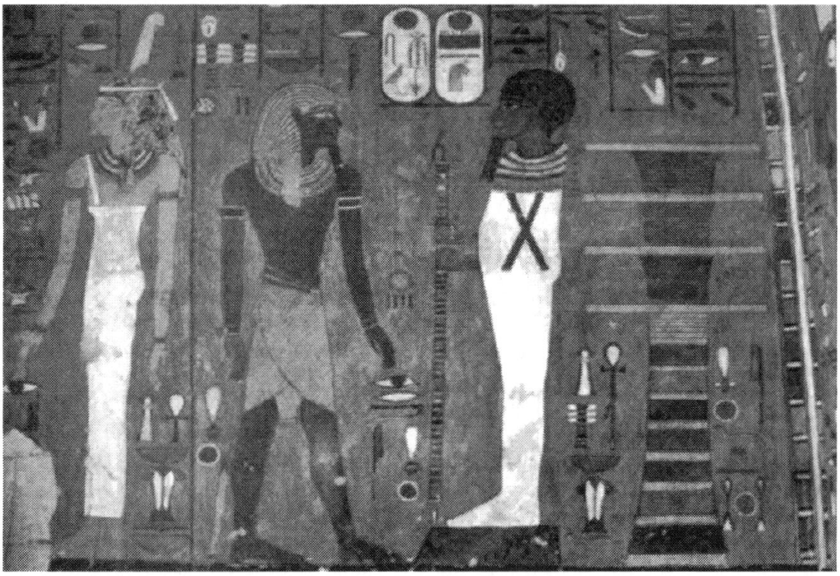

Painting from the Tomb of Rameses I, Valley of the Kings, West Thebes, in Egypt.

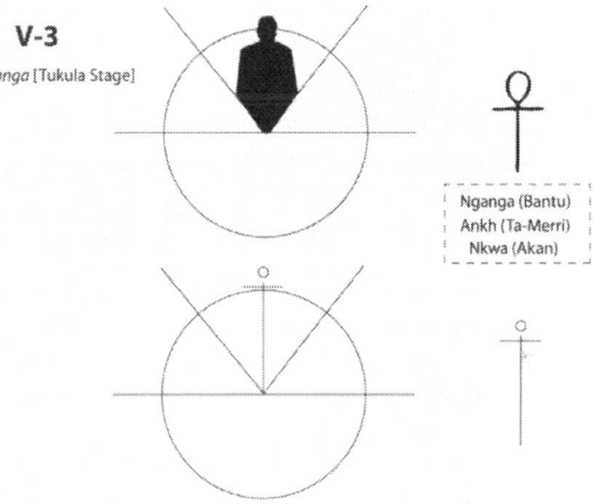

Osiris (*Wsr, awujale, Orìṣá, Ras*)

The story of Yeshua is none other than an ancient story of *Èṣú,* which was carried out of Egypt by the Chaldeans who entered Canaan and later became the Hebrews (*Iber'iym, Fula-ni*). The story of Jesus is a about a master teacher who was murdered for his revolutionary character and charges against the Roman state. The story of his crucifixion tells of Jesus' "ancestralization" and his subsequent mummification as he was wrapped in "white linen" cloth. This topic is further explored in Imhotep (2011).

Author D.M. Murdock in her book *Christ in Egypt: The Horus Jesus Connection,* posits that Jesus is associated with the Egyptian deity *Hrw* (Cheru, Zulu, Horus). We have already posited that Yeshua (Jesus) is a later form of Egyptian *Šw* and the Yoruba *Èṣú* (*Ayeshu* in the Akan). In Greek Yeshua is rendered *Iesous* or *Iasous*. In Arabic it is *Issa*. A title associated with the Egyptian *Hrw* is *Iusa*. Gerald Massey rendered the meaning "the coming son" from Egyptian *iy, iw, ii, jj, jw* or *jwj* meaning "to come;" and *sa, or za* meaning "son." I find this to be folk etymology. I find the 4th century archbishop of Jerusalem St. Cyril's rendering to be more plausible for the definition of Jesus.

St. Cyril posits the meaning of the Greek *Iesous* to mean "healer." We have already posited that Jesus is an *nganga* priest and one of the titles is that of a *healer* (which we know Jesus did a lot of healing according to the Bible). He posits that the term derives from the Greek word *iasomai* meaning "to heal." Arthur Drews[30] states, "Epiphanius (*Haeres*, c, XXIX) clearly perceived this connection when he translated the name Jesus 'healer' or 'physician'(*curator, therapeutes*)."

I argue that the name *Iesous* is built off the consonantal root *-s-* correspondingly in the Yoruba word *Èṣú*. The root *-s-* in *Èṣú* is the same root for *aṣe* which is typically used to mean, "the power to bring things into existence through sound" in liturgical Ifa. In Yoruba *aṣẹ* means "order" or *a ṣẹ* "it will happen." Its cognate in Hebrew is *siwwah* "command." In the Amarigna language it is *ez* "command." In the ancient Egyptian its cognate is *s3* "ordain, order." As Oduyoye (1996:53) notes:

> The concept of *ase* in Yoruba prayers can be seen from the concept of *afose* "the act of uttering in such a way that the words have unfailing effect." The power of *afose* is thought to be possessed by some men who have potent powers to bless or to curse irrevocably. **Such men are medicine men, the priest-herbalists whose blessings are sought during religious festivals and whose curses are feared**. (emphasis mine)

This quote accurately describes a priest, an *nganga*, medicine man, a healer. It is common knowledge that in African tradition healing is not only done with physical concoctions and instruments, but is aided by spoken words (spells, Egyptian *ḥk3*). This is a common practice and it is believed that all efforts will render impotent results if not accompanied by the right words. Sound is the agent/force used to activate the potential of the invisible world (*orun*) and make it manifest in the physical (*aiye*). Is this not a major characteristic of Yeshua (Jesus, Iesous)? Are we not to call on his name to be healed (Acts 4:10, Mk 9:38-39)?

The word *Èṣú* and *Aṣe* are built on the "Afroasiatic" root *ṣwh*. Observe the following chart (Saakana, 1991: 75):

	Hebrew	**Yoruba**	**Mende**	**Tiv**	**Nupe**	**Chuchewa**
To come to pass	*swh*	*se*				
To command	*siwwah*	*Se (ekpe)*				
To cause to come to pass	*Saw (imp.s)*					
A command, authority	*mi-sewah*	*ase*				
The power to cause to happen		*ase*		*tsav*		
magic			*sawa*	*tsav*		
witchcraft				*tsav*		*Ma-sawe*
Ruler					*Etsu*	
The angel who holds God's staff of authority		*Esu*				

30 Arthur Drews, *The Witnesses to the Historicity of Jesus*, tr. Joseph McCabe, Watts, London. 1912. p.196

In Yoruba cosmogony, *Ẹ̀ṣú* is the force that carries one's prayers to the right forces (*òrìṣà*). He uses the power of *aṣẹ* to make it happen. Yeshua plays the same role as intermediary between man and the Creator and he too uses the power of the word to get things done. By contemporary standards Jesus would be known as a Vodou priest, Babalawo, Hogon or a Sangoma. A Babalawo is someone who has mastered and knows how to harness his own *aṣẹ* to heal and bring balance to a community. Remember also that the ciLuba word *NeNga* means "without end" and in this case, in relation to our comparison with *Ẹ̀ṣú*/Jesus, would speak to their promise of "eternal life" (*ankh, nkwa, nga*). Either way it goes, the cross associated with Jesus is a sign that he is a wise master, a healer, one who can command the forces of nature to bring blessings. These are ancient concepts that predate the Hebrew myths by thousands of years. Only when we engage Africa deeply can we gain a better understanding of the ancient Egyptian symbols and their deep underlying messages. The philosophy behind the Biblical narrative becomes clearer as well with a thorough engagement with Africa. Plain and simple, all African symbols are mnemonic devices that remind the wisdom seeker of how he/she's supposed to act.

Conclusion

In this paper we have presented iconographic, cultural and linguistic evidence that supports our view for a reevaluation of the *ꜥnḫ* symbol and its associated meanings. We have confirmed that the *ꜥnḫ* is a symbol not only of life in the physical sense, but a life of service, of vitalism, of health and healing, of wisdom, infinite love, solidarity, eternal life, power and authority. The *ꜥnḫ* symbol is also a sign of a master teacher: an *nganga* or *nkaka*. It is a creative synthesis of terms which betrays the limited Egyptologists' notion of *ꜥnḫ* simply meaning "life" or "person." Africa explains clearly the conceptual elasticity of this term and symbolism and it holistically reminds us of our obligations as leaders on earth. More importantly is provides us with a criteria by which to evaluate a leader in the community.

One will notice in Egyptian reliefs that only persons of high rank or royalty within the Egyptian society were shown receiving or holding the *ꜥnḫ* symbol (priests, gods, administrators, etc.). These members all belonged to or have gone through the **pr-ankh** (*mbidi-nganga*): society/school of initiated masters. This reaffirms the notion that the *ꜥnḫ* was not only a concept but a title or rank within Egyptian society: a term for someone who has been initiated.

The *ꜥnḫ* symbol is a reminder of how we are supposed to act and our responsibilities as leaders and teachers of our communities. It reminds us that mastering the art of being human, by knowing life to the highest degree, will equip us with the tools (our bags of wisdom) to tower over life's one thousand and one challenges. It is no wonder why the *ꜥnḫ* symbol was used as a key for locked doors in ancient ciKam (Egypt). It is telling us something in symbolic code: that the key to a full and successful life is good character and service (*ka-t, bakaa, ghanga*) in your community. It is good character and service that will continually open doors of opportunity for you in life. When you have mastered yourself, then you can stand powerfully (vertically) as a pillar in your community. Good character leads to good health, vitality, prosperity and abundant blessings and this, my friend, is living (*ankhw*).

REINTERPRETATION OF THE ANKH SYMBOL PART II

Introduction

In part one of this series, we suggested new interpretations for the meaning of the ancient Egyptian ꜥ*nḫ* (ankh) "life" symbol ☥ as an emblem for a master teacher or doctor (*nganga*). This was established by examining various African languages and cultures who, to this day, still utilize this symbol and its associated terminology to represent various aspects of *life*. In this essay we will expand our initial findings and present new data that will now help us to understand the initial shape of the ꜥ*nḫ* and how it became associated with various aspects of *life*: especially the *breath of life*.

Many people have interpreted this sign to mean "life, eternal life, an utterance of life, etc." All of these are viable, but as part-one of this series has demonstrated, there is more to this emblem than simply "life" as has been taught in the Egyptological literature. In regards to its shape, there are numerous interpretations for the inspired design. One interpretation is of the sun moving across the horizon line: 𓈌. This interpretation doesn't explain the vertical "leg" of the image. Another explanation claims that the oval loop at the top of the ꜥ*nḫ* is representative of a woman's womb and the vertical shaft is that of a male phallus. Together they unite and thus *life* is possible. This, however, doesn't explain the vertical bars. One interpretation exclaimed that each letter in the word ꜥ*nḫ* represented a word that related to each of the deities in the Ogdoad.[1] An article can be written alone on the errors in this interpretation. Another claim is that it is representative of an Ethiopian *messob* table. This is a table used to serve food. An image can be seen below.

Figure 1: Messob Table from Ethiopia

1 See "Secrets of the Ankh" by *Bro. Reggie*: http://www.secretoftheankh.com/ (retrieved 7/29/2013).

Although the *messob* resembles the *ʿnḫ*, it however doesn't resemble its unique characteristics in regards to the oval top and vertical shaft. Therefore, I do not find this correspondence tenable: plus I doubt the Egyptians used a table to represent "man" as *ʿnḫ* also means "man."

NKWA

Ancient Egyptian *ankhu* = man
Budge 124B

It is my belief that I have stumbled across the true inspiration behind the *ʿnḫ* symbol in my recent eBook titled *Passion of the Christ or Passion of Osiris: The Kongo Origins of the Jesus Myth* (2011: 95). It is clear from my initial findings that the *ʿnḫ* symbol was inspired by the human body and no external items can be its source. The information has been staring us in the face this whole time. We just have to look below the surface of one's self to see the inspiration. The following explanation also elucidates as to why the *ʿnḫ* is often depicted close to the nose of deities and officials in ancient Egyptian artwork: it is literally associated with the breathing process, something quite essential to the maintenance of *life*.

The Anatomical Inspiration for the Ankh

There is an ancient Egyptian proverb that states, "Know thyself and thou shalt know the gods." They meant this literally. It is my contention that the *ʿnḫ* symbol is simply the *thoracic complex* of the human body.[2] This interpretation finds support in actual Egyptian iconography. The compared image on the right below is of the *ʿnḫ* that is super imposed with the *ḏd* 𓊽 pillar and the *wʿs* 𓌀 scepter.

Figure 2: Human thorax compared to Egyptian *ʿnḫ*

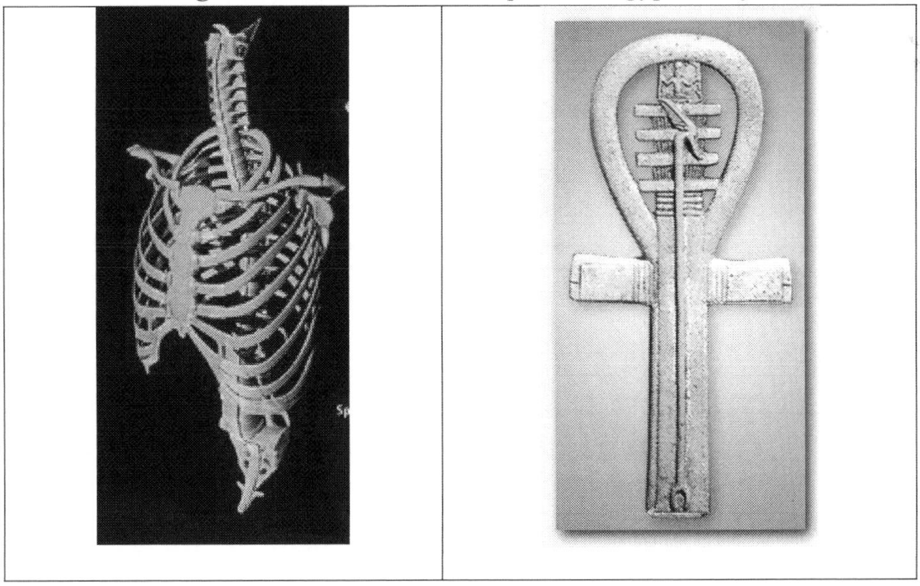

2 The *thorax* (from Greek "θώραξ" - thorax, "breastplate, cuirass, corslet"[1]) is a division of an animal's body that lies between the head and the abdomen.

Thorax bones in the center with "loop" surrounding the spine. The "arms" are the shoulder blades (*mškt*) or collar bones (*ḫ3b, bbwy*).	Ancient Egyptian fusion of the ʿ*nḫ* and the *ḏd* pillar, which is the spine. We could then interpret the *wʿs* symbol in the center as the brain stem.[1]

What reinforces our interpretation here is the placement of the spinal column (*im3ḫ*) in relation to the loop in the ʿ*nḫ* image above. The ʿ*nḫ* is nothing more than a stylized depiction of the thoracic bone structure. Because of the ʿ*nḫ*'s shape, it was hard for researchers to see its true image. The Egyptians try to depict items in the best view possible, often betraying its actual likeness. A case in point is the *htp* (*hotep*) 𓊵 image which is a cake loaf on top of an offering mat).

While we could better see the mat looking from the top down, we could not distinguish the cake from that angle. So the ancient Egyptians decided to use the side-view of the cake since the emphasis was on "offerings" and not the mat for which offerings were displayed on. In the case of the ʿ*nḫ*, they decided to use an aerial view of the thorax so that the loop is flatly visible. In its normal context, the loop (the first rib) is more horizontal (with a slight tilt up), not vertical as depicted on the ʿ*nḫ*. The word ʿ*nḫ* is present in a few terms that relate to this part of the body in the Tshiluba language:

Nshinga	"Neck"
ma-Sang(u,o)	"Interval between the shoulders; junction point of two shoulders or two arms= *nTangani/diTung (U, A)* - a-mapa/makaya/mapwapwa"
di-/ma-Sanga	"crossroads, confluence, junction, joint, node" (Kalamba and Bilolo, 2009: 131)

There are three primary ways in which the ʿ*nḫ* is depicted:

- A common depiction is of a god or goddess holding the ʿ*nḫ* in their hands, usually by the loop "handle."
- Another common depiction is of the gods purifying a priest or king by anointing him with life-giving water represented by the ʿ*nḫ* symbol.[3]
- The third depiction is of the gods holding the ʿ*nḫ* to the noses or the mouths of Egyptian royalty.

Connecting the ʿ*nḫ* with the human thorax helps us to explain the following images:

3 In my book *Passion of the Christ or Passion of Osiris*, I linguistically and conceptually connect the ʿ*nḫ* with the god *Wsr* (Asar, Osiris). *Wsr* is often associated with water in the Egyptian texts. The *s-r* root of *Wsr's* name means "life" and this is why he is associated with the life-force and other items in nature essential to *life*: water, plants, the sun and air.

Figure 3:

Many Egyptologists understood that the *ʿnḫ* was associated with the breath but now we know why. The primary function of the thorax is *respiration* (breathing). The *ribs* (*spr*) and the *diaphragm* (*ntnt*)[4] move so that the thoracic cavity increases and decreases in size during the *inspiratory* and *expiratory* phases of respiration. Doctors note that the thorax probably aids in returning venous *blood* back to the heart because of the negative pressure produced with respiratory movements. This is going to be vitally important for our second interpretation of the *ʿnḫ* symbol later on in our discussion. The thorax also serves to *protect* the organs located within its cavity, plus some organs of the abdominal cavity. In other words, the thorax is our internal *savior* (a savior is someone or something that protects).

The Structure of the Thorax

The primary organs and structure of the thorax consist of the following:

- lungs (*smꜣ*)
- heart (*ib, ḥꜣty*)
- aorta and its branches
- superior and inferior vena cavae
- trachea (*ḫḫ*) and primary bronchi
- sympathetic trunks and their associations
- azygos and hemiazygos venous systems

The bony boundaries of the thorax consist of:

4 Apparently the Egyptians knew the diaphragm was connected to breathing as the word *nti* "breath, air" is related to *ntnt* "diaphragm."

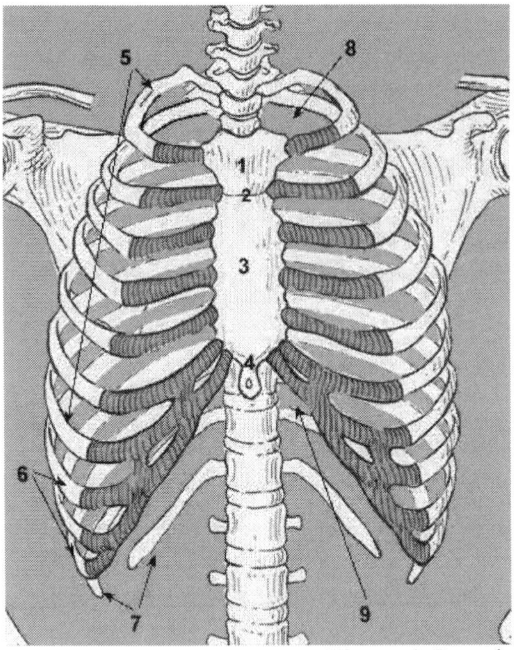

- sternum
    - manubrium (1)
    - sternal angle (2)
    - body (3)
    - xiphoid process (4)
- 12 pairs of ribs
    - 6 or 7 pairs of true ribs (5)
    - 3 or 4 pairs of false ribs (6)
    - 2 pairs of floating ribs (7)
- thoracic inlet (superiorly) (8)
- thoracic outlet (inferiorly) (9)
- thoracic vertebrae, posteriorly

Figure 4: Bony boundaries of thorax

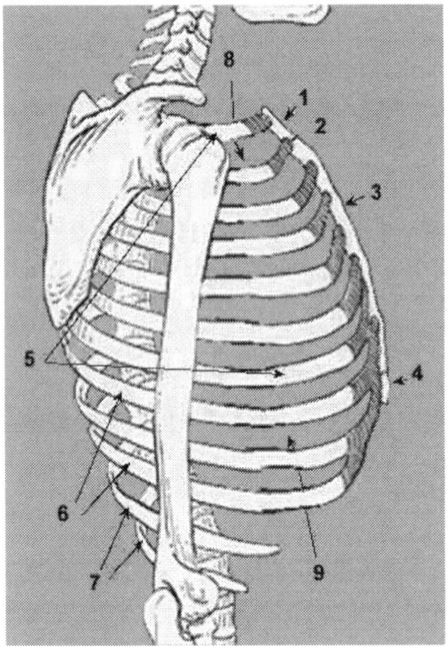

Figure 5

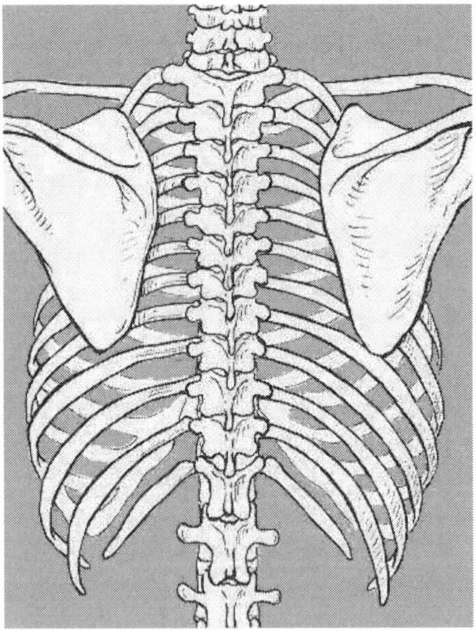

Figure 6

What doctors call the "True Ribs" are ribs that have a direct attachment between the vertebrae and the sternum. Each rib attaches to the sternum by its own costal cartilage. The "False Ribs" attach to the sternum by way of the costal cartilage above it. Floating ribs do not have an anterior attachment at all. The vertical bar of the *ʿnḫ* symbol is the sternum (Egyptian *ḳ3bt*) or at times can represent the trachea.

Sternum

- jugular notch (1)
- facet for head of first rib
- manubrium (2)
- facet for head of second rib
- manubriosternal joint (sternal angle) (3)
- body (made up of several fused sternabrae) (4)
- xiphoid process (5)

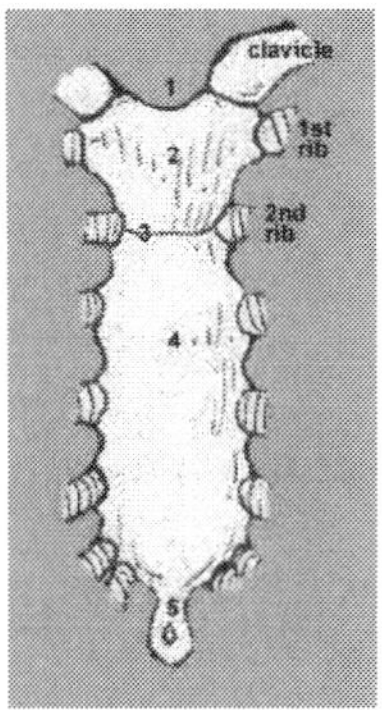

Figure 7

The "loop" on the *ʿnẖ* would correspond to the thoracic cavity. Looking at the thorax through a cross section, we notice that the loop is almost kidney shaped. Below is a traverse section view.

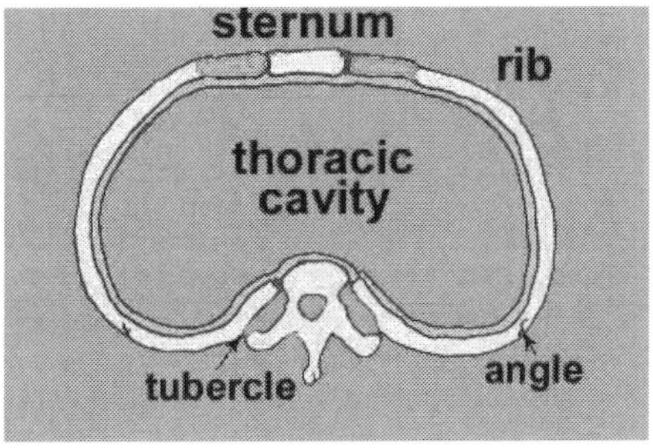

Figure 8

We are reaffirmed in our interpretation of the *ʿnẖ* being the thorax because all three sections of the sign ☥ is given in ciLuba as *nkonko* "ring, collar, sternum." The "ring" would be the thoracic cavity (the top rib); the "collar" would be the *collar bone* and the "sternum" is simply the *sternum*. The ciLuba *nkonko* is simply the word *ʿnẖ* reduplicated.

To get a greater appreciation of the thorax, we must examine the thoracic wall. The thoracic wall is made up of the sternum, ribs plus three layers of intercostal muscles, diaphragm and the intercostal vessels and nerves.

Muscles of the Thoracic Wall

The muscles of the thorax consist of the *intercostals* and *diaphragm (ntnt)*. The *intercostal* muscles are arranged as three layers between the ribs: external layer, internal layer and an incomplete innermost layer. The diaphragm closes the thoracic outlet and separates the thoracic cavity from the abdominal cavity. The three layers of the *intercostal* muscles are:

- external layer -- *external intercostal*
- internal layer -- *internal intercostal*
- innermost layer -- *transversus thoracic* (anterior), *innermost* (lateral) and *subcostal* (posterior)

The most important muscle of the thoracic wall is the *diaphragm*. During normal respiration, this muscle is the primary component. The diaphragm pulls air down into your lungs. As you can see in the images below, the innermost layer is split into three differently named muscle groups. The *transversus thoracis*, innermost *intercostal* and *subcostal* muscles make up the deepest layer of muscles from anterior to posterior, respectively.

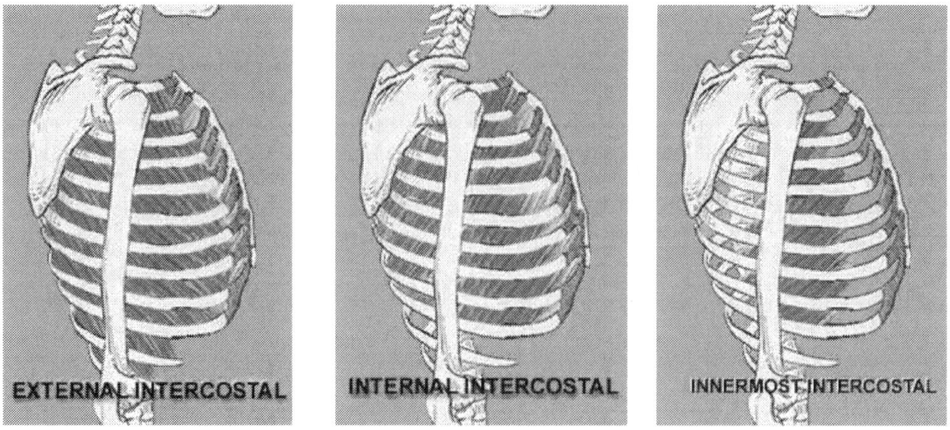

Figure 9

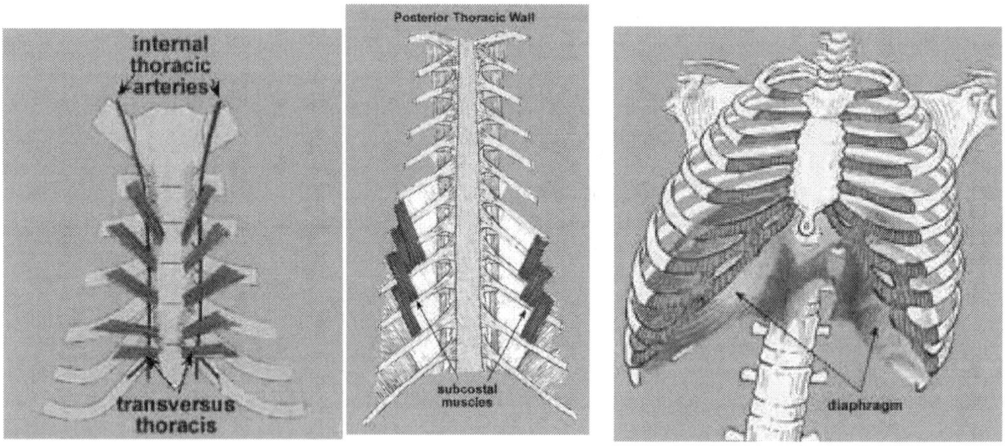

Figure 10

The Respiration Process

All of this detail is critical in the understanding of the breathing process for human beings. The ʿ*nḫ* is a symbol for the respiration (breathing) process and although the bones are the primary structure of the emblem, it speaks to all that is involved in the breathing process.

Respiration is the process of exchanging O_2 (oxygen) with CO_2 (carbon-dioxide). Molecules of oxygen and carbon dioxide are passively exchanged, by diffusion, between the gaseous external environment and the blood. This exchange process occurs in the alveolar region of the lungs. In order to get the oxygen into the lungs, all of the structures that we have discussed previously (and others not mentioned for the sake of space) act together to increase the area of the thoracic cavity.

The respiratory system is like an upside down *tree*. When air enters your body, it goes down your *trachea*. This would be the trunk of your tree: the one airway at the beginning of the process. This one-way process quickly then divides into two airways to feed into two lungs; these are your *bronchial tubes*. And just like tree branches, those airways break off into four, then eight, then hundreds of thousands of little airways in each lung.[5] Those airways are your *bronchi*. At the end of each of these airways are tiny sacs called *alveoli*. You could think of them as leaves at the end of branches. A healthy lung has hundreds of millions of these alveoli. Each alveolus is covered with a thin layer of fluid that helps you breathe. It does this by keeping the alveoli open so oxygen is absorbed and carbon dioxide is excreted. Thus, we take in oxygen and release carbon dioxide as a waste product.

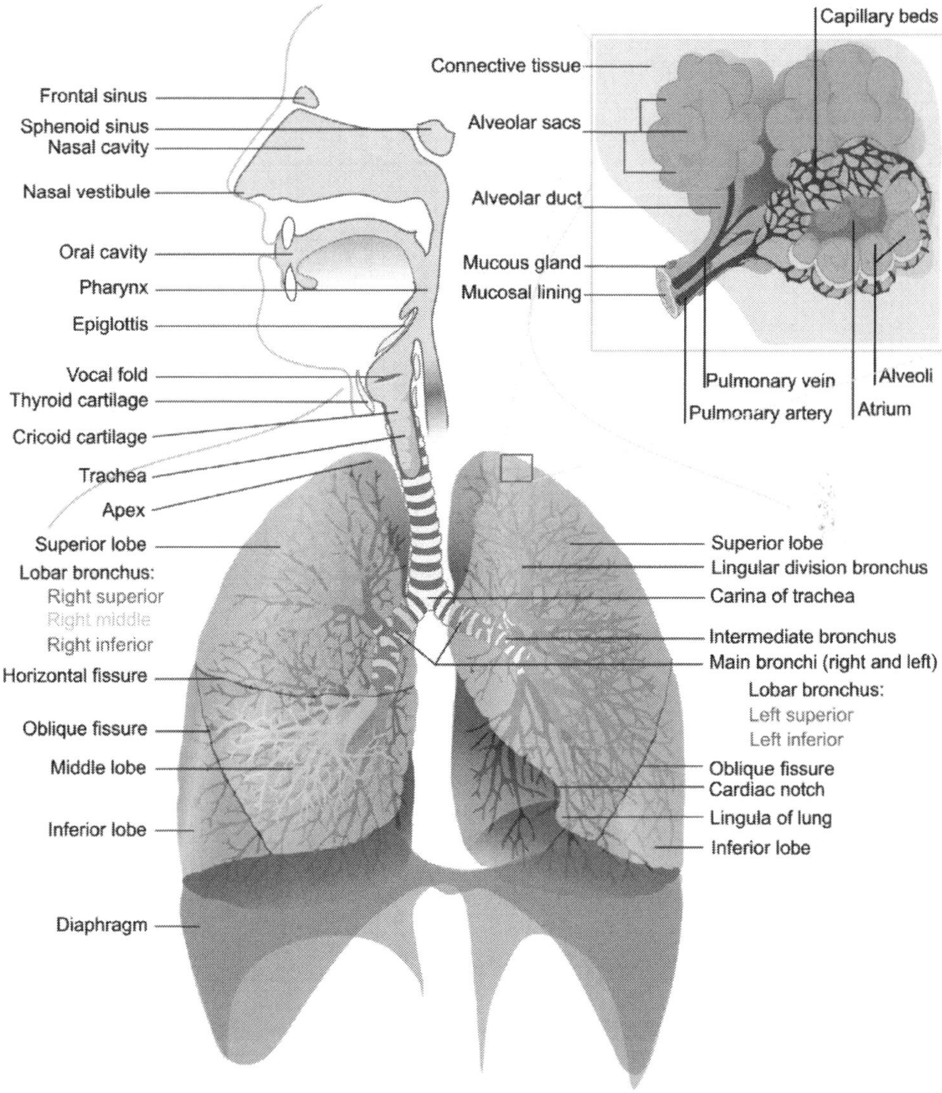

Figure 11

Getting back to the bronchial tubes, they are responsible for cleaning out your lungs. They are often covered in mucus, dirt and germs. This is why your lungs has millions of these tiny hairs called *cilia* that act like brooms that sweep away all of the stuff caught by the mucus

5 It would be interesting to discover that this numeration follows the 2^n series which is the basic binary counting system in Africa: 2, 4, 8, 16, 32, 64, 128, etc. This numbering system is essential to the Yorùbá system of Ifa and for ancient Egyptian building and even market calculations. See Dr. Charles D. Finch's The *Star of Deep Beginnings: The Genesis of African Science and Technology* (1999). Khenti Publishings.

(which is a trap for dirt). They move very fast, like windshield wipers, clearing your lungs with every single breath. This is why it is important not to smoke because smoking kills these cilia fibers. The aging process is affected as well, so the city you live in can affect the way you age; especially if the city is highly toxic due to pollution.

In respiratory physiology, *ventilation* (or ventilation rate) is the rate at which gas enters or leaves the lung (oxygen is a gas). Ventilation occurs under the *control* of the *autonomic nervous system* from parts of the *brain stem*, the *medulla oblongata* and the *pons*. This area of the brain forms the respiration regulatory center, a series of interconnected brain cells within the lower and middle brain stem which coordinate respiratory movements. The sections are the *pneumotaxic* center, the *apneaustic* center, and the *dorsal* and *ventral respiratory* groups. It is this autonomic nervous system that I believe the *wꜥs* scepter is meant to represent in the superimposed *ꜥnḫ*.

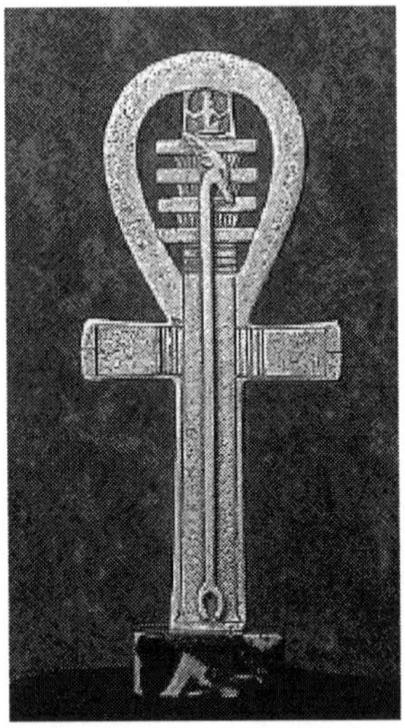

Figure 12: *ꜥnḫ*, *ḏd*, and *wꜥs* scepter super imposed

Inhalation is initiated by the diaphragm and supported by the external intercostal muscles. Normal resting respirations are 10 to 18 breaths per minute, with a time period of 2 seconds. During enthusiastic inhalation (at rates exceeding 35 breaths per minute), or in approaching respiratory failure, accessory muscles of respiration are recruited for support. These consist of *sternocleidomastoid, platysma*, and the scalene muscles of the **neck**. Pectoral muscles and *latissimus dorsi* are also accessory muscles. Under normal conditions, the diaphragm is the primary driver of inhalation. When the diaphragm contracts, the ribcage expands and the contents of the abdomen are moved downward. This results in a larger thoracic volume and negative pressure (with respect to atmospheric pressure) inside the thorax. As the pressure in the chest falls, air moves into the conducting zone. Here, the air is filtered, **warmed,** and humidified as it flows to the lungs. During forced inhalation, as when taking a deep breath, the external intercostal muscles and accessory muscles aid in further expanding the thoracic cavity. After this process begins exhalation. This is generally a passive process but with forced exhalation the abdominal and the internal intercostal muscles get involved.

The major function of the respiratory system is gas exchange between the external environment and the body's circulatory system. In humans and mammals, this exchange **facilitates oxygenation of the blood** (Egyptian *snfw* "blood") with an affiliated removal of carbon dioxide and other gaseous metabolic wastes from the circulation. As gas exchange occurs, the acid-base balance of the body is maintained as part of homeostasis. If proper ventilation is not maintained, two opposing conditions could occur: *respiratory acidosis*, a life threatening condition, and *respiratory alkalosis*.

The *Ebers Medical Papyrus* (1557-1530 BCE) informs us that the ancient Egyptians were very familiar with the circulatory system, its importance and its proper functional characteristics.[6] For instance (pEbers 99, 1-12):

> *ḥ3t-ʿ m sšt3 n swnw*
> Introduction to the secret lore of the doctor
> *rḫ šmt h3ty rḫ ḥ3ty*
> Knowledge of the heart's movement, and of the heart.
> *iw mtw im.f n ʿt nbt*
> There are vessels inside it leading to each member.
> *ir nw rdiw swnw nb sḫmt-wʿb nb s3w nb*
> Thus, when any doctor, surgeon (literally, priest of Sekhmet), or exorcist
> *ʿwy dbʿw.f ḥr tp*
> places his hands or fingers on the head,
> *ḥr mkḥ3 ḥr drwt hr st ib*
> on the back of the head, on the hands, on the position of the heart itself
> *ḥr ʿwy ḥr rdwy nb*
> on the limbs or on any other part,
> *ḫ3i.f n ḥ3ty*
> in so doing he in fact examines the heart,
> *ḥr ntt mtw.f n ʿt.f nbt*
> because the heart's vessels lead to each of the (patient's) members;
> *nt pw mdw.f ḫnt mtw nw ʿt nbt*
> in other words, the heart speaks within the vessels of each member[7]

The *Papyrus Ebers* is humanity's first medical encyclopedia. In the above passage is the first historical reference for taking a pulse. This text demonstrates that the Egyptians had discovered that the heart was the main motor of the human body and it is the starting point for the irrigation of the whole organism. The blood needs oxygen to help get rid of metabolic waste in the circulatory system. That's where the processes mentioned above involving the thorax come into play. It also speaks to why we need pure oxygen in our bodies. If our air is toxic, the oxygen can't properly cleanse our system.

The Ankh and the Blood

In the upcoming publication *Ogun, African Fire Philosophy and the Meaning of KMT*, I discuss, in part, the possible relationship between the *ʿnḫ* symbol and the blood (so essential to *life*). Because it is a minor point within a larger context of the book, I will expand my initial findings here as it is even more relevant to this discourse.

The association of the *ʿnḫ* and blood comes from an unlikely source: the ancient Greeks. In the Minoan *Linear A* script (on the island of Crete), many of the signs derive from African pictographs, especially the ancient Egyptian hieroglyphs. Various traditions of writing developed in different areas, among peoples speaking related but different dialects, and using different scribes (Campbell-Dunn, 2006: 75). As Campbell-Dunn (2006, 2008) has demonstrated, the

6 However they considered this a one-way process.
7 Cited in Obenga (2005: 371-372)

early Minoans derived from West Africa (a good number coming from Nigeria). With this said, the ʿnḫ ☥ symbol is also present in the *Linear* script. Like the ancient Egyptian pictograph, the *Linear* glyph also means "life," but it has a different pronunciation: *za*. This may prove that there were at least two pronunciations of the thorax symbol in Egyptian: ʿnḫ and sʿ.

Griaule (Huyghe ed. 1957: 81) describes a Keita (Mandingo) woman drawing a sign:

> *"First of all the woman responsible for the work faced east and painted a black circle; then, turning to the north, she painted another circle at the top of a vertical line, followed by a similar figure, but including a transverse line forming the arms; in a fourth figure another bar representing the legs..." (cited in Campbell-Dunn, 2006: 68).*

It is clear that from this description that the woman is drawing a variation of the ʿnḫ or "life" sign. Among the Keita it is called the "Life of the world." It is related to the Dogon symbol with the same application. This sign is given two meanings that are in line with our above meanings for *nkwa* or *ankh*. The first meaning is 'humanity' and the celestial placenta (the upper ellipse). The second meaning is the earthly placenta (the open ellipse). The cross in the center represents the four cardinal points.[8] Griaule notes that this symbol is not only found among the Mandingo and the Dogon (of Mali), but is found as far away as Cameroon which is "Bantu" country.

Aduno Kine

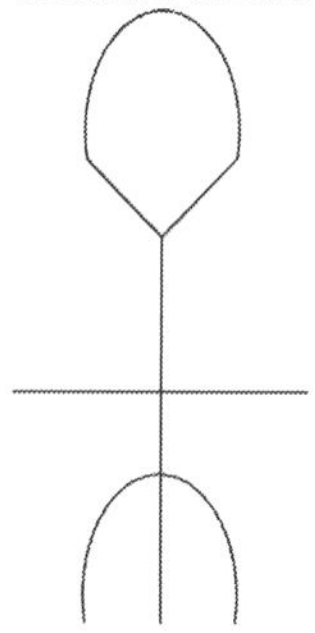

Dogon symbol for the "life of the world"

In the *Passion of the Christ or Passion of Osiris* book, I demonstrated how linguistically the concept of "life" is conveyed using terms that are based in the *s/j*, *s-r* or *s-l* root in many African languages (including ciKam/Egyptian) and how this is embedded in the name Wsr/Jsr (Osiris). The essence of *Wsr* is based off the *-s-* root which essentially means "to activate, the power to cause to be." This /s/ alternates with /j/. Given these two things, I believe we can associate the Yorùbá terms *Òjè* "life" (after death) and *èjè* "blood" (*êjë* "vow," blood oath?)[9] as related to our *-s-* root in *Wsr*. This root can be seen in Yorùbá *Ò jé* "He was/He is – He happened to be," *jí* "Wake up from sleep" (back into consciousness and life).

Compare with Westermann's Proto-Niger-Congo reconstruction **za/dza* "blood." Nupe

---

8 See Marcel Griaule, "*L'Image du monde au Soudan*," in *Journal de la Societe des Africanistes*, Volume XIX, Paris. pp. 81-88

9 It should be noted that the word ʿnḫ in Egyptian also means "oath." This could be further proof that the ʿnḫ symbol could carry more than one sound value.

has *e-dza*, Guang *obu-dza*, Lefana *ubu-dza*, Ahlo *obi-dza*, Ewe *ku-dze*, Kilimonjaro (Caga) *samu, sau*, Sumerian *sa*, Yorùbá *e-dze* "blood." Blood is *life*, the blood is soul. In Yorùbá we have *sí* "to be" which is cognate with Hebrew *yesh* "there is" (=Assyrian *su* "to be, to have").[10] We should also note that among the ancient Greeks the term *zoe* (s>z) is "*life* personified" (usually paired with *logos* "the word"). In Kiswahili *eshe* also means "life." In part one of this series, we noted the *ꜥnḫ* sign represented a master teacher or healer and in Africa this healer is called *nganga* which is *ꜥnḫ* reduplicated. If the *ꜥnḫ* also was pronounced *za*, then we may have another correlation as a doctor or priest in Egyptian was called *sꜣ, sꜣw, swnw*.

As we can see above, blood is related to life and is captured in various cognate terms: *sa, za, dza, dze*, etc. The support for the association between the *ꜥnḫ* and blood comes from the thorax once again. The following image displays the blood supply to the thoracic wall.

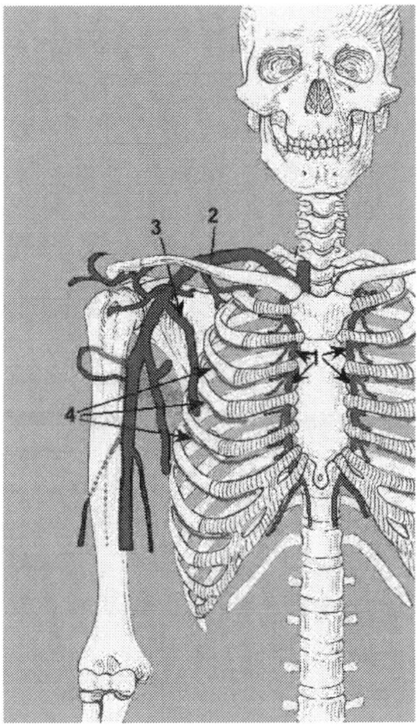

Figure 13

The thoracic wall is supplied by three sources of blood supply:

- axillary
  - supreme thoracic (2)
  - lateral thoracic (3)
- subclavian
  - internal thoracic (or mammary) artery (1)
    - anterior intercostal branches
- aorta

intercostal arteries (4)

In Imhotep (2011), I also demonstrate how *Wsr* (Yeshua, Eshu) is related to "paths" or "channels" for which fluid or other things travel. I also mentioned that *Wsr* and his sister/wife *ꜣst* are the exact same deity (force or concept) expressing itself, conceptually, as masculine and feminine. With that said, *ꜣst* (Isis) is associated with the *ti.t* (*tiye*(*t*), *thi.t*) emblem  known as the "knot of Isis." Budge interprets this sign as "an amulet symbolic of the uterus of Isis" (Budge 847b). This would still be in alignment with *ꜣst*'s many attributes as she is the great mother, the womb from which all derived. In the *Book of Coming Forth by Day* it is known as "the name of *Mwt*[11]" (*cyMawu* in Tshiluba). At times the loop at the top was replaced with the head of *Ht Hrw*, thus identifying her with *ꜣst*.

---

10 This -s- root is found in the Yorùbá phrase *dá wa sí* "Keep us alive" (Preserve us); *Kúda yi si* "Death kept this one alive." The term *sí* means to have "life," to "exist;" in other words, "to be."

11 After a transliteration and German translation on the *Thesaurus Linguae Aegyptiae* website, B. Backes (ed.) Totenbuchprojekt, Nordrhein-Westfälische Akademie der Wissenschaften => pTurin Museo Egizio 1791 Tb 114-165 => pTurin Museo Egizio 1791 Tb 114-165, Tb 164. Accessed June 29, 2010

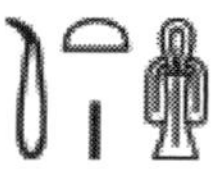

tj.t "amulet"

tj.t "amulet, Isis blood"

The origin of this emblem appears to be unknown and may be a variation of the *ʿnḫ* ☥ symbol. The difference between the two being that the *tj.t's* "arms" are folded downward and the "arms" on the *ʿnḫ* are raised horizontally. The hieroglyph is usually translated as "life" or "welfare." The *tj.t* has been displayed alongside the *ʿnḫ* ☥ and the *ḏd* 𓊽 pillar signs as early as the third dynasty. Because it is associated with "the blood of Isis," it is often depicted in a red color and was often fashioned from red stones such as carnelian, jasper, and from red glass. The feminine *–t* suffix was often dropped during the middle kingdom period, so the root is *tj* "life." The *t* may have been more closely pronounced as either a /ts/ or /dz/ sound which would match our *sa, dza, dze* terms above. The Egyptian *tj*/*tj.t* matches more closely the Yorùbá *si* "life, to exist, to be."

If we pay attention to the emblem, we see that the "knotted ropes" follow the same path as the blood supply to the *thoracic wall.* Because the *tj.t* symbol is seen alongside the *ḏd* and the *ʿnḫ*, this further provides evidence that this *tj.t* sign (blood) is connected to the *thorax*. It is my belief that there is enough evidence to not only associate the *ʿnḫ* with the thorax (and by extension oxygen), but with blood and the circulatory system itself.

We spoke briefly about the *ʿnḫ* symbol being directed at the noses of patrons in the Egyptian reliefs. Given our association with the *ʿnḫ* and blood (*za*), we may also speculate that the *ʿnḫ* is not only associated with oxygen to the nose, but also blood vessels in the nose. The pEbers 854b speaks directly of vessels supplying blood to the nose, and even the eyes (pEbers, 854c). In other words, the *ʿnḫ* supplies blood (life) to all major organs.

Even if we restricted the *ʿnḫ* to the bones, it is bones that create blood. Blood is created in the *bone marrow* which is a flexible tissue found in the interior of the bones. There are two marrow types: red and yellow marrow. Red marrow consists of hematopoietic tissue and yellow marrow consists mainly of fat cells. Red blood cells, platelets and most white blood cells arise in red marrow. Red blood cells are primarily for carrying oxygen and some carbon dioxide through the use of heamoglobin. White blood cells are part of the innate immune system. The platelets are involved in blood coagulation and derive from stem cells. Both red and yellow marrow contains numerous blood vessels and capillaries. What's interesting is that in case of severe blood loss, the body can convert yellow marrow back into red marrow to increase blood cell production. Talk about a back-up plan.

The Ankh and other Energy Sources

As we can see from the information presented thus far, the respiratory process involves a lot more than simply taking in oxygen. What we will discover below is that breathing helps with the generation of energy in a process called *cellular respiration.*

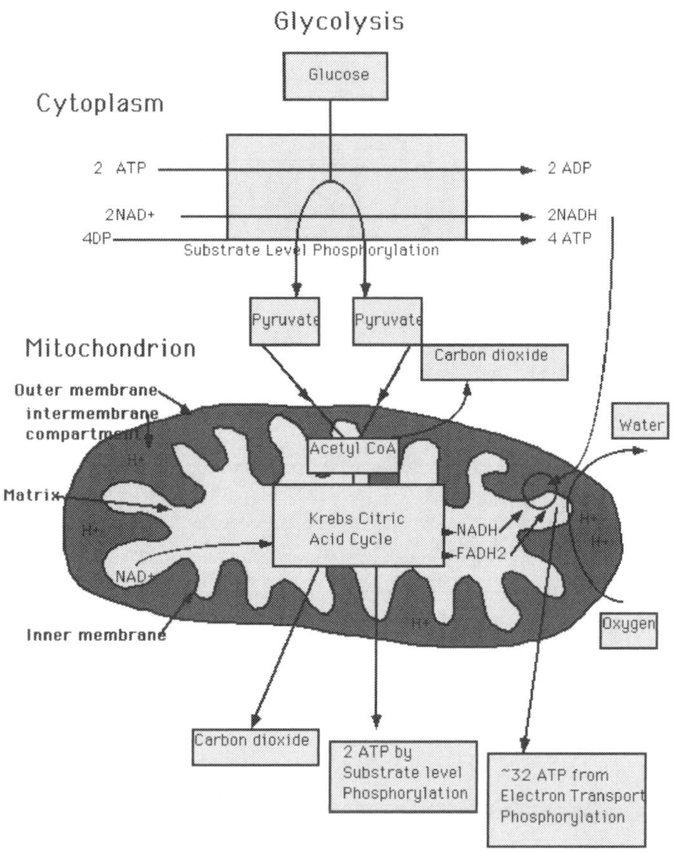

Figure 14: Glycolysis

Cellular respiration is the set of the metabolic reactions and processes that take place in the cells of organisms to convert *biochemical energy* from nutrients into *adenosine triphosphate* (ATP), and then release waste products. The reactions involved in respiration are catabolic reactions that involve the redox reaction (oxidation of one molecule and the reduction of another). Respiration is one of the key ways a cell gains useful energy to fuel cellular reformations.

Nutrients commonly used by animal and plant cells in respiration include sugar, amino acids and fatty acids. Molecular oxygen (O_2) is a common oxidizing agent (electron acceptor). Bacteria and archaea can also be lithotrophs and these organisms may respire using a broad range of inorganic molecules as electron donors and acceptors, such as sulfur, metal ions, methane or hydrogen. Organisms that use oxygen as a final electron acceptor in respiration are described as *aerobic*, while those that do not are referred to as *anaerobic*. The energy released in respiration is used to synthesize ATP to store this energy. **The energy stored in ATP can then be used to drive processes requiring energy, including biosynthesis, locomotion or transportation of molecules across cell membranes.**

Aerobic respiration requires **oxygen** in order to generate **energy** (ATP). Although carbohydrates, fats, and proteins can all be processed and consumed as reactant, it is the preferred method of pyruvate breakdown in glycolysis and requires that pyruvate enter the mitochondrion in order to be fully oxidized by the Krebs cycle. The product of this process is *energy* in the form of ATP (*Adenosine triphosphate*), by substrate-level phosphorylation, NADH and $FADH_2$.

In other words, oxygen enhances energy generation. To give a layman's example, I used to run track in high school. I ran the 100 meters, the 400 meters, I did hurdles, long jump and either was the second leg or tail in the 400 meter relays. One thing our coach (Coach Turner, who was also the biology teacher) always stressed was our breathing. By learning how to breathe properly while running, we maximized our energy output and would do better than those who did not know how to breathe correctly. The oxygen combined with biochemical energy stored in our muscles allowed us to go longer and run faster. When the mitochondrion in the muscles does not get the oxygen it needs, it goes into what is called a *lactate acid fermentation.*

Without oxygen, *pyruvate* (pyruvic acid) is not metabolized by cellular respiration, but undergoes a process of fermentation. This fermentation process is responsible for the muscles aching (with components calcifying) while running (because we don't normally take in as much oxygen when running). This is also why after a run, a runner feels a lot better after taking in large amounts of oxygen because oxygen is being restored back into the muscles giving it the energy it needs to continue. Fermentation is less efficient at using the energy from glucose since **2 ATP are produced per glucose**, compared to the **38 ATP per glucose produced** by aerobic respiration. This is because the waste products of fermentation still contain plenty of energy. This is why learning how to breathe during sports activities is so important. The less oxygen you take in, the less ATP per glucose (a sugar) you produce. The more oxygen you can take in, the lesser the chance of fermentation and the longer one can sustain oneself during high energy activities. Remember ATP is involved in locomotion and drives processes needing energy. Running is an activity that you need a lot of energy for.

Without all of the technical details, the ancient Egyptians summarized this whole process in a salutation given to the kings.

NKWA, WAJU, SIMBA

Ancient Egyptian *ankh, udja, snb* = life, prosperity and health
reinterpretation = life, vitality and health
Budge 124B

The salutation is usually given the meaning of *life, prosperity and health.* I think given our analysis of the *ʿnḫ* that we can be a bit more precise in relation to the human body. We have already connected the *ʿnḫ* with oxygen, respiration and the blood. But what we haven't done is connect it with the foods we eat. Remember that cellular respiration involves converting biochemical energy from nutrients into ATP (another form of energy). Those "nutrients" come from food and the *ʿnḫ* is also associated with food.

ʿn ʿnḫ	"Sustenance"
ir ʿnḫ	"make provisions"
ʿnḫ nsw	"king's victuals"
ḫt n ʿnḫ	"(a type of plant) embodiment of food, staff of life, tree of life"
ʿnḫ	"garland" (a plant)
ʿnḫt	"corn"

The food we eat derives from plants which captures sunlight and stores it as energy during a process called *photosynthesis*. As plants and trees grow, they absorb carbon dioxide in the atmosphere and store it as carbon in their biomass. Humans can only absorb carbon through plants.

The word *wḏ3* (waju) is usually rendered "prosperity" but I think we are justified in relating it to energy.[12] The term *wḏ3* also means "salvation." When we look at the term *waju* or *wajo* in a few of the Afro-Asiatic languages, its message becomes clearer. In Ethiopic the term *waju* or *wajo* means to *heal* or *recover health. Wajo* also refers to a person who *roasts* and distributes meat at ceremonial meals. A dialectical variant is pronounced *waya* which means "heat, warmth"; *wayyaa*, "recovering from illness." *Wayu* means "fire-brand." In the Yindin language the word *waju* means to *burn* or *cook.*[13] Among the Kuku Yalanji of Australia *waju* also means *to burn* (not related to Afro-Asiatic). The glyph used to convey the word *wḏ3* is a fire drill or an instrument used to start a fire or the commencement of the burning process. As will be detailed in *Ogun, African Fire Philosophy and the Meaning of KMT* (forthcoming), across Africa fire is used as a symbol of *vitality* and is why I interpret this word to mean *vitality*. In modern times we can use this symbol to mean "the burning of calories" through exercise.

Snb is known better among Niger-Congo speakers as *simba*. In Dr. Fu-Kiau's 2006 work *Simba Simbi*, he informs us that *simba* means "to hold up, to keep, to bless, to treasure, to touch, to retain." This gives way to a variant *simbi* which means "a keeper, a watch over; someone with power to protect; a living energy that holds up everything." *Simbi* is the power behind life and the secret behind all growth and development. It is the mother principle that nurtures all. It is also the God principle, the living principle that holds up everything.

Used in this manner, the idea that is given is that the Divine Life Process, *ʿnḫ,* engenders a fire (*waju*) which courses through the body and promotes health (*simbi*): a balanced environment of energy that holds up the human being. This is more than a benediction, but describes the respiratory process. By inhaling oxygen (*ʿnḫ*) and eating food (*ʿnḫ*) the *ʿnḫ* (thorax) sends the oxygen to the blood (*za, ʿnḫ*) by the *cellular* and *aerobic* respiratory processes that send energy (collected from plants through photosynthesis) to much needed areas of the body providing optimal vitality (*wḏ3*) and protection (*simbi*) against illnesses.

Vitality is what gives the impetus to life. Vitality is the force which sustains and vies a person the will to live (*ʿnḫ*). It is vitality that sustains the immune system and it is the immune system that keeps external (bacteria, viruses, poisons, waste material, etc.), as well as internal agents (chemical, emotional, psychological, etc.), from disturbing the course of *life* (Ashby, 2001: 179). The thorax and all of its components is responsible for circulating the life force from the sun, which is then captured by plants in carbon form and consumed by animals and human beings. A formula that can make it easier to understand is: vitality = immunity (protection) = health = life. If we equate *wḏ3* with "the burning of calories" in modern times, we could say that *ʿnḫ* (oxygen, food) + *wḏ3* (exercise, calorie burning, metabolism) = *snb* (health, immunity)

This interpretation is reinforced in the iconography of Ancient Egypt as concerns the *ʿnḫ* (*nkwa, nga, ka*). In the image below, the *ʿnḫ* is shown with the god *ḫpr* rising from a lotus plant with two uraeus serpents, one on each side of it. On top of the serpents and the beetle (*ḫpr*) are sun disks which are being raised. To the average person this may seem like some neat religious artwork. But to an African priest this means much more. The connection to the breath and the thorax is made much clearer with the help of Bantu languages.

12 The word *wḏ3* also means "pectoral" which may be relevant to our discussion of the thorax (chest)

13 See *Ergativity* (1994:120 fn 11) by Robert M. W. Dixon. Cambridge University Press.

Figure 15: Mirror-case of King *twt-ʿnḫ-Ỉmn* (Tutankhamen) of the 18th Dynasty

In the center of the loop of the *ʿnḫ* symbol is a winged beetle whose Egyptian name is *ḫpr*. The most common definition of this term is "existence" or "transformation." But many have not considered what the actual symbol means. Why would a dung beetle have wings on its side? And why would it be carrying the sun? As I discussed in *Passion of the Christ or Passion of Osiris*, the many meanings of a character in a myth derives its associations by the unification of similar terms that have the same consonantal root and meaning. In other words, the character in the myth represents a "theme" which in linguistics we call the "associative field" of meaning. We see this play out among the god *ḫpr* of ancient Egypt.

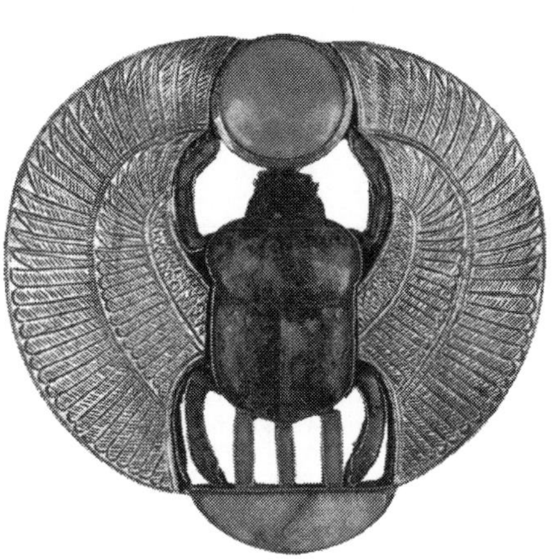

Figure 16: Lapis Winged Scarab from the Global Museum, with King Tut's coronation name—Neb-Kheperu-Re (*nb-ḫpr-rʿ*)

Let's first examine the word *ḫpr* in the Tshiluba language. The *kh-* sound is actually a prefix. The *ḫ* sound often corresponds to /*k*/ or /h/ in Niger-Congo languages. The Tshiluba prefix *k-* can also be *ci-*. We first examine the ciLuba form of the word *beetle* (*Scarabaeus sacer*).

ḫprr

kapepu, kapepwela, kapepula, kapulupulu, kaholoholo, kampulu, cipepu, cipepwela, cipepula, ciholoholo, cipulupulu; cimpulu[2]

We note that the image of *ḫpr* is of him raising the sun (Ra) in the eastern horizon. There are a few terms in ciLuba that are of importance for us here. To "raise," in ciLuba, is *shu-la*. The root of the word *ḫpr* has the meaning of "wind" or to "blow." In ciLuba "blown" is *pupa, peeps, pepula, pupwila*. In Luba *Cipepu* or *Cipepewela* can also be rendered *ku-ku-Pepa* or *pepula* "blow, being carried by the wind." We should note that *Cipepu-la* means "strong wind," "Breath bearer of Ra." The key words are *Pa* "to give, to sponsor, to award; blow *Pe/Pa* "wind" (also *cipepa, cipepela*) and *Pela-Ditem* "friction or making fire by rubbing with stone or wooden flint." The root *-p-* is reduplicated in ciLuba. The *ku-* prefix (Egyptian *ḫ-*), as noted by Webb and Sure (2000: 230), is a noun-class marker that "...contains nouns created from verbs that use the prefix indicating the infinitive marker to express the act of doing, becoming, or the state of being." This *pe/pa*, *pepu*, etc, root is an ancient Niger-Congo root meaning *wind* or to *blow*.[14]

> PWN *PHET* "blow," *PHUPH* "wind, blow", *PHUP* "pigeon, dove" (flap wings), I Yorùbá *a-fefe* "wind," III Lefana *o-fe-fe* "wind," V Temne *a-fef* "wind," VI Mende *fefe* "wind, breeze," Mangbetu *mbimbato* "wind," Bantu *pepo* "wind", Swahili *upepo* "wind," Bantu (Meeussen) *peep* "blow." Fula *fufede* "blow" (forge).[15]

This very root is also in the term meaning "wing" or to "fly." A matter of fact, the very English word "fly" (and Yorùbá *Ifa*) derives from this ancient African root.

14 See Westermann's Index B (1927 : 310 f) for reconstructed PWS and Bantu roots; **pap* "wind."

15 See GJK Capbell-Dunn (2006: 88). *Who Were the Minoans: An African Answer*. Author House Publishing. Bloomington, IN.

FLY **Sumerian** *dal* "fly"

DA "fly, go" **-l**

PWS *pi* "to fly", *pí* "to throw", "feather"
PWS *pap* "wind"
PWN *PAPA* "wing"
PWN *PÍAP* "wind"
Bantu *padad* "fly"
Kongo *epapi* "wing", Ngala *lipapu* "wing" etc
Mande *pã* "to fly" (with wings), also *dama* "to fly"
Mangbetu *oda* "go ahead"
PCS **la* "motion"

***D = d** ***A = a** ***D = l ?**

WING **Sumerian** ^{ĝis} *pa* "wing"

BA, PA "wing", "feather"
PWS *pap, pep* "wind"
PWN *PAPA* "shoulder, wing"
PWN *PÍAP* "wind"
PWN *BÁMBÀM* "wing"
Bantu (Meinhof) *pepo* "wind"
Bantu *baba* "wing", *papá* "feather"
Bangi, Ngala *lipapu* "wing"
Mande *dāmba, dāba, dāma* "wing"
Mangbetu *babara* "large, broad, flat"
Mangbetu *kupapa* "wing"

***P = p** ***A = a**

The ciLuba language informs us that the target is not the beetle, but the action of "blow," "to lift or move through," the "wind." As we mentioned previously, the Egyptian scarab beetle is seen carrying the sun through the sky. *Ḫpr* is at once the "wind" that carries (Egyptian *fꜣy* "to carry, to lift") the light from the sun and the "breath" (*Kepepa*) of *Ra*, the very heat of the sun. This very "breath" is the same "breath" that human beings take and this is what is being signified by having the scarab beetle in the center of the *ꜥnḫ* symbol (air). A matter of fact, the word *ꜥnḫ* can also mean "beetle," so we see a double association here.

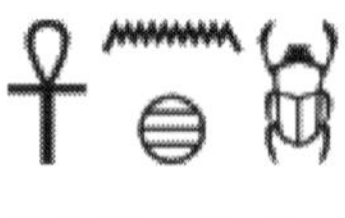

ꜥnḫ "beetle"

The following table provides an expanded range of meanings for the *-p-* root in the ciLuba language that directly corresponds with our discussion and assumptions on the meaning of the *ꜥnḫ* symbol.

ciLuba	Meaning
Peepa ≋ -puupa	blow hard, be impetuous, shake under the effect of wind, blow
pee ☛ der.:-Peepa	wind
Peepuka	be carried by the wind
Peepulula ☛ Syn.:-Sàngulula,	treat others regardless, winnow, sift again
Peepela ≋ puupula	breathe
Pùmuna	spread, exhale, breathe, breath, feel at peace
-Pùmuka *-Pùmwina, -Pùmwisha*	be poured into, spread
Puupa	blow
Punja	breathe (said of the wind), be impetuous
lupeepèlà lwa mpuupija	tornado
Puupala	blow, be lightweight, easy
-Peepela ≋ -puupala	be or become light, decrease; be or become easy
Puuya	blow, breathing (*mpuuyaa dilààla* "someone who breathes in their sleep)
Puuyakana	Pant, highly desired
-Pwìla≋-pwìdila, -pwìja	blow, whisper, inspire
Peepula	remove by blowing, blowing; empty; *kupeepula mbilu* "flee"
cipeepudi	precursor
Dìpeepula	swell with pride
Pwìja	breathe

This *-p-* root not only deals with the "wind" and "breathing," but in Bantu is associated with the instrument of breathing, the lungs, as can be seen in PB (from the BLR3 database):

DER	9443	papu		N 3	lung	E G
DER	9444	pàpʉ́	LH	N 5	lung	N S
DER	9445	papua		N 5	lung	G M
DER	9426	pàpá	LH	N 7	lung	J

This root dealing with "breath" and "lungs" can be seen in Egyptian as follows:

tpi	"breathe"	(ciLuba *-pùnja* > *di-punja* "breathe"; *pwìja* "breath")
tpr	"breathe"	
ffii	"lungs"	[Meeks: AL 771545]
wfꜣ	"lung "	[Wb I 306]

As we can see here, the proto-Bantu *p-p* root for "lungs" becomes *f-f* in Egyptian (p>f). However, the /p/ sound is retained in the forms *tpi* and *tpr*. The usage of the *ḫpr* beetle inside the loop of the *ʿnḫ* symbol reaffirms our interpretation which argues the *ʿnḫ* symbol is the thorax bone and the symbol is directing us to the process of *breathing* (the quintessential indicator that life is present).

Symbolism of the Snakes

The two snakes on the side, it is my belief, are used to represent the nerves within the thoracic complex. These represent the components of the brain stem and the central nervous system. The thoracic wall is supplied by the intercostal nerves which are the anterior primary rami of **spinal nerves**. The nerves of the thoracic walls are the:

- spinal cord (1)
- dorsal (sensory, afferent) root (3)
- ventral (motor, efferent) root (2)
- spinal nerve (4)
- dorsal primary ramus (mixed) (5)
- ventral primary ramus (mixed) (6)
- white communicating ramus (8)
- gray communicating ramus (7)
- sympathetic ganglion (9)

When the spinal cord is examined in cross section you can usually pick out two colors on its surface: white and gray. This is called the white matter and the gray matter of the spinal cord. The gray matter forms a butterfly-like image with dorsal horns and ventral horns. The white matter is made up mostly of nerve fibers running up and down the spinal cord. The gray matter is made up mainly of cell bodies of nerve cells, this giving a grayer appearance.

We are familiar with various ancient signs that use the snake to represent the nerves of the spinal cord.

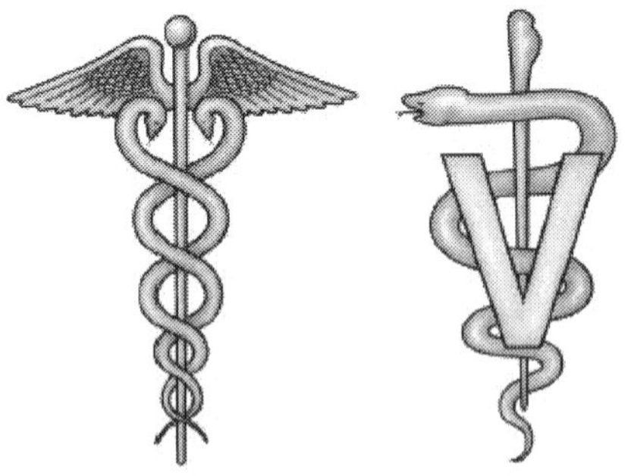

Figure 17: Modern Caduceus

The very signs used in our modern medical associations derive from ancient Egypt. They are called a *caduceus*. The image on the left originated in the hermetic period and the one on the right is a modification used by veterinarians. The center pole represents the spine and the snakes represent the nerves that circle the spine. We can also see the "sun" represented by the ball on top of the spine and the "wings," which I associate with the god *ḫpr*—who we see in

Fig. 15 above carrying the sun on its head and flapping its wings. This symbol (the caduceus) is directly taken from the ancient Egyptians who creatively generated various ways to convey this aspect of the human anatomy and its related processes. A few representations for the ancient inspiration are given below.

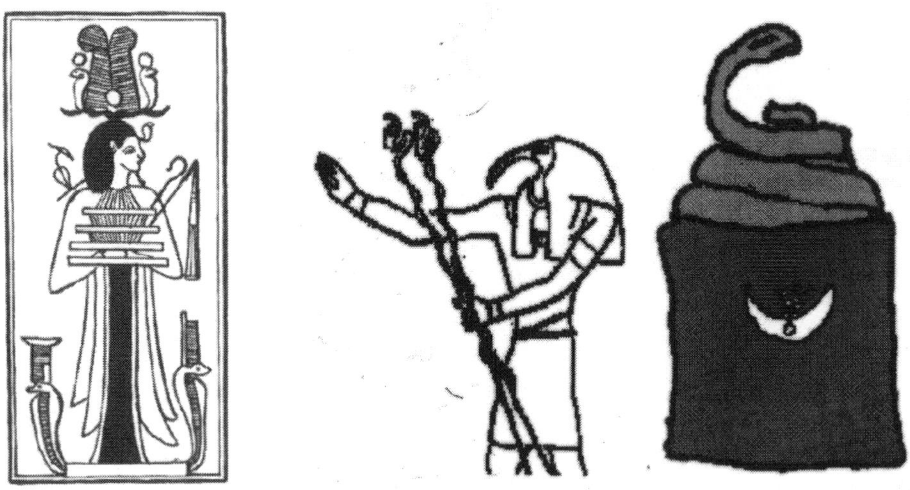

Figure 18

On the left is the god *Wsr* (Osiris, Washil, Eshu, Yeshua/Jesus) displaying the *ḏd* pillar (the spine) for which he is famous. The two serpents represent *Nb.t ḥwt* and *ꜣs.t* who we can identify by the crowns on the top of the heads respectively. In the center is the god Djehuti/Thoth with the ancient form of the caduceus staff. And on the far right is the "Basket of Aset" showing the Arat serpent with the classic 3 ½ turn that one associates with Indian Yoga and the concepts of Kundalini life-force. All of these images are conveying the same thing: the channels of energy that move up and down the spine. This is what we see in the version of the *ʿnḫ* symbol seen with the god *ḫpr* and the two uraeus serpents in the center of the loop. What's interesting here is that the uraeus snake is also associated with the word *ʿnḫ*:

ʿnḫ nṯr "uraeus snake" (as amulet)[16]

The two uraeus serpents around the spine are also connected with the pineal gland. The ancient Egyptians were very familiar with this gland in the brain and even associated Wsr with the pineal.

16 The Bantu word *nyoka* (*ʿnḫ*) means "snake."

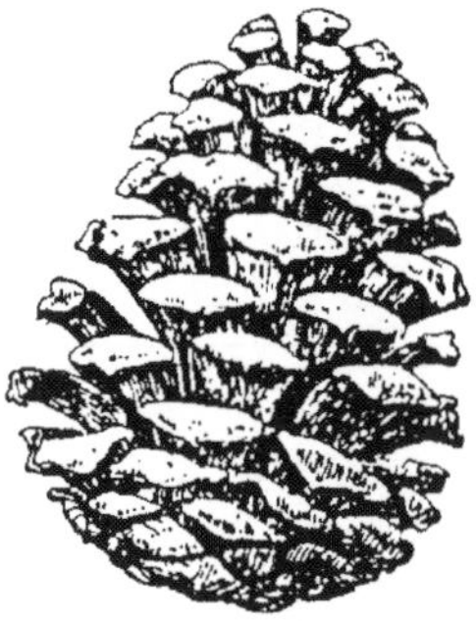

Pine cone

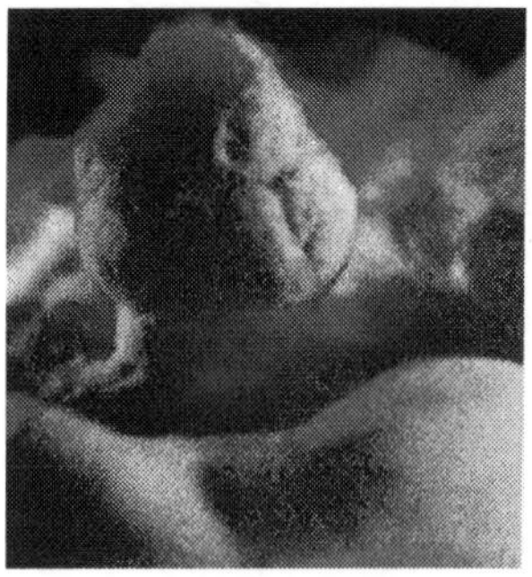

Pineal gland

Osiris in between 2 uraeus serpents.
From the Egyptian Museum Turin, Italy

Figure 19

The pineal gland is a small endocrine gland in the vertebrate brain. It produces melatonin, a hormone that affects the modulation of wake/sleep patterns and photoperiodic (seasonal) functions. It is shaped like a tiny pine cone (hence the name) and is located near the center of the brain between the two hemispheres, tucked in a groove where the two rounded thalamic bodies join.[17] Another hormone, serotonin, is also secreted during the day. Both melatonin and serotonin have their own path and is represented by the two snakes around the brain stem for which the pineal is attached. Aset and Nebehet could possibly represent these two hormones. An expanded discussion of these associations will take place in a forth-coming publication titled *Osiris Decoded: Tracing an Egyptian God Through the Yorùbá System of Ifa*. Space will not allow for an expansive discussion here.

An Alternative Pronunciation?

I mentioned earlier that the word *snb* (Kikongo *simbi/simba*) can mean "protection" and I interpret this to mean "immunity" or the "immune system" in our modern language, so vital to "health." This association between the *ꜥnḫ* and protection is confirmed in the *ꜥnḫ* image (the thoracic complex) as the snakes are holding up the *šn* sign which is a symbol for "eternity" and "protection."

As we discussed in the *Passion of the Christ or Passion of Osiris* (2011), the *šn* (from *šni* "to encircle, embrace, enclose, envelop", "to surround"; ciLuba *šing, nshing, cing*) is just the loop of the *ꜥnḫ* without the vertical bar at the bottom. The *šnw* is just an elongated version of the *šn*.

Figure 20: Variations of the *šnw*

Ankh (old kingdom) / *ꜥnḫ*	*šn*	*šnw*
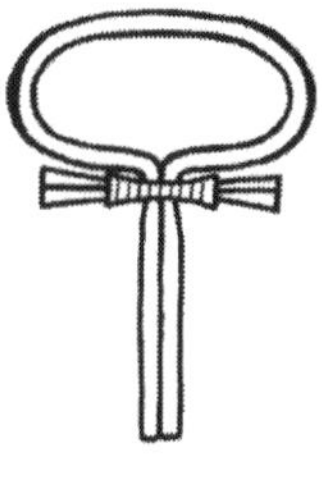		

17 Wikipedia.com (retrieved August 17, 2008)

We should note the following in the Egyptian language:

šnꜥ "breast, upper body, thorax"

sn "to breathe, to kiss, to smell"[18]

Essentially the same root for "eternity" and "protection" in Egyptian is the same root for "thorax, breast and upper body." When we compare the symbols in the table above, with knowledge of the meanings of *šnꜥ*, we find support in the Egyptian language for our thorax interpretation for the *ꜥnẖ*'s design. It should be noted that the word *šnꜥ* can also mean "turn back, repulse, repel, police (district), to hinder, constable, custom's officer, patrolman." Each term is within the semantical field of "protection" for which the thoracic complex is designed for.

I suggest here that the real pronunciation of the *ꜥnẖ* symbol, when depicted using the rope loop, is either *snẖ* or *šnẖ*. We find support in the Somali language of East Africa. In the Somali nomadic culture—a culture akin to the ancient Egyptian in language, material culture and religion—a looped knot of the main robe is called *caynka*.[19] This is usually paired together with the *baydda* and *kabaalada* which holds and stabilizes a camel load. Compare to ciLuba *šing, -cìnga* "fence, surround, enclose, circle"; *nyunga* "move in a circle; *nshinga* "thread, wire, braided rope, metal cable, telecommunications line (telegraph, telephone, internet), phone"; *MuShinga/ ka-Nzinga* "Newborn with the umbilical cord rolled up"; *muJinga* "cord, reel; braided rope"; Kikongo *singa* (pl. *misinga*) "a rope, a cord"; Kikongo *zinga* (pl. *zingidi*) "to encircle, to put around, to bandage, to furl a sail, to twine rope or string, to pack a parcel"; Kalenjiin *syaang'an* "rope," *syaang'aneet* "rope braided securely for tying animals."

The root is present in the Egyptian words *ꜥḥ* "rope"; *ꜥḳꜣ* "a rope"; *kꜣw* "a ship's rope."[20] The *s-* prefix is not a causative affix, but a word which means "to tie": PWS *ka* "hand" > Nupe *so* "to tie" (action of hand); Yoruba *so* "to tie"; Soko *isoso* "to tie" > Sumerian *sa* "cord" > (Afro-Asiatic) Hausa *sak?a*, Angas *sak*, Musgu *sasaka* "weave."

The *s-* prefix is suffixed in some related Egyptian words: *wgs* "tow rope"; *ḳꜣs* "cord, rope, binding, string (bow), tie (rope ladder)." We should keep in mind that the Egyptian word *šnw* means "rope, cord." The /ẖ/ sound interchanges with /š/ in Egyptian, thus *ꜥnẖ* and *šnw* may be a product of metethesis. The word *ꜥnẖ* (depicted as a rope) may also be a reflex of the word *nkt* "fetters, rope"; *ỉnki* "Ropes to the ship" [Wb I 101]; *ꜣẖꜣẖ* "Rope, Fibers" [Meeks:

---

18 Kikongo *nsunga* "a scent, a pleasant smell"; ciLuba *nsunga* "smell"; *-nunka* (*nunkila*)"exhale, spread a smell, feel, smell"; *cinunkilu/lununkilu* "sense of smell." Johnson (1922: 38) has for Bantu *şi* "nose" (131), *sini* "nose" (268). One is also reminded of Afro-Asiatic: Klesem *siŋ*, Suku *šin*; Cushitic: Kamir (C) *esiŋ*, Afar (E) *san*, Egyptian *snsn* "to smell." We also have in Lolo *jici* "smell", Ngombe *su* "smell", Kele *liti* "smell and in Kongo *zunu* "nose" (see Campbell-Dunn, 2009a: 53).

19 See my discussion in Imhotep (2011: 93-95) on how the ropes around the waste are used to determine the "health" of a person in central Africa.

20 Compare to Sumerian *gu* "cord, wool, linen"; PWS *gu* "cotton plant", Yoruba *e-gu* "cotton tree"; PWS *gua* "hand"; PWS *kuà* "to have", "to give"; Bantu *kua* "Hand anlegen", *kuata* "to hold"; Ngala, Poto *mokulu* "cord"; Kele *ikulu* "thread," Mande M *kutu* "cotton"; Mangbetu *hu* "cotton plant." The suffix to this root may be: PNC **li*, **ri* "tie"; PNC **ri* "rope", Grebo *li* "rope", Bini *iri* "rope", Idoma *oli* "rope" etc. (Campbell-Dunn, 2009b: 42). The original meaning of the word "rope" in African languages may have been, "twisted/woven cotton" or "twisted/tied cord/linen."

AL 780082]; *fnḫ* "Rope" [Meeks: AL 781573]. We have a reflex in ciLuba in the word *niNga* "twist, squeeze, bind strongly" which must be done in order to make a rope (ciLuba *muJinga* "cord, reel, braided rope"; *nshinga* "thread, wire, braided rope").

Given the information above, we note again that the Egyptian *ꜥnḫ* "life" may have been pronounced something like *snḫ* or *šnḫ* as can be observed in Kikongo *zingu* (var. *zangula*) "life," *zanzingila* "vitality" (Eg. *snḫḫ* "rejuvenate" [Wb IV 170] < *nḫḫ* "be reborn" ?); *luzingu* "material life"; *nzingulu* "living"; *zingu* "biography" (see Fu-Kiau 2003: 115). The Egyptian has the form *sꜥnḫ* "to bestow life, to perpetuate, make live, preserve, revive (dead), nourish, feed, perpetuate, nourish, support." The s- prefix, however, may not always be a causative.

The Sun in the Loop of the Ankh

It is my contention that the suns depicted earlier inside the *šni* of the *ꜥnḫ* mirror of Tutankhamen represents *energy* or could represent *electricity*. This image seems to be telling us that *light energy* from the plants, food (possibly symbolized by the lotus plant) and oxygen (symbolized by the winged scarab beetle) are processed inside the *ꜥnḫ* (the thorax) and it is converted into to the kind of energy that the body can utilize which helps to maintain the vitality of the organism (the person) and protects it from internal and external dangers (strengthens the immune system). The lotus plant may also represent the arteries or channels for which blood and oxygen flow throughout the body. A more modern depiction of this process (aerobic respiration) can be seen below.

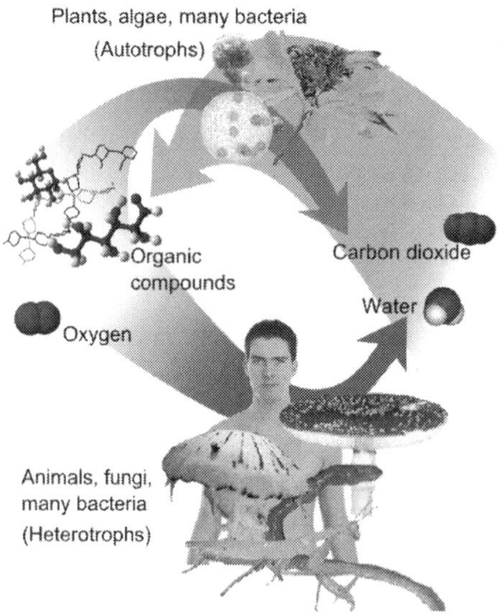

Figure 21

Aerobic respiration is the main means by which both plants and animals utilize energy in the form of organic compounds that was previously created through photosynthesis

Other Breathing Connections

We note that the *ꜥnḫ* symbol is often depicted as a looped knotted rope. We also connect the *ꜥnḫ* with the various processes of respiration located in the thorax. The ancient Egyptians also connected the breathing processes with "tying" in their symbol for the unification of Upper and Lower *Kmt* (ciKam, iKame, BuKam) 𓋬. This symbol is a combination of the lungs with various plant-stems acting as the valves which carry either blood or oxygen to various organs. The lung is called *smꜣ* 𓄥 in Egyptian. The glyph depicts the trachea (*ḫḫ*) and the left and right lung. The image below of the gods *Hrw* and *St(k)* show them both unifying Upper and Lower Egypt by tying the symbols of Upper Egypt (lotus plant) and Lower Egypt (papyrus plant) around the trachea.

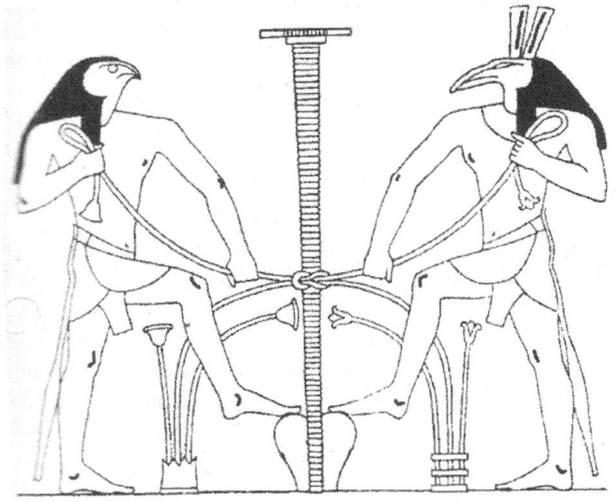

Figure 22

Here we see the two gods "making a covenant" by tying the knot around the lung. In Imhotep (2011) I go into an expanded discussion on how the tying of knots are used in Africa to represent a covenant or a contract that has been made between two parties whose situation has been arbitrated by an *nganga* (*ꜥnḫ*). This image appears to represent the same concept. Tying knotted ropes in Africa was an ancient practice that ritually bound the persons tying the knots to the commitments they have made. It should be noted that the Egyptian word for "vertebra" *ts* literally means "knot."[21] This may be relevant given our connection between the *ꜥnḫ* and the spinal column and why the *ꜥnḫ* is depicted as a knotted piece of rope.

In terms of the process of breathing, I offer the following as a possible interpretation. It is my current belief that the above image, outside of its political connotations, simply speaks to the process of respiration and how blood, oxygen, the lungs and arteries work as a coherent system to maintain life. Given our understanding of how African myths are created in Imhotep (2011), what I would suggest is that one pay attention to "who" is doing the tying as this can be very important in terms of a proper interpretation.

Heru and Set may represent important features in the process of breathing for which I cannot decipher at this time. Set in the above image is holding the lotus plant (*Nelumbo nucifera*) which allegedly was introduced from Persia. The *Blue Lotus* (*Nymphaea Caerulea*) is native to Egypt and has been proven to have some psychoactive and physiological effects on the body. It was used as a "visionary" enhancer and was taken either by way of smoking it or brewing it in teas or alcohol (wine being the favorite). It was seen as the key to good health, sex and rebirth. The *Blue Lotus* was an aphrodisiac and enhanced sexual vigor like Viagra, was used as a pain killer like Arnica, a tonic like Ginseng, and **circulation stimulant like Ginkgo**

21 *ts n psd* "dorsal vertebrae"; *ts n nhbt* "cervical vertebrae"

Biloba.[22] With this in mind, what we could be looking at is a possible recipe used to invigorate one's sexual life, unblock blockages, or ingredients used to promote optimum health. The key is in researching the possible health benefits of the papyrus plant if it was ever consumed to see if it had in medicinal purposes. One could be reading too much into this, but it wouldn't hurt to explore the possibilities.

Figure 23

In Fig. 23 above, we can see another version of this relief where the *ʿnḫ* association is more vivid. As we can see, the *šnw* acts as the "loop" aspect of the *ʿnḫ* and the trachea acts as the vertical bar of the *ʿnḫ,* verifying and confirming our association between the *ʿnḫ* and the thoracic complex. The word *šnʿ* is simply the word *ʿnḫ* backwards: e.g., Egyptian *ʿnḫ* "vow, swear, oath"; Coptic *anaš* (SB), *anaḫ* "oath, something you are bound too." The *ḫ* and *š* sounds interchange in Egyptian.

There is another version of this same image, but the gods *Hrw* and *St* are not doing the tying: it is the god *Hapi* (Abbey), which is a personification of the Nile River.

22 *Nymphaea caerulea* - Water Lily / Blue Lotus http://www.entheology.org/edoto/anmviewer.asp?a=65&z=6. See also, Nymphaea caerulea http://en.wikipedia.org/wiki/Nymphaeacaerulea

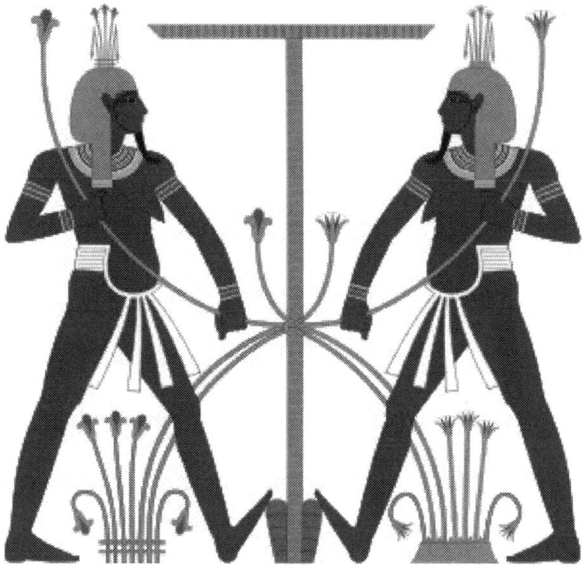

Figure 24

In this version one could say that it is the very Nile River that *unites* all of the polities of Egypt (*tꜣ-mry*). The god Hapi is depicted as a male with female breasts. This, to me, is symbolic of the flow of the river (which is seen as masculine in African traditions), but also the nurturing aspect of the flooding which gives birth to vegetation along its banks (which would make this a feminine attribute). In terms of the body, it could simply be making a reference to the importance of water to the body and its circulation points represented by the lotus and papyrus plant stems. More investigation is needed here.

The Ankh and Trees

In Imhotep (2011), I presented a hypothesis about the relationship between the *ꜥnḫ* symbol and trees, in that on some level the *ꜥnḫ* was representative of a tree or plant. Given our correlation between the *ꜥnḫ* and the breathing process, there may be further correspondences between the *ꜥnḫ* and trees/plants that would strengthen this hypothesis. Trees, like human beings, also go through a respiration process. The anatomy of the tree has striking similarities to that of the human being. As mentioned in Imhotep (2011), in many African cultures, trees are seen as human beings. There may be something to this idea not apparent on the surface.

A tree is a woody, upright plant with three main parts: root, trunk (stem, bole), and crown (branches). Tree roots have two key functions: they anchor the tree to the ground and absorb the water, minerals and oxygen that are essential to growth. Like human beings, trees need oxygen too. However, trees absorb oxygen from the roots which absorbs oxygen from the gaps between soil particles. Oxygen diffuses into the root through the root hairs. If the soil gets too wet and becomes waterlogged, the roots cannot easily get oxygen from the soil. The tree will not grow in such conditions.

Trees are usually broken down into hardwood or softwood trees. Hardwood trees usually have broad leaves and are either *evergreen* (for example, eucalypts) or *deciduous*, shedding their leaves in the autumn (for example, oaks and elms). The foliage of the tree is responsible for three main processes: transpiration, photosynthesis and respiration. On the bottom of leaves are openings called *stomata*. Water evaporates from the leaves via the stomata and that is what is called *transpiration*. Transpiration is important because it maintains a supply of water to the cells – essential for the cell processes to continue. A tree takes up a lot more water than it actually needs and the excess is used to carry the dissolved minerals from the roots to the leaves. The watery solution created is called the *sap*. The tree extracts the minerals from the sap and all that is left is the water which is removed by transpiration.

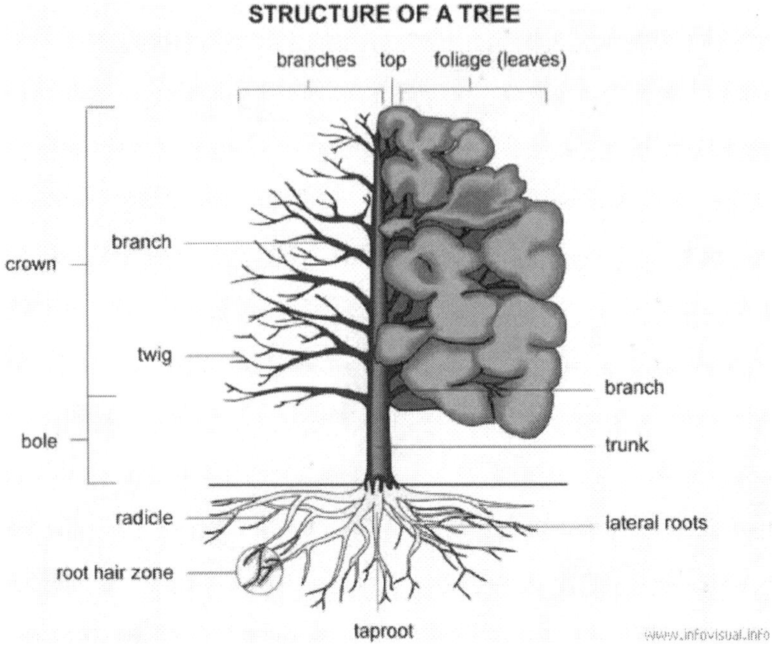

Figure 25

The most important chemical reaction on earth is photosynthesis. It is the initial energy source for all food chains on the planet. Trees make their own food through photosynthesis. Leaves absorb carbon and oxygen through the stomata in the form of carbon dioxide. Inside the chloroplast in the cells, the chlorophyll molecules (the plant's green pigment, its life blood) uses energy from the sun to make the hydrogen from the water combined with the carbon and oxygen and from the soluble carbohydrate: i.e., sugars. The sugars can then be made into starch for storage. Carbon atoms are the food of all organisms. **Photosynthesis is the only way that nature can trap the carbon molecules in the air and convert them into food**, which is then transferred through food chains into other organisms. This is very important to note because if you kill off all the trees and plants, you kill off man's food supply.

Trees, like all organisms, need energy to grow. This energy is released from the food made by photosynthesis in a process of *respiration*. This process occurs in the **mitochondria of the tree's cells** 24 hours a day**.** Some of the food is combined with oxygen and the reaction releases stored energy for growth. Respiration uses oxygen and releases energy, carbon dioxide and water. This is the reverse of the photosynthesis which collects the sun's energy, combines it with carbon dioxide and water and releases oxygen.

This is important for us here because the human body essentially goes through the same process as mentioned in previous sections. It is the respiration (*ˁnḫ*) process that releases the energy stored in food in both humans and plants. Plants make their own food through photosynthesis and humans get food from plants (or animals that eat plants). Just eating the food is not enough as you need something to kick the stored energy in the food out so the energy can be transported to areas that need it. That is what respiration does and why it is so important for runners to take in lots of oxygen while running. It takes a lot of energy to run and it is through respiration that we get access to that stored energy in food to replenish that energy we are exerting during the running process.

In both humans and trees, this process occurs in the mitochondria. Remember that in humans, the energy released in respiration is used to synthesize ATP to store this energy. The energy stored in ATP can then be used to drive processes requiring energy, including biosynthesis, locomotion or transportation of molecules across cell membranes.

Further connections between human beings and trees can be seen in the actual shape of a tree and that of the lungs. The center image below is of the structure of the tree flipped upside down, and in many respects, it resembles the human lungs. Here, the roots would be the opening of the trachea that takes in oxygen just like the roots of a tree takes in oxygen from the gaps of the soil. The trunk would be the *trachea* of the human being for which oxygen (and food) is transported to the lungs (and other needed areas). The lungs on the left and right of the trachea would be the foliage of the tree. Just like a tree, the trachea splits into "branches" called *bronchial tubes*. And just like tree branches, those airways break off into four, then eight, then hundreds of thousands of little airways in each lung. Those airways are your *bronchi*. The "leaves" attached to these bronchi would be the *alveoli*. Each alveolus absorbs oxygen and carbon dioxide is excreted. The opposite happens with trees: they release oxygen as a waste product and "breathe in" carbon dioxide from the atmosphere.

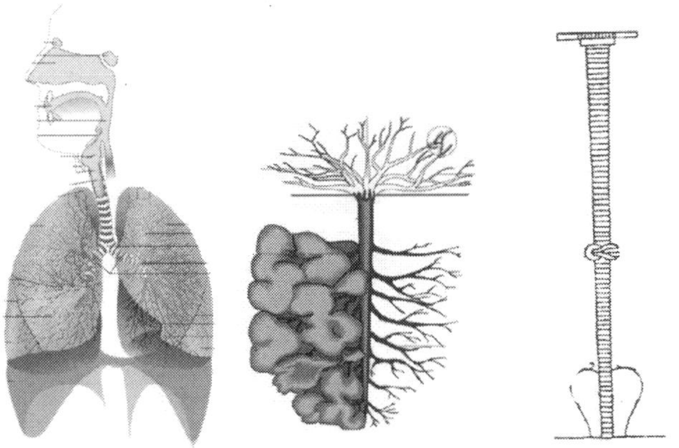

Figure 26

As we can see here, a tree and the human being share a similar physiological feature. In terms of the *ʿnḫ*, it may turn out that the ancient Egyptians noticed these similarities as well. To what extent I cannot tell at this time. But one thing is for sure, the ancient Egyptians understood what parts of the body were involved in the breathing process and they created various symbolic representations to convey this message to initiates (*ʿnḫ*, *sm3*, *ḏd*, etc); often in combination with other symbols to drive home the point. It may turn out that humans didn't evolve from ape-like ancestors, but from trees. Sounds like a good movie script idea to me.

Conclusion

As we are beginning to understand here, the *ʿnḫ* represents the whole system responsible for the maintaining of life in the human being. What the different variations of the *ʿnḫ* inform us is that the spine, the lungs, the nerves, the diaphragm and the heart are important in the sustaining of life. The *ʿnḫ* doesn't represent one item, but a system of processes and components of the body that are dependent on each other and is fueled by the oxygen we breathe in from the atmosphere.

The ancient Egyptian "artwork" can no longer be seen simply as "religious" texts, but scientific treatises on various aspects of knowledge known up until the time of the pharaonic records. These scientific expositions were codified in a way that it was easier to understand the processes by conveying them through anthropomorphic figures and by borrowing images from the environment in order to act as mnemonic devices so the priest doctors could see how their "insides" worked by observing their "outside" representations in nature. The writings on the walls may simply be large medical encyclopedias. The various items that one sees attached to the foreheads of the "gods" and priests, or the items that they are holding in their hands, may represent for the reader that these individuals have a good "grasp" on particular scientific concepts for which those items (a snake, an *ꜥnḫ*, a vulture, etc) represents.

It is a known fact that Egyptian doctors were highly skilled and specialized in definite domains. Herodotus (484-420 BCE) provides direct testimony to this fact as he lived and travelled the length of Egypt. He tells us:

> *In Egypt, medicine is subdivided in this fashion: each doctor treats one illness, not several. The place is full of doctors; some are eye doctors, some treat ailments of the head, some specialize in dentistry, some treat illnesses of the abdomen, and yet others specialize in illnesses of unspecified parts of the body. (Obenga, 2005: 401)*

All of the different "priesthoods" were just different wisdom traditions that focused on a particular science. The "gods" of that science/craft were the personification of the focus of that practice. So, for instance, if someone is a "son of Ptah" they could be one of two things: a medical doctor or an architect (or general craftsmen). Imhotep, the famous vizier of the 3rd Dynasty, was both. *Ptḥ* ("break open, open to work, carve, god of craftsmen, to create, to shape") in the Tshiluba language is *PaDika* "open, burst, tear,"; *PaTuk*(a) "spring forth, arise, out"; *KuPanda* "build"; *Pandish* "save," *Mu-Pandish* "savior"; Amarigna *baTS'hae* "carve, engrave"; Kiswahili *patua, pasua* "to split open." One key term here is *Mu-Pandish* "savior" and in Africa this is a term associated with medical doctors or wise sages who are the community's arbitrators (between fellow man or between the human and spiritual communities).

Figure 27: The god Ptah holding the *ḏd* pillar, the *wꜥs* scepter and two *ꜥnḫw*. All of these are symbols associated with the thoracic complex and by extension respiration.

In relationship to trees, the *ḏd* pillars are representative of trees. The *ḏd* pillar was originally a symbol of Ptah before it was associated with Wsr (Washil, Mujilu, Ashil) who is also symbolic of trees (see Imhotep 2011). One of the titles of Ptah is *ḫry-bꜥk-f* "He who is under the maringa tree" (Wilkinson, 2003: 124) which refers to an ancient tree god that was absorbed by Ptah at an early date in the city of *Mn Nfr*. One may ask how is a god of architects and craftsmen associated with medical doctors? My answer is that in order to be an architect in ancient Egypt, one not only had to master general architectural principles, but had to have a deep familiarity of the human body and what makes it work.

The reason for this, as R.A. Schwaller deLubicz has pointed out in *Temple of Man* (1998), is that the temples were representations of the human body. In order to mimic the science behind the human canon, one had to study it and apply it to architectural forms. Nothing on earth has a better design than the human body. This is why Imhotep, the son of Ptah, was an architect and a physician (also a poet and astronomer): he had to understand the functioning of both the body and its design. This concept is rooted in the ancient African belief of, "As above, so below. So below, as above." This proverb simply refers to the belief that the human being is a microcosm of the greater macro-universe. If we want to understand the greater cosmos, we should study well the human body. Using this as a pedagogical framework, the ancient Egyptians used the information gathered from the study of the human body and applied it to all social spheres, including architecture. deLubicz (1998: 335) presents us with an example of this principle concerning the Iput Isut temple of Luxor.

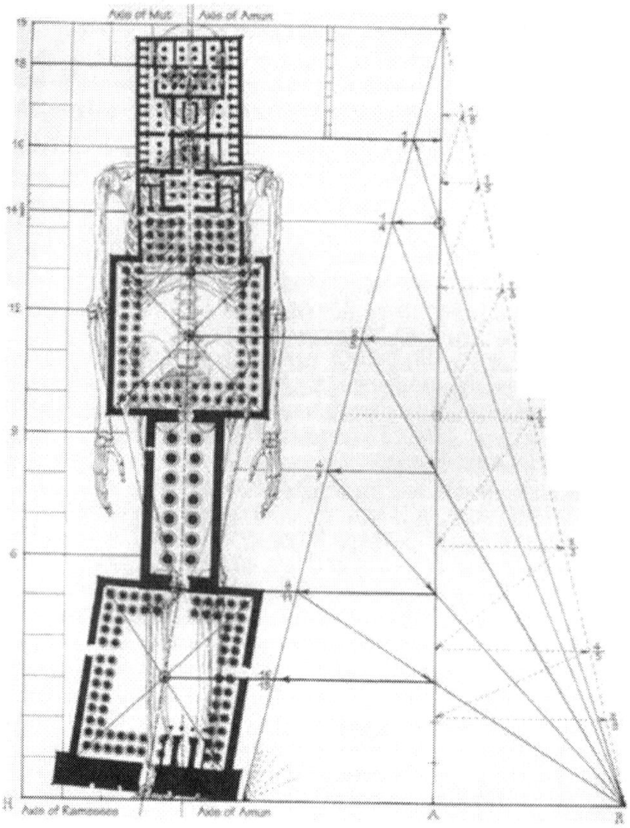

Figure 28

Given what has been revealed in this text, it should give us a starting point for future studies. Instead of, for instance, looking at ancient Egyptian zootypes in their artwork as external objects of worship, one should look for their internal representations in the human body to ascertain exactly what were the Egyptians trying to convey by using that animal in the myth. We should be asking ourselves, "Why would the ancient Egyptians use 'that' object to represent 'this' concept? What part of the human body does that object in nature represent internally?"

Nature is an external representation of an internal reality for African doctors and scientists. So to better understand ourselves, we must look at our "external selves" in nature; the same with ancient Egyptian artwork. This study also may provide evidence that the practice of mummification may not have truly been associated with religious connotations (at least initially), but with medical autopsies and the study of the human anatomy. In the desert, in 2500 BCE (for example), there were no refrigerators to preserve the bodies. How can you have a prolonged study of the insides of a person's body without 1) opening the person while alive, or 2) waiting until they are dead and rushing through the material before decomposition? Mummification is the answer. It allows the doctors to study the insides of the human being at no risk of injury to the person. Medical doctors still preserve the body in modern times for study; they just use refrigerators to conserve the body parts, which the ancient Egyptians did not have.

What this preliminary study has also brought to light is the importance of breathing in relation to the body's vitality and health. This study also should inspire the reader to take up Yoga. Dr. Muata Ashby has a whole series of books dedicated to Egyptian Yoga. What we call Yoga (what Ashby calls *Sema Tawy*) may have been prescribed by Egyptian doctors to increase vitality and strengthen the immune system and as a general healing modality. Theophile Obenga is also convinced that the study of ancient Egyptian statuary can provide an inexhaustible source of information on the practice of Yoga (Obenga, 2005: 394). Breathing properly is the corner stone to successful Yoga practices. Drs. Roizen and Oz, in their work *You: The Owner's Manual* (2005), gives deference to Yoga throughout the text and prescribes many Yoga techniques in order to live a healthier life.

Learning to breathe deeply and properly has many benefits. For one, it helps transport nitric oxide—a very potent lung and blood vessel dilator that resides in the nasal passages—to the lungs. Remember the ancient Egyptian reliefs that show the *ʿnḫ* being directed towards the nose? Deep breaths make your lungs and blood vessels function better. Taking in deep breaths helps your lungs go from 98 percent saturation of oxygen to 100 percent saturation of oxygen. Also, breathing deeply helps improve the drainage of your lymphatic system, which removes toxins from your body. We all should be familiar with the stress relief benefits. This is why in a heated situation it is recommended that you step back and take deep breaths. It could save you from a weekend in jail. Shifting to slower breathing in times of tension can help calm you and allow you to perform (mentally or physically) at higher levels. With that said, I'm going to work on my movie script where humans derive from trees....after some Kemetic Yoga!

NKWA, WAJU, SIMBA

Ancient Egyptian *ankh, udja, snb* =life, vitality and health

(Table Footnotes)

1 The brain stem is connected to your spinal cord. It's responsible for controlling many involuntary functions, such as breathing, digestion and heart rate.

2 Kalamba and Bilolo (2008: 201).

Towards a Better Understanding of Hotep in the Ancient Egyptian Language

Introduction

This is a preliminary paper on the meaning of the word *ḥtp*  in the ancient Egyptian language. Many historians and philologists have commented on the meaning of this term, but it is not quite clear as to how the word is constructed and if there are any other possible meanings to the term which may expand our knowledge of its usage and better clarify certain texts in the ancient Egyptian records.

To help us achieve our goal, we will seek help (primarily) from the Yorùbá language of Nigeria and the ciLubà-Bantu language of Congo and Angola. Over the years I have found these two languages to be of the utmost help in clarifying the structure and expanded meanings of ancient Egyptian lexemes. This is in part due to the fact that these languages belong to the Kongo-Saharan language family. As currently classified by mainstream linguists, the ancient Egyptian language belongs to a family called Afrisan or Afro-Asiatic. The validity of this language family has been in dispute by a few linguists such as Dr. Theophile Obenga and Dr. Cheikh Anta Diop. We don't have space to address the issues of this language family, but it should be noted that Afro-Asiatic derives from the Kongo-Saharan languages (Campbell-Dunn, 2009a: 5-6). This is evident from the structure of words that are no longer analysable[1] in Afro-Asiatic, but analysable in Kongo-Saharan as we will see throughout this text.

This knowledge allows us to get to the real roots of words and to better ascertain their meanings. This is because early human languages were mono-syllabic (Campbell-Dunn 2009a) and many Kongo-Saharan languages still retain their mono-syllabic structure with additional noun-class prefixes. In Afro-Asiatic these agglutinated terms become the basis of its bi-consonantal and tri- consonantal word structure. Many of the infixes, noun-class prefixes and verbal suffixes are no longer operative in many of the Afro-Asiatic languages. These once independent words have become lexicalized and treated as a single lexical item. Antonio Loprieno (1995: 57) speaks about this phenomenon as it pertains to compound nouns in Egyptian. But with a systematic comparison of cognate terms in Kongo-Saharan languages, we can get to the real roots of words in Afro-Asiatic.

The ancient Egyptian word *ḥtp* or *htp* is what we call a triconsonantal word. This means that the root consists of 3 consonant phones (*ḥ-t-p*) and often the change of vowel changes

1 Capable of being partitioned.

the dynamic of the word (or the whole word altogether). However, as we will discover, this verb really consists of a mono-syllabic root (*-p-/-b-*) behind a causative morpheme (*t-*) and a prefix (*ḥ-*). Before we can get started with our comparison we must properly define the various meanings of *ḥtp* in the ancient Egyptian language.

Meaning of the triliteral *ḥtp* 

The following table provides us with an operative set of definitions from which to start our comparison. When people think of the word *htp* (often vocalized by Egyptologists as hotep/hetep) the primary definitions that come to mind are "peace" and "offerings." But as we will discover there are many definitions of this triconsonantal term and these not-so-often mentioned definitions help to expand our discourse for which to posit new interpretations to terms we thought we fully understood.

Table 1: *ḥtp/htp* in Egyptian

Word	Translation	Reference
ḥtp-ḥr-mw	someone being devoted to	Wb III 190
ḥtp-dj-nswt	funerary offerings	Wb III 187
ḥtp	[name of the blessed dead]	Wb III 195
sḥtpj	censer	Wb IV 222
sḥtpj	[Title of Osiris]	Wb IV 222
sḥtp	offering table	WB IV 223
sḥtp	wild catch	Wb IV 222
sḥtp	[name of incense]	Wb IV 223
dbḥt ḥtp	Food needs	Wb V 440
m-ḥtp	happy, peaceful	Wb III 193
r-ḥtp ytn	until sunset/sundown	Wb III 192
sḥtp	[bread]	Wb IV 223
sḥtp	satisfy	Wb IV 221
st-ḥtp	resting place	Wb III 191
sẖt-ḥtp	food box(in the Hereafter)	Wb III 184
ḥtp-n-wnm	food basket	Wb I 320
ḥtp-nṯr	God sacrifice	Wb III 185
ḥtp-wr	excrement	Meeks: AL782 871
ḥtpjt	lady (of uraeus)	Wb III 194
ḥtpjw	peaceable	Wb III 194
ḥtpj	gracious, merciful (of God),	Wb III 194
ḥtpj	[furniture]	Wb III 196

ḥtpj	[priest]	Wb III 195
ḥtptjw	Bring sacrifice end	Wb III 195
ḥtpt	Federation (vegetables)	Wb III 196
ḥtpt	peace	Wb III 194
ḥtpt	offering table	Wb III 183
ḥtpt	food	Wb III 183
ḥtpt	station, stop (in procession)	Meeks: AL772 893
ḥtpt	[bread]	Wb III 195
ḥtpt	[measure, part of itrw{river}]	RdE30 (1978)S16; Meeks:AL782 878
ḥtpt	[priestess]	Wb III 195
ḥtpt	female genitals	Wb III 195
ḥtpwj	is satisfied with	Wb III 192
ḥtpw	good weather	Wb III 194
ḥtp	flowers (to the deceased, offerings)	Wb III 195
ḥtp	blood	Wb III 196
ḥtp	peace	Wb III 194
ḥtp	grace	Wb III 192
ḥtp	basket	Wb III 195
ḥtp	mat with bread	Wb III 183
ḥtp	food	Wb III 184
ḥtp	downfall, setting (Sun)	Wb III 192
ḥtp	incense	Wb III 196
ḥtp	[name of the blessed dead]	Wb III 195
ḥtp	[God]	Wb III 195
ḥtp		
	evil plot	RdE29 (1977) p. 10; Meeks: AL772 900
ḥtp	pacified	Wb III 194
ḥtp	satisfied	Wb III 188
dbḥt ḥtp	"funerary meal, altar, offering table"	Mark Vargus Egyptian Online Dictionary (for the rest of the following entries)
m ḥtp	"come in peace, arrive safely"	

ḳd ḥtp	"administration"	
m ḥtp	"welcome"	
ii m ḥtp	"come in peace, arrive safely"	
ḥtp di nsw	"an offering the king gives"	
šmʿt ḥtp	"bundle of sedge"	
st n ḥtp	"resting place"	
ḥtp	"boon, offering, meal"	
ḥtp	"rest in (tomb), assume (titulary)	
ḥtp	"satisfy, make content, pacify, occupy (throne)"	
ḥtp	"pardon" (someone)	
ḥtp	"be pleased (with), be happy, be gracious"	
ḥtp	(subdivision of a phyle)	
ḥtp	"fall out (of hair)"	
ḥtp	"peace, mercy, favour"	
ḥtp	"set, setting (of sun)"	
ḥtp	"to dwell"	
ḥtp	"basket"	
ḥtp nṯr	"oblations, divine offerings"	
ḥtp wr	"excrement"	
ḥtp	"food offerings, meal"	
ḥtp	"harmful action"	

As we can see from **Table 1**, the triconsonantal root *ḥtp* can mean a wide variety of things. Space will not allow us to explore every possible form this word can take. We will, however, focus on two underlying themes for this root: *offerings* and *peace*.

ḥtp as offerings

In relation to the theme of "offerings," *ḥtp* can have the following meanings:

ḥtp	"food offerings, meal, basket (of food?), name of the blessed dead (ancestors; those for who which the offerings are for)
ḥtp	"boon (help, godsend), offering, meal, the Divine (God)"
ḥtp di nsw	"an offering the king gives"
dbḥt ḥtp	"funerary meal, altar, offering table, food needs"
ḥtp.t	"food, offering table, bread"
sḥtp	"offering table"

htp-nṯr	"oblations, divine offerings"
sḫt-ḥtp	"food box (in the Hereafter)"
ḥtp-dj-nswt	"funerary offerings"

As we can see from the above, this term relates to food, the act of offering the food, that which the food is offered on and/or contained in, the ancestors and the Divine itself. But looking at cognate terms in related languages we come to discover that its verbal form *sacrifice* has a more violent root for which its present sense derives.

As William W. Hallo noted in his paper "A Ugaritic Cognate for Akkadian *ḫitpu?*" concerning the word *ḥtp*:

> The root *ḥtp* is familiar in Arabic, Hebrew and Aramaic in connection with slaughtering or hunting and occurs already in a Ugaritic text in the specific context of a sacrifice. We read, in a prayer to Ba'al, "A bull, oh Ba'al, we consecrate (to you), a votive offering, oh Ba'al, we dedicate (to you), the first fruits, oh Ba'al, we consecrate (to you), the booty, oh Ba'al, we offer (to you), a tithe, oh Ba'al, we tithe (to you)." The word translated 'booty' here is *ḥtp*, comparable to the *ḥetep* ('prey') of Proverbs 23:28. Given the context, however, the word may already foreshadow the connotation of a kind of sacrifice. That is surely the meaning of Akkadian *ḫitpu* which occurs in monthly sacrificial lists of the late first millennium.[2]

As can be gleaned from the above cited text, *ḥtp* derives from a root that means "to hunt, to slaughter." I argue that this term ultimately derives from a monosyllabic root that means to "cut, slice and burn." It is believed that from this act of killing/slaughtering that the very item being killed became the word for offerings (food = sacrifice). But I'm here to suggest, also, that within this paradigm exists two different roots and that *ḥtp* "offerings" and *ḥtp* "sacrifice" are two separate words (homonyms) that eventually became synonymous with each other (by way of paronymy). The *ḥtp* that means "offerings" comes from a root that means "to give, to present" and the *ḥtp* that means "sacrifice" derives from a root that means "to cut, slice, pierce" and "to burn, cook."

The Egyptian *ḥtp*—as already mentioned—has cognates in the Semitic languages. Before we examine these cognate terms, we must refamiliarize ourselves with common sound mutations. I will argue that the *ḥ-* in *ḥtp* derives from a *k-* sound (*k<ḥ*) as can be attested in Tshiluba-Bantu. This can be gleaned from Akkadian *ḫitpu* "offering," as the *ḫ-* is more of a guttural /h/ sound. This /k/ sound often is palatalized to become /s/, /š/, /z/, /c/, /j/ and /t/. From the /t/ sound we get /d/ as *t's* and *d's* often interchange between languages and these two phonemes can also produce /s/, /š/, /z/, /c/, /j/ and even /l/. The /p/ sound, we will see, is often vocalized in other languages (and within the same language) as /b/ (see Kalenjiin for instance; p<>b). With this understanding of common phonological changes between phonemes, it will be easier for the layman to see how the terms to be compared are essentially the same terms: just morphological variants of each other.

The word *ḥtp* "sacrifice" in Hebrew is *zebah* "sacrifice," which itself is an alternate of Hebrew *tabah* "to slaughter." Every slaughtering of an animal for food was originally done as a religious act. Here we see that in the word *zbh* (*zebah*) the /z/ takes the place of /t/. The historical root of *ḥtp* is *tp* as can be seen in Hebrew. This is confirmed in Aramaic *debah* "sacrifice" and Ugaritic *dbh* "sacrifice." Whether the initial *ḥ* in *ḥtp* has been dropped, or moved into final consonant position in Semitic (metathesis), I cannot say at this moment. Semitic tends to add *h's* at the beginning and ends of words where its cognates in Kongo-Saharan rarely possesses

2 William W. Hallo, "New Moons and Sabbaths," 8; repr. in *Essential Papers*, 319. Cited in Chazan, Hallo and Schiffman (1999: 44)

this feature (i.e., Yorùbá *El, Olu, Oluwa* "God"; Arabic *Allah* "God"; Hebrew *Eloh* "God").[3] The /h/ phoneme is a highly amissable first and final consonant.

By looking further west into the Yorùbá language of Nigeria, we come to understand that this root (*tp*) is actually further reduced to *-p-*. The Egyptian word *ḥtp* "offering, sacrifice" in the Yorùbá language is known as *ẹbọ* (also *ṣẹbọ*) "sacrifice." A verb that goes with *ẹbọ* is *rù* (*rù'bọ* "to offer sacrifice"). Yorùbá *ru* is cognate with the Hebrew noun *'olah* "whole burnt offering,"[4] and related to the hiphil verb *ha'aleh* "to sacrifice." It is said that Hebrew *'olah* is related to Hebrew *'alah* "to go up," since the smoke of burnt offerings rises up to God (*Eloh*) (Oduyoye, 1996: 52).

Sacrifice and Offerings in African Tradition

Before we go any further on exploring this term, it would be beneficial for us to examine the purpose and nature of sacrifice within the larger African context. Philip Neimark in his book *The Way of the Oriṣa* (1993: 33) informs us that a sacrifice:

> ...is an avenue for restoring whatever positive process has been disrupted in your life and for acquiring general well-being from Olódùmarè (our God).

He goes on further to describe *ẹbọs*, which are:

> ...the practical offerings of sacrificial elements to the orìṣà, the divine designates who carry our pleas or wishes to Olódùmarè. For example, offerings may be made to Ogun, Obatala, Esu, Ifa, Osun, Ori. The specific offerings one would make to a particular orìṣà would depend upon the problem being approached and the orìṣà to be appeased.

There are two other kinds of sacrifices made in the Yorùbá system of Ifà: *etùtù* and *ipese*. *Etùtù* offerings are for the ancestors (*egúngún*). It is through *etùtù* that spiritual linkage is achieved. The other type of sacrifice is *ipese* and they are offered to the *aje* (goddesses of riches) and *ajogun* (both good and bad energies controlled by the *orìṣà* deity *èṣú*). As noted by the late Babalawo of Ifà Dr. Ifalobi Epega—in his work *Ifà: The Ancient Wisdom* (2003: 86)—sacrifices are made to save one's self and one's family. It is used to ward off misfortunes and to help others: especially the poor, needy and the sick. By making small sacrifices, human beings can achieve their destinies and avoid pre-mature death.

The late Dr. E. Bọ́lájí Ìdòwú, in his classical work *Olódùmarè: God in Yorùbá Belief* (1994: 121-125), presents us with seven types of offerings in the Yorùbá tradition which I will summarize below:

a) *Meal and Drink Offerings* (Egyptian *ḥtp* "food, bread, oblations") – begins with customary libations offered at the shrine of the divinities. Meals are also offered on special days in which the devotee also takes part of the offering and consumes. The offerings are a means of communion between the *orìṣà* and the worshippers.
b) *Give or Thank-Offering* – These are sacrifices that are offered as gifts to the divinities. Often, offerings are made to the *orìṣà* in appreciation of some success in, or prosperous issue of, an enterprise. Women who have sold well in the market, the person who has been blessed with child, etc., all want to show their thanks (Yorùbá *dúpẹ́*) to the *orìṣà* whom they believe to be the dispenser of their special blessings.
c) *Votive Offering* (*ẹbọ ẹ̀jẹ́*) – This is an offering made to the spirits for some supplication,

3 See *Chapter 2* this volume for a possible derivation of /h/ from /s/.
4 We note the added *-h*: *ru* vs *olah*; *r<>l* interchange.

and in return for granting what has been requested, the devotee vows to do some action.

d) *Propitiation* (*ẹbọ etùtù*) – This is an offering of appeasement to avert disaster such as illness, epidemic, drought, or famine (often believed to be the wrath of spirits). The underlying belief of the ritual act is that after such a sacrifice, the manifestation of "the wrath" will be withdrawn.

e) *Substitutionary* (*a-yẹ̀-pin-ùn* "that which alters an agreement") –This agreement alters an agreement made between a person and his "companions." These companions are wandering spirits that "prank" by entering a woman's womb only to be born to die shortly thereafter. In such a case a sacrifice is made to prevent this from happening by making an agreement with the spirit to not prank.

f) *Preventative* (*ogun kòjà* "that which wards off attacks") –Such a sacrifice is either public or private. It is often a precautionary measure to ward off evil or misfortune. Also, it is offered when there is definite knowledge of an impending disaster.

g) *Foundation* – Sacrifice in this category combines the nature of propitiation and preventative. It is to appease the spirit of the earth in order that all may be well with that which is being founded. The sacrifice is offered at the foundation of a house, village, or town.

With this understanding—from the examples given from the Yorùbá tradition of Ifà—we know that a sacrifice is used to bring about balance and blessings in a person's life. It is a process in which energy (good or bad) is redirected in particular areas in a person's life. This will become very important throughout this text.

A cognate term for *ẹbọ* in Yorùbá is *bọ* "to worship, to deify." It belongs to the same consonant root as the heteronym *bọ́* "to feed." In Tshiluba we have *-pa* (≈*pèèsha*)[5] "give, award, provide, to give sparingly"; *dipà* "giving"; *dyùpa* (<*-uupa*) "to discharge" (a gun or battery); in other words to "release" something. An offering is the giving away of something valuable as a gift or tribute. But it is also used to discharge/release negative energy surrounding one's life.[6] The idea is that when you sacrifice and give something of value (to someone else, to the ancestors, or to the Divine), in the spirit of reciprocity (Egyptian *m3ʿ.t*; ciLubà *Balelela, Cyama*), more blessings and protection from harm will come your way.

The *tp* root of *ḥtp* in the kiKongo language is *simba* (t > s). The word *simba* in kiKongo means "**to hold up**, to keep (something), **to bless**, to treasure, to touch, to retain" (Fu-Kiau, 2006:1). Again this root is present in Yorùbá as *bọ́* "to feed, maintain, support, cherish, nourish, or foster." The Yorùbá term can also mean "to beat the mud floor of a house (a form of maintenance); to wash slightly" (Egyptian *wʿb* "to cleanse"). The *-b-* root in KiKongo and Yorùbá respectively morphs into *-f-* (b > p > f) in Egyptian: *f3y* "raise, lift up, carry, support, weigh, present, deliver (taxes, tribute); *f3i* (alternate form); *f3y.t* "reward."

This is important to note. In African tradition, sacrifices aren't always used to request something from spirit, but to feed spirit itself (to add life, as a form of blessing). Sacrifices "maintain" and "nourish" spirit. An example from the Amazulu of South Africa will illuminate this point for us. Credo Mutwa, a Zulu Sangoma (priest), in his work *Indaba My Children* (1964), introduces us to the reality of ancestors and their need for nourishment in order to survive. In Zulu tradition, the soul of a person is not an ancestor. What is an ancestor is the *spirit double* of a once living human being (the accumulated experiences and personality of a person). In Zulu tradition this double is called the *ena*.

5 The suffix *esha* in Tshiluba is equivalent to the causative *s-* prefix in the ancient Egyptian language: i.e., *wʿb* "pure"; *swʿb* "to purify."

6 In the case of a negative point in one's life, this is achieved by the animal being sacrificed absorbing the negative spirit of a situation and taking it with its spirit as it dies into the spirit realm to be dealt with by the patriarchs there.

> When a baby is born, it is born with a body, a mind and a soul, but not with an Ena [double]. The Ena grows like a flower as the child is formed and nourished by the experiences of the growing child. It is shaped by the child's own character and also the characters of those whom the child chooses to imitate, such as parents or tribal hero (Mutwa, 1964: 569).

In the ancient Egyptian tradition, I argue that this function was served by the *b3* as the *b3* needed food and water to survive like the *ena* of the Zulus (unlike the *k3*) and was believed to be the personality of the human being by many scholars. These spirits live only a short time after death unless they are nourished with sacrifices. As Mutwa further notes:

> An *Ena* must eat to grow and live, the same as you must eat to grow and live. While you live you eat for both your body and for your *Ena,* but when you die your *Ena* will also die unless it can continue to eat. If we do not sacrifice cows and goats regularly so that the *Enas* of these animals can go to feed our ancestors' spirit, they will go into a state of non-existence. Our ancestors' spirits must remain alive because we must regularly ask their advice about problems we encounter, and they must take our problems we encounter, and they must take our problems and plead for us with the gods – just as the common people must have the *Indunas* who can plead for them with the chiefs. (ibid.)

This excerpt helps us to understand why we present offerings to the ancestors (the *enas*): it is to help them live. They in-turn provide us with valuable information which could improve our lives and help us tower over obstacles. Many African-Americans think that simply "calling out the names" of our ancestors forever keeps their spirits living. This is incorrect from a traditional standpoint: one must also physically feed them. Understanding this very fundamental aspect of African ontology, we now know why the ancient *baKame* (Egyptians) made such a big deal about "living for eternity." It wasn't their souls (*ka*) they were fighting for, it was their doubles (*ba*), the holders of the individual personality, that they wanted to live forever. They wanted to protect their personality.

All beings possess the same soul (Mutwa 1964, de Lubicz 1981), but the double is unique to each being and it is this individual personality that they wanted to live forever (I mean you worked so hard to develop it, why not?).[7] During Credo Mutwa's initiation into sangomahood, his elders told him the importance of sacrificing to the ancestors (the *enas*). They encourage him to:

> Urge the people, Oh my son, urge them always to slaughter a goat or a cow for the helpless spirits of their ancestors. Tell them that a man who tries to live without his ancestors is like a tree struggling without its roots, and that a man who is ignored by his ancestors is a disgrace in the eyes of the gods. His conscience will haunt him until his dying day and he will die weeping like a lost hyena in the darkness.
>
> My son, you know that when a man sacrifices regularly to his ancestors, the *Enas* leave the land of Forever-Night and come to live in that man's kraal always. They live there and repay his adherence by protecting him and his children and wives from harm, by interceding with the gods on his behalf, and by giving him luck in all he does. They also help him by sending him advice by dream messages in his hour of trouble. They not only shield him from harm, they make him the dread of his enemies (ibid. 570-571).

7 I will expand more on this topic in an upcoming work titled *The Ena, The Ancestors and the Papyrus of Ani.*

In his quest for evidence of the importance of the ancestors, Mutwa finds a legal basis for communion with the ancestors.

> This belief that a man lives solely to serve his ancestors is one of the most deep-rooted beliefs in the whole of Africa, and tribal unity is based on this. The tribe as a whole must keep the spirits of its founders alive—every tribe in Africa believes this (ibid. 573).

Now that we have properly situated the ritual of sacrifice in its proper African context, we can continue with the linguistic aspect of our discourse. Here it should be noted that when comparing terms in Egyptian that begin with an /h/ or a /w/ to cognates in Yorùbá, these matches usually render "zero" in first consonant position (C_1). Yorùbá nouns do not usually begin with an /h/ or h-type sound. So looking for cognates for the Egyptian *ḥtp* triconsonantal root in Yorùbá, one would have to look for a *t-p* consonant root or its equivalent alternate forms (e.g., *d-p*/*d-b*).

By studying the Yorùbá language, and understanding that the real root of *ḥtp* is *-p-*, we should be able to find this root in Egyptian. If the real root of *ḥtp* is *-p-*, then we should be able to find Egyptian words with just the *-p-* root with the same meanings as the triconsonantal form. We discover that the Egyptian language indeed has this monosyllabic root. However, the voiceless plosive /p/ has become voiced /b/ for these roots. The following table should make clear this discovery. **Table 2** below shows the primary root in Egyptian along-side the expanded form. The expanded forms will also show the alternative renderings of the same root. So we discover that *ḥtp* is not always vocalized as *ḥtp*, but has various dialectical and morphological forms.

Table 2

Yorùbá	**ciLubà**	**Egyptian** (monoliteral root)	**Egyptian** (bi- or tri-literal)
ẹbọ "sacrifice, offering"		*ꜥbw* "offerings"; *bw* "offering"	*ḥtp* "food offerings, meal"; "boon, offering, meal";
		ꜥbꜣ "offering stone, memorial stone, altar"	(*ḥtp.t* "offering slab, offering")
bọ́ "to feed, maintain, support, cherish, nourish, or foster"	*-pèèbwa* "be a gift, receive"; *pa* "to give, provide, award"	*iꜥb.t* "offering"; *tꜣ ꜥb.t* "offering festival"	*ḏp.ty* "an offering" [t > d] (alternate form without the *ḥ-* prefix)
	-tàpa "lend help, give a helping (hand)"		
	Cidììbwà "food, foodstuff"	*bꜥꜣ* "foodstuff"	*ḥtp* "food"
		pꜣ.wt "offerings, cakes"; *pꜣ.wt* "offering loaves"	*ḥtp.t* [bread];
		bꜣ "fruit, seed, grains";	
àdàbà "a dove" (metathesis?) [sacrificed to Obatala)			*ꜣpd* "fowl"; used on the *ḥtp* offering table)

Yorùbá	**ciLubà**	**Egyptian** (monoliteral root)	**Egyptian** (bi- or tri-literal)
ṣẹbọ "sacrifice"		*wꜥb.t* "meat offering"	*šꜣbw* "meat offering" (as food); *sb* "piece of meat" (as sacrificial offering); *sbw* "food offering"; (*sbw* "spoils of an army" may be related here; Ugaritic *ḥtp* "booty")
adẹ́bọ (Carabalí *andabo*) "an idol-worshipper" (the word means "friend, follower, admirer," in other words a "devotee.")	*mbwa* "friend, comrade"; *mukuba* "priest"	*wꜥb* "Wab priest"; *wꜥb.t* "female priesthood" [a sorority?]; *wꜥbw* "priests"	*ḥtp* [God], *ḥtpj* [priest], *ḥtp.t* "priestess"
ibò/dibò "cast lots" (an act of a priest)			
bọ "to worship, to deify."			
adupẹ "thank you, gratefulness" (*dupẹ* "give thanks" [*da ope*]; *ìdúpe* "thanks, thanksgiving, Eucharist")[1]	*mwabi* "happy"		*ḥtp* "be pleased (with), be happy, be gracious"; *m ḥtp* "welcome"; *ḥtp* "pacified, grace"; *ḥtpj* Gracious, Merciful(of God),
adába "proposer, mover, suggester, one who attempts"; *idába* "proposal, motion";		*wꜥbw* "plea, appeal"[2]	
tuba, tunba "to repent, surrender" [sense evolution?]			*ḥtp* "pardon" (someone) Pardon "to grant, forgive"; "give, present"
àtẹ̀pa "medicine which renders a poison which has been trodden on ineffective."	*ondapa* "treat, cure"; *ciShipa* "antidote" (medicine)	*ꜣbw* "a medicine" (an active medicinal ingredient)	*sp* "medicine, dose, portion (of food), remnant (of food), residue" [*sẖbw* "draught (of medicine)?] (t > s)
bọ́ "to beat the mud floor of a house (a way of tidying the place up); to wash slightly"		*wꜥb* "to cleanse"; *ꜥbw* "purification"	

Yorùbá	ciLubà	Egyptian (monoliteral root)	Egyptian (bi- or tri-literal)
	Nkambwà "ancestor, grandfather, great-grandfather" (<*fwà* "die, no longer exist"		*ḥtp*[name of the blessed dead] *ḥtp.tyw* "the peaceful ones" (the blessed dead)

What we are witnessing here is evidence of a multiple-stage linguistic relationship between Yorùbá, ciLubà and Ancient Egyptian. The relationship is not single-stage. There are multiple reflexes to match various time depths. By understanding common morphophonology, especially in a language whose written history spans more than 3000 years, we can anticipate certain changes and look for those sound changes to reaffirm and establish certain hypotheses as it pertains to word formation and meaning in the language under examination.

To further confirm that the root of *ḥtp* is *-p-*, we can look for another common sound mutation to reaffirm our earlier assumptions. The /b/ [+voiced] sound often devoices and becomes /p/ [-voiced]. The /b/ also morphs into /m/ [+LABIAL, -continuant, +voice]. If *-p-* is the root of *ḥtp*, we should find evidence of this where p <> b, and from this sound change we should also see b > m. The following table may support such an assumption.

:

Table 3

Egyptian (full form)	m- stem	b- stem	ciLubà
ḥtp "food offerings, meal"; "boon[3], offering, meal";	*m3ʿw* "products, offering, tribute, gifts"	*ʿbw* "offerings"; *bw* "offering"[4]	*-pèèbwa* "be a gift, receive"; *pa* "to give, provide, award"
	m3ʿ "fit to be offered"	*iʿb.t* "offering" *t3 ʿb.t* "offering festival"	*ambika* "someone help take a load on the head or shoulder"; "make responsible, entrusted with change"; "to give, present, offer" *ambikila* "in addition to" *ambikisha* "place in a cross-shaped manner" *cyambikilu* "how to give" *uupuluja* "submit to, put in the hands" *ambika*[2] "attached, devote, apply" *-lubula* "advertise, communicate"; "present"; "provide" (*muluba* "spoksperson") [*ba/mba/bu* being the root in each term]
	m3ʿ "present, offer, make presentation"		*pa* "to give, provide, award"

Egyptian (full form)	**m- stem**	**b- stem**	**ciLubà**
ḥtp [name of the blessed dead]; *ḥtp.tyw* "the peaceful ones" (the blessed dead)	*mꜣʿ.tyw* "blessed spirits, the Just, blessed dead"		*akambwa* "ancestor"; *fwa*(b > p > f)
ḥtp [God], *ḥtpj* [priest], *ḥtp.t* "priestess" [no doubt the leaders in any traditional African society]	*mꜣʿ* "leader"(<ʿꜣ"leader, chief workman, commander, Elder, Noble, Master")		*mulopò(ù)* "chief, lord, God" [t > d > l] *nsambu* "greater, more"[5] [t > s] *-à/-antàpu* "special, extraordinary, determining, decisive"
kṯmw "divination, omen" (k-t-m) [if indeed a match, the /m/ could have derived from /b/ (<p).	*mꜣꜣ* "a seer, one who sees" *mk* "lo, behold, look, see" (b > m)		*lubùku* "divination, consultation of fate" *kutempa* (k-t-p)/ *kubuka lubuku* "view the lot" *buka* "see the fate, spirits" *tempa* "examine, inspect, seek" (t-p) YORÙBÁ: *dibò* "cast lots" (an act of a priest; to see the unseen)
ḥtpj "gracious, merciful"; *ḥtp* "grace, be pleased, be happy"	*mꜣṯ* "proclaim, think up, devise, announce, name" [metathesis? *m-ṯ<ṯ-m*?; m<b] [*ṯm* "to think up, invent, imagine" may be relevant here]	*ỉb* "think, suppose, believe, feel, fancy, perceive, heart, soul"	*meeji* ≋ *menji* "intelligence, think, reflect" *mwoyo(i)* ≋ *mooyo(i)* "heart, life, mind, soul, courage, will, desire, inclination, mood, feeling, greeting, thought." (metathesis *ib>bi>mwoyo*) **Yorùbá** *dabá* "think, hope, imagine, speculate, conjecture" *adupẹ* "thank you, gratefulness" (*dupẹ* "give thanks"; *ìdúpe* "thanks, thanksgiving, Eucharist")[6]

As we can see from this section, understanding common sound mutations can be very rewarding when doing comparative work. Once a sound takes on a particular morphology, it then begins to take on its own set of mutations as time passes in each given direction. These are sometimes hard to spot because of additional prefixes, infixes and suffixes. What we end up having in the language is what linguists call a "doublet": that is, two or more variations of the same term in the present language with the same or similar meanings. This is necessary to bring about slight semantic distinctions that could not be adequately expressed using the one term (Lord 1966). Once confusion is apparent with homonymic lexemes, slight differences in spelling and articulation begin to develop (e.g., English *cloth* vs. *clothes*).

The Violent Origins of Sacrifice

As mentioned earlier, *ḥtp* "sacrifice" comes from a root that means "to kill, to slaughter." As we have demonstrated throughout this text, the root of *ḥtp* is *t-p* or *-p-*. If the root is indeed *-p-* in Egyptian, then we should find this same root in Yorùbá and ciLubà as in the case with the examples above. This is verified in Yorùbá with the root *pa*:

> *pa* (primary idea: "to make to feel" or suffer; extensively used in composition); to kill; murder; put out of existence; ruin; stay; betray; quench fire, extinguish; bruise; rub, scrub; cut (yam seed or calabashes into halves); break any hard nut; peel the bark of a tree; win a game; hatch; tell fables [around a campfire?]; cultivate a new grass field; be drunken.

Part of this analysis informs us that "cutting" may be at the source of this term. A reflex of this term in Yorùbá is *be* "cut, peel"; *bọ̀* "to insert, pierce, boil, seethe, coddle or parboil"; *bu* "to bake under ashes, broil, to dive, to hide under the sand." The terms "cutting" and "piercing" (inserting) belong to the same semantic field.

This root in ciLubà is represented, in part, by the sound mutation p > f. The word *fwà* means to "kill, extinguish, die, no longer exist." A few examples from across Africa will help us to see the semantic range of this root:

PWS (Proto-Western-Sudanic) *bì* "wound", Ewe *a-bì* "wound", Nyanbo *ki-bi* "wound"
PWN (Proto-Western-Negritic) *BI* "war"
Bantu *puta* "wound"
Soko, Kele *bita* "war"
Mande *so-so* "talon"
Mangbetu **bi* "wound"
PCS (Proto-Central-Sudanic) *b*i*, *b*e* "to open"
PCS **fu* "kill" ?[8]
<u>AXE</u> Sumerian *bar* "to split" (axe)

BA, PA* "arm", "split", "axe"** ***-r

PWS *bà* "two" (*búá* ,*(ba)* "hand, arm") **Sumerian** *bal* "axe, hatchet"
Kongo *pasa* "to split", Lolo, Ngala, Poto *epasu* "to chip"
Bantu *band, pac* "to split"
"Bantu" *pel', pale* "knife" (120), *beri* "knife" (190), *balω* "knife" (5a)
Bola, Sarar *u-mban* "knife"
Bulanda *mban* "knife"
Mande *paka* "knife"

8 Campbell-Dunn (2009: 40, 46)

Mangbetu *mba* "knife"
PCS **mba* "cut, knife"

AXE **Sumerian** *dur*$_{10}$ "axe"

TU "strike" (head) **-r**

PWS *tu* "knock, strike", Grebo *tunu* "push", Temne *t.un* "strike"
PWN *THUBH* "pierce" **Sumerian** *udug*$_{2}$, *(utug*$_{2}$*)* "weapon"
Bantu *tuŋga* "to pierce"
Bangi *etomba* "pierce" **Sumerian** *nú(g)* "kill" (sub voc)
Bantu *tuut* "to strike"
"Holoholo" *tuut* "to strike"
Mande *su* "corpse", Susu *tu* "dead man"
Mangbetu *adu* "detach"

[Linear A has *TUNU* "strike" written on an axe]. [Maori has *toki* "axe"][*u-* is prefix or reduplication].
[The *–r* may be "tie", axes were bound with rope]. [Final *–g* may be ergative, or *ka* "cut"].[9]

The *t-p* in the word *ḥtp* may represent a serial verb. That is, a verb composed of two different roots with the same or similar meaning. If so then *ḥ*-is a prefix. The *t-* could be PWS *ta, tu* "knock, strike." So the act of sacrifice (hunting, slaughter) in the ancient mind was articulated something like: "strike-cut, knock-pierce, hit-kill."

I would argue that both phonemes derive from an ancient word for "hand" expressed as **tV* or **kV* (where *V* represents "any vowel"). The earliest human languages were not lexically rich—which is why tone, inflection and agglutination were key to expressing human thought. A look into the Yorùbá word *da* (t > d) will provide insight for our endeavor.

> *da* "the primary idea of this verb is "to make or create" [it's signification is modified by the noun with which it is used in combination]

This term can be seen in various forms, all with a common theme:

dà	"to cast, fuse, pour, betray a trust, to slip a child under the arm from the back"[10]
de	"reach"
da	"give"
dì	"tie, bind, unite, freeze, congeal, coagulate, dense"
di	"become" [(<*da*) *d'* "become" (also "until")]
dẹ	"to set a trap; ensnare; tempt; bait; allure; decoy; hunt")
dè	"bind, put in shackles, screw together, rivet, tie, put in fetters"
dé	"come, arrive, reach, cover"
dabọ̀	"cease"
edi	"the act of tying or binding" (also *èbo, àbo*)

9 Campbell-Dunn (2009: 24)
10 *ore mi da mi* "My friend betrays me" (lit. - pours me out); "to be acceptable as a sacrifice (because the blood of the sacrifice is poured on the ground) "to become"; When it is used in this sense it is changed into *di* for the sake of euphony before e, i, o and all consonants.

The earliest verbs derived from nouns (Campbell-Dunn 2009a). In this case the word for "hand" is the same word used to denote "actions done with the hand." It is the "hand" that "gives, binds, unites, pours, strikes, tears, stops, covers, throws, places, uncovers, reaches, casts, allures, etc." In other words, it is our "hands" that "bring things into being" (makes or creates). This same root is present in Egyptian (some with a pre- or suffix):

di	"to give, to grant, to allow, to cause, to make"
rdi	"put, place, appoint, send (letter), cause, permit, grant"
dw	"give, place, put, implant (obstacle), strike (blow), cause"
wdi	"throw, shoot (an arrow), commit (offense), deal (harm, injury)
wdi	"present (*m3ˁt*), give (balm, make up)
diw	"gift"
ḏ3	"spread righteousness"
ḏ3	"to show forth, to reveal (uncover), to extend, to carry over"

The form *di* in Egyptian derives from *iri/ri* "to do, to act" (ciLubà *eela* "to do, act") [r/l/d is a common sound shift]. The Kongo-Saharan rule states: [l+i>di] and this phenomenon is witnessed throughout the Egyptian language. This word for "hand" became the sign for the phonetic sound /d/ in Egyptian represented by the hand hieroglyphic sign: *da =/d/* →  [D46]. Variants of this root became lexicalized in the grammar and it is the source of the "causative" morpheme in human languages (losing its status as a full word). The /d/ comes from /t/ (d > t); the /t/ further morphs into /s/ and this is where we get the causative [s] in Egyptian (ciLubà *esha*). This [s] can also derive from the palatalization of /k/ (PWS **ku, *ka* "hand, to cause").[11] We can see the lexicalized form in Yorùbá in the following names.

Ògún d' èjì	Ògúndèjì	"Ògún becomes two"
Ògún d' ìran	Ògúndundìran	"Ògún becomes hereditary"[12]

The *d'* signals "become" and derives from the word for hand. This *d'* "causative"[13] can also be seen in the name Modúpẹ́:

Modúpẹ́	Mo dúpẹ́	"I give thanks"

The word *dúpẹ́* is actually two words: *da ọpẹ́* "give thanks/gratitude." That same *d'(a,i,u)* is present in Yorùbá words like *dibò* "cast lots" (*lit.* hand-throw lots); *ṣẹbọ* "offering/sacrifice" (*lit.* hand-give present /hand-cut kill); *àtẹ̀pa* "to crush" (*lit.* hand-strike crush). The Niger-Kongo word for "hand" possibly merged (by homonymy) with the word *àṣẹ* "the power to make things happen" in the Yorùbá language (commonly said after prayers). This same root is behind the meaning of the deity *Èṣú* in the Ifà tradition; it relates to *raw power*, the power to create or make something happen (authority, from the "head"). This was expressed traditionally with the use of the hands and this, I argue, is the source of the /t/ morpheme in the word *ḥtp* in the

11 Bender (Heine & Nurse, 2000: 283) gives examples of the **k* causative suffix in Nilo-Saharan languages. Thus, for example, **ṣ'ú:k* 'to drive (animals)' [PNS **ṣu* 'to lead off, start off' plus old **k* causative]; Kunama *sugune-* to cultivate, to raise animals [back-formation from noun, consisting of stem plus **n* noun suffix]; Kanuri *sùk* 'to drive (many things), to speed horse'; Dongolawi *šu:g* 'to drive along, off'. The suffix *-ika* "to set" also appears in some Bantu words as a causative suffix (Torrend, 1891: 278).

12 Oduyoye (2001: 13)

13 Yoruba also has a *mu* causative (<PWS *búá* "arm")

ancient Egyptian language, which we also saw interchanged with /d/: *dp.ty* "offering meal."[14]

The following glosses demonstrate the many sound changes in Kongo-Saharan (and Sumerian) languages for the word for hand (Campbell-Dunn, 2009b). This list will also demonstrate various applications of the root as a result of the many conceptualizations of what can be done with the hand.

PWS *lá* "make"
PNC **la* "hand"[15]

<u>HAND</u> **Sumerian** *šu...bar* "to release"

TU "hand", "take"
BA "hand", "put away", "not"
-r

PWS *nú* "hand" < *tu
PWS *nú* "five", Yorùbá *m-a-nu* "five", *a-nu* "five" (passim)
PWS *tú* "to take" (action of hand)
PWS *búá* "arm" etc
PWN *BA* "put away" **Sumerian** *šu* "hand"
PWN *TU* "pound", *TU* "shoot" (actions of hand)
Bantu *tiud* "take"
Swahili *twaa* "take"
Mande *bolo-ba* "hand", *bolo-muso* "left hand"
Mangbetu *ebara* "to flatten", "to extend" (hand)
Mangbetu *osua* "to chase clapping the hands", *ésu* "to pierce", "to pour" (action of hand)

***T = š** ***U = u** ***B = b** ***A = a**

This is seen not only in Latin *ne,* but Greek *mē* "not" < PWS *ma,* itself from **mba, ba* "hand" (Sumerian *bara* "vetitive"). Yorùbá has *m-a-nu* "hand" <*mba* + **ntu* (Sumerian *šu* "hand" <**tu*). [Words for "to be" are often related to words for "eat", "hand", PWS *búá*]

<u>DATIVE</u> **Sumerian** *na* "give"

NA "give"

PWS *ná* "to give"
PWS *ta* "to give"
Bantu *nink* "to give"
"Bantu" *na, nyana, ana* (134), *na* (248), *nts'a* (74) "give"
Kongo *vana* "give"
Mande *ni* "give"
Mangbetu *nio* "nourishment"
[Compare PWS *ta* "hand"= "give"].

***N = n** ***A = a**

14 The root derives from *dp(t)* "to taste, bite, experience, little fish, bread, fish, piece of meat, kidney, loin."

15 The form *la* derives from *da* "hand" which itself has an alternate form *ta(u)* "hand" (t > d > l).

<u>DO</u> **Sumerian** *du, dudu* "do"

DU, TU "do" **[R]**

PWS *tum* "to work"
PWS *lù* "to weave, *lu, (du)* "to plant"
PWN *TU (TUN)* "to build"
PWN *DUT* "to pull"
Bantu *ding* "to do", *gid* "to make"
Bantu *di,t* "to work"
Mangbetu *adu* "to finish"
ES Barea *doko, toko* "one" (hand, task)
PCS *d*o* "to work, cultivate"

***T = d** ***U = u** **or** ***D = d** *** U = u**

<u>AGENT, ERGATIVE</u> **Sumerian** *e* "do, make"

KA, KIA "hand", "make"

PWS *ka* "hand"
PWS *kia*(>*ke*) "make" (action of hand) **Sumerian** a_3"make"
PWN *KA, (KYA)* "hand"
Bantu *kít* "do", *gid* "act"
Bantu *gi* "go", *(k)a*"go"
Bantu *ka* "hand"
Bantu *ka* "hand"
Mande *kè* "to make"
Mangbetu *âki* "to cause"

***K = #** ***IA = e** ***K = #** ***A = a**

In the case of *ḥtp* in Egyptian, the term can broken-down as: *ḥ*- prefix, *t*- causative and -*p*- root. In various ways this term has taken on different morphologies and each has gone through their own mutations to form slight semantic variants. The ciLubà-Bantu language provides us with plenty of examples to demonstrate that *t-p* is the root and *ḥ*- (<*k*-) is the prefix.

Table 4: *ḥtp* in ciLubà

Vocabulary Roots: *t-p* : *k-t-p* : *c-t-p* (Egyptian *t-p* : *ḥ-t-p*)	**Meaning**
-tàpa	(a) "knock, slug, inflict, jolt, click"; "lend help, give a helping (hand)" (b) beat the game, winning (victorious) [*kutàpa makàsà* "win the game"] (c) "gnaw, invade" 1. *Bundu kutùtàpa* we have been ashamed 2. *Nzala mmintàpa* I very hungry (d) hurt (e) injury, death, kill, slay
kutàpa nsàlu	"Tattoo" (from the root meaning to cut/slice)
citàpilu	"stroke"
citàpilu cimwe	"at once, one stroke, all of a sudden, in one fell swoop"
kutàpa dipi	"give a blow, slap"
mutàpi	person who strikes, cuts or kills
mutàpi wa nkòsolu	person (who) coughed
ntàpa *-à/-a ntàpa kùbìdì*	"double-edged"
ntàpilu	(A) how to hit, hurt, etc.. *kutàpa muntu ntàpilu munga* give a second blow to someone (B) typography
ntàpu	(A) tattoo instrument (B) chisel
-tàpangana	"harm each other, kill each other"
-tàpika	"to hurt"
-tàpila	"to begin, to start"
kutàpila muntu kîyi/kêyi	"say something to someone"
kutàpila Mukaj	"woo a woman"
Tàpulula	"reprint, republish by improving"
Tàpa	"hatch, appear to break, to develop"
ditàpa (<-tapa)	
Tàpila	"start, begin to"
tàpa [3]	"successful strikes/blows, (to be) chastised"
Tàpa [4]	(A) draw (a liquid) (B) harvest (palm beer, honey ...)
Tàpulula	available separately, divided into different categories, sorting, classifying
ciTapa	(A) rack (B) grill on which meat is to smudge, or cassava to dry
ciTàpu	"small knife for tattooing"; "chisel or masonry"
	(b) "used to transfer"; "in the hair ornament or through the nasal septum"
tàpula	"tapping off, empty by tapping" (*kutàpula nshima* "transfer "nshima" from pan to plate or bowl"); "extract"

As we can see the *t-p* root can be used to express different ideas all derived from a common theme of "cutting, hitting, piercing and striking." Early writing was done by cutting, slicing or scratching into wood or stone. It is easy to see how this root can be used for terms like: *ntàpilu* "typography" (*lit.* hand-cut/chisel); *citàpilu* "stroke"; *Tàpulula* "reprint, republish by improving"; *kutàpa nsàlu* "tattoo." Even the word "write" in English belongs to a root which means "to cut."

> **Write**: O.E. *writan* "to score, outline, draw the figure of," later "to set down in writing" (class I strong verb; past tense *wrat*, pp. *writen*), from P.Gmc. **writanan* "tear, scratch" (cf. O.Fris. *writa* "to write," O.S. *writan* "to tear, scratch, write," O.N. *rita* "write, scratch, outline," O.H.G. *rizan* "to write, scratch, tear," Ger. *reißen* "to tear, pull, tug, sketch, draw, design"), outside connections doubtful. Words for "write" in most I.E languages originally mean "carve, scratch, cut" (cf. L. *scribere*, Gk. *grapho*, Skt. *rikh-*); a few originally meant "paint" (cf. Goth. *meljan*, O.C.S. *pisati*, and most of the modern Slavic cognates).[16]

As we can see the *t-p* root has developed, semantically, in many different directions over a long period of time. While one direction veered towards *writing*, another direction veered towards *sacrifice*, *war* and *destruction*. **Table 5** below presents some proposed cognates and related terms for this *t-p* root in *ḥtp*.

Table 5

Egyptian	Yorùbá	ciLubà
wpw "cut off, cut up, open" *sf* "cut up, cut off, cut" *sfsf* "slaughter, massacre" (sound mutation? t > s; p > f); *sf<u>t</u>* / *sft* "slaughter" (animals), "make sacrifice, cut up"; *sf<u>t</u>t* "a slaughter offering" *sf<u>t</u>* "knife, sword"[7]	*bọ̀* "to insert, pierce, boil, seethe, coddle or parboil"; *be* "cut, peel"; *bu* "to bake under ashes, broil, to dive, to hide under the sand"[8] *pa* "to kill, murder, cut, scrub"	*-pempa* "cut the tip ends, cut, cut to equal lengths"; *-bèya* "raze, shave" *-fwà* "kill" (PWS **fu* "kill") *-seba* "weeding, cut grass"
dbḥt ḥtp "funerary meal, altar, offering table"; *ḥtp.t* offering table"; *sḥtpj* "censer" (an incense pot)	*pẹpẹ* "altar" (reduplication?)	*ciTapa* (reflex)[9] (A) rack (B) grill on which meat is to smudge, or cassava to dry
ii m ḥtp, m ḥtp "come in peace, arrive safely"	*àtibọ̀* "coming; returning"	
	ìpadàbõ, dé, bõ "arrive"; *bọ̀* "to return, to arrive, to travel towards"	
ḥtp "harmful action, evil plot"	*tipá-tipá* "with force, violently"	*-tàpa* "knock, slug, inflict, jolt, click"; "lend help, give a helping (hand)"
	ijaba "trouble" (*ija* "strife, war, fight, quarrel")	*-shipa* ≋ *-shipaya, -shibaya, -shibeya, -shebeya* "to kill, to murder"

16 See OED: http://www.etymonline.com/index.php?allowed_in_frame=0&search=write&searchmode=none

ḥtp "blood"[10]		*pitula* "to fall to the ground, spill"; "to cause death"; "twist" Syn.: *-shipa, -bùtula*
	tàpá "to kick"; *tàpási* "to kick against, to spurn"	*citàpilu* "kick, blow, shot, hit"
ḥtp "the blessed dead"; "God." (one appeals to the ancestors and the Creator to come to one's defense. In other words, to provide protection from life's ills) *ibw* "refuge, shelter" [other may be relevant terms] *stp* "cut up (animal), butcher, cut off (limbs)" *stp* "be dismembered, ruined" *stp ꜣḫ* "protect, carry out protection" *stp sꜣ* "to extend (protection) *stp sꜣ* "protect, do escort duty, protector, bodyguard" *stp* "noble, outstanding"	*adábòboni* "defender, succourer, protector, guardian" (*idābò, idābobo* "refuge, protection")	*dikùba* "protection, care"; *-kùba* "to protect" *kutàpa* "cut down"
	adẹpa "an appropriate salutation to one going out hunting"	
	dipò "to succeed" (to win) (<*pa* "win a game")	*-tàpa* "beat the game, winning" (victorious) [*kutàpa makàsà* "win the game"]
	àtẹpa "that which is crushed to death."	

There is a particular set of definitions that I think may be applicable to the ancient Egyptian. Given the Yorùbá *dipò* "to succeed" (to win) (<*pa* "win a game") and ciLubà *-tàpa* "beat the game, winning" (victorious) [*kutàpa makàsà* "win the game"], maybe *ḥtp*, on some level, could also be interpreted as "to win, be victorious, to succeed/success, to accomplish something." If so, this may have some interpretive value for the name *jmn ḥtp* (Amenhotep) which could mean "Amen is victorious" (*Imana-a-tàpa*); or "Amen is our Champion." More investigation is needed here, but I think this is a good start.

The ciLuba word *mutàpi* "person who strikes, cuts, or kills" informs us of the meaning of the great leader of the Monomotapa kingdom in Zimbabwe. The king was named *Mwene Mutapa* which would mean something like "Champion of War" or "Victorious King" (*mwene* "lord, ruler, owner"). You could not be a king in antiquity without being a fiery warrior (think Tshaka Zulu of the Amazulus). This is why in Yorubaland, kings would often take on the name of *Ṣàngŏ* "The god of lightening" to denote that the king is the kind of military leader that "strikes like lightening and booms like thunder"; the same with the name *Ògún*.

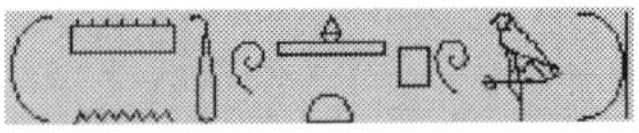

mnṯw-ḥtpw "the victorious one?"

MUNTU KATAPA (Mentuhotep III of the XI Dynasty in the *Nganga/ Sangoma* (*ꜥnḫ*) pose of a master.

ḥtp as Peace

It is interesting that *ḥtp* can at once derive from a root that means "to kill" and another that means "peace." That is because *ḥtp* "offering" and *ḥtp* "peace" (for all intents and purposes) are homonyms (or at least homographs). In this aspect of *ḥtp* "peace," we are presented with these other connotations: "contentment, good pleasure, set (of the sun), to dwell, mercy, favor"; *hptyt* "calm, mild, clement." It appears that there is an underlying theme dealing with "settling/ going down, falling, rest, tranquility, peace of mind." This can be seen in this Egyptian reflex: *ḥtp* "fall out (of hair)."

In regards to the settling/going down aspect of this term, the Yorùbá language has the following reflexes[17]*dúbu* "to lie across or athwart" (diagonally, crossways); *ṣubú* "fall down" (d > s); *dubulẹ̀* "to lie down"; *Dọbalẹ* "to prostrate on the ground (*le/ile* "ground"); to lie flat on the stomach (with arms close to side)." It is a form of salutation: *ìdọbalẹ* "prostration, falling on the face; a mark of respect to a superior by a male"; *idabu* "breadth, latitude, that which is placed athwart." It appears that the root is **bu* and over time the phenomenon of metathesis has occurred (b-t > t-b).[18]

<u>LIE</u>	**Sumerian** *uš*$_2$"lie"
BU "stoop"	**-š**

PWS *bù* "bow down" etc, Tschi *butu-w* "turn upside down", Ga *butu* "to overthrow"
PWN *BU, BUT* "bow down, crouch"
Bantu *but* "lie down"
Mande *suru* "to stoop"
Mangbetu *bu* "corpse"
Mangbetu *buru*"on the ground"
Mangbetu *buburu* "under"
Mangbetu *pu*"ashes"
PCS **pu, *bu* "earth, dust"
PCS **vuru* "earth, mud"
ES Dongola, Kenuzi *bu* "lie down"
CS Mangbutu *ubu, abu* "to sleep", Efe *abuabu* "sleep", Lese *(k)abu* "sleep" (Greenberg)

17 Remember that the root is *t-p/d-b* with *ḥ*- yielding *zero for* C_1 in the triconsonantal form.
18 There is evidence of early free-word-order in early human languages. See Campbell-Dunn (2009a).

[Initial loss of *b,* common in Sumerian :*t* > *š*]

***B = #** ***U = u** ***T =š** *** U = u ?**[19]

As we can see from the data above, the same word used for "crouch, stoop and lie down" is the same word used for "sleep." It is from the "calm" nature of "sleep" (rest) from which we derive the meaning of *ḥtp* "peace." This is reflected in Egyptian *ḥtp* "rest (in tomb), assume (titulary)." The following reflexes in ciLubà provide additional applications for this root.

Table 6: ciLubà reflexes

Vocabulary	Meaning
-pòòka(with-*ka* suffix)	"fall, break, drop by maturity date or old age (fruits [off of a tree], flowers, teeth ...)"
-dìpuka	"out all of a sudden, fall" (*-dipuu* "rush out")
kùdimaja ≋ kùdimika	"make flat, bed, sleeping"
-kùdimana	"to be lying flat" [<*-kùdimana Panjshir*> to lie belly to the ground]
-tàbala	"laying down with eyes open"
budìpòpe(a)	"modesty, quiet, recollection, selected"
dipoa	"to keep quiet, quiet, collect (one's thoughts), meditate"
bupwekèle (a)	"humility, modesty"
lubàcì [t + i > ci] (possible metathesis: tb > bt> baci)	"appeasement, calm, serenity, silence, peace, attention."
⟨-à/-a lubàcì⟩	"careful"
ḥtp **"to dwell"**	
-sòmba	"sit, sitting, to cause to sit, live", resting, retiring,
cisòmbelu	"living room, residence"
lusòmbèlà	"where you sit"
-sòmbela (verbe intransitif Appl.) *-sòmba*[1], *-sòmba*[2]	"talk, discuss"
Nsòmbelu ≋ nsòmbedi [l+i>di], *nsòmbèlà,*	"how to behave, conduct" (home training?)
-sòmbesha, sòmbelela	"companionship, conversation, chat"

The Egyptian word *ḥtp* meaning "peace" derives from a root meaning to "sit, rest, fall." The concept of "peace" is a secondary meaning derived through a linguistic process called *metaphoric extension.* This process of metaphoric extension has expanded this root into other conceptual areas. This can be seen in the Egyptian word *tpj* "he who is *ON*, over, above someone or something" (a leader, chief, captain) (Budge 828b). To "sit" you must sit "ON" something; you must be "above it." Something must be "below" you in order to "fall down, sit, rest, etc."

A procedure I like to do is to see if a dialectical variation can be found where the primary phonemes have morphed into known sound changes which reinforce these concepts. From here I then compare them in other related languages. In Egyptian *ḥtp*[20] is also rendered as *ḥdb* "sit (on), seat (oneself), stop off" (t>d, p>b) (Mark Vygus, 2012: p2006). The Kalenjiin language (Nilo-Saharan) will provide us with some cognate terms that will reinforce that *ḥtp* and *tpj* are

19 Campbell-Dunn (2009b: 85)

20 See also (M.E.) *ḥtp* = "be gracious, contented, pleased, be at peace, become calm, go to rest, etc." (Faulkner, p190)

from the same root.

tep-sii [21] "place on top of" or "cause to be placed on top" or "cause to sit down/enthrone."
tepii or *tep* "stay"
tep-ooten "sit down"
ti emptoon "sit down" (Coptic)
tep-een ng'echereet "sit on throne, chair" (Sambu, 2008: 8)

teb "rest, stay, sit."
tembes "relax/rest"[22]

In Africa, titles for kingship are often connected with being "seated" on a throne. This is why the Q1 𓊨 "throne" determinative is associated with someone in power. In Ghana the Asantehene is king because he has been "enstooled" as such and has gone through a "seating ceremony." Even in the English language we say things like, "He is currently in the SEAT of power." This would explain why we have the following entries for *ḥtp* in the Egyptian lexicon:

ḥtpj = "furniture" [Wb III S 196]
ḥtp = "occupy a seat" (Mark Vygus, 2012: p1532)

As stated previously, in order to "sit" one must be above something and it is this logic for which Egyptian *tpj* "he who is on, upon, above something/someone" (a leader, chief, captain) and Kalenjiin *tep-sii* "cause to sit down, caused to be placed on top, to be seated/enthroned" derive.

The /*ḥ*/ sound in Egyptian often corresponds to Kongo-Saharan /k/. This was demonstrated with ciLuba above and is also true for Kalenjiin in regards to the word *ḥtp* (<*ktp*). In Kalenjiin we have the following:

ketepi "to sit"
ketepi ng'echereet "to sit on the stool"[23] (Sambu, 2008: 208)

As we can see here, all morphemes are accounted for and both renderings stand on both legs (form and meaning): *ḥtp* (*ḥ-t-p*) = *ketepi* (*k-t-p*). The Kalenjiin, Yoruba and ciLuba languages reinforce the notion that *t-p* is the root of *ḥtp* and the /*ḥ*-/ sound is a prefix.

Conclusion

We have taken a long/round-a-bout journey to discover that the word *ḥtp* in the ancient Egyptian language derives from different sources for which two of them, ironically, mean the same thing: "hands." It is with the gifts of our hands, the fruits of our labor, that we show our appreciation to the spirits and ancestors that direct our lives and work on our behalf on the other side. It is this communion with the spirit-world that ensures our success in this world. It is within this dimension of offerings—and its rootedness in the linguistic core that can denote a successful battle—that I believe it is worth expanding the notion of *ḥtp* to include the meanings of "success, winning, to champion, and to be victorious." This is the aim and purpose of sacrifice: to gain favor from the spirit world; to gain victory over circumstances; to open

21 The *-sii* suffix in Kalenjiin is a causative and cognate with Egyptian's *s-* causative prefix and ciLuba's causative suffix *-esha*.
22 Kalenjin – English Online Dictionary: http://africanlanguages.com/kalenjin/
23 This is in reference to an elder couple's marriage ceremony in which they basically renew their vows.

spiritual channels for which blessings can flow so that we may obtain the necessary life-tools to succeed and to be able to create in an atmosphere that enables us to tower over the one thousand and one challenges here on earth in our pursuit for perfection.

(Table Footnotes)

1 A linguistic case of *sense evolution*.

2 One could argue that an *ḥtp* is an "appeal" to the spirits to work on one's behalf. It is a motion to take action in a particular direction. In the case of a *Votive Offering*, the devotee would be proposing something in return for spiritual favor.

3 *Boon* means "gain, benefit, bonus, advantage, windfall, help."

4 As mentioned earlier, this -b- root becomes -f- in Egyptian: *fꜣy* "raise, lift up, carry, support, weigh, present, deliver (taxes, tribute); *fꜣỉ* (alternate form); *fꜣy.t* "reward."

5 Most words for authority in world languages derive from words for "head" or "great/big." *mꜣꜥ* "leader" in Egyptian derives from *ꜥꜣ* (*/ꜣ/* can also equal /l/) "leader, chief workman, commander, Elder, Noble, Master" (ciLuba *mwadi* "chief, leader, president"; l + i>di), but also *ꜥꜣ* "great (of size), many, greatly, greatness, influence"; "distinguished, genteel, noble"; *ꜥꜣ.t* "a great thing"; *ꜥꜣỉ* "big, important, heavy, sublime, plentiful, much, rich, senior." *m-* is a prefix.

6 A linguistic case of *sense evolution*. The word "thanks" derives from a root that means "thought, gratitude, to think, to feel." It is this sense of "thought, thoughtfulness, gratitude and feeling" for which one gives "thanks" and shows appreciation.

7 The final *-ṯ* can be a suffix. There is a rendering *sfḫ* "to cut up" that may support this theory.

8 This term is included to highlight that offerings were often "burnt offerings." So to "bake, boil, broil" is relevant in this sense.

9 This is a case here of secularization. This root represents anything that holds or cooks food (i.e., Eg. *ḥtp* "basket, offering table")

10 This is an important aspect of animal sacrifice. See Neimark (1993) for a prospectus. The term could read "to pour blood" or "to draw blood" (actions of the hand).

TYING KNOTTY ROPES AS A WAY OF KNOWING IN ANCIENT EGYPTIAN

Introduction

This essay attempts to make a connection between the concept of "knowing" in the Ancient Egyptian language and a symbol used as a determinative [Gardiner sign V12 𓍼] in a few words for "knowing" in the *mdw nṯr* (hieroglyphic) writing script. The V12 sign is that of a twisted or folded piece of rope or string and it carries the consonant values of either *ʿrḳ, fḫ,* or *šfdw*. There are other variations of rope signs in the *mdw nṯr*—such as 𓍱 [V6] with the consonant sound values of *g, sš, sšr*, and 𓍢 [V1] with the consonant sound values of *šnt, št* and the numeric value of 100—that are also used in words for "knowing" in Egyptian.

In some ancient societies, before the phenomenon of writing as we know it became the primary means of record keeping, people used to communicate and keep records of major events and lineages through the tying of *knotty ropes*. Each knot, tied in a specific manner, represented important events. People had to be trained to be able to "tie" and "untie" knotty ropes and their symbolic messages. This means that there was a class of specialists who were able to "code" and "decode" the language of knotty ropes and those that could do it were considered to be persons who "knew" the underlying spirit of the society, and in many cases the world at large.

This notion of "tying" and "untying" knotty ropes—by way of metaphoric extension—became synonymous with having "knowledge" in general. A person of great knowledge is someone who is able to *codify* (systematize) accumulated data, as well as *decode* (unravel) life's mysteries. It is these symbolic characteristics of knowing that I argue are fossilized in many of the terms in the Egyptian *mdw nṯr* script for "knowing."

To help us make the connection between tying knotty ropes, knowledge and wisdom, we will first examine this phenomenon as experienced through the culture of the people of Kongo in central Africa. From there we will make some cultural, as well as linguistic connections between the Kongo-Bantu and ancient Egyptian languages that will lend support to the notion that this idea and association was fossilized in the *mdw nṯr* script in a few words for "knowing."

Tying Knotty Ropes

To get a better understanding of this phenomenon under examination, we will now look into the practices of the people of the Bantu-Kongo as told to us by the eminent scholar of Bantu culture, Dr. Kimbwandende kia Bunseki Fu-Kiau of Kongo. Our summary information for this section primarily comes from his principle works *Mbongi: An African Traditional Institution* (2007: 27-32), *African Cosmology of the Bantu Kongo: Principles of Life & Living* (Tying the Spiritual Knot) (2001), *Self-Healing Power and Therapy: Old Teachings from Africa* (2003) and many of his public lectures.

In the rural areas of the Kongo cultural regions of central Africa, there is a common "shelter" called an *Mbôngi* that one finds in the center of almost every village. The construction is the physical living symbol of one of the most important African political institutions. The word *mbôngi* in Kikongo derives from the root *bônga* meaning "to take, to seize, to accept, to make one's possession, to own." It can be understood by the phrase *bônga yeko* which means "to take a responsibility" and is associated with a person or institute that is supposed to lighten the weight and relieve its members of socio-economic problems of the community. From *bônga* we get *bôngi* or *M'bôngi* "the one who takes (responsibilities, etc.). One could argue that Yeshua (Jesus) the Christ could be considered an *M'bôngi* as he, according to the Biblical text, took on the 'burdens' of mankind in order to relieve them of its weight.

The *Mbôngi* is the location where all issues of public interest, be they social, political or economic, are publically and openly discussed. One could consider the *Mbôngi* the "White House" of the village. Like any governmental institution, there are important roles and positions that are held by prominent people of the community. Space will not allow us to go through each of these positions, but one of these roles is important for our current discourse.

In each *Mbôngi* there is a clandestine group of individuals who have diverse responsibilities for the security of the community and its members. These individuals are called *N'swâmi* or *Muswâmi* "authorities operating in secret." The job of the *N'swâmi* is to "spy" or collect information around the *Mbôngi* and its constitution. Within this group one finds watchmen, investigators, detectives as well as spies. Each of these 'agents' have the responsibility of counseling the community and its leaders of Mbongi.

The watchmen known as *N'kengi* have an integral role to play in the *Mbôngi*. These individuals are responsible for the behavior among the community members of the *Mbôngi*. Out of this group of *N'swami* is *N'langi* (<*langa* "to inquire") who is an individual whose greatest responsibility it is to keep a close watch on the boundaries of the community lands and to report to the council of the *Mbôngi* any possible violations. The *N'langi* has to know precisely who does what and where on the lands as well as in the community forests and waters. As such he knows almost everything going on in savannahs as well as in the forests of the community. It is his job to "know" things. As a result of his knowledge he is also known as *Me-Zûmbu*, the authority responsible for all questions related to community real estate. The *Me-Zûmbu* is often also a skillful hunter or a great collector of *Nsamba* (a vegetal milk from the palm-tree).

Each of these occupations requires him to have continual contact with all community properties (water, lands and forests). Fu-Kiau informs us that:

> Me-Zumbu, the authority responsible for community land property, is a **wise** and **intelligent** individual. He knows the name of almost all animals, plants, birds, snakes, mushrooms, fruits, and fish found in community lands. He can distinguish them by their voices, cries, motions or by their footprints left on their pathway. He tells stories about them or imitates their voices and acts." (Fu-Kiau, 2007: 28) (emphasis mine)

This emphasis on *wisdom* and *intelligence* will become very important for us later on in our discourse.

Another position within the *N'swâmi* is that of *N'suni* (<*suna* "to observe closely").[1] He is a skillful individual who can follow or detect through footprints or *lôbula* (directional information provided by the grass touched by a passer-by) of any person suspected of causing disorders within the community. In other words, this person is a tracker. Beside the *N'suni* is the *N'neki* who are the "spiers." The *N'neki*, however, gathers information outside of the community to report back to the *Mbôngi*. Outside of their jobs of collecting information outside of the *Mbôngi*, they are also petty travelers and traders which make them ideal for gathering information beyond their borders.

In the recent past one could see an individual in the *Mbôngi* called *Na Makolo* or *Makolo* in short. This person was the keeper of "knotted information," i.e., symbolically written information (an archivist). Anytime a decision related to numbers of days, weeks, or months, price setting or dates, the *Mbôngi* asked the *Na Makolo* to *braid a cord* and *tie the number of knots* which would represent the date set up for the next debate or meeting. Contracts (*mandaka/ngwizani*), often in alliance with other *Mbôngi*, were also "knotted" with the braided rope.

The *Na Makolo* was obliged to know in detail the meaning symbolized by each knot. He was also required to decipher or decode the message symbolized by each knot on his knotty ropes. This was a common practice among the *Ngânga-nkondi*, the specialists in "problem hammering" among the Kongo.[2] If cuts (on wooden sticks) or knots on braided ropes are made to represent recorded events, contracts or numbers related to the community well-being, these sticks or ropes are given to the *Ne-Masamuna* (<*samuna* "to speak out") who is the community griot (information and record recaller) or deposited in *nzo-n'kisi* (also called *nzo-bakulu*) "the house of the ancestors" (i.e., "the house of history"; *bakulu* "ancestors," *kikulu* "history"). If these sticks or ropes were given to the *Ne Mabika* (<*bika* "to announce"), the announcer would recall these coded messages at an *Mbôngi* meeting which he would then cut or untie a knot at the end of every day or week according to the unity of the agreement until the last knot which represents the symbolic date of accord was reached.

In summary, the *Mbôngi* is a political institution where community concerns are addressed and community problems are resolved. There are many positions and roles that various community members play in the functioning of the community *Mbôngi*. Various members of the *N'swami* information gathering committee collect information on foreign relations, ecological conditions, boundary security, social relations and economic matters to the community *mbongi*. Decisions are made on next steps forward and these decisions are then archived by the *Na Makolo* who makes special knots on braided ropes. In future meetings these knotty ropes are then untied (deciphered) and read to the public as contracts and other dates have been completed and/or have passed.

These knotty ropes become a source of knowledge and history and becomes the symbol of not only records of one's past, but of the connection between community members, living or

1 Kikongo *suna* "to observe" may be related to Egyptian *ṯnḥ* "to observe, to look" by way of palatalization of /k/ > /ṯ/. More investigation is needed here.

2 The *nganga* (Egyptian *ʿnḫ* reduplicated) is a specialist or master healer or wise man. An *nkondi* is a "problem-nailing-recorder-object" which is often a wooden carved statue by which knotted ropes are "hammered" with nails when contracts or agreements are rendered between parties.

dead (*n'singa dikânda* "the biogenetic rope of the family or clan").[3] In other words, the rope is a symbol of one's family tree. When community waves are 'shaken' (by social disruptions of any kind), community leadership calls for a reconciliation meeting (*mu kangulula)* to "tie again" (to *re-ligar*/religion) the community relationships. Once these broken relationships are reestablished, then the community bio-spiritual rope will be strengthened and the balance between man, God and nature will be restored. The rope becomes a symbol of gathering, unity and information and we will see how this all comes together throughout our discourse.

Knotting: An Ancient Tradition

Using knotted ropes as a means to record history and thoughts is not an exclusive practice of the Kongo. In South America there is a type of rope writing called *quipu,* a Quechua word for "knot." Quipus (or *khipus*), sometimes called *talking knots*, were recording devices historically used in the region of Andean South America by the Inka people. A *quipu* usually consisted of colored, spun, and plied thread or strings from llama or alpaca hair. It could also be made of cotton cords. The cords contained numeric and other values encoded by knots in a base ten positional system. Quipus might have just a few or up to 2,000 cords. Archaeological evidence has shown that systems similar to the *quipu* were in use in the Andean region from c. 3000 BC. They subsequently played a key part in the administration of *Tahuantinsuyu*, the empire controlled by the Incan ethnic group, which flourished across the Andes from c. 1450 to 1532 AD. After the Spanish invasions of South America, this form of 'writing' fell out of disuse to be replaced by European forms of writing.[4] Spanish observers of Inka record keeping at the time of the conquest stated that this knotted-cord device was also used for recording narrative events of the past.

The Chinese also had knot-writing. According to *The Complete Book of Chinese Knotting: A Compendium of Techniques and Variations* (2007: 9) by Lydia Chen, early knots (outside of typical constructional use) became developed for communication purposes, to exchange letters and numbers and to record events. An early scholar by the name of Zhou Yi commented about the trigrams of the *Yi Jing* or *Book of Changes,* which is the oldest of the Chinese classic texts. It describes an ancient system of cosmology and philosophy that is at the heart of Chinese cultural beliefs. He informs us that "in prehistoric times, events were recorded by tying knots; in later ages, books were used for this." In the second century CE, the Han scholar Zhen Suen wrote in his book *Yi Zu,* "Big events were recorded with complicated knots, and small events with simple knots." The chapter on "Tufan," in the *New Tang Chronicle,* reveals that due to a lack of writing, the ancient Chinese tied cords to make agreements like we saw among

3 The Dogon of Mali has a similar conceptualization as that expressed in the Kongo. Griaule & Dieterlen in their book *The Pale Fox (*1986: 452-453), in discussing Nommo's ark, informs us about these symbolic ropes which are punctuated by a series of knots called "knots of the great Amma" or "knots that do not break the rope (of the ancestors) of the womb (i.e., of the generations). Each knot in itself represents the ark, and the rope represents the descent of the ark. It is the quasi-unbreakable, close tie established by Amma (God) between the ancestors and the descendants. So just like in the Kongo, the rope is symbolically used to represent that agent that binds the living community to its ancestors. On page 452 of Griaule & Dieterlen (1986) is a picture of the ropes and its knots (fig. 154). It resembles very closely the double-helix found in DNA. Were the Dogon aware of DNA and its shape? DNA is literally the "rope" that binds all human-beings to their ancestors (the biogenetic rope: *n'singa dikanda*). The double-helix shape of DNA was discovered in 1953 by James Watson and Francis Crick. *The Pale Fox*, however, was written in 1965. Griaule died in 1956 and had been studying the Dogon since 1935.

4 See http://en.wikipedia.org/wiki/Quipu (retrieved March 8, 2013). See also the *Khipu Database Project* http://khipukamayuq.fas.harvard.edu/ (retrieved April 21, 2013).

the Bantu-Kongo. Special government officials were available to explain the knots. Family genealogies were also recorded by knotting ropes. Danny Boey, in his article "Jia Pu (Chinese Genealogical Record): An Introduction," informs us that "Prior to the invention of writing, Chinese genealogical information was recorded by tying knots on ropes."[5]

In other parts of Africa knotted writing was also used. Jean-Pierre Hallet and Alex Pelle, in their book *Pygmy Kitabu* (1973: 211), provides images of the Efe-Batwa people of the Ituri forest of Zaire and their elaborate knotted ropes in the Avogbaya village. As noted by Hallet & Pelle, "Pygmy women say that these knotted cords are 'writing', but cannot explain how the system works."

Hermel Hermstein, in his book *Black Sumer: The African Origins of Civilisation* (2012: 114), provides an example of such a practice among the Ijebu people of Nigeria who are closely related to the Yorùbá. He informs us that:

> ... the so-called aroko of the Jebu people living in the hinterland of Lagos consists of a reed cord, two red knots, four cowrie shells and a piece of fruit-peel (...). This is a letter a very sick person might send to a friend and it reads: 'The illness is getting worse, our only hope rests with God'. *Literacy and the Politics of Writing* by Albertine Gaur, Intellect Books 2003 p32

In other words, the cord, the knots, fruit peel and the additional cowrie shells all had meaning and each item (with a specific configuration) was attached to a vocabulary term.[6] This form of communication is based on the *rebus* principle. The most common example usually given in literature to explain the rebus principle is presented below:

> To name one custom, the Yorùbá of Africa have always used pebbles as indexical symbols; these could even assume homophonic value (an important component of some phonetic writing), whereby one word sounds identical to another with a different meaning. To arrange a tryst[7], for example, A Yorùbá man would leave six pebbles for a woman to find – Yorùbá *efa*, or 'six', also means 'attracted'. If the woman was willing, she left eight pebbles as an answer: Yorùbá *eyo*, or 'eight', also means 'agreed'. *History of Writing* by Steven Roger Fischer, Reaktion Books 2001 p21

As we can see, this is an ancient practice and the rebus principle, in actuality, is the basis of *mdw nṯr* and its 'apparent' polysemy as it regards certain hieroglyphic signs. This will be the focus of our next section as we now have the context by which to further speculate in regards to the association of "knotting ropes" and "knowing" in the ancient Egyptian hieroglyphic writing script.

Knowing in Egyptian

A fundamental question to address in this discussion is, "What do Africans mean and understand when they say that they *know* something?" This is a question of *epistemology*, that is to say, the branch of philosophy concerned with the nature and scope of *knowledge*. It questions what knowledge is, how it is acquired, and the possible extent to which a given subject or entity can be known. To my knowledge, the ancient Egyptians did not have a one-to-one matching term for epistemology. But I would argue that the focus of one's intellectual efforts, in Egyptian

5 See full article at http://genealogy.about.com/library/authors/ucboey1a.htm (retreived March 8, 2013).

6 We will further explore the Yorùbá form of writing called *aroko* later on in our discourse.

7 A *tryst* is a "rendezvous" or a "meeting."

times, was to become a *sage* or *wise* person: in other words, a philosopher concerned with *truth* and r*eality* (Egyptian *mꜣꜥ.t*; ciLuba *bulelela*).

It is argued by Obenga (1992: 54-57) and Bernal (2006: 262-267) that the Greek word *sophos*, from where we get the word *philosophy* (lover of wisdom), derives from the ancient Egyptian word *sbꜣ* "wise, intelligent, judicious, teach, teaching, school, guidance, direction, to tend, and surveying instrument" (Coptic *sbō* "teaching, education, intelligence"; *sabe* "wise, intelligent, judicious"; *sbui* "disciple, apprentice"; *seb* "intelligent, cunning"; *sbo* "to learn, teach"). In Bambara we have *subaa* "initiated teacher and student, one versed in hidden knowledge only known to initiates"[8]; Bantu *ziba, libe, dziba, zhiba, seba*, etc., "knowledge, wisdom, diviner, physician, one who knows, is an expert in, teach, have intercourse, converse with the spirits, priest, magus" (see Wanger, 1935: 202-204); Egyptian *sꜣbwt* "intelligence, knowledge, cleverness, wisdom, ability."[9] The earliest definition for a sage or philosopher can be found in the ancient Egyptian text of Antef of the 12th Dynasty. The German Egyptologist Hellmut Brunner translates a passage of Antef's writings and he informs us that a philosopher (*sbꜣ*) is one:

> ...whose heart is informed about these things which would be otherwise ignored, the one who is clear-sighted when he is deep into a problem, the one who is moderate in his actions, who **penetrates ancient writings**, who is sensible enough to **unravel complications**, who is really **wise**, who instructed his own heart, who stays awake at night as he looks for the right paths, who surpasses what he accomplished yesterday, who is wiser than a sage, who brought himself to wisdom, who asks for advice and sees to it that he is asked for advice. (from the inscription of Antef, 12th Dynasty; Middle Kingdom, 11th and 12th dynasties 2052-1778 BCE) (emphasis mine)

I bolded some key terms and phrases above as they are pertinent to our discussion. As stated earlier, *wisdom* is the key objective of ancient Egyptian intellectual pursuits and this is reinforced in the *Instructions of Antef*. In the Egyptian language we have the following related terms: *sꜣi* (Coptic *sŏi*) "to be wise, prudent"; "to be satisfied" (The pyramid Texts, 551, etc.); *sꜣ.t* "prudence, wisdom" (Sinouche, B 48); *sꜣꜣ* "wise man"; ciLuba *disòòlakaja* "discernment, prudence" (<*sòòlakaja* "clarity, space, separate, judge, analyze").

A person is wise, in part (according to the Egyptians), because one *penetrates ancient writings*. In the ancient writings are wise instructions and knowledge on all things known up to that time. Knowledge is not simply a collection of facts, but it is a system of thought with its own internal logic and epistemology. Knowledge is the means by which we direct our behavior to achieve our ends most efficiently and successfully. So it is important that one have access to and a desire for books with the intent of penetrating its pages in an attempt to gain information that can help one tower over life's one thousand and one challenges.

8 See Amadou Hampâté Bâ's article "The Living Tradition" in J. Ki-Zerbo (Ed.). (1981). *UNESCO General History of Africa, Vol. 1: Methodology and African Prehistory*. Heinneman Educational Books, Ltd. London. p. 191.

9 The *s-b* form of the word in Niger-Congo is a loan. The word in Egyptian, *sbꜣ*, consists of two morphemes: the *s-* causative prefix + the root (*b-l*). The *s-* causative is fossilized in this Egyptian term since predynastic times. The root can be seen in PAA **bar* "see, know"; Semitic **bVrVy-* "see, examine" (Akkadian: *barû*; Arabic: *bry* [-i-]; Jibbali: *ebrer*); Egyptian *br* "see" (Coptic: **belle* 'blind': Bhr *belle*, Shd *bolle*); C.Chadic **bur-* "think, consider, remember" (Gude: *bəərə* 1, *bəərə-tə* 2 [Hs]; Gudu: *bùr-ínà* 2 [Kr N390]); Saho-Afar: **bar-* "learn" (Afar (Danakil): *bar*); Lower E.Cushitic **bar-* "learn" (Somali: *baro*); Dahalo (Sanye): *ḅar-* "know." In Cushitic the causative is *-is* and it is suffixed to the root: Cushitic *baris*. In ciLuba-Bantu it is *–pàdisha* "teach, learn, instruct, view, introduce." The causative in ciLuba is *-ish* and is suffixed in Bantu. This is a clue that the *s-b* form is a loan. To "teach" in the African mind is to "cause" (*s-*, *-is*, *-ish*) + "to see, know" (**bVr*).

A true philosopher is someone who has a critical awareness of the intellectual and cognitive traditions of both his or her own society and that of other societies. For the ancient Egyptians, wisdom was to be found in the mysteries of nature, but also in the accumulated wisdom of one's ancestors as laid out in books. The ancient Egyptian language has several important words as it regards writing. A few can be seen in the table below.

sš "to write, to write down, to inscribe" [verb]	
sš "write, inscribe, paint, draw" [verb]	
šw "blank papyrus roll" [noun]	
sš / sḫ3 "writing" [noun]	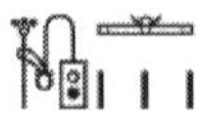

Notice that the words *sš* and *šw* have the V12  tied or folded rope determinative. When I first looked at these words I had to ask myself, "Why would a tied piece of rope be used as a determinative for writing?" At first I thought that the rope symbol may be used to reinforce the consonant sound values of the leading glyphs. This is common in Egyptian writing. For instance, the word *3d*  means "alligator" (ciLuba *ng-Andu, g-andu*, (Lingala: *gando, nkando*) "alligator"). As we can see, the determinative is that of an actual alligator and that glyph has the *3d* sound value. So when we see the alligator determinative in a word like *3d*(*w*) 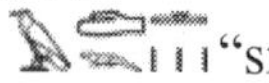"smoothing down (of clay)?, unkneaded clay," we know the determinative has nothing to do with the actual word itself other than to reinforce the sound value of the leading glyphs.

The V12  tied rope determinative cannot be used in this manner because it carries three different sound values: *ʿrḳ, fḫ,* or *šfdw*. None of these values are *sš* or *šw*. So what could they possibly mean here? It would have to be some other conceptual modality at play in this instance. I began to investigate further and went about to look for words where the V12 sign is either the lead glyph or was isolated by itself with a meaning relevant to writing. I instead found the following terms:

šfdw "papyrus roll, register, calligraphy?" [noun]	
šfdw "book" [noun]	
fḫ loosen, release [verb transitive]	

The word *šfdw* has the meanings of "papyrus roll, register, calligraphy and book." Calligraphy is another word, essentially, for "writing" and now it makes sense as a determinative for the words *sš* and *šw*. *Šfdw* is also a word for "book" and the V12 glyph is also used in *fḫ* "loosen, release." The ancient Egyptians didn't have books bound like we see today, but instead had papyrus rolls (*šfdw*) that one had to "tie" and "untie" with string or rope as we see in this determinative: .We see this determinative used in the word for "scribe," *sš* . This determinative is primarily used to represent "abstraction" or an "idea." It is fitting for a sign that represents intellectual thought and ideas. Could this sign be hinting to an idea of "tying" and "untying" knotty ropes as a way to convey the notion of "unraveling" complications? It appears that this may be the case. We will revisit this question a little later on.

The question now becomes, "is the rope sign connected with books and writings simply because they share the same phonetic values?" Or is there a deeper meaning that is commonly being overlooked? I decided to see if more could be gained if I looked at other terms with a different rope hieroglyph determinative or leading glyph. I record the following:

sšrw "linen" [noun - clo.]	𓍱
šs "rope" [noun]	𓍱
šs (plant ?, tree ?) [noun - flora]	𓍱𓈖𓈒𓏥
šs "cord, rope" [noun]	𓍱𓈖𓍢

As noted earlier, the 𓍱 [V6] glyph has the consonant sound values of *g, sš, sšr*, and 𓍢 [V1] carries the consonant sound values of *šnt, št* and the numeric value of 100. What I am finding consistently in these terms associated with ropes is the phoneme /*š*/. It is my contention that this is the primary root and all of the other phonemes are grammatical features or other words agglutinated to the root. It would be consistent with the following (from Campbell-Dunn, 2009b):

<u>(TIE), CORD</u> **Sumerian** *sa* "cord"

<u>KA</u> "tie"

PWS *ka* "hand"[10]
PWS *ta* "hand",
Proto-Akanic *-*sã* "tie up" (< **ta*).
Ewe (Rongier) *sà* "tie a knot".
Nupe *so* "to tie" (action of hand)
Yorùbá *so* "to tie"
Soko *isoso* "to tie"
Kele *bosamba* "hand"
Mande *koro* "cotton"
Mangbetu *akoko* "plier"
ES Alur, Shilluk, Luo *tol* "cord", Berta *tsera* "cord"
Afro-Asiatic : Hausa (1) *sak?a,* Angas (1) *sak,* Musgu (7) *sasaka* "weave"

[Linear A has *sa* "flax"]

***T = s** ***A = a**

Relevant to this discussion may be the Yorùbá terms: *kókó, ìdìjú, ìsolù* "knot," (v) *dìsoṣe kókó* "tie" and *koríko* "grass." It's possible that the rope was also named after the material used to make ropes.

---

10 Many verbs derive from nouns. In this case, the word for "hand" also came to denote "the action of the hand."

sšr nsw / šs nsw "royal linen" [noun - clo.] PB *-*cua* "grass" PB *-*koka* (short) "grass" [k-k > s-s ?]	
šnp "reed mat" [noun - furn.]	
sš "cut" (linen, papyrus) [verb]	
sš "linen pad, (linen covered splint ?)" [noun]	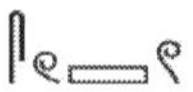
swt "scirpus reed, emblem of Upper Egypt" [noun - flora][1]	

A possible connection could be made by the observation that the same name for "rope" is the same name for the Goddess of writing: *sš3t*.

sš3t "tow rope" [noun - boat]	
sš3t "Seshat" [noun - div.]	
sš3t "Seshat" [noun - div.]	

Seshat (literally, "the female scribe") was the goddess of all forms of writing and notation, including record keeping, accounting and census taking as well as being *'she who is foremost in the house of books'*: the patroness of temple libraries and other collections of texts (Wilkinson, 2003: 166).

It could be a coincidence that a word for a type of "rope" is the same word for the goddess of writing and record keeping. However, other terms seem to reinforce this correlation. The word *štyw / štw* "to tie, bind" has a variant *sti* "attach, knot, tie up, *inscribe*." We also have *ṯy* "band, tie"; *ṯy* "learned man, the scribe" (Budge, 852b). Again, scribing/writing appears to have an association with tying/binding.

By way of extension of the concrete and action themes, we see this same -*šs*- root expanded to encompass the ideas of "knowledge and wisdom." We note the following:

šs3/sš3 "know, to be wise, be aware, clever"	
šs3/sš3 "to be skilled, experienced, cleverness"	
šs3/sš3 "to take counsel, mediate, consider, think about"	
šs3w "healing arts, medicine, pathology, diagnosis"	

As we can see here, the goddess *sš3.t* is in reality the personification of "knowledge, wisdom, excellence, and cleverness (*šs3/sš3*)" as can be found in writings or books (*sš/šw*). The word *šs3/sš3* "to be skilled, experienced, cleverness," even has a rope determinative  which doesn't carry the *šs* sound value. So we see an association with *reading* and *wisdom* and it is my contention that there was a correlation between *tying* and *untying* ropes as a metaphor for being able to *write* (tie) and *research* (untie; "unravel complications") information.

Each kind of word history in some manner reveals a portion of the human history of the speakers of the language. Some words that are occurring today in daughter languages will prove to have the same meanings, unchanged, since ancient times. In contrast, the semantic derivations of words often reveal older, now lost, ways of thinking or former ways of thinking and doing things. Christopher Ehret, in his article "Language and History" (in *African Languages: An Introduction* ed. by Bernd Heine & Derek Nurse (2000)), provides such an example of this phenomenon in language.

> [I]n the proto-Mashariki language, a daughter language of proto-Bantu spoken near the great Western Rift valleys of Africa at around 1000 BC, a new word for "to plant (crops)" came into use. Because this verb previously in Bantu history meant 'to split', its new meaning tells us that the proto-Mashariki people continued to emphasize an earlier rainforest-based agricultural technique, protective of fragile soils, of cutting a narrow slit in the ground and planting a new cutting from a yam or other similar food plant in the slit. In the next several centuries after 1000 BC, the settlement of Mashariki people in lands with richer soils, along with changes in their crops led to the complete loss of this practice among their descendants. Without this piece of linguistic testimony, an insight about earlier agricultural technology might have been lost. (Heine & Nurse, 2000: 278)

This is essentially what we argue is going here in the Egyptian hieroglyphs. Before the written word took precedence in human societies, the oral tradition was the primary way to record and transmit information. Noting the limitations of human memory, human beings found other ways in which to record major events and one of those ways was the tying of ropes made from various materials. The words for "tying" and "rope" were transferred to the process of "writing" at the time of the development of the hieroglyphic script. We continue to do things like this today. In the future, while I am in the community promoting this book, I will more than likely say something like, "I wrote this book because....," knowing full well that I technically did not "write" anything with my hands: I *typed* everything out. No one writes books anymore, literally, however we still use the terminology for the process although the means by which we record and print thoughts have now changed (via *typing*).

The Egyptian Origin of the Logos?

There appears to be further support for our correlation between tying ropes and knowledge with other examples of terms that utilize the V12  determinative. As stated earlier, the V12 determinative also has a sound value of *ˁrḳ*. This consonant combination can represent many ideas in Egyptian (as a result of homonymy), but the ones that are relevant to this discussion can be found in the following table:

ˁrḳ "to know, to be wise"	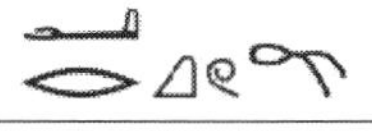
ˁrḳ "to swear, to abjure, to renounce"	

ꜥrḳ "to be versed, to be adept"	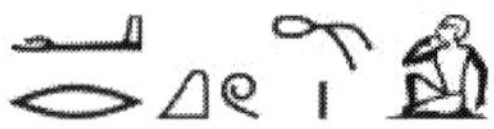
ꜥrḳ "basket, weapon case"	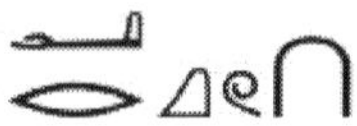
ꜥrḳ "bind" (Kalenjiin *kwaar* "tie with a rope an animal, rope, teether")	
ꜥrḳ "swear (an oath)"	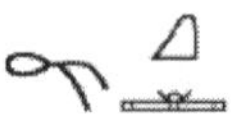
ꜥrḳ "to complete" [verb] (Kikongo *kalunga* "to complete"; Kalenjiin *rook* "be complete, concluded, finish")	
ꜥrḳ "the end, limit"	
ꜥrḳ "know, perceive, gain full knowledge of, be wise, skilled (in)"	

As we can see here, the rope signs are used in conjunction with the themes of "knowledge" and "wisdom." However, it could be argued that the association is simply present because the determinative carries the sound value of ꜥrḳ. One would have to explain then why the Z7 glyph is also attached to the word ꜥrḳ 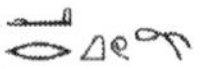 when it doesn't carry this sound value. The Z7 "coil"  glyph is a variant of the V1  hieroglyph, but this glyph carries the sound value of /*w*/. I argue that this is the case because of the etymology of the word ꜥrḳ, for which I further argue is also the origin of the Greek word *logos*. A quick search on Wikipedia for the definition of *logos* provides us with the following:

> Logos (pron.: /ˈloʊɡɒs/, UK /ˈlɒɡɒs/, or US /ˈloʊɡoʊs/; Greek: λόγος, from λέγω *lego* "I say") is an important term in philosophy, psychology, rhetoric, and religion. Originally a word meaning "a ground", "a plea", "an opinion", "an expectation", "word," "speech," "account," "reason," it became a technical term in philosophy, beginning with Heraclitus (ca. 535–475 BC), who used the term for a principle of order and knowledge.

These definitions may in fact be derived from two separate linguistic roots in Africa. The confusion comes as a result of believing that Indo-European is an isolated language family with no parent of its own. As a result, researchers do not look into African languages for loans into IE or inherited lexemes. The *online etymological dictionary (OED)* provides the following data for our word *logos*:

> *logos* (n.): 1580s, *Logos*, "the divine Word, second person of the Christian Trinity," from Gk. *logos* "word, speech, discourse," also "reason," from PIE root **leg*- "to collect" (with derivatives meaning "to speak," on notion of "to pick out words;" see *lecture* (n.)); used by Neo-Platonists in various metaphysical and theological senses and picked up by New Testament writers. Other English formations from logos include *logolatry* "worship of words, unreasonable regard for words or verbal truth" (1810 in Coleridge); *logomania* (1870); *logophobia* (1923).

> *logic* (n.): mid-14c., "branch of philosophy that treats of forms of thinking," from O.Fr. *logique* (13c.), from L. (ars) *logica*, from Gk. *logike* (techne) "reasoning (art)," from fem. of *logikos* "pertaining to speaking or reasoning," from logos "reason, idea, word" (see *logos*). Meaning "logical argumentation" is from c.1600.
>
> *logarithm* (n.): 1610s, Mod.L. *logarithmus*, coined by Scottish mathematician John Napier (1550-1617), lit. "ratio-number," from Gk. *logos* "proportion, ratio, word" (see *logos*) + *arithmos* "number" (see arithmetic).
>
> *lecture* (n.): late 14c., "action of reading, that which is read," from Medieval Latin *lectura* "a reading, lecture," from Latin *lectus*, pp. of *legere* "to read," originally "to gather, collect, pick out, choose" (cf. election), from PIE **leg-* "**to pick together, gather, collect**" (cf. Greek *legein* "to say, tell, speak, declare," originally, in Homer, "to pick out, select, collect, enumerate;" *lexis* "speech, diction;" *logos* "word, speech, thought, account;" Latin *lignum* "wood, firewood," literally "that which is gathered"). To read is to "pick out words." Meaning "action of reading (a lesson) aloud" is from 1520s. That of "a discourse on a given subject before an audience for purposes of instruction" is from 1530s.

The OED traces the word to PIE **leg* "to collect, pick together, gather." The fact that they trace this word to PIE, but can give only one branch of IE to inherit the term, doesn't instill confidence for me that it is in fact an IE word. It is highly possible that the Greeks 'borrowed' this term from the Egyptians when the Greek philosophers went into Egypt to study *sbꜣ* (philosophy). Or it is an inherited term from its African parents which possessed the most expansive senses.

PIE **leg* is cognate with Egyptian *ꜥrḳ* "bind, basket, weapon case"; "ribbon" (Meeks: AL 780762); "corner, twist, bend, angle" (Meeks: AL 780760); ciLuba *lunga* "bind, connect"; "something folding on itself and join, make ends meet"; "weaving, making chains" (*diLunga, llunga, lungakaja; ndungabilema* "person who repairs, mender, repairer, doctor, shoemaker, therapist, mechanic"). Other forms in ciLuba-Bantu are reflected as: *-luka* "braiding, weaving" (der. *-lukila*); *banda* "braid"; *ciluka* "network"; *joba* "braid"; *lukakaja* "form projects, plan"; *-lukakanangana* "be interspersed, be complex"; *-lukulula* "repair" (e.g., "a thread"); *nunga* "braid."[11]

Heraclitus used *logos* in the sense of "order and knowledge" because he was probably familiar with the concept of "tying knotty ropes" and knowledge being the *collection* and *synthesis* (binding/tying) of data as expressed in the hieroglyphic language. Knowledge in its simplest explanation is a *collection* of facts that have been arranged in logical *order* for better comprehension (ciLuba *-lukila meeji* "combine, to make combinations in the mind/spirit, look for a combination"). In modern times, information is primarily arranged in books. In more ancient times, before writing was the norm, it was more so arranged in speech (oral tradition).[12]

Assuming that our correlation is correct—that the concepts of tying and binding are equated with knowledge and wisdom—there may be an association between the Egyptian terms *ṯs* "to tie, to bind*"* and *ṯs* "speech, utterance, phrase, sentence, maxim." Notice that both the word for "to tie/bind" and "speech" has the coiled rope determinative. Tying is a form of writing and writing and speech are seen as synonymous. Campbell-Dunn (2009b) equates writing and speech and provides the following examples:

---

11 CiLuba suffixes include the following: -ij, -ik, -am, -at, -in, -ibu, -ish, -ulul, -il, -angan, -akaj, -akan, -akanangan.

12 See Amadou Hampâté Bâ's article titled "The Living Tradition" in UNESCO's *General History of Africa Vol. I: Methodology and African Prehistory*, ed. J. Ki-Zerbo, 1981, pp. 166-205.

WRITE **Sumerian** *sar, šar* "to write"

TA "write" **-r**

Sumerian *šar*$_8$ "to explain"

PWS *tá* "to tell, to relate", Atjulo *ta* "to speak", *ta-re* "to speak", *o-ta-re* "word"
PWN *THÁLA, THÁLI* "stone" (used to scratch, write)
Kele *ta* "write" Bangi, Poto, Ngombe *sono* "write"[13]
Mande *sèbè* "to write", *sèbè-ri kè* "to write"
Mangbetu *te* "hand"

***T = s** ***A = a** ***R = r**

We are reaffirmed in our association of the idea of the "word" and the concept of "binding" when we examine the Egyptian term *brṯ*  "contract, covenant, agreement, treaty." The determinative is of a seated man with his hand to his mouth signaling that this term has something to do with *speech* (or actions of the mouth). In other words, this expression—as depicted by the hieroglyphs—denotes that a man's word is his "bond." It appears that contracts were made by word of mouth and not detailed contracts on paper like we see today (at least initially as there are other forms of this word with the book determinative). We will explore other correlations between ropes, knowledge and speech a little later on in our discourse.

The word *lecture*, as stated by the OED, derives from Latin *lectus/legere* "to read," originally "to gather, collect, pick out, choose" (cf. *election*), from PIE **leg-* "to pick together, gather, collect." To convey this sense of "gathering" or "collecting," the Africans simply used the sign of a rope  which was a tool for bundling and uniting things together (especially papyrus scrolls). This is verified in Egyptian with the word *šdi*  "to exact, to collect," and *ink*  "unite, gather together, collect, embrace." Both of these terms use a rope/cord determinative to convey the idea of collecting (PIE **leg* "gather, collect"). It is with this knowledge that I argue PIE **leg* should also mean "to bind, unite."

The extended meanings of "knowledge" and "wisdom" is a result of this fact gathering (**leg*) process. To **leg/ʿrḳ/lunga* is to "study or research" and this is why we use this root in English to mean "the study of" in such words as socio*logy* "the study of social systems," dermato*logy* "the study of skin," epistemo*logy* "the study of knowledge."[14] We were introduced earlier to a term in the Kikongo language called *n'langi* (<*langa* "to inquire") "one who inquires, an investigator" as it regards the Bantu-Kongo concept of *Mbôngi* (Fu-Kiau, 2007: 28). This is from the same root as Egyptian *ʿrḳ* "to be versed, to be adept, know, perceive, gain full knowledge of, be wise, skilled (in)." This root is reflected in ciLuba as *longelu* "school."

Keeping in mind homonymy and paronymy, one root of the word *ʿrḳ* is *ʿr* and it has two primary associations. The first is *ʿr*  "a pen made from a simple reed, used as a paintbrush by scribes." The second is *ʿrt* 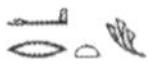 "a scroll of papyrus or leather." There is also *ʿrw* 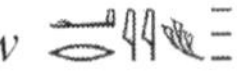 "read brush, rush brush." Another variation is *ʿrt*  "papyrus roll, scroll, list, tablet" and it has our rope/cord/string determinatives seen throughout our other examples. Both of these are tools to record information and by adding the *-ḳ* suffix we get abstractions like "know, be wise, to be versed, to be adept, perceive, be skilled in, and gain full knowledge of." Here the association is being made between the "tools" for recording information (i.e., "a rope, a pen and a pad") and the results of the constant interaction with these tools in conjunction (i.e.,

---

13 We should note that in Kikongo *kusona* is to "engrave," *masono* "engraving" (-> writing, art) and *nsoneki* "the engraver."

14 *log, logo, ology* "word, study, say, speech, reason" > catalog, prologue, dialogue, zoology, logo." http://www.prefixsuffix.com/rootsearch.php?navblks=1011000

"knowledge and wisdom").

We mentioned earlier the Yorùbá writing system called *arókọ̀,* and as we can see it has the same consonant root as our Egyptian term *ꜥrḳ* and PIE **leg*. It is a writing system that uses ropes and cowry shells to communicate (often between priests and kings). However, *arókọ̀*, as a non-verbal communicative system, can utilize many objects as vehicles for meaning among the Yorùbá people. As noted by M. S. Abdullahi-Idiagbon in his 2010 article titled, "African Traditional Semiotics: The Example of 'Ar'oko' in Yorùbá Tradition," *arókọ̀* can take any of the following forms:

- The skin of a monkey;
- Comb;
- Cap or ring (known with a person);
- Whisker;
- Fruits like pineapple, orange, etc.;
- 'Esuru' (a specie of potato) and a left over, of un-hatched incubated eggs of a fowl;
- A specific number of items;
- A feather;
- Putting a stone in a junction/cross road;
- A stick of broom;
- Cam

The choice of a particular form will strictly depend on the intent of the sender as well as his relationship with the receiver. *Arókọ̀* could be sent by a traditional ruler or chief, Ifa priest, *ogboni* cult member, hunter, artisan or an ordinary person to a counterpart or any other person, group or body. Although many objects can be used in the art of *arókọ̀*, it is my contention that its expanded modalities are rooted in the process of tying "knotty" ropes.

Theophile Obenga discusses the Yorùbá knot writing and argues that *arókọ̀* is a genuine writing script in his book, *L'Afrique dans l'Antiquité* (1973). In this work (pp. 360-378) he informs the reader about its most ancient uses as an actual writing script utilizing a series of cowry shell combinations to represent words and phonemes. As it regards the meaning of the word *arókọ̀*, Obenga provides the following explanation (my translation):

> The fuller and [more] primitive form of *arókọ̀* is *aparoko*: the latter can be broken down as follows:
>
> *a*: "the act of" (here that particle changes the verb name)
> *pa*: "things attached, linked together (interconnected)"
> *rọ̀*: "thought" (*rirọ̀* "reflection")
> *kọ*: "write"
>
> Thus, *aparoko ->parókọ̀ -> arókọ̀* signifies "the act of writing thoughts by joining each other," "the act of thinking and writing what you think"; or, in a word, "writing." Similarly, the Yorùbá say that dictation is "the writing that someone pronounces or states in a loud voice": *apeko* (*a*: "the act of", *pe*: "call, say aloud", *ko*: "write"). This here is tangible information that allows us to consider the strings in the Yorùbá cowries as a true graphic system (*arókọ̀*). (Obenga, 1973: 369-370).

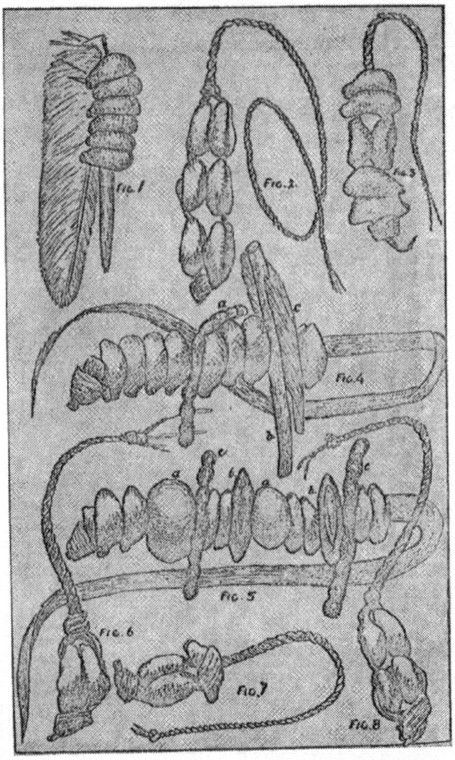

LETTRES ÉCRITES EN *arókò* (YORUBA).

The Egyptian language, however, may help to support Obenga's analysis. A drawback to his investigation of *arókọ̀* is that he didn't check to see if the term was present in related languages and if this term is analyzable in those languages as well.

As we have seen, words meaning "rope, tie, bind" also have "speech" and "writing" associations. For instance, in Yorùbá we have the word *okùn* "rope" (something that is *ohun* "a thing made"). We also have *ohùn* "speech" (Egyptian *ẖnw* "utterance, words, speech"; *hn* "speech, utterance, shouting, cheering"; *ḥn* "to command, to regulate"; *ḥnw* "commands, orders, ordinances"; *hni* "to play music"; *hnw* "musicians"); *ìhìn* "news"; *ìhìn rere* "good news"; *ròhìn* "relate news"; *ohùn* "tone, tune."[15] We note also in Egyptian *ẖnr* "restraint, lock up, shut out"; *ẖnd* "bend (wood), twist together (flower stems)"; *ẖndwt* "female weavers."

When we look at the following words in Yorùbá, as compared to *arókọ̀*, we get a better understanding of the underlying theme.

àròká	"the business of a news monger"
àròkán	"reflection on painful experience"
àròsọ	"a rumor; a whim; an invented tale"
aroye	"explanation, complaint, excuse, debate, reasoning, plea, expostulation, advocacy, allegation, controversy, loquaciousness"
arọ̀kin	"one who tells ancient stories as a profession" (=>*ròhìn* "relate news")

15 There is a dialectical interchange in Yoruba between /k/ and /h/. We see this in the word *kiní* "things" (inanimate objects) and in the Oyo/Ibadan dialects, *ohun* "things." This same interchange exists in the ancient Egyptian language as well.

aròhìn "advertiser, story-teller, newsmonger, narrator"

Notice that these terms have to deal with "speech" in some form or fashion and may be related to this notion of "tying" (concatenating words together in coherent sentences). The *-r-* morpheme, however, derives from *rò* "to tell; relate; conceive; imagine; meditate; think; deeply; stir up; plague; trouble"; *ró* "to sound; place in erect position; excite"; *ọ̀rọ̀/ede* "speech"; *òrò* "speech, word" (Egyptian *r* "word, mouth, language, speech"; *rw/r3w* "words, sayings, utterances"); *èrò* "thought" (< *ró* "think").

Obenga argues that the *-kọ* ending means "write." As we argue here "writing" and "tying" are conceptualized the same in African languages. Thus, in Yorùbá we have: *kókó* "knot"; *koríko* "grass" (often used for ropes); *dìsọ̀e kókó* "tie" (v); *kọkọ́wéhàntúrú* "write"; *kọ, kọwe* "write"; *akọwe* "writer"; *ikọwe, iwe* "writing." One has to ponder that if the Yorùbá are not known (historically) for "writing" (in the modern sense), what did the term now used for "writing" mean originally? In light of our larger discussion, the following Yoruba terms may shed some light:

kó	"to gather, to take a large quantity, to rob, forage"
kò	"to hold together, draw together, darn"
kò	"to sew, tack, baste, seam, stitch"
kojo	"to collect, aggregate"
kojopo	"amass, gather together"
kọ	"to emit flashes of light (as lighting); be vivid, yell, crow, to call to one at a distance, write, make marks upon, tattoo."

The latter word *-kọ* emerges from within a greater theme of "making signs" or "to signal." One can make a signal either by "calling, emitting flashes of light, or making a mark on something." I would argue that tying ropes would fit into this theme as the knots (and shells) were used to make "signs" in *arókọ̀* and these signs were used for communication." In other words, these "signs" were a different form of "speech."

It is obvious when comparing the Yorùbá and Egyptian forms that these words consist of monosyllabic roots which appear to have free-word-order forms. Again, we argue that paronymy may be at play here with words for "rope" and "speech." Compare Yorùbá *paroko* (the communication method which utilizes ropes and cowries) with Egyptian *ḥr*  "a rope" (aboard a ship); *ḥbr*  "rope"; *ẖr*  "to say" (=> *k3* "to say"; *g3*  "to chant, sing, whistle"); *ẖrp*  "to direct (a project), control (affairs)"; *ẖrpt*  "guide rope." As we can see there is a little bit of metathesis going on here.

As noted by Obenga, the *-p-* in *aparoko* is *pa* "things attached, linked together." In Egyptian this would be (p>b):

ꜥb "unite" [verb]	
ꜥb "join, unite, present" [verb]	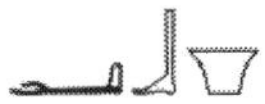
ꜥb / ꜥb3 "unite, present (to)" [verb intransitive]	
iꜥb "join, unite" [verb intransitive]	

iꜥb "assemble" (of persons) [verb]	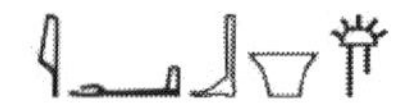

The /*ẖ*/ or /*ḥ*/ morpheme may be the actual word for rope:

ꜥḥ "rope" [noun]	
hy "secure a rope, tie up (boat)" [verb]	
ꜥḳ3 (a rope) [noun] (see also *k3w* "a ship's rope")	
ẖ3/ẖ3y "measuring cord, scales pendulum, plumb line"	
ng3 "cord, constraining noose"	

A word like *hp* "rope"  may actually be two words "bounded/threaded rope." A variant form of this term would be *nḥb*  "unite, link together, equip (with)." We mentioned previously a form of knot/rope writing in South America called *quipu* "talking knots" that may be of interest here (Egyptian *hp* "rope" *h-p*; *quipu* "talking knots" *q-p*).[16] The triconsonantal form of the Yorùbá p-r-k root may be represented in such words as (by way of metathesis):

3bẖ "link (arms), festive movement of arms"	
3bẖ "unite, mix, mingle"	

Therefore, the Yorùbá words *arókọ̀*, *aparoko*, *àròká* may all just be variants of Egyptian *ꜥrḳ* "bind, to swear, to renounce, to know, to be versed, adept" and *ẖrp* "to direct," *ẖrpt* "guide rope."

Knots, Wisdom and the Akan

This association between "ropes, knots" and "wisdom" can be seen in the Akan adinkra symbol known as *Nyansa Po* "Wisdom Knot."

Nyansapo "wisdom knot"; symbol of wisdom, ingenuity, intelligence and patience

The Akans revere the *nyansapo* symbol which endorses the understanding that wisdom solves all problems. This symbol conveys the idea that "a wise person has the capacity to choose the best means to attain a goal. Being wise implies broad knowledge, learning and experience, and

16 This could be chance coincidence or a global root. More investigation needed here.

the ability to apply such faculties to practical ends."[17]

Logos and the Word

The idea of *logos* being associated with "the word" stems from a separate etymological root than PIE **leg* "to collect." Although the word *logos* has come to mean *word* in the Greek language, it wasn't used in the grammatical sense as they used the word *lexis* for common usage. However, both *logos* and *lexis* derive from the same root. This root is the suffix in the word *dialogue* which is composed of *dia* ("through, across") + *log* ("word") which connotes a conversation (exchange of words) between two or more people.

We see the association between *logos* and the *word* in the Egyptian terms *ʿrḳ* "to swear, to abjure, to renounce"; *ʿrḳ* "swear (an oath)." These are semantically specific connotations of the word, but they both deal with a form or manner of speaking. In ciLuba we have *-langa* ≈ *-nanga* "exhort, to lecture, instruct"; *mulangu* ≈ *munangù* "exhortation, admonition, lesson"; *nanga* "exhort, teach, to lecture" (Kikongo *nongo* "proverbs").

These definitions are more in alignment with the Greek from where we get the term *lecture,* which deals with the exchange of knowledge and wisdom via word of mouth. Reflexes can be seen in Proto-Bantu (Meeussen) as *-*dong* -L "speak"; *-*dong* -H "insult, lie"; *-*ded*- "speak" (Egyptian *ḏd* "statement, words, to command, to assert, to maintain, say, speak, speak of, utter (speech), recite (spell), tell (to), expect, mean (something)"); *-*jad*- L "speak, give advice"; *-*jad*- L "spread"; *-*búud*- "speak, talk, say, tell"; *-*búud-id*- "speak, announce"; *-*búud*- "ask (question)" (Egyptian *bdḥ* "ask for, beg, to request, pray for, petitions"): (l>d).

This notion of "speech," as it pertains to knowledge, is also present in another Egyptian term *rn* "name." Calling upon a name, in the African sense, is to invoke the spirit of the thing when its name is uttered. This is why in the ancient Egyptian texts there was an emphasis on the initiates knowing the names of the *nṯrw;* as to know the name of something is to have the ability to control it through *ḥk3* "words of power, bewitch, spell" (<*k3* "to say"); ciLuba *akula* "oral"; *-aakula* "talk, speak, utter, express"; *mwakulu* "language."[18] This word is similar in sound to the word *ḥḳ3* "govern, ruler, rule over"[19] (ciLuba *-aakwila* "rule over, govern") and thus the notion of being able to use words to rule or control things for which one knows its true name (*ḫrp* "direct, to lead, govern, control).

The Egyptian term *ḥk3* "words of power, spell, magic, magical influence" is cognate with ciLuba *cibìikidilu* "name, substantive, designation"; *biikila* "call, to bring, invoke, name, describe"; *-iinyika* "call, give a name, name" (var. *-iidika*). We noted that a name is the spirit of the thing and this is reinforced in the Egyptian language in the word *k3* "soul, spirit, essence (of a being), personality, name." *k3* is the root of *ḥk3* where *ḥ*- is a known prefix on the root. So this is telling us that a name is the "soul" or "personality" of a thing; it is an attempt to describe the core essence of a thing, the source of its character. One can say, then, that *ḥk3* is the "the power to invoke/activate the spirit/soul of a thing."

The name of something is a source of knowledge and information; as it is the name that describes the character of the thing being invoked (and also the history of the person and his/her

17 See http://www.adinkra.org/htmls/adinkra/nyan.htm (retrieved March 23, 2013)

18 This root is where we ultimately get the word "call" in English. It has a global spread.

19 It's possible that the word *ḥḳ3* "ruler" is composed of two primary words: *ḥw* "authoritative utterance, dictum, command" and *ḳ3* "high, exalted, intense (of storm), strong (of light)." Therefore, a *ḥḳ3* would be someone of an exalted position who has the authoritative rank to give commands (someone with a powerful voice).

family).[20] The name is also a mnemonic device to help recall a thing in memory. The Egyptian word *rn* "name" is cognate with the Yorùbá word *rán* in *rán ti* "to remember"; (Ijebu) *níran* "to remember." A name is a linguistic way of remembering a person (Oduyoye, 1996: 64-5). In Hebrew the name is associated with "remembering" as noted in A.G. Herbert's article "Memory, Memorial, Remember, Remembrance":

> The modern notion of remembering, psychologically viewed as the act of an individual mind, is quite alien to the Hebrew conception, which is in the first place communal, and closely related to the idea of the name.[21]

All of this comes together when we understand the connections between "call, invoke, remember, name and knowledge." In the Yorùbá language we have the word *orúko* "name." A variant of this term is part of a literary genre which is described in Yorùbá as *oríkì* "praise name." The latter is a literary form by which you remember the person within the history of his/her family, clan and tribe; hence the genealogical content of *oríkì*. If one was to try to find a cognate in Semitic, for example, of this consonant root for "name" (r-k), one will not find it. However, ask a Yorùbá man to give you the Yorùbá for "to mention" and "to mention the name of," and you will get a variant of the same word: *dárúko*. In Arabic the word *dakara* is a verb meaning "to mention"; it has a cognate in Assyrian *zikaru* "to mention, to name" and this shows up in Hebrew as *zekar* "to remember."

Oduyoye believes that this word (*orúko*) is the product of backformation from the word *dárúko*. Given our data on the *r-k* root in regards to Greek *legein* "to say, tell, speak, declare"; *logos* "word, speech, thought, account;" this may not be the case. The *dá-* prefix had a grammatical property that was fossilized in the word which Oduyoye denies a grammatical role.[22] The two forms in Yorùbá could simply be doublets (PB *-*dUk*- "name").

It is my contention that the ultimate root for *logos* "word," *dárúko* "name," *oríkì* "praise name," can be found in ciLuba as *eela* (-*le*-)"send away, or exit from the self (a sound, an idea, word, object...), transmit, show, express, speak" (Egyptian *ʿr* "to leave, to go out, to quit, to lead, to carry away"; *rw* "word, speech"). *Eela* can also mean "introduce, put/set/make, push"; "dispose, arrange, lay, apply, put out, place."It is the root to such words in ciLuba as *cila* "cry, cry out"; *diyi* "voice, word, order, act" [l+i>di] (Egyptian *iri* "act, do"); *kalele*(a) "make a communication shouting loudly"; *lubila* "call, cry" (*kwela lubila* "shout, a call")"; *mulunga* "howl" (*kwela mulunga* "scream"); *mulengu* "flute"; *aalula* "say, explain, detail" (Egyptian *rr* "a magic word"). This root is in the Egyptian word *mꜣṯ* "to proclaim, to announce out loud (as a means of invoking into being)" (*m*- is a prefix). Anything that has to deal with an object, sound or idea *exiting* from the self has this root and thus the expanded associations with "words" which propagate from the mouth, or ideas written on paper (projected from the mind to the paper).

20 See Samuel Gyasi Obeng. (2001). *African Anthroponymy: An Ethnopragmatic and Morphophonological Study of Personal Names in Akan and Some African Societies*. Lincom Europa.

21 See Alan Richardson, ed., *A Theological Word Book of the Bible*, S.C.M. Press, 1959, p. 142.

22 Oduyoye (1971: 62) finds issue with E.C. Rowland's commentary in *Teach Yourself Yoruba* for which he argues that *dá-* in *dárúko* is a verb that he glosses as "make." Oduyoye asks the question, "Would *dárúko* then mean 'to make a name'?" I think it would be more appropriate to treat *dá-* as a fossilized ergative meaning "to cause," thus *dárúko* would mean "to cause to mention"; to mention the name of." The *Dictionary of Yoruba Language* (1913) notes that *dá* is a verb with the primary idea of "to make or create" but its signification is modified by the noun with which it is used in combination. It is also a particle with a ***causative force***, and when used with other words has the meaning of "to cause to have." This is exactly the function as expressed in the Egyptian *s*- in *sḫꜣ* "to mention, remembrance, memory."

As we can see from these few examples, many terms can be made from the root *eela* (Egyptian *ꜥr*) by adding various affixes. The word *dárúko* (<*orúko*(*i*)) in Yorùbá is just the root *eela* with grammatical affixes that have been fossilized and are no longer productive in Yorùbá. As noted, we see this term reflected in other languages such as Egyptian *ꜥrḳ* "to swear, to abjure, to renounce, to be verse"; Greek *legein* "to say, tell, speak, declare"; *logos* "word, speech, thought, account;"ciLuba *biikila* "call, to bring, invoke, name, describe." Egyptian *ꜥrḳ* is just a reversal of the term *kꜣ* "to say"; ciLuba *akula* "oral"; *-aakula* "talk, speak, utter, express"; *mwakulu* "language." The *ku-* prefix is the infinitive meaning "to," thus *ku-* (to) + *-eela-* (speak, say, express, sound).

In the Egyptian language we have the word *sš/sẖꜣ* 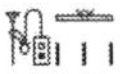 "writing." There are two pronunciations for this hieroglyph as can be seen here. The second variation (*sẖꜣ*) is similar in sound to the word *sẖꜣ*  "to mention" (as writing is a form of recalling and mentioning information in texts > "speaking"). As we noted before, this idea of "to mention" is connected to the idea of "remembering" which is exactly what a *name* helps human beings to do. We therefore have the variants: *sẖi / sẖꜣ*  "remember, call to mind, think about, mention"; *sẖꜣw / sẖꜣ*  "remembrance, memory, memorial." The initial *s-* is a grammatical prefix called a "causative" that "brings about - makes - occasions - produces - induces" a phenomenon to be. The term *dárúko* is a word that has been affected by metathesis on the root.

Yorùbá	*dárúko*	(d-r-k)	"to mention, to mention the name of"
Arabic	*dakara*	(d-k-r)	"to mention"
Assyrian	*zikaru*	(z-k-r)	"to mention, to name"
Hebrew	*zekar*	(z-k-r)	"to remember"
Egyptian	*sẖꜣ*	(*s-ẖ-ꜣ*)[23]	"remembrance, memory, call to mind, mention"

Another example can be given to demonstrate this point as it regards the Yorùbá forms. Observe the following:

Arabic	*gafara*	(g-f-r)	"forgive"
Yorùbá	*foríjì*	(f-r-j)	"forgive"
Arabic	*kafara*	(k-f-r)	"to cover, to hide"
Hebrew	*kapar*	(k-p-r)	"to atone"
Aramaic	*k^epar*	(k-p-r)	"to wash away, to rub off"
Egyptian	*krp*	(k-r-p)	"to scrape out"
Yorùbá	*paré*	(k-p-r)	"to rub off" (*kparé*)[24]

Each of these terms are variations of the same theme: to run off—to rub off stain—to wipe off stain, taint, blemish, sin—to forgive (i.e., to wipe clean one's wrongs). It should also be noted that the phenomenon of metathesis is common when /r/ or /l/ is one of the consonants (see Lord, 1966: 92): e.g., Yorùbá *erùpé*, Hebrew *'apar* "dust." This is what is going on with our word *oríkì* (r-k). It is also possible that: 1) the *k-* initial or *-k* ending is a separate affix on the root *-r-* and thus not the product of metathesis when we see these phonemes switched, or 2) the switch is a result of old free-word-order in Kongo-Saharan as grammatical morphemes were once full words in times past (see Campbell-Dunn, 2009a). Homburger (1929: 333) informs us that in Niger-Congo the same morphemes occurred "sometimes as prefixes, sometimes as suffixes, sometimes as infixes." The Yorùbá word *o-rúk-o* is cognate with Proto-Bantu **-dUk-* "name" (PB **-dɔng-* "speak, teach"; Sumerian *dug* "speak, talk, say"). So the *orúko* form is not a

23 We note here that the /ꜣ/ sound value was an /l/ sound in its initial stages.

24 Simultaneous articulation of the /k/ and /p/ sounds in the Hebrew and Aramaic examples above.

back-formation.

Egyptian tells us that the *s*- initial (in *sḫ3*) is a causative morpheme and this was fossilized in Yorùbá through sound mutation as *dá*- (a causative). Ultimately, *s*- (palatalized from /k/; Yorùbá *ṣe* "do") and *da*- derive from a word meaning "hand" and the "action of the hands" which became the grammatical "causative" in African languages.

DO **Sumerian** *ki* "do"

KI "do"

PWS *kia* "to do"
PWN *KIT* "to end"
Bantu *gid* "make", *kít* "to make"
Mande *kè* "to do"
PCS **ki* "to break"
Mangbetu *âki* "to break", "to cause, invent", "to destroy" etc
Khoisan : Hatsa *cikina* "make"

*K = k *I = i

MAKE **Sumerian** *dím* "to make"

LI, DI "hand"
-m

PWS *li* "to dig" (*d.i*), *lì* "to eat" (with hand), *lim* "to put out fire" (*dim*), action of hand.
PWN *DI* "to eat", *DÍ , DIO* "right hand", *DIM* "extinguish"
PWN *LÍMA* "tongue" (thought of as hand)
Bantu *dío* "right hand"
Bantu *dinga* "ring" (worn on right hand)
Mande M *tiké* "hand"
Mangbetu *-di* "various actions"
ES Mahas, Fadidja *eddi* "hand"
ES Kenuzi, Gondola *id* "man"

***D = d** ***I = i** ***M = m**

MAKE **Sumerian** *aka* "make"

KA "make" **[R] or a-**

PWS *ka* "hand", "open"
PWN *KA* "hand, arm"
PWN *KHANT* "cut" (off)
Bantu *ka* "hand"
Bantu *gado* "arm"
Bantu *kat, kant* "cut"
"Holoholo" *kal'* "to cut", *ha* "to give"
Gur **ŋa* "make"
Mande *kè* "to make"

Mande *tigè, tikè* etc "cut"
Mangbetu *éki* "to introduce"
Mangbetu *éhi* "to cause to move"
Mangbetu *ose* "to mix"
Mangbetu *ogo* "cut"
PCS **ga* "cut"

[Compare Maori *whaka* "make", from **baka*].

K = k ***A = a**

<u>**AGENT, ERGATIVE**</u> **Sumerian** ***e*** "do, make"

KA, KIA "hand", "make"

PWS *ka* "hand"
PWS *kia* (> *ke*) "make" (action of hand) **Sumerian** a_3 "make"
PWN *KA, (KYA)* "hand"
Bantu *kít* "do", *gid* "act"
Bantu *gi* "go", *(k)a* "go"
Bantu *ka* "hand"
Bantu *ka* "hand"
Mande *kè* "to make"
Mangbetu *âki* "to cause"

*K = # *IA = e *K = # *A = a

The Egyptian word *ʿrḳ* (*r-ḳ*) and *sḫꜣ* (*ḫ-ꜣ*) are both variants of the word *rḫ*(*t*) "knowledge" (Greek *logos*). The following chart shows its many manifestations.[25]

rḫ "wisdom, experience, opinion, find out"	
rḫ "know, be aware of, Inquire !, learn, diagnose"	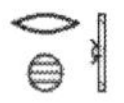
ʿrḳ "know, perceive, gain full knowledge of"	
rḫ "copulate, to know a woman sexually"	
rḫ "wise man, scholar"	
ʿrḳ "to know, to be wise"	
rḫ sw "wise, clever"	
ʿrḳ ib "clever"	

25 Some may see the interchange between /x/ and /q/ problematic. However, Orel and Stolbova (1995: 433-7) see it as a standard alternation in Afroasiatic.

rḫ "to be able"	
ꜥrḵ "to be versed, to be adept, skilled (in)"	
rḫ "to list"	

The Yorùbá word *oríkì* "praise name" and the Egyptian *rḫ* "to list,"[26] *rḫt* "amount, enumerate, number, list, knowledge" are variants of the same word. As Oduyoye noted, the word *oríkì*'s relatedness to the idea of remembering is indicated in the fact that praise names are almost always *genealogical* (Oduyoye, 1996: 64). In other words, *oríkìs* are often praise names for dead ancestors. To do an *oríkì* is to "recall" or "list" one's ancestors. This is reinforced in S.A. Babalola's *The Content and Form of Yorùbá Ijala* (1966), as he informs us:

> [I]t is traditionally believed that the correct performance of oriki in honour of a progenitor gladdens that progenitor in the world of the spirits and induces him to shower blessings on his offspring on earth. (Babalola, 1966: 24)

We mentioned the Yorùbá word *rán tí* "to remember" with its cognate in Egyptian *rn* "name" (ciLuba *dina, rina* "name"). There is also the variant *ìran* which means "generation, antecedent, ancestral generations." This is reflected in Egyptian as *rn rn* "list, name list, roll call" (reduplication); and just like our other term *ꜥrḵ*, *rḫ* carries meanings associated with "wisdom, inquiry and knowledge."

Oríkì (rḫ "to list,"*)*, therefore, is the knowledge of and ability to recite one's ancestral lineage and deeds. To have information on and the ability to recite the wisdom of the ancestors is considered to be the basis of knowledge and wisdom in African pre-Western societies. We note all of this in detail because, as we mentioned earlier, family genealogies were also recorded by knotting ropes and we see the rope sign determinatives in our Egyptian words *ꜥrḵ* and *rḫ,* which have to deal with memory, mentioning and listing.[27]

Recitation was highly encouraged in ancient Egyptian society as a method to keep information in memory for easy recollection.

> *Mry sšw msdw ib3w*
> Cherish study, avoid the dance,
> *iry.k sr iḳr*
> So you'll become an excellent official
> *m rdit ib.k n t3 bw3t*
> Do not yearn after outdoor pleasures, hunting and fishing;
> *mk ḥ3 ḳm3w šspw*
> Shun boomerang throwing and the chase.
> *wr šw sšw m ḏbꜥw.k wšd m grḥ*
> **Write diligently by day; recite at night.**
> *snsny n.k t3 wsty p3 gsty*
> Let your friends be the papyrus roll and the scribal palate;
> *nḏm sw r šdh*
> such work is sweeter than wine
> *ir sšw n p3 ntty rḫ sw 3ḫ sw r ir i3t nbt nḏm sw r ꜥḳw*

26 We also take note the rope determinative here.

27 We mentioned, as an example, Danny Boey, in his article "Jia Pu (Chinese Genealogical Record): An Introduction," who informed us that "Prior to the invention of writing, Chinese genealogical information was recorded by tying knots on ropes."

> Indeed writing, for one who knows it, is far better than all other professions, pleasanter than bread and bear
> *rḥbsw r sgnn*
> more delightful than clothes and perfumed ointments,
> *sbḳ sw r iwꜥt [ḥr] Kmt*
> more precious than a legacy in Egypt
> *r miḥꜥt ḥr ꞽImntt*
> than a tomb in the west (pLansing, 20th Dynasty; British Museum 9994)

Because this root (*eela*) is grounded in the concept of knowledge and all of its applications, we find many terms in ciLuba related to this lexeme:

eela	"send away, or exit from the self (a sound, an idea, word, object...), transmit, show, express, speak."
lunga	"expand, make an effort to reach, extend your arms to reach, extend, lengthen"
meeji ≋ menji	"intelligence, think, reflect, give advice"
lungènyi	"intelligence, mind, because, ability, mindset, apply to, contrive to, carefully, with skill, meaning, mental, mentally"
landa	"reflect, meditate"
langa	"meditate, reflect, project"
màyeelè (a)	"trick"
bungèèlàmèèjì ≋ bungèèlà	"philosophy"
dyeji	"idea, intelligence"
bweji	"rationality"
lweji	"reason" (*-à/-a lweji* "rational")
lumvwilu	"understanding, intelligence"

The *r-k* root may also be present in these ciLuba terms: *-pilùke*(a) "scientist"; *-piluka* "exceed"; "be competent"; *mupilùke*(a) "scholar, expert" (*rḫ*  "wise man, scholar").

Yoga and its Egyptian Context?

There have been many proponents in the Afrocentric community who have asserted that the concept and practice of Yoga existed in ancient Egypt. The more well known advocates of this theory are Dr. Asar Ha-pi, Dr. Muata Ashby[28] and Yiser Ra Hotep.[29] The Dr. Hapi/Ra Hotep camp asserts that the evidence for Egyptian Yoga can be seen on the back of a 18th Dynasty chair of king Tutankhamen which depicts the god *šw* in a 'yogic' position. The *nṯr šw* represents the concepts of *air* or *breath* and since Yoga is connected to breathing techniques, there has been a connection made between the deity, breathing and the practice of Yoga. The Dr. Ashby camp believes that the philosophy of Yoga can be connected to the Egyptian phrase *smꜣ tꜣwy* "The Union of the Two Lands." For Ashby, this not only speaks about the confederation of Nilotic kingdoms that became Egypt, but is metaphorically applied to the notion of uniting one's personal consciousness with that of a perceived universal consciousness. I ultimately

28 http://www.egyptianyoga.com/
29 http://www.kemeticyoga.com/

agree that the concept of Yoga existed in ancient Egypt, however, I do not accept the primary evidence given for the practice as given by Dr. Hapi, Dr. Ashby or Hotep. I think that there is a more solid case for its existence in Egypt and comparative linguistics provides us with a tool to extract this information from ancient Egyptian texts.

My method, when comparing cultural artifacts from two distant cultures in space and time, is to first examine, linguistically, the terms used to represent the concepts in the respective cultures. I do this to see if there is: 1) a cognate relationship between the representative terms, or 2) a conceptual relationship between the terms not necessarily based on linguistic cognates. This allows us to see if it is possible to accurately compare the underlying themes of the concepts that inform the practices. We therefore first have to examine the word Yoga to see if there is at least a cognate in the Egyptian language. If it is found that there is a linguistic relationship, then we can go further to see if the two or more lexemes were *attached* to similar *practices* in both traditions. I argue that such a relationship exists and that the Egyptians indeed had 'Yoga'.

Yoga (Sanskrit, Pāli: योग, /ˈjəʊgə/, *yoga*) is a commonly known generic term for a series of physical, mental, and spiritual disciplines which originated in ancient India.[30] In modern times it is commonly associated with a series of exercises and stretches used to improve the relationship between the mind, body and soul. The word *yoga* is Sanskrit and derives from a PIE root **yewg* "to join, union, to yoke." In Vedic Sanskrit, the more commonly used, literal meaning of the Sanskrit word *yoga* ("to add", "to join", "to unite", or "to attach" from the root *yuj*) already had a much more figurative sense, where the yoking or harnessing of oxen or horses takes on broader meanings such as "employment, use, application, performance" (compare the figurative uses of "to harness" as in "to put something to some use").

There are very many compound words containing *yog* in Sanskrit. Yoga can take on meanings such as "connection", "contact", "method", "application", "addition" and "performance." For example, *guṇá-yoga* means "contact with a cord"; *chakrá-yoga* has a medical sense of "applying a splint or similar instrument by means of pulleys (in case of dislocation of the thigh)"; *chandrá-yoga* has the astronomical sense of "conjunction of the moon with a constellation"; *puṃ-yoga* is a grammatical term expressing "connection or relation with a man", etc. Thus, *bhakti-yoga* means "devoted attachment" in the monotheistic Bhakti movement.

It is my contention that the reconstructed PIE root **yewg* "to join, union, yoke" is just a variation of the PIE **leg-* "to pick together, gather, collect" by way of a slight semantic shift, however all related to "tying, binding." The word *yoke* in English derives from this root **yewg*/**yug*. This is important to note because the /y/ sound often derives, morphologically, from a /g/ or /k/-type sound (g/k>y). Mallory & Adams—*The Oxford Introduction to Proto-Indo-European and the Proto-Indo-European World* (2006: 248)—expands our discourse with the following commentary on our PIE root as it regards the word *yoke*:

> One word for 'yoke', **yugo´m*, is widespread (e.g. OWels *iou*, Lat *yugum*, NE *yoke*, Lith *ju`ngas*, Grk *zugo´n*, Arm *luc*, Hit *yukan*, Av *yugam*, Skt *yuga´m*, all 'yoke') and derives from **yeug-* 'join, harness' (see Section 22.5).[31]

---

30 See http://en.wikipedia.org/wiki/Yoga (retrieved March 28, 2013).

31 Mallory & Adams posit that the -*g* in **yewg* is a suffix with **yew* being the root. "**yeu-* 'bind, join together' Skt *ya´uti*"; "The basic root **yeu-* 'bind, join together' (e.g. Lith *ja´utis* 'ox, steer' [<*'that which is yoked'], Skt *ya´uti* 'binds, unites') is more widely found in the extended form **yeu-g-* 'yokes' and yields that meaning in Italic (Lat *iungo¯*), Baltic (Lith *ju`ngti*), Grk *zeu´gnu¯mi*, and Skt *yuna´kti* (see also Section 15.5)" (Mallory & Adams, 2006: 381). The African languages confirm this as we have seen throughout this discussion. See *Chapter 6* this volume for a discussion on "ropes, tying" and its monosyllabic root -*k*- or -*s*- which derives from a word for "hand" with the derived verbs denoting the "action of the hand."

As we can see here the /y/ in the *y-k* root can be rendered as a /j/ sound as can be seen in the Lithuanian dialectical variation *ju'ngas*.[32] I argue that this /j/ is a palatalized variation of a /k/ or /g/-type sound found in the African variations. The *Online Etymological Dictionary* provides more variations of the word *yoke*:

> Old English *geoc* "yoke," earlier *geoht* "pair of draft animals," from Proto-Germanic **yukam* (cf. Old Saxon *juk*, Old Norse *ok*, Danish *aag*, Middle Dutch *joc*, Dutch *juk*, Old High German *joh*, German *joch*, Gothic *juk* "yoke"), from PIE **jugom* "joining" (see *jugular*). Figurative sense of "heavy burden, oppression, servitude" was in Old English.

We are reaffirmed once we begin to look at the African evidence and cognates for this term. The following is from the Proto-Bantu BLR3 database.

> **gàng* "tie up, hang"; **káángl*káng* "tie up, seize"; **kúng* "gather up, assemble, tie up"; **kúngá* "umbilical cord"; **kúngá* "fish; eel"[33]

The /k/ and /g/ became palatalized in the C_1 position and is reflected in the following terms in PB:

> **-dùk-* "plait, braid" **túng* "put through, thread on string, plait, sew, tie up, build, close (in); **tóngá* "basket"; **túngá* "country, village"[34]

Here the /k/ and /g/ sounds became /t/ and /d/. In Niger-Congo, the /l/ and /d/ sound interchange. But /d/ and /j/ are common sound shifts as well. This is why the following reflexes in PB are relevant to this entire discourse:

> **dùng* "join by tying"; **dùng* "season food"; **dùngò* "joint, genou"; **dùngé* "seasoning; seasoned food"[35]; **dùngò* "knee" (from the concept of bending); **jùng* "cure fracture" (in other words, join fracture together); **dùng* "be straight, right, put straight, fitting, adjust"

With Sumerian being a Niger-Congo language (Hermstein 2012, Cambpell-Dunn 2009a, 2009b), we see a variant of this term reflected in Sumerian as *lug* "twist, be crushed." As it regards the PIE **y-g* root meaning "unite, tie, bind, collect," we see various sound morphologies as it regards the initial consonant: *k*, *g*, *j*, *y*, *t*, *d*, *z*, and *l*. A [dz], [dj] or [ts] sound wouldn't be out of order either. We see the initial consonant as a /s/ sound in these reflexes: ciLuba *šing, -cìnga* "fence, surround, enclose, circle"; *nyunga* "move in a circle; *nshinga* "thread, wire, braided rope, metal cable, telecommunications line (telegraph, telephone, internet), phone"; *MuShinga/ka-Nzinga* "Newborn with the umbilical cord rolled up"; *muJinga* "cord, reel; braided rope"; Kikongo *singa* (pl. *misinga*) "a rope, a cord"; Kikongo *zinga* (pl. *zingidi*) "to encircle, to put around, to bandage, to furl a sail, to twine rope or string, to pack a parcel"; Kalenjiin *syaang'an* "rope," *syaang'aneet* "rope braided securely for tying animals." In Afro-Asiatic we have Hausa *sak?a*, Angas *sak*, Musgu *sasaka* "weave." We may have an example of metathesis in the

32 Note j>y is common in world languages: e.g., Egyptian *jmn* "right side" > "west"; Semitic *ymn* "right side" > "south" (Loprieno, 1995: 34).

33 An *eel*, in many respects, is shaped like a rope or cord.

34 Compare **túngú* "village, community" (conceptually) with Egyptian *m3ʿ* 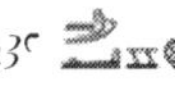 "village" and *m3ʿ* "rope."

35 The word for "seasoning" may come from the notion of "combining" or "mixing" spices. I am not quite sure the reference in this case.

Egyptian words: *wgs* "tow rope"; *ḳ3s* "cord, rope, binding, string (bow), tie (rope ladder)."

With these variations of the root, we shouldn't have a problem comparing PIE **yug* "to join, union, yoke" to Egyptian *ʿrḳ* "bind." In Egyptian the /r/ or /l/ sound was often written as /i/: e.g., *sb3/sbi* "play flute." The Germanic school of Egyptology often transcribes the /i/ sound as /j/. On that note, a reflex for *ʿrḳ* in Egyptian is *iḳ* "fetters, shackles." Another variation is *3k* "bind." Reflexes of this theme (of binding, constraining), by way of metathesis, can be seen in the word *krj* "to be restrained, caged"; *krj* "prison."

Andrew Sihler, in his book *Language History: An Introduction*, in discussing the phenomenon of infixes (an affix inserted into the middle of a word), discusses our term under examination:

> **infix**: a bound morpheme that interrupts a morpheme. (Cf. prefix and suffix) In a few language families like Austronesian infixes are abundant; in most Indo-European languages they are rare or non-existent. English and most modern Indo-European languages do not have any. Proto-Indo-European had one infixing verb stem marker *-*ne*- alternating with *-*n*-. For example, the root *yewg-/yug-* 'link, join; yoke' the present imperfect finite stems were **yuneg-/*yung-* componentially **yu-ne-g/*yu-n-g-*. Crucial is that **yug-* is a single element, not a sequence of elements **yu-* and *-*g*-... (Sihler, 2000: 259)

Sihler (2000) differs with Mallory & Adams (2006) in asserting that the final consonant -*g* is not a separate element, but is part of the root. A look into African languages may clarify the discrepancies between these two works. However, we find the PIE **yung*-form in Egyptian: *ink* "unite, gather together, collect, embrace"; *inki* "ropes to the ship" [Wb IS 101]; *inḳi* "a ship's rope"; *3h3h* "rope, fibers" [Meeks: AL 780082]; *fnḫ* "Rope" [Meeks: AL 781573]. The final -*g* sound could just be the result of nasalization on the /k/ which weakened the /k/ into /g/. We see here that the three phonemes are a match: PIE *y-n-g*, Egyptian *i-n-k*, PB *d-n-g*; *j-n-g*.

The Egyptian word *ʿnḫ*, I argue, is also of the same root. Early depictions of the *ʿnḫ* symbol consisted of a loop and tied piece of rope as can be seen below.

Many are familiar with the more popular meaning of *ʿnḫ* relating to "life." However, this word can also mean "vow, swear, oath" (Coptic *anaš* (SB), *anaḫ* "oath, something you are bound too"). Bernal (2006: 638) also notes *ʿnḫ* "to link, imprison, bind" which gives us the meaning of "oath" by way of metaphoric extension (an oath being a "binding" social agent). We see this notion of "constraint" (being bound to) in the reflex *ʿnḫ* "captive, prisoner." It is this notion of "binding" that gives us the notion of "writing" as we discussed throughout this text. From there it extends into "books" and we see this same association with the word *ʿnḫ* "document." Note the string determinative at the end of the word *ʿnḫ*, which is associated with various words dealing with "writing, books and knowledge."

As we noted earlier, there is an interchange between the Egyptian sounds /*ḳ*/ and /*ḫ*/ as can be seen in *ꜥrḳ* "to be wise, know" and *rḫ* "wisdom, wise man, to know." We can see this interchange again with *ꜥnḫ* ☥ "oath, swear, vow" and *ꜥrḳ* 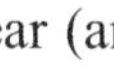 "swear (an oath)."[36] Note the borrowing from Egyptian in Greek with the word *opkoς* (H) "to bind, swear, oath" (Coptic *ōrk*).

It is important to note the variations in pronunciation and the semantic range of the core theme: "binding, uniting." The purpose of yoga is connected to this notion of "uniting" with spirit or universal consciousness. As noted by Wiki, the ultimate goal of Yoga is *moksha* ('liberation'; from the cycles of rebirth) though the exact definition of what form this takes depends on the philosophical or theological system with which it is conjugated. Bhakti schools of Vaishnavism combine yoga with devotion to enjoy an eternal presence of Vishnu. In Shaiva theology, yoga is used to unite *kundalini* with Shiva. Mahabharata defines the purpose of yoga as the experience of Brahman or Ātman pervading all things. In the specific sense of Patanjali's Yoga Sutras, the purpose of yoga is defined as citta-vṛtti-nirodhaḥ (the cessation of the perturbations of consciousness). This is described by Patanjali as the necessary condition for transcending discursive knowledge and to be one with the divinely understood "spirit" ("purusha"): "Absolute freedom occurs when the lucidity of material nature and spirit are in pure equilibrium."

One can only stop the cycles of rebirth by becoming one with the universe and to become "enlightened." The goal of Egyptian 'yoga' is very similar to that of the Indians. The objective was to become one with the *nṯrw*, but more specifically to be an *ꜣḫ(w)* "a luminous being/ spirit" (a "star"). The following excerpt comes from the Pyramid of Pepi I, north wall, mortuary antechamber corridor (columns 15-20). It provides us with a context by which we can argue for Egyptian 'yoga'.

> *nn n.k ꜥꜣwy pt*
> The gates of heaven open for you;
> *sn n.k ꜥꜣwy ḳbḥw*
> the gates of the firmament draw apart for you,
> *ipw ḥsfw rḫwt*
> (the same gates) that shut out rebels.
> *nwiw n.k mnit ḏsww n.k ḥnmmt*
> Those gone before hail you; the Sun people hail you;
> *ꜥḥꜥ n.k iḫmw-ski*
> the everlasting stars rise for you.
> *f̱w.k snṯr mḥyt.k iḫt*
> Your wind is incense; your north wind is smoke.
> *ṯwt wrrti m tꜣ-wr*
> You are great in Thys;
> *ṯwt sb pw wꜥti prr m gs iꜥꜣbty n pt*
> You are the unique star that rises in the eastern sky
> *n iwti rdi.n.f ḏt.f n ḥr dwꜣti*
> and does not go to Horus of the Dwat
> *ḳꜣi wrt m m sbꜣw iḫmw-ski*
> Ah, you rising so high among the imperishable stars,
> *nski.k ḏt*
> You will never, never fade. (Obenga, 2004: 239-240)

This old kingdom text, from the 6th dynastic period, talks about a deceased king, Pepi I, who in order to enter the world beyond, had to undergo ceremonial cleansing rituals with water for purification. The goal of these purification rituals was resurrection. Once purified, the king is

36 Note that r>n is a common sound change. We also note that in Egyptian the /l/ sound is often represented by /n/, /r/, and more rarely by /ꜣ/ and /j/ (Loprieno, 1995: 33).

resuscitated and morphs into a star ("you are the unique star that rises in the eastern sky"). This is Egyptian apotheosis. We see the same practice among the Efé people of the Ituri forest of Zaire who believe that a blessed soul is transformed into a star after death. Hallet & Pelle, in their book *Pygmy Kitabu* (1973: 225), note that: "The Efé Pygmies believe that the vital force or immortal constituent of the human personality 'returns to heaven, where God transforms it into a star'." This concept is also present among the Yoruba of Nigeria. The following was said at a hunter's funeral:

1. Mo pọsẹsẹ- pọsẹsẹ
2. Ọwọ̀ọ̀ mi ọ̀ bÁkànbí mọ́
3. Babaá wá diná ọ̀run kò tiẹ̀ kú mo
4. Babaá wá si tiẹ̀ dòòrùn
5. Eyí ta ó fi sásọ gbẹ kalẹ̀
6. Ákànbí ire lálẹ̀dé ọ̀run

1. I trotted and trotted,
2. I couldn't reach Ákànbí anymore.
3. Our father has been transformed into a heavenly light which never dies
4. Our father has even been transformed into a sun,
5. Whose rays shall dry our clothes.
6. Ákànbí, rest in peace. (Barnes, 1995: 194-195)

The language in this passage is very pharaonic in nature. As discussed in the text, the deceased hunters who become ancestors are thus a source of light; they permit no obscurity. The "sun" refers to all of those souls who have displayed sufficient energy while on earth that they may thereafter illuminate the spirit world. In other words, "the stars are souls which have evolved to supreme perfection." The soul is a reservoir of energy that enables human beings to reclaim perfection in the realm of eternity. Therefore, the soul is a form of energy that enables people to transcend death and reach the abode of eternity, the fields of enlightenment.

The deceased who is transformed into a unique star among the Egyptians is called an *ꜣḫ* (Yoruba *aiku* "immortals"). This word *ꜣḫ* has the same phonemes (essentially) as our words *ʿrḳ* and *rḫ* and we can see that there is some punning going on in these associations (by way of paronymy). The word *ꜣḫ* can have the following meanings:

ꜣḫ	𓅜𓐍 "spirit, successful, right, be beneficial, useful, profitable, glorious one, good, beneficial, advantageous, fame, worthy of, devoted to, to please"
ꜣḫw	"benefactions, good, excellent things, glorifications, ability, mastery"
ꜣḫw	"power (of god/spirit) [Wb I 15], magic, magical words, useful knowledge, master"
ꜣḫt	"horizon"

In ciLuba-Bantu, the above is cognate with:

-lenga	"beautiful, good, to improve, be good, be beautiful, be advantageous, be at peace, be sure"
-lengele	"good, nice, pleasant, beautiful, useful, advantageous, course"
cilengà	"fine clothes, ornament, adornment, jewel, finery"
-lèngama	"abound, be abundant"
lengàlengà	"very many, very large amount, overflowing"
bulenga	"beauty, goodness, quality,"
-à/-a Bulenga	"saint, holy"
ntungù	"gratuity, benefit, bonus, advantage, reward, compensation, payment"

lungènyi "spirit, mind, intelligence, because, ability, mindset, for, meaning, mental" (*mu lungenyi* "carefully, with skill")
lukèndù "horizon, row, stacked rows, superimposed rows" (PB *déng* "go beyond, fade from the horizon")

As we can see this term has a wide range of meanings and associations. In some African languages the /ꜣ/ sound, in the word *ꜣẖ*, has lost it consonantal value: e.g., Bwiti *kouck*, *kouk*, or *ku*; Mbochi *le-ku*, *ikuu* and *okué*; Kalenjiin *aiik/oiik* "departed souls, spirits"; Yorùbá *aiku* "immortal." We can see further evidence of this association with the stars after death in the *Rꜥw Nu Pr.t m ḥrw* "Words for coming forth by day,"[37] Chapter 176, when Ani states:

> I abhor the eastern land, I will not enter the place of destruction, none shall bring me offerings of what the gods detest, because I pass pure into the midst of the Milky Way, one to whom the Lord of All granted his power on that day when the Two Lands were united in the presence of the Lord of Things… (Wasserman, 2008: 130).

As we can see here, when Ani says "I pass pure into the midst of the Milky Way," he is talking about a region of stars for which it is believed a great number of ancestors resided. In Chapter 174 he is a bit more explicit in his association with the stars. He states:

> I will raise up Atum, for my words are great; I have issued from between the thighs of the Ennead, I was conceived by Sekhmet, it was Shesmetet who bore me, a star brilliant and far-travelling, who brings distant products to Re daily. I have come to my throne upon the Vulture and the Cobra, I have appeared as a star. (ibid.)

In many ancient traditions it is articulated that the spirit, or spirit world, is composed of "light." If the spirit world is made of light, then the inhabitants, it can be assumed, also must be made of light. We see this kind of association in Egyptian by way of another term, *bꜣ*. The *bꜣ*  is the "spirit, soul or double" of the person in Egyptian ontology. This *bꜣ* "comes out" of the body of the deceased at the moment of death. This entity is represented often as a tiny bird in Egyptian texts and sometimes as a shaft of *light* rising from a vase of oil (Obenga, 2004: 236).

The association between "light" and "spirit" is due to Egyptian punning as it regards the word *ꜣẖ*. The word *ꜣẖ*, with its associations with "light," has the following reflexes:

ꜣẖ "flame, fire" [Wb I 17]
ꜣẖw "sunlight, sunshine, radiance"
ꜣẖꜣẖ "stars"
jꜣẖw "shine (the sun)" [Wb I 33]

This root is present, by way of metathesis, in the Egyptian term *tkꜣ* "flame, light, torch, wick, taper, illumine, burn, illumination."

In practically all human languages, the concept of "education, knowledge and wisdom" is metaphorically associated with "light." In common thought, "darkness" represents ignorance and "light" represents knowledge. Knowledge is the light of the mind. It 'reveals' that which has been hidden to our consciousness. Light makes us aware of our surroundings and it allows us to "know" that which is around us. Light, then, becomes synonymous with knowledge.

37 I render this phrase in ciLuba-Bantu as *Bwalu bwenu civwilu mu bukulu*; in Yoruba *Òrò ni Ifa/fo mú Òrò* "Commands/Science for transforming into a star"; "Words/spells/commands for coming home (to heaven) [*dyUlu, KwUlu/ Kulu* "heaven," *diKolo, ciKulu, ciEla, ciLunga* "homeland"]"; "The process (act, steps, necessary work) for transforming into an ancestor (a divine being, "god")"; "The science of transforming into light."

For the ancient Egyptian we can see the basis for the play on words: *rḫ* "knowledge, wisdom"; *ʿrḳ* "to know, wise man"; *3ḫ* "spirit, luminous one"; *3ḫw* "master, magic, useful knowledge." One doesn't have to die to become an *3ḫw*. All one has to do is to be of good character, a person of service and a person of immense knowledge and wisdom. The latter develops as a result of study and experience. It is through the process of 'Yoga' (Egyptian *ʿrḳ* "bind" > "to know, to be wise, to perceive, gain full knowledge of, be skilled, to be versed, to be adept") that one becomes an *3ḫw* (both in life and after death).

The relationship between "knowledge" and becoming an "enlightened" being (in life and in death) can also be seen with the Egyptian word *sb3*. The word *sb3* can mean  "wise, guidance, teach, instruction, student"; *sb3*  "star"; *sb3jjw* "Star Gods" [Meeks: AL 773485].

Both the Indian and African traditions assert that a person was to become *one* with the cosmos after one has reached enlightenment. The African articulated it specifically as becoming a *star*. For the African, this was a logical process, and as we have seen, the very concept of *logic* (from root *-log-*) derives from this same process of "tying and untying knotty ropes."

In both the African and Indian forms of yoga, "meditation" and "deep reflection" are the exercises by which one reaches a state of enlightenment. In ciLuba this concept of "meditation" is again reflected with our *r-k* root: *-langa* "reflect, meditate, project" (var. *-landa*). I see this as a variant of the Egyptian word *nk3* 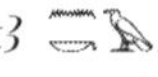 "meditate on, think about, take counsel"; *k3i*  "think about, plan, to reflect" by way of metathesis (*k-3* < *3-k*?). In light of our overall discourse, compare *nk3* to *ng3*  "cord" (constraining noose). Again, the same word for "rope, cord" is the same word connected to themes associated with "knowledge" and "wisdom."

Another point of correspondence between Egyptian and Indian yoga is the belief in reincarnation and the halting of reincarnation being the ultimate objective of each tradition. As noted earlier, in Indian yoga the objective of yoga practices was the concept of *moksha* ('liberation'; from the cycles of rebirth). We find a similar attitude in ancient Egypt and an example can be seen in a hymn to Amen-Ra.

> Amen-Ra who first was king,
> The god of earliest time,
> The vizier of the poor.
> He does not take bribes from the guilty
> He does not speak to the witness
> He does not look at him who promises,
> Amun judges the land with his fingers.
> He speaks to the heart,
> He judges the guilty
> He assigns him to the East,
> The righteous to the West. (P. Anastasi II.6, 5-7)[38]

For the ancient Egyptians, the East represented "rebirth" while the West represented the final resting place of the righteous. This east-west orientation is inspired by the apparent movement of the sun. The rising and setting of the sun becomes the source metaphor for the birth, living and dying stages of all life in general. Reincarnation is the repeated coming back of the soul on earth to experience existence with the aim of chipping away the gross fetters that keep souls experiencing these cycles of life. One has to purify oneself through the development of good character and right actions in order to reach a level where one would not be required to repeat life and gain more lessons.

The Egyptians have a few terms that represent the concepts of reincarnation. The first is

38 M. Lichtheim *Ancient Egyptian Literature*, Vol. II, 1978, p.111.

 *mstyw/msṯyw* "reincarnation, rebirth, new body, descendant, offspring." This term is in alignment with many African traditions—such as the Yorùbá, Dagara and Kalenjiin, for example—that assert that one is reborn through one's ancestral and family lines. Therefore, the 'offspring' of a family line is the reincarnation of an ancestor of times past. The second term is  *wḥm ꜥnḫ* "repeating life" (living again).

Maulana Karenga, in his book *The Husia: Sacred Wisdom of Ancient Egypt* (1984), provides us with an example from the "Book of Coming Forth By Day" that echoes this notion that souls come to earth to purify their character in hopes of an immortal existence among the stars. In this section of the text Ani states:

> My name does not pass away. I am the soul that created the deep, that makes its seat in God's domain. My nest, *my place of birth*, is hidden and my egg has not been broken. I am Lord of the heights and **I have made my nest in the sky. But I come down to earth that I may do away with my uncleanliness**. O Lord Osiris, come then and establish me and make me strong. Grant that I may enter the land of everlastingness as you have done along with your father Ra, whose body never passed away and who is one who indeed does not die…May your spirit love me and not reject me. And may you not let my body decay, but deliver me as you did deliver yourself. Let life rise out of death. Let not decay make an end of me or my enemies come against me in their many forms. (Karenga, 1984: 108) (bolded emphasis mine)

Ani states in the bolded above, "I have made my nest in the sky." This means that his "home" is in the heavens. He then follows with, "But I come down to earth that I may do away with my uncleanliness." In other words, he comes to earth so that he can work on his character. In the Ifa tradition of the Yorùbá, we have a saying that "Heaven is our home. Earth is the market place." Earth is the place we come to work on ourselves (to conduct business), but our ultimate home is in the heavens (*ciLunga, diKolo, ḥr.t*). The meaning behind this statement is in alignment with what Ani states in his plea for immortality (Egyptian *ꜣḫw*; Yorùbá *aiku*).

Not only do I argue that the Egyptians had yoga (*ꜥrḳ, rḫ*) and that the goal was the liberation of the soul from the fetters of reincarnation, I also argue that accompanying the desire for immortality was the aspiration for *free-will* and to maintain one's *identity* in the process. You will see in certain Egyptian texts a request to appear in any form as one desired when one reached the West. For instance, Ani in the *Book of Coming Forth By Day*, as cited in *The Husia*, reaffirms his desire for immortality when he states, "Let me proceed in peace to the West." This is then followed by, "And may I assume whatever form I want in whatever place my spirit wishes to be" (Karenga, 1984: 106). This is very telling in that it assumes that human beings are in essence a slave to the cycles of reincarnation and the forms by which they find themselves on a daily basis. By becoming one of the blessed ones (*ꜣḫw*), by purifying one's heart and actions on earth (through living a *mâatic* life), one then earns the right and ability to come in-and-out of form as one sees fit. This is the difference between the Indian and the Egyptian objectives within their own 'yoga' traditions. The Indian desires to become one with the universe while losing their identity. The Egyptian wanted to maintain their identity and move in-and-out of form as they saw fit. So the ultimate desire in Egyptian *ꜥrḳ/rḫ*/yoga was to obtain free-will.

As noted, the requirement for such a lofty state of existence is the purity of one's heart, mind and actions. This is why in the 125th chapter of the *Book of Coming Forth By Day*, the deceased declares that "I am pure, I am pure, I am pure, I am pure" (*iw.i wꜥb.kwi sp*; said 4 times). One must be pure like the *nṯrw* "divinities" in order to operate and live like the *nṯrw*. The only way one can be of pure heart and mind is to live a life of *mꜣꜥ.t* "righteousness, justice, truth, fraternity" instead of *isft* "evil, wrongdoing" (Amazulu *uzibuthe* "spirit of conflict"). We see here another play on words as the word *nṯr* can also mean "pure."

To be pure is to be without blemish or foreign elements. This notion of purity is given in Egyptian as *twr* "show respect to, hold sacred, to cleanse, to purify [verb]; *twr, twrj,* (later *tui*) "to be clean, to cleanse, to purify, to celebrate a ceremony of purification, purified, pure, to pray with a pure heart, clean handed"; *ntr* "natron"; *ntrjt* "natron"; *nṯrj* "natron, soda, trona" (sodium bicarbonate carbonate); *ndr* "natron" (see Budge 409b),[39] *nṯr* (*nthr* in Greek times) "natron" (Budge 408b); *nṯrj* "purified, cleaned, clean, pure" (from natron soda). From Egyptian the word was borrowed into Semitic languages - Akkadian *nit(i)ru*, Aramaic *nithra*, and Hebrew *neter* נתר. Other examples of this root in other languages are: Hebrew *ṭḥr* "to be pure" (*ṭᵉḥor-ah* "purification"); Twi *dwira* "purify" (*Odwira* "festival of purification"); Yorùbá *tòrò* "clean"; Kalenjiin *tiliil* "holy, clean" (*Netiliil* "Holy one, sacred one").

The Amarigna language of Ethiopia provides us with some expanded examples for our *n-t-r* triconsonant root: *NeTere* - vt: bounced (a ball); refined (by melting, e.g. gold); *NiTir* - adj refined; *Tnte nTr* - n. Element (chemical); *NTr qbe* - refined butter; *Ntr werq* - n. refined gold; *teneTere* v.i. was refined; *AneTere* v.t. refined; bounced; *AnTari* - n. refiner; *werq anTari* - n. goldsmith; *AnT'renya* – silversmith; *ManTeriya* - refining flux; *AnaTere* - v.i. acted flamboyantly; *AsneTere* v.t. had refined; *AnäTära* – pure.

To become a *nṯr* (ciLuba *ntalù* "excellence, excellent" (<*talama* "be smart, be attentive, be focused"; *-à/-a ntala* "crafty"; *CiTelu* or *CiTeelu* "exemplary, exemplary woman, beautiful, good (do), an excellent reputation"), one must refine (Amarigna *AneTere* "refined") one's character ("But I come down to earth that I may do away with my uncleanliness" -Ani). This is achieved through *yoga* which is at once the ***process*** (*rḫ* "inquire, find out, learn, diagnose"; *ꜥrḳ* "gain full knowledge of, perceive"; *nk3* "meditate on, think about, take counsel"; *k3i* "think about, plan, to reflect"; *logos*; *logic*) and the ***goal*** (*3ḫ*(*w*) "spirit, master, light"; *rḫ* "wisdom, experience, to be able,"; *ꜥrḳ* "to be versed, to be adept, to know, to complete [one's mission in life?]") of all spiritual aspirants in the ancient traditions.

Yoga (*ꜥrḳ/rḫ*) is achieved through study and reflection; through "tying knotty ropes" and binding (*ꜥrḳ*, **yug*) the accumulated data from a primary study of nature and ancient wisdom contained in books and tradition. With the knowledge revealed throughout this essay, we should now have the proper basis to reevaluate the word *religion*. The *Online Etymological Dictionary* argues the following for the word religion:

> **Religion**: c.1200, "state of life bound by monastic vows," also "conduct indicating a belief in a divine power," from Anglo-French *religiun* (11c.), Old French *religion* "religious community," from Latin *religionem* (nominative *religio*) "respect for what is sacred, reverence for the gods," in Late Latin "monastic life" (5c.). According to Cicero derived from *relegere* "go through again, read again," from *re-* "again" + *legere* "read" (see *lecture* (n.)). However, popular etymology among the later ancients (and many modern writers) connects it with *religare* "to bind fast" (see *rely*), via notion of "place an obligation on," or "bond between humans and gods." Another possible origin is *religiens* "careful," opposite of *negligens*.

I think that both the modern definition and the 'folk-etymology' are in fact correct because the root, in both senses (to *read* or to *bind*) all derive from the same root PIE **leg* "to collect, gather, unite" as we have seen with the word *logos* meaning "word, read, reason." Religion, linguistically speaking, is Yoga and both are rational processes, methods for achieving enlightenment through logic, reasoning, study, meditation, reflection and application. The prefix *re-* "back, again" essentially informs us that religion is "ongoing study." One must not be

39 Natron is a cleansing agent.

satisfied with surface appearances but must get "deep" into a problem.[40]

An additional note on the prefix *re-* may shed some light on its usage in the word *religion*. As noted by Angela Della Volpe—in her article "Shall we "re-consider"? A look at the pragmatics of the semantics of re-" (2011)—notes that re-, in essence, means to "repeat" an action. Because repeating an action may result in reversing it, the Latin re- prefix, in some instances, acquired the additional meaning of 'un-': i.e., *re-velare* "to unveil," or *re-cludere* "to disclose." The OED defines re- as:

> *re-*: word-forming element meaning "back to the original place, again," also with a sense of "undoing," c.1200, from Old French and directly from Latin *re-* "again, back, against." Often merely intensive.

The same source, under the entry of the word *reveal*, states that *re-* means "opposite of." With this in mind, the word *religion* can simply mean "to unveil" or literally "to untie" or "unbind." If **leg* is the process of "binding, gathering and collecting," or the "uniting, codifying" of facts (knowledge), then *religion* would be the systematic approach to "decoding" (untying) the hidden jewels within a body of knowledge collected over a period of time. The ancients used to codify the accumulated knowledge by way of "myths." The priesthood education system taught initiates how to properly "untie, decode" the myths and this is why *myths* are often associated with *religion*.

Conclusion

This essay has attempted to make viable connections between the ancient practice of tying 'knotty' ropes and the acquisition of knowledge. This former association was fossilized in the ancient Egyptian *mdw nṯr* writing script, graphically, in words dealing with writing, books, speech, knowledge, wisdom and skills. Scrolls (books) and the rope used to tie them together were often made of the same material. So both objects became symbols for the process and product of learning. There is also a strong genealogical component embedded in these themes. We come to better understand that *wisdom*, in part, is associated with knowing about and having the ability to recall the wisdom of one's ancestors.

As noted by Obenga (2004), although there were specialized institutes for learning, most often, specific trade and life wisdom was passed down through one's family line by the father. Because there was never a claim of "revealed texts" in ancient Egypt, wisdom was often passed down from father to child in the form of a document called a *sb3yt*. It is a will of sorts, that instead of passing down property through one's lineage, one passed on wisdom through these writings. A few relevant reflexes are given in the table below.

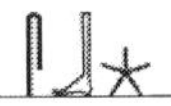	*sb3* "pupil, student"
	*sb3* "supervision, guidance, direction"
	*sb3* "teach, teaching, instruction, tend,"
	*sbḳ/sb3* "wise"
	*sb3yt* "written teachings, instructions, guidance"

40 One can argue that the "blind faith" aspect of modern 'religion' is actually "anti-religious." To be religious is to approach the Divine with reason, with an uncanny ability to be able to "tie" and "untie" the knotty ropes of life.

	*sb3yt* "chastisement, punishment"
	*sb3yt* "education"
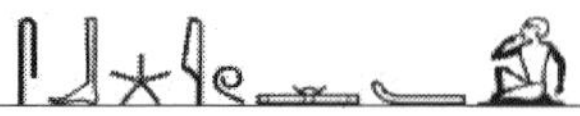	*sb3yt/sb3* "teaching, learning"
	*sb3yt* "book, book of instruction"

There may be a play on words as it regards this process of passing down wisdom from father to son in the ancient Egyptian tradition. It can be argued that a root for *sb3* is *b3* which one can find cognate in the Canaanite language as *ba'al* "lord, master, husband." Reflexes can be found in Luganda *lu-baale/ba-lu-baale* "divinities"; Hebrew *b^{e}'al-iym* "divinities," *ba'al* "husband"; *ba'al hah-bayit* "landlord"; Yorùbá *baálé* "husband, father," *baálé ilé* "landlord," *baálé* "chief of rural settlement"; Egyptian *b3*  "soul," *b3*  "might, power," *b3w*  "glory, respect, authority, power, strength, fate, might, impressiveness, will." The word *sb3* "teach" and the word *sb3yt* "chastisement, punishment" have the same determinative of a man holding a striking stick. Discipline in the classrooms was strict and punishment was not unusual for unruly students as can be seen in the *Papyrus Lansing* (20th Dynasty) where it states "Because you beat me on the back, your teaching entered my ears" (Obenga 2004: 570). In the New Kingdom the *Papyrus Sallier I* states, "I strike you a hundred times, but you pay no heed at all." The *Papyrus Anastasi* describes a schoolboy playing truant and a father's response towards his behavior:

> A stupid son, badly reared by his father, is a statue of stone. A son who remembers what he is taught, and has a strong desire to learn, has a splendid destiny; his character will help bring blessings upon him. Where the learner's attitude is hostile, no instruction can succeed. He who heeds a first reproach is spared a second. If a child's character is wanting, it is because he is disobedient. Thoth, the great god (of writing), gave the earth the whip to help educate fools. A child who steers clear of scandal will never be hit a regrettable blow. No child dies from a beating given by his father's hand. (Obenga, 2004: 271)

A father is seen, then, as someone who teaches as well as disciplines a child (anyone who is a respected authority figure).[41] A son who adheres to his father's teachings will grow up to be wise and succeed in life. Also noted in the excerpt above is the fact that the god Thoth gave mankind the whip to educate fools. It is possible that many of the whips were made out of rope, and if so, it would give us a new dimension for the association between ropes and knowledge.

Not much is known about the material used for the whips in ancient Egypt, but there may be a clue in the word *krṯ* 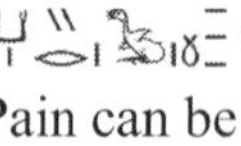 "strap, (whip) lashes" which utilizes the tied rope glyph  [V6] as a determinative. Pain can be a strong motivating factor for learning information (think of old-school pledging processes of college fraternities for example). You'd want to get the information in your head as quick as possible to avoid getting struck for incorrect responses to charges. Therefore, the rope/cord/whip would have a different conceptual relationship to learning, knowledge and wisdom than what we have associated earlier with tying knotty ropes.

All-in-all, knowing in the African context is intimately related to the accumulated knowledge of one's ancestors. It is the obligation of the student to get to know one's family line because within that line is a storehouse of knowledge. Just as we are the recipients of the long-developed, ancient customs and beliefs of our ancestors, so our descendants will receive

41 In African societies, the word for priest, teacher and even king is simply the word for "father": e.g., Yorùbá *babalawo* "father of mysteries" (a priest).

whatever tradition we hand on to them. This bonding that unites the living with the dead and the generations to be born is symbolized by rope in the Bantu-Kongo tradition (see Fu-Kiau, 2001) and this concept may be fossilized in the *mdw nṯr* script. Each living person is a *knot* on the *rope* of life and is the regeneration of souls who have come with the gifts and potential for discovering new more satisfying dimensions for being human.

Christopher Ehret, in his book *The Civilizations of Africa* (2002), reaffirms—in many ways—the sentiments expressed above. In describing the Bantu conceptualization of community, Ehret notes that:

> The people in such a village saw themselves as part of a mutually recognized wider grouping of many villages, which they called **-lungu*. This word derives from a proto-Bantu verb, **-lung-*, meaning "to join by tying." The metaphor encoded in the word shows that even though the earliest Bantu people based their rights in the local village community on kinship, they saw their wider society or ethnicity as a joining together of separate kin groups—as something mutually entered rather than imposed by birth. (Ehret, 2002: 111-112)

The BLR3 database reaffirms the sentiments expressed in the excerpt above. We see reflexes in Bantu such as: **-dùk-* "plait, braid," **túng* "put through, thread on string, plait, sew, tie up, build, close (in); **tóngá* "basket"; **túngá* "country, village" (ciLuba *musoko, diTunga* "village"; *ciMenga, ciHunda* "large collection of, metropolis"). We see these same associations in the ancient Egyptian language with the word *mr*  "to tie, to bind, fasten, be bound, join, collect, connect, bundle." It has a by-form: *mꜣꜥ*  "rope" (at front of ship), *mꜣꜥ.t* "towing rope" (r > *ꜣ*). The same root is used for the word  "*mꜣꜥ* "village." A variation of this root could be *ꜣbt*  "family" (metathesis; m>b). This root is also found in the word *smꜣ* "unite, to join, associate (with), arrive (in), to sleep (with female), combinations, assemble." It is also found in *smꜣw* "confederation, association." This allows us to get a better meaning for the phrase *smꜣ tꜣwy* "the uniting of the two lands." In essence, *smꜣ tꜣwy*  or *tꜣ-mrj*  is really a word for "confederation; the land of bounded families/villages; the collective." The same type of association between "tying/binding" and "family/village" that we see in Bantu is present among the ancient Egyptians.

I end with the following excerpt from a New Kingdom *sbꜣyt* that I think summarizes this whole paper quite nicely in light of the revealed data.

> The wise scribes from the time following the age of the gods, those whose prophecies came true, their names remain for eternity. Their names are mentioned because of the books they wrote in their lifetimes. The memory of those who wrote them remains beautiful for all eternity. Become a scribe. Fix this plan in your heart, so that the same might happen to your name. A book is more precious than a painted stele, more valuable than a wall covered with inscriptions. A book erects mansions and pyramids in the hearts of those who pronounce (the author's) names. Truly, a name in the mouths of men is an asset in the city of the departed. (Excerpt from a New Kingdom *Instruction* [after Siegried Schott], cited in Obenga, 2004: 569)

(Table Footnotes)

1 Kalenjiin: *suuswoot* "a blade of grass, a lot of grass"; *soosyoot* "a type of palm assigned the botanical names *Phoenix redinata* and *Hyphaene thebaica;* ciLuba: *bisoosà* ≈ *bisonsà* "grass, legumes"; *cisoosà* ≈ *cisonsà* "brin d'herbe"; *biseki* "legumes."

APPENDIX A: The Complexity of Meaning

One of the underlying premises of this book is that the study of *semantics*[1] can better help us to understand the deeper aspects of ancient Egyptian concepts as expressed through its language. When confronted with the major ideas of ancient Egypt, understanding the concept of *meaning* is essential. The focus of this Appendix is *meaning* and is meant to be a supplement to the information on semantics given in *Chapter 2* of this volume. Because of space limitations and the focus of that chapter, we could not get into the heart of the subject there, but I felt it pertinent to the overall theme of this volume, so I decided to discuss it more in-depth here.

I have found the discussions on the topic of *meaning* in linguistics very helpful in the following works: *A Basic Course in Anthropological Linguistics* (2004: 99-120) by Marcel Danesi; *Semantics* by John I. Saeed (1997, 1st Ed.); *Translation and Translating: Theory and Practice* by Roger T. Bell (1991); and *Comparative Linguistics* (1966: 231-258) by Robert Lord. In this section I will synthesize and draw primarily from these sources. Our objective is to critically examine how meanings are encoded in words, sentences and utterances. This is a study of semantics.[1]

Meaning

The objective of defining *meaning* has been elusive for researchers and many have come to the conclusion that it cannot be defined: at least accurately. Meaning is something that people understand intuitively, but defies a precise definition. Because of this dilemma, linguists have devised techniques for fleshing out the meaning of linguistic forms, to get around this question of what meaning is in any absolute sense. The most common method for fleshing out meaning in related languages is the *comparative method*.[2] Semantics typically has two branches of study: *historical semantics*, which is concerned with diachronic semantics or change of meaning; and *descriptive semantics* which attempts to describe the *conditions* of meaning relationships and change of meaning (synchronic semantics).

Semantics is concerned, amongst other things, with the description and origin of the diversity of meaning clustering around a single lexical unit or word. Looking at the word "head" can provide us with pristine examples of the diversity of the usage of a term. Head can mean: (a) the physiological head; (b) the intellect or mind; (c) chief, or head of an organization; (d)

1 *Semantics* (from Greek sēmantikós) is the study of meaning. It typically focuses on the relation between signifiers, such as words, phrases, signs and symbols, and what they stand for.

2 In linguistics, the *comparative method* is a technique for studying the development of languages by performing a feature-by-feature comparison of two or more languages with common descent from a shared ancestor, as opposed to the method of internal reconstruction, which analyzes the internal development of a single language over time. Ordinarily both methods are used together to reconstruct prehistoric phases of languages, to fill in gaps in the historical record of a language, to discover the development of phonological, morphological, and other linguistic systems, and to confirm or refute hypothesized relationships between languages.

head of a vegetable (e.g. cabbage); (e) head of a chapter; (f) head of a jetty; (g) head of cattle; (h) head of a coin (as opposed to tails); (i) head of water (technical term); (j) head of steam. The underlying meaning of all of these associations is "something that leads," "something that guides," or that which is in "the forefront/the upper most region."

When studying meaning, it is imperative that we start by noting that every word, phrase or sentence is a *sign*—it is something that stands for something other than itself. The word *cat* is a sign because it doesn't stand for the phonemes that comprise it, /kæt/, but rather for a "feline mammal." The latter is known as the *referent*. Two types of referents are encoded in signs: *concrete* and *abstract*.

- ***a concrete referent***, such as the animal designated by the word *cat,* is something existing in reality or in real experience and is normally available to direct perception by the senses (a cat can be seen, touched, etc.);
- ***an abstract referent***, such as the meaning captured by the word *idea,* is something that is formed in the mind and is not normally available to direct perception by the senses (an idea cannot be seen or touched physically). (Danesi 2004: 100)

The sign allows the mind to conjure up the things to which it refers even though these might not be physically present for the senses to perceive. This is important to understand for this discussion; for just because the word *cool,* for example, can refer to a relative temperature, it doesn't necessarily mean it is used in this temperature context in every instance.

There is a key feature of a sign known in psychology as *displacement*. By simply uttering the word *cat*, for instance, people understand what is being singled out in the world of experience, even though an actual *cat* may not be present for the person to observe. In a similar fashion, if someone was to say the phrase *bright idea*, people will still understand what is being implied, even though no such thing is available for the senses to detect. It is this feature that has allowed mankind to be able to refer to anything at will, even to something that is made up completely by human imagination. This is what separates us from the animal kingdom (along with other characteristics).

Our ability to talk about the world depends on our mental models of it. In this view a language, therefore, represents a *theory about reality*: about the types of things and situations in the world (Saeed, 1997:24). We note then that different conceptualizations influence the description of the real world situations.

The bridge that connects a sign and its referent is what is intended with the word *meaning*. This encompasses all of the possible meanings of the sign. There are essentially three types of meaning. The first type of meaning is known as the *literal* or *denotative meaning*. For instance, a cat is a small carnivorous mammal domesticated since early times as a catcher of mice and rats, and as a pet, exists as different breeds. The second type of meaning is known as *connotative*. This type of meaning is extended to embrace other referents that are seen to have something in common with the basic referent. So when someone says, "that boy is cold," they aren't referring to the body temperature of the person. They are speaking about the amazing talent of the person and how witnessing this talent makes them *shiver* as if they were *cold*. The third type of meaning is *figurative*, that is, it is known by it associations with other signs and their meanings. For instance, if someone "let the cat out the bag," we know there is no real cat, but the association is to the word "secret" which was revealed by someone.

As Danesi notes:

> Since the use of the sign is what determines its meaning, the linguist will always have to keep in mind: (1) the pragmatic or contextual conditions that hold between

> speakers and signs; and (2) the rules of discourse, which govern relations among the elements within utterances. (2004: 100)

It's not enough to simply read word definitions in a dictionary and declare victory in meaning. The whole cultural context must be taken into consideration when investigating key terms. One must see the world from the view-point of the people under examination as much as possible.

Types of Meaning

We've already discussed the two types of meaning: *denotative* and *connotative*. We are going to briefly expand on our preliminary account as it is essential to this discourse.

Denotation is the meaning that a sign is designed to encode initially: it is the relationship between an *expression* and its *extension*. It is a prototypical exemplar of a *category*. A cat refers to a category of animal that we recognize as having the quality of "catness." "A creature exemplifying catness" is the denotative meaning of cat. A set of semantic features specifies what a cat is: [+mammal], [+retractile claws], [+long tail], etc. By understanding these features in combination as the essence of "catness," we are able to determine if a being (imagined or real) falls within this category (= [+mammal], [+retractile claws], [+long tail], etc.).

The meaning of a sign can be extended to encompass other kinds of referents that appear, as a matter of inference or analogy, to have something in common with the original referent. We see such associations with the word "house" as its denotative meaning refers to any, more or less, "free standing structure intended for human habitation." We note that the term house can be used to refer to things like:

1. the *house* is in session = "legislative assembly, quorum"
2. the *house* roared with laughter – "audience in a theater"
3. they sleep at one of the *houses* at Howard University = "dormitory"

The extensions of the word house are not random or disconnected to the semantic features that make up the initial referent which has the following features: [+structure], [+human], [+habitation], etc. A house can refer to anything that involves or implicates humans coming together for some specific reason.

Connotation, therefore, can be defined as the mapping of the semantic features of a sign onto a new referent if it is perceived to entail these features by inference or analogy (Danesi 2004: 103). A manifestation of connotation is Zipf's law. In exploring our examples of *cat* and *house*, to cover the connotative meanings of these terms would require the coinage of at least six new words. This would require much more effort in terms of memory, lexical choice and so on. Through connotation, Zipf's law[3] ensures that we will make use of a finite set of linguistic resources to encompass an infinitude of meanings, thus decreasing cognitive effort in matters of reference.

This is apparent for anyone who has examined ancient African languages. Ancient African languages are not vocabulary rich. They rely on an array of connotative meanings deriving from the same root with slight vowel alterations in many cases. For example, the root **ka* is used for "fire, life, human being, authority, burnt, earth, to sit, country, land, hands, to cut (with hands), axe (which you use with hands), etc."

3 The principle suggests that the ways in which human beings organize their linguistic systems and exert themselves in speaking tend towards least effort. Zipf developed his principle on the observation that there is a manifest correlation between the length of a specific word (in number of phonemes) and its rank order in the language (its position in order of its frequency of occurrence). (Danesi 2004: 12)

The demarcation between denotative and connotative is not straightforward, and as it turns out, denotative meaning can hardly ever be determined without reference to connotation and other processes (Danesi 2004: 105). Danesi also notes that when studying languages of different cultures, different semantic feature arrays may have to be drawn up, since distinctions as to what is meaningful will vary. This is important as our *house* example above will further illuminate later on in this discussion. What is the root feature in one language family (i.e., a structure<home) is not the root in another language family (i.e., fire<home); although the terms may derive from the same source.

Associative Field Theory

Words that share one or more features together is called a *lexical field.* The great linguist Ferdinand de Saussure has demonstrated that each word in a language is surrounded by a network of associations which connect with still other forms. Therefore, a given term is like the center of a constellation. The center point is where other coordinated terms converge and their sum is indefinite. To illustrate this thesis, Saussure drew up the following diagram (Lord 1966: 238):

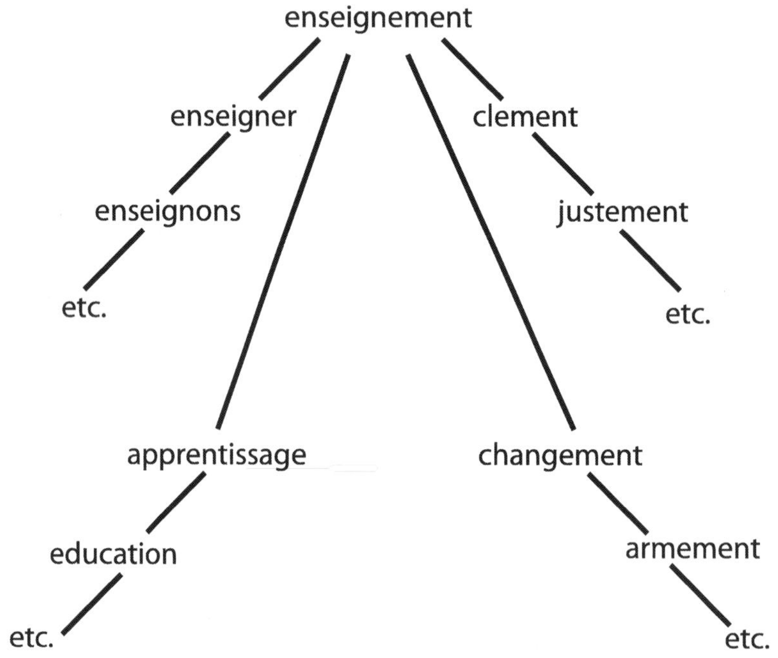

In the first leg of this diagram are the following terms: *enseigner* "to teach," and *enseignons* "we teach." These are linked by similarity of grammatical form, or *paradigmatically*. The second leg (*apprentissage*, *education*) are linked to the noun *enseignement* by synonymity or semantic relationship. A suffix (*-ment*) links the third and fourth legs. The *changement* and *armenent* lexemes are nouns and are kept separate from the fourth leg which comprises miscellaneous, accidental grouping, comprising nouns, adjectives and adverbs, sharing only the element *–ment.*

Saussure's pupils have expanded his work and expressed the associate field as "a halo which surrounds the sign and whose exterior fringes become merged." This field is formed by a network of associations: *contiguity, similarity, sensation* and *name*. No finite limits can be assigned to any field; thus why it is considered *open*. So we note that lexical units cannot be viewed in isolation (what Modupe Oduyoye (1996) calls mono-language etymolizing). Instead, these lexical units form a closely knit and articulated lexical sphere, where the significance of each unit is determined by its neighbors, their semantic areas reciprocally limiting one another. I relate this to the African proverb which states, "*I am, because we are. We are, therefore I am.*" This simply means that my personality is a result of growing up in a given community. This community has shaped me in all types of ways, and in turn, I help to shape it. Linguistically this can be seen in the associative field where a lexical item derives its meaning from "growing up" in a given "community" (field). These units are found in all cases to be indissolubly bound up with the social or cultural context mentioned earlier.

Words belong to never-ending chain sequences, to phrases, sentences, contexts to the fabric of the entire language (Lord 1966: 241). Words have no meaning until they become joined together in a linguistic whole. As long as there's no clash of context, this range of associations can coexist (like in the case of homophones). Whenever homophones exist, the homophones will acquire different spellings wherever possible (i.e., person—parson; soul—sole; maze—maize; bell—belle). When homonyms threaten to arise, the two forms will diverge phonetically or morphologically (i.e., cloth—clothe; brothers—brethren; shade—shadow). A word will either adjust itself dynamically in a field or be rejected. Meanings build up composite meanings in a larger "field of tension."

This building of composite meanings is seen in this day and age not in terms of feature differentiation, but rather degree. The lexical fields are characterized by distinctive semantic features that differentiate the individual lexemes in the field from one another, and also by features shared by all the lexemes in the field (Danesi 2004: 106). The example given by Danesi is one of [+seat] (i.e., something in which to sit), such as a *chair, sofa, bench*, etc. All of these belong to the same semantic field. One way in which to distinguish the type of seat is in how many people can sit in the seat, whether a back support is included and so on.

The open nature of the associative field poses problems for those wanting to neatly classify features which are constantly changing to meet new social needs. This makes it virtually impossible to develop a core set of features for describing them. This technique, according to Danesi, is limited to determining literal meaning. Because of the dynamics and open-endedness of the field, it is virtually useless for figurative meanings. In traditional semantic approaches, figurative (also known as metaphoric) meaning was considered ornamental. But since the 1970's it is not only seen as systematic and regular, but also central to language.

Abstract concepts are linked systematically to concrete ones via metaphor (from Greek *meta* "across" + *pherein* "to bear"). A metaphor is a cognitive strategy that allows people to portray and understand abstract concepts in terms of concrete reality. Ideas and feelings are experienced as if they were sensations and are named as such. I argue that much of the debates on Egyptian concepts suffer from researchers not understanding the metaphoric meanings and associations of such concepts. Thus, we have researchers who never penetrate their deeper meanings and associations, because they stay on literal meanings (e.g., *Rᶜ* = "sun god").

However, defining metaphor poses a certain dilemma. Danesi (ibid) demonstrates this dilemma with the following metaphor: *the professor is a snake*.

- There is the primary referent, *the professor,* which is known as the *topic* of the metaphor.
- Then there is another referent, *the snake,* which is known as the *vehicle* of the metaphor.
- Their correlation creates a new meaning, called the *ground,* which is not the simple sum of the meanings of the two referents.

When examining the process of associating the two referents in the example above, it is not the denotative meaning of the vehicle that is transferred to the topic, but rather its connotation: it is the culture-specific characteristics perceived in snakes—danger, slyness, slipperiness, cunningness, etc. It is this complex of connotations that produces the *ground.*

George Lakoff and Mark Johnson (American linguists) refer to the result (the ground) of the linkage as a *conceptual metaphor*. A conceptual metaphor has two parts in our phrase "The professor is a snake." Each part is called a *domain*: for which [people] is called the *target domain* because it is the abstract concept itself. It is the *target* of the conceptual metaphor. The second domain is [animals] and is called the *source domain* because it encompasses the class of vehicles that *deliver* the intended meanings (the slyness, cunningness, etc.) to the *target domain*.

There are many more layers to the associative field that space will not allow for here. Our purpose in discussing this aspect of semantics is to remind the researcher that they cannot determine meaning of a lexical unit in isolation: there is always a cultural context for which a term is used and we must utilize techniques that will allow us to penetrate that cultural core. The best way is through the eyes of the people. Among Africans in particular, this is best illustrated in poems, proverbs and mythology. We will now examine *word meaning* as the last leg of this section.

Word Meaning

The primary technique used for establishing word meaning is by comparison as words can be seen to relate to each other in specific ways. One such way is *synonymy*. Synonyms are words having the same or nearly the same meaning in one or more of their uses (i.e., near-close, far-distant). Another way to determine meaning is through *antonymy*. Antonyms are words that are opposite in meaning: night-day, up-down. Both methods are not completely reliable as some words can be used in the same context, while others cannot, although they are synonyms for example.

Another method for ascertaining meaning is through *homonymy*. Homonyms are words with the same pronunciation and/or spelling, but with different meanings. When the homonym is purely phonetic it is known as a *homophone* (i.e., hair-hare). If the homonym is orthographic,[4] then they are known as *homographs* (*play* as in a Tyler Perry *play* vs. *play* as in My child likes to *play*).

An additional type of relation that is known between words is *hyponymy*, which is the process by which the meaning of one sign is included in that of another (i.e., the meaning of *scarlet* is included in the meaning of *red*; *tulip* in that of *flower*). This is related to our associative field discussed earlier. With hyponymy we are able to relate word meanings to the overall meaning of lexical fields, thus focusing on those specific features that keep words within the field distinct.

Another feature of meaning to note is that in African languages, nouns in remote ancient times, were not nouns that we would recognize today. Today we define the noun by contrast with the verb. The "primal" noun knew of no such contrast. For example, the ARM was used alike for a limb of the body and for ACTIONS OF THE ARM. The HEAD was used alike for the physical organ and for the ACTIONS OF THE HEAD: eating, drinking, etc., even for the water that was drunk (Campbell-Dunn, 2009a: 148). Each primal noun was a cluster of associations. Some of these associations were more concrete than others. We note that concepts

4 The orthography of a language specifies a standardized way of using a specific writing system (script) to write the language. Where more than one writing system is used for a language, for example Kurdish, Uyghur or Serbian, there can be more than one orthography. Orthography is distinct from typography.

were not discrete units but they overlapped and flowed into each other. The MOUTH was part of the HEAD. The terminology used for the SKY was also used for the HEAD as the sky was the *head* of the world from which the RAIN fell. To demonstrate this convention, we can take the Niger-Congo root PWS **li, *lu* "head" (also *di, du* "head") to form Niger-Congo *di, d.i* "to eat," *dum* (*dumu*) "to bite" (with *d.u* "to bite"). Stapleton (1903) argues that Niger-Congo words are formed from a very small number of roots. This is apparent in Egyptian as well.

Concluding Remarks

Much of the debate in Egyptological circles, as it regards major Egyptian themes, has suffered much due to 1) mono-language etymolizing, 2) the insistence on perfection (exact word matches) and 3) a lack of understanding the cultural contexts and the associative fields in which lexical units live. As Campbell-Dunn (2009b) notes, the reconstruction of the details of past civilizations over thousands of years can only be partial at best. Trying to enter into the minds of people who inhabited a world that we no longer know intimately, with a vastly different mindset, poses difficulties and sets limitations for our current tools of analysis. Researchers must take note of this. Language is the carrier of culture and the languages we speak today are legacies of our remote and mysterious past which still carries features that find their explanation in it. *Language is the oldest living witness to history.*

Demanding exact replication, as noted by Campbell-Dunn (2009b), of meaning is an exercise in futility. Words change meaning over time. For the comparativists, difficulties may arise due to semantic slippage. Words have different suffixes and prefixes and one must be able to discover these root forms to do a proper comparison. Old basic nouns generally hold their meaning almost unchanged, but these same nouns may be used connotatively and as we have discussed previously, this open-ended phenomena extends its associations indefinitely and makes it virtually impossible to narrow down a core set of features due to new social contexts. In this volume we have examined several different features of our signs in various African languages and spiritual contexts in order to get a better understanding of the meanings associated with the terms, to hopefully discover their core themes from which its other meanings derive. By expanding our research parameters to the Niger-Congo and Nilo-Saharan proto-reconstructions, we have a deeper well in which to draw comparisons that will allow us to gain clarity about the various shapes and forms words has taken over the millennia.

Unlike in European languages, where the tendency for word-meanings is mapped to a one-to-one/sign-to-meaning basis, in Africa the lexemes are in of themselves "themes." In other words, the lexemes represent an underlying theme for which many items are associated, and with the same lexeme. For example, in the Ga language of Ghana, the word *la/lala* can at once refer to the "sun," to "blood" and "singing." The underlying theme that connects them all is the principle of "vitality" and "life." Each of these concepts, in one way or another, represents the principle of vitality and life; whether through the life giving rays of the sun, or the life present in blood, or the expression of life and vitality through singing. All of these concepts are represented by the same term and are not homonyms in the traditional sense. We see these types of examples all throughout the ancient Egyptian language and this, we posit, is one of the major characteristics that links Egypt with the rest of Black Africa.

APPENDIX B: The Sounds of Cilubà

Family: Niger-Congo Subfamily > Benue-Congo Genus > Bantoid

Tshiluba is a member of the Bantu language family spoken by about six million people in the Democratic Republic of the Congo, where it is one of the national languages along with Lingála, Kiswahili and Kikongo. It is spoken mainly in Western and Eastern Kasai. Other names for the language include Cilubà, Luba, Luba-Kasai and Luba-Lulua. The official language of the DRC is French. Recent population statistics are not available, but it is generally accepted that there are at least six million speakers of Cilubà. In Guthrie's classification of the Bantu languages, the Lubà language is labelled as the 1st language of the 3rd group of zone L, thus L31 (Guthrie 1948: 54). In addition, Guthrie distinguishes between three dialects: L31a, L31b and L31c (see map below).

Geographic distribution

The geographical areas where Cilubà is spoken can tentatively be pinpointed as shown in the map below, taken from De Schryver (1999: 11).

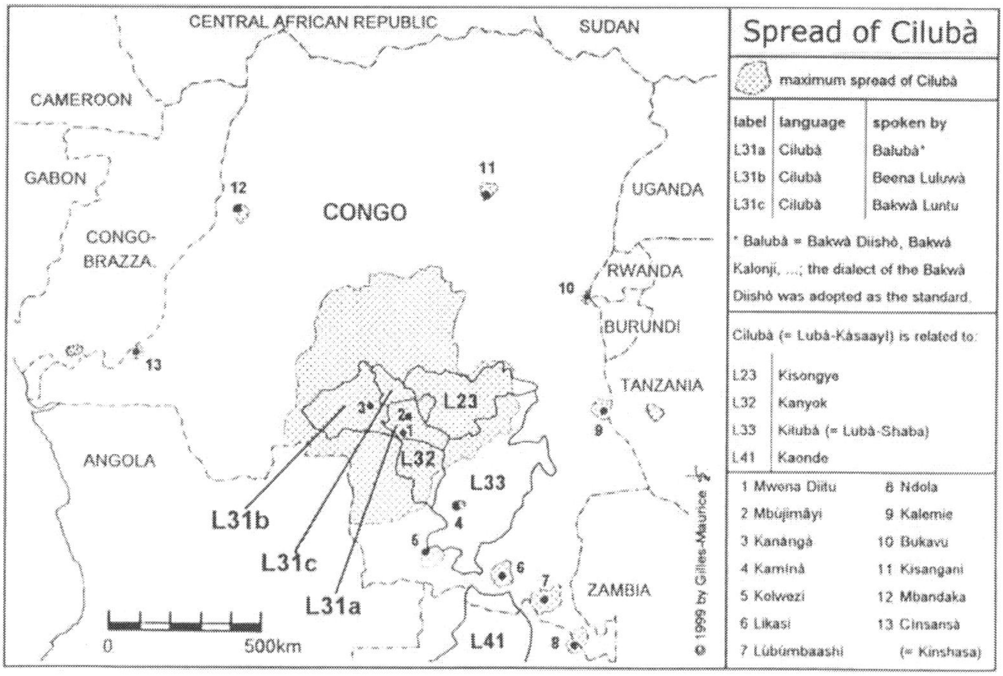

The following is an adaptation of notes from Dr. Ngo Semzara Kabuta on the ciLuba language, creator of the www.ciyem.ugent.be website (originally written in French).

Introduction

There are three categories of sounds: 5 vowels, 2 glides (or semi-vowels) and 18 consonants. Each vowel can be short or long and can carry a high, low, rising or falling tone. Furthermore, any vowel can be nasalized before a consonant.

1 Vowels: i, e, a, o, u.

Each vowel can be short or long. It (the vowel) carries a *high-tone* (which is not represented in the spelling, since it is the most common), *low-tone* (represented by a low-pitched accent), *rising-tone* (represented by a circonflexe accent reversed) or descending (represented by a circonflexe accent).

i : *milice (militia)*	: micì	*arbres(trees)*
e : *sel (salt)*	: kutèèla	*citer (quote)*
a : *malade (sick)*	: kubala	*lire (read)*
o : *épauler (shoulder)*	: mòna	*regarde (see)*
u : *courant (current)*	: muntu	*personne (person)*

1.2 In some contexts, the joining of two vowels (*a, i*) produces a new vowel, always long (*ee*):

ma-ìsu > mêsu "eyes" ; ma-ìku > mêku "families."

1.3 At a different vowel, *i* and *u* becomes *y* and *w* respectively:

bi-anza > byanza "hands" ; u-àka-fùnd-a > wâkafùnda "you wrote"

1.4 *i* becomes *e* when preceded by *e* or *o*:

ku-pòòl-il-a > kupòòlela "pick" + preposition
ku-tel-il-a > kutelela "sewing" + preposition

1.5 *u* becomes *o* when preceded by *o*:

kukòs-ulul-a> kukòsolola "cut, splitting, carving"

1.6 Has the form of the vowel that follows:

bà-eel-a > bèèla "putting"
ma-ìmpè > mîmpè "good, beautiful" [Egyptian *nfr* "good, beautiful, perfect"]

2. Glides: y, w.

y: yen: yaya "big sister"
w: watt: wayi "she /he has gone"

3. Consonants : m, n, ny, ng, b, v, 1, d, z, j, p, f, t, s, sh, k, c

m : *maman "mother"*
n : *nier "deny"*
ny : *oignon "onion"*
ng : *parking*
b : *bureau "office"*
v: *vent "wind"*
1 : *loi "law"*

d : *donner "to give"* (it is not clear, however, what is before *i* and after *n*) : dîsu *oeil "eye"*, bundù *honte "shame"*
z : *zéro*
j : *jurer*
p : has no equivalent in French. It is pronounced leaving a slight opening between the lips (unlike the French, they are totally against one another), so that the sound evokes the sound *f*. It can also be outright pronounced as an aspirated *h*. After *m*, it is pronounced as in French.
f : *finir "end"*
t : *tout "all"*
s :*sel "salt"*
sh : *choix "choice"*
k : *quiconque "anyone"*
c : *match* [these are still represented by *tsh*]

3.1 Followed by *i*, certain consonants change as follows (the infinitive in brackets):

l + i> di:	wălààdi (kulààla) *she fell asleep*
n + i> nyi:	wănyaanyì (kunyaana) *she lost weight*
z + i> ji:	wăzaajì (kuzaaza) *has crashed*
t + i> ci:	wătuucì (kutuuta) *she hit*
s + i> shi:	wăkòshi (kukòsa) *she cut*

3.2 Preceded by a nasal, two consonants change as follows:

n + l> nd: ndòmbèlà (kulòmbela) "asks for me" /n - lòmb- ìl – à/ moidemande-for the verb-final)
m + p [Φ]> mp [p]: mpèèshà [mpèèshàj (kupèèsha [kuΦèèsha]) "gives me"

3.3 *l* preceded by *n, m* or *ny* is pronounced *n*:

kutùm-il-a > kutùmina "send"+ préposition ; kukàn-il-a > kukànyina "utter of menances" + preposition

3.4 Given some suffixes (in general -*il*-), *l* or *n* preceded by a vowel different from *i* is dropped:

kusungul-il-a > kusungwila "choose" + preposition (choose for, by)
kusumpakan-il-a > kusumpakeena "worry "+ preposition

4. Tones

Tones have a distinctive function as essential as that of consonants and vowels. It is therefore necessary to master the operation. Vowels may be pronounced in a registry *high* or *low*. Two different tones can be combined with rising tone (low-high, noted [ˇ] in the spelling) or falling tone (high + low, denoted [ˆ]). In the diagrams below, [/] is the rising tone and [\] the falling tone; points indicate the limits of syllables.

mwêndù mujimà [\ . _ . ¯ . ¯ . _]   *a fully [lit] lamp ;*
mwêndù mujìma [\._.¯ . _ . ¯]   *a lamp [that has been] turned off*
Ndaayà [¯ . _] (name of a woman) ; Ndààyà [__ . _] (name of a man)
wăyi [/ . ¯] *he/she is gone* ; wâyi [\ . ¯] *you went away*

Intonation. In reality, the pitch of notes is relative. In general, we can say that in a statement, a second high tone is less than the previous high, and a second low tone, is lower than the previous. Thus, the following sentence: "*Pangààkabàmbilà bwalu abu bààkasànka bikolè*" [When I shared with them this story, they were very pleased] pronounced approximately as the tonal scheme (a) in 12 levels and not according to the diagram (c) on two levels. In diagram (a), there is often neutralized low tones and successive highs, so that levels 10-11, 8-9, 6-7, 4-5 and 2-3 are often made about the same height, as in the diagram (b).

(a)

12	pa											
11			ka									
10		ngàà										
9					mbi							
8				bà								
7							bwalu ebu					
6						là						
5									ka			
4								bàà				
3											nka biko	
2										sà		
1												lè

(b)

7	pa						
6		ngààka					
5			bàmbi				
4				là bwalu ebu			
3					bààka		
2						sànka biko	
1							lè

(c)

2	pa		ka		mbi		bwalu ebu		ka		nka biko	
1		ngàà		bà		là		bàà		sà		lè

Table 1: Sound interchanges in CiLuba-Bantu[1]

n ↔ *m*	*np* ↔ *mp*	*p* ↔ *f* ↔ *v*	*r* ↔ *l* ↔ *d*	*sh/š* ↔ *s* ↔ *z*
m↔ *b*	*w*↔ *b*	*p*↔ *h*	*rn* ↔ *nl* ↔ *nd*↔ *d*	*f* ↔ *v*↔ *pf*
m↔ *mb*	*s* ↔ *z* ↔ *j*	*p*↔ *b*	*d*↔ *t*	*t̲/č* ↔ *t*

Table 2: Verbal extensions in Tshilubà[2]

Tshiluba extensions	**Definitions**	**Reconstructed forms in Proto- Bantu**
-il- / -el- / -in- / -en-	Applicative	* -ID-
-ish- / -esh- / -ij- / -ej-	Causative	* -I- / * -ICI-
-angan-	Reciprocal	* -AN-
-ibu- / -ebu-	Passive	* -U- / * -IBU-
-ik- / -ek-	Neutro-Passive	* -IK-
-ik- / -ek-	Neutro-Active	* -IK-
-am-	Stative	* -AM-
-ul- / -ol- / -un- / -on-	Reversive	* -UD-
-ulul- / -olol- / -unun- / -onon-	Repetitive	* -UDUD-
-akan-	Extensive	?
-at-	Contactive	* -AT-

Bantu Noun-Class Prefixes

Bantu noun class systems can be roughly characterized in the following typological terms: First, noun classes tend to be realized as grammatical morphemes rather than independent lexical items. However, these grammatical morphemes were once independent words (Torrend 1891, Campbell-Dunn 2009a, 2009b). Second, they function as part of larger 'concordial' agreement systems, where nominal modifiers, pronominals, and verbs are all morphologically marked with the same noun class (gender) feature. Lastely, although productive semantic classes have been reconstructed for Proto-Bantu, much of the semantics of current Bantu noun classes is no longer productive, and in some languages the number of classes has been morphologically reduced (we argue the same for ancient Egyptian). Nonetheless, noun class systems are *grammatically* productive in most Bantu languages, and *semantically* productive to some degree (Senft, 2000).

Proto-Bantu Noun Class Meanings

Noun Class Meanings

1/2 humans, other animates
1a/2a kinship terms, proper names
3/4 trees, plants, non-paired body parts, other inanimates

1 The following table taken from Mubabinge Bilolo: *Tuleshi Kapya Ne Dyanga Mu CiKam: Mishi Ya CiKam Mu Cyena Ntu* (2008).

2 The following table is take from, "Bantu verbal extensions: a cartographic approach" by Gloria Cocchi in: V. Moscati & E. Servadio (eds.), *Proceedings of the "XXXV Incontro di Grammatica Generativa"*, CISCL Siena: STiL - Studies in Linguistics, Vol. 3 (2009): 91-103.

5/6 fruits, paired body parts, natural phenomena
6 liquid masses
7/8 manner, varied, diminutive
9/10 animals, inanimates
11 long thin objects, abstract nouns
12/13 diminutives
14 abstract nouns, mass nouns
15 infinitive
16,17,18 locatives (near, remote, inside)
19 diminutive
20/22 augmentive (diminutive)

Another way of saying it is:

Meanings of prefixes:

1. person
2. people
3. animate agent
4. plural of 3,
5 singular of 6,
6. paired things, multiples
7. custom, method, tool
8. pl of 7
9. animal
10 pl of 9
11. One of many things
12 pl of 13 & 19
13. small thing
14 abstraction
15. verb infinitive
16. "on" - Locative
17 "outside" - Locative
18 "in" - Locative
19. diminutive
20. pejorative
21. augmentative

Table 3. Various Niger-Kordofanian Noun Class Systems[3]

	**PB*	*Setswana*	*Sesotho*	*W. Ejagam*	*Cross River & Kru*
1	mo-	mo-	mo-	N-	x
1a	ø	ø	ø		
2	va-	ba-	ba-	a-	
2a	Vò-	bo-	bo-		x
3	mo-	mo-	mo-	N-	
4	me-	me-	me-		
5	le-	le-	le-	e-	
6	ma-	ma-	ma-	a-	
7	ke-	se-	se-		
8	Vi-/di	di-	di-	bi-	
9	n-	N-	(N)-	N-	x
10	di-n-	diN-	di(N)-		x
11	lo-	lo-			
12	ka-				
13	to-				
14	Vo-	bo-	bo-	o-	
15	ko-	γo-	ho-		
16	pa-	fa-			
17	ko-	γo-	ho-		
18	mo-	mo-			
19	pi-	i-			
20	γo				
21	γi				
22	γa				
23	γe				

3 This table is taken from K. Demuth (2000). "Bantu noun class systems: Loan word and acquisition evidence of productivity." In: G. Senft (Ed.), *Classification Systems*. Cambridge University Press. pp. 270-292.

Cilubà Noun-Class Prefixes

Table 4: Cilubà noun-class system

Milongo	Mitù yà bibìikidilu	Mitù yà bifìleedi, mifìdi nè mibadiki
1	**mu**-/N-mù-, ø	mu-
2	**ba**-/bà-, baa+	ba-
3	**mu**-/mù**mi**-/	mu-
4	mì-, N, ø	mi-
5	**di**-/dì**ma**-/	di-
6	mà-, maa+	ma-
7	**ci**-/cì, cii+	ci-
8	**bi**-/bì-, bii+	bi-
11	**lu**-/lù	lu-
12	**ka**-/kà-, kaa+	ka-
13	**tu**-/tù-, tuu+	tu-
14	**bu**-/bù-, buu+	bu-
15	**ku-**	ku-
16	**pa**-/+	pa-
17	**ku**-/+	ku-
18	**mu**-/+	mu-

1/2 : mulundà/balundà, mùmpêlà/baamùmpêlà, mààmù/baamààmù, Maweeja Nnangila
1/4 : ngomba/ngomba, nnyòka/nnyòka, nkwasa/nkwasa, sàtèlità/sàtèlità
3/4 : mucì/micì, mùpanù/mìpanù
5/6 : dikaaya/makaaya, dîsu/mêsu, dìkalù/màkalù, kaadìkalù
5/0 : dipaala, diibila, didyunda
0/6 : mashi, mabèèla, maluvu, mâyi, mashìka, mafi
6/6 : màshinyì/màshinyì, meetèlà/meetèlà, mèèsà/mèèsà
7/8 : cintu/bintu, ciidìkalu/biimàkalù
7/0 : citòòka, cifìika
8/8 : bidyà/bidyà, bìro/bìro
11/4 : luumù/nguumù, lungènyi/nngènyi, lumwènu/mmwènu
11/0 : luuyà, lûsù
12/13 : kantu/tungu, kaamàshinyì/tuumàshinyì, kàye/tùye
0/13 : tuminu, tuseku, tulù, tûmvi
14/6 : bùlokù/màlokù, bulundà/malundà, bwowa/mwowa
14/0 : buumùntù, busenjì, bukùnza
15/0 : kuseka, kumvwa, kwowa, kwenda
16/0 : pa mèèsà, pambèlu, pêku
17/0 : ku mèèsà, kumbèlu, kwîsu
18/0 : mu nzùbu, munda, mwitu

Egyptian and Ciluba Sound Correspondences

Table 5: Basic Egyptian Signs and their Phonemes[4]

Gardiner Sign Coda	Symbol	Description	Proposed Sound Value	ciLuba	Other possible vocalizations
G1		vulture	*ȝ*	a	r/l
M17		Reed leaf	*e/i/j*	i	gi, bi, ci
		Double reeds	*e/y*	y	g>y
D36		Arm	*ꜥ*	a, e(n)	ka, ba
G43,		Quail chick/ rope	*u/w*	u	b, swa
D58		Lower leg/foot	*b*	b	p, k
Q3		seat[1]	*p*	p	b
I9		Horned viper	*f*	f	b
G17		Owl/carpenter's level	*m*	m	b, p
N35,		Water/white crown	*n*	n	m, mb; ng, nk > ny
D21		mouth	*r*	l	
O4		courtyard	*h*	h, k	
V28		Twisted flax	*ḥ*	ng, nk, sh	s
Aa1		sieve	*ḫ*	ng, sh	
F32		Belly & udder	*ẖ*	sh, nk, h	x
O34		Bolt/lock	*s/z*	s, sh, z	t, j, k
S29		Folded shawl	*s*	s, sh, z	
N37		Pool of water	*š*	sh	
N29		Hill slope	*ḳ*	k, q	
V31		basket	*k*	k, g	t

4 The column for ciLuba comes from Bilolo (2011: 236). The "Other possible vocalizations" column is from Imhotep (2012b).

W11	𓎼	Jar stand or stool	*g*	g, ng, nk	
X1	𓏏	Bread loaf	*t*	t	d
V13	𓍿	Tethering rope	*ṯ*	tsh, ci	t
D46	𓂧	hand	*d*	d, t, ci	
I10	𓆓	cobra	*ḏ*	dj, nd	d, j, k

Also, when understanding dialects and change over time, one has to be familiar with the common morphology of phonemes. For this study I have adopted the *Table of Equivalent Consonants* created by Alexander Aberfeldy.[5] As noted by the author:

> Before we can understand the wordlist we need to understand something about consonants. The new approach has one tool, the Table of Equivalent Consonants or TEC, and the TEC has one application, the wordlist. The TEC was inspired by Soundex, a phonetic indexing system devised early in the twentieth century by Robert C. Russell and Margaret K. Odell. They called their invention the Soundex system and patented it in 1918 and 1922. It has been used, successfully, ever since to bring order to the spellings inflicted on immigrant surnames by English-speaking clerks and, often, by the owners of the names. In a similar way, the TEC has brought order to several million everyday words. The main feature of both systems is a reduction in the number of effective consonants from the dozens used in European languages to six effective consonants. Vowels are ignored. Both systems are effective because these variant spellings are not the result of sloppy speech, imperfect education, or laziness: they represent what actually happens to sounds when they are passed, many times, from mouth to ear and then written down, usually by a clerk who does not speak the same language. Every word in our dictionaries was transmitted orally for most of its existence and then transcribed in a similar way.

Here is the table below:

Fig.1.1 The TEC

1 B Mb P F V W
2 M N Ng Gn F V
3 C G J K Q S X Y Ch Sh H
4 D T Th Z
5 L LL
6 R RR

Fig.1.2 The 36 disyllabic roots

1 BB, BM, BC, BD, BL, BR
2 MB, MM, MC, MD, ML, MR
3 CB, CM, CC, CD, CL, CR
4 DB, DM, DC, DD, DL, DR
5 LB, LM, LC, LD, LL, LR
6 RR, RB, RM, RC, RD, RL, RR

5 http://lochearnhead.wikidot.com/ (retrieved September 3, 2013)

One can visit the material for more details on how it is organized. For now, the table above shows certain primary consonants and their common dialectical variations; the results of internal and external agents of morphological change over time. It helps us to anticipate the different spelling of words across space and time and can be applied to African languages, especially Egyptian with its known life of over 3000 years.

(Table Footnotes)

1 Some argue that this is a sign for a *mat*. See *p* "mat" (as covering for furniture), (statue) base, throne" ▯.

BIBLIOGRAPHY

ACHAMPONG, Nana S. (2011). *Adinkra (i'kon')-concepts: Concept icons of the Ashanti Akan of West Africa.* Achampong & Sons. Baltimore, MD.

ADESOLA, Oluseye. (N.D.). *Yorùbá: A Grammar Sketch Version 1.0* (unpublished paper)

AIYEJINA, Funso. (N.D.). "Esu Elegbara: A Source of an Alter/Native Theory of African Literature and Criticism."

ALDER, Margot. (1986). *Drawing Down the Moon.* Beacon Press. Boston, MA.

ALLEN, James P. (2005). *The Ancient Egyptian Pyramid Texts.* Society of Biblical Literature.

______ (2010). *Middle Egyptian: An Introduction into the Language and Culture of Hieroglyphs*, 2nd Edition. Cambridge University Press. Cambridge.

ALLYN, Legesse. (2009). *Amarigna & Tigrigna Qal Hieroglyphs for Beginners.* AncientGebts.org Press. Los Angeles, CA.

ANSELIN, Alain. "Signes et mots de 'ecriture en Egypte antique." In *Archeo-Nil* n11, 2001, pp. 136-164.

ASANTE, Molefi and Mazama, Ama. (Eds.). (2009). *The Encyclopedia of African Religion.* Sage Publications, Inc. Thousand Oaks, CA.

ASHBY, Muata (2001). *The Egyptian Book of the Dead, The Book of Coming Forth By Day: Mystical Philosophy of the Pert m Heru The Kamitic Book of Enlightenment.* Cruzian Mystic Books. Miami, FL.

______. (1996). *Resurrecting Osiris: The Secret Mysteries of Rebirth and Enlightenment.* Cruzian Mystic Books.

BA, Amadou Hampate. (1981). *The Living Tradition.* In: *General History of Africa Vol. 1: Methodology and African Prehistory.* Heinemann/UNESCO. University of California Press: 166-205.

______ (2008). *A Spirit of Tolerance: The Inspiring Life of Tierno Bokar.* World Wisdom.

BADAWI, Elsaid M., Haleem, Muhammad A. (2008). *Arabic-English Dictionary of Qur'anic Usage.* Koninklijke Brill NV, Leiden, Netherlands.

BALDICK, Julian. (1997). *Black God: The Afroasiatic Roots of the Jewish, Christian and Muslim Religions.* I.B. Taurus Publishers. London. New York.

BALG, G.H. (1887). *A Comparative Glossary of the Gothic Language with Especial Reference to English and German.* Denton, Waldo & Co. Mayville, WI.

BANGURA, Abdul Karim. (2011). *African-Centered Research Methodologies: From Ancient Times to the Present.* Cognella. San Diego, CA.

BARNES, Sandra T. (Ed.). (1997). *Africa's Ogún: Old World and New, 2nd Edition.* Indiana University Press.

BATES, P., Chiba, M., Kube, S. & Nakashima, D. (Eds.). (2009). *Learning and Knowing in Indigenous Societies Today.* UNESCO: Paris, 128 pp.

BAUER, Laurie. (2007). *The Linguistic Student's Handbook.* Edinburgh University Press. 22 George Square, Edinburgh.

BEKERIE, Ayele. (1997). *Ethiopic: An African Writing System.* The Red Sea Press, Inc. Lawrenceville, NJ.

BELL, Roger. T. (1991). *Translation and Translating: Theory and Practice.* Longman Group UK ltd. London & New York.

BENGTSON, John D. (Ed.). (2008). *In Hot Pursuit of Language in Prehistory: Essays in the four fields of anthropology.* John Benjamins Publishing Company. Amsterdam and Philadelphia.

_____ (2008). "Materials for a Comparative Grammar of the Dene-Caucasian (Sino-Caucasian) Languages." In: *Orientalia et Classica XIX. Aspects of Comparativistics.* Moscow. pp. 45-119.

BENGTSON, John D. & Ruhlen, Merritt. (1994). "Global Etymologies". In: M. Ruhlen (Ed.), *The Origins of Languages: Studies in Linguistic Taxonomy.* Standford University Press. Standford, CA. pp. 277-366.

BERNAL, Martin. (1987). *Black Athena Vol. 1. The Afroasiatic Roots of Classical Civilization.* Rutgers University Press. New Brunswick, NJ.

______(2006). *Black Athena Vol. III: The Linguistic Evidence.* Rutgers University Press. New Brunswick, NJ

BILOLO, Mubabinge, and Kalamba, Nsapo. (Eds.). (2009). Renaissance *of the Negro-African Theology: Essays in Honor of Professor. Bimwenyi-Kweshi.* Academy of African Thought. Munich, Freising, Kinshasa

BILOLO, Mubabinge. (2010). *Invisibilite et Immanence du Createur Imn (Amon-Amun-Amen-Iman-Zimin): Example de la Vitalite de l'Ancien Egyptien ou CiKam dans le Cyena Ntu.* Publications Universitaires Africaines. Munich-Kinshasa-Paris.

______ (2008). *Meta-Ontologie Egyptienne du –IIIe millenaire Madwa Meta-Untu: Tum-Nunu ou Sha-Ntu* (APA. I.8). Munich-Kinshasa-Paris.

______ (2003). *Les cosmo-théologies philosophiques de l'Egypte antique: problématiques-Premisses hermeneutiques-et-problemes majeurs.* Menaibuc. France.

BLENCH, Roger. (2008). "The Problem of Pan-African Roots." In: J.D. Bengtson (Ed.), *In Hot Pursuit of Language in Prehistory*. John Benjamins. Amsterdam and Philadelphia. pp. 189-209.

BLENCH, Roger. (1995). "Is Niger–Congo simply a branch of Nilo-Saharan?" In: R. Nicolai and F. Rottland (Eds.), *Proceedings: Fifth Nilo-Saharan Linguistics Colloquium, Nice, 1992*. RüdigerKöppe. Köln. pp 83-130.

______ (1993). "New Developments in the Classification of Bantu Languages and their Historical Implications." In: D. Barreteau, & C. v. Graffenried (Ed.), *Datation et Chronologie dans le Bassin du Lac Tchad*. pp. 147-160. Paris: ORSTOM.

BOMHARD, Allan R. (1984). *Toward Proto-Nostratic: A new approach to the comparison of Proto-Indo-European and Proto-Afroasiatic*. John Benjamins Publishing Company. Amsterdam.

______ "On the Origin of Sumerian." In: *Journal of the Association for the Study of Language in Prehistory, Issue III* (December 1997).

BOMHARD, Allan R. and John C. Kearns. (1994). *The Nostratic Macrofamily: A Study in Distant Linguistic Relationship*. Mouton de Gruyter. Berlin.

BOWEN, T.J. (1858). *Grammar and Dictionary of the Yorùbá Language*. Smithsonian Institute. Washington, DC.

BUDGE, E.A. Wallis. (1904). *The Gods of the Egyptians: or Studies in Egyptian Mythology*. 2 vols. Open Court. London and Methuen and Chicago.

______ (1908). *The Book of the Kings of Egypt: Dynasties I-XIX*. Kegan Paul, Trench, Trubner & Co., Ltd., London.

______ (2003). *Egyptian Hieroglyphic Dictionary, Vol.1 and II*. Kessinger Publishing, LLC. New York, NY.

BUNSON, Margaret. (2002). *Encyclopedia of Ancient Egypt. Revised Edition*. Facts on File, Inc. New York, NY.

BURKERT, Walter. (1985). *Greek Religion*. Harvard University Press. Cambridge and Massachusetts.

BUSIA, K. A. (1968). *The Position of the Chief in the Modern Political System of Ashanti*. Frank Cass. New York, NY.

CAMPBELL-Dunn, GJK. (2006a). *Who Were The Minoans: An African Answer*. Author House. Bloomington, IN.

______ (2006b). *Comparative Linguistics: Indo-European and Niger-Congo*. Author House. Bloomington, IN.

______ (2007). *Maori: The African Evidence*. Penny Farthing Press. Christchurch, NZ

______ (2008). *The African Origins of Classical Civilization*. Author House. Bloomington, IN.

______ (2009a). *Sumerian Comparative Dictionary: Sumerian Part I*. Penny Farthing Press. Christchurch, NZ

______ (2009b). *Sumerian Comparative Grammar: Sumerian Part II*. Penny Farthing Press. Christchurch, NZ.

CARROLL, Karanja K. (2008). "Africana Studies and Research Methodology: Revisiting the Centrality of the Afrikan Worldview." In: *The Journal of Pan African Studies*, Vol.2, No.2, March. pp. 4-27.

CHAMI, Felix A. (2006). *The Unity of African Ancient History: 3000 BC to AD 500*. E & D Limited. Dar es Salaam, Tanzania.

CHEN, Lydia (2007). *The Complete Book of Chinese Knotting: A Compendium of Techniques and Variations*. Tuttle Publishing. North Clarendon, VT.

CHILDS, George T. (2003). *An Introduction Into African Languages*. John Benjamins Publishing Company. Amsterdam/Philadelphia.

CHRISTALLER, Johann G. (2012). A *dictionary of the Asante and Fante languages called Tshi (Chwee, Twi) With a Grammatical Introduction and Appendices On the Geography of the Gold Coast and Other Subjects*. Nabu Press.

COMRIE, Bernard. (1998). "Regular Sound Correspondences and Long-Distance Genetic Comparison." In: J.Salmons, B.Joseph (Ed.), *Nostratic: Sifting the Evidence*. University of Southern California, Amsterdam and Philapelphia. pp. 271-276.

DANESI, Marcel. (2004). *A Basic Course in Anthropological Linguistics*. Canadian Scholars' Press Inc. Toronto, Ontario.

DARKWAH, Nana Banchie. (2005). *The Africans Who Wrote the Bible: Ancient Secrets Africa and Christianity Have Never Told*. Aduana Publishings. Russellville, AR.

DAVID, Rosalie and David, Antony E. (2003). *A Biological Sketch of Egypt*. Seaby Publishings. London.

DAVIDSON, H.R. Ellis. (1988). *Myths and Symbols in Pagan Europe: Early Scandinavian and Celtic Religions*. University Press. Syracuse.

DE LUBICZ, R.A. Schwaller (1998, <1957). *The Temple of Man*. Inner Traditions International. Rochester, VT.

DIOP, Chiekh A. (1991). *Civilization or Barbarism: An authentic anthropology*. Lawrence Hill Books. Brooklyn, NY.

______ (1977).*Parenté génétique de l'égyptien pharaonique et des langue snégro-africaines: processus de sémitisation*. Les Nouvelles Éditions Africaines. Ifan-Dakar.

______ (1987). *Precolonial Black Africa: A Comparative Study of the Political and Social Systems of Europe and*

Black Africa, from Antiquity to the Formation of Modern States. Lawrence Hill Company. Westport, CT.

______ (1989).*The cultural Unity of Black Africa: The Domains of Patriarchy and Matriarchy in Classical Antiquity.* Karnak House. UK.

DIOP, Chiekh A. (Ed.) (1978), *The peopling of ancient Egypt and the deciphering of Meroitic script: proceedings of the symposium held in Cairo from 28 January to 3 February 1974*, UNESCO. Subsequent edition (1997) London: Karnak House.

DIXON, Robert M. W. (1994). *Ergativity*. Cambridge University Press.

DOUMBIA, Adama and Doumbia, Naomi. (2004). *The Way of the Elders: West African Spirituality & Tradition*. Llwellyn Publications. St. Paul, MN.

EGLASH, Ron. (1999). *African Fractals: Modern Computing and Indigenous Design*. Rutgers University Press. New Brunswick, NJ and London.

EHRET, Christopher. (2002). *The Civilization of Africa: A History to 1800*. University of Virginia Press.

______ (2000). "Language and History." In: B. Heine and D. Nurse *African Languages: An Introduction*. Cambridge University Press. United Kingdom. pp. 272-297.

EPEGA, Afolabi A. (2003). *Ifa The Ancient Wisdom*. Athelia Henrietta Press. New York, NY.

ERMAN, Adolph & Grapow, Hermann. (1971). *WÖRTERBUCH DER AEGYPTISCHEN SPRACHE im Auftrage der deutschen Akademien hrsg Bd. I-V*. Unveränderter Nachdruck. Berlin.

EXELL, Karen. (Ed.) (2011). *Egypt in Its African Context: Proceedings of the Conference Held at The Manchester Museum*. Archaeopress. London.

FATUNMBI, Awo Fa'lokun. (N.D.). *Awo Yorùbá: The Language of Ifá, Glossory of Terms Used in Divination*. Unpublished.

FAULKNER, R.O. (1962). *A Concise Dictionary of Middle Egyptian*. Griffith Institute, Ashmolean Museum. Oxford.

FINCH, Charles S. (1998). *The Star of Deep Beginnings: The Genesis of African Science and Technology*. Khenti, Inc. Decatur, GA.

FOXVOG, Daniel A. (2009). *Introduction to Sumerian Grammar*. University of California Berkley.

FRANCI, Massimiliano. "Egypto-Semitic Lexical Comparison - 2 Some Considerations in the Lexicon of Physical Environment, Spontaneous Vegetation and Wild Animals." In Popielska-Grzybowska,J., Białostocka. O., & Iwaszczuk. J. (Eds.).

______ (2009). *Proceedings of the Third Central European Conference of Young Egyptologists. Egypt 2004: Perspectives of Research. Warsaw 12-14 May 2004*. The Pułtusk Academy of Humanities. pp. 61-68.

FRIEDMAN, Florence D. (1981). *On the meaning of AKH (3H) in Egyptian mortuary texts*. Thesis (Ph.D.)-- Brandeis University.

FU-KIAU, K. K Bunseki. (2006). *Simba Simbi: Hold up that which holds you up*. Dorrance Publishing, Inc. Pittsburgh, PA.

______ (2001).*African Cosmology of the Bantu Kongo: Principles of Life & Living*. Athelia Henrietta Press. Brooklyn, NY.

______ (1991).*Self Healing Power and Therapy: Old Teachings from Africa*. Inprint Editions. Baltimore, MD.

GADALLA, Moustaffa. (2004). *Sacred Geometry and Numerology*. Tehuti Research Foundation. Greensboro, NC.

GARDINER. Alan H. (2007). Egyptian *Grammar: Being an Introduction to the Study of Hieroglyphs*, 3rd edition. Friffith Institute Oxford. Cambridge.

GARELLEK, Marc. (ND). "Glottal stops and prosodic strengthening of voice quality." http://www.linguistics.ucla.edu/people/grads/mgarellek/Garellek_2012_ms.pdf

______ (2013). *Production and perception of glottal stops*. PhD Dissertation, University of California. Los Angeles, CA.

GERALDINE, Pinch. (2002). *The Handbook of Egyptian Mythology*. ABC-CLIO. Santa Barbara, CA.

GONZALES, Rhonda M. (2008). *Societies, Religion and History: Central East Tanzanians and the World They Created, c200 BCE – 1800 CE*. Columbia University Press.

GOODENOUGH, Erwin R. (1953). *Jewish Symbols in the Greco-Roman Period, 12 Vols*. Pantheon Publishing. New York, NY.

GREENBERG, Joseph. (2005). *Genetic Linguistics: Essays on Theory and Method*. Oxford University Press. Oxford, NY.

______ (1963). *The Languages of Africa*. Indiana University Press. Bloomington: pp. 6-41.

GREGERSEN, Edgar A. (1972) 'Kongo-Saharan'. *Journal of African Linguistics*, 4. pp 46-56.

GRIAULE, Marcel. (1965). *Conversations with Ogotemmeli: An Introduction to Dogon Religious Ideas*. Oxford University Press. Oxford and New York.

GRIAULE, Marcel and Dieterlen, Germaine. (1986). *The Pale Fox*. The Continuum Foundation. Chino Valley, Arizona.

______ (1949). "L'Image du monde au Soudan." In: *Journal de la Societe des Africanistes*, tome n°2, vol.19, Paris. pg 81-87.

GRIFFIN, J. (2001). "Introduction." In: G. Boardman & Murray, (Eds.), *Oxford Illustrated History of Greece and the Hellenistic World.* Oxford: Oxford University Press. pp. 1–12.
HALLET, Jean-Pierre and Pelle, Alex. (1973). *Pygmy Kitabu.* Random House, Inc. New York, NY.
HALLOWAY, Joseph, Ed. (2005). *Africanisms in American Culture.* Indiana University Press. Bloomington, IN.
HANNIG, R. (2000). *Die Sprache der Pharaonen: Großes Handwörterbuch Deutsch-Ägyptisch (2800 - 950 v. Chr.).* (Lexica 3). Kulturegeschichte der Antiken Welt 86. Mainz: von Zabern.
HARRISON, S. P. (2003). "On the limits of the comparative method." In: B. Joseph and R. Janda (Eds.), *The Handbook of Historical Linguistics.* Blackwell. Oxford. pp 213–43
HARVEY, Graham (Ed.). (2000). *Indigenous Religions: A Companion.* Wellington House. New York, NY.
HATTO, A.T. (1944). "The Name of God in Gothic." In: *The Modern Language Review*, Vol. 39, No. 3. July. Modern Humanities Research Association. pp. 247-251.
HEINE, Bernd & Kuteva, Tania. (2004). *Language Contact and Grammatical Change.* Cambridge University Press. Cambridge, New York, Melbourne, Madrid, Cape Town, Singapore, Sao Paulo.
HERMSTEIN, Hermel (2012). *Black Sumer: The African Origins of Civilisation.* Pomegranate Publishers.
HICKEY, Raymond and Puppel, Stanislaw (Eds). (1997). *Trends in Linguistics: Studies and Monographs 101. Language History and Linguistic Modelling: A Festschrift for Jacek Fisiak on his 60th Birthday Volume II.* Walter de Gruyter & Co. Berlin
HOMBURGER, Lilias. (1929). "Africa" in EB ps. 333f [cited in R. van Bulck, *Les RecherchesLinguistiques au Congo Belge*, Libraire Falk fils, Burxelles. 1948: 63].
ÌDÒWÚ, E. Bólájí. (1994). *Oludumare: God in Yoruba Belief.* Africa Tree Press. NY.
ILLES, Judika. (2009). *Encyclopedia of Spirits: The Ultimate Guide to the Magic of Fairies, Genies, Demons, Ghosts, Gods & Goddesses.* HarperCollins Publishers. New York, NY.
IMHOTEP, Asar. (2011a). *Passion of the Christ or Passion of Osiris: The Kongo Origins of the Jesus Myth.* MOCHA-Versity Press. Houston, TX.
______ (2012). *Ogun, African Fire Philosophy, and the Meaning of KMT.* MOCHA-Versity Press. Houston, TX (unpublished).
______ (2012b). "Egypt in its African Context Note 3: Towards a Method for Vocalizing *mdw nTr* Symbols."
______ (2010). "Reinterpretations of the Ankh Symbol: Emblem of a Master Teacher."
______ (2011c). "Reinterpretations of the Ankh Symbol Part II."
______ (2009). *The Bakala of North America – The living Suns of Vitality: In Search of a Meaningful Name for African-Americans.* MOCHA-Versity Press. Houston, TX.
______ (2008). *Esodus: Internal Reflections and Conversations with the Sun.* MOCHA-Versity Press. Houston, TX
ISSA, Jahi and Faraji, Salim (2006). *The Origins of the Word Amen: Ancient Knowledge the Bible Has Never Told.* Amen-Ra Theological Seminary Press. Los Angeles, CA.
JOHNSTON, Harry H. (1919). *Bantu and Semi-Bantu Languages.* Oxford University Press. London.
JORDAN, Michael. (2004, [1993]). *Dictionary of Gods and Goddesses, 2nd Ed.* Facts on File, Inc. New York, NY.
KAJANGU, Kykosa. (2006). *Wisdom Poetry.* Blooming Twig Books. East Setauket, NY.
KALAMBA, Nsapo and Bilolo, Mubabinge. (Eds). (2009). *Renaissance of the Negro-African Theology: Essays in Honor of Professor. Bimwenyi-Kweshi.* Publications Universitaires Africaines. Munich, Freising, Kinshasa.
KAMALU, Chukwunyere. (1998). *Person, Divinity & Nature: A Modern View of the Person & the Cosmos in African Thought.* Karnak House Publishings. London.
KARENGA, Maulana. (2006). *Maat: The Moral Ideal in Ancient Egypt.* Sankore University Press. Los Angeles, CA.
KARENGA, Maulana and Carruthers, Jacob H. (Eds.). (1986). *Kemet and the African Worldview: Research, Rescue and Restoration.* Sankore Press. Los Angeles, CA.
KEITH, Arthur B. (1989). *The Religion and Philosophy of the Veda and Upanishads (part 1).* Motilal Banarsidass Publishers. Delhi, India.
KLIEMAN, Kairn A. (2003). *The Pygmies Were Our Compass: Bantu and Batwa in the History of West Central Africa, Early Times to c. 1900 C.E.* Heinemann Press. Portsmouth, NH.
KUYK, Betty M. (2003). *African Voices in the African American Heritage.* Indiana University Press. Bloomington, IN.
LAM, Aboubacry Moussa. (1994). *Le Sahara ou La Vallee du Nil?: Apercu sur la problematique du berceau de l'unite cuturelle de l'Afrique Noire.* Editions MENAIBUC. Dakar.
LASOR, W.S. "Proto-Semitic: Is the Concept No Longer Valid?." In: [ed.] E.M. Cook, FS S. Segert, Maarav 5-6. 1990, 189-205.
LEVINE, Baruch A., Hallo, William W., Schiffman, Lawrence H. (Eds.).(1999). *Ki Baruch Hu: Ancient Near Eastern, Biblical and Judaic Studies in Honor of Baruch A Levine.* Eisenbrauns.
LICHTHEIM, Miriam. (1978). *Ancient Egyptian Literature, Vol. II: The New Kingdom.*

University of California Press. Berkeley, CA.
LOPRIENO, Antonio. (1995). *Ancient Egyptian: A Linguistic Introduction.* Cambridge University Press. New York, NY.
LORD, Robert. (1966). *Comparative Linguistics*. David McKay Company. New York, NY.
MAAT, Sekhmet Ra Em Kht and Carroll, Karanja K. (2012). "African-Centered Theory and Methodology in Africana Studies: An Introduction." In: *The Journal of Pan African Studies*, Vol. 5, No. 4, June.
MADAN, AC. (1902). *English-Swahili Dictionary 2nd Edition.* Oxford at the Clarendon Press. London.
MALLORY, J.P and Adams, D.Q. (2006) *The Oxford Introduction to Proto-Indo-European and the Proto-Indo-European World.* Oxford University Press. New York, NY.
MARSHALL, Jonathan. (2001). "The sociolinguistic status of the glottal stop in Northeast Scots." In: Reading Working Papers in Linguistics 5. 49-65.
MASSEY, Gerald. (1975). *Book of the beginnings* (Vol. 1). University Books. Secaucus, NJ.
MBITI, John S. (1989). *African Religions & Philosophy.* Heinemann Educational Publishers. Oxford.
MEEUSSEN, A.E. (1967), "Bantu Grammatical Reconstructions" in Africana Linguistica, 3 (*), ps. 79-121).
MILAM, John. H. "The Emerging Paradigm of Afrocentric Research Methods." Paper presented at the Annual Meeting of the Association for the Study of Higher Education (Minneapolis, MN, October 28-Novemer 1, 1992).
MILESTONE Documents. "Nebmare-nakht: A Scribal Schoolbook." Accessed March 10, 2013. http://www.milestonedocuments.com/documents/view/nebmare-nakht-a-scribal-schoolbook/text
MILLER, Cynthia L. (Ed.). (2007). *Studies in Semitic and Afro-Asiatic Linguistics Presented to Gene B. Gregg.* Oriental Institute. Chicago, IL.
MISSIONARY Book Shop Church. (1913). *Dictionary of Yorùbá Language*. Lagos.
MKABELA, Queeneth. "Using the Afrocentric Method in Researching Indigenous African Culture" in *The Qualitative Report,* Vol. 10, No. 1, March 2005, pp. 178-189. Retrieved May 27, 2013, from http://www.nova.edu/ssss/QR/QR10-1/mkabela.pdf.
MORRISON, W.M. (1906). *Grammar and Dictionary of the Buluba-Lulua Language: As Spoken in the Upper Kasai and Congo Basin*. American Tract Society. New York, NY.
MUHAMMAD, Wesley. (2009). *Black Arabia & The African Origin of Islam.* A-Team Publishing. Atlanta, GA.
MURDOCK, D.M. (2009). *Christ in Egypt: The Horus Jesus Connection*. Stellar House Publishing.
MUTWA, Vusamazulu C. (1964). *Indaba, My Children: African Folk Tales. Grove Press*. New York, NY.
NIEMARK, Philip J. (1993). *The Way of the Òrìṣà: Empowering your life through the ancient African religion of Ifa.* HarperCollins Publishers.
NGARA, Constantine. (2007). "African Ways of Knowing and Pedagogy Revisited." In: *Journal of Contemporary Issues in Education*, 2(2), pp. 7-20., University of Alberta, http://ejournals.library.ualberta.ca/index.php/JCIE.
NDIGI, Oum. (1993). "Le Basaa, l'egyptien pharaonique et le copte: premiers jalons revelateurs d'une parente insoupconne." In: *ANKH, revue d'egyptologie et des civilisations aficainse*, n2, avril. pp.19-27.
OBENGA, Theophile. (2004). *African Philosophy: The Pharaonic Period 2780-330 BC.* Per Ankh Publishing. Senegal.
______ (1992). *Ancient Egypt & Black Africa: A Student's Handbook for the Study of Ancient Egypt in Philosophy, Linguistics & Gender Relations*. Karnak House. London
______ (2007). *Ancient Egyptian and Modern Yorùbá: Phonetic Regularity.* In Ankh Journal #16. Per Ankh. Paris, France.
______ (1973). *L'Afrique dans l'Antiquité*. Présence Africaine, Paris
O'CONNOR, Michael P., and Freedman, David N. (Eds). (1987). *Backgrounds for the Bible.* Eisenbrauns.
ODUWAFUN. (2007). "Ewe Orisha: A Treatise on the Role of Plants in Yorùbá Religion." Self-published paper.
ODUYOYE, Modupe. (1996). *Words and Meaning In Yorùbá Religion: Linguistic Connections Between Yorùbá, Ancient Egyptian and Semitic*. Karnak Publishing. London.
______ (1984). *The Sons of the Gods and the Daughters of Men: An Afro-Asiatic Interpretation of Genesis 1-11*. Oribis Books. Maryknoll, MY
______ (2001). *Yorùbá Names: Their Meaning and their Structure.* Sefer Books LTD. Ibidan, Nigeria.
OREL, V. and Stolbova, O. (1995). *Hamito-Semitic Etymological Dictionary*. Leiden: Brill.
OSUNDIYA, Baba. (2001). *Awo Obi: Obi Divination in Theory and Practice.* Athelia Henrietta Press. New York, NY.
OYIBO, Gabriel. (2001). *Highlights of the Grand Unified Field Theorem: Formulation of the Unified Field Theory or the Theory of Everything*. Nova Publishers. Hauppauge, NY.
PAUL, Shalom M. "Daniel 6:20 : an Aramaic Calque on an Akkadian Expression." *In Scriptura : International Journal of Bible, Religion and Theology in Southern Africa*, 2004, Volume 87. pp.315-316.
PERIOS, Ilia. (1999). "Family Evolution, Language History and Genetic Classification." In: V. Shevoroshkin & P.

J. Sidwell (Eds.), *Historical Linguistics and Lexicostatistics. AHL Studies in the History of Language 3.* Melbourne. pp. 260-306.

PFOUMA, Oscar, (1993). "Culturelle Histoire de l'Afrique Noire," chap. Publisud, 1993, chap. 1: *L'Egypte pharaonique: une Éthiopie* , pp. 1: *L'Egypte pharaonique: une Ethiopia,* pp. 8-33.

PUHVEL, Jaan. (1987). *Comparative Mythology*. The John's Hopkins University Press. Baltimore, MD.

QUIRKE, Stephen. (2001). *The Cult of Ra: Sun-Worship in Ancient Egypt.* Thames & Hudson, Inc. New York, NY.

RA, Ankh Mi. (1995). *Let the Ancestors Speak: Removing the Veil of Mysticism from Medu Netcher.* JOM International INC. Temple Hill, MD.

RINGE, Don. (2006). From *Proto-Indo-European to Proto-Germanic: A Linguistic History of English, Vol. I.* Oxford University Press. New York, NY.

ROIZEN, Michael F. & Oz, Mehmet C. (2005). *You The Owner's Manual: An Insider's Guide to the Body That Will Make You Healthier and Younger*. Harper Resource. New York, NY.

RUHLEN, Merritt. (1992). "Multi-Regional Evolution or 'Out of Africa'?: The Linguistic Evidence." In: T. Akazawa & Em″oke J. E. Szathmary (Eds.), *Prehistoric Dispersals of Mongoloid Peoples*, Oxford University Press. Oxford. pp 52–65.

SAAKANA, Amon Saba. (Ed.) (1991). *African Origins of the Major World Religions, 2nd Edition.* Karnak House Publishers. UK.

SAEED, John I. (1997). *Semantics*. Blackwell Publishers. Oxford, UK.

SAMBU, Kipkoeech A. (2008). *The Kalenjiin People's Egypt Origin Legend Revisited: Was Isis Asiis?* 2nd Edition. Longhorn Publishers. Nairobi, Kenya.

______ (2011). *The Misiri Legend Explored: A Linguistic Inquiry into the Kalenjiin People's Oral Tradition of Ancient Egypt.* University of Nairobi Press. Nairobi, Kenya.

SCHENKEL, W. (1980) "Horus" in W. Helck and W. Westendorf, eds. *Lexikon der Agyptologie.* III: cols 14–25.

SCRANTON, Laird. (2006). *The Science of the Dogon: Decoding the African Mystery Tradition.* Inner Traditions. Rochester, VT.

______ (2010). *The Cosmological Origins of Myth and Symbol: From the Dogon and Ancient Egypt to India, Tibet, and China.* Inner Traditions. Rochester, VM.

SOMÉ, Malidoma. (1994). *Of Water and the Spirit: Ritual, Magic, and Initiation in the Life of an African Shaman.* A Jeremy P. Tarcher/Putman Book.

STAROSTIN, Sergei A. *A Concise Glossary of Sino-Caucasian* [Appendix to "Sino-Caucasian]. (no date)

STEWART, John M. (1976) *Towards Volta–Congo reconstruction: a comparative study of some languages of Black-Africa.* (Inaugural speech, Leiden University) Leiden: UniversitairePers Leiden.

______ (2002) "The potential of Proto-Potou-Akanic-Bantu as a pilot Proto-Niger–Congo, and the reconstructions updated." In: *Journal of African Languages and Linguistics*, 23, 197-224.

TAKÁCS, Gabor. (1998). "The Law of Belova in Work." in: Rocznik Orientalistyczny 51/2, 1998, 115-128.

______ (2000). "Towards the Afro-Asiatic etymology of Egyptian zš 'to write'." In: *Bulletin of the School of Oriental and African Studies*, 63, pp 261-273. doi:10.1017/S0041977X00007229.

TAKÁCS, Gabor and Vycichl, Werner, Eds. (2003). *Egyptian and Semito-Hamitic (Afro-Asiatic) Studies in Memoriam W. Vycichl: In Memoriam W. Vycichl (Studies in Semitic Languages and Linguistics)* [Library Binding]. Brill Academic Publishers. Leiden, NL.

TAYLOR, John R. (1995). *Linguistic Categorization: Prototypes in Linguistic Theory, 2nd Edition.* Clarendon Press. Oxford, UK.

THOMASON, Sarah G. and Kaufman, Terrence. (1988). *Language Contact, Creolization and Genetic Linguistics.* University of California Press. Berkeley, Los Angeles, Oxford.

THOMPKINS, Peter and Bird, Christopher. (2000). *The Secret Life of Plants: A Fascinating Account of the Physical, Emotional, and Spiritual Between Plants and Man.* HarperCollins Publishers. India.

THOMPSON, Robert F. (1995). "Faces of the Gods: the Artists and their Altars." In: *African Arts*, Vol. 28, No. 1, (Winter). pp. 50-61

______ (1984). *Flash of the Spirit: African & Afro-American Art & Philosophy*. First Vintage Books. London.

THUNDY, Zacharias P. "God: A Short Study in Etymology." Undated article.

TORREND, J. (1891). *A Comparative Grammar of the South African Bantu Languages: Comprising those of Zanzibar, Mozambique, the Zambesi, Kafirland, Benguela, Angola, the Congo, the Ogowe, the Cameroons, the Lake Region, etc.* Kegan Paul, Trench, Trubner & Co., LTD. London.

TOWEET, Taaita (1979). *A Study of Kalenjiin Linguistics*. Keyna Literature Bureau. Nairobi, Kenya.

VAN BINSBERGEN, Wim M.J. (2009)." The continued relevance of Martin Bernal's Black Athena Thesis: Yes and No." African Studies Centre, Leiden

VERNET i Pons, Eulàlia. (2008). "Formació i estructura de les arrels verbals en semític: comentari etimològic dels determinatius radicals presents en els verba tertiae infirmae de l'hebreu bíblic masorètic" [on line]. Ph.D. Dissertation. Universitat de Barcelona. Departament de Filologia Semítica

http://www.tdx.cat/TDX-0212109-111510. Barcelona.
VON Warburg, Walter (1969). *Problems and Methods in Linguistics.* Basil Blackwell. Oxford.
VYGUS, Mark. (2011 – July). *Ancient Egyptian Dictionary.* (downloadable .pdf).
WALKER, Robin. (2006). *When We Ruled: The Ancient and Medieval History of Black Civilizations.* Black Classic Press. Baltimore, MD.
WANGER, W. (1935). *Comparative Lexical Study of Sumerian and Ntu ("Bantu"): Sumerian The "Sanscrit" of the African Ntu Languages.* W. Kohlhammer. Stuttgart. Berlin.
WEBB, Vic and Sure, Kembo. (Eds). (2000). *African Voices: An Introduction to the Languages and Linguistics of Africa.* Oxford University Press. South Africa.
WELMERS, William. E. (1973). *African Language Structures*, UCLA Press. Berkeley, CA.
______ (1971). "Niger-Congo, Mande." In: Thomas A. Sebeok, Jade Berry, Joseph H. Greenberg et al. (Ed.), *Linguistics in Subsaharan Africa*, (*Current Trends in Linguistics,* 7), The Hague. Mouton. pp 113–140.
WESTERMANN, D. (1927), *Die westlichen Sudansprachen und ihre Beziehungen zum Bantu*, de Gruyter, Berlin.
WINN, Shan M. M. (1995). *Heaven, Heroes, and Happiness.* University Press of America, Inc. Lanham, MD.
WILKINSON, Richard H. (2003). *The Complete Gods and Goddesses of Ancient Egypt.* Thames & Hudson. New York, NY.
WILKINSON, Toby. A. H. (2001). *Early Dynastic Egypt.* Routledge, Inc. New York, NY.
______ (2003).*Genesis of the Pharaohs: Dramatic new discoveries that rewrite the origins of ancient Egypt.* Thames and Hudson, Ltd. London
YAKUBOVICH, Ilya. (2010). "The West Semitic God El in Anatolian Hieroglyphic Transmission." In: Y. Cohen, A. Gilan, and J. L. Miller (Eds.), *Pax Hethitica: Studies on the Hittites and their Neighbours in Honour of Itamar Singer*, Harrassowitz Verlag, Wiesbaden. pp. 385-398.
ZABKAR, L.V. (1988). *Hymns to Isis in Her Temple at Philae.* Brandeis University Press. London.

Websites

Beinlich Egyptian Online Dictionary
http://www.fitzmuseum.cam.ac.uk/er/beinlich/beinlich.html (German)

Canaanite Dictionary
http://canaanite.org/

Dictionnaire ciLuba
http://www.ciyem.ugent.be/ (French)

GOTHIC DICTIONARY with etymologies by András Rajki 2004
http://web.archive.org/web/20100416081032/http://etymological.fw.hu/Gothic.htm

Health and Yoga
http://www.healthandyoga.com/

How Trees Function
http://www.insights.co.nz/magic_habitat_htw.aspx

Kalenjiin Online Dictionary
http://africanlanguages.com/kalenjin/

Khipu Database Project
http://khipukamayuq.fas.harvard.edu/

Kinyarwanda Dictionary
http://www.freelang.net/dictionary/kinyarwanda.php

Kiswahili
http://africanlanguages.com/swahili/index.phpl=en

Luganda Dictionary
http://www.gandaancestry.com/dictionary/dictionary.php

Meeussen's Proto-Bantu Reconstructions
http://linguistics.berkeley.edu/CBOLD/Docs/Meeussen.html

Online Etymological Dictionary
http://www.etymonline.com

Proto-SBB (P. Boyeldieu, P. Nougayrol & P. Palayer 2004); La liste de Swadesh pour le proto-SBB (Sara-Bongo-Bagirmi, branche Soudan Central des langues Nilo-Sahariennes)
http://sumale.vjf.cnrs.fr/NC/Public/pdf/swadesh_SBB.pdf

isiNdebele Dictionary
http://africanlanguages.com/ndebele/

Sesotho sa Leboa Dictionary
http://africanlanguages.com/sdp/

Setswana Dictionary
http://africanlanguages.com/setswana/

Sheng-English Dictionary
http://africanlanguages.com/swahili/sheng/index.php?l=en

The General Shona Dictionary
http://www.dokpro.uio.no/allex/gsd.html

"The Semiotics of Aroko in Yorùbá Tradition" --M.S. ABDULLAHI-IDIAGBON
http://www.unilorin.edu.ng/publications/idiagbon/THE%20SEMIOTICS%20OF%20AROKO%20IN%20YORUBA%20TRADITION.htm (retrieved 4/13/2013)

Tower of Babel
http://starling.rinet.ru/

Wikipedia
http://www.wikipedia.com

Wulfila Project
http://www.wulfila.be/

Yorùbá Dictionary
http://www.Yorùbádictionary.com/

Index

Symbols

A

B

C

D

E

N

O

P

Q

R

S

T

U

V

W

X (transliterated in Egyptian as /ẖ/)

Y

Z